# MY FATHER'S GUN

# MY FATHER'S GUN

ONE FAMILY, THREE BADGES,
ONE HUNDRED YEARS IN THE NYPD

## Brian McDonald

A DUTTON BOOK

DUTTON
Published by the Penguin Group
Penguin Putnam Inc., 375 Hudson Street, New York, New York 10014, U.S.A.
Penguin Books Ltd, 27 Wrights Lane, London W8 5TZ, England
Penguin Books Australia Ltd, Ringwood, Victoria, Australia
Penguin Books Canada Ltd, 10 Alcorn Avenue, Toronto, Ontario, Canada M4V 3B2
Penguin Books (N.Z.) Ltd, 182–190 Wairau Road, Auckland 10, New Zealand

Penguin Books Ltd, Registered Offices:
Harmondsworth, Middlesex, England

First published by Dutton, a member of Penguin Putnam Inc.

First Printing, May, 1999
10  9  8  7  6  5  4  3  2

REGISTERED TRADEMARK — MARCA REGISTRADA

LIBRARY OF CONGRESS CATALOGING-IN-PUBLICATION DATA:
McDonald, Brian (Brian Vincent)
  My father's gun / Brian McDonald.
    p.    cm.
  ISBN 0-525-94396-X (alk. paper)
  1. Police—New York (State)—New York—Biography.   2. Irish Americans—New
York (State)—New York—Biography.   3. Irish American families—New York
(State)—New York.   4. Fathers and sons—New York (State)   I. Title.
  HV7911.A1M33   1999
  363.2'092—dc21
  [B]
                                                                98-51156
                                                                     CIP
Printed in the United States of America
Set in Janson

*For Mom*

I would like to express my gratitude to the many people whose guidance, knowledge, and candidness helped make this book possible. First, I'm indebted to the police officers who worked alongside the members of my family. In my mind, they are heroes all. I would also like to thank archivist Daphne Dennis, the Bronx Historical Society, Inspector Michael Collins, and authors Thomas Repetto, Robert Daly, Luc Sante, and Peter Maas whose research made my job infinitely easier. I was blessed with the extraordinary assistance of editor Rosemary Ahern, Jane Dystel (the Jerry McGuire of literary agents), Sam Freedman, and Miriam Goderich.

Most important, I would like to thank my family, especially my father and my brother Frankie. I love them. Warts and all.

# CONTENTS

# PROLOGUE

On the evening of January 18, 1987, my brother Frankie sat at a desk in the 48th Precinct house, the borough command center for the Bronx Task Force, and absently gazed out the window at the crawling traffic on the Cross-Bronx Expressway. The snow, which had begun falling lightly the day before, had taken on a steady slanting trajectory and the fat, swirling flakes clicked against the window. He thought of the young patrolman's body lying in the foyer of the building on Fordham Road. He thought of the surrounding neighborhood. He'd run past that building a thousand times as a kid. He played Johnny-ride-the-pony on those sidewalks every day. Yet this neighborhood no longer even remotely resembled the one that lived in his recollections.

My brother and his partner, Detective Edward Blake, had worked three solid days on the investigation into the murder of off-duty patrolman Michael Reidy. Both of them had been assigned to the Major Case Squad, a kind of detective all-star team. My brother was frequently picked for this elite squad, and routinely worked high-profile and high-priority cases. In November

1986, he, along with one hundred other detectives, was assigned to the case of Larry Davis, the drug dealer stickup artist who shot and seriously injured six cops and initiated the largest manhunt in the history of the NYPD. Now, it was a cop-killer the Major Case Squad was after.

At first, their information was thin. They knew Reidy, a rookie cop assigned to the 41st Precinct, had been shot and killed as he was robbed in the vestibule of his mother's building across from St. Nicholas of Tolentine Church. They knew that Reidy had cashed his paycheck at a check-cashing place on Fordham Road. They surmised that someone had followed him home. They knew, too, that there had been a struggle, and that Reidy had emptied his five-shot revolver. But, they had no witnesses, and three days into the investigation, very few leads.

Then a patrolman named Powers walked into the office with his girlfriend. He had asked to see the detectives assigned to the Reidy case. It seemed to my brother and Blake that Powers had an agenda, that the patrolman wanted to use his girlfriend's information as currency, to trade for a possible promotion into the detective division. In a way, you couldn't blame Powers. For patrolmen, opportunities like this one didn't happen often. It was a golden opportunity. After Powers made his opening play, he stood for a few moments in an uneasy silence. He was well aware that my brother and Blake were the ones who would let the appropriate bosses know how important his information was—if, in fact, it was important. But what the patrolman didn't know was that he couldn't have made a worse choice in picking a champion for his cause. My brother took on just about every case— especially the killing of a cop—on the deepest of personal levels. In his job, in his life, he always led with his heart, the way Muhammad Ali led with his left—a personality trait that made him a great cop, led to mistakes, and, ultimately set him up for disappointment after disappointment. The NYPD is the all-time heavyweight champion of disappointing people. My brother pushed the cold container of coffee across the desk and sat on the desk's corner and felt his stomach turn—from the bad coffee, Powers' blatant careerism, or both. I'll promise him anything, he thought, hear what the girl has to say, then forget him like yesterday's New York *Post*.

Initially, it seemed what the girlfriend had wasn't really much. She said that her brother overheard someone bragging about murdering a cop. Frankie and Blake were leery, but interested. As seasoned detectives, they knew many murders were solved on such seemingly vague information; criminals like to brag, their fatal flaw. Yet countless other investigations are steered down the wrong street when detectives take these kinds of tips too seriously. Still, after three days of absolute nothing, my brother and Blake were willing to grab on to even the most tenuous of threads. They pulled their coats from the backs of their chairs and headed to the address of the brother of Patrolman Powers' girlfriend.

The brother told the detectives that he knew the man who had bragged about killing a cop only by his street name, Ski. But, he said, he knew that Ski had a half-brother, with a different last name, who was in prison upstate.

By ten p.m. the detectives were back in the office, canvassing the upstate prison system by phone. In those days, before computer links, such work was arduous. They called dozens of prisons, without success. At this time of the night, most of the prisons' administrative offices were manned by skeleton crews. Some officials they reached that night didn't have access to files; others told the detectives to call back the next morning. My brother didn't have time to wait.

The break in the investigation came when a watch warden from an upstate prison, who'd promised to phone back after he looked through his files, did. It was six a.m. My brother well remembers the exact time. He had looked at his wristwatch often during those early morning hours because he had an eight a.m. appointment at One Police Plaza—the most important trip to headquarters in his police career. Now, with the fresh lead, he wondered if he'd make the appointment at all. He wondered, as he and Blake again grabbed their coats, if he really wanted to make it.

Under "Siblings" the prison files on the half-brother listed Ski's full name, Angel Maldonado. It also listed his last known address. The building superintendent answered the bell, dressed in raggy jeans and wearing an undershirt. He wiped sleep from his eyes as he looked at my brother's shield through the glass of the building's front door. Yes, the super said through the glass, he knew who Maldonado was; but no, he didn't live in the building anymore. The super turned and began to shuffle down the hall. My brother slammed his shield against the glass and screamed to the man in the undershirt to open the door.

"He moved out two weeks ago," the super said over his shoulder, unimpressed by my brother's credentials. In this neighborhood, in those years when crime was more regular than trash collection, a police badge, even a gold one, had about as much juice as an expired credit card.

From experience, having witnessed his anger, I can see, in my mind's eye, my brother's face, fiery red, like a full summer setting sun, the veins in his neck like cord, as he continued to slam the window with the gold shield, screaming at the super: "To where?"

For a moment the man hesitated in the hallway, his back to my brother. Finally, he turned and opened the door.

Back at the Command Office there was much activity. Quickly a stakeout was planned at the address the superintendent had grudgingly given, 190th Street and Morris Avenue. The captain of the Task Force, John Ridge, called my brother and Blake into his office to congratulate them. He told the two detectives that a press conference was planned for later that morning, as soon as they brought Maldonado in, and that he wanted them there. My brother looked at his watch; it was nine a.m. "I'm going to have to

4

miss it," he told the captain. "I'm already an hour late for my appointment downtown."

As he drove his ten-year-old Nissan through the heavy snow down the East Side Drive, my brother thought back over the past twenty years of his life. The storm provided extraordinary solitude; the crunch of the snow underneath the tires, and the squeaking beat of the wipers, which fought in vain to keep up with the flakes smashing against the windshield, added a rhythm to his thoughts—memories, which came to him revised, edited like a eulogy. In them there was no frustration, no bureaucracy, no demotions or heart-wrenching unsolved cases; just the pure contentment he had always felt as a cop.

He had been to his share of cop retirement parties held in rooms above fake Irish bars. He had even made some of the farewell speeches himself: What a great guy, a terrific cop, and the rest of the happy horseshit that goes along with such oratory. He had chipped in many times for the cheap-gold shield ring, the parting gift, and had slapped the retiree on the back and promised to keep in touch, to meet regularly for a few beers. But after each of these parties, my brother knew that the relationship would just not be the same. He was about to leave a job that not only defined him as a man, but also delineated his world. Many years later, he told me that a cop was the only thing he'd wanted to be; in many ways—tradition, circumstance, environment—it was the only thing he could have been.

He turned off the Drive at the Houston Street exit, far north of the exit for One Police Plaza, and pulled the car over to a phone booth. Money had been the determining factor in his decision, and he hated that. I'll call them, he said to himself, just tell them I've changed my mind. But as he sat there in his Nissan, his thoughts went to his wife, Pam, and their two daughters. For so much of the past twenty years they had struggled together just to get by. The offer he had would mean the struggle would be over. He realized that he had no choice. He had to do it, for them. He tugged at the wheel of the Nissan and made a slow U-turn back onto the Drive.

Later that morning, about the time that Angel Maldonado was being arrested in the Bronx for the murder of Michael Reidy, my brother handed in his gold shield, Kevlar vest, and service revolver to the pension check at police headquarters and retired. And so ended nearly one hundred years of police service in my family.

I was not one of them, although I took the entrance exam to the New York City police department in the mid-1970s. Whether by fate, or, more likely, because of the city budget crisis then, which caused layoffs and a freeze on hiring cops, my life unfolded in a completely different direction. But I don't know whether I would have taken the job had it been offered. Looking back, I see I was much more involved in rebelling against tradition, family or otherwise, than in joining it. Still, more than twenty years later, when I see a beat cop walk by, or watch the news tape of the latest sensational crime or scandal, or listen, enraptured each time, to my brother and father's remembrances of the job, I am haunted by thoughts of how things might have been.

Though, because I never put on the uniform, I stood just outside their insular circle, I was very much a part of the cop society. And, in many ways this vantage point offered me a better view.

What lies ahead is a memoir of three generations of New York City cops in my family. My grandfather was a patrolman and traffic cop at the turn of the century, the time of the very birth of the modern department; my father was a policeman for twenty-three years, the last fourteen as a detective-lieutenant squad commander in possibly the most infamous of precincts—the 41st, Fort Apache. As an undercover cop and later a Bronx detective, my brother was involved in scores of cases that have been fodder for a myriad of cop books, movies, and TV shows. The place in which I grew up, Pearl River, became a bedroom community for hundreds of commuting city cops, and it indelibly dyed everything within its boundaries in the blue of the NYPD.

In the telling of this story, I take a risk, for in cop families "not airing your dirty laundry" is a sacrament taken somewhere between baptism and first holy communion. The "blue wall of silence," is as much in place in the cop home, where doors and windows are shut so "the neighbors won't hear," as it is in the precinct house. But the insular nature of my world has always left me screaming behind the gag. Cop stories are at root really just family stories, filled with secret conflicts, shame, desire, and humor, only dressed up with sirens and flashing lights. They deserve to be told, no matter the risk.

Partly, this book is a record of on-the-job tales—"war stories," as cops call them—taken from a trunk full of remembrances. Whether it was as a kid overhearing my father's conversations with his cop friends or his dinner table talks with my mother, or listening as my brother Frankie told his tales of peril and parable culled from the New York City streets, I found that these stories captured my imagination and transported me back through time to my father's office in the 41st Precinct squad room or to the backseat of the undercover taxicab my brother rode working the streets of Times Square.

But I don't rely on imagination, for, as my father is fond of saying, the drama of cops' war stories increases in direct proportion to their time away from the job, and the number of cocktails they've had. What follows is a researched social history of the New York City police department and the eras and events surrounding each of the cop members of my family. Though this is a family memoir, my approach is journalistic. I serve as both narrator and character. The perspective is uniquely mine and begins from my earliest memories.

One Saturday, when I was eight or nine, and my parents were out shopping at the Finast supermarket, I took it from my father's closet. I was surprised how heavy it was. The leather of the holster felt smooth and hard. It slipped out easily into my hand. The steel snub-nosed barrel and cylinder were cool against my palm. Currents of power and fright surged through me. But the fear I felt was not of the gun itself, but of the scolding I was sure to take if my father ever caught me. My curiosity, however, demanded to be satisfied.

I had watched his ritual a thousand times. At night, when he came home from work and stood in front of the hallway closet, my childhood imagination saw a Wild West gunslinger. I can still hear the slap his belt made as he whipped it off, his left hand at his side, holding the holster. I watched him—through the screen door as I stood on the stoop or peering over my comic book as I sat in the living room—while he snapped open the cylinder and let the bullets drop into his hand. I watched as he locked the bullets in a metal box, then wrapped the belt and holster together and placed them deep on the top shelf of his closet and shut the door.

I held the gun only a minute or two, aiming it at an imaginary bad guy, as I watched my reflection in the living room mirror, all the time listening for his car to pull into the driveway. I remember how the .38-caliber Police Special fit perfectly in my small hand.

# CAMELOT

*Pearl River*

*In short there's simply not a more congenial spot ... than here in Camelot.* —Alan Jay Lerner, *Camelot*

# 1

My mother didn't want to move out of the Bronx. Period. She was more than content in the Fordham neighborhood in which we lived. When my father brought up the subject, my mother became quiet or began to talk about the weather or the nosy downstairs neighbors. She was a city kid, born and bred. All she had ever known was the Bronx. She liked that her friend Theresa lived one floor below. She liked that Alexander's was a few blocks away at Fordham Road and the Grand Concourse. In the Bronx, her first question to a new face at Devoe Park at the bottom of Sedgwick Avenue was "Are you from this parish?" St. Nicholas of Tolentine, gothic and cathedrallike, was more than just her church; it gave her her identity. For my mother, a move to Pearl River might as well have been a move to Russia. It was a foreign land—far too spread out, and far too far from the Bronx. "Do they even have Catholics there?" she had once asked my father, only half jokingly.

But by 1954, my father began to tell my mother that he was concerned for the safety of my older brothers, Frankie and Eugene, then nine and eleven. Neighborhood gangs, like the Scorpions, the Golden Guineas, and the Fordham Baldies, had begun to make their criminal presence felt. Though at that time, Fordham gangs were little more than juvenile delinquents, with most of their nefarious activities conducted between the factions (rumbles and the like), my father knew how quickly that could change. In the 41st Precinct, where he worked, just two miles or so south and east of Fordham, the seriousness of teenage gang crime was already in evidence. The Puerto Rican Lightnings had members just a few years older than Eugene. And, though he wouldn't broach the topic with my mother, who thought the Irish were the true chosen people, the Gents, a South Bronx Irish gang, had a division called the Junior Gents that *were* Eugene's age.

He had witnessed the handiwork of these pint-sized gang members, who gathered, sometimes thirty strong, in front of Eddie and Miriam's candy store on the corner of Hoe Avenue and West Farms Road. He saw the gaping wounds ripped in young flesh by car aerials (then the weapon of choice). One night, a young mother who lived over Eddie and Miriam's dumped a pot of cold water on the young toughs for making too much noise and keeping her baby awake. The Junior Gents retaliated by decapitating a stray cat, shoving a broomstick in the bloody corpse, and firing it like a lance though the woman's window. The Junior Gents were already using zip guns and marijuana. For most of those kids, heroin and revolvers were just around the corner.

Though his children's safety was undoubtedly of paramount importance, it wasn't my father's only motive for moving from the Bronx. Unlike my mother, he hadn't been born in New York City, but grew up in a small coal-mining town in eastern Pennsylvania. Though he moved to New York when he was only eighteen, and had, by 1954, been a city cop for twelve years, his allegiance to the Bronx wasn't anywhere close to my mother's. His dream was the garden-variety American version—a house, with a driveway and a backyard.

Even my mother had to admit that a home in the "country," as they called Pearl River at the time, would be a luxury of space. With four boys then (I was born in 1954), a move out of the cramped two-bedroom apartment at 2300 Sedgwick Avenue had become a necessity. But my mother's solution to the problem lay right across the street. She would take the stairs up to Tar Beach and look longingly at the newly erected apartment house, which advertised "studios," not the no-bedroom city apartments of today, but three-bedroom flats, with two—my God, two!—bathrooms. In the hopes of dissuading my father's intentions, my mother concocted a scheme with her friend Theresa to buy a coin-operated Laundromat, then a futuristic idea. My father humored her for a while, until it came time to fork over the down payment. He wasn't about to let her anchor him to the Bronx with a business. He wasn't going to gamble their savings. That money was going to be a down payment on a home.

Though my mom gave in to my father's wishes for a move out of the city, she didn't cave easily. During the spring of 1955, my parents took several car trips to Rockland County looking for houses. With each new house they considered, my mother would formulate some sort of excuse. It's right in front of a mountain, she said of one. The mountain, my father remembers, was little more than a hill. Another, in the neighboring town of Tappan, was in a community without a Catholic church or school—a sacrilege, she said. Others just gave her a bad feeling. When they looked at the house on the corner of Blauvelt Road and McKinley Street, my mother was caught in her own trap.

With my father walking ahead, angry and frustrated at her lack of cooperation, my mother chatted with the sales agent, who told her that this house was already promised to a doctor. But, the sales agent said, this was the model; there were other identical homes in the development that weren't taken. Mom saw this as an opportunity to prove that she wasn't being stubborn. After taking the tour of the house, she told my father that she liked it, and would be interested if this house, and only this house, was available. The builder, Mr. Lombardi, happened to be working in the yard that day, and my father went to speak to him. From the window in the kitchen, my mother smiled with approval at my father and then at Mr. Lombardi, all the time confident that the house was already sold.

In the yard, Mr. Lombardi told my father that the doctor had yet to come up with a binder for the home, and that if he really wanted it, it was his. In near despair, my mother watched as my father and Mr. Lombardi shook hands on the deal.

A little over three months later, on a blistering July day, the Seven Santini Brothers moving truck pulled in front of 2300 Sedgwick. As we drove over the George Washington Bridge, my mother cried; leaving the Bronx was a hurt she would never really get over. Yet, when the whole family walked (and carried me) into our new home, the first order of business was to hold hands and jump up and down listening to the beautiful silence of no one knocking back.

It was almost as if developers like Lombardi had civil servants in mind when they built their houses. They were ugly, cheap, and all looked the same. Asbestos-shingled Cape Cods and split-levels, carbon-copied twelve and fifteen at a clip, each with its own weedy and stony half-acre, sold on the average for $15,000. With as little as $500 down, and mortgages of thirty years obtained with the G.I. Bill (most of the buyers were World War II or Korea veterans), lifelong city apartment dwellers could be home owners. No more paying rent. No more trying to find the building super to fix the toilet. No more city buses blowing their horns below your bedroom window. With the completion in 1955 of the Tappan Zee Bridge over the Hudson River, and the extension of the New York State Thruway, cutting the commute from Rockland County to New York City to less than half an hour, people could keep their civil service jobs and still live like country lords.

It was a carrot hung from blue-collar heaven, and the houses sold like sheet sets at a white sale. Between 1950 and 1960 over 50,000 people moved to Rockland County.

In my memories from our early days in Pearl River, my father is standing somewhere in the background. Freshman lanky, but with a prodigious beer belly that made him look like a kid smuggling a basketball out of a gymnasium. He would pat it often and say: "Cost me plenty." His hair was coal black, thick and swept back. His face was long and his nose was just a size or two too wide for it. Most of the time his expression was dour, the corners of his mouth turned down. But when he did laugh it resonated with a deep baritone, and his stomach would shake.

The reason my father isn't in the forefront of my memories is simply because he wasn't around all that much. It wasn't that he spent all his off time in the bars, like some cops did. No, it was his job that kept him away. Often, the phone would ring at dinnertime or afterward and I'd listen to his all-business detective-boss voice. When he hung up the phone he would go to his closet, strap his gun back onto his belt, put on his suit jacket, and after a short muffled explanation to my mother, head out the door. Once in a while, I would answer the phone when one of those calls came for him. The gravelly voices on the other end would sometimes say: "Could I speak to your daddy?" Sometimes, disregarding my age, they would just ask for Lieutenant McDonald.

But even when my father was there, at home, he erected a wall between himself and his family. Each evening I'd watch for him to pull into the driveway. I didn't run to him and jump in his arms the way some kids did when their fathers came home from work, the way you'd see on television shows like *Father Knows Best*. Instead, I'd peer out of my bedroom window, or from the side lawn, where I played whiffleball, sometimes just by myself, pretending I was Ed Kranepool launching homers into the big pine tree on the corner of our property. My father's long legs would fold from the car and he would stand on the driveway for a moment and stretch his back. He wore tortoise-shell sunglasses, the kind you see in photographs of John F. Kennedy on his sailboat off Hyannisport. He would rub the back of his neck before climbing the brick steps to the house. Inside, he would fix himself a scotch and sit silently in his chair in the living room.

When I did hear him talk about his work, the words bubbled up uncontrolled, like gas from a corned-beef-sandwich lunch. From these utterances I knew his precinct was a "jungle," and that it was filled with "Mau-Maus." I knew that the word "junkies" was always preceded with the imprecation "goddamned." I knew, too, that he was "in the chorus," the euphemism he used for the police department, although this was at first confusing. "Why do policemen sing?" I asked my mother.

I somehow knew his job was important. But I came to this conclusion not because of anything he said, but because of what he wore. Meticulously hung in the vestibule closet, over his neatly positioned size eleven "David" wing-tip shoes (two pair, one black, one brown; stretched with shoe trees, polished regularly, and resoled and reheeled once a year), his suits had "weights" for summer and winter. Some of them came with two pairs of pants.

But it was his expression rather than his clothing or few words that told the full story. With each year, his face became more stoic until it looked as though it had been chipped from pale rock. The details of what went on each day and night at his job aside, the result of that struggle—even to a six-year-old—was obvious. The cops were losing.

# 2

Pearl River prior to the suburban explosion of the 1950s might well have been a country town in any number of places in rural New England. It was heavily wooded with birch, pine, and elm, dotted with cattail-filled marshes and undulating hills. There were orchards—apple and peach—and fields of corn, cabbage, and tomatoes naturally irrigated by tumbling streams. Even after we moved into the house on the corner of Blauvelt Road and McKinley Street, I can remember deer and red foxes scampering through the backyard, and, of course, raccoons who welcomed suburbia and the garbage that came with it with open paws. One of the favorite pastimes my friends and I had was to search for arrowheads in the woods of a section of the town called Naurashaun, which, three hundred years before, had been inhabited by the Lenni-Lenape Indians. Though we found plenty of rocks, we unearthed no trace of the tribe.

Throughout southern Rockland there were pre–Revolutionary War homes, and graveyards with crumbling and tilted tombstones, that dated back to the 1700s. George Washington's Continental Army had once made camp in Orangeburg, a town bordering Pearl River to the east. In 1781, Washington celebrated his victory over Cornwallis at Yorktown in Mabie's Tavern in the neighboring town of Tappan, not far from where, in a farmhouse owned by a family named Bogart, General Lafayette had once set up headquarters. Major Andre, the British spy, was tried and convicted of treason in a tavern in Tappan, now a restaurant called the 1776 House.

In 1890, an industrialist named Braunsdorf purchased a parcel of southern Rockland named Muddy Creek, after a lazy brook that wound through the area. He built a sewing-machine factory and then enticed the New York and New Jersey Rail Road, a subsidiary of the Erie line, to build a line of tracks nearby by erecting a train station, which still stands in the middle of what is now Pearl River. Early lore has it that railroad workers or local residents (or both) found pearls in freshwater oysters embedded in Muddy Creek. But more likely, Braunsdorf changed the name of the community to Pearl River as an early public relations move, to entice business and settlers to the growing community. Braunsdorf was a visionary. He built stores and the first post office in

Rockland County. He was also an inventor. If it weren't for Thomas A. Edison's idea some years later, Braunsdorf's electric arc light might have made him a household name.

In the fall of 1942, the Army Corps of Engineers, along with several local contractors, built a troop staging camp on farmland in Orangeburg. With its proximity to the Hudson River, and thereby to New York Harbor, Camp Shanks became one of the two largest GI embarkation facilities in the country (the other was a sister camp, Camp Kilmer, at New Brunswick, New Jersey). Through the barracks of Camp Shanks, 1.3 million U.S. soldiers passed on their way to Europe to fight the war. Thousands more were processed through the camp on their way home; most of these were frontline soldiers.

In the years after the war, stories in the *Journal-News*, the local paper, told about G.I.s from around the country who first saw Rockland County during their time at Camp Shanks, liked it, and returned to settle there. The camp was also used as a processing facility for German and Italian prisoners, both those on their way to internment in POW camps in the United States and those being repatriated back to their homelands. There was even a story in the paper of a German POW who first saw the lush, rolling hills of the county through the barred windows of Camp Shanks and returned to Rockland after the war, where he made his living as a Volkswagen mechanic.

One of the American soldiers who passed through Camp Shanks on his way to Europe but did not return was army lieutenant Vincent Skelly, my uncle. He was killed in action in Saint-Lô, France, a few weeks after the Normandy invasion.

In 1956, the 1,300 acres that made up Camp Shanks was sold to housing developers, and the land became part of the suburban explosion.

The multitudes of city cops who eventually moved to Pearl River actually began with just a small group of apostles. In 1955, there were only about a dozen city cops living in the area. Some of the earliest, along with my family, were Edward "Tink" Bentley and his brothers, Walter and Andrew, who were radio car partners on the West Side of Manhattan; Frank Eckart, also a cop on the West Side, who moonlighted as a lifeguard at Nanuet Lake, the swimming club to which we belonged; and Ed McElligott and Ray Sheridan, detective partners in the 48th Precinct in the Bronx, who bought homes right next to each other in Pearl River. The reason cops were such a small percentage of this initial migration was simple. For them, it was illegal to live in Rockland County.

Back in the Depression, the longtime Bronx borough president, James J. Lyons, had championed a law requiring municipal city workers, such as cops and firemen, to live within the five boroughs of New York City. His rallying cry was "Local jobs for local boys." Although exemptions to the law were passed in the late 1950s—and by then, for the most part, police brass tended to ignore the regulation (probably because more and more of the upper echelon of the NYPD was moving out of the city, too)—the Lyons Law was still very much in effect when my family moved to Pearl River. My father, like the other early cop settlers, had to "maintain a residence" in New York City. On tax forms and other official papers, he used the address of my mother's sister Ruth, who lived in Parkchester.

For my father, the move to Pearl River was something of a gamble and very uncharacteristic. He was a stickler about adhering to the rules of the police department. Once, as a patrolman, during the first days of World War II, he and a small squad of other rookie cops were assigned to guard the reservoir in Central Park as rumors swirled that the Japanese were planning to poison the city water supply. It was a late December night, and the temperature dove to near zero. There was a windowless pump station near the reservoir that was heated, but he refused to even warm himself for a minute, because his explicit orders were not to leave his post. He might have frozen to death had it not been for a grizzled old patrol sergeant who pulled him off the post and drove him back to the station house to thaw out. One of my father's favorite expressions was "play by the book," and he did, throughout his police career. Apparently, however, his desire to get out of the Bronx was so strong, he was willing to do so at the risk of his career—one that was filled with promise. In 1955, as a detective-lieutenant squad commander, my father had arguably the highest profile—and undoubtedly the highest rank—of all the city cops in Rockland. For the first few years we lived in Pearl River, he rarely drove his own car to work. Fearing being spotted by either a boss or a shoofly (an Internal Affairs investigator), my father took a lift with a Con Edison worker who lived in town and worked near his precinct in the Bronx. Perhaps there is no one better at hiding from investigators than cops, and my father was no exception. When a case made him miss his lift home, he would borrow a car from a used-car dealer near the station house. We never knew what kind of broken-down heap would pull in to the driveway. It could be an old round DeSoto or big-finned Chrysler. But he wasn't only fearful of shooflies and bosses. He was also worried about the native neighbors, who didn't exactly roll up the welcome wagon to the homes of any of the new arrivals from New York City. Though some native Rocklanders, especially the businessmen and merchants, were happy with the encroachment of suburbia, some saw it with the enthusiasm of a Parisian watching the Germans march through the Arc de Triomphe.

By the late 1950s, though it was still illegal for them to live in Rockland (exemptions in the Lyons Law allowed for cops and other city workers to live in counties that, like Westchester and Nassau, were contiguous with the city limits), the number of New York policemen in the county increased dramatically. Because of the clandestine nature of the situation, official records of how many city cops actually lived in Rockland were not kept. But to offer some insight, three of the twelve homes in the development where we lived were owned by city cops. Given the fact that there were hundreds of new housing developments throughout lower Rockland at the time, and although the ratio of cops to non-cops varied throughout, at the very least the original twelve had grown by twelvefold.

As each day the shadow of New York City crept closer to their bucolic way of life, the suburbanites feared that lurking in that darkness were all of the city's ills. Sometimes these suspicions boiled over into pure resentment. The people who lived across the street from us wouldn't let their children play with my older brothers, because Frankie and Eugene were "city kids." But nowhere was this animosity more in evidence than in the relationship between the local police and the city cops.

As it had been from its earliest existence, the New York City Police Department of the late 1950s was the most insular of societies. In a paramilitary organization, with overwhelmingly homogeneous ethnicity and culture (read: Irish, Catholic) the danger of the job and a common enemy (criminals) encouraged a locker room–like camaraderie. For the city cops living in Rockland County at this time, this brotherhood was intensified even further by their secretive living situation. They car-pooled and socialized together. They joined fraternal organizations like the Knights of Columbus. Their families—our families—went on vacations together to the Police Camp in the Catskills. For city cops, there was no good reason to venture outside their circle. In their minds, the outside world was a place they had little in common with, a place that did not operate under the same rules and codes. In those years, Rockland County was the outside world.

Before the Palisades Interstate Parkway was completed in 1958, offering an exit to Pearl River and Orangeburg, city cops would drive home from work on the winding two-lane country road Route 9W. Just off 9W in Tappan stood two taverns, Sullivan's and the Orangeburg Hotel. It was here that the two cop cultures first collided.

Perhaps, on the part of the Orangetown cops, there was a feeling of being outgunned—a pure machismo type of thing. By 1957, 1958, the twenty-four-man force of the Orangetown Police Department was outnumbered five to one by the big-city counterparts living in their jurisdiction. After day shifts and midnight tours, Sullivan's and the Orangeburg Hotel would be thick with the cigar smoke of city cops sitting shoulder to shoulder at the bar. As at Rick's Café Américain in *Casablanca*, nothing infuriates the locals more than when the saloons fall to the occupying army. What irritated the Orangetown cops even further was the use of the local ball fields.

For years before city cops came to the county, the high school field in the middle of Pearl River had been a favorite spot for Orangetown police and other native Rocklanders to play softball. The city cops practically took over the field. They had enough players for two teams to play against each other, with a third full team waiting to play the winners. It was after losing the softball fields that the Orangetown police had a meeting at which they decided not to extend any professional courtesy to the city cops. During this time, my father was pulled over for a broken taillight on one of the junk heaps he had borrowed from the used-car dealer. When he told the Orangetown cop he was a lieutenant on "the Job" in the city, the local officer was unimpressed. Though my father wasn't issued a ticket, the local cop gave him a stern warning (what any other citizen would be allowed), and promised the next time he saw him, he would write him up. Other city cops weren't as lucky. Their cars parked near the ball field routinely received tickets for the most inconsequential of offenses. Some were pulled over for minor traffic violations and given summonses. Certainly, in looking back, these indiscretions on the part of city cops—matters of softball fields and bars—seem trivial. But, perhaps, for the Orangetown cops, ball fields and bars repre-sented resentments that ran much deeper.

City cops were better paid; the detectives wore better suits, and they worked in a job that was world renowned. In 1960, the pay for Orangetown cops was less than $5,000 yearly, far less than the city cops made, and that salary came without medical benefits or a pension. All of the Orangetown cops had to work second jobs. For them, the New York City cops were not only an occupying army, but their guaranteed twenty-year pension plans meant they were going to be in Rockland County forever. What's more, Or-angetown cops were often the target of ridicule by the city cops. Then, there was essentially no crime in Rockland County, save the occasional drunk driver and teenage prankster. City cops joked that their country cousins shot a squirrel once in a while just to make sure their guns worked. But the rift between the two police departments didn't last forever. And, ironically, it was a scandal involving an ex–New York cop that marked the end of the division.

On Thursday, March 26, 1959, with hatchets and sledgehammers in hand, a task force of twenty-one law enforcement agents, in-cluding members of the New York State Police and the State Crime Commission, and agents from the Rockland County dis-trict attorney's office, broke through the front door of the Com-fort Coal building in Piermont, executing a midnight gambling raid. What had tipped off the local authorities was the preponder-ance of "gangster cars," black Lincolns and Cadillacs, parked throughout the sleepy hamlet on specific nights of the week. Pier-mont, just a few miles from Pearl River, was like the town time forgot. So unusual was its Depression-era look, Woody Allen would years later use it as the backdrop in his period piece *The Purple Rose of Cairo*. In 1959, a black Lincoln parked anywhere in Piermont went about as unnoticed as a farm tractor pulling into an IRT subway station.

Once inside the building, the agents arrested forty men and confiscated some $6,000. Orangetown cops who had staked out the building for some weeks prior said that the gambling operation's weekend take reached $50,000 and more. The night of the raid, most of the gamblers were found sitting around plywood tables playing three-card monte and gin rummy. Though the accommodations were rustic, they were also quite genteel. On a plywood buffet table sat platters of fried chicken and sliced watermelon, and bottles of anisette. Most of those arrested had New York City addresses. The raid was conducted without notice to the local police chief, John J. Smith.

Smitty, as he was known, had been the police chief of Piermont for less than two months. Before his short tenure as chief, he was a New York City plainclothes policeman assigned to the 10th Division vice squad in Harlem. In April 1958, less than a year before the Piermont raid, the Tenth Division had been disbanded for ties with "KGs," police parlance for known gamblers. Smitty and others from his unit were packed off to the Bronx Park Precinct—in exile, to be sure. In August of that year, after Piermont residents had voted to form their own police department (they had been under the jurisdiction of the Orangetown police), the Piermont Village Board began conducting a search for a police chief. The job paid $5,500 a year and came with the responsibility of heading a force of four officers.

Just how Smitty became a candidate for the position I'm not sure. I do know, however, that his subsequent appointment was fought by the Rockland County Police Benevolent Association. They contended that Smitty, still a member of the New York City police department while he was under consideration for the Piermont job, was required to live in New York City, and so couldn't possibly have fulfilled the Piermont job's requirement of six months' Rockland County residency. Still, in January 1959, the state civil service commission approved Smitty's appointment, over the PBA's objections.

The night of the raid, Smitty resigned his post, but that bit of theatrics didn't solve his problems. Three months later, he was indicted by a Rockland County grand jury on gambling charges. At first, Smitty contended that he was not involved in any way with the gambling operation. But as time went by, and information was gathered—mainly from the gamblers themselves—it became known that Smitty was not only aware of the game, but was involved in its operation.

What frightened the local residents, fueled the investigation, and ultimately put Smitty in an untenable situation was not the size of the game, but the players involved. One of the men arrested that night was Michael "Big Mike" Pinetti, from East Harlem, Smitty's old beat. Pinetti was a real-life Nathan Detroit. He ran crap games and other gambling enterprises all over Manhattan. He also had close ties with Willie Moretti, a high-ranking member in what was then the Luciano crime family. For native Rocklanders, Pinetti was their worst fears made real, and in Smitty they saw the personification of the slick big-city cop who thought they were all rubes. Because of this, Smitty took the worst of the punishments handed down by the grand jury. While Pinetti was sentenced to two months in jail, the ex-chief was given one year. His crime was officially "neglect of public duty." But for most city cops, including my father, Smitty's crime was much more grievous: he had stained the reputation of all the cops who lived in Rockland, and, for that matter, of every good cop in the entire department. In my father's view, there was only one thing worse than a bad cop: a bad cop who made good cops look bad. But besides besmirching good reputations, Smitty's actions also drew a spotlight on the city cops living surreptitiously in Rockland County. Though none of the city cops had to leave their homes and move back to the Bronx, the last thing they wanted was publicity, which is exactly what the Piermont raid brought. For two solid months, Smitty was the headline in the local *Journal*

*News.* He even made, the day after the raid, page one of *The New York Times*.

Still, in some ways, Smitty's transgression helped heal the break between the Orangetown and New York City cops. For one thing, it took the wind out of the more blustery city cops. It turned out the Orangetown police didn't only shoot squirrels. They were trying to do their job and weren't as naive as their big-city counterparts thought them to be. And, on the part of the Orangetown cops, even for the most hostile of them, a year's jail sentence gained Smitty a certain amount of sympathy. Orangetown cops knew he was a father with a house full of children. They also knew that jail time, for a cop of any stripe, was an unthinkable punishment.

But perhaps what gained Smitty the most sympathy—in time, even from the city cops—was that it was just hard not to like him. In the years that followed the raid, Smitty's personality overshadowed his crime. He later became a bartender, working in a number of taverns in Pearl River. Smitty had the perfect temperament for behind the bar, gregarious and fast with a funny line. As each generation of Pearl River teenagers reached drinking age—many (myself included) New York City cops' children—Smitty kept watch over them like a defrocked priest in a Jimmy Cagney movie. So, too, did Orangetown cops flock to the other side of the bar from Smitty. There they confided to him that card and crap games had in fact existed in Piermont for years before he arrived, albeit in a more localized form, in the back of the barbershop and the grocery store.

But there was another reason why the rift between the two departments disappeared. As the number of city cops in Rockland County increased, they moved to houses across the street and down the block from Orangetown cops. When they became neighbors, a familiarity grew between the two police departments. They had plenty in common—the struggles of home ownership and putting children through school. Not too long after the Piermont raid, a popular New York policeman named Gately was killed on the way home from work when his car crashed on the Tappan Zee Bridge. His funeral was held at St. Margaret's in Pearl River, and the church overflowed with New York City cops. On the steps of the church stood a color guard sent by the Orangetown Police Department. If there was any animosity left on either side, it was dispelled that day.

# 3

Although he hung up his suit jacket each night, my father kept his tie on tight to his collar. At the dinner table, he would fold it inside his shirt. Right up until he undressed for bed, he wore his tie. I once told the mother of a friend of mine on the block that my father wore a tie in the shower. She laughed and asked where I got my sense of humor from, as if it was known that my father was devoid of one.

He wasn't. But he seemed the butt of the joke much more than the teller. My parents belonged to a card group that met every Friday night. For the most part, the players were city cops and their wives. When the game was held at our house, I would listen from my room to raucous laughter and banging on the table, part of a card game called Bernie, Bernie. I never heard my father's voice. When the gathering was held at houses other than ours, my father was always the first to leave. He earned the name "Mr. Coats" because he would gather his coat and my mother's and wait impatiently for her to hurry her good-byes.

In personality, my mother and father were polar opposites. Fiery and emotional, traits that showed in her intense blue-green eyes, my mother was as demonstrative as my father was self-contained. She had an explosive temper, inherited from her Irish-born mother and handed down to her sons. Most of her ire seemed to be directed at my father. My parents' arguments were always one-sided. My mother would rant at him: "Jesus, Mary, and Holy

Saint Joseph, once in while think about someone besides your-self." I suppose most of her anger toward him was residual, from the move out of the Bronx. But there were other underlying resentments—never mentioned even during the screaming.

Sometimes, in the middle of her tirades, my father would look up the stairs and see me standing there watching: "Let's go to Dairy Queen, Bri. I have the collirobbles," he'd say, using his term for the ripping pain in his stomach. In his Volkswagen on the way, he'd chew the end of an unlit cigar. I wanted to know why he didn't stick up for himself in arguments with my mom. But I didn't say anything. Neither did he.

They didn't argue all the time. And, although I can't remember many intimate moments between them—tender touches, or any-thing more than perfunctory kisses good-bye—there were some clues to the affection they had for each other. On my mother's birthday or Christmas, my father would go to the Pearl Shoppe, a quaint little store in Pearl River, and buy her a silk scarf or a pair of earrings. His gift would always be accompanied with a card, which was then displayed on the shelf under the bow window in the living room. He signed the card in the same manner every time: "Love, Franko"—which, no doubt, was her term of endear-ment for him. But I can't remember ever hearing my mother call him that. Most times, when they were together in the house, my mother would sit in her reclining chair doing a crossword puzzle, separated from my father by the oak table—and about a million miles—both of them silently facing the bow window like some mismatched pair of officers on the bridge of Jules Verne's *Nautilus*, burrowing through the soundless sea.

My mother tenaciously held on to her Bronxness, and she had lit-tle to do with anyone in Rockland County who could not recall the opulence that once was the Grand Concourse. As it hap-pened, by 1960, she was surrounded by people who could. The development on McKinley Street was almost wholly made up of families from the Bronx, and they wore their old neighbor-hoods—and parishes—like name tags at a sales convention: High-bridge, Kingsbridge, and Throgs Neck; Sacred Heart, St. John's, and St. Francis, to name a few. Some old Bronx habits lived through the suburban transition. People sat on their front stoops in the summer, though now separated by lawns and driveways. Fathers played stickball on the weekends, with the three-sewer home run rule surviving the move. We even had Bronx-like block parties. Still, for my mother, these familiarities were nothing more than cheap imitations, and she desperately missed her Bronx friends and old home.

In Pearl River, the friendships my mother did make were with the wives of other city cops. Like their husbands, they kept to themselves. My mother belonged to the sister organization of the Knights of Columbus, the Columbiettes, whose members were mostly cop wives. Most of these women had young, growing families, and accordingly, a great deal of their time was spent in St. Margaret's School–related activities. In our early years in Pearl River, before I was old enough to go to school, my mother would take me along to the Columbiette meeting room in the basement of the K of C hall. The din of conversation in that room was sharp with nasal Bronx accents. The ashtrays were filled with white-filtered cigarettes, all with deep red lipstick stains.

In those years, I formed a special bond with my mother; it hap-pens when you're the youngest. My older brothers were all in school: Tommy at St. Margaret's; Frankie at Pearl River High School; and Eugene away at the State University of New York Maritime College at Fort Schuyler, Queens. Together we'd go on shopping trips to Alexander's in Fordham or to meet her best friend, Nora, at the Automat on Fordham Road. They would sit, drink coffee, and talk for hours and I would eat lemon meringue pie and tour the little compartments looking at the treats behind the glass doors. For me, these trips were like secret missions, a glimpse into my mother's real happiness. Even at five or six, I knew that my mother flowered against the gray backdrop of the Bronx.

During the summer, on weekdays, my mother sat in a circle of beach chairs with the other cop wives at Nanuet Lake. On the weekend, their husbands, our fathers, had their own circle. With their white skin, and outfits of bathing suits, knee-high black nylon socks, and brogan shoes, you could have picked them out from the window of an airliner. All of my friends at the lake were the sons and daughters of New York cops: Michael Skennion, Gerard Sheridan, the Baumann girls, and others. Even on our vacations we were surrounded by cop families.

The Police Camp in the Catskills had been given to the New York City police department in the early 1920s by David Kaplan, a wealthy New York financier. Once Kaplan's country estate, the land consisted of 600 acres of dense wood and clearings veined with crystal streams that spilled down the side of the mountain. When the NYPD took it over, they called it the Police Recreation Farm, and used it for the rehabilitation of policemen and members of their families who had taken ill with consumption or pneumonia. But mostly it was used for cops who needed the fresh mountain air to dry out.

By the mid 1920s, the center was already being used more for recreation than rehabilitation. The police commissioner at the time, Richard E. Enright, ordered policemen, including the Riot Battalion, to help in building sewers, a reservoir, and bungalows, to modernize the camp for pleasure use.

By the early sixties, there was a waiting list to reserve a week at the camp, which lodged a hundred cop families in bungalows or in the main hotel, Kaplan's old large and sprawling house, built at the highest vantage, with a wraparound porch and a vista of lush green magnificence.

The last time we went to the camp was in 1960. On that trip it was just me, Tommy and my mother. My father had to work, as did my brothers Frankie and Eugene. One night after dinner, I played flashlight tag with some friends in the darkness that engulfed the grounds surrounding the main hotel. I could hear the clink of cocktail glasses and loud cop conversation from the front porch. I heard my mother telling a story of ordering oysters that night at dinner. All of the waiters at the camp were the sons of cops, and most of them became cops themselves. One even became the police commissioner—Robert J. McGuire, who had worked at the camp in the 1950s. My mother said that the young man who was taking care of her table returned with a message from the chef, who said that if she wanted oysters she should go to Sheepshead Bay. I can still remember the laughter from her story floating on the still summer night air. That night, the sky was littered with sparkling stars. My friends and I lay on the grass and picked out the constellations. To us, that everything we did involved other cops' families was the most natural thing in the world—our orbit in a solar system held in place by the gravity of the New York City Police Department.

In November 1960, my mother was absolutely aglow when John F. Kennedy was elected president. But even my parents' political affiliations kept them at odds. My father voted for Nixon, and he wasn't alone among the New York cops living in Rockland. The attachment of the New York City police department to the Democratic party, a partnership that dated back to the very beginning of Tammany Hall, didn't survive the move to suburbia. The saying went: "As soon as a cop buys a power lawn mower he becomes a staunch Republican."

Because it was such a loaded subject for both, my parents made a deal early on in Kennedy's term that political discussions were verboten. Still, my mother couldn't help but remind him every now and then who had won the election. But, in time, even my father softened toward JFK. I can remember his laughter wafting up the stairs from the rec room as he sat watching the young president's beguiling press conferences. But perhaps the most obvious area in which Kennedy's presidency affected my father, and every other New York City detective, was fashion. Since the inception of the detective bureau, its members had always been identified by the hats they wore. My father's was one of the more popular styles, a plain Dobbs fedora. But other detectives wore homburgs, even porkpies (the hat that Gene Hackman's movie character, Popeye Doyle, wears in *The French Connection*). Detectives in Manhattan's 14th, 16th, and 18th Detective Squads, especially those near the Theater District, were known for flipping up the front brim of their fedoras, a style that Mickey Spillane's Mike Hammer made famous. But with Kennedy's thick, uncovered locks, detectives' hats became a relic, like the bobby-style helmets the cops at the turn of the century wore. Luckily for my father, he had a Kennedy-like head of hair. There were plenty of detectives who didn't, and from that point on, their baldness was exposed for the world to see.

The Kennedy years marked the end of the successful transition to America's suburban way of life. City cops in Pearl River measured this success in the most modest, practical ways. Through the miracle of immigrant Italian masonry and cheap wood paneling, built-in garages were turned into rec rooms. Cement was poured for patios and redwood decks were affixed to the backs of houses. For the most part, city cops weren't the handiest of groups. Most, having grown up in apartments, hadn't picked up a hammer in their whole lives, unless it was to hit someone over the head with it. Hadler's, a hardware store in town, became a popular meeting spot for city cops who imposed upon the proprietor, George Hadler, for instructions on basic home-improvement projects—simple electrical wiring and how to mix cement.

Like most of that Depression, World War II generation, they also measured success in the opportunities given to their children. Bragging rights came along with the enrollment of cops' kids in private high schools in northern New Jersey, such as Don Bosco and Bergen Catholic, which my brother Eugene attended. Later, colleges such as Fordham University and NYU provided the same chest-thumping platform.

But ultimately, success was measured purely along civil service lines, and rank was the great divider. Even as a young kid, I knew the chain of command: patrolman, sergeant, lieutenant, captain, deputy inspector, full inspector, and so on, and I knew the subtle differences between them: Patrolmen's kids wore hand-me-down clothing and inherited their older siblings' bicycles. Lieutenants' kids got their own bikes and shopped at Robert Hall for new Easter suits or dresses each year. Perhaps the biggest jump was from lieutenant to captain.

One of my father's friends in town was James Skennion. After his first wife died, Mr. Skennion married a New York City police-woman, whom everyone called Mary, including her stepchildren, Jimmy and my friend Michael. If you had to pick a poster family for New York cops living in Pearl River, the Skennion family would be it. They lived in a fine brick home with a built-in pool on a cul-de-sac. Mr. Skennion was an affable man who talked out of the side of his mouth, the side that didn't hold the cigar. Whenever I saw him—at Nanuet Lake, or at pool parties held at his home for his cop friends' families—he would tousle my hair and in a growl like a friendly lion ask, "How are you, lad." But aside from his built-in pool and good-natured way, what made Mr. Skennion quite possibly the most popular of the cop fathers was his job.

One of the few memories I have of being alone with my father was the day he brought me to a Yankee game. We didn't even need tickets: My father showed his badge to get us in the stadium, and Mr. Skennion, as captain in charge of the detail at Yankee Stadium, arranged for our seats behind home plate. We stopped in his office in the bowels of the stadium before the game. While we were there, a tall black man dressed in a suit walked in the door. Mr. Skennion greeted the man with a roar of hello and a

slap on the back and then turned to me: "Lad, I'd like you to meet
Big Ellie," he said. "Big Ellie who?" I replied. That I didn't know
Elston Howard, the then All-Star catcher for the Yankees, was
cause for a big laugh all around. "You must be a Mets fan," the
catcher said, smiling. Actually, I was. I had Mets pennants in my
bedroom, and my brother Eugene had, the year earlier, in 1962,
taken me to the Polo Grounds to watch them play, an event that
instantly formed me as a fan for life. In spite of my allegiance to
the crosstown team, Elston Howard signed a baseball for me, and
I decided right then and there that being a captain was much
more important than a lieutenant.

By 1963, there were over a thousand city-cop families living in
Rockland County. Though this number represented a fraction of
the then 28,000 members of the NYPD, by no means did 1963
mark the end of cops moving out of the city. The number of commuting city cops increased by hundreds, thousands, over the ensuing years.

And as more and more city cops moved to Rockland, and as
those cops moved up the ranks of the police department, a political power base developed. This was an arena in which my father
was well versed—put him in a room filled with cigar smoke and a
politician or two, and he was at his best. He had spent a good part
of his police career involved in the Detective Endowment Association, a line organization and quasi union of New York City
detectives.

As members of the Knights of Columbus the city cops had lob-
bied several county politicians, including a state senator named
Joseph Nowicki, for exemptions to the Lyons Law. To concen-
trate their political punch even further, city cops splintered off
from the Knights of Columbus and formed a chapter of the Ancient Order of Hibernians, an Irish fraternal organization. The
charter membership of the Pearl River chapter of the AOH read
like a verse from "McNamara's Band": Sheridan, Dunn, Moran,

O'Brien, and McDonald. My father was the first president of the chapter, and wrote the bylaws on the typewriter on his desk in the 41st Precinct squad room.

There is nothing like a parade to draw the attention of politicians. In 1962, along with my father, Ray Sheridan, the Bronx detective who lived next to his partner, organized the first St. Patrick's Day parade in Rockland, which was held in New City, the county seat. Except for a few logistical problems (the small streets in New City and not being fully prepared for the crowds) the parade was a resounding success, with thousands of people watching. The event empowered city cops in the AOH as a political entity. That same year the "Lyons Law" was repealed.

In March 1963, on the Sunday after St. Patrick's Day, the AOH parade, having been moved to the wide streets of Pearl River, marched down Middletown Road and turned onto Central Avenue, led by Finbar Divine of the New York City police department's Emerald Society Pipe Band. Six foot four, with a waxed handlebar mustache soaring from his face like the wings of a black hawk in full flight, his chest thrust forward, pumping his five-foot-long crosier, his noble chin an icebreaker slicing through the cold March winds, he fronted the bagpipes wailing "Garry-Owens." Behind the band, little boys and girls, dressed in Catholic school uniforms, the girls' knees rosy from the cold, followed, as though Finbar were a fearless giant leading them through the safe green fields of Pearl River. It mattered little that twenty-two miles south a coming funnel cloud was forming that would spiral crime rates to the city's all-time high. It didn't matter that the move of white policemen from the city they were charged with protecting exacerbated a racial division that was already exploding in riots. No. For my father, and the other city cops who proudly watched, the parade was a manifestation of their dreams. It was the same dream that, fifty odd years earlier, my grandfather had

had when he moved his family to a neighborhood in Brooklyn—then suburban itself—filled with cops who commuted on the newly built subway. It was a dream my brother Frankie, surrounded by cop culture and infused with familial instinct, would inherit, and struggle to keep alive. Along the route, New York City cop parents: fathers wearing green tam o'shanters, faces red from an earlier-than-usual scotch, mothers with Kelly green scarves and guilty eyes hiding truths of unhappy homes or too much St. Patrick's celebration the night before, clapped and smiled, secure in the knowledge that this their town was as insular and magical as Brigadoon. Or better yet, with Kennedy in the White House, Camelot.

# 4

The following summer, 1963, was the last time all of my brothers lived in the house in Pearl River with my parents. Eugene was on summer break from the Maritime College; Frankie was working two jobs—construction and the Honey Wagon, as my father called the garbage truck Frankie hung off early each morning; Tommy, then thirteen, was playing Babe Ruth League baseball; and me, nine years old. Most of my memories of those years were of Frankie. My other two brothers were important presences, but Eugene was much older and a mystery to me, defined more by his absence than any quirks of character, while Tommy was just enough older than me to consider me a pain in his ass. When we were leaving the house to go out and play, my mother would yell those words to Tommy that would make me shiver: "Take your brother with you." For Tommy, this was the greatest of burdens, and he never shied away from letting me know it. Frankie, however, was a different story.

Under the pine trees, I would watch him wash his car, a Malibu Super Sport with baby moon hubcaps. When I tried to help, he would spray me with the hose or grab me by my hands and spin me until I walked like my uncle Joe coming home from the American Legion Hall. At night, we'd shoot sock basketballs into a hamper placed on my desk, a nickel a game. Having practiced all day, I'd beat him most of the time, firing caroms off two walls, using the shade on the window as a backboard. But I'd play him double or nothing, until he got even (most times I'd miss on purpose). I knew his rituals by heart. Getting ready for a date with his girlfriend, Carol, he'd press his chino pants to a razor-sharp crease and hang them by the cuffs from the top drawer of his bureau. He paid me a quarter to buff his loafers until they shined like the Malibu, but I would gladly have done them for nothing. He'd spend an hour in the shower, then wipe a hole in the fogged-up bathroom mirror, and spend forever shaping his hair with Georgia Peach—the front into a pompadour, the back into a ducktail. Though not handsome in the classic sense, he had rough good looks with intense eyes like his mother's, and a single deep dimple in his chin that looked as though, as a baby, he had fallen asleep on the point of a pencil. For hours after he left, the bathroom would be thick with the sweet fragrance of Old Spice aftershave.

One night that summer, when my parents had gone out for the evening, Frankie had a party at the house. From my bedroom, I heard some loud shouting and came out to see what was happening. My brother was standing in the living room facing a teenager with broad athletic shoulders. His name was Bobby, and he was screaming in Frankie's face, the argument over their girlfriends. Frankie glared at Bobby. When my brother became angry, all other emotion was displaced, his eyes glazed, his outward demeanor would seem calm, almost serene. Plenty were fooled. For Frankie was like a shark feigning indifference to his prey. But I knew what was about to happen.

I had watched, peeking out the kitchen window, his fights with Eugene on the side lawn. At one time, Eugene, two years older, always had the better of Frankie, who couldn't seem to infiltrate his older brother's superior reach. Still, no matter how bad a beating he took, even with tears streaming down his cheeks, his lips fattened and bloody, or his shoulder pinned to the ground by Eugene's knees, Frankie would not give up. "You punch like a girl," he would say defiantly. But as they grew older, as Frankie developed a barrel chest and bulging arms, not even Eugene would take him on. By the time he was in his late teens, even my father tiptoed around his anger. The night he graduated from high school he was involved in an accident while driving my mother's car. I saw the flashing lights of the police car in our driveway from my bedroom window, then saw my father, wearing only his boxer shorts and sleeveless "guinea" T-shirt, as he called it, talking to the cop on the front steps. At first, the conversation was muffled. Something about Frankie running a stop sign and smashing the car into a utility pole. The young Orangetown policeman knew my father was a detective-lieutenant in the Bronx. By this time, the local police treated city cops, especially those with rank, with a mixture of envy and respect. The patrolman stood on the steps holding his hat behind his back. He told my father that though Frankie had been drinking, no charges would be filed. My father thanked him, but his tone was commanding, dismissive.

When the patrolman left, the screaming started. At first, Frankie sat on the couch, his head down, as my father lit into him. The car, a two-tone white and aquamarine Chevy Bel Air, had been totaled. Carol had suffered a broken arm. As my father riddled him with white-hot words, I saw it begin. As always, the first sign came in my brother's eyes: a stare focused on a spot on the floor somewhere near his feet. I saw my father's eyes go wide. He, too, knew Frankie's anger, and at that moment looked afraid. Had it not been for my mother, awake now, dressed in a nightgown and having closed the doors so the neighbors wouldn't hear, wedging herself between them, Frankie would undoubtedly have done something he would have felt very sorry about. Instead, he turned away and with frightening fury punched the kitchen wall, caving in the plaster. My father stood there, more shocked than angry, as Frankie slowly walked out the front door.

At the party that night, the punch was a lightning-quick left hand that literally lifted Bobby off the ground. He slammed against the wall, the snap of his head breaking the thermostat. There was a gasp among the others in the living room. Frankie himself seemed taken aback by the viciousness of the blow. He quickly turned and walked out of the house and onto the front lawn. I ran down the stairs and went to him. He blew the smoke from a Lucky out in a stream, as if trying to exhale a demon that lived within him. His face now was soft, his eyes repentant. He put his arm around me and we walked under the big pine on the corner of the property. Though I was frightened of many things then, I was not afraid of my brother's anger. Of course, when I was a child, it was never directed at me. But more than that, I understood it. Like the anger of the Incredible Hulk in my Marvel comic books, Frankie's rage was a superpower, one he didn't ask for or want. And each time it arose, and changed his very physicality, it extracted from him an emotional price. Only I knew that the aftermath of one of his explosions was when Frankie's soul was most exposed. More than any other time, it was here where my hero worship began.

On November 22, 1963, my father drove from the 41st Precinct to meet Eugene in lower Manhattan. My oldest brother had broken his arm in a touch football game and was having the cast removed. That day, Frankie, home from the Brooklyn Navy Yard—having enlisted in the Navy a few months before—drove with his friend Artie Norton to pick up tuxedoes for Artie's wedding. Tommy and I were in class at St. Margaret's when the news came. Sister Marie Gabriel announced it over the loudspeaker on the wall at the head of the classroom.

We were let out of school early, and when I arrived home, my mother was sitting in the living room holding her head in her hands. I went to her and touched her lightly on the shoulder; for a moment, she looked at me without recognition, her eyes red spiderwebs, with heavy dark circles underneath. Then, as if the realization of who I was at once descended upon her, she grabbed me and pulled me to her chest, her action giving way to the deepest of sobs. Eleven years earlier, two years before I was born, she had lost a child, my sister, Mary Clare, just four years old. The unspeakable grief of that loss, buried in the Gate of Heaven cemetery and the years that had passed, had been again released by the tragic events in Dallas. For my mother, all hope was lost, sealed in a coffin and accompanied down Pennsylvania Avenue by a single riderless horse.

My father was called into work that evening, the brass of the NYPD fearing chaos in the streets, an overreaction. There would be no chaos. For the South Bronx, like the rest of the country, stood silently numb that night, as if it had been engulfed by the most frigid air—the big policeman, as my father called the coldest of winter crime-free nights.

The Camelot of Pearl River, too, began to die that day. The innocent facade, slowly at first, started to peel like cheap wood panel. Our town was not magical, nor was it insulated from the eruptive events of the country in the coming years: the assassinations, the threat of nuclear war, the war in Vietnam, and the coming plague of drug abuse that would spread like an airborne virus, float over the moat of the Hudson River, and settle like a fine toxic dust on the neatly kept back lawns.

Often, during those next few years, the last of my father's police career, I would be awakened at two or three in the morning by the click of his pipe tapping against the glass ashtray. Silently, I would creep to the door and peer down into the darkness of the living room to see him sitting again in his wing chair, the smoke from his pipe rising, metallic blue in the shaft of light from the lamp on the table, surrounding him like a ghostly wagon train keeping the demon Indians at bay. Next to him was a half-empty glass of buttermilk, drunk to coat the internal bleeding. "Goddamned scotch," I'd hear him mumble, a self-admonishment for the three he would allow himself when he came home from work. The scotch was needed, and not the culprit. Not the only one, anyway. The stabbing pain in his stomach was from the knife wounds, and bullet wounds, and every kind of wound a human can suffer. By 1963, there were almost two murders a week in the 41st Precinct, better known as Fort Apache. And each killing ripped open his stomach a little wider. And each, it seemed, took him farther away from me.

The next day, as a result of military concerns that the assassination had national security implications, Frankie was put on active duty and sent to Key West for advanced training, then on to Jacksonville, Florida. From the window of his bedroom, the one with the flower box of geraniums, the one that I would be given, I watched him on the steps saying good-bye to my father and mother. My mother pushed the tears in her eyes away with her palm; my father stiffly shook my brother's hand. Just before Frankie ducked into the backseat of his friend's car, he looked up at me and waved. I started to cry.

# TAMMANY

*Thomas Skelly*

*There is more law at the end of the policeman's nightstick*
*than in all the decisions of the Supreme Court.*
                                    —Alexander "Clubber" Williams

# 1

My maternal grandfather, Tom Skelly, was born on the Upper East Side of Manhattan in 1868. His parents, Jane Wheeler and Matthew Skelly, emigrated from Ireland during the great potato famine of the 1850s. Like most of the famine refugees, they arrived in the new land with practically nothing. But, as a young boy, my grandfather didn't experience the hardships his parents endured, nor did he know the squalor of the tenements on the Lower East Side, the home of the second wave of Irish immigrants in the 1890s. He had the great good fortune to be American born, and with that came the inherent right to the bounty that was and is this country. Because of that stroke of luck, combined with the fact that his father worked his skinny Irish ass off building a small horse-drawn trucking company, my grandfather grew up in a family that was relatively financially secure.

Beginning with just one rig, my great-grandfather built the business; eventually he owned a half-dozen rigs, with as many drivers working for him. He tended to hire "off-the-boat" Irish, and on their backs, and with his own sweat, he became successful enough to afford a private home in the "suburbs" of East Sixty-first Street and Third Avenue. It wasn't Fifth Avenue, but it wasn't bad. And it was a world away from the tenements.

But in 1878, my great-grandfather fell off a rig, dead of a heart attack. Perhaps my grandfather would have never become a policeman had his father lived a few years more, until Tom was old enough to run the family business. The New York City police department of his time was a vehicle of societal acceptance for Irish immigrants. The department was nearly 50 percent immigrants, the overwhelming majority of them Irish. Unlike other jobs Irish filled—masonry and construction—the police department, with its uniform and tight brotherhood, gave them a sense of belonging and purpose, perhaps even a little superiority. But my great-grandfather had already reached a level of acceptance with his business, and my grandfather was an American. Certainly, there was discrimination, even toward American-born Irish. But it was not nearly as harsh as it was toward recent Irish immigrants, those who met with the now often talked about sign "No Irish need apply."

My great-grandmother tried to run the trucking business for a while, but, according to my mother, the drivers stole from her, and she was forced to give it up. She took the little money she had left and opened a candy store on Second Avenue and Eighty-fifth Street. There, in an apartment above the store, she lived with her three children. In the 1880 census, my great-grandmother is listed as a white female, forty-eight years old and widowed, her occupation "storekeeper." Her daughter Mary is seventeen, single and working as a drip maker (candles? or drapes?). Her sons, Thomas and Joseph, are twelve and eight.

My great-grandmother's life had gone from bad to good to bad again. She had survived the potato famine and the crossing. She worked as hard as her husband, not only raising a family, but working on the rigs herself. Four of her children had died, including young Matthew, two years older than my grandfather, who died at ten, just two months after Matthew Senior passed away. But while her husband was alive, she had enjoyed her new land and her fine home. Her letters back to Ireland enticed much of her clan to follow her to America, where dreams were a reality, not peat fire variety the way they were in Ireland. Then, the day her husband died, all of it was snatched away.

In his youth, my grandfather Tom went to the "Brothers' school," as my mother called Catholic school, a local grammar and high school. In his late teens and early twenties, he drove a rig for his sister Mary's husband, Larry Redmond, who was in the trucking business for a while. He also worked on and off as a stevedore along the riverfront.

At the age of twenty-five, sometime in 1893, Tom Skelly joined the New York City police department, then called the Metropolitan Police. The exact date of his entry into service is somewhat of a mystery. City records give several dates, including March 15, July 10, and November 15, 1893, and March 27, 1905, the last undoubtedly wrong because that date would have made him ineligible for the pension he received when he retired in 1919. What is perfectly clear is the dishonesty of the organization he joined.

So corrupt was the department of my grandfather's time, the *Mail and Express*, a newspaper of the day, called it "a ghastly sinkhole of official impropriety." *The Brooklyn Daily Eagle* spoke of it as even more infamous, calling it "the most corrupt, brutal, incompetent organization in the world." The going rate for a badge then was $300, a veritable fortune considering the average weekly wage in the tenement community, where most of the Irish-born cops lived, was around $5. Those who didn't have the financial resources to pay for the badge outright borrowed the money from the local Tammany Hall politician, to be paid back with interest. Tammany Hall was the crooked Democratic political machine that ran New York City for the last half of the nineteenth century and into the twentieth. For most of those years, the police department operated as Tammany's graft collection agency. The system worked from the bottom up. Patrolmen who were in the pocket of the Hall looked the other way as wardmen collected graft from businesses like barrooms and gambling halls. There was a saying in the police department then that summed up the duties of a patrolman: "Hear, see, say nothing. Eat, drink, pay nothing." The captain of the precinct then would take his slice, kicking back a small percentage to his collector; the local Tammany boss would then take his, with the rest filtering back to the Hall itself. It was a lucrative business. One published report of the day estimated the graft collected in a Sixth Avenue precinct called the Tenderloin at $75,000 to $100,000 a month. Within the department, promotions were bought: $3,000 for precinct detective, as much as $15,000 for the position of precinct captain. Captains ruled like feudal lords.

I have no way of knowing whether my grandfather paid for the then square badge of the police department. I do know, however, that such a practice was the rule rather than the exception. Tom did have to fill out an application and take an entrance examination. But these tasks were perfunctory and had little to do with whether or not you were appointed. In memoirs published in a 1905 *Cosmopolitan Magazine*, a retired police captain listed some of the questions asked on his entrance exam: "What direction is Sydney from the South Pole?" "What is a straight line?" "What poet is called the 'Bard of Avon'?"

If my grandfather did have an angel, it would have been someone like Whispering Larry Delmore, the illiterate Yorkville Tammany heavyweight, who could sign his name only with an "X"; or Mike Cosgrove who owned a saloon on East Eighty-seventh Street, right next to the Algonquin Club, Tammany headquarters in Yorkville. Cosgrove, first a ward heeler, and later mentor to Senator Robert F. Wagner, had ties to Big Tim Sullivan, who oversaw Tammany interests in the gambling halls on the Bowery and was the unofficial political boss of all the districts south of Fourteenth Street. (He later became a state senator and congressman, but those jobs actually carried less weight than his former position.) If Mike Cosgrove opened the door to the police department for my grandfather, then it follows that Tom would have been assigned to a precinct within Sullivan's domain.

He was. City records say that my grandfather was first assigned to the 10th Precinct, which lay south of Houston Street and east of the Bowery. This district was populated mainly by Germans and Polish Jews, and the individual neighborhoods were named accordingly: "Jewtown" and "Little Germany." The Jewish quarter was centered at Hester and Essex Streets. There, the five-story tenements—where at night families would sleep lined up next to each other in one-room apartments—were, during the day, transformed into individual factories called "sweater shops." Women worked sewing machines making knee pants, coats, and other garments. On the sidewalks, in front of small stores, men in long black coats and beards would outbargain each other to compete for customers, the clicking of passing horse hooves keeping beat to the haggling in Yiddish. An outdoor shopping bazaar, called the Pig Market (undoubtedly an ethnic joke), lay at the corner of Hester and Ludlow Streets. There, hats, suspenders, pants, poultry, fruits, eyeglasses, baked goods, and cigars were sold, the best bargains to be had on Friday, just before the Sabbath.

As a patrolman, my grandfather was assigned a beat, a few square blocks that was walked clockwise, with the right shoulder nearer the buildings. Roundsmen (later renamed sergeants) walked in the opposite direction, their left shoulders to the building, so they would come upon the patrolman doing his rounds. During the nighttime, a patrolman's duty was mostly to check the locks on doors and windows, move vagrants and drunks along, and look in on the open businesses, mostly bars and gambling halls in my grandfather's precinct, to make sure nothing was amiss.

Throughout his precinct the fumes of breweries and illegal stills mixed with the smell of fish and onion that emanated from the Jewish tenements—and the horse manure that covered most of the streets. There were perhaps 500 bars east of the Bowery and south of Fourteenth Street then, and most of them made their own whiskey.

At night, the streets were rife with small-time criminals and fences. In the parlance of the day, the 10th Precinct was "the crooked ward"; the Bowery, lined with bawdy saloons, gambling joints, and whorehouses, was called Thieves' Highway. Playing the numbers, then called policy betting, was the most prevalent form of gambling. But dogfights, cockfights, and boxing matches were also popular, along with procuring the services of transvestites and other prostitutes of every age. The whiskey in the Bowery was most times laced with camphor or other toxic additives. Cops called some of the saloons "sleeping cars," a reference to the fact that disreputable barkeeps administered "knockout drops," chloral hydrate, to some patrons, and then robbed them while they were unconscious, according to *Low Life* by Luc Sante. One hall on the Bowery, McGurk's, became infamous and a tourist attraction for headquartering a suicide craze. McGurk's clientele was partly longtime prostitutes from the strip. These down-and-outers, too old and ugly to make a living at their trade, would find final solace in McGurk's by drinking carbolic acid, then the transportation mode of choice to the next world. McGurk made no attempt at concealing the morbid allure of his saloon. On the contrary, above his doorway an electric sign—the first on the Bowery—garishly blared "McGurk's Suicide Hall." In 1899, seven suicide attempts were made at McGurk's, six of them successful. McGurk himself was even known to offer impromptu eulogies over his just-former customers' bodies. But suicides were not confined only to McGurk's. The term "the Dutch act" was coined because of the frequent suicides in the German quarters of the 10th Precinct ("Dutch" being a term for German, i.e., "Deutsch").

# 2

In my grandfather's day, the captain of the 10th Precinct was one William Devery. Perhaps there has never been a cop as powerful and corrupt as Devery. His ties to the political machine were as thick as the blocks of the very hall of Tammany itself. His father, a mason, helped in the construction of the Tammany building on Fourteenth Street. As a child, Devery would deliver his father's lunch pail. Like my grandfather, he was a born and bred New Yorker. There, however, any similarity between the two ended.

A bear of a man, weighing 250 pounds, Devery was known for his white-hot temper, colorful personality, and blatant and unrepentant corruption. While my grandfather would sit in the cheap bleacher seats at the old Polo Grounds to watch his beloved Giants play, Captain Devery and his partner, the gambler and bookmaker Frank Farrell, owned the New York Highlanders, a team later sold to Colonel Jacob Ruppert and renamed the New York Yankees. Devery's own fortune was once estimated at $300,000, more even than the aristocrat Teddy Roosevelt had.

Devery would rise to the highest rank in the department, chief of police, after a Tammany coup broke Republican control of the police board. Yet even at that lofty perch, he would operate his network of police protection each night from a West Side street corner. A steady stream of gambling bosses, pimps, and criminals of every imaginable type would report—with envelopes stuffed with cash—to him personally. When the *Mail and Express* printed a menu of prices police charged for protection, including $50 a month for pool-hall gambling houses, $25 a month for rumrunners, 80 percent of thefts, and $3,000 a year for an illegal abortionist to ply his trade, one of Devery's inner circle suggested that Devery assign a detective to find out where the leaks where coming from. Devery responded in his usual irreverent way: "A detective? We need a plumber!"

As is the case today, cops, especially corrupt ones, made great copy. Lincoln Steffens, then a police-beat reporter, referred to Devery once as a "lovely villain." One of Devery's duties as chief of police was to preside over departmental trials, which often he did drunk. The defendant was usually one of his minions brought up on charges of corruption. Devery was known to advise them from the bench. One of his favorite sermons—"When ye're caught with the goods, don't say nothin' "—was perhaps the foundation of the NYPD's blue wall of silence. To Devery, the sin wasn't the crime itself, but getting caught.

By all accounts, my grandfather had an easygoing, mild temperament. My mother says that he was soft-spoken, with a dry wit. She remembers one story he told about a cop who had to write a report of a horse that died on Kosciuszko Street. The cop couldn't spell the location, so he dragged the animal around to Smith Street.

My grandfather thought of himself as something of a boulevardier. He would dress in a fine tweed suit, wear a flower in his lapel, and frequent the dance halls around the city. Before he was married, he dated a number of women he met at those halls. But, as is often the case with Irishmen, even Irish Americans, he remained the devoted son. He lived with his mother, above the candy store, until he was married at twenty-eight. His gentle nature, however, was not the best of fits for the head-breaking ways of the police department in those days. Probably the cop of that era best known for ruthlessness was Alexander "Clubber" Williams.

Born in Canada of Irish descent in 1839, Williams worked as a shipbuilder in Key West and Japan and as a ship's carpenter and longshoreman in New York before he joined the police department in 1866. A towering, powerfully built man, Williams immediately earned a reputation for taking on the toughest characters in his precincts. His first day on the job, in a Brooklyn precinct, he entered a saloon to arrest two known criminals. When they resisted, he threw both of them through the saloon's plate-glass front window. His reputation served him well, and he quickly rose through the ranks of the department. In 1876, he was assigned the captain's post at the 29th Precinct, the Tenderloin, a name that Williams himself bestowed upon it. Of all the precincts then in the city, the Tenderloin, filled with every conceivable establishment of vice (along with legitimate entertainment like the Metropolitan Opera House and the Broadway theaters) was by far the most lucrative for corruption. Upon learning he was to be transferred there, Williams remarked, "All my life I've never had anything but chuck steak; now I'm going to get me some tenderloin." Even as captain, Williams was known to prowl the street, holding his nightstick over his shoulder, ready to administer a beating to anyone he deemed deserving. And no one was exempt. Augustine E. Costello, a newspaperman and author, who wrote a flattering ode to the police department called *Our Police Protectors* but also published Clubber Williams's famous tenderloin remark, was beaten senseless in the 29th Precinct house after Clubber arrested him without charge.

Though Williams became a kind of poster boy for the rough cop of the day, he was by no means the only one. Jacob Riis, a photographer and journalist who became famous for his exposés of tenement life, reported an example of an average cop's handiwork. A crowd of onlookers had gathered to watch a building fire. A beat cop approached and attempted to disperse the crowd by singling out a particularly interested citizen and cracking him full force across the back with his nightstick. The man, stout, with a full beard, buckled in pain and quickly obeyed. Riis, who was watching at a close distance, approached the policeman and informed him that he had just clubbed the former president of the United States, Ulysses S. Grant.

During his term as police board president, a position later

called commissioner, Teddy Roosevelt often made midnight excursions to the seedier precincts in the hope of exposing police corruption and dereliction of duty. Usually accompanying him were Riis and Lincoln Steffens. One of Roosevelt's favorite destinations was the 10th Precinct. One night, in the 10th, he came upon a cop in close conversation with a prostitute. When the commissioner asked the cop what he thought he was doing, the officer threatened to "fan" him with his billy club. When Roosevelt identified himself, the officer turned and ran at full gallop down the street, with the prostitute in hot pursuit.

Still, the public at large seemed complacent about police brutality. Each year in May, the department held a parade down Broadway. Behind a full brass band, thousands of cops—sometimes as much as a third of the entire force—marched in uniform, led, in Devery's day, by the fat chief on horseback. Along the route, tens of thousands would watch and shout, "The finest!" as the parade passed. Their laudatory cheers became part of the city's nomenclature. Even today, the NYPD is often referred to as New York's Finest. The only problem was, back then some of the criminals cheered as loud as the honest citizens.

In 1894, a partisan Republican commission headed by Clarence Lexow, a New York state senator from Rockland County, was formed to investigate election abuses by Tammany but evolved into a scrutiny of police corruption. The commission was established after several sermons—more like searing attacks—on the department and its vice-fueled graft by the Reverend Charles Parkhurst. Parkhurst, the minister of the staid (and mostly Republican) Madison Square Presbyterian Church, was also the president of the New York Society of Prevention of Crime, an organization devoted to closing whorehouses and other lurid establishments in the city. The Reverend's homilies made front-page news (Parkhurst himself had notified the press that his speeches would be newsworthy), and swelled antipolice sentiment among the more powerful and rich New York City Republicans. The police fired

back by demanding Parkhurst provide evidence of police impro-
prieties, and that he deliver such evidence in front of a grand jury
made up of Tammany sympathizers. Parkhurst set out to do exactly that. He hired a private detective named Charles Gardner to
personally guide him through the underbelly of the New York
night. What Parkhurst witnessed repulsed him. One establishment offered the services of male prostitutes to homosexuals; another featured gambling on matches between wild dogs and rat
packs. All of the vice-laden institutions Parkhurst witnessed operated with seemingly little concern for anonymity. He presented
his proof to a grand jury, which, because of the attending publicity, was more independent than the one first formed, and forced
the transfer of all but one of the precinct captains in the districts
he had toured. Those transfers, however, did nothing to change
things—and, in fact, were a boon to the replacements, because it
was customary for vice operations to pay $500 to new precinct
commanders.

Though in some circles Parkhurst was elevated to the exalted
level of a "saintly" reformer, among the denizens of the night, and
even the regular working class, Parkhurst was a joke. Many of
these saw his crusade against the police and vice as more an ethnic
attack on German and Irish immigrants than the righteous battle
against evil that the reverend professed to be waging. The police
department and Tammany, whose constituency was made up
wholly of immigrants and the children of immigrants, used their
leverage with the lower classes in a publicity war against Parkhurst. Before the grand jury assembled, Devery arrested Gardner,
Parkhurst's detective, for procuring the services of prostitutes and
attempting to bribe a madam. According to police testimony,
Gardner was seen playing "leapfrog" with a prostitute during one
of Parkhurst's tours, with the good Reverend looking on. The
story was quickly entered into folklore of the street, but with one
little change. This variation of the ditty "Ta-Ra-Ra-Boom-De-
Ay" was a big hit in the dives of the Tenderloin:

*Dr. Parkhurst on the floor*
*Playing leapfrog with a whore,*
*Ta-ra-ra-boom-de-ay,*
*Ta-ra-ra-boom-de-ay.*

The later Lexow Committee's findings, however, wouldn't be as lenient as the grand jury's, and as a result of the commission many members of the New York City police department's upper echelon, including William Devery, were fired. Some even faced jail time. Still, none of these punishments stood on appeal, and two years later, in 1896, Devery was reinstated.

To my knowledge, my grandfather didn't commit many sins as a young policeman, at least not sins of the magnitude of Devery and his lot. There are no records of departmental disciplinary actions taken against him. (Though the police department was permeated with corruption, it did go through the motions, as exemplified by Devery's court, to give the appearance that it policed itself. "Clubber" Williams, for example, was brought up on departmental charges 358 times, even fined 224 times. Each of these actions, however, was strictly ornamental, and the fines were minuscule compared to the amount Williams was making off the streets.) Nor was my grandfather involved in any sensational arrests. In fact the most dramatic event that happened to him in his early years on the beat had nothing to do with the police department at all. It was an event, however, that changed his life forever.

# 3

As he stood at the altar in 1895, he might not have realized it, but my grandfather was marrying not only the Erin beauty beside him but her family as well, and, for that matter, the whole of Ireland. His new bride might have immigrated to America a few years before, but as far as she was concerned, she brought the Old Sod with her.

Julia Murphy was born on St. Patrick's Day, 1875, in County Kildare, Ireland. When she was fifteen, she emigrated to the United States, following her older sister, Mary, who had come over a few years before. Often, older brothers or sisters would make the voyage from Ireland to America first to set things up, then send for their younger siblings. From what my mother says, her Aunt Mary was independent and strong-willed, characteristics that helped her to survive in the new land. By the time Julia arrived, Mary was already "forelady" in a millinery company on East Ninth Street.

Mary was an artist, and one of her duties was to go to the stores on Fourteenth Street and Broadway to sketch the expensive hats in the windows. Back downtown, milliners would make cheaper versions. According to my mother, artists ran in the Murphy family. A sister, Nora, who stayed in Ireland, was an art teacher and something of a Bohemian. During the summer, she would travel to the south of Ireland. There, our family lore says, she became friendly with George Bernard Shaw.

Julia had made the voyage with her sister Bessie. Mary had arranged jobs for them both: Bessie was to be a seamstress in a company called Swartz that made uniform pants (policemen were among their most frequent customers), and Julia would have a place in the millinery company where Mary worked. The three sisters lived together in an apartment on East Seventh Street. Like most new immigrants, they needed to pool their wages to afford housing, and they needed to be within walking distance of their jobs.

Julia, it seems, hated New York. It was far too crowded and smelly, with foreigners speaking languages she had never heard and dressing in ways that she had never seen. What's more, even at fifteen, she found herself fighting off the advances of lascivious men almost every day. Julia was both blessed and cursed with astounding beauty. Her neck was long and graceful, her features perfect, her face softly angular, her eyes hypnotically dark.

Mary protected her younger sister with ferocity. During the day, at work, she kept a watchful eye on her, and at night she forbade her to leave the cramped and stuffy apartment. Perhaps because of her confinement and uncomfortable feelings in her new environment, Julia became more and more unhappy. When she was seventeen, Mary arranged a job for her, away from New York, as a chambermaid for a wealthy family in Bar Harbor, Maine. In the summer of 1892, Julia packed her suitcase, said a tearful goodbye to her sisters, and boarded a train north. But the change in scenery did little to perk up her spirits, and she found that she couldn't run from her beauty. The family in Maine had a Filipino houseguest who stayed most of the first summer Julia worked there. He would leave amorous notes under lamps and cushions for her to find as she cleaned. Several times, Julia found herself alone with the houseguest in close quarters—in hallways or in the pantry—and narrowly escaped his advances. She complained to the head housekeeper, who at first disregarded her tale as the fantasy of a young girl—that is, until she found one of the houseguest's notes. One day soon after, the housekeeper, a bull of an Irishwoman with burning red cheeks, confronted the man. "You keep your yellow hands to yourself," she warned him. And from then on the Filipino left Julia alone.

For Julia, Maine was only a little better than New York. And it was still not Ireland, for which she was desperately homesick. What's more, she missed her sisters terribly. After only a year and a half, she returned to New York and again lived with Mary.

If there was any solace in New York for Julia, it was the number of Irish who lived there. And when she returned, now nearly nineteen, she began to socialize at church gatherings and Irish ladies'-society dances. Though Mary looked upon Julia's newfound independence with a jaundiced eye, her younger sister had matured while she was away, and a rebellious streak, not unlike Mary's own, had awakened.

One of Julia's favorite dances was held at Webster Hall, not far from Mary's apartment, on Thursday nights. The dance was called maid's night out, because of the preponderance of single domestic servants who attended. Though, at one time, social functions such as these were restricted to native-born Irish (and were usually run by Irish county societies like the Limerickmen, Meathmen, and Wexfordmen), by Julia's day the doors were open to first-generation Irish-Americans. Still, the overwhelming majority of those who frequented the dances were Irish born. The music was gay, even raucous, with virtuoso step-dancers, and set dances consisting of four couples whirling around the floor. But there were also the more intimate partner dances, called couple dances or two-hand dances, to a waltz or a polka.

Julia was extremely popular, and seldom did a set go by that she wasn't escorted onto the floor. One night, a man with a jaunty mustache and a mischievous glint in his eye approached her and asked for a dance. As he spoke, she was quite surprised that he didn't have an Irish brogue. And on the dance floor, she was impressed with his mastery and grace, and a bit amused when he whispered in her ear if he could call on her at home.

"Well, now. That depends," she said, eyeing him coyly. "What is it that you do for work?"

"I'm a policeman," came the answer.

"Thomas Skelly the policeman, is it?" Julia said capriciously.

In 1896, my grandfather was transferred to the 13th Precinct. The 13th bordered the 10th, extending east to the East River. The characteristics of the two precincts were pretty much the same except, as you neared the river, the population in the tenements became even denser. Germans and Jews still dominated the inland neighborhoods, but the buildings along the river were heavily Irish. The smell of lager beer and fish and onions gave way to that of boiled cabbage, and, of course, there was still the odor of distilled whiskey. The transfer also came along with a raise in pay: Tom's salary was now $1,150 a year. He and Julia could have afforded an apartment in just about any section of Manhattan save Fifth Avenue and its environs. But Julia was not willing to give up her family, even if seeing them only meant a short ride downtown.

In her defense, being a cop's wife in those years meant spending much of your time alone. Cops then worked nine-hour shifts, and most often were required to remain "on reserve" in the station house for an additional six hours. Usually, patrolmen were given one day and one night off in eight-day rotations, and their time off hardly ever fell the same way two weeks in a row. It was commonplace for cops to work thirty-six hours straight, and not unusual for them to sleep on a cot in the dormitory of the precinct house for four or five nights running.

In October 1896, Julia gave birth to the Skellys' first child, Walter. Born prematurely and nursed in the cold, drafty tenement, Walter didn't have much of a chance. He died one year, three months, and twenty-seven days after he was born. Walter had contracted bronchopneumonia and, according to his death certificate, had convulsed for five days before he expired.

Devastated after the death of her child, Julia gave in to her husband's urgings that the tenements were no place to begin a family. She agreed to move uptown, to 106 East Eighty-ninth Street. One year later, in 1899, my grandfather was transferred to the 28th Precinct in Yorkville. He was now living and working where he had grown up. He knew the shopkeepers and the neighborhood folk. The new apartment was airy and bright, in a fine building not too far from Park Avenue. Julia gave birth to two healthy babies, Marion, called Mazzie, in 1898, and Tom Junior in 1900. And even though Julia's sisters and other family members made the journey uptown far too often for his liking, my grandfather had every reason to believe his life was in perfect order.

# 4

The side-wheel steamboat called the *General Slocum* had been hired for Wednesday, June 15, 1904, by St. Mark's Evangelical Lutheran Church on Sixth Street between First and Second Avenues, the spiritual center of a densely populated German community called Weiss Garten (White Garden). The outing involved a short cruise to the north shore of Long Island, where a picnic was to be held. At nine o'clock that morning 1,300 churchgoers, mostly women and children, boarded the vessel at the Third Street pier. According to newspaper reports of the day, the children's laughter could be heard for blocks.

Named after a Civil War officer who went on to become a congressman, the *General Slocum* with its great paddles was a familiar sight on the river. The captain, William Van Schaick, had the year before been given an award for safely transporting 35 million passengers. The June 15, 1904, fire started in a forward hold called the lamp room, in which were stored a barrel of kerosene, a barrel of benzene, and glassware packed in hay. Investigators believed that a kerosene lamp exploded in the hold, setting the hay ablaze and then igniting the kerosene. The fire is believed to have started as far south as Fifty-fifth Street and was burning out of control by the time the boat had steamed abeam Blackwell's Light, on a dot of an island across from Eighty-sixth Street. The engineer and mates on the steamer futilely fought the blaze as worn fire hoses burst from the water pressure. What's more, the captain was not notified for seven precious minutes. During that time the *General Slocum* sailed into the treacherous currents of Hell Gate, sealing the fate of many aboard. When finally notified, Van Schaick made the disastrous decision to try and make North Brother Island, a two-and-a-half-mile-square patch of land in the arm of the East River that leads to the Long

Island Sound. During the mile-and-a-half-long trip through the racing waters, the *General Slocum* burned like a bonfire. Passengers who jumped into the water were swallowed by the currents. The canvas of their life preservers was ripped and worn, the corking inside crumbled like stale bread. But an even worse fate awaited those who chose to stay aboard.

As the alarm sounded in the Eighty-eighth Street station house, my grandfather and two dozen other patrolmen, including Thomas Cooney, scrambled into wagons that headed north along the Manhattan shoreline. Tugboats and other vessels shuttled the police to North Brother Island. The river tug my grandfather and Cooney boarded was called the *Wade*. As it neared the burning wreckage, Cooney dove into the river. Newspaper reports said that he single-handedly rescued ten people from the gurgling water, swimming back again and again to the tug with hysterical survivors clutching him around the neck. My mother said that Tom stayed on the tug, pulling aboard those whom Cooney and others saved from the river. Meanwhile, the steamer was an inferno. From the deck of the *Wade* my grandfather and crew members watched helplessly as people were burned alive. At one point, a deck buckled and snapped, catapulting passengers into the river, some with their clothing ablaze, like fiery human arrows.

With confusion and death all around him, my grandfather didn't notice that his partner, Cooney, had been swallowed by the water. No one on the *Wade* did. Only when the tug, filled with survivors barely clinging to life, headed back toward North Brother Island, did my grandfather realize that Cooney was missing. Frantically, he and the mates searched the tug, and the black waters strewn with bodies and burning debris, but Cooney was nowhere to be found.

Much later that afternoon, his body, along with hundreds of others, was pulled from the water.

All that night of the *General Slocum* disaster, and throughout the following day, river vessels and horse-drawn hearses shuttled the bodies to the Twenty-sixth Street Pier in Manhattan. Relatives lined up for blocks to identify the bodies laid out in rows on the pier. That Friday there were hundreds of services in thirty-seven different churches, including 114 at St. Mark's Evangelical Lutheran alone. For days afterward, police officers and volunteers on river vessels searched for the dead. Each day, the gruesome body count in the newspapers rose, finally reaching over one thousand.

Captain Van Schaick faced criminal charges. He was found negligent in his duty and sent to Sing Sing prison after being sentenced to ten years. Blinded in the accident, the captain was pardoned by President William Howard Taft after serving three and a half years. The disaster shattered the community of Weiss Garten. In the following years most of the residents, unable to live with the horrible memory of the *General Slocum*, moved out of the Lower East Side, a great number of them settling in the Yorkville section, which remained a German enclave for the next seventy years.

I imagine my grandfather was a hero the day of the *General Slocum* disaster. I can imagine his heroism a lot easier than I can imagine him. He left no letters, scrapbooks, or even photographs. I did locate a photograph of him in the archives of the Museum of the City of New York. The group shot, streaked and faded with time, was taken in 1912, in front of the 13th Precinct, which housed Traffic Squad B, his assignment at the time. The bottom part of his face, just below his mouth, is hidden by the high, rounded police hat on the officer in front of him. All the men look pretty much the same: Most have bushy handlebar mustaches; all wear a dark frock coat with a double line of copper buttons. My grandfather's mustache is the most neatly trimmed, and it turns slightly upward at the corners of his mouth. He wears a thin, almost imperceptible smile. There seems to be a glint in his eye.

Almost one hundred years ago, he lived and worked in the same neighborhood I live in now: Yorkville. The old Eighty-eighth Street precinct house—now an upscale redbrick building filled with young professionals who pay thousands a month in rent—stood on the next block behind my apartment; his beat could have brought him right past my front stoop. Once in a while, mostly at night, I walk to his old precinct's address, 432 East Eighty-eighth Street, and close my eyes and pretend that I've been transported back in time. And, if the street is quiet enough, I can almost see the cops mustered out in front, each of them wearing bobby-style hats and navy blue coats. In my mind's eye, I can see Tom Skelly, my grandfather, his finger pulling on the end of his dapper mustache as he whispers an amusing story to the cop standing next to him.

Two blocks from the station house are Carl Schurz Park and a promenade that overlooks the East River. At night, the lights from Gracie Mansion, the mayor's home, cast jagged shadows across the walkway from the trees and fence that surround the mansion. The river is a wide ribbon of oily blackness on which gracefully slide weighty tankers nudged by tugs. The grace of these big ships belies the ferocious currents beneath. A tidal river, the East flows alternately in both directions with an amazing force. A cop from the NYPD's scuba unit once told me that on a simulated rescue maneuver he jumped in the river at Fourteenth Street and was swept north to Ninety-sixth Street, over four miles away, in less than ten minutes. The swirling currents at the confluence of the East and Harlem Rivers are some of the most dangerous in the United States. There, off the shore of Wards Island, once was a favored dumping spot for mob hit men, their victims bound with masking tape in the trunks of Ford Galaxies and Chevy Novas, their final resting place waiting soundlessly at the bottom of the river.

When I think of my grandfather on the tug that day, and of Cooney's ultimate sacrifice, a welling begins at the bottom of my lungs. The feeling is a familiar one to me. Throughout my life, every time I read a story about hero cops or see sad news footage of them, I experience it. The written history of the New York City police department has always been punctuated with scandal, brutality, and the most criminal of actions, perhaps more in some eras than others, but still as consistent as commas. But throughout those pages of its history, the police department has also been as consistent in incredible heroism. When I look at photographs of the soot-covered policemen holding the crumpled, blackened bodies of the seamstresses who died in the 1911 Triangle Shirtwaist Factory fire; or listen to Police Officer Stephen McDonald, paralyzed in a wheelchair and hooked to a respirator, forgive the young black man whose bullet put him there; or watch the news footage of the World Trade Center bombing and the blue shirts carrying people to safety; or see any news story of the funeral of a cop killed in the line of duty—the images of the grieving widow and children—my soul clenches. But, until now, I have always kept those feelings to myself.

# 5

Though the mayoral election of 1901 (Seth Low, a former mayor of Brooklyn and president of Columbia University, was elected mostly on his promise to reform the police department) brought sweeping changes, and finally the end of William Devery's reign, the NYPD of the early part of the twentieth century was still rife with corruption. Tammany politico-cum-gangsters like Big Tim Sullivan were still very much in charge. In an April 2, 1902, telegram to *The New York Times*, the Reverend Parkhurst described the situation this way: "We had supposed that the administration was going to reform the police. It looks as though the police were going to reform the administration."

In early 1905, my grandfather was offered the position of doorman at a Tammany-run betting shop. It might have come as a reward for his taking part in the rescue on the river. Though the
post meant working throughout most of the night, and though he
would be surrounded by hard and sordid characters, it was a lucrative job. Not only would he continue drawing a salary from the
police department, he would also be paid as much, if not more, by
the gambling establishment.

In all respects, that year should have been a banner one for my
grandfather. He now had over five years at the 28th Precinct, and,
no doubt, had settled into a familiar routine. As a result of the
*General Slocum* tragedy, he had proved his mettle as a policeman,
and was well respected in his precinct. He had moved his family
to a bigger apartment, around the corner from Eighty-ninth
Street, on Lexington Avenue. And, to top it off, the Giants won
the 1905 World Series, beating the Philadelphia Athletics on the
strength of three shutouts by Christy Mathewson. Things were
moving along just fine. That was, until he turned down the doorman position.

As a young father then, Tom Skelly had matured out of his
boulevardier days. At night he would sit in his parlor, wearing a
velvet smoking jacket (the annual Christmas gift from Julia and
the children), a Camel cigarette burning on an ashtray next to
him, reading the sports section of the *Evening World* to see how
his Giants had fared that afternoon. Unlike his father, who was
endowed with an immigrant's motivation to succeed in the new
land, my grandfather was content with a policeman's salary—it
was quite enough to keep his family warm and healthy, with a few
dollars left over for a night or two a week at the local tavern. He
was of the first generation of New York's civil servants, a forerunner of generations to come who would live within the financial
bounds and constrictions of their careers, trading any dreams of
riches—at least of honest ones—for job security and a pension.

Years later, he told my mother that he turned the offer down because he simply didn't think policemen should be involved with gambling. But he also knew quite well that once he was on the Tammany payroll there was no turning back. Though many cops filled their pockets with graft, many more lost any vestige of a pension while in the clutches of the Hall. For cops who fell from favor but retained their jobs, though, the fate might have been even worse.

By one news account of the day, after arresting the keeper of a Tammany-protected saloon for opening on Sunday, a patrolman was transferred, or "railroaded," six times in four months. According to *The Police Establishment*, by William Turner, a patrolman named Jeremiah Moran, who had refused to contribute to various Tammany-held organizations, was, in the space of one year, transferred from 126th Street in Manhattan to Astoria, Queens, then to Flushing, and finally to the recesses of Whitestone in the Bronx. Turner wrote, "Moran no longer bothered to unpack." It was not at all uncommon for cops to pay a "protection fee" of $25 a year to guard against being transferred, but even that was of little help if you were on the bad side of the Hall. In refusing to toe the Tammany line, my grandfather must have known he had taken quite a risk. Perhaps, having lived in Yorkville his whole life, he thought that his deep roots in the neighborhood would provide protection against any Tammany repercussions. It didn't.

Almost immediately after he turned down the offer, he was sent to the 3rd Precinct on Greenwich Street in Greenwich Village. His commute to the Lower West Side, the opposite corner of the island of Manhattan from where he lived, was, on good days, an hour by trolley car. Add two hours a day for travel to the already inhuman hours cops then worked, and my grandfather hardly ever saw his wife and children's faces. But Tammany's wrath didn't end there. By the time Tom's twenty-six-year police career was over, he would work in seven different precincts: the 10th, 13th, 28th, 3rd, 2nd, Traffic A, and Traffic B. What's more, he would stay at the same salary, then $1,400 annually, for the next sixteen years. It was 1918, a year before he retired, by the time he received his next raise—$50 a year.

My grandfather endured these hardships because he had no other option. At the time of his Greenwich Village transfer, he had already served twelve years in the department, just eight years short of retirement and pension. He was also nearing forty. For a man that age, in those times, starting over would be just about impossible.

Just as my grandfather became accustomed to the long trip to Greenwich Village, he was transferred again, this time to the precinct that operated out of City Hall—still not an easy commute from the Upper East Side. But, by the time he was sent to the City Hall Precinct, technology had jumped one step ahead of even the malevolent minds of Tammany. In 1904, the Interborough Rapid Transit subway opened, making the commute to City Hall from Brooklyn a breeze. In 1905, my grandfather moved his family to Brooklyn.

The house he bought was on Fifty-fifth Street, some distance from the brand-new subway station, but easily accessible to it by trolley car. Though his finances were such that he had to take a considerable mortgage on his purchase, the house had an apartment on the first floor, and the rental income would help considerably with the payments.

As the Tappan Zee Bridge and Palisades Parkway would do fifty years later, the subway kindled a migration of cops who worked in lower Manhattan, to Brooklyn neighborhoods like the one in which my grandfather settled. The trend also mirrored the Pearl River phenomenon in other ways. It was the forerunner to the later American dream, of houses with backyards and, for cops, insulation and isolation from the stress and seediness of the places where they worked. My grandfather's next-door and down-the-block neighbors were both assigned to the City Hall Precinct, and the three of them (whenever they worked the same shifts) would ride the newfangled contraption together as it rattled its way underneath the East River.

The move to Brooklyn, my mother says, brightened my grandfather's view of his job, and his life. Not only was he now a home owner, but he also had distanced himself—despite the subway—from his wife's family. Throughout the time they lived in Yorkville, Julia had held open their apartment doors to her relatives newly arrived from Ireland. My grandfather had once remarked to his wife: "Do the Irish even know what a hotel is?" My mother's oldest sister, Mazzie, often said that my grandfather's first order of business in Brooklyn was to hang the pictures of his wife's family—which covered the walls of the apartment in Yorkville—in the bathroom of the new home. My grandfather delighted in needling his wife about her heritage. Sometimes, after a few drinks, he would sing:

*My name is O'Brien, I'm from Harlem,*
*I'm an Irishman as you can see,*
*I can sing like a thrush or a starlin', or the little bird up in the tree,*
*They tell me to go over to England,*
*And pay a short visit to France,*
*And there to bring out my new fashion,*
*And call it the high-water pants. . . .*

Still, my grandfather was careful to take his raillery only so far. Julia had the quintessential Irish temper, and ultimately, at home, she was the boss. The pictures didn't hang in the bathroom for long.

Julia also took responsibility for finding a tenant for the apartment, which she did, only a week or so after her family moved in upstairs. My grandfather came home from work that day to find his wife sitting with a young couple in the backyard having tea. My mother says he wasn't thrilled with Julia's choice of tenants. The couple's name was Baruch, and they were Jewish.

During the early years of the twentieth century, hundreds of thousands of Jews emigrated to the United States from Eastern Europe. This tidal wave of people had followed a similar flow of Irish a few years before. This dynamic caused a natural animosity between the two ethnic groups. Language barriers and suspicion of different customs and beliefs formed walls behind which Jews and Irish (along with Germans and Italians) huddled tightly in isolation from each other. For the Irish cops, this division was farther exacerbated by the distrust the Jews had for the new land's legal system (perhaps for good reason). In the Jewish wards of the 10th and 13th Precincts, people believed fervently in policing themselves. Criminal justice was handed out not in city courts but by elders in temple. But as the influx of Jews continued, their criminal element spilled from the insular community to the city at large. In 1908, Police Commissioner Theodore A. Bingham wrote in *The North American Review* that fully half the criminals in New York were Jewish. His remarks were considered inflammatory and out of proportion by the Jewish community, but undoubtedly there was a burgeoning Jewish criminal problem. Ruthless Jewish gangs like the Eastmans, named after their leader, Edward "Monk" Eastman (born Osterman), prowled the Lower East Side. Though Big Tim Sullivan was still the overall crime boss of the East Side, and Eastman and other gangs paid the appropriate homage to him, Sullivan fully realized that Jewish gangs were a growing force to be reckoned with. He even took to wearing a yarmulke and attending Jewish services as an act of gangland diplomacy.

The Baruchs, however, were far from being criminals. The downstairs apartment was often filled with the graceful notes of classical music played on a Victrola or the muted sounds of the piano playing. They were educated and sophisticated to a level that Julia—and later, even my grandfather—admired. They were also family oriented. While they lived in my grandfather's house, the

Baruchs raised a son named André, who grew up to become a radio personality and star in early television.

Julia didn't give a second thought to renting the apartment to Jews. As far as she was concerned, it mattered little what ethnicity her tenants were, as long as the rent was on time and they were clean and quiet. As in all of their family squabbles—though my grandfather would grouse for a while—Julia would ultimately have her way.

In 1910, my grandfather was transferred again, this time from the 2nd Precinct to Traffic Sub Division A. He would spend the last nine years of his police career as a traffic cop. By all accounts, he was perfectly content with his new assignment. He didn't have to walk a beat in the crime-infested tenement neighborhoods. He didn't have to sleep on the lumpy cots in the station house. In the Traffic Division, he wouldn't have to answer to crooked captains or Tammany bosses. But perhaps most important, he wouldn't have to witness graft among his brethren in the rank and file.

In the police code of the day, William Devery's code, a canon that would survive throughout the history of the NYPD, the worst offense any cop could commit—even an honest cop—was to inform on other policemen. In one published report from my grandfather's day (reprinted in *The Blue Parade* by Tom Repetto), an honest policeman was asked whether, if he had witnessed a cop take a bribe, he would report it. The honest cop answered: "I wasn't born in Ireland, but my father and mother were, and thank God! none of my name were ever informers either in the old country or in this. I would be ashamed to look my children in the face if I turned informer. . . . My father was ninety years of age when he died and he used to tell us children of the fate that followed informers in Ireland—the devil would sometimes claim their bodies even before they got to the graveyard and to the tenth generation ill-luck, misfortune and a curse went with them. . . . Show me a 'squealer' . . . and I will show you a fella who had a heart of a coward and a disgrace to the police."

Though Tom enjoyed a joke at the expense of his Irish in-laws, his devotion to his mother and reverence toward his father's work ethic imbued him with the deepest respect for the Irish and the hardships they endured. And, aside from their lighthearted bickering, and along with her beauty, it was his wife's strong Irish will that drew him to her. He supported Julia when she began to collect nickels and dimes, kept in a coffee can in the cabinet over the stove, for Irish Freedom, an organization that funded the Irish struggles against the English, and he never tired of Julia telling the story of her father being jailed by the English for harboring Fenian rebels. Though my grandfather had every reason to resent the Irish Tammany regime, this animosity did not filter down to the cops with whom he worked day in and day out, even when his refusal to toe the Tammany line meant shunning by some in his ranks. For my grandfather, an assignment to the traffic squad was an oasis, as far from the Tammany graft machine as he could get and still be able to wear the blue uniform of the police department.

The traffic squad also meant steady workdays and regular days off. His schedule was eight a.m. to five p.m. Monday through Friday, and half a day every other Saturday. His free Saturday afternoons were frequently spent at the Polo Grounds. In the teens and twenties, baseball games rarely took longer than two hours, not like the three- and four-hour marathons of today. Players would run on and off the field like they had dinner reservations. My grandfather would usually be on the train by five o'clock and home for dinner.

This is not to say that it was a cushy job. To be a traffic cop in 1910 was to be in the midst of insanity. The streets were a riotous mix of skittish horses and unreliable early automobiles. There were no crosswalks, no traffic lights, no traffic signals at all. In 1912, 38,000 automobiles were registered in New York; they were still the exception rather than the rule. The biggest problem with automobiles in that day was an epidemic of runaways—cars that, left idling because of the difficulty in starting them, had slipped into gear. But trying to control horse-drawn traffic was harder by far than any problem even today's automobile traffic poses. Tom Skelly's first traffic post, on lower Broadway, was a main trucking and passenger route to downtown Manhattan. A traffic cop standing in the middle of the street staring at a team heading toward him, full gallop, was, to say the least, in a precarious situation. Only two years before he arrived in traffic were the first rudimentary regulations put into effect, requiring drivers to raise the whip to signal a stop, and keeping slower traffic to the right. In 1905, special legislation, with the backing of the courts, empowered traffic cops, and drivers started to take them seriously. Before then, traffic violations were considered a nuisance by the courts and were most times dismissed. Often magistrates would administer stern warnings to traffic cops not to clog their schedules with such trivialities. Disputes between horse-drawn truck drivers were commonplace, and fault in an accident was sorted out with fists on the street. Some years earlier, as police board president, Teddy Roosevelt had introduced a twenty-nine-member bicycle unit, known as the Scorcher Squad, to apprehend speeding horse-drawn trucks and carriages. The squad made over 1,300 arrests in its first year.

Besides vehicular traffic, the other serious concern was pedestrians. In those years, crossing a busy thoroughfare was a life-or-death proposition. For a while, traffic cops gave preferential treatment to pretty girls and important people. Because of this, an order was imposed "that under no conditions would traffic men take hold of any person by the arm for the purpose of escorting him or her across the street, except a blind person." Cops were then issued semaphore disks marked "Stop" and "Go" to control traffic.

My grandfather's last command was Traffic Sub Division B, where he stayed for six years. The fixed post was on Thirteenth

Street and Fourth Avenue, just a block south of Tammany Hall; his career had come full circle.

Though Tammany's influence with the police department would continue until Mayor Fiorello La Guardia's tenure thirty years later, the Hall's foundation had already begun to crack. One by one, the reigning lords of corruption left the police department. After his police career, and, without Tammany's backing, a failed attempt at a political one, William Devery lived in opulence in a townhouse on East Tenth Street and kept himself busy with significant real-estate interests in the beachfront community of Rockaway. Clubber Williams, too, lived well after his police career, spending most of his time in his Cos Cob estate, or in leisurely cruising on Long Island Sound on his steam-powered yacht. Big Tim Sullivan, however, wasn't so lucky. In 1912, while a congressman, he was committed to a private asylum for a mental breakdown. Some time later, he escaped the asylum and was run over by a train—a gruesome event that led to suspicions of foul play, which were never confirmed. For ten days his body lay in the morgue at Bellevue before a policeman recognized the former Tammany king of the Bowery underground.

The Thirteenth Street traffic post was on the main thoroughfare for wealthy bankers and financiers heading from their homes on Park or Fifth Avenue to Wall Street. My grandfather became friendly with a number of these princes of finance; at Christmastime the chauffeurs would stop the limousines, and gloved hands would appear out of back windows with envelopes for him, a few dollars in each. By today's standards this would be thought of as graft. But then, giving the beat or traffic cop a Christmas envelope was no different from giving a holiday gift to the postman or doorman. One Christmas, an executive of F.A.O. Schwarz on East Fourteenth Street gave Tom a wooden elephant on wheels. The toy was the high point of his children's Christmas that year, and, for years after, made the rounds, handed down from sibling to sibling.

By the late teens, my grandfather had witnessed a complete

changeover from horse-drawn transportation to automobiles. In the spring of 1919, a Wall Street banker he had become friendly with had his chauffeur pull the car over at Grandfather's post. The banker asked him if he planned to be a traffic cop the rest of his life. Tom considered the man's words carefully. He had been a policeman then for twenty-six years. For most of that time, he had struggled within a corrupt system, and was treated by it vindictively. Still, he had always found pride in wearing the uniform of the NYPD. As a little girl, after the family moved from Brooklyn to the Bronx, my mother waited at the central rail station for him to come home. "He always looked so spit-and-polished," she said. "His shoes had a glossy shine, and his gloves were so white. He would hold my hand as we walked together back to the apartment. Everyone seemed so friendly to him. People in the neighborhood would wave at him and say hello. People looked up to him, and respected him for being a policeman."

In June 1919, at the age of fifty-one, my grandfather took his wealthy friend up on his offer, and went to work as a bank guard for the Bank of New York on Fifth Avenue. The staid environment of banking was quite a change from the rough world of the police department. If there was corruption in the banking business, and undoubtedly there was, it was on a level that my grandfather would not be privy to, nor would it affect his life. He spent his next fifteen years wearing the bank guard's uniform, standing erect on the glimmering tile floor in the cavernous bank office, and smiling at the customers—men in high collars, women wearing fashionable bonnets. At night he would come home, now at the regular, respectable hour of just after four p.m., take off his still-shiny shoes, and rub his feet. Twenty-six years of walking a beat, directing traffic, and standing at a bank guard's post could be counted in bunions, calluses, and ingrown toenails.

For a while Tom owned a car, an Essex, and sometimes on weekends he would drive to Long Island to visit some of his old chums from the police department who had moved there when they retired. He stayed faithful to his Giants, and once in a while would attend a game. But as he grew older, his Sunday afternoons at the Polo Grounds became more and more infrequent.

Thomas Francis Skelly, my grandfather, died on June 6, 1935, at the age of sixty-seven. The wake was held, as wakes often were back then, in the parlor of his Bronx home. Some of his old neighbors from Yorkville came to pay their respects, as did several of the cops he had worked with over the years. Julia prepared ham and cabbage and bought plenty of booze—for in her hands, of course, it was an Irish wake. Gone was all my grandmother's youthful beauty. The years had left her heavy with jowls, and she had great, sad eyes. My mother remembers that her uncle Joe, my grandfather's younger brother, arrived at the wake carrying a giant arrangement of white carnations in the shape of a cross. She seldom saw her uncle. He was a big man, much bigger than his older brother, with a full, bushy mustache and great big hands. He, too, was a cop, but he was a first grade detective and worked in the "Silk Stocking District" of Park and Fifth Avenues. All my mother knew about him was that he owned a boat, which he kept on Long Island; that he lived in a nice apartment on the East Side; and that he was married to a German lady.

At the wake, he came to my mother and held her for a moment in his big hands. His eyes welled with grief, or remorse, or both, and his voice shook in a soft, deep timbre: "Your father was an honest cop" were the only words he said to her.

In late October 1997, I received an envelope from the New York City police department, finally a response to my many inquiries about my grandfather. Inside was the entire official record of Tom Skelly's police career—one sheet of paper, his pension certificate. On it are printed his date of entry into service, July 10, 1893; his retirement date, June 21, 1919; his badge number, 2790; and his annual pension, $825. Listed are the names and birth years of his wife and five children: Julia, 1875; Marion, 1898; Tom Junior, 1900;

Ruth, 1907; Eleanor, my mother, 1910; and Vincent, 1914. The certificate is stamped in large, hollow block letters, "DEAD"—his police career summed up in a few dry facts. Having lived with two more generations of New York City cops, and having been surrounded by hundreds of them my entire life, I wasn't surprised by the recorded indifference.

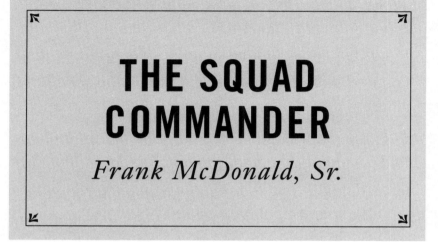

# THE SQUAD COMMANDER

*Frank McDonald, Sr.*

# 1

I am driving with my father across Route 84 in Pennsylvania toward Archbald, to see, in his words, where it all began. Eighty years old now, my father hasn't been there in many years, and in that time an extension to the highway has been built. When we took our exit the roads were unfamiliar to him. "Jaysus," he said, affecting his father's Irish brogue, as he did often when talking about his childhood. "You'd think I'd know the way. I sure as hell knew the way out of here."

I reassure him that his memory is not at fault, but progress. We pull into a gas station to ask directions to the Red Hill cut, the road through the mountains to the town where he grew up. When I ask the attendant at the station the way to Archbald his face breaks into a grin: "What do you want to go there for?" he says.

A coal-mining hamlet carved out of the anthracite-rich hills of northeastern Pennsylvania, Archbald had been built out of the sweat and stubbornness of miners at a time, the mid to late 1800s, when coal ran this country. The town lived by the union: first the

Knights of Labor, and later the United Mine Workers of America, which fought in legendary labor disputes, often went on strike, and eventually gained better working conditions and wages for its members. But it was the union's greed that led to the demise of the mining industry, and ultimately, to the decimation of Archbald. Strikes during the First World War necessitated the use of alternative fuels—most prominently, petroleum products. By the Great Depression, Archbald, and its coal-mining industry, were choking on the dust of poverty and despair.

As a child, I went with my family to Archbald once or twice, on trips to the Pocono Mountains. I laughed at the size of the house on Cemetery Street where my father lived with his younger brother, Joseph, and his mother and father. It seemed a quarter the size of our house in Pearl River, and lay on a plot of land no bigger than a throw rug. My father said the house was originally a one-room school, and had been converted into a home with a tiny parlor and a small kitchen downstairs, three bedrooms upstairs. Two of the bedrooms were so small, he explained, that you couldn't stand up in them, as they followed the contour of the steeply pitched roof.

I yawned at the stories of the Depression my father told on these trips or at the dinner table: The soup meat his mother would buy on Saturday, and how she would miraculously stretch it into meals for most of the week. Or how his house was heated only by an open hearth in the kitchen. You might as well have slept out of doors, he said, for all the heat in the bedrooms. And the house didn't have indoor plumbing until he was in high school. As children, he and his brother would bathe in a galvanized tub in the kitchen, the water heated on the hearth. My father said he remembers Pete, my grandfather, coming home from the mines and soaking his feet in the tub, his long johns pushed up to his knees and down to the middle of his ass as Mary, my grandmother, scrubbed the black soot from his back with a stiff brush. As my father and Joe grew older, they would shower at the shifting shanty, a communal shower room where the miners washed the black coal dust from their bodies after work. The shanty was a half-mile from home, and the brothers would make the trek carrying a towel and a bar of lard soap.

I never knew my paternal grandparents, Pete and Mary. They were both dead long before I was born. There were pictures of them in the house, though. In one, Pete is tall and gaunt, wearing round-framed glasses, looking like the man holding the pitchfork on the Kellogg's Cornflakes box. His ears are very large and shaped like a Chihuahua's. His nose is thin at the bridge, but flares wide at the nostrils. Though his mouth is turned down at the corners, it gives the impression that he is smiling, or rather, keeping something amusing to himself. There is also something mischievous in his coal-black eyes.

Mary is a very large woman, with great heavy breasts covered in a frilly blouse with puffy sleeves. She wears her hair neatly piled in a bun, which crowns a round, sweet face. Her lips are slightly pursed and her smile seems a little sad. I imagine her rising each morning at five a.m., stoking the fire, removing the socks, work shirts and long johns hung over the hearth to dry, then cooking breakfast, making Pete his lunch, and walking, stooped slightly forward from the weight she carries, the three quarters of a mile to St. Thomas Aquinas Church for six o'clock mass. I also imagine her rocking Pete, home from a two-week drunk, like a baby, weaning him off the horrors with a bottle of warm ale, stroking his matted hair and saying: "There, there. All done now, Pete. All done."

According to family lore, Pete's immigration from Ireland to the United States in 1883 had little to do with the poverty and oppression that afflicted most of the legions of Irish who arrived on these shores in the nineteenth century. Pete's father, Jerome McDonald, was a shopkeeper in Carrickmacross, County Monaghan, on the northern border of what is now the Republic of Ireland. He was also an exclusive distributor of Lipton tea—as you might well imagine, an enormously important commodity there. Pete's six brothers and sisters who remained in Ireland were all well educated and would never experience the hardship that Pete endured in the United States.

Now by modern standards, the events of that morning at Ballymackney school in Carrickmacross, which Pete and his younger brother Owen attended, would not have dictated the geographical relocation that Pete planned that evening as he stuffed his cloth bag with a few shirts, a change of underwear, and the statue of the Virgin Mary his mother had given him for his Holy Communion. But in the Ireland of those days, punching the schoolmaster, a person held in the utmost esteem—as important as any county official—was an offense of the highest order. And even though the schoolmaster, Snoodles McNally, wasn't a popular man and possessed a temperament that was irascible at best and especially rancid when he took a drink, which was most of the time, the townspeople would have never forgotten the incident, and a stigma would have been attached to Pete. He would forever be the boy who gave Snoodles McNally what-for.

The story goes that Pete had come to the aid of his younger brother, who was receiving a savage beating from the schoolmaster. But whether the punch, righteous as it may have been, was the only reason Pete decided, at that precise point, to come to America is not completely clear. More likely, the landing of Pete's straight right hand squarely on Snoodles McNally's nose was the crowning event of a series of indiscretions. By all family accounts, Pete was the most rebellious of the Carrickmacross McDonald clan, and because of these shenanigans, he was not his father's favorite. Whatever the precipitating reasons, that very evening, carrying his few belongings, Pete found his way to the port of Dundalk with just enough fare (his own savings and some money from his mother) for the voyage to America.

Pete entered himself on the ship's passenger list as a twenty-one-year-old laborer, which was a lie on both counts. The ship was filled with hundreds of other Irish. He passed the time of the voyage, which first stopped at Liverpool, then went on to New York, listening to the other passengers' tales of hopes and plans, and these undoubtedly lifted Pete's dampened spirits.

He wasn't completely alone when he arrived in America. Friends of the family, and a cousin or two from his mother's side, had made the voyage before him. But Pete once told my father that when he stood alone in Castle Garden at the southern tip of Manhattan, then the immigrants' portal to the new land, he cried for his mother and his home.

Pete might well have become a policeman, my father once told me, had he stayed in New York. Several of his cousins were then members of the police force. But at sixteen, he was far too young for police work, and lying about his age was likely to be more difficult there than it was on shipboard, where nobody cared as long as he paid his way. So one of his cousins found him a job as a gardener. By the time Pete was twenty-one, old enough to be a cop, he was far from New York.

His first job in America was at the Johnson estate in the Riverdale section of the Bronx. Wealthy landowners, the Johnsons held title to most of Riverdale and parts of Manhattan. Pete spent his time grooming the vast lawns and gardens of the estate; he lived in the caretaker's shack with several other gardeners. His three years at the Johnson estate were more of an adventure than a means of survival. Though he was paid little, he had a warm home, hot meals each day, and good company.

There he met an Irish-American girl by the name of Mooney who was visiting the Johnson estate with her family. Though she was far above his station, the Mooney girl was charmed by Pete— his Irish guile and youthful sun-browned body, lithe and muscular from the hard work on the grounds. She invited him to visit her at her home in Mount Vernon. The very next weekend, and on many subsequent weekends, Pete did exactly that.

Fulfillment of his teenage hormonal urges did not come without a price. The trip to Mount Vernon included the crossing of the Harlem River in a rowboat and then a ten-mile walk. But according to stories handed down by Pete himself, the journey was well worth it, as Miss Mooney's liberal standards left him absent of want and girls like her in that day were hard to find. On the way home, his story went, Pete would, more often than not, "borrow" a horse from an unwitting Mount Vernon farmer.

Soon Pete became restless at the Johnson estate. He took a job across and up the Hudson River, in a rock quarry in Haverstraw, New York. Miss Mooney, merely the first of Pete's many conquests, was quickly discarded, and Pete began what would be his life's work, tunneling into the earth and breaking rocks. It was while he was working the quarry that Pete first heard of the job opportunities in the Pennsylvania coal mines. Less than a year later, he was off to Archbald.

As Pete labored under English foremen and bosses, he cursed his dumb luck at having traveled 3,000 miles from his famously beleaguered homeland only to be oppressed by the Brits in Archbald, Pennsylvania. Though Irish were among the earliest settlers of Archbald, in the 1840s, it was English and Welshmen who owned the land. Miners back in the old country, the English and Welsh first discovered and mined the anthracite coal in the Lackawanna Valley, where Archbald lay. A miner's life is a hard one whether conducted in the British Isles or America; although conditions here were somewhat easier and resources were more plentiful, the English landowners gained power while the Irish broke their backs; thus an old world dynamic was imported to these shores.

But this was America, not England. And the natural contempt the raw Irish laborers, like Pete, felt toward the English foremen and bosses of the Pennsylvania coal mines was the genesis of the United Mine Workers Union, in which Pete remained active for the rest of his life. Though his education did not extend beyond primary school, he was still far more literate than most of the Irish who worked the mines. Because of his writing skills, he was elected the first recording secretary of the local union chapter under the first United Mine Workers Union president, John Mitchell. In the dimly lit clapboard houses of the union men, where meetings were held, Pete, his round-rimmed glasses reflecting the low light, would keep the minutes of the meetings in a strong, looping script. Pete also wrote long, lyrical letters home for the illiterate Irish coal miners, happily offering this service for the opportunity to exercise a creativity that welled within him.

In 1902, the year of the great mineworkers' strike, Pete became a naturalized citizen. That winter, led by John Mitchell, 147,000 members of the United Mine Workers walked out demanding pay increases, an eight-hour workday, and other concessions from the mine owners. As the strike—and the winter—wore on, the entire country felt its effects. Large industry and basic services such as home heating and travel on locomotives were significantly reduced by the short supply of hard coal. In Archbald and nearby Eynon there were frequent union demonstrations, even riots. During one of these, the National Guard fired into the crowd, seriously wounding a man. Meanwhile, fearing an explosion of civil disorder, President Theodore Roosevelt appointed a commission to arbitrate the dispute. The union's team of lawyers was headed by Clarence Darrow. Knowing that the strike had captured the attention of the country, and sensing that public opinion lay with the miners, Darrow staunchly held his ground, refusing to give up any of the miners' demands. In an eight-hour closing argument worthy of a Hollywood screenplay, Darrow said the strike was "one of the important contests that have marked the progress of human liberty since the world began." Darrow told the commission that the mine operators were fighting for "slavery . . . for the rule of man over man, for despotism, for darkness, for the past." Darrow's eloquence was handsomely rewarded. In March 1903, the commission granted the miners almost everything they had wanted. Darrow, of course, would go on to further acclaim in a storied career as a lawyer. In 1925, he defended the right to teach Darwin's theory of evolution in the Scopes trial. But by then, his victory for the miners twenty-two years earlier was barely a memory in Archbald.

It was 1916 when Pete waited at the altar of St. Thomas Aquinas Church for Mary Sweeny to walk down the aisle. By then he was forty-four, his hands gnarled and rough as rock, his lungs, like the houses, trees, and streets of Archbald, coated with coal dust and the rest of his insides stewed in Irish whiskey.

Mary Sweeny, fifteen years younger, no doubt married Pete to escape her surroundings. She grew up the youngest of twelve siblings in a boardinghouse and bar that her father ran in Simpson, Pennsylvania. It was no place for a woman to visit, never mind live and work. And, by all accounts, Mary's childhood was horrible. Her father was a tyrannical drunk who beat her mercilessly, sometimes in front of drunken coal miners who would urge him on. She was a heavy girl, nearly obese by young womanhood. The coal miners called her names and told jokes about her weight, loudly enough for her to hear. Her father worked her like a coal miner's mule. She spent her days scrubbing and wringing out the miners' coal-caked shirts and pants and their shit-stained underclothing, sweeping and mopping their rooms, making sure there was brown paper in the horrid foulness of the outhouse. Still, she was good-natured, known to hum to herself as she cooked dinner for the dozen miners and the dozen members of her family. And she started every day at mass, where, perhaps, she prayed for a better life. For better or worse, her prayers were answered in the form of Pete, a sometime lodger and frequent drinker at the boardinghouse, who proposed on one knee in the kitchen.

Pete's drinking caused as much hardship in my father's family as did the Depression. Though he wasn't drunk all the time—in fact, he took the pledge on several occasions and stayed sober for long stretches, sometimes as long as a few years—it seemed he never missed an opportunity to sabotage his career or his family's fortunes by going on a binge. Coal miners were paid by the pound of coal they produced; the richer the chamber, the more money they would earn. Each time Pete worked his way up to a fine chamber, a punishment for being drunk and missing work would send him to the most infertile reaches of the mine. Once, after being dry for two years in the Temperance Society, the A.A. of its day, Pete was in line for promotion to foreman at more than double his miner's pay, only to have the promotion taken away when he went out on a two-week drunk to celebrate.

Partly the allure of the drink for Pete was that it dulled the pain of his job and released him—albeit temporarily—from the residual guilt of running away from his homeland and the fresh guilt of not being able to provide for his family during mining strikes and the Depression. I now wonder how he felt, what Irish demons roamed his thoughts, as he waited on line at the local parish for government surplus cheese or at the borough building for the relief check. But outside influences can never completely justify a drinking problem. For Pete, and in varying degrees for generations of my family, it is more an inside job—a hole in the Irish soul in the shape of a shot glass, one that has a cracked bottom and can never be filled no matter how much whiskey is poured into it.

The biggest career disappointment caused by Pete's drinking came in union politics, where his most fervent aspirations lay. He was passed over time and again when he ran for higher office. He was popular with the workers in a joker's role. But that same reputation held them back from casting their vote for him in the serious atmosphere of the unions.

Despite the trouble produced by Pete's periodic inebriation, Mary stayed the doting, loving wife. "He has the heart of a poet," she'd say. And so he did. In the barrooms of Archbald, Pete would stand and recite "The Diamond D," an ode to a coal miner, or, though he never took a lesson, sit at the piano and play a raucous drinking song or a sweet and haunting Irish lullaby. And even three sheets to the wind, Pete was able to make people laugh. My father remembers one day during the Depression when Mary sent my uncle Joe to fetch Pete from Moran's, a speakeasy in a private house not too far from Cemetery Street. When Joe walked into the barroom, Pete was dead drunk, his face on a table. As Joe shook him awake, Pete looked at his son through whiskey-blurred eyes, and though he'd never owned a vehicle more extravagant than a bicycle, said, loud enough for the whole bar to hear: "Did you bring the car, Joe?"

For my father, Pete's drinking was the source of ridicule and humiliation by Archbald's small-town gossips. It was hard for my father to hate Pete, though. When his father was sober, Frank saw in him an intelligent, caring man. Pete's eyes, my father said often, had a sparkle, a life force that engaged those in his presence and drew them in with a sorcerer's spell. Pete's sober personality had the beauty and glimmer of an icicle hanging from the porch of his home, but it was only a matter of time before whiskey, like a quick rise in temperature, dislodged it to fall and shatter before his family's eyes. Waiting for the crash steeled my father's feelings. But it was a certain deadness in his mother's eyes, a never-talked-about unhappiness, that bothered him the most. Often, when Pete was out on one of his roundelays, as Mary called his drunks, Frank would sit next to his mother on the tiny gray porch (all porches in Archbald were then painted battleship gray) of their home. She would stroke his hair and look longingly at the surrounding mountains of Archbald. "Someday," she'd say, "I'd like to follie the Red Hill Road and see what lay on the other side of those hills." In her whole life, she had never traveled farther than twenty miles from Simpson, the town where she was born. She would gaze down at my father, who sat at her feet, and again up at the mountains, but her eyes would ultimately always settle on Cemetery Street, in anxious wait for the sight of her husband staggering home.

"Promise me you'll never drink, Frank," Mary asked of my father once.

On our recent trip, I stood with my father on that same porch. He knocked on the door, but no one was home. The house, though still small, had been re-sided and there was a small flower garden in front. Indeed, all the homes in Archbald are now brightly painted and vinyl-sided, with neatly kept lawns and gardens. The last of the coal breakers, those towering structures that incessantly spewed coal dust day and night, has been closed for some twenty years, and Archbald is now a bedroom community for the growing high-tech firms in nearby Scranton and Carbondale. As we drove the streets of his childhood, my father pointed out where Moran's, the speakeasy, once stood; and where now stands a large ranch-style house. We went to the shifting shanty, which still stands, but in disrepair: crumbling brick walls, the inside draped with cob-webs. Our last stop was the cemetery, only steps from the porch where my father once sat with his mother. We stood over the un-marked plot where both his parents are buried. The afternoon had turned crisp and a chilly wind rustled up Cemetery Street. I waited quietly, watching him from the corner of my eye, his head bowed, his eyes closed. When he finally raised his head and looked toward me, I saw that his eyes were moist with tears. I pre-tended not to notice. Clumsily, I went to him and draped my arm around his back. "Come on, Pop," I said. "It's getting late."

# 2

In 1935, right after he graduated from high school, my father left Archbald for the same reason the immigrants left Ireland: there was no future there. Pete spent most of a relief check for his ticket to New York. On the porch they said their good-byes, Mary crying and Pete stiff and sober: "Good luck, boy" were the only words his father could muster. A few blocks from his home, in front of the Alco barbershop, my father boarded the trolley to Scranton, Pennsylvania, then a train to Hoboken, New Jersey, and last a ferry across the Hudson River to West Twenty-third Street in Manhattan. When he arrived in New York he had one suitcase, one fried-bologna sandwich (one having been eaten on the trip), and $2.

In New York, he lived with his aunt Mary, her son Frank McCabe and an Irish cousin with the same name as my father—Frank McDonald. With three Franks living together, they called my father by his middle name, Jerome. Aunt Mary's apartment was on Thirty-sixth Street and Second Avenue, a railroad flat. My father slept on a lumpy couch under a window that looked out onto Second Avenue and a small park across the way. Because he slept in the living room, where most of the household activity was centered, he was always the last to bed. Some nights, if Mary was entertaining a relative or neighbor, Frank would struggle to keep awake in a chair, silently praying that his aunt wouldn't offer her guests another cup of tea. Even when he did get the room to himself, he lay awake, listening to the cars and the shouts of the city night outside, so unfamiliar compared to the quiet of Archbald.

Frank McCabe found him a job as a clerk for a company called the National Credit Office, a subsidiary of Dun & Bradstreet, a credit investigation firm. The first day on the job, he was sent to make collections on West Thirty-seventh Street, in the Garment District. There were more people on that one street than he had ever seen in his life. The buildings were a towering maze of elevators and room numbers that left him wandering and wondering whether he would ever finish his rounds. It took him most of the day to complete an assignment that should have been done in an hour. When he finally returned to the office, his boss told him that he had better become more familiar with the city, or else look for another job. Each day, Frank became more seasoned, making mental notes of building numbers and shortcuts, until he knew every back alley and service elevator on the street. His pay was $12 a week, $8 of which he gave his aunt for room and board.

For fun, he'd go to the cinemas in Times Square or play basketball in the park across Second Avenue. He had played basketball in high school, even a few semipro games in his senior year. On the court, he made his first friends in New York. One of them was a wiry young man named Billy Graham, who had a thick East Side New York accent, and whose father owned a saloon on Thirty-sixth Street. Frank and Billy would battle under the backboards each evening, a classic struggle of my father's height and expertise against Graham's scrappy, street-fighter tenacity. One night, the two sat on a bench in the park and talked about their plans for the future. Graham had his all mapped out. He was going to become a professional fighter. He had already fought a few local club fights and had shown some promise. "I'm going to be the champion of the world some day," he told my father. When Graham asked about Frank's plans, my father said: "I'm thinking of taking the police exam."

"Well, you'll always have shiny shoes and a paycheck, Jerome," Graham said.

My father took the entrance examination for the police department on April 4, 1939. It was the largest police civil service examination in the history of New York City. My father was one of 30,000 applicants. The Depression had made civil service attractive to people of the most diverse ethnic and social backgrounds ever. For the first time, universities and colleges such as NYU, St. John's, Fordham, and City College all offered classes in police procedure. The mayor of New York, Fiorello La Guardia, began a campaign for what he called the professional police force. Extra credit would be given on final exam grades for people with college experience. "In the Police Department we need chemists,

93

mechanics, accountants, electricians and engineers. We need them every day for the efficient and well-balanced work of the department," the mayor said in a speech one day. Three fourths of the 30,000 applicants had some college credits. Of the 1,200 who were ultimately appointed to the police department, nearly 1,000 had college experience; of those, 289 had law degrees.

Although a graduate of what he called a soup school, Archbald High ("soup" was a reference to the free lunch that came with the limited educational environment), my father was a pretty fair student, and he retained his scholar's habits well into adulthood.

He loved going to the library, and when he wasn't playing basketball, he spent hours picking volumes from the shelves and reading until the librarian would shake his shoulder and say she was closing up. In preparation for the civil service exam, three nights a week he attended Delahanty's, a prep school for the police test. Most of the other evenings he shunned the basketball court and pored over the police textbook with questions from past exams.

The test was held in Commerce High School on the Lower East Side of Manhattan. My father was one of the first to arrive, his pencils sharp, a good hot lunch, fixed by Aunt Mary, in his stomach. The testing room, a gymnasium, was filled with wooden desks and chairs. Frank fidgeted with his eraser and looked around the room, sure that everyone else was smarter than he, although he noticed one or two who seemed at least as nervous. The monitor handed out the test pamphlet. On it was printed, "The Municipal Civil Service Commission," along with a note that warned: "This is a difficult test." Frank opened the pamphlet, scanned the first page, and noticed a question that made him wonder if he had studied the right books:

Suppose that while you are patrolling your post you observe a woman, clad only in what seems to be a sheet, strolling along Madison Avenue. The woman is leading a doe by a chain. A

crowd is beginning to collect around the woman. You should (select from the following):
(a) Take the woman and the doe to the precinct. (b) Telephone the ASPCA to take the doe and disperse the crowd. (c) Summon another patrolman to take care of the doe, then compel the woman to return to her home. (d) Remove your coat to cover the woman and then compel the woman and the doe to return to her home. (e) Pay no attention to the incident because it is probably a publicity stunt.

He took a deep breath and thought for a moment, and then the absurdity of the question dawned on him: No doubt a publicity stunt, he thought. He marked "e," and moved on. Unlike prior civil service tests for patrolmen, which rewarded those who could memorize the most cram information, the 1939 test aimed to measure commonsensical judgment and reasoning, along with testing applicants in traditional academic areas like mathematics and word definitions. With each question Frank answered, his confidence grew. Three and a half hours was allotted for the test, and after three hours, during which he went over his answers to the one hundred multiple-choice questions twice, he was finished. He took the trolley back to Aunt Mary's, confident that he'd done his best. Though he knew the odds against him, nearly thirty to one, he thought he had a chance.

It would be five weeks before the test results were announced. During that time Frank worked for the NCO in their main office, as he had now been promoted to file clerk. He no longer had to navigate the buildings and the mass of people in the Garment District; rather, he worked in a clerk room, clothespinning credit slips to an elaborate set of wires and pulleys—the interoffice communication mode of the day.

In the meantime, he moved with Aunt Mary to the Bronx; the apartment house on Second Avenue was being razed to build the Midtown Tunnel. Just the two of them lived in an apartment on

Loring Place. Frank McCabe had moved out, and Irish Frank had been kicked out for doing too much carousing in the Bronx bars.

As the weeks went by, each day after work, my father would stop at Delahanty's to see if the results had been posted. Sometimes he would stay at the school to play basketball; other times he went with his friends from the credit office to the movies. As the days went by, he became more and more anxious about his results. More than just the security of a civil service job now fueled his desire to become a policeman. He watched the cops walk into Delahanty's in uniform, cops studying for the sergeant's test or higher, and he saw in them a certain confidence, almost an arrogance. Their swagger was intoxicating. He saw the uniform as armor. If he was wearing it, no one would laugh at him as they had at his father.

Finally, the results of the test were posted. The question concerning the woman and the doe had been inspired by the real-life experience of a patrolman on a Madison Avenue beat, who encountered the pair a few weeks before the test. It was a publicity stunt for the World's Fair, which was being held in New York at the time. My father had marked the right answer. More important, he had also marked most of the other questions with the right answer. My father's name was on the list of those who had passed.

Although he knew he'd passed, he still wouldn't know how he'd placed on the list until the official notice arrived at Loring Place a few days later.

For a few moments, my father held the letter from the civil service commission in his hands, unopened.

"Go ahead, Jerome," his Aunt Mary urged. "I'm sure it's only the best of news."

He scanned the letter for the all-important number. It was 804; he had made the top 1,200 with room to spare.

# 3

In those days, if young Frank McDonald's head had glowed, he could have been a lamppost. At six feet three inches, he weighed 158 pounds, and that was with a Manhattan telephone directory under each arm. He was in fairly good shape from playing basketball and living the life he'd promised his mother, no drinking or smoking. But he was seven pounds under the police department weight requirement for his height.

In my grandfather's Tammany days, though there were also height-for-weight requirements, cops who didn't fit into the envelope got around the regulations in the most inventive ways. In one published memoir of that time, a fat cop wrote that he put a wad of chewing gum on the counterweight of the scale when the doctor wasn't looking. But with Mayor La Guardia's election, Tammany and its disregard for rules were all but dead. (Tammany Hall actually died as a result of yet another scandal. Judge Samuel Seabury directed what was first an investigation into organized crime's influence with New York magistrate's court judges, but the inquiry evolved to target a city contract payoff scheme to then mayor James J. Walker. Jimmy Walker, the darling of Tammany, decided discretion was the better part of valor and in 1932 resigned, but did so with his usual panache. With photographers' flashbulbs exploding around him, the dapper Walker waved good-bye as he walked up the gangplank to a ship sailing to Europe. With him sailed the last of Tammany's significance in New York City; in 1933, La Guardia was elected mayor.)

Colorful, honest, and forceful, La Guardia was the perfect mayor for the times. As the Depression demoralized the common man, "the Little Flower," as La Guardia was called, aggressively reorganized city government, vigorously battled corruption and gambling, and exerted his considerable influence with Franklin

Delano Roosevelt to get the city millions in federal funds to build highways, hospitals, and airports. By 1939, he had turned his attention to the NYPD. His aim was to build a super police force. With a majority of college men on the list to be appointed, the mayor now wanted the brawn to go along with the brains.

The physical exams for what would become known as the Class of 1,200 were given at the NYU gymnasium and athletic fields in the University Heights section of the Bronx. They were presided over by a panel of athletic directors and coaches from city colleges and universities: the football coach at City College, the track coach of NYU.

Frank McDonald passed the physical exam with the proviso that he gain seven pounds within a month or be dropped from the list. For the next thirty days he drank milk by the gallon and ate everything in sight: chocolate cakes by the dozens and the hearty, potato-laden meals his Aunt Mary made. But despite the enormous caloric intake, by month's end he had gained only four pounds. When the day came to be reweighed, he sat in City Hall Park, across from the civil service building, and ate ten bananas. Almost bursting, he went into an Automat and drank as much water as he could hold. The lengths people went to pass that year's police department entrance physical were extraordinary. As my father walked into the civil service building, a cab stopped and two men emerged, carrying a third man strapped to a board. He had been stretching on it for two weeks to make the height requirement. This may seem preposterous, but desperate attempts to make the grade—including that of the man on the board—were reported in numerous newspapers. (My father says that the man on the board made the requirement and years later rose to the rank of a deputy chief inspector.) When my father stepped on the scale, it registered the minimum—exactly 165 pounds. That day, he made himself a promise that he would never eat another banana as long as he lived.

* * *

The police academy training was held in a precinct in Brooklyn and presided over by a drill-instructor type named John Murray. The recruits called him Father John because of his patrician looks and no-nonsense demeanor. At the Academy, Frank McDonald learned how to shoot a pistol, what to expect on the streets of New York, and how to defend himself with a billy club and his hands. One of the rituals was boxing matches between the recruits. One day, my father was pitted against a young recruit named Mike Codd. When they entered the ring, the first punch Codd threw landed well below my father's belt, and he collapsed on the canvas. Just like that, the fight was over. When he regained his breath, my father staggered over to Codd and whispered: "If you ever do that again, I'll knock your teeth out." One night, years later at a function honoring Mike Codd as the new police commissioner, my father reminded him of the story.

The competition was stiff in the Academy, and although there was a line drawn between the college men and those, like my father, who had only high school educations, the Depression was a great equalizer. No matter who you were or where you came from, all the recruits were working for a common goal: the job. For Father John, a college degree meant little as far as police work went. And the academy instructor relished dispersing the college men to remote precincts when recruits were sent out in the "field" with patrolmen.

On September 4, 1941, the day he graduated from the Academy, my father was assigned to the 28th Precinct. The salary was $1,500 yearly, only $50 more than the rate my grandfather Tom Skelly had retired at twenty-two years earlier. Still, my father felt flush. He had just left the credit company, where he'd been making $18 a week; before that, he and his family had depended on public assistance. When he donned his uniform, a baggy fit over his gangly frame, strapped on his service revolver, and reported for work that first morning, the sergeant at the desk said: "Welcome to Harlem, son," and smiled. Harlem or hell, my father thought, it was a step up from Archbald.

When he received his first paycheck from the police department he sent two train tickets to Archbald, for his mother and father to come visit in New York. My father said that when he met his mother at the Twenty-third Street ferry port, her eyes were the size of tea saucers. She had never been on a train before, nor had she been on a boat of any kind, and how must she have felt, my father wondered, when she saw the sight of Manhattan rising to the heavens before her?

My father rented a room at McAlaster's boardinghouse on the beach at Ninety-sixth Street in Rockaway, and there, he and his parents had a big seafood dinner before he was off to the city to work. The next morning he went to McAlaster's again to meet them for breakfast. There, his mother still wore an amazed expression. She said that the storm the night before was one of the worst she'd ever heard, and that it kept her up most the night. There hadn't been any storm, my father remembered. His mother had never heard an ocean before. She thought the waves crashing against the shore were the roll of thunder.

My mother had listened to the Rockaway waves years before my father ever set foot there. A four-mile barrier beach on a peninsula that juts from the southern shore of Queens, Rockaway became known as the Irish Riviera, thanks to investors and developers like the infamous William Devery. The silky sand beach, dotted with colorful umbrellas and filled with the laughter of youth, fronted a boardwalk lined with graceful rooming houses, small hotels, and Irish bars. But for my mother, the allure of Rockaway was more than the gaiety of sight and sound. She had once fallen in love, deeply in love, there. And this, too, was long before she met my father.

She was nineteen and had gone on a week-long holiday to

Rockaway Beach with some friends and her sister Maz. While there, she met a boy, a lifeguard by the name of Timothy Carey. Each day she spread a towel on the sand beneath his chair, at night they walked the noisy streets holding hands.

I have a picture of my mother at a beach about that time—1929 or 1930. In the photograph, she stands with her older sister and two friends, the Lindinger girls. She wears a loose-fitting one-piece bathing suit, and her legs are slender and athletic. Her long, curly hair is swept back over her shoulder. Her eyes have a devilishly seductive look.

When Julia found out about the lifeguard, she forbade my mother to see him. Julia was protective of all her children, but Eleanor was her youngest daughter, and she wasn't about to give her up at the age of nineteen. Desperate, lovesick, my mother went to her father for support. But by then he had had his fill of arguments with Julia, most of which he lost. He refused to take his daughter's side, and my mother never forgot his failure to stand up for her.

Eleanor and her lifeguard lover decided to elope. She knew she would be the talk of the neighborhood. She also knew that Julia would be furious and disown her. Yet her heart leaped as she stood on the platform of Grand Central Station with her lover holding her arm and two tickets for Ocean City, Maryland.

They would marry in Ocean City; Tim would find work as a lifeguard, and she as a secretary. Made shortsighted by desire, they didn't even think as far ahead as the coming winter, when my mother's new husband would be out of a job.

But, at some point during the train ride, her thoughts went to her parents. The idea of never speaking to her mother again made her sick to her stomach. By the time she arrived in Ocean City those feelings were just too painful to ignore. She took the next train back to New York and cried the whole way.

Eleanor didn't try to keep in touch with the lifeguard after that, and she kept the hurt and her resentment toward her parents inside. The lifeguard undoubtedly spent that summer in Ocean City. The following year my mother did take a trip back out to Rockaway and ask about him, but she was told by the other lifeguards that Tim hadn't returned for his job that summer.

Years later, when my father was a young desk sergeant in Harlem, a somewhat older than average patrolman was transferred to his precinct. His name was Tim Carey, and it seemed vaguely familiar to my father (my mother having once told him the story of her young love). When Patrolman Carey reported to the desk, my father asked him if he had ever worked in Rockaway as a lifeguard. The patrolman enthusiastically answered that indeed he had, undoubtedly thinking my father knew him from there. When he "turned out" assignments to the patrolmen for that tour, a midnight–to–8 a.m. shift on a February night, my father gave the newcomer a "fixer" (a stationary post) at the edge of the Polo Grounds, on 155th Street and Eighth Avenue—"the North Pole," as the cops from the precinct called it. Patrolman Carey never had the slightest clue what he had done to deserve such an assignment.

When my mother met my father she was nearly thirty, eight years older than he, and somewhat scandalously single, given the place and time: the insular Irish neighborhood of Fordham in the early 1940s. Once, when I asked about her late-in-life marriage, she paused, looked across the living room at my father sitting in his chair, wrinkled her nose, and said in a giggling whisper: "Maybe I should have waited a little longer."

Although she lived with Julia up until she married my father, my mother was stubbornly independent and undoubtedly had her own plans for the future. Times were changing for women. Although many girls of her era still thought marriage the ultimate goal, even in these just pre-war-industry times, it was becoming increasingly acceptable for women—albeit with a very low glass ceiling—to build their own careers. Eleanor worked in a stenography pool for the Mutual Insurance Company in downtown Manhattan, having learned her trade at Grace Institute, then a well-known secretarial school. She had gone to Grace after only one year at Theodore Roosevelt High School, and against the wishes of her father. She often told me, in a pat motherly way, that her happiest moments came when her children were born. But, had her life gone in a different direction, she might have been just as happy being a single career woman. Her best friend in the world, Nora Banks, was single her whole life.

Like my grandparents Tom and Julia, my parents met at a dance. It was held at the YMCA on Lexington Avenue in Manhattan in June 1941, while my father was still in the police academy. Frank went there that night at the urging of a friend from the credit office, Bill Kelly, who had promised him that there would be plenty of girls from the big insurance companies in attendance, all of whom were great dancers.

When my father approached the girl in the pillbox hat—a Fordham neighborhood girl, he knew, because Fordham girls, the single ones with their own money, dressed to the nines—he affected his father's brogue and said: "Are you doing any dancing a'tall, a'tall?"

My father says that my mother blushed and accepted his offer. My mother, however, says that she had her suspicions of him right off. He seemed a bit young to her, he was about as wide as a mop handle, and she thought his confidence was just an act. She did dance with him, but there her doubts about him grew even stronger—he didn't even know how to do the Lindy. When he told her he was from a place called Archbald, she nearly—her "big-city girl" attitude in full bloom—walked away.

For his part, my father didn't waver. Still riding the high from passing the police exam and entering the Academy, he tried to impress her by whispering: "You know, I'm a police officer."

"So what," my mother said. "So was my father, and my uncle, too."

Later on that night, my father asked the Fordham girl out for a cup of coffee. He had hoped it would be only the two of them, but on agreeing to go, my mother invited all of her friends to come along. As luck would have it, they sat next to each other in the crowded booth in a coffee shop on Third Avenue. Perhaps it was there that she began to see something appealing in the country boy. She giggled with her girlfriends when someone said that my father had ears like two open doors on a taxicab. She liked that he didn't seem sensitive about the needle the girls were giving him, and when they were getting ready to leave, and my father asked if he could see her again, she flashed a demure smile and said positively, "Maybe."

My mother declined several times when Frank first began asking her out. My father wasn't the only suitor she had, and besides, she was deeply involved in her job and a bevy of causes, like the America First antiwar movement. She often attended rallies at places like Madison Square Garden to listen to Charles Lindbergh and others speak against America's involvement in the war in Europe. But my father remained persistent. And one night, my mother invited him to her house for dinner. As with the lifeguard years before, Julia wasn't so thrilled with my father. Perhaps it was because he was a policeman: resentment still festered from the department's treatment of her husband. More likely, it was because Julia was afraid my mother would become seriously involved. By then her other children were married, and her youngest son, Vincent, had enlisted in the army. It was only Julia and my mother living in the apartment. If my mother were to get married, Julia would be all alone, a point she made often to my mother with more than just innuendo. This Irish guilt, a skewed sense of filial responsibility, was, undoubtedly, another reason my mother stayed single so long.

Julia spent most of that meal in sullen silence—that is, until after dinner, when my father asked if there would be any dessert. Julia scolded him for being rude and stormed out of the kitchen in a huff. My father thought that he had permanently damaged any chance of getting Julia's blessing on his relationship with her daughter.

One of their first real go-out-for-dinner dates was on December 7, 1941. As they sat enjoying a luau buffet at Mayer's Parkway Inn in the Bronx, there was a commotion near the bandstand. An "extra" edition of the *Journal Tribune* had been delivered, and the Hawaiian band members had gathered around to read about the attack on Pearl Harbor. As the news spread through the dining room, a combination of fear and anger gripped my father. His younger brother Joe was in the army, stationed at Shoffield Barracks at Pearl Harbor. My father slammed his hand on the table and announced his intention to enlist the next morning. My mother, who also had a brother in the army, calmed my father down.

"Let's first find out how Joe is before you go off to save him," she said. My uncle Joe did survive Pearl Harbor; my father took my mother's advice and didn't enlist. Instead, he stayed in the police department (New York City policemen were offered an exemption to the draft), and the following June they were married. That summer, they rented a small apartment in a house on Ninety-sixth Street in Rockaway. Though the world was turned upside down by the war, for the newlyweds, the summer of 1942 was a kind of extended honeymoon. My mom spent her days at the beach, while my father commuted into the city to work. At night he would come home exhausted and fall asleep next to his new bride, listening to the ocean waves crashing against the shore and dreaming of the staged explosions in Madison Square Garden.

As a rookie policeman during wartime, my father was assigned to go from apartment house to apartment house trying to enlist people in the air raid warden program initiated by Mayor La Guardia. The mayor was so afraid of an air attack on New York (perhaps rightly so) that he recreated the Battle of Britain in

Madison Square Garden. My father and a thousand other rookie cops play-acted the city's emergency response plans.

In Rockaway, my mother befriended a woman staying at the same apartment house. Ruth Mackey's husband was also a policeman. My father and Charlie Mackey were introduced by their wives, and though Mackey was much farther along in his career—he ran the NYPD's celebrated bomb squad—he took to the young patrolman. The two spent many happy evenings chatting about police work on the porch, with its view of the laundry lines that hung between the Rockaway bungalows.

"The flags of Ireland," Mackey once said of the laundry.

When the summer ended and my parents moved to the Bronx, my father kept up contact with Mackey, often visiting him at his office in the police headquarters annex at 400 Broome Street.

Besides running the bomb squad, Charlie Mackey had another talent, one he was loath to advertise. In those days, a warrant wasn't needed for wiretaps. In fact, there was little regulation of wire taps at all. Private organizations sprung up offering the service to anyone—and on any phone—for a price. Police used them frequently in investigations, mostly of illegal gambling enterprises. Most of the time, in those days, wiretaps had to be installed in the basement of the same building where the phone to be tapped was located. The placing of a wiretap required not only technical expertise, but burglarlike cunning to get in and out of basements undetected. Among those who knew him, Charlie Mackey was thought of as the best wire man in the department. Many years later, that expertise would almost place him in the middle of one of the most infamous events ever to occur in our nation's capital.

In the early seventies, well after he had retired from the police department, Mackey was approached by a retired cop he knew was working for the government in Washington, D.C. The ex-cop told him that he had a wire job for him in the Capital that would involve very little work and would pay handsomely. It was a bugging job, the acquaintance said, not a wiretap, and a one-shot deal. As a seasoned ex-detective, Mackey was skeptical from the outset. He told the acquaintance he'd have to think about it and get back to him. Mackey didn't bother calling back, but the ex-cop was persistent, calling him on several other occasions. "It's only a hotel room," the ex-cop pleaded. Mackey had to admit the offer was tantalizing, and he could have certainly put the money to use. But, finally, he followed his initial instinct and told the contact that he was just not interested. Over the next several months, Mackey realized he had made the right decision. The article that caught his attention was in *The New York Times*. It was about a burglary at Democratic party headquarters, in the Watergate Hotel.

In the parlance of cops, Charlie Mackey became my father's rabbi. But the first favor Mackey arranged for my father, as it happened, was not in the police department. During one of their porch chats the summer after the Japanese bombed Pearl Harbor, Mackey told my father that he had a nephew who was a captain in the Office of Naval Intelligence. He said that they were looking for cops, especially New York City cops, to work in the division stationed at the Brooklyn Navy Yard. A few weeks later, my father went to 50 Church Street, the headquarters of the Third Naval District. Policemen admitted into the ONI were automatically made navy third-class petty officers. Thanks to Mackey—and his nephew—not only was my father given this rank when he joined the ONI, he also spent the first year and a half of his military service in Brooklyn, close enough to commute home.

In December 1942, my father began his wartime naval career. By then, my mother was almost six months pregnant with their first child, my brother Eugene. Although she was never in favor of the war, with her brother, Vincent, a lieutenant in the army, and my father's brother Joe in the South Pacific, she proudly taped a flag with blue stars on the apartment door, indicating family members involved in heavy fighting.

On March 2, 1943, Eugene was born. Even Julia congratulated

my father on a job well done. That night he had his first drink, a weak scotch and soda, which went right to his head.

Less than a week later, he received a telegram from Pete.

My father was granted leave from the ONI when he learned of his mother's illness. When he arrived in Archbald she was lying on a bed in the living room of the home on Cemetery Street. She had had a stroke, and was barely conscious when my father walked in the room. He leaned close to her, held her hand, and whispered to her that she was now a grandmother. Mary weakly squeezed my father's hand to let him know she understood. His leave was only for two days, and my father stayed that night in his old home. The next day he took the train back to New York.

Less than a week later, he received another telegram from Pete saying that Mary was dying. He arrived at Peckville Hospital the next day, just in time to hold his mother's hand once more before she passed away. Pete sat in the hospital room, propped up against a wall, so drunk he had no idea what had just transpired. Of all Pete's benders my father had been witness to, this one hurt him the deepest. Still, the next day he weaned his father off the horrors with a bottle of warm ale, as he had seen his mother do countless times, so Pete would be at least half presentable at the wake and funeral.

Two weeks after Mary died, Pete showed up at the door at 2300, dressed in his Sunday suit and holding a busted suitcase. "The people in Archbald said I should come live with my son," he said.

My mother wasn't altogether thrilled.

In the late winter of 1944, my father received orders to report to San Francisco, from where he would be sent to the 7th Fleet in the South Pacific. But the head of the San Francisco Office of Naval Intelligence, a man named William Quinn who was a former chief of police of San Francisco, changed the order; my father and two other New York City cops were assigned to him. My father fought the remaining year of the war on the shores of Treasure Island in San Francisco Bay, locking up sailors who stole from footlockers and chasing down AWOL cases.

The week after the D-Day invasion, my mother's brother, Vincent, was killed in action by a sniper as he tried to carry a wounded soldier to safety.

My father's brother Joe was at this time engaged in combat on several islands in the South Pacific. My father had no contact with him for months—in fact, Joe wasn't notified of his own mother's death until a month after it happened, when he finally received the crumpled letter from my father. Through the Red Cross, and his contacts in Naval Intelligence, my father had tried to arrange a leave for Joe to attend his mother's funeral. But Joe was involved in such heavy fighting, a leave was out of the question.

(Joe ultimately did return home after the war. He was placed in the Fort Devins army hospital near Worcester, Massachusetts, for treatment of shell shock and hepatitis. After having survived the bombing of Pearl Harbor, after four years in the armpit of the Pacific theater—four years of witnessing the most unspeakable horrors—and after six months in an army hospital, he returned to Archbald to live with a friend's family. At the train station, the only familiar face there to greet him was that of an old Irish railroad worker, who asked: "Have you been out of town, M'Donald?")

The day my father returned to New York after his discharge, he called my mother from Grand Central Station, expecting to hear shrieks of joy and a voice overcome with emotion. What he heard was an order to pick up some milk on the way home. Often, during wartime rationing, an enlisted man in uniform was the only person able to obtain such precious commodities. My mother had given birth to two wartime babies: Eugene, undoubtedly conceived during that first summer in Rockaway, and Frankie, during my father's weekend leaves from the Brooklyn Navy Yard. For my

mother, there was no time for sentimental reunions. For my father, there was a lot of catching up to do in the world of dirty diapers and early-morning feedings.

# 4

On January 1, 1946, a bitter cold night, Frank McDonald was
back in a police uniform in the 28th Precinct in Harlem. As he
began his tour that night, a beat on a cold, quiet street, a man
stumbled toward him and collapsed at his feet. Having just served
nearly four years in the navy during World War II, my father hadn't
witnessed so much as one shot fired in action. Now, not twenty
minutes after he arrived in Harlem, there was a man lying on the
street in front of him dying from a gunshot wound. The next day
my father paid a visit to his rabbi on Broome Street.

Mackey knew a Brooklyn captain in plainclothes named John
Martin, and was sure he could get my father assigned to him.
Though my father wanted out of Harlem in the worst way, it wasn't
only Harlem that impelled him to seek out his rabbi. My father's
experience in the navy had given him a taste of what it was like to
hold rank, and he brought this gathering ambition back to the police department. Unlike my grandfather Tom, Frank McDonald
wasn't about to remain a patrolman the rest of his career. Still, he
was leery of the plainclothes division, which had been rife with
scandal and corruption from its inception.

There is a popular misconception that plainclothes policemen
are part of the Detective Bureau or its more modern version, the
Detective Division. Plainclothesmen were not detectives. (There
is no longer a plainclothes division. In the years after the 1972
Knapp Commission investigation it was disbanded. Charge of investigations into gambling, vice, and narcotics was given over to a
newly formed unit called the Organized Crime Control Bureau
[OCCB].) In the organizational chart of the New York City police

department, plainclothesmen were under the auspices of the uni-
formed arm. The genesis of the plainclothes division perhaps
dates back to the wardmen, the bagmen for the crooked precinct
captains of the nineteenth century. Often wardmen dressed in civilian clothing so as not to draw attention to their graft-collecting
activities. By the 1940s, the plainclothes division, which dealt exclusively in investigations into gambling and vice, was a cesspool
of corruption. A joke circulated in the police department after
one of the many gambling scandals tied to the plainclothes division: St. Peter is at the Pearly Gates when twelve plainclothesmen
appear before him. Peter goes in to see God and says, "I have a
problem; there are twelve plainclothesmen at the Pearly Gates
looking to come in all at once." And God says, "Well, just treat
them like anyone else—find out one by one if they're worthy of
heaven, and if they are, let them in. And, Peter," God says, "come
back and tell me how it works out." Peter leaves but returns almost immediately. "They're gone," he says to God. "The plainclothesmen?" God asks. "The Pearly Gates," Peter says.

My father's instincts told him to turn down his rabbi's offer, but
it was hard for him to say no to Mackey, who had already steered
him in the right direction once. Not knowing what to do, my father asked if he could sleep on it.

"Sure, Frank," Mackey said in a soothing voice. "Take your
time."

That night, he went home and asked my mother what she
thought. A city kid, the daughter of a cop, and now the wife of a
cop, my mother was more savvy than my father in many ways, at
least back then, even when it came to his job. Though she clearly
remembered the unfair treatment her father received after he
turned down the Tammany offer to be a doorman, she said: "Say
thanks, but no thanks, Frank. Something else will come along."

Something did. The next day, when my father went back to
Mackey's office, he told his rabbi that he was passing on plainclothes. Mackey smiled. "I thought you might," he said. He then

told my father that he also knew of an opening in the detective district captain's office in Harlem, and if my father wanted, he would make a call.

Two weeks later Frank McDonald was a detective, assigned to the 6th Detective District headquarters in Harlem, as secretary to the district captain. My father held this position for nearly four years and was secretary to several district captains, of whom Hughie Sheridan was the most memorable. Tall, silver-haired, and elegant, Sheridan looked more like an ambassador than a policeman. He went to a Harlem barber each day for a shave, and his hair was always neatly coiffed. He wore immaculate Savile Row suits and Turnbull & Asser dress shirts. He drank old scotch at the Artists and Writers club. "Top drawer, Frank," he would say to my father. "Always buy top drawer." (Though my father never could afford Savile Row, he did follow Sheridan's advice as much as he could, buying Hickey Freeman suits, Stanley Blacker blazers, and such.)

Sheridan liked my father, and the feeling was mutual. They shared a love of reading and, as a good clerical man—a fast typist with a flair for writing that brought life to the dull reports and letters of the office—my father was an asset to his boss, and Sheridan knew it.

While he was working at the district office, my father became the delegate from Harlem to the Detective Endowment Association. He was a natural politician. Towering, his weight finally catching up with his height, with midnight-black hair parted just to the right of middle and thick enough to comb back with an open hand, he had the kind of presence that made even a roomful of detectives stop and take notice. He was a voracious reader, which endowed him with a professorial vocabulary. And he also had experience, of sorts, in politics. In his senior year at Archbald High School he'd run for class president and been elected; his dominion comprised all of forty-eight students.

Frank's first year in the police union, the president of the DEA was a legendary Runyonesque character named Denis "Dinny" Mahoney. Because my father was the delegate from Harlem, Dinny, who grew up on West 118th Street, and whose closest police friends worked in the Harlem precincts, took a special shine to him. In the realm of police politics, Mahoney's blessing was like that of a pope.

Officially, Mahoney was assigned as a detective to the pick-pocket squad, but it was said that he spent most of his working hours in the saloons along the Great White Way. He was a familiar figure at Billy Rose's raucous Diamond Horseshoe, and one of the few who could hold his own matching wits with Texas Guinan, the razor-tongued nightclub impresario. By all accounts, Mahoney was as brightly lit as the theater district itself. Chipmunk-cheeked, with a sharp pointed nose and small gleaming eyes, he acted as if he owned Broadway. He often wore a tuxedo, even a Prince Albert coat, and a variety of rakish hats including a white homburg and a silk plug that earned him the nickname Silk Hat Dinny. In the early 1920s, a news account of Mahoney's election to the ceremonial post of mayor of Harlem ran in the *New York Globe*:

> Perhaps there are no flags flying to the breeze in Harlem. Perhaps there is no blare of trumpets to mark the joyous occasion. But what of it? Harlem is still furiously celebrating, in its solid mental way, the election of one of its favorite sons as the Mayor of all one can survey uptown.
>
> Yes, mates, it was a real old fashioned election that catapulted "Silk Hat Dinny" into the mayoralty office. The new Mayor of Harlem is a detective-sergeant in real life and is connected with the One Hundredth Street police station.

The biggest event of the year for the DEA was their annual dinner-dance, held at the Hotel Astor in Times Square. The Harlem "mayor" was in charge of booking the entertainment.

There wasn't a theatrical agent on Broadway who could have done a better job. Mahoney grew up with the comedian Milton Berle on 118th Street. In those days, Berle's *Texaco Star Theatre* was the highest-rated show on television. Each year, as a favor to Dinny Mahoney, Berle served as emcee for the dinner-dance. But Uncle Miltie was only the beginning of the talent Mahoney paraded onto the Astor's bandstand: Benny Goodman's band would provide the swing, Jack Benny or Jackie Gleason the laughs, and Bing Crosby the voice.

One night, in 1942, just a week or so before the big dance, Dinny was sitting with a couple of his cronies at a table in Leon and Eddy's, a famous Broadway watering hole, when he noticed a great commotion at the door. The stir was caused by the entrance of a skinny kid in a tuxedo, with slicked-back black hair.

"Who's that?" Mahoney asked of one of his cronies.

"Frank Sinatra," came the reply.

Mahoney summoned Sinatra over to his table with a wink and a sideways tilt of his head. The next week, instead of singing to the horde of bobby-soxers at the Paramount Theatre, Sinatra was cradling the microphone at the DEA dinner-dance.

Needless to say, the ticket for the dance was the hottest in town. Along with just about every one of the city's VIPs, 600 New York City detectives and their wives, most of the men in tuxedos, all of the women in gowns, packed the huge ballroom and balconies of the Astor, while being entertained by the biggest names in show business. Mayor William O'Dwyer wouldn't have thought of missing the event; neither would any other top politician or New York businessman—all thanks to the connections of Dinny Mahoney.

For my father, those days of the DEA were heady times, a fulfillment of his Academy dreams. The stringbean of a boy from Archbald, all assholes and elbows, as he would say, was now mingling with the powerful and famous of New York. In his new surroundings he developed a certain confidence and cockiness. Detectives, he found, were treated with a respect he had not known as a patrolman and certainly not as a coal miner's kid. And the respect came not only from policemen, but from the city at large. Then, to be a detective in New York was to be something special, and while he drove Milton Berle or Sugar Ray Robinson home after the dinner-dance Frank would wonder what his friends back in Archbald would say if they could see him.

In September of 1948, while my father was still working for Hughie Sheridan, my mother gave birth to her third child. By all accounts, Mary Clare was a perfectly healthy baby. She had curly hair like her mother's, cornflower-blue eyes, and a rosy complexion. She hardly ever cried, but cooed, chortled, and smiled most of the time. Although she would never admit this, my mother was absolutely thrilled to have a baby girl come into her life, and not another boy. She stretched the family budget on pink baby suits and nightclothes. She'd bundle Mary Clare in blankets and a woolen bonnet and bustle her downstairs to visit Theresa or lay her in the stroller and proudly parade down Sedgwick Avenue to show her off to the other young mothers gathered in Devoe Park.

Late one night, when Mary Clare was just four and a half months old, my mother was awakened by a soft but deep cough coming from the baby's crib, next to her bed. The child had spat up a dark gray fluid, which covered her face and the front of her nightclothes. My mother was alarmed. Though she had seen plenty of every imaginable kind of regurgitation with her other children, she had never seen anything the color of what now covered her daughter. Early the next morning, without even calling to make an appointment, my mother dressed Mary Clare, now wheezing and coughing harder, in warm clothing, wrapped her in blankets, and rushed to the family physician. Though the office was busy that morning, a cold January day in the midst of the flu season, the doctor made time to examine the baby. With a waiting room filled with sick patients, the doctor quickly wrote out a prescription for a sulfa drug, the penicillin of its day, and told my mother to fill it as soon as possible.

My mother hurried to the druggist on the corner of Sedgwick Avenue and Fordham Road holding Mary Clare, still wrapped in blankets, and handed the prescription over the counter. Doc Applebaum, a diminutive man with a balding head and wire-rimmed glasses, had been the family druggist since my mother and father moved into 2300. He greeted my mother by her first name and asked about Mary Clare's condition. He knew all the neighborhood folk and had a genuine concern for each of them. As he started to fill the prescription, he raised his head over the counter and asked my mother, in a mildly perplexed tone, if she was sure the doctor knew the medication was for Mary Clare.

Yes, my mother said, she was sure. She told him that she had just then come from the doctor's office.

"It seems an awfully large dosage for an infant," he said.

For a moment, Doc Applebaum's words worried Eleanor. But Mary Clare had been wheezing and coughing with greater discomfort, and she wanted to bring her home to the warmth of the apartment. Besides, Theresa was watching Eugene and Frankie, and she had enough on her hands with her own baby in diapers. Again my mother told the druggist she was sure, and Doc Applebaum filled the prescription.

Eleanor rushed home, past Shultz's candy store and the dry cleaner, past Tony the greengrocers' and up the incline of Sedgwick Avenue. As she passed the alleyway to the carriage room she barely noticed the boys of the building holding their secret meeting. The bell in the tower of St. Nicholas of Tolentine rang as it did every hour, but my mother didn't notice. Up the steps of 2300 and through the large foyer she held Mary Clare ever tighter to her chest. The words of Doc Applebaum resonated in her thoughts.

In the elevator rising to the fifth floor, she decided to call the doctor, just to be sure the prescription was correct. Inside the apartment, she laid Mary Clare in the crib in her bedroom, being sure to change the blanket in which she had wrapped the baby for the trip to the doctor's office with a fresh one from the shelf over the radiator, built to keep the baby's bedclothes warm and dry. She then walked to the hallway where the telephone sat on a small round table and called the doctor, whose number she knew by heart. The nurse who answered said the doctor was too busy to come to the phone, but she would relay my mother's question. Over the phone, my mother could hear what sounded like agitated voices in the background—something about druggists doing doctors' jobs, and such. The nurse returned to the line and said the prescription was right and that the doctor said she should start Mary Clare on the medication as soon as possible.

The sulfa drug did little to improve Mary Clare's symptoms. Two days after her doctor's appointment, my parents brought Mary Clare to the hospital. There she was diagnosed as having double pneumonia and chickenpox, a viral disease for which sulfa drugs are useless. Though the infant mortality rate in those years from such a condition was extraordinarily high, Mary Clare survived after an extended hospital stay. But soon after, my mother became convinced that there was something very wrong with her child. At first, she thought it was just the illness working its way out of her system. But as the days folded into weeks, Mary Clare's complexion, once a healthy pink, took on an ashen cast. She seemed listless and unaware of her surroundings. There is a family snapshot of my father holding Mary Clare before she became ill. It was taken on the sidewalk near Devoe Park. He is tall and slender, dressed in a raincoat, wearing a fedora; his expression is the very essence of smiling proud papa. Mary Clare is wearing a wide-brimmed bonnet and a sweet small smile, perfectly safe in his arms. One night, a few weeks after she became sick, Frank

117

came home and lifted Mary Clare from the crib. There was no recognition in his baby's eyes. She didn't reach and grab at his nose as she liked to do in the past. She didn't cry and reach for her mother. It was as though he was holding a lifeless doll in his arms.

Each morning my mother would wake from her fitful sleep and rush to the crib, expecting each day to be greeted with the smile she had once known. But each day the same dull eyes looked back at her. The baby would have spat up most of what she ate. The crib was smeared with thick, gooey vomit. Each night my mother knelt on the hardwood floor next to her bed and prayed to the Virgin Mary for a miracle. But as the weeks went by, Mary Clare slipped farther and farther away.

Six weeks after she became ill, my parents took Mary Clare to be examined at the New York Medical Center. There, the worst of their fears were realized.

The doctor's diagnosis was that Mary Clare had developed brain damage as a result of the viral infection. A year later, with most of the hope for a miracle drained from my mother, Mary Clare was admitted to Willowbrook State School, a hospital on Staten Island for severely mentally retarded children. The entry that day on her medical chart read like this:

April 12, 1950:
Mother, who was upset, but appeared intelligent and reliable, re-turned to the school (hospital) today and gave the following in-formation: Patient is third of three children, two brothers, 7 and 5 years respectively. Pregnancy and birth normal. Developed ap-parently well up to 4½ mos. of age. Was able to turn over, to hold her head up. Vision and hearing keen. At that age child con-tracted pneumonia and subsequently chickenpox. Following these conditions, child regressed obviously. She lost interest in her en-vironment and did not recognize her parents anymore. At 6 mos. of age, diagnosis of post-infectious encephalopathy was made at Medical Center. At present, child sits only when propped up, hearing impaired, vision unchanged, does not speak.

Each day, my mother drove to Staten Island to be with Mary Clare. Most days Frankie would go with her. Eugene had started school at St. Nicholas of Tolentine and would go to his grandmother's or Theresa's for lunch. Understandably, my mother was sullen and moody. At night she'd sit on the floral-patterned couch and smoke cigarettes. When my father came home—he was out with his detective friends more and more frequently—my mother would lash into him. The trip to Staten Island each day was too much of a strain on her. She seemed to argue with her husband all the time now.

On July 12, 1950, my parents went to Willowbrook together to take Mary Clare back to the Bronx. In an archaic tangle of bureaucratic red tape, Willowbrook required, in order for Mary Clare to be certified by the state, that the child be readmitted after a "home stay" of two weeks. On the Staten Island Ferry, Mary Clare began to shake violently as she lay in my mother's arms in the backseat of the car. The convulsion lasted over ten minutes. Afraid to jeopardize the state certification, my father drove all the way to Morrisania Hospital in the Bronx, with my mother clutching Mary Clare, trying to keep the extreme tremors from happening again.

After Mary Clare was released from Morrisania Hospital and brought back to Willowbrook, my father rented a cottage on Staten Island. My mother stayed there with Eugene and Frankie for the rest of the summer and into the fall. My father would visit only on the weekends. During the week, at night, he stayed alone at 2300.

For my father, in those days, the prospect of running a detective squad seemed about as realistic as being appointed the next police commissioner. You just didn't walk into a job like that. Squad commanders were crowned, not promoted. He would see them glide into division headquarters, dressed like mobsters: the finest homburgs, topcoats with felt collars, pinkie rings. They ate dinner at the Stork Club, were given the best tables at the Copacabana and Colony. They were gods. They knew everyone and answered to no one, and were treated with impunity and respect. They called everybody "kid," no matter their age or position. Just maybe, after ten or fifteen years in the bureau, maybe then, if he was lucky, he would get a shot at a squad. But not at only thirty-two, he thought, not even if he was the only horse in the race. But a funny thing happened in the starting gate.

In July 1948, Dinny Mahoney had died of what was called in one obituary a "complicated illness." The infirmity, no doubt, had its inception in Broadway scotch and Cuban cigars. In 1949, my father took and passed the sergeant's exam, and was on a list waiting for appointment. He had studied for the test mostly at night, with a friend and DEA cohort named Joe Harley, sometimes in one of the empty rooms in the chief of detective's office at police headquarters, where Harley worked. With Eugene just barely out of diapers and Frankie still wearing them, and then with the arrival of Mary Clare, the apartment at 2300 was a chaos of whines and cries and runny noses and smelly diapers. And even though Pete had since moved in around the corner with my uncle Joe (who had moved to the Bronx a few years before), the apartment was no place to memorize police procedure and sergeant's responsibilities. Though my mother understood how important the promotion was—with three children now, there was not much left at the end of the pay period—she couldn't help but resent her husband's absences from home.

In 1950, as Mary Clare was being admitted to Willowbrook, Joe Harley ran for the DEA presidency, with my father on his ticket as overall secretary. They won in a landslide victory. Their friendship became stronger as they worked side by side on the monumental task of filling Dinny's shoes. Harley was a quiet, even-tempered man, stout in stature, with handsome dark-Irish features and black hair combed back on the sides. Though he and my father lacked Mahoney's jaunty style—and his connections—

the DEA functions remained successful under their watch. Milton Berle was still stalwart at the dinner-dance, and my father was able to arrange for the Ink Spots, Mel Tormé, and others to perform. He and Harley worked long hours, sometimes late into the night, lobbying for extended benefits for police officers. Once a month, they would hold a dinner at the Belvedere Room at the Astor and invite congressmen and state senators. It was during these dinner meetings, the "rubber chicken circuit," as it was called, that the DEA first began to prevail upon politicians to vote for Social Security benefits for municipal employees (they were not, under the federal social security law, eligible in those years).

Harley's clerical job with the chief of detectives made him privy to the decisions and workings of the top echelon of the Detective Division. In 1950, the office in which Harley worked was a place under siege.

In September of that year, under the orders of Kings County District Attorney Miles F. McDonald (no relation), a major bookmaker named Harry Gross was arrested. The arrest was a result of an investigation into alleged police graft in connection with Brooklyn gambling. Gross rocked the city with allegations that he paid to the police $1 million of his $20 million yearly take for protection of his rackets. Those rackets included twenty-seven horse-betting rooms, dozens of sports bookmaking locations, and untold numbers of card games, crap games, and policy (numbers) operations.

But even more remarkable than the sums Harry Gross said he paid the police were the ranks of the police he said he was paying. Though the names of these ranking officers would not be officially tied to the scandal until two years later (when Gross testified in front of a Brooklyn grand jury), the very week after the bookmaker was arrested, Police Commissioner William P. O'Brien, Deputy Commissioner Frank C. Bals, and Chief of the Department William T. Whalen all resigned. And on August 31, 1950, as

Jimmy Walker had done eighteen years earlier, the mayor of New York City abdicated his office. Though William O'Dwyer had suffered a heart attack a few months earlier and was never officially implicated in the scandal, there were those who believed the mayor as guilty as any of his subordinates, and thought his leaving office was more an escape than a resignation.

When the rumblings of the Harry Gross scandal were first felt through the department, months before O'Dwyer resigned, my father, Joe Harley, and other officers of the police line organizations were summoned to city hall for a meeting with the mayor. A meeting between O'Dwyer and the police union officials was not unusual. The mayor had a close relationship with the police, having walked a beat himself as a young cop in Brooklyn. Most of the top echelon of the police department were his personal friends. Some of these friendships, like the one with Chief Whalen, dated back to when both men were rookies in the Police Academy. But even the rank and file thought of O'Dwyer as one of their own. My father called him the Bohola Boy, in reference to the town in County Mayo, Ireland, where he was born.

Family ties aside, O'Dwyer's good relationship with the police unions—a voting block, then some 20,000 strong, with wives and other voting-age relatives—was also good politics, even if it did hark back to the dark days of Tammany Hall.

From 1898, when the five boroughs were consolidated into the municipality of New York City, until the time of Jimmy Walker's resignation in 1932, the relationship between the mayor's office and the police department had by turns been one of allegiance or enmity. Most of this shifting had been dictated by political affiliation, most prominently Tammany Hall and Republican reformers. La Guardia was the first mayor of New York to have a hands-on relationship with the police department without totally being an indentured servant to a political machine. Though the old Tammany tiger had been defanged by La Guardia's election,

O'Dwyer's relationship with the cops was in many ways a revival of the Hall.

During the 1946 mayoral campaign, Judge Jonah J. Goldstein, one of O'Dwyer's opponents that year, addressed a meeting of the Patrolmen's Benevolent Association. During his speech, Goldstein said that he would conduct a "relentless barrage of police investigations" to drive out any underworld influences in the police department—a thinly disguised attack on O'Dwyer. In 1940 and 1941, O'Dwyer had been the Brooklyn district attorney, where he was lionized by the press as the second coming of Eliot Ness. While holding the D.A.'s office—for just two short years—O'Dwyer successfully headed more than eighty murder investigations. Most of these killings were by "Murder Incorporated," the Brooklyn dock mob. O'Dwyer's key witness in these investigations was Abe "Kid Twist" Reles, a Brooklyn thug and sometime associate of Murder Inc. A conscienceless killer himself, Reles had been convicted of stabbing to death a parking attendant who hadn't retrieved his car quickly enough. It seemed that once Reles started talking he couldn't stop. He implicated politicians and policemen as providing protection for the Brooklyn mob, and named Albert Anastasia as the "lord high executioner" of Murder Inc. But not one politician or policeman was subjected to the D.A.'s investigation. And when pressure from the public and the press forced O'Dwyer to act against Anastasia—who, for some inexplicable reason, seemed to have been granted immunity by the D.A.—Reles conveniently fell out of a fourteenth-story window at the Half Moon Hotel in Coney Island, despite the fact that he was there under the protection of six policemen including O'Dwyer's friend Captain Frank Bals, later the deputy commissioner. Without Reles as a witness, the investigation into Murder Inc. was over, and no charges were brought against Anastasia.

When Judge Goldstein finished his speech he received a hearty ovation from the audience of patrolmen. But as soon as he walked out the door, the PBA voted unanimously to back O'Dwyer for mayor.

From the looks of O'Dwyer during that meeting with my father and the other line organization officials, it was obvious that the mayor was agitated over the state of his police department and all the newspaper talk of scandal. O'Dwyer was a towering man with a great white head of hair and a florid Irish complexion. But on the day of the meeting, his face was a road map of bursting capillaries. At one point he slammed the oaken desk in his office, sending a pipe stand flying.

"There is more money to be made in concrete than there is in cops!" my father remembers the mayor yelling.

At that moment, a thought flashed through Frank's mind, of Charlie Mackey and his offer to send my father to the plainclothes division in Brooklyn, the very nexus of the rumors of scandal that now swirled. With scores of cops losing their jobs because of the scandal, and with Mary Clare sick at home, my father exhaled in relief that he had decided to talk the offer over with his wife. When he went for a late lunch with Harley and some of the other line organization officers, my father clucked and shook his head in agreement with the rest at the table when someone said: "A few otherwise fine policemen take a couple of bucks from a Jew policyman and the whole department has its knickers in a twist. Even a good man like O'Dwyer is hiding like a hen in a fox house." But inside, my father's thoughts were all about his wife and her advice.

On December 18, 1950, my father was officially promoted to sergeant. The ceremony was held at city hall; Mother went in a stylish dress with a lace collar and wore a wide-brimmed hat. In the picture taken that night, she is holding on to my father's arm. She has a thin smile as she looks at him. He wears his new sergeant's stripes; his uniform is too snug around the middle, and he has started to gain a double chin.

Vincent Impellitteri, who as City Council president gained the acting mayoralty when O'Dwyer resigned, gave a speech that night. Fifty-two sergeants, along with a dozen lieutenants, two captains, two deputy inspectors, and two full inspectors, were promoted that day. Chief of Detectives August Flath was promoted to William T. Whalen's old position as chief of the department. But, besides my father's own, the promotion that would affect his career most was the one given to the man who became the new chief of detectives.

Like most of his fellow cops, my father was in awe of Conrad Rothengast. A native New Yorker with a brusque demeanor and a Prussian general's posture, the new chief of detectives had come up the hard way, serving in every civil service rank in the police department. He had even been busted from the Detective Bureau once, early in his career, and had worked his way back. The demotion was more a result of politics than a disciplinary matter. Rothengast had been a protégé of Richard Enright, the police commissioner from 1918 to 1925, when John F. Hylan was mayor. He worked directly for Enright in what was then known as the Commissioner's Squad, a precursor of the Internal Affairs Division. When Hylan lost the election to Tammany candidate Jimmy Walker in 1925, the new mayor appointed "King" George McLaughlin police commissioner. Boisterous and controversial, McLaughlin got his nickname because of his monstrous ego and lavish lifestyle. When he left the department he was presented with a solid gold detective shield encrusted with diamonds and rubies and inscribed "With appreciation, from the heroes of the bureau." On his appointment to commissioner, McLaughlin made it his first order of business to clean house. Rothengast was sent packing to the Bronx to walk a beat. From first-grade detective to patrolman is quite a tumble, but the event taught Rothengast a valuable lesson: Civil service was the safest road to advancement in the police department. He passed the sergeant's exam in 1928, the lieutenant's three years later, and the captain's in 1937. It was the kind of rise in rank my father admired and dreamed of—and tried to emulate.

After my father's promotion to sergeant, he was assigned briefly to the 32nd Precinct. Though he was now out of the Detective Bureau, and had to step down from his post as secretary of the DEA, my father remained close to Joe Harley, who now worked for Rothengast. As a sergeant, my father got his first taste of being a boss, and he liked it. He also found out he was good at it. He took comprehensive notes of his rounds supervising the patrolmen. He didn't take any nonsense, even though most of the men he supervised were older than he. One night, he found one of these old-timers drunk at his post. The cop's beat was a particularly crime-infested block and the drunken cop was a hazard not only to the people it was his job to protect but to himself. My father wrote the cop up—not a popular decision with some of the man's fellow patrolmen. But others, including the lieutenant and captain of the precinct, respected my father for it. He began to build a reputation as a tough—but fair—boss. But being a police sergeant was not always a serious business.

Each week the plainclothesmen would march a parade of Chinese gamblers into the station house. It was a ridiculous ritual of building up arrest statistics. For the most part the gamblers, generally waiters from Chinatown restaurants, didn't speak English. The plainclothesmen would make up the arrest reports with inventive names and places of birth. Once in a while, my father would be assigned as desk sergeant, where he'd have the job of entering the arrest information into a ledger. Young Ho, Old Ho, and One Hung Lo would all have been born in Shanghai. The gamblers would be hustled off to night court, where they paid the allotted fine, and they'd be back at their crap game before the night was over.

My father was less than a year into his time as a patrol sergeant when Joe Harley called and invited him for lunch near police headquarters.

During Rothengast's tenure as chief of detectives, the last vestiges of the O'Dwyer regime and the Harry Gross scandal were swept out the door of police headquarters. Changes were made in the Detective Division with lightning speed. Rothengast's mandate was clear: There would be no scandals while he was in charge.

Joe Harley had formed a close relationship with his boss. Both native New Yorkers from big families, they related on an intimate level. For Harley, it was an exciting time, working for a dynamic chief whose honesty was impeccable. And Rothengast was a powerful ally. According to Harley, it was as simple as this with Rothengast: If you were on his good side, he'd do as much as he could for you; if you weren't, watch out—no matter who you were.

During his time as chief of detectives, and later as chief police inspector, the highest rank in the department, Rothengast pursued a secret vendetta against J. Edgar Hoover. Although the chilly relationship between the NYPD and the FBI was caused more by a power struggle than anything else (New York city police brutality cases were investigated by the FBI, and other federal statutes also gave FBI agents, most of whom were non–New Yorkers, jurisdiction over the NYPD), perhaps the discord between the two law enforcement agencies can be traced back to Rothengast's grudge. At the advent of World War II, Fiorello La Guardia set up a clandestine unit called Special Squad One, which was to serve as a liaison between the NYPD, federal law enforcement agencies, and military intelligence. At the time, Rothengast was a highly decorated captain and was regarded with respect by both La Guardia and his police commissioner, Lewis Valentine. Fiercely patriotic, Rothengast wanted to lead the squad, and La Guardia thought him the perfect choice. But when Rothengast's name was sent to the FBI for a routine clearance check it was rejected by Hoover himself, because of Rothengast's Bavarian ancestry. According to the story, Rothengast never forgot this, and his resentment festered over the years. What had made Hoover's decision all the more bitter was that Rothengast's brother, U.S. Army Staff Sergeant John S. Rothengast, was killed in action in Germany just before the end of the war.

When Rothengast was promoted to chief of detectives he assigned two of his men to follow Hoover whenever the director came to New York. From the racetrack with mobster Frank Costello, to the Stork Club with Walter Winchell, detectives Willie Mulligan and Paddy Hogan tailed Hoover wherever he went. Rothengast was so admired by detectives that his secret investigation of Hoover became a bureau-wide cause. Even retired detectives helped out. The doorman at the Stork Club was ex-detective Harold Magee; retired detectives ran the security for the New York Racing Association. Retired detectives and moonlighting cops functioned as bartenders and limousine drivers, and thus Rothengast was kept apprised of every move Hoover made in New York. Rothengast built a dossier on Hoover that the FBI director himself would have been proud of.

According to my father and other sources, on leaving the police department in December 1953, Rothengast destroyed the file by setting it afire in a metal wastepaper basket. It's doubtful he ever intended to use the file against Hoover; more likely it was an insurance policy. Although, by all accounts, Rothengast's character was unimpeachable, rumors swirled that a member of his immediate family had a gambling addiction. When it came to his position in the NYPD, a job he loved, Rothengast was not about to leave anything to chance. After being burned by something as inconsequential as a German-sounding name, he put nothing past Hoover's wanton vindictiveness.

Perhaps only coincidentally, a little over a year after Rothengast retired, Hoover named a native New Yorker, James J. Kelly, as special agent in charge of the New York area. The FBI director finally realized the folly of having non–New York agents interacting with the NYPD. As time went by, and city cops of Rothengast's era sent their children through college and on to law schools at Fordham and St. John's Universities, the rolls of the FBI became filled with the names of city cops' kids—and Rothengast's grudge, and the rift between the NYPD and the FBI, were all but forgotten.

On a late winter afternoon in 1951, my father met Joe Harley around the corner from police headquarters in a restaurant on Kenmare Street named Patrissy's. Considered one of the better Italian places in the neighborhood, Patrissy's was frequented by the brass of headquarters. The restaurant had one big dining room, paneled in rich, dark wood and filled with tables covered with red-and-white-checked tablecloths. Joe Harley sat alone at a corner table and waved my father over. At first the two friends engaged in small talk, chitchat: Harley bringing his old buddy up-to-date on happenings in the DEA, my father regaling Harley with stories of Chinese gamblers. My father kidded Harley when, untempted by the various Italian delicacies on the menu, Joe ordered his usual lunch of a Western egg sandwich and a cup of coffee. My father ordered veal scaloppini, and, because it was his day off, a Dewar's scotch, served with a small bottle of club soda on the side. By the time the lunch was served my father had noticed a gleam in Harley's eyes. He had known Harley long enough to know when his friend was bursting with some juicy news.

"Do you have something you want to tell me?" Frank asked, eyeing Harley with good-natured suspicion.

"Nothing much," Harley answered, coyly dabbing his mouth with a napkin, "just that Rothengast wants you in his office on Wednesday."

Traditionally, in the police department, official word comes only after sufficient time for unofficial word to be given. Though Harley wouldn't come right out and say what the chief of detectives wanted to see my father about, even after intense prodding, my father knew from his friend's expression that it had to be good news. Still, a voice in the back of his mind, a voice born in Depression-era Archbald, was tapping out a distress signal. What if it wasn't such good news? Or what if things changed in two days?

The day of the meeting with Rothengast, my father sat in a luncheonette down the block from police headquarters trying to drink a cup of coffee and looking at his watch every minute or so. He had arrived a full hour early. He wore his best suit, one that he bought from a tailor in the Bronx, and one that he thought Hughie Sheridan would have been proud of. He was too nervous to eat, and just a sip of the coffee made his stomach sound like someone was shaking a sheet of aluminum in it. His watch finally read ten of nine, and he put a dime under the saucer and walked down the street toward police headquarters.

The front of the old building at 240 Centre Street still evinced some of its original elegance. The centerpiece of the limestone facade was a four-story clock tower topped with a dome that had once been gilded, but now was chipped and faded. The stairs leading to the entrance were flanked by stone lions and Corinthian columns. Inside the cavernous foyer, awash with bronze and iron grillwork, the marble staircase lay before him. Rothengast's office was on the second floor, and Frank walked slowly up the stairs looking at the brass plaques that lined the walls, dedicated to officers killed in the line of duty. Each time he walked up these stairs he looked for the name of Francis McKeon, whom he had known at the Academy. McKeon was shot and killed with his own gun on November 17, 1945, after a struggle with someone whom *The New York Times* described as a "crazed Negro janitor." It had been McKeon's first day back on duty after serving four years in the Navy during the war.

My father could hear his heart beating, and was sure the lapel on the new suit was bouncing up and down to the thumping muscle in his chest. He got to the stair where he knew McKeon's plaque hung, and stopped to look. The memory of the fresh young face, with a smile as quick as a cigarette lighter, came flooding back to him, and he imagined McKeon saying "Go ahead, Frank," urging him up the stairs.

Joe Harley sat at his desk in the anteroom of the chief's office as my father walked in. Harley greeted him with a wink of the eye and a strong handshake, then disappeared behind the smoked-glass door of the chief's office. A moment later, he returned and held open the door for my father to enter.

Rothengast sat behind a desk large enough to set for dinner. He was in his shirtsleeves and his tie was loose around his collar. His trademark double-breasted suit jacket hung on a clothes tree behind the desk. The chief motioned my father to sit, and, as was his wont, came right to the point.

"Frank, I'm going to give you the Four-One squad," said the chief.

My father's smile must have been infectious, because for a moment—and only a moment—Rothengast smiled back. In that moment, as my father digested the chief's words, the nagging voice that told him that something might go wrong evaporated like the smoke from one of his cigars. He thought of the cramped apartment at 2300. Then he thought of the tiny ramshackle house in which he grew up, and of his first days in New York, when he slept on the couch at Aunt Mary's. He thought of the first pay envelope, from his days at the credit union, which he kept in with his personal papers, and of the $12 he'd made that week. He thought of the squad commanders, the ones in the felt collars, whom he'd watched in awe while he worked for Hughie Sheridan. He knew that it was undoubtedly Harley's whispers in Rothengast's ear that had cemented the contract, the biggest of his police career, one that meant a significant raise in pay, one that signaled his star in the department was rising, one that would make his dream of a home for his family—which now included

Tommy, the fourth child—a reality. As these thoughts tumbled in his mind he realized that the chief was still speaking, and he forced himself to listen.

"I have full confidence in you, Frank," Rothengast said. "But there are a few things you should know."

He explained that the Four-One was a fairly busy detective squad, and one that seemed to get busier every day. Most of the thirty or so detectives who would work for my father had been at the Four-One quite a while, some of them sent there for disciplinary reasons: men with drinking and gambling problems, men caught in compromising positions with prostitutes, and some who had beaten confessions out of suspects. This squad, the chief cautioned, had for years been the carpet under which the department's fallen angels were swept. My father was to be the "new broom" that would sweep the place clean. It was important that the squad commander be someone not beholden to Bronx brass, not inculcated in the inbred ways of the Bronx Detective Division. What Rothengast didn't say then, but what my father found out later, was the Four-One detective squad, fifteen years prior, had been Rothengast's. In the chief's eyes, it was a special assignment.

Rothengast stood and shook my father's hand. "Remember, Frank," the chief said deliberately, "no scandals." At the door Rothengast told him that if any problems arose, he should call the chief directly. Then he asked my father if he had any questions. Frank had just one—one he wouldn't ask the chief. He needed directions to the 41st Precinct. He didn't know how to get there.

At the beginning of her stay at Willowbrook, the entries in Mary Clare's chart are almost daily. By late 1951, they are separated by months. Some refer to my mother's visits. There are no references to my father. The picture they paint of Mary Clare's short life is heart-wrenching and gruesome. Her temperature sometimes climbs to 105, and she seems to be suffering from viral infections all the time. She spits up any food she eats; the word "vomiting" is in nearly every entry. Her hands are encased in mittens, to keep her from putting her fingers in her mouth, which induces the vomiting. In one entry, she has been put in isolation—for fifteen days. She had developed ringworm and mumps. She convulsed often.

On the last page of the chart, in July 1952, my mother appears again, requesting that Dramamine, the motion-sickness drug, be administered to Mary Clare. On August 6, treatment with Dramamine is instituted, but the chart says that vomiting has continued.

The last entry, on August 8, 1952, is headed with the word "EXPIRED"—just as I have written it, in capital letters and underlined. The entry reads:

At 11:15 P.M. last night child was found by the attendant without pulse or respiration. Artificial respiration was instituted and the doctor on call was notified. At 11:30 P.M. Aug. 7th, child was pronounced dead by Dr. Fleischer. A telegram was sent to the parents. The body was examined and found to be without bruises or recent injuries. On order of Dr. Fleischer, body was removed to the morgue.

The cause of death was listed as bilateral pulmonary atelectasis. Mary Clare died choking on her own vomit.

There was no one home at 2300 to receive the telegram. My family had gone to New Hampshire to visit my mother's sister Mazzie at her farm. From a window in the old farmhouse, my father saw a New Hampshire state trooper's car pull in to the long gravel driveway. When the telegram went unanswered, Willowbrook contacted the NYPD, which sent word to the troopers to contact my father. Frankie, Eugene, and Tommy stayed with my aunt, and my father and mother drove in silence back to New York.

The day of my sister's funeral mass, thirty detectives stood on the steps of St. Nicholas of Tolentine, on Fordham Road, as the little coffin was carried to the hearse. It was a tradition in the police department of those days—when almost all cops lived in the city—to show support when family members died. How strange it must have been to see them there. A funeral mass for a four-year-old girl, guarded as if she'd been the mayor of New York. For my mother, truly, a part of her died that day, and sadness took up residence in a corner of her soul.

Every year, on the Sunday before Christmas, the whole family would go to visit Mary Clare at the Gate of Heaven Cemetery in Westchester County. Of my many childhood memories of this day, the clearest came when I was five. We drove through the wrought-iron front gate and past the wooden guardhouse to the parking lot, crowded with cars—the Sunday before Christmas is a big day for visiting the dead. My father had to park far from the cement paths through the cemetery's grounds. Dark gray clouds, like sagging stained mattresses, hung from the sky. My hands stung from the cold because my mittens were stuffed in my pockets. I was too old for mittens, I'd told my mother that morning.

We walked a great distance on the winding paths, my mother and father up ahead, leading the way; Eugene walked with his girlfriend, Diane, whom I liked because she played badminton and often had a catch with me in the backyard. Tommy walked by himself, reading the names off the headstones. I walked next to Frankie. We came upon our marker, a huge tree, barren and forlorn in its winter slumber. The rest of the way was on crusty snow, past headstones and monuments.

"Don't step on the graves," Frankie warned me. "You'll disturb the dead."

I tiptoed my way, careful to not bother the dead. My father stopped and looked around like an ostrich peering over the herd.

"Are you sure this is the right way, El?" he asked my mother. She paused, too, doubting her instinct, which would have found the grave in the middle of the night. Eugene reassured my parents that we were on the right path. Eugene's memory is like a Polaroid camera, and we continued silently on, the only sound the icy snow crackling beneath our feet. We looked for the name Duran on a headstone, as Mary Clare did not have a headstone and Duran was buried right beside her. I wondered if Mary Clare and Duran spoke to each other under the ground. When we finally reached the plot, my mother laid the Christmas ivy and poinsettias she carried on the undisturbed snow.

We stood in a circle and prayed. I didn't know what to say in my prayers, as I never knew my sister. So I said, I'm sorry I never knew you, and then my prayer was finished. My father looked down at his feet, which he stamped back and forth, a habit he'd acquired from standing fixed posts on winter nights in his early days as a patrolman. My brothers and Diane also bowed their heads. After a short while, my father lifted his eyes and gave us a quick tilt of his head, the signal to give my mother time alone. We waited in a bunch, twenty steps or so from her, our breath coming out in white puffs of smoke, our hands rummaging for warmth in the pockets of dress overcoats. I looked at my mother as she stood with her shoulders hunched, her back heaved in short, rapid sobs. She stood there for a long time, and I was most anxious to leave because I knew we were going to Patricia Murphy's restaurant for dinner afterward and Patricia Murphy's had a Christmas princess who wore a glimmering white gown and sat in an old-fashioned sled in the lobby and gave out candy canes to all the children. I pulled at my father's coat and asked when we were going to go.

"When your mother's ready," he said, as he stood there at attention. Finally my mother turned to us, dabbing the corners of her eyes with a handkerchief, her tears having left streaks from her mascara that looked like finger marks on dirty windowpane.

At the restaurant, Eugene and Frankie made a trip to the bathroom, then came back to the table bursting with laughter. Frankie told us that they'd met an elderly man whose hat had fallen into the toilet. He repeated what the man had said: "First my wife leaves me, then I lose my job, and now this!" I imagined the man's hat bobbing in the porcelain sea. My mother laughed hardest of all of us. But her laughter stopped suddenly, and I saw her fighting back tears. I went to her, and she clutched me, so tight I almost couldn't breathe. It was as though she was afraid that something would come to snatch me away from her, and this time, she would not let her child go. I saw that my father's expression was uncomfortable, nearly guilty. For what? I now wonder. For letting Mary Clare die? As if, as a cop, he had failed at his charge to keep his child safe from harm? Even if that harm was a disease? No. He shouldered the fault, because my mother needed to blame someone. For years it was her undying belief that the sulfa drug caused Mary Clare's condition, even after the doctors told her it was the viral infection. And even if it had been the sulfa drug, my mother needed some*one* to blame, not some*thing*. I knew, as only a child knows these things, that Mary Clare's death formed a chasm between my parents, and in that moment, in my mother's grasp, I knew too that that fissure also separated me from my father. He would give me up, to ease some of my mother's pain.

# 5

At the Bronx Historical Society, a real estate atlas from 1911 shows 1086 Simpson Street, then under construction, occupying lots 17 through 20, square in the middle of the block between 167th Street and Westchester Avenue. According to the atlas, the street front of the station house measured one hundred feet. On the south side of the building is a ten-foot-wide alley.

The station house took over two years to build and opened in 1914. The facade that faced Simpson Street was three stories high and made of limestone, which on the ground floor was rusticated in grand arches around the large and low windows and the doorway. The roof was terra-cotta, an elaborate assemblage of a forest-green tile that, at a certain time of the morning, glimmered in the sunshine. It was built by the reputable architectural firm of Hazzard, Erskine & Blagden. The design was called beaux-arts, or renaissance revival, and was to evoke, with its cornice and broad-hipped roof, the early-sixteenth-century palaces of Florence and Rome.

On the left side of the doorway, etched into one of the large foundational blocks, was the inscription "Police Department, City of New York, R. Waldo, Police Commissioner, MCMXIII."

Under Mayor William J. Gaynor, who had survived an assassination attempt in 1910, Rhinelander Waldo's term as commissioner—from 1911 to 1913—was considered quite an innovative time. It was then that the rank of "roundsman" was abolished and the modern "sergeant" took its place. Waldo oversaw the use of the first automobile in the police department, ordered new uniforms with heavy coats and large pockets to keep his men warm in the winter months, and instituted the three-shift platoon system. And he was a visionary when it came to municipal buildings.

While fire commissioner, a post he held before he was police commissioner, he devised an elaborate plan to build twenty-five additional firehouses in outlying areas of the city to quicken response time. As police commissioner, he initiated a similar, though scaled-down, proposal for police stations in the Bronx, to accommodate what Waldo foresaw—the coming population explosion of the borough. The Simpson Street building was to be the prototype for all those built in the Bronx after it. By 1911, plans were in the works for three new station houses and the rebuilding of two more.

But, except for the Simpson Street station house, Waldo's vision would not come to fruition. Perhaps, too involved in the grand scheme of things, the commissioner had lost touch with the everyday workings of his department. A scandal, which involved a small-time gambler named Rosenthal (who blew the whistle on the police department's involvement in gambling enterprises) and a dashing, crooked lieutenant named Charles Becker (who ordered Rosenthal's murder), brought about the commissioner's ultimate downfall. The Curran Committee, formed to investigate the scandal, found Waldo unfit and incompetent. The Simpson Street station house was the only one of its distinctive style built.

On the real estate atlas, the rest of Simpson Street is designated as residential, with building shapes colored in deep red to signify brick apartment houses, most with the code "5B" indicating a five-story building with a basement. On the far northwest corner of the block, several lots are taken up by Public School No. 20. An elevated subway station is marked at the intersection of Simpson Street and Westchester Avenue. The atlas shows the raised elbow of track where the train turns to run above Southern Boulevard directly behind the station house.

What the atlas didn't show is that in those five-story tenement buildings lived Irish, Germans, Italians, and the beginnings of the Jewish population that, with the completion of that elevated subway in 1905, grew by the tens of thousands each year. It didn't show that for the Jews and the Irish who lived in the squalor of the Lower East Side of Manhattan, the South Bronx was the real America, the place they had dreamt about on their voyage over, where harmony and opportunity lay.

When the station house opened, the entire population of its precinct was a suburblike 48,000. Over the next two decades, coinciding with the largest period of immigration of Jews from Eastern Europe, and the subsequent overcrowding of the tenement neighborhoods of the Lower East Side, the Jewish population of the Bronx would grow to 600,000, with the majority settling in the southern portions of the borough.

Even with the bulging population, the crime rate stayed remarkably low. Police blotters of the early 1920s from what would become the 41st Precinct (it was first designated the 62nd Precinct), read like those from an ideal midwestern town. Owners of unlicensed dogs, drivers speeding at a thirty-two-mile-an-hour clip along Southern Boulevard, and teenage boys roughhousing in the streets were the lawbreakers of the day. Yes, it was Prohibition, and raids on speakeasies were cited, and every once in a while there was a record of a cop discharging his weapon. Usually a rabid dog or a lame horse was the recipient of the bullet.

Thirty years after that atlas was made, during World War II, further waves of immigration to the South Bronx would occur. Blacks from the southern states and Caribbean people, mostly from Puerto Rico, flocked to the area to find wartime jobs in the factories of Hunts Point. (Northern blacks had lived in the Bronx since the 1600s, when they were brought as slaves to work the farms in the Morrisania area.) The war also brought with it rent control, first federally orchestrated, then run by the state.* Though once viewed as the height of egalitarianism, rent control and other influences would polarize the South Bronx and ultimately lead to its devastation.

But the Bronx was still a thriving place when, on a bright spring morning, my father drove his maroon '49 Nash Rambler down Southern Boulevard, under the elevated subway tracks, on the first day of his new assignment: April 2, 1951. Following the directions he'd been given at Bronx Detective Bureau headquarters, he passed Jennings and then Freeman Streets, where stout Eastern European women sold fruits and vegetables from wooden carts. Farther down, he passed the kosher chicken stores that lined the boulevard, and still more sidewalk vendors. He turned on Westchester Avenue, where the scent of Jewish delicatessens filled the air. The streets were teeming with people, Yiddish mixed with Spanish, forming a continuous hum.

He parked the Nash in the alleyway next to the station house and walked through the front entrance. He didn't notice that the archway around the door was rusticated; he didn't see the inscrip-

---

*In the 1960s, charge of rent control was taken over by the city.

tion on the cornerstone. My father *had* noticed the roof, and thought it a bit much for a police station.

Inside, he walked through the foyer and up to the desk sergeant and asked where he could find the squad room. He was directed up a flight of stairs to his right. The walls in the stairway were cracked and chipped. A waist-high wooden gate separated the squad room from the landing. Behind the gate, a bald man with a gin-ruddy face was seated at a desk typing a report with a deliberate two-finger style. At first, the detective didn't notice my father standing in front of him. After an awkward moment or two, he finally looked up at the tall young man dressed in a fine suit, and with only the slightest of interest asked:

"Can I help you?"

"I hope so," my father answered. "I'm your new boss."

The squad room was lined with a half-dozen or so wooden desks, on each a typewriter. The plaster on the walls, like that in the stairway, was chipped and the color of a nicotine stain. Inside the room, the first thing that caught my father's eye was a picture of George Washington hung rather oddly near the far top corner. The detective at the desk, noticing my father's questioning expression, shrugged and said "Bullet hole," and offered no further explanation.

In very little time, Frank realized that Rothengast's assessment of the detectives in the Four-One squad—that they were the fallen angels of the department—was, if anything, an understatement. One morning, early on in his new job, my father was standing at the top of the stairs by the gate to the squad room as a new uniform lieutenant was addressing the patrolmen mustered together on the main floor. Through the front door of the station house walked one of my father's detectives, Mike Hickey. The other detectives in the squad, my father knew, called Hickey the Inspector, because of his penchant for fashionable attire: natty hats and vests, always with the gold chain of his pocket watch fashionably displayed. Frank also knew that Hickey was considered the court jester of the squad.

In a moment, Hickey sized up the situation unfolding in front of him: the unseasoned lieutenant, the lines of patrolmen, most of whom were well aware of Hickey's reputation. Hickey winked to the desk sergeant, who immediately announced, in a commanding baritone, "Inspector in the station!" The lieutenant snapped to attention, greeting Hickey with a crisp salute. Hickey put his hands behind his back and walked slowly back and forth, inspecting the troops.

"Men," he said, deadly serious, "we have a situation. It seems a truck filled with Karo syrup has crashed into a chicken market on Westchester Avenue. There are syrup-covered chickens running wild in the street down there."

The patrolmen who knew Hickey tried to keep straight faces, but a few of them couldn't and spat out laughter. Those who didn't know him, including the lieutenant, stood agape, in astonished silence. Hickey didn't notice that my father was watching from the top of the stairs.

"I want you to approach the chickens with extreme caution," he continued. "They are extremely dangerous in this condition. So let's hop to it, the neighborhood depends on you."

Hickey dismissed the men, then spun on his heel and marched right past the befuddled lieutenant and up the stairs to the squad room. My father stepped into the doorway of his office and pretended to read a report, as the raucous laughter from below wafted up the stairs behind Hickey.

Though my father shrugged off Hickey's performance, there were other events that caused him to wonder what he had ventured into. One of the first murders that occurred during his time at the 41st was of a woman named Eugenia Fargus, who was killed in the basement of her apartment building. The police were notified by her husband, who said he'd found his wife dead around one o'clock in the morning. When Bill Carren, the detective assigned to the case, arrived at the scene, the victim was lying on the floor of the basement, naked, with a two-inch-wide knife wound in her forehead. Carren reported that the husband and wife had been drinking heavily that night. He also wrote that the husband's alibi was flimsy at best—he had told Carren that he left the apartment at eleven p.m. and returned two hours later. Carren told my father that the husband was his prime suspect. Carren had good reason for believing Fargus to be guilty: The husband had a prior arrest record, for robbery, and there were no witnesses who could corroborate his alibi. But the main reason Carren thought him the killer was the husband's occupation—he was a house painter.

Eugenia Fargus's body had been painted from head to toe with a dark-green enamel.

The husband was brought into the squad room numerous times and interrogated for hours, but didn't admit to the crime. Carren tried every trick he knew to elicit a confession. He threatened, he consoled, he even brought a Bible in one day and knelt and prayed with the husband. But still Fargus didn't break. Carren became so emotionally involved in the case, my father strongly suggested that he take his vacation—which he did, to a summer house in the Catskill Mountains. When he returned to the squad room a week later, he did so carrying a large cardboard box, which contained a three-foot-long blacksnake he had captured near his mountain cottage.

"I'm going to bring the husband in one more time," Carren told my father. "I'm going to lock him and this snake in the interrogation room until he confesses."

Carren never got the chance. My father remanded the snake to the New York City sewer system. The murder of Eugenia Fargus was never solved.

\* \* \*

One of a squad commander's primary functions is the charge of scheduling and the assignment of cases. On the wall of the squad room, between the crisscross wire door of the holding cell and a sign above the fingerprint desk that read, "All officers must remove their revolvers before fingerprinting prisoners and must be accompanied by a backup officer, NO EXCEPTIONS," hung a blackboard lined in chalk. The days of the week were printed across the top, the names of detectives in pairs down the side. For the detective partners, the work week was five days. Each day included two tours—eight a.m. to five p.m., "day duty"; five p.m. to eight a.m., "night duty." The group of the detectives working a tour was called a team. Each tour was divided into individual time slots, with partners assigned to each slot. If a crime occurred during your time slot, you were assigned to it. This was known as "catching." If you caught a homicide or other major crime, you could be taken off the schedule, at the squad commander's discretion, to work the case to its conclusion. The squad commander had absolute and final say on anything concerning the chart.

Throughout his first month running the Four-One squad, my father was an enigma to his men. He arrived each morning before day duty started, and left each evening well after night duty began. But he seldom engaged the detectives in conversation and mostly stayed behind his desk (carved with the initials of past occupants, like an oak tree at a lovers' lookout), the office door halfway closed, readying the chart for the week, reviewing the crime cases being worked, and reading back records of others that were closed. His cool and distant demeanor was no doubt a cover for his uncertainty. He had gone from patrolman to detective squad commander in four years, a huge jump in rank and responsibility. He was only thirty-three, the youngest squad commander in the city. The natural trepidation he felt expressed itself, as it did most times with my father, inwardly.

Also, he took Rothengast's warning, "No scandals," very seriously. And he now knew that the sordid reputation of the men in the squad was deserved. Some of the reports he reviewed were shoddily written, others incomplete. The squad's arrest performance was mediocre at best. He thought that, individually, some of his men were savvy, street-hardened detectives. But an overall malaise, a lax attitude, seemed to permeate the squad as a whole.

The worst thing he could do, he thought, was give his men the impression that he was concerned with his popularity.

As a boss, my father was a natural. He had, for lack of a better word, balls. Maybe this boldness came from his instant rank in the navy or his time in the Detective District office. Or maybe it was born out of defiance, from years of seeing his father's servitude to the foremen in the mines. Wherever it came from, he had it. And he was about to show his squad that he did.

A month into his command, Frank reassigned his detectives to new partners. When the schedule went up, there was a great commotion, with loud, heated conversation and low grumbles. Some of the detectives had worked with their partners for years; in the police department, there is no more sacred a union. A detective named O'Brien stormed into my father's office and demanded to know what was going on.

"Things are going to change around here" was all my father said.

A few of the detectives complained directly to the bureau chief, who demanded an explanation. Chief Edward Byrnes had already made it clear that he was not in my father's corner. That first day of his assignment, just before driving to the 41st Precinct, Frank had stopped at the chief's office. "Don't make any mistakes," Byrnes had said coldly.

On a tribal level, the New York City police department has always run on an elaborate system of contracts—not the kind printed on paper and signed on dotted lines, but verbal ones sealed with a handshake or the clink of a glass of scotch. This can be dated back to the days of Boss Tweed and the beginnings of the corrupt Tammany regime, when promotion and desirable assignments were first offered for a price. Throughout most of the history of the police department, nepotism and ethnicity (for the most part Irish "taking care of their own") were the criteria by which sought-after assignments were granted. Chief Byrnes, diminutive in stature, with a halting, blunt delivery, was Bronx born and raised, and had spent his whole police career there. He wanted the Four-One squad for one of his own protégés. The thought of an outsider—a hayseed, for Christ's sake!—was a personal insult to him. But with Rothengast on my father's side, there was nothing Byrnes could do. When my father explained that he'd made the partner changes because he was unhappy with production, Byrnes, regardless of how he felt, couldn't countermand him. But, over the coming weeks, the 41st Precinct squad room was a very unhappy place, and my father a very unpopular boss.

# 6

Though in the civil service records, Frank McDonald was still officially a sergeant, his appointment as squad commander of the 41st Precinct brought with it the title of acting lieutenant, a rank created in 1925 by Commissioner Enright in order to bestow the appropriate authority and respect on detective squad commanders. My father had already begun work on losing the "acting" portion of his title, by readying for the lieutenant's exam.

He had discovered the fast track in the police department: pass the tests and have friends in high places. He had both the smarts and the access. He had placed in the top 10 percent in his first two civil service tests; the patrolman's and sergeant's exam. He had every reason to believe he would do as well on the lieutenant's test. But his vision of his future did not stop there. After lieutenant, the last level of civil service is captain. Higher ranks are bestowed by appointment. Just two more tests, he thought, and with the backing of people like Conrad Rothengast, who was about to be appointed chief police inspector, Frank McDonald's future in the police department was limitless. But my father's ambition only further exacerbated the division between him and his detectives.

As the president of the police board, from 1895 to 1897, Teddy Roosevelt oversaw a campaign to put an end to advancement by favoritism and graft. The first civil service exam for patrolmen was given in 1895. Roosevelt championed written tests and background checks for promotions. When he moved on to bigger things, and the corrupt machinery of the department began to grind once more, most of his reforms remained in place. But the model he created rewarded book smarts, not street smarts. There has long been a breach, in the police department, between commanders and their subordinates. Like battle-seasoned veterans receiving instructions on how to fight from army officers who had never been to the front lines, street-smart cops looked upon their book-smart bosses with sarcastic contempt. My father's early success and quick climb up the ranks included one little glitch: When he arrived at the 41st Precinct, he had absolutely no real experience as a street detective. His time in the Detective Division had been spent wholly in clerical, administrative, and political positions. He also lacked the intimate local knowledge possessed by the men who now worked for him, most of whom had grown up in neighborhoods of the Bronx. But this would change. It had to.

In preparing for the lieutenant's test, my father joined a study group that met in one of the midtown hotels, like the Astor, and took cram courses together at Delahanty's, the civil service exam school. In 1953, he took the test and aced it. He was thirty-five, and his career was proceeding as planned. The captain's test was next, and so were what Frank called the halcyon days.

The stories of the Rat Pack, the name sarcastically hung on the study group by one member's wife because of their late-night carousing, lived on for years in my home. After a few hours of study, they would go for dinner, and then continue late into the night at one of the hot spots of the day. They walked into restaurants and nightclubs like the Copacabana and Toots Shor's, and the sea parted. At Toots Shor's, Jackie Gleason would send them a round of drinks, or Phil Silvers would pull up a chair and sit with them, testing out his latest routine. When the check came at the end of the night—if it came at all—it would represent a fraction of what they had actually spent.

I have a photograph of the Rat Pack, taken in May 1956 in a place called Joe King's Rathskeller on Third Avenue in Manhattan. Seven men, all in finely tailored suits, are sitting on a banquette around a table draped in a checkered cloth. On the table sits a bottle of J&B scotch, and before each man is a small, straight glass. My father's arms are stretched along the banquette, around Jack Kelly and Frank Weldon, both squad commanders.

They were an impressive group. Two of them, Walter Fenn and Andy Leddy, had been B-17 pilots during World War II. Gus Harms, towering, with thick, blond hair, had been a member of the 1939 U.S. Olympic water polo team, and had won the Latin prize at Fordham University despite the fact that he was not Catholic. He also had his law degree before he took the entrance exam to the police department. Other members' reputations were formed during their police careers. Jack Kelly grew up in the Chelsea section of Manhattan, where his father owned a pet store and sold pigeons to West Side mobsters, some of whom took a shine to the friendly young man behind the counter. Before the advent of the Organized Crime Control Bureau, Kelly was considered one of the department's foremost experts on crime families. Mario Biaggi was well on his way to becoming the most decorated policeman in the history of the NYPD. And finally there was Frank Weldon, perhaps the closest of the group to my father. Soft-spoken, suave, with matinee-idol looks, Weldon might have been the best detective of the bunch. As heroin became the number one cause of crime in New York City, Weldon's investigations into the drug trade were legendary. He was also credited with solving the Wiley-Hoffert murders. Two women in their early twenties—one the daughter of a prominent surgeon, the other of a well-known writer—were butchered in their Upper East Side apartment. Before Weldon took over the investigation, the wrong man was indicted in the murders. As a result of Weldon's arduous detective work, the man responsible for the killings was caught and the wrongly accused man exonerated. The pilot for the *Kojak* television series was based on the case, with Telly Savalas playing Frank Weldon. (Quite possibly, this was the only time in television history when the real cop was better looking than the actor playing him.)

In the photograph, my father's face is full, nearly fat. His broad smile says there's no place in the world he'd rather be. Filled with confidence, he and his detective cronies were the young lions of the department. And though several of them worked in the Bronx, Manhattan, it seemed, was their private club.

One night, early in his time at the 41st Precinct, my father and several of the Rat Pack sat ringside to watch his old basketball pal Billy Graham fight Kid Gavilan for the welterweight title in Madison Square Garden—a fight Graham lost in a controversial decision. In a Greenwich Village bistro called the Bon Soir, the Rat Pack sat and watched as a young songstress from Brooklyn named Barbra Streisand made her professional debut. On another night, they went to the midnight show at the Copacabana, where Sammy Davis, Jr., was performing. Ushered down front by the maitre d', they were seated at a table next to Yankee stars Mickey Mantle, Hank Bauer, Whitey Ford, and Billy Martin. Just as the show started, Martin began to argue with a man at the table on the other side. Frank Weldon recognized some of the men Martin was screaming at as wiseguys from the Bronx. The shouting escalated into a wrestling match and few weak punches were thrown. Mantle and Bauer rushed to Martin's aid. Right in front of my father, one of the tuxedo-clad bouncers grabbed Martin from behind and in a low but authoritative voice explained to him that if he ever wanted to play baseball again he'd better leave right that moment. The next day, the fight was a front-page story in all the New York papers, the news accounts calling the table Martin had argued with "a Bronx bowling team." Frank Weldon called my father at his office the next day and said, "They're the kind of bowling team that drills holes in the balls with .38 caliber revolvers."

For Frank McDonald, these were the days and nights of being absolutely bulletproof. Nothing, it seemed, could slow down the juggernaut of his career. Very early one morning, after a night out on the town, he and five of the Rat Pack were riding home along the Bronx River Parkway. Frank Weldon was at the wheel, driving extremely fast, and didn't notice the garbage truck lumbering in the lane in front of him until he was almost upon it. Weldon slammed on the brakes and cut the wheel, but clipped the back end of the truck. Their car caromed out of control, flipping over, and ending upside-down in a ditch along the drive. Perhaps it was providence, or maybe it was the fact that there were six wide bodies filling every space in the car, but the most serious injury was to Frank Weldon, who broke a toe. My father didn't get a scratch. Not even a tear in his suit. He walked to a nearby gas station and called two of his detectives to come pick them up. The detectives chauffeured the lieutenants home. Life in the police department was that easy for my father; with a snap of his fingers, problems would vanish. The week after the crash, the study group met at Toots Shor's, and named the gathering "the wake," which it was called from then on. At the table they observed a moment of silence for Frank Weldon's toe, then lifted their glasses of good scotch for a toast.

Even my father's nascent investigative skills seemed predestined to greater things. On August 22, 1953, he was notified of the apparent suicide of a fairly well known doctor and his wife, who lived in a Parkchester housing development. Although Parkchester lay in the 43rd Precinct, one weekend a month, on a revolving basis, squad commanders in the Bronx would cover two precincts. Because running a detective squad was a twenty-four-hour, seven-day-a-week job (often my father would be awakened in the middle of the night at home by a phone call telling him he was needed at the office) the system was instituted to assure the commander at least one weekend a month of peace and quiet.

At the scene, my father saw that the doctor's wife was slumped on the couch in the apartment; the doctor lay on the floor near the doorway to the kitchen. Both bodies had foam around their mouths. On a coffee table sat two champagne glasses. The couple's twenty-one-year-old son and a male friend were also at the scene. It was they who had called the police. When the Bronx medical examiner, Charles Hochman, arrived, he determined that the couple had died from cyanide poisoning and that it was indeed a suicide pact. Hochman knew the couple—the doctor, William Fraden, worked for the city health department.

Hochman was well respected by detectives in the Bronx. Every year, the Bronx squad commanders would throw a birthday party in his honor. As the borough M.E., Hochman inspired many a story. He was known to perform autopsies holding a scalpel in one hand and a half-eaten Danish in the other. At one autopsy, of a prostitute who was murdered in Hunts Point, his dictation to the stenographer read: "A female, Negress, approximately twenty-five, five foot two inches, one hundred and twelve pounds, narcotics tracks on both arms, and well-traveled fore and aft."

In the Parkchester apartment that day, my father asked Hochman why, if it was a suicide pact, hadn't the couple both died on the couch? Why was the doctor's body on the floor near the kitchen? Hochman explained that cyanide poisoning causes inordinate thirst, and the doctor had most likely tried to crawl to the kitchen for water. Still, my father had his suspicions, not the least of which fell upon the couple's son and his friend. He thought their attitude too cavalier in the face of what had happened. In spite of his respect for Hochman, my father decided to open a murder investigation.

Nine months later, Harlow Fraden, the couple's son, confessed to killing his parents. The friend, Dennis Wepman, had been his accomplice. The two men were believed to have been in a homosexual relationship. The night of the murders, Wepman had stood at the doorway to the apartment, taking notes to be used in a novel he was writing.

Though the stars then seemed aligned in my father's favor, the future of the South Bronx didn't look as promising. In the decade after the war, when landlords became fed up with the rent ceilings imposed by state law, their frustration began to show in the upkeep of their buildings, which fell into disrepair. Throughout the 1950s, older residents of the Bronx were reluctant to leave their rent-controlled apartments; young ones, with the automobile and highway explosion in America, moved their new families to the North Bronx, Westchester, and, by the mid 1950s, Rockland County.

Meanwhile, inside the 41st a truce of sorts had been called. About a month after my father had reassigned the detectives to new partners, he reunited them. This about-face did not indicate that he succumbed to pressure from either his detectives or the Bronx brass. Younger than any of the men who worked for him, my father had made the move purely to send the message that he was the boss. The message was received. Although none of his men were about to ask him over to their houses for dinner, respect for my father began to grow in the squad room, and a transformation occurred in the detectives' attitude toward their jobs. Though a large percentage of the men did have sordid pasts, Frank's original assessment that most were good detectives was correct. For years before my father arrived, the inmates ran the asylum of the Four-One squad. Now they had a boss who asserted structure and chain of command, and the inmates became detectives again, and their inherent talents began to show.

In my father's first few years in the 41st Precinct, most of the homicides there were crimes of passion: drunken escalations of neighborhood grudges and outstanding debts; domestic quarrels, like the Eugenia Fargus case, that ended tragically. But, by the mid-1950s, with the infusion of heroin and the growth of teenage gangs, murders in the precinct not only came with alarming frequency, they were horribly arbitrary. One day, my father sat at his desk looking at crime scene photographs, the face of Mary Rozincoff staring lifelessly back at him. In one photo, she lay on her bed, her nightgown pushed up to her waist, her head positioned in the grotesque angle of death. He passed that face almost every morning on Jennings Street as he drove to work. In the winter months, she'd wrap her legs in burlap against the cold. Like the other street vendors, selling fruit and vegetables, she stood close to a trash can ablaze with a wood fire to keep warm. From the crime report on his desk, my father knew she had a son, a doctor who lived on Long Island. He imagined her saving each dime she made to send the son through medical school.

The crime report was an all too familiar story now: The intruder, a heroin addict, had popped the window of her ground-floor apartment on Southern Boulevard and, as she slept, smothered Mary Rozincoff with her own pillow.

During the investigation, Mrs. Rozincoff's son came to the squad room to speak to my father. As Frank began to express his sympathies, the son stopped him in mid-sentence:

"Where's the money?" he demanded. He had come not out of concern about the progress of the investigation into his mother's murder, but because he was convinced that police officers, and not the murderer, had taken her money. The two detectives working the case were standing at the door to my father's office and overheard the entire conversation. Frank looked at the detectives and then stared coldly at the doctor.

"Get the fuck out of my office," my father said, "or I'll have you arrested for interfering with a criminal investigation."

Whether or not he was within his rights to arrest the doctor didn't matter. What did was that the doctor believed him—he scurried past the now beaming detectives, and down the stairs. The detectives didn't say anything to my father, but they didn't have to. Their expressions told the whole story. My father was no longer the cold, distant squad commander. By 1954, three years into his tenure at the 41st Precinct, Frank McDonald was a boss for whom you wanted to work, and that loyalty showed in the performance of his squad. The "fallen angels" of whom Rothengast had warned had begun to build a different kind of reputation.

Mike Hickey once told my father that, years before, he had quit drinking for good when he found himself one midnight, dressed in full uniform, directing traffic in Teaneck, New Jersey. Hickey was also an inveterate gambler. This he didn't give up. He spent most days off at Aqueduct or at the New Jersey shore, at Monmouth Racetrack. One summer, my father and mother took a vacation in Spring Lake, New Jersey, and stayed at the Breakers Hotel, where Hickey always stayed. A perennial bachelor, Hickey spent each morning perfecting his golden tan on the beach. In the afternoon, it was on to the track. At night, Hickey would play poker with a group of guys on the porch of the hotel. One of Hickey's card-playing buddies was a knock-about actor named James Gregory. Years later, Gregory played the part of "Inspector Luger" on a TV sitcom called *Barney Miller*, about a New York detective squad. My father saw Hickey's mannerisms in Gregory's portrayal.

But when it came to work, Hickey was the consummate professional. Despite the Hollywood glamorization, detective work is for the most part painstaking and systematic. The investigation of a crime can mean hundreds of interviews, knocking on doors, talking to everyone and anyone, who might have a shred of valuable information. The detective then assembles this information—along, of course, with any evidence—and formulates a list of suspects. The part that comes next is what you mostly see on television—when the suspect is interrogated in the squad room. But before that ever happens, hours upon hours of detective work have been done.

Hickey had his own system of canvassing for information. His favorite saying was "Always look for the yenta," the neighborhood busybody who would sit in the window of her apartment and watch and see everything that happened on the block. Hickey's yentas helped solve a good portion of his investigations.

Mike Hickey and the other detectives who worked for him gave my father a detective squad ultimately regarded as one of the best in the Bronx (from 1958 to 1962, their arrest-to-crime ratio was at or near the top in the borough). But they also brought humor to their work without which the job would have been impossible to perform.

My father often told stories about Hickey. There was the time he assigned Hickey to investigate a series of robberies at Howard's, a clothing store. He said Hickey was the right detective for the job, given his fondness for fashion. The thieves were lowering themselves through the skylight of the store with a rope. Hickey decided to lie in wait for them, and sure enough, the first night he spent in the store, a rope dropped from the skylight.

The next day Hickey brought the suspects into court for arraignment. The magistrate, whom Hickey knew from Greenwich Village, where they had both grown up, was hard of hearing. On the stand, the D.A. asked Hickey to relay what he had witnessed the night of the robbery. Hickey began to answer in a normal tone of voice, but, every other sentence or so, he would just move his lips. The judge began to tap his hearing aid, becoming ever more frustrated as Hickey's testimony continued. An irascible character, he yelled at Hickey to speak up, at which Hickey again just pretended to talk. Finally, the magistrate came out from behind the bench and demanded that Hickey show him what had happened. From the evidence table, Hickey took the rope the thief had used and began to wrap it around the judge's legs, then around his arms, as he elaborated the thief's method. The whole courtroom was in stitches. Even the defendant was laughing so hard, tears were streaming down his face.

By the early 1960s, white flight from the Bronx was extremely fast. From 1960 to 1966, 205,000 whites moved out. In their wake, blacks and Puerto Ricans moved en masse from less desirable housing in Harlem and other areas, looking, as the Irish and Jews had decades before, for a better place to live. But for blacks and Puerto Ricans, the South Bronx was no longer the oasis it had been for the early immigrants. Throughout the 1950s wartime industry abandoned the Hunts Point factories. By the early 1960s, other industries were packing up the truck. From 1960 to 1966, 216 companies, manufacturing everything from apparel to machinery, left the South Bronx.

As their constituencies disappeared, Bronx politicians turned their backs on the community, and services vanished. As the 1960s approached, federally financed bulldozers razed block after block of tenement housing in the neighborhoods surrounding the 41st Precinct, and city-run housing projects were built. "Come one, come all" was the advertising catch-phrase of the day. But for those who came, there was little work. At the same time, an amazingly complex welfare system was instituted. Heroin addiction grew to epidemic proportions, and teenage gangs fueled the spiraling crime rate. From 1950 to 1960 murder-homicide arrests in the Bronx grew by 66.7 percent. By 1965, that number had more than tripled.

One by one, the delicatessens on Westchester Avenue, the kosher markets on Southern Boulevard, began to close, their owners fleeing a neighborhood that was deteriorating before their eyes. Clothing stores, like Howard's and Crawford's, were first gated; then they left and the premises became check-cashing stores, or they were simply torched, their charred remains used as shooting galleries. The stately apartment houses on Fox and Kelly Streets first became run-down and eventually were abandoned. Police wore air-raid hard hats, and later, riot helmets as protection from copings and bricks thrown at them from rooftops. Hunts Point, once a bustling industrial area, became a wasteland; packs of wild dogs roamed the lots of deserted factories. Drug pushers and prostitutes lined Southern Boulevard and Westchester Avenue where pushcart vendors once hawked their wares. The murders piled up, becoming, to my father, anonymous faces in crime scene photographs and numbers to be added to statistics. Some of them, like Mary Rozincoff, stood out as exclamation points in the volumes of murders. By the early 1960s, the 41st Precinct led the city in virtually every major crime statistic.

At the beginning of his tenure at the Four-One, my father acted as the administrative boss, assigning his detectives to cases. But as the 1960s began and the sheer number of crimes began to overwhelm his squad, more and more he found himself at crime scenes, in abandoned buildings, in ramshackle apartments, and, in February 1962, in the dank, dark basement of 1171 Bryant Avenue.

On that cold winter day, as my father walked from a delicatessen around the corner from the station house, he was approached by a building superintendent from Bryant Avenue. The super knew my father, as most of the neighborhood did by then. The station house and the squad room had become a refuge from the onslaught of crime and predators. The super was nervous, agitated. He said that there were four or five men in the basement of his building with guns and that he had heard them plotting a robbery and murder. Nothing was implausible then in the 41st Precinct. And just the week before, there had been a major gun bust in the basement of another building in the precinct. My father went back to the squad room and rounded up two detectives to go with him to investigate.

My father, followed by the two detectives, all three men with guns drawn, eased open the door to the blackness of the basement. The only sound was the clanking of the boiler. Then something rustled in the darkness, and then there was the sound of metal dropping to the floor. My father crouched into shooter position, the technique he had learned twenty years before in the police academy. He held the Police Special with two hands, just as the instructors had taught. Up to this point in his career, he had never discharged his weapon on duty, and right then he said a little prayer to keep that streak alive. He heard the sound of a door creak before he saw the movement from the corner of his eye. Silently, he signaled to the two detectives. There was just enough light for Frank to make out the figure standing just a few feet away, holding a revolver pointed directly at him.

For a split second there was only deadly silence. Then, from the dark recess behind the man, he heard his name: "Frank, holy shit. Frank! Don't shoot, Eddy, don't shoot. . . ."

The seven men in that basement that day were all cops. The man who recognized my father was Vinnie Hawks, a lieutenant in the narcotics squad. He and my father had been in the academy together. The man holding a gun on my father was a detective named Eddy Egan. Frank knew Egan and had no use for him. One day, my father had walked into the squad room to find a prisoner hung by his wrists with handcuffs in the lockup cage. The prisoner had been put in that position by Egan, who had arrested him for narcotics possession and was trying to coerce him to inform on his supplier. My father had the prisoner taken down and ordered Egan out of the squad room, telling him that he never wanted to see him in the precinct again.

In the basement, my father was furious with Hawks. "Why wasn't I notified?" he screamed. Hawks tried to explain, but my father wasn't about to listen. He knew the thoughts that had surged through his own mind. One quick movement, by anyone, and he certainly would have fired. Had that happened, in all likelihood an all-out gun battle would have ensued. My father stormed from the basement, with Hawks apologetically following after.

Back in the squad room, my father called his boss, Red Walsh, then the detective district commander. Walsh told him that Hawks and Egan were working on a narcotics smuggling case and had asked for, and been granted, absolute anonymity. "It wouldn't have been so anonymous had seven cops killed each other in that basement," my father shouted as he slammed the receiver.

The stakeout in the basement of 1171 Bryant Avenue was part of an international heroin smuggling investigation. A mobster by the name of Tony Fuca lived in the building, and in the carriage room of the basement New York City narcotics detectives and federal agents had found nearly forty kilos of heroin, which had been smuggled into New York from France. Fuca had been arrested, but was released on bail. The narcotics cops and agents were lying in wait for Fuca's connections to come pick up the package.

The total amount of heroin was some 118 pounds, then the largest quantity ever seized in the United States; the case spurred a best-selling book and an Academy Award–winning movie. The French Connection case, however, came within a hair of being the biggest massacre of policemen in the history of New York City.

In the early 1960s, the burning in my father's stomach was constant. By then he fully realized that his once bright career had dimmed like a gray Bronx dusk. Often, in the middle of a shift, he would leave his office and walk to a luncheonette on Southern Boulevard to drink a milk shake, the lactose doing more harm than good. Sometimes, he would just walk around the neighborhood— down Simpson Street and across Fox Street. He remembers the overpowering odor of urine coming from the foyers of each of the buildings. He remembers the hollow deadness in the eyes of the junkie prostitutes and the frightened expressions of those who were chained to this neighborhood by poverty. There was also the look of anger in the eyes of some he passed. He had known poverty, of course, but what he now saw was far different from the whiskey-soaked version of his youth, the one wailed in barroom songs. In 1963, there was a murder in the precinct where a man stabbed his brother in the jugular vein with a fork. The argument was over a piece of chicken. Though it would take a decade for the South Bronx to die—the corpse set ablaze in a funeral pyre—by 1963 the bleeding within had begun. By then there was no longer any hope in the 41st Precinct. There was no longer any sense.

Later that year, my father went to the medical office in police headquarters. There an X ray showed that he had developed stomach ulcers. He too had begun to bleed. And for him, there was no longer any sense to being a cop.

In 1964, Mike Hickey died of a heart attack at Aqueduct racetrack with, as my father always remembered to note, two winners in his pocket. In some ways, Frank's last ounce of enjoyment in the police department went to the grave with Hickey. By then, he had taken the captain's test three times and failed. On the first test he had missed passing by a single point.

I never fully understood why my father failed the captain's tests. His preparations for the first of his attempts, in 1956, came before my recollection, but I do remember how, before his last try, he rarely read the thick exam textbooks, the ones that lay next to his gun on the top shelf in the hallway closet. Undoubtedly, the disappointment of so narrowly failing shook his confidence—it was the first scholastic exam of any kind he had failed in his life. But perhaps the reason for his subsequent failures lay deeper. If my father had become a captain, his police career would have been extended by five, even ten years. His time in the 41st Precinct had exacted a price, both emotionally and physically. Perhaps he just didn't want to be a cop any longer.

By the middle of 1964, the blustery days of the Rat Pack had faded to anecdote, told with a nostalgic air. Like someone left behind at a train station, my father watched as his study group, without him, climbed to the very top echelons of the police department: Jack Kelly would run the Bronx homicide squad; Gus Harms rose to the rank of deputy chief inspector and was, at one point, seriously being considered as a candidate for police commissioner; Mario Biaggi had begun laying the foundation for a second career as a congressman from the Bronx. The rest—except for Frank Weldon, who died in 1966 from a combination of ailments (he had his first stroke at a Rat Pack "wake" at our home in Pearl River)—reached at least the rank of captain and some rose as high as full inspector.

Several times during his last years on Simpson Street, my father requested a transfer. Each time his request was turned down. His tenure as squad commander of the 41st Precinct lasted for fourteen years, the longest anyone had held that position. Years after my father retired, Chief of Detectives Fred Lussen told him that the brass didn't want to move him, that the volatility of the precinct was such they were afraid a new squad commander would either fold under the pressure or stoke the flames that were then consuming the South Bronx. Fourteen years. Almost a death sentence.

In late 1964, though, my father finally received a transfer, to the Property Recovery Squad in downtown Manhattan, a desk job a universe away from Simpson Street. The man who took over the Four-One squad held that position for less than a year. Over the next half-dozen years there were at least four different squad commanders in the 41st Precinct.

My father retired from the police department on January 1, 1965. Some of his old gang threw him a racket, actually more a quiet dinner, at Tony Amandola's restaurant in the Bronx, the event about as festive as returning a library book. He was home early that night, poured himself a glass of buttermilk, sat in his chair in the living room, and read. "Damn guinea food," he mumbled.

A week later, he started his second career, as a security manager for Eastern Airlines; his office was at Kennedy Airport. If he talked about missing the police department, I didn't hear him. Rarely, in his cocktail hour or dinner table conversations with my mother, did I hear the names of his old Rat Pack comrades, or the other detectives who had worked for him. Instead, there was a new set of names mentioned: Howard Brunn, an ex–FBI agent who worked alongside him for the airline, and, later, Frank Borman, the one-time astronaut who became president of Eastern.

His new job took him to the skies often: to Boston, Chicago, Miami, and San Juan. On his return flights, when the pilot would settle the jet into a landing approach over New York City, and the South Bronx, my father didn't even look out the window.

Save the glory years of the Rat Pack, his time in the airline business was the happiest of my father's working life. As the years went by, he and my mother took full advantage of employee flying privileges, and saw most of the world. In 1968, Eastern Airlines was given the contract to transport the Vince Lombardi Super Bowl trophy from New York (where it was made) to wherever the game was being played. From 1968 to 1979, my father and mother attended ten Super Bowls, and all the festivities that surrounded the event.

Our first family vacation after my father took the job with Eastern was to Acapulco. In a pink Jeep with a striped surrey top, I rode with my brother Tommy, then sixteen and having just received his license, for miles along the Pacific coast, watching as a brilliant crimson sun slowly dropped into the turquoise water—a sight that is as clear now in my thoughts as it was thirty-some years ago. In some ways, the jet we boarded for that flight to Mexico was a kind of rocket ship that flew Tommy and me out of the cop universe, out from under that canopy of stars over the Police Camp. But for my mother—born into it, married to it, and, when Frankie joined the force, mothering it—the police department would always remain in the deepest level of her being. For my father, neither distance nor silence could separate him from the department. It was too much a part of him, it had taken too much from him, to forget that easily.

# 7

Just before Christmas a few years ago, I received a package in the mail. It wasn't a surprise. My father had called me several days before to tell me it was on the way. "I'm writing your book for you," he said.

In his familiar, strong, looping script—handwriting that was almost identical to his father's, and that I had once, as a kid, tried to forge for a note to my teacher, failing miserably—was fifty pages of his life; not just events and episodes, but feelings that made me weep several times at his tenderness. He wrote about my mother and their early life together, about the Rat Pack, all but a few now gone, "too soon," as he wrote. With fondness and respect, he wrote about Hickey and the other men who worked for him. In my mind's eye, I saw him sitting at the kitchen table, his glasses on, the only light on in the entire house the one hanging from the ceiling above him, the bargain-brand bulb bathing him in dull white, his pen flashing across the legal pad as the memories flashed across his mind. There was a scotch in front of him on the table. This I knew. I could tell when the scotch began to blur his still-fertile brain—the writing became just a bit larger and slightly sloppy. Still, he knew when to stop—writing, at least—as he would then sign off with a crooked "Keep the Faith, Dad."

The package also contained a large manila envelope of pictures. As I dumped them out on my bed, they spilled like pieces of a broken mirror onto the covers—fractured reflections of my family's history: my father with Eugene and Frankie, then just kids, on the roof of 2300; my parents at their wedding reception, a table with ten or so friends in the crowded Mayer's Parkway Inn; my mother, young and lovely, at Rockaway beach; my father in his police uniform at a St. Patrick's Day parade. As I looked at my father's young face I realized that the picture showed a man I never knew—startling black hair, almost handsome features, eyes that gleamed.

My thoughts went back to the one and only time I went with him to his job. The trip was to buy an Easter suit for me on Orchard Street, but he had to stop at the 41st Precinct on the way. Partly as joke and partly to keep me from wandering away, he put me in the lockup cage. Through the crisscross of wires I could see men in short-sleeve shirts, their ties loose around their necks. They smoked cigarettes and cigars. They called each other Hickey and Hoy, Squires and Martin. They sat at desks with old-style Underwood typewriters and rotary phones. They all wore guns on their belts.

One of the detectives, a man with a nose spread across his face as if he had been hit with a frying pan, asked me what I was in for. I blushed and said nothing. Through the half-open door, I could see my father standing in his office. I could hear his deep voice—a baritone sax, confident, in charge, rising above the chatter in the room. Several times he looked at me, but he didn't smile. I wasn't scared. Many times I'd overheard mention of the cage in his stories.

I stood quietly at attention, like a little soldier. My hair, freshly cut that morning at Enio's Barber Shop, was Vitalis-slicked to my scalp, my hands were at my sides, holding the bottoms of my short pants, my shirt was buttoned to the collar, my eyes were wide-open, inquisitive sponges, soaking in everything around me. There was something familiar about being locked in, watching my father through the cage.

I was his youngest child. My earliest memories of him are from the end of his police career, a time when most of his dreams were already dead. I wonder now how different things might have been had he never become a cop.

About the same time I received the package from my father, I was given permission to search back case files in the basement of the 41st Precinct station house. The precinct is no longer housed in the once grand structure on Simpson Street; the new vermilion-brick and dark-tinted glass building on Southern Boulevard looks more like an HMO than a police station. I was led down a staircase to a cinder-block hallway with thick metal doors painted red. My sergeant guide unlocked one of the doors. Inside, the walls were lined with metal shelves. Every inch of the shelves was taken up with thick cardboard boxes the size of large microwave ovens, squeezed one on top of the other. Each was marked with dates and type of crime. My eyes greedily searched for the era when my father ran the detective squad. At first, I saw nothing earlier than the late 1960s, a time when the 41st Precinct was burned to the ground. Most were marked with dates from the mid 1980s to the early 1990s, the crack cocaine era of devastation—box upon box with "Murder," "Rape," "Robbery" emblazoned on it in red Magic Marker. There were hundreds of boxes; thousands and thousands of individual records of still open cases.

They don't keep records that far back, my sergeant guide told me. I begged for one more look. On the top shelf of the far recess of the room, I saw the corner of a box I hadn't yet checked. I stood on a stepladder and pulled away the boxes that hid it. "Murders 1950s" was written on its side. My hand shook as I opened it. Inside were a dozen legal file folders—murders that had gone unsolved. My father's signature was on each DD 5, detective case report. The names that lived in his stories—Mike Hickey, Larry Squires, Bill Hoy—appear over and over again. The files also contained personal items from the victims and other articles of evidence: a small leather-bound address book, keys to a home, a crime tip written on toilet paper that crumbled in my hand. There were also crime scene photographs, each a graphic glimpse into my father's job:

In 1954, Samuel Tannenbaum, seventy-seven, the owner of a toy store on Freeman Street, stabbed forty times during a robbery.

In 1958, twenty-six-year-old Rosa Hernandez and her two-year-old daughter, murdered in their apartment at 660 Dawson Street. Both were beaten with the steel end of a mop handle, then drowned in a bathtub filled with scalding water.

In 1959, Nicholas Serico, sixty-nine, pistol-whipped to death as he pleaded for his life in the vestibule of his apartment house. The murderer made off with the $7 in his wallet.

The box also contained Eugenia Fargus and Mary Roznicoff's folders. The face in the Mary Roznicoff crime scene photo stared back at me just as it had to my father those many years earlier. Intently I read each file, and tried to imagine my father in this world of murder, one so different from anything I had ever known. My thoughts went back to a time when I was growing up in Pearl River. A boy a few years older than I had drowned in Nanuet Lake; his body lay near the diving board. My friends and I went to take a closer look as Mr. Eckart, the city cop and part-time lifeguard, covered the boy with a coarse green blanket. As I watched the scene, transfixed—it was the first time I had ever seen a dead body—I felt a hand on my back. My father had followed me, and he put his arm around me and led me away. I had no way of knowing it then, but this was the reason my father had moved his family as far as he could from the world in which he worked: to keep his children from seeing what he saw all the time—cold bodies covered by coarse blankets.

Less than one year after my father retired from the police department, I stood in the garishly lit hallway of Columbia Presbyterian Hospital as nurses wheeled him by on a gurney. He had been rushed there for an emergency operation that removed three quarters of his ulcerated stomach and part of his ruptured esophagus. Nora, my mother's friend, held my hand as Eleanor walked alongside the gurney, her eyes moist and worried. Later, doctors told Frank that he had come perilously close to dying on the operating table.

When he returned home, he was gaunt and looked very old. He was forty-seven. For months afterward, he ate nothing but farina and oatmeal. He sucked on lollipops instead of cigars. Once in a while my mother would broil a steak for him, but my father could only chew it like bubble gum, then remove the pieces from his mouth and place them on the corner of his plate, which he hid, embarrassed, with a cupped hand.

That fall, after his operation, I played Mighty Midget football in Orangeburg. Most of the kids who played with me were the sons of New York City policemen. Both my coaches were city cops: Larry Kasperac, a traffic cop on Delancey Street, and Burton Armus, who had once worked for Frank Weldon and was then a detective in Manhattan. (Later he was the technical adviser to the *Kojak* television show.)

Still pale and frail, my father came to a couple of my games, and from the field I could see him standing off by himself, away from the rest of the city cops who came to watch their sons play. After the games, as he walked me to the car, some of the other cop fathers would approach to say hello. In their words, in their demeanor, there was respect. Even in his emaciated condition, even though he was now nearly a year retired from the department, in the other cops' eyes he was still a squad commander. But more than that, their respect came from the knowledge of where my father had worked, how he had done his job, and the price he had paid in doing it.

In his police career, Frank McDonald took the Roosevelt reforms and turned them upside down. He went from book cop to a street cop, and, as most of these cop fathers knew well, no one spends fourteen years as a street cop in the South Bronx and comes out whole.

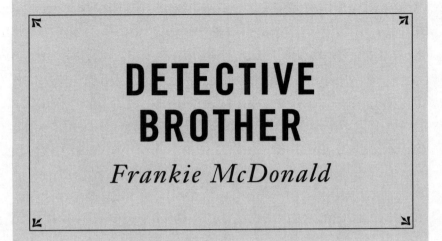

# DETECTIVE BROTHER

*Frankie McDonald*

*There is no saint without a past—no sinner without a future.* —Ancient Persian mass

# 1

At the departmental hearing, I sat waiting for my turn to testify. My hands were sweating; my tie and collar felt tight around my neck. I had never been on a witness stand before. The attorney representing Frankie had coached me on what questions to expect. I had told him the same words that I so often had told myself: "All my brother saw was a cop in trouble." The attorney's efforts only made me all the more uncomfortable, because they brought the night vividly back to my thoughts.

In the early winter of 1972, Frankie had stopped into Chuck's, the tavern where I worked at the time. Sitting at the bar, my brother seemed out of sorts, sullen and preoccupied. Perhaps he had had a fight with Pam, his wife, but he didn't say. Maybe it was the job, the recent cop assassinations at the hands of the Black Liberation Army, the ultra-militant splinter group of the Black Panther Party. Or perhaps it was money. The house, the kids, the bills were strangling him, and he just couldn't seem to get ahead

I wasn't working that night; I had stopped in to Chuck's, as I often did on my night off. I liked the attention my friends and customers gave me on my "busman's holiday." It was a weekend night, and the bar was filled with woozy coeds and long-haired college guys, usually fodder for Frankie's cynical humor. But he sat quietly.

Our plan was to find a place to hold a bachelor party for our brother Tommy, who was to be married the following month. I had suggested Gulliver's, a loud nightspot in Pearl River where I knew some of the employees. We only had one drink there, because the place was too crowded and besides, the bartender, a friend of mine, said that they didn't hold bachelor parties. But while there, Frankie met a city cop named Larkin whom he knew casually. The three of us left the club together.

Outside, Larkin, who lived a few towns away in Spring Valley, suggested we go to his house to play cards. At the time, I thought of myself as something of a cardsharp. I played in a weekly game where you could easily win or lose several hundred dollars. The truth was, I lost far more times than I won, but on several prior occasions I had bragged to Frankie about my cardplaying prowess. We agreed to pool our money, with me playing the cards. We left Gulliver's in two cars, Larkin driving ahead, and Frankie and me following. It was unusually warm, and the night was shrouded with a thin fog. As we followed Larkin along the back roads toward Spring Valley, I saw, in the darkness ahead, flashing lights that left streaks on the fog like the tails of Fourth of July fireworks.

The Spring Valley police car was stopped at an odd angle to the side of the road. In front of it was a large white sedan, an Oldsmobile or a big Buick, perhaps a Continental. As we slowly passed, Frankie's eyes were riveted to the scene: a lone cop was surrounded by six men, the occupants of the sedan. The six men were black.

I stayed in the car and watched the events unfold through the window: Frankie jumping out and running across the street to where the men stood in a circle around the Spring Valley police officer. At first he didn't know that the cop was an underclassmate of his from high school, until he was almost face to face with him. I watched as Frankie said something to the cop, and as one of the men grabbed his arm. There were shouts, heated words exchanged, but they were muffled by the distance, the fog, or my reluctance to hear them. Then I saw Frankie take out his gold shield, and hang it around his neck, as if to say, "That's who the fuck I am. . . ."

The flashing lights, the scene of the men surrounding the policeman, the still-bleeding memory of cop assassinations—all this, and too many beers—swirled like a vortex. It was as though, for Frankie, this was happening on the streets of Times Square or in Bedford-Stuyvesant, Brooklyn, the areas he worked as an undercover detective, and not in suburban Spring Valley. His two worlds had dangerously melded into one. Chin to chin with one of the men, Frankie screamed like a baseball manager fighting with an umpire over a bad call at the plate. For a moment, I sat frozen in dread, praying that he would just walk away. Finally, he did walk away, but not without parting words. I didn't hear him say *the* word; the lightning rod of a word that, in the early 1970s, when racial tension in New York City was stretched as tight as the skin of a snare drum, would blow everything out of proportion; the same word that I had heard come from the lips of every white cop I had ever known. But I made it a point not to listen.

Later, as we drove to Larkin's house, my brother sat in remorseful silence. I could tell he knew he had screwed up. We played cards most of the night in Larkin's finished basement, the walls hung with an extensive gun collection. But the laughter and conversation were forced, and for most of the night Frankie sat looking at the same can of beer in his hand.

That night, the Spring Valley officer wrote a report and left it on his captain's desk. The next day, the captain read the report and wrote a letter to the New York City police commissioner's office.

The commissioner's office filed interdepartmental charges and scheduled a hearing—an event that would change Frankie's life.

# 2

It seemed, while he was growing up, that Frankie would become anything but a cop. It wasn't the job itself that seemed so remote; rather, what was unfathomable was the thought that Frankie would follow his father's path. During his teenage years, the late 1950s and early 1960s, Frankie's relationship with our father ranged from antagonistic to outright hostile. Most of this discord revolved around Frankie's loathing of school and his rebellious nature. My father often lamented his lack of a college education. A natural student, he would've relished being in the company of those as devoted to books and learning as he was. The last thing Frankie relished was school. Eight years after he just barely graduated from St. Margaret's, the grammar school he was enrolled in when we moved from the Bronx, I was approached there by a nun named Sister Blasius, a square stump of a woman, who asked me if I had a brother named Francis. When I told her I did, her lips turned as white as a dying pope's:

"I guess I can expect you to be the same sort of bold article," she hissed.

What made the rift between my father and Frankie even more pronounced was the comparison my father made between his two oldest sons. The difference between my two oldest brothers is remarkable. It's hard to imagine that they came from the same family. By the time they were in their teens, Eugene—fair-haired, with clear azure eyes—was towering. Frankie wasn't short by any standard, except when he stood next to his older brother. Eugene had classic handsome features. Frankie's face was slightly pock-marked; his hair was reddish-brown, the color of the mud you see around the construction of a brick house, his complexion ruddy.

But greater even than their physical contrast was the difference in their personalities. Like my father, Eugene was inward-looking, contemplative, and analytical, while Frankie's emotions were mercurial. Eugene's feelings weren't easy to read; Frankie's were as obvious as neon signs. They both had tempers, a trait they (all of us) inherited from our mother, but Eugene's anger smoldered, while Frankie's was volcanic in its eruption.

When we moved from the Bronx, both Eugene and Frankie were enrolled in St. Margaret's. Some of the nuns there, a Dominican order, had come from the St. Nicholas of Tolentine school in Fordham. Just like the cops, they had made the escape from the Bronx to the suburbs. For Eugene, two years older than Frankie, and at that awkward age of twelve, when new friendships are hard to make, the nuns offered a familiar environment, and one in which he excelled. In Eugene, my father saw the scholastic opportunity he himself had longed for.

Frankie, on the other hand, spent much of his time devising ways to infuriate the nuns. Even before we moved to Pearl River, Frankie had begun to build a churlish reputation with them. One nun at St. Nicholas of Tolentine regularly hit him on the knuckles with a heavy wooden ruler. When he came home from school he'd keep his hands in his pockets so my mother wouldn't see the bruises. One day, the nun, who knew our father was a policeman, told him: "I wish I had your father's nightstick to hit you with."

By the time he was at St. Margaret's, Frankie had perfected the fine art of flatulent noises, using the one-hand-under-a-flapping-arm technique. He became so proficient with spit balls, he could hit the back of a nun's head from the last row of the classroom, where he always managed to sit. One time, he and a school pal, Willie Salvador, booby-trapped a nun's closets with piles of book bags. When she opened the door she was pummeled by the ensuing avalanche. But at St. Margaret's too, he paid a dear price for his antics; often Sister Therese Bernard would kiss her knuckle before administering a noogie to the back of his head.

When it came time for Eugene to choose a high school, my mother, of course, wanted him to go to a Catholic school. My father agreed, but there were certain hurdles that stood in the way. One was distance. The closest Catholic high schools, Bergen Catholic and Don Bosco, in Bergen County, New Jersey, were a twenty-minute car ride away. In addition, there was no school bus service from Rockland. But what presented the biggest hurdle was money. With four children and my parents' mortgage on the new home, there wasn't a whole lot left over. Though Eugene took the entrance exams for Don Bosco and Bergen Catholic, both of which he passed easily, my parents were resigned to the fact that they just couldn't afford the tuition ($25 a month) for a private school. In the fall of 1955, they enrolled Eugene in Pearl River High School.

When the pastor of St. Margaret's, Monsignor Toner, found out about my parents' plans, he paid a visit to our home. Toner had a commanding presence, despite his stooped posture, slight build, and generally wizened appearance, which made him seem older than his sixty years. His words that evening, though spoken with confessional softness, came right to the point:

"Eugene has too much ability to be wasted in public high school," he said as he sat in the living room drinking coffee from the good tea service.

My father tried to explain the family's financial situation. Toner, looking over his glasses at him, said: "There is always a way." My mother needed little convincing. They would find a way, she promised the monsignor. Two weeks later, Eugene was in Bergen Catholic.

To meet the cost of Eugene's tuition, my father took a second job, selling check-writing machines. Like the move to Pearl River, moonlighting was against police department regulations. But, for my father, Eugene's education outweighed any risk. Frank Mc-Cabe, the cousin my father lived with when he first came to New

York, sold the machines in his spare time, and did rather well. My father, however, was just not cut out to be a salesman. Accustomed to being the boss, he couldn't master the hat-in-hand posture. He ended up selling only about five or six of the machines: one to a liquor store in Rockland County, and the rest to businesses in his precinct. One of the machines sat in the attic of our house for years after. Still, my parents were able to cut enough corners to pay the tuition. My father brown-bagged his lunch instead of buying his usual corned-beef sandwich from one of the Jewish delicatessens on Westchester Avenue; my mother clipped coupons and invented new ways to turn canned tuna fish into family dinners.

Their financial sacrifice didn't go unappreciated. Eugene was awake before dawn each morning, studying his thick algebra, history, and Latin textbooks, the light over his desk cutting a triangle in the darkness of his room. In the winter months, before the sun rose, he would walk the mile across town to Bonamolo's, a candy store near St. Margaret's, where he would meet his friend Jimmy Moriarity and his car pool to school. He thrived in the strict atmosphere maintained by the Christian Brothers who taught at Bergen Catholic. Rarely was he the target of their discipline (except for the time he misplaced his tuba when the school band marched in the St. Patrick's Day Parade). And, as he had in St. Margaret's, Eugene finished his first year in high school at the top of the class. My father basked in his academic success.

There was no intercession by the monsignor when Frankie graduated from St. Margaret's. Undoubtedly, Toner was relieved to see him go. Still, my mother insisted Frankie have the same opportunity as his older brother. My parents chose Albertus Magnus for Frankie, a newly built school in Bardonia, New York, just a few towns from Pearl River in Rockland County. Despite his strenuous objections, Frankie was enrolled in the first class of the new school.

But although he showed up at Albertus each day, he rarely did any homework or even went to classes. Instead, he hung around the grounds, smoking Luckies. Maybe he'd sneak into the gym and shoot baskets. My father was furious when he found out, and several huge screaming matches in the living room ensued. Frankie didn't care how much his father yelled. Even then, no one, not even his father, could make him do what he didn't want to do. The school, however, settled the arguments—the administration asked Frankie to leave halfway through the first semester of his freshman year.

In October 1958, Eugene's junior year at Bergen Catholic, an event occurred that signified a rare collision of father and son's worlds.

Jimmy Moriarity, the designated driver of Eugene's car pool, was a notoriously late riser, and often the trip to school was a road rally so they'd arrive on time. Moriarity would barrel through the northern Bergen County towns of Montvale, Park Ridge, and Woodcliff Lake, alternately glancing at the road in front of him and at his wristwatch. One misty, gray morning that year, going at breakneck speed, Moriarity turned onto Broadway in Park Ridge, a sleepy road covered with a canopy of maple trees that ran alongside a reservoir. As he did, a white Lincoln Continental raced past in the oncoming lane, almost forcing him off the road. Moriarity got a quick look at the occupants of the Lincoln, two men in leather jackets. Eugene and the other students let go a torrent of choice words as Moriarity gunned the gas in pursuit. They lost sight of the Continental as it rounded a curve on Broadway; then they heard what sounded like an explosion.

On the other side of the bend, a blue Ford sedan was on its roof, its tires still spinning, smoke rising from the hood. Moriarity stopped the car and Eugene and his classmates piled out to see if the driver was all right. He wasn't. As Eugene approached the

Ford he could see the man hanging upside down in the car, blood dripping from his face, his neck at a forty-five-degree angle against the car's roof. At first, Eugene and his classmates thought that the Continental had cut off the Ford too. But then my brother noticed a three-inch round hole in the driver's side window. Moriarity ran to a nearby house and called the police.

That night, home from school, Eugene received a call from the Bergen County prosecutor, a man named Gil Gilissi. What Eugene and his classmates came upon that morning was not a traffic accident at all, but a mob rubout of man named Johnny "Baseball Bat" Scanlon. Scanlon was a convicted enforcer for a union goon squad on the West Side docks of New York. He had earned his nickname by beating two men nearly to death with a bat in a West Side bar. The prosecutor asked Eugene to come down to his office to look through mug shots of known mobsters in the hope of identifying the men in the Lincoln. My mother called my father at work.

"He's not going anywhere," my father said on the phone. "I'll be right home."

During his police career, my father had known his share of mobsters. With his Bronx squad commander pals, he often went to Joe Cago's Lido restaurant in the Castle Hill section. Better known as Joe Valachi (*The Valachi Papers* by Peter Maas), Cago's testimony in front of a Senate subcommittee documented the existence of the Mafia for the first time. From his days of walking a beat in Harlem, my father knew Tony Bender, Valachi's boss in the Luciano-Genovese crime family. Often, he and his Rat Pack were seated at tables next to mobsters at the Latin Quarter or the Copa. In the code of organized crime, at least in those days of "honorable" mobsters, being a cop's son brought with it a certain amount of immunity from reprisal. Though honorable on its surface, this professional courtesy was at root strictly business. In the late 1950s, when most crime families still shunned the lucrative distribution of heroin and other drugs, organized crime's main sources of income were illegal gambling and vice. These operations depended on the cooperation of the police. This cooperation, generally given by crooked plainclothesmen, was paid for. But, because of the sheer proliferation of daily numbers outlets and houses of prostitution, and because they were busy enough with more serious crimes, even honest cops, for the most part, looked the other way. That is, however, until investigations into murders and other major crimes necessitated information that only those involved in organized crime possessed. On these occasions, it was not at all unusual for detectives to exert pressure on the mob by closing down the vice operations, and even though they would quickly reopen in other locations, such crackdowns would cost the mob days of revenue. The threat of crackdowns placed policemen, and their families, in an untouchable position. Still, my father was not about to let Eugene be mixed up in any prosecution of a mob hit.

"Over my dead body will he look at any pictures," my father told Gilissi when he called that evening.

"I can subpoena him," Gilissi said.

"Go ahead and try," my father warned, "and I'll do everything I can to keep him out of this."

Because of my father's strenuous objections, and perhaps because of his position as a detective-lieutenant in the NYPD, Gilissi didn't press the matter and Eugene never looked at any pictures. Jimmy Moriarity, who had gotten the best look at the men in the Lincoln, was brought into the Bergen County D.A.'s office. But as a witness, Moriarity proved to be of little help. For some reason his recollection of the event became clouded. Perhaps only coincidentally, on graduating from Bergen Catholic, Moriarity, who according to Eugene was only a fair student, received a full scholarship to the University of Bogotá in Colombia, South America.

The following year, 1959, the main topic of discussion at the dinner table was which college Eugene would attend. His top three choices were Fordham University, Yale, and the Naval Academy. He was accepted by both Fordham and Yale, but not Annapolis. This probably had more to do with our family's lack of political pull than with any deficiency in Eugene's academic ability. At one point Fordham was his top choice. In his high school yearbook, under "Future Plans," he had written, "Fordham, to study law." But by the time he sent in an application and took the entrance exam, he had cooled to the idea of becoming a lawyer. Though Yale would have made both my father and Eugene happy, it was far too expensive, and too far above his station, to even consider. Although Eugene undoubtedly had the smarts to fit in at Yale, socially he would have felt out of place—he had a kind of civil service inferiority complex that permeated my family. My father started championing the State University of New York Maritime College at Fort Schuyler. For Eugene, it was an easy sell. In high school, his strongest subjects were math and sciences, and, from the time he was eight or nine, he was interested in ships. For a few years, our grandfather Pete was a caretaker at the Webb Institute on Sedgwick Avenue, one of the leading schools of naval architecture in the country. Pete often took Eugene on guided tours of the school and grounds. The thought of being a naval engineer felt natural to Eugene, and thrilled my father. In 1960, he was off to Fort Schuyler.

Meanwhile, Frankie literally labored through Pearl River High School. From his freshman year on, he worked two jobs. After school and during the summer, he'd work for a landscaper or a construction company, and each morning he awoke before light and went to work on the "honey wagon," the garbage truck. He took hour-long showers before he went off to school. He might not have even bothered (to go to school, not take the shower), if he hadn't noticed the attention the pretty girls were paying to the guys wearing the Pearl River Pirates football jackets.

In the classic underdog manner, a pose my brother Frankie

brought to an art form, he tried out for the football team at the beginning of his sophomore year, at the last possible minute. In the Bronx he had played his share of sidewalk games: stickball, Johnny-ride-the-pony, even a little basketball on the sidewalk with a half-deflated ball and the bottom rung of a fire escape ladder as the hoop; and though he had played football a few times, once in a semi-organized game on a hill in Valhalla (the team headed downhill was given the advantage), football wasn't really a city game. But in Pearl River then, it was big stuff. In 1959, the high school team won the county championship (the last time it did).

Frankie arrived at the first practice looking like a kid dressed up as a football player for Halloween. The only equipment left for him was a pair of pants at least two sizes too big, tiny leather shoulder pads, and a leather helmet, the kind you see in pictures of Red Grange. He wore high-top sneakers, because Mel's Army and Navy was already sold out of football spikes.

The captain of the team looked like a poster boy for high school athletics: six foot two, an Adonis build, ruggedly handsome, with reddish-blond hair. The coach, Max Talaska, a balding drill sergeant of a man, thought he would make an example of the latecomer in the baggy pants. He rounded the team into a circle and matched Frankie one-on-one against the captain.

As Talaska's whistle blew, the captain exploded out of his stance, knocking Frankie, who had to hold his pants up with one hand, on his ass. The whole team laughed, a sadistic grin cut Talaska's face, and the captain stood over Frankie like Cassius Clay later would over Sonny Liston. His face crimson, Frankie thought to himself: That will never happen again.

The second time, they met in a resounding crunch. Neither moved an inch, and the team responded with oohs and ahhs. The captain glared at Frankie. Frankie glared back.

The third time Frankie hit the captain so hard he stumbled

backward into Talaska, both of them winding up in a tangle on the ground. Humiliated, the captain ran from the practice field into the locker room, changed to his street clothing, and never returned to the team. Frankie started that year at offensive and defensive tackle, and the next year was the captain of the team.

In 1962, Frankie's senior year at Pearl River High School, I went with my brother Tommy to watch him play against the team from Tappan Zee, a neighboring town. The week before, in a game against Nyack, Frankie had dislocated his shoulder. Pearl River lost soundly to Nyack, 34–0, but Frankie made fifteen tackles on defense—half of them with only one arm. For the Tappan Zee game, my father taped a foam rubber pad to his shoulder and bound his arm flat against his side. Pearl River fell behind in the game, 20–0, but with one hand—literally—tied behind his back, Frankie made a dozen tackles. Early in the second half, he made a ferocious hit on a Tappan Zee halfback that caused a fumble and started an incredible comeback. Pearl River tied the score in the last seconds of the game, and when the gun sounded, the fans streamed from the bleachers to the field as though the Pirates had won the national championship, even going so far as to tear down the goalposts and hold a parade up Central Avenue after the game. A U.S. senator from New York, Kenneth B. Keating, happened to be in Pearl River that day for the opening of a local Republican club. He attended the second half of the game and afterward asked to be photographed with Frankie. In the photo—which ran in the next day's paper—the senator's arm is around my brother's shoulder and his eyes are on the young player in an adoring gaze. Frankie's expression seems to say he's not impressed by the attention: He's looking off to the side, at neither the senator nor the photographer. Later that year, he was voted All-County.

By then, Frankie had joined up with a quasi gang that called itself the Brothers. Nine or ten strong, all, like Frankie, were displaced city kids. Although they spent most of their energies on souped-up cars and shaping their pompadours, and although they paled in comparison to the Bronx gangs—the ones my father was so concerned with—the Brothers did have their share of rumbles, late-night carousing, and altercations with the law.

In 1963, the summer after they graduated from high school, the Brothers decided to take a trip together to the Jersey shore. They met on a Friday night in the Commodore Bar and Grill, a tavern in the middle of the town. The plan was to have a few beers and then drive down the Garden State Parkway in several cars. By the time they actually left, the time allotted for a "few beers" had grown by several hours. It was almost eleven p.m. when they began the caravan. Needless to say, when they arrived in the beach town of Wildwood, finding a motel that would rent a room to the ten of them—in their condition—presented a problem. To increase their chances, they decided to split up. Frankie rode with his friend Bobby Dunn and another teen named Louie, who was the driver of the car. As they cruised down the main drag in Wildwood, they saw two girls hitchhiking. They stopped the car and asked the girls if they knew of a motel with vacancies. Ten minutes later, they pulled into the motel's parking lot, with the hitchhiking girls in the backseat. In front of the motel were half a dozen guys drinking cans of beer. Just as soon as the girls stepped from the car, Frankie knew that picking them up had been a mistake. As he climbed from the car in the hope of mitigating any overreaction on the part of the girls' boyfriends, he was charged by one of them and the rumble began. Though outnumbered, Frankie and Dunn held their own (Louie, who never left the car, screeched out of the parking lot, leaving his two friends behind). Frankie threw a punch that landed square on the nose of the kid who'd charged him. The fight finally stopped when two Wildwood police cars showed up—all of them were arrested and placed in the town jail house overnight.

The next morning, the local magistrate looked at the lineup in front of him. The shirt of the kid Frankie had punched was covered in his own blood. Eyeing him, the judge said:

"Now that I know who lost the fight, someone tell me what happened."

Everyone began talking at once. The judge ordered silence, and picked Frankie as the spokesman for his side. Frankie relayed the story of the hitchhiking girls and their boyfriends' ire.

"We didn't want any trouble," Frankie pleaded to the judge. "I'm going to be a policeman."

The judge leveled a glare at Frankie and said: "Son, I'd be willing to bet you will never become a cop."

Frankie's declaration to the judge in Wildwood was perhaps the first time he told anybody his dream of becoming a cop. He certainly hadn't discussed it with his father. Their relationship, unlike the one my father had with Eugene, remained tenuous at best. And when Frankie joined the navy, right out of high school, my father seemed happy to see him go. It might straighten him out, he said. Frankie's car accidents, his brushes with the law, and his volcanic temper caused, for my father, too much disharmony, and—his ultimate accusation—too much unhappiness for our mother. My father always deflected his own feelings onto his wife: "You're breaking your mother's heart," or "I won't have you hurting your mother this way," he would often say when Frankie came home late or in trouble. Utter falsehoods. My mother's heart could never be broken by Frankie: he was so much more *her* son than my father's. That anger, that independence—these were all things Frankie inherited from her, along with her sense of humor. My mother didn't condone Frankie's wildness, but she accepted it. But for my father, Frankie was the black sheep of the family. And as Eugene fulfilled all of my father's expectations, the distance between Frankie and our father lengthened.

I have two photographs from that time. In one, Eugene wears

the dress whites of the Maritime Academy, a pristine poster boy with sleek lines, razor edges, and a cream-colored complexion. In the other, Frankie, ruddy-faced, wears his navy uniform: a boxed, stiff sailor hat, bellbottom pants with buttons, clumsy mirror-black shoes. Eugene is the officer, Frankie the swabbie.

The navy did not straighten Frankie out. At least not right away. While on shore leave, a month after he was assigned to Jacksonville, he got into a fight over a girl in a sailor bar. The Shore Patrol was called and he ended up spending Christmas in the brig. Soon after, an official-looking letter from the navy arrived at the house. In it, Frankie's captain explained that he was writing because he knew my father had been in the navy and was a lieutenant in the New York City police department, and that he therefore would appreciate the severity of Frankie's insubordination. My father read the letter at the kitchen table and shook his head in disgust, then carefully put it back in the envelope and placed it where he would see it every day: in his closet, up behind his gun.

Frankie sent me postcards from places like Madrid, Rome, and Hamburg. I pinned them to the wall next to my bed. At night, I would listen to Marv Albert's "Scoop" and "Yes!"—his radio play-by-play of the Knicks games—and pretend I was Cazzie Russell hitting a jumper from the corner, keeping sharp for when Frankie came home and we would play sock basketball again.

Frankie also wrote to our father. It was in one of these letters that he first told him that he wanted to become a policeman. When my father read the letter, he shook his head, folded it back into the envelope, and stuck it deep on the top shelf of his closet, right next to the captain's letter.

Though my father maintained his suspicions of his second son, Frankie had begun to change. He wrote to a high school English teacher named Miss Warren, whose class he had rarely attended, and asked if she could suggest books for him to read. Lying on his bunk, rocking to 45-degree angles in a "tin can" destroyer called the U.S.S. *Bigelow*, Frankie, for the first time, discovered treasures like *Crime and Punishment, Our Town*, and *A Connecticut Yankee in King Arthur's Court*.

His newfound serious attitude kept him out of further trouble, but fun was still on the agenda. While in port in Germany, he and two of his mates took shore leave and found themselves in a nearly empty beer garden with a handful of other sailors and locals listening to an oompah band. When the band took a break, one of Frankie's mates asked the members if they would mind if he and his friends played a few songs. Frankie climbed onstage and sat behind the drum set, and the two other sailors, after hurrying back to the ship to retrieve their electric guitars, quickly set up next to him. They began the set with "Wooly Bully" and followed with "I Want to Hold Your Hand" and several other Beatles tunes, then the new rage in rock and roll. On hearing the familiar music, sailors wandering past the beer garden began to pile in, and by the end of the first set the place was packed with navy men dancing with the local girls. They played late into the night, and even a few members of the Shore Patrol came in to listen.

In March 1966, Frankie was honorably discharged from the navy and began classes at the Delahanty Institute. Twenty-five years earlier, my father had sat in the same classrooms in the Delahanty building on Thirteenth Street and Fourth Avenue—the same corner where for seven years my grandfather had worked as a traffic cop.

The night he graduated from Delahanty's, Frankie went to his old haunt, the Commodore, to celebrate, but none of the Brothers were around. A few had gone on to college, but most hadn't, working in construction or in gas stations. By 1966, at least six of the original ten Brothers were in the marines and the army, seeing heavy action in Southeast Asia.

The Commodore was just not the same without his friends, so Frankie headed to a bar called the Deer Head in West Nyack, a few towns away. There he sat alone, looking out the window as it began to rain, when he noticed a girl step from a car. She wore a tan raincoat and had her hair up. She was pretty, with round eyes that twinkled and a small, sweet smile set in a jaw that perhaps was a touch too pronounced but gave her face an overall happy expression. Frankie's eyes were fixed on the front door as he waited for the girl to enter. When she did, he realized he knew her. That's Pam, he said to himself. She had dated a guy he played football with in high school. He remembered that Pam and a group of her friends had been at every one of his games. He caught her eye and gave her a little wave. Pam waved back, and Frankie turned back to the bar, feeling the blood rush to his face. While he sipped his beer and gathered his courage to approach her, Pam walked over to him.

After they talked for a while, he asked if she would like a lift back to Pearl River. "Sure," Pam said, with a smile.

Gallantly, he opened the door to the Impala for her, hopped in himself, and gunned the gas, leaving a testosterone spray of gravel behind. A half-mile or so from the bar, with one hand on the steering wheel and the other stretched out on the back of the bucket seat where Pam sat, he took a turn too quickly and the car hydroplaned off the road and into a ditch. A tree limb cracked the windshield, and smoke poured from the engine block.

Pam, unhurt and totally calm, said: "I guess you're not the best driver in the world. You've given me a ride twice, and both times you got into an accident."

Frankie looked out over the hood of the Impala at the rising steam, and then quizzically back at Pam.

"The night of your graduation?" Pam said, trying to engage his memory.

"Jesus," Frankie muttered, holding his face in his hands, remembering then that Pam was his friend Willie Ahlmyer's date, and that both of them were in the backseat of my mother's car when he crashed it.

Like Frankie, Pam was a transplanted city kid; she had lived in Brooklyn until she was ten. She even had cops in her family. Her grandfather, on her mother's side, had once been the chief of police of Savannah, Georgia, but, she confided to Frankie, his primary source of income was a very lucrative bootlegging business. Her paternal grandfather, Joseph Lawler, owned a famous restaurant in the Singer building in downtown Manhattan. His customers were Wall Street financiers, Tammany politicians, and Broadway actors. Two of the bartenders who worked for him went on to fame as legendary New York saloonkeepers: Sherman Billingsley, who ran the Stork Club, and Toots Shor. Pam's grandmother was a Broadway actress who went by the stage name Lucy Lord and performed in musicals and light operas.

But when Pam's grandfather retired from the restaurant and handed the reins over to Pam's father, Michael, and his three brothers, the business began to decline. Pam told Frankie that her father and uncles ran the place into the ground. One time, at the restaurant, Pam's father stuck a fork in a small-time bookmaker to whom he owed several thousand dollars. A lieutenant from the 1st Precinct by the name of Hiller, a customer and a man who knew the price of a drink—and the money he was saving by not paying for it—was more than happy to make the incident magically disappear from the police files. After Michael paid him off, the bookmaker was happy to keep his mouth shut.

Soon after the restaurant closed, Pam's mother filed for divorce and moved to Montvale, New Jersey, with Pam and her brother, Clem. There she worked as a waitress in a restaurant called the Steak Out, popular with the New York City cops living right across the state line in Pearl River.

The young romance burned bright and hot, and even though Pam's mother looked at Frankie suspiciously when he came to pick her up—no doubt convinced that he was some sort of demolition derby driver, bent on steering her only daughter into a twisted-metal wreck—she eventually became resigned to, if not happy about, the fact that Pam and Frankie were a steady item.

The following May, Frankie took the police entrance exam at George Washington High School in upper Manhattan. He had crammed every night for weeks, sitting at the same desk his brother Eugene, doing his high school studies, had used. At night and early in the morning, before he left for his construction job, the same triangle of light cut through the darkness over it. Frankie's face was tight with worry when he returned to the house the day of the exam. He had little faith in himself as a student, and no experience that hard study paid dividends.

A couple of months later, while he waited for the results of the police exam, Frankie married Pam in a ceremony at St. Margaret's, followed by a small reception in the back room of a modest restaurant called the Old Hook Inn. They spent their honeymoon moving into a tiny one-bedroom apartment behind an Esso station in Pearl River. Pam had a calming effect on Frankie. They held hands and giggled together. He bought a Volkswagen Beetle—which, compared to the muscle cars of his past, made me laugh.

About a month later, Frankie drove the Volkswagen to the George Washington Bridge bus terminal to pick up a copy of *The Chief*, a civil service newspaper where the answers to the exam were published. His hands trembled as he sat in a coffee shop there and compared his answers with those in *The Chief*. By his count, he scored 92. When he received the official result, he found his actual score was 94. With the 5-point bonus given to veterans, his final mark was 99.

# 3

Although my father still bathed in the glow of his oldest son's success (Eugene had graduated Fort Schuyler with a degree in nuclear fission; then he married his head-turningly beautiful high school sweetheart, Diane Schurerer, and took a job in Newport News, Virginia, where he worked as an engineer on a crew that was replacing the reactor core in the nuclear-powered aircraft carrier U.S.S. *Enterprise*), the subtlest of changes occurred within my father while Frankie was in the Academy. Perhaps he became caught up in his son's enthusiasm; maybe the sight of Frankie in the gray Academy uniform stoked memories of his own youthful optimism as a rookie cop. Frankie, too, seemed to warm in their relationship. He would often stop at the house on Blauvelt Road on the way home from the Academy. I would see his Volkswagen pull in the driveway from the window of my bedroom, and run to the front door. On hearing Frankie's car, our father would put down the book or paper he was reading and wait expectantly for the door to open. They would sit across from each other in the living room: Frankie drinking a beer, my father sucking on hard candy in lieu of the cigars he could no longer stomach. As Frankie would relay the day's events, my father would intently measure each of his words, and judiciously produce statements like "Make sure you keep your nose clean."

Though Frankie would bristle a little at such comments, he seemed happy to have someone with whom he could talk about "the Job." It was on this common ground that Frankie and my father forged a new connection.

My mother would bristle too and, as she always had, come to Frankie's defense. "You don't have to tell him that," she would say to my father. "Frankie knows what to do."

There had always been a deep connection between Frankie and

my mother. Her love for him—for all of us, her boys—was obvious and fierce. Yet I never truly knew how she felt about Frankie becoming a cop. She was proud, of course, but would have been proud no matter what his career choice. Still, I remember something melancholy about my mother then. Sometimes, as she listened to her son's cop talk, she would put down her crossword and close her eyes like someone listening to a sad aria on a radio. I realize now that that song had played for the whole of my mother's life, and, for her, it was both painful and impossible not to listen to.

Frankie's first friend in the police department was a fellow recruit named Jimmy McDermott. They actually met while they were both walking from Grand Central Station on the day they were to be sworn in, the first day in the Academy. Like most of the close friends Frankie would make in the department, McDermott was something of a character. Tall and slim, with a wide, freckled face that would be right at home in County Cork, McDermott thought of himself, in Frankie's words, as an instant "hairbag," police parlance for a cop who has been in uniform for a long time. As the two young recruits walked into the elevator in the Academy building on Nineteenth Street, Frankie pressed the button for the second floor, where he knew the swearing-in was being held. "Where do you think you're going?" McDermott asked as he pushed the button for the eighth floor. "The ceremony is all the way upstairs." As Frankie began to disagree, McDermott stopped him in mid sentence. "Listen, I was already on the Job, it's on the eighth floor," he said, filled with bluster. McDermott's confident demeanor made Frankie doubt his own information. When they got off the elevator on the eighth floor there was nothing but a large, empty room. By the time they got back to the second floor, the recruits had already been seated in alphabetical order. All 600 of them had to stand to make room for the latecomers, who, because of the closeness of their last names, sat right next to each other. As they did, the first deputy in charge of personnel shook his head and sarcastically announced: "You two are really starting your career off on the right foot."

As it turned out, Jimmy McDermott hadn't actually been a member of the NYPD; rather, he had worked as a policeman on the New York Central Railroad. When Frankie learned this, he called Jimmy "Choo-choo," a name that caught on with the rest of the Academy cops.

Often, Frankie would meet McDermott at a soda fountain near his home in the Bronx, comparing notes on their nascent police careers and drinking egg creams. The setting was appropriate. For they were kiddy cops, both with innocent visions of what lay ahead for them in the Job: saving the city and the like. And, though Frankie was already well indoctrinated into the world of saloons, he was content passing the time in soda fountains with Jimmy, who didn't drink. Besides, Jimmy was as funny as anybody he had ever met in a bar. Funnier.

One day, Jimmy invited Frankie and another friend up to meet his wife and children. On the train uptown, he warned Frankie not to stare at his wife. "She has this nervous twitch," he said, vaguely explaining that she had been in some kind of accident before they were married. "When people stare at her, it kind of kicks up," Jimmy said. "What the hell are you talking about?" Frankie asked. But Jimmy was adamant. "Please, for my sake, don't stare." Frankie shrugged and promised he wouldn't stare.

On the sidewalk outside his apartment, Jimmy's wife, a pretty girl with dark hair and a round Irish face, stood holding on to a baby stroller with one hand, and the hand of a small child with the other. As Jimmy introduced them, Frankie smiled thinly, then quickly averted his eyes. For a moment she looked at him quizzically, then knowingly at her husband, and then back to Frankie. "He gave you the twitch story, didn't he?" she said with resignation. "I don't have a twitch, he tells everybody the same thing."

* * *

Though, in Frankie's era, the Academy term was only supposed to last six months—910 hours of intensive classroom, physical, and firearms training—he wouldn't actually graduate until May 15, 1968, one year to the day from his swearing-in. Several times during that period, his class was assigned to bolster the manpower in precincts and other units. Less than a month into the Academy, Frankie was assigned to the 47th Precinct in the northeast Bronx. Fearing a reprise of the 1964 and 1965 Harlem race riots, the police brass had decided more cops were needed at the precinct level throughout the city. During his four months at the 47th, Frankie saw little action. The 47th Precinct then was a relatively peaceful command, a residential Italian-American enclave. Plus, the police department's paranoia about riots proved just that, paranoia. Mostly, Frankie was assigned either to be the third man in a patrol car—sort of a watch-and-learn position—or to stand a post on a quiet block. Even though the recruits were allowed to wear blue uniforms—summer-weight shirts and pants—and the lapel pin of the precinct, rather than the traditional Academy grays, Frankie couldn't help but feel like an uninvited outsider. For the most part, he kept his mouth shut and did as he was told.

At the end of that summer, Frankie and Choo-choo McDermott were assigned on a barrier detail for the West Indian Day parade in Brooklyn. When the parade was over, the two Academy rookies began to load the blue wooden sawhorses back onto a truck. They were dressed in civilian clothes—T-shirts and jeans—but both wore their service revolvers on their belts. As they were finishing up, a clearly shaken man approached and told them that someone had been shot just a block or so away. McDermott leaped from the back of the truck, and both he and Frankie ran, following the man to the scene. There a victim lay on the sidewalk, alive, but with a gunshot wound to the chest. The people gathered around on the sidewalk explained that the person responsible for the shooting was in the building in front of which the man lay. Frankie and McDermott unholstered their guns and ran up the stairs. As they reached the third-floor landing, an apartment door opened and a rifle appeared—not pointed at the rookie cops, but barrel first. Frankie grabbed the rifle, and Choo-choo cuffed the man holding it. Just as they began to march their prisoner down the stairs, a group of people arrived, whom Frankie and McDermott believed to be precinct detectives. Later, Frankie found out that in fact they were plainclothes policemen in a detective training unit and still patrolmen in rank. But at that moment, the rookies had every reason to believe that these were detectives, and when the plainclothesmen told Frankie and McDermott to escort the victim to the hospital, while they brought the suspect into the station house, the recruits followed orders.

In the Academy, off-duty guns and a statue called the Mayor's Trophy are awarded to recruits who prove the best in academics and physical condition, and (this category was the most prestigious) make the best arrest. Though they didn't say it at that moment, both Frankie and McDermott believed that they had made the arrest that would secure them the ultimate Academy prize.

In the back of the ambulance, on the way to the hospital, the victim told the two fledgling cops what had happened. He was sitting on the stoop when a man who lived in the building told him to move. When he refused, the man went up to his apartment, returned with the rifle, and shot him point blank. As the man told the story, obviously in shock from his wound, his eyes began to roll up in his head. Frankie held the man's hand as he was wheeled into the emergency room, reassuring him that everything would be all right. But though the doctors valiantly tried to save him, they couldn't. The man died right there on the operating table, with my brother still holding his hand.

A couple of hours later, Frankie and McDermott returned to the station house. As they reported to the desk, a sergeant handed

McDermott an envelope that contained his handcuffs. McDermott asked the sergeant what had happened to the man he and Frankie had arrested. The sergeant told him that the man had already been processed into the system and was at that moment being arraigned in court. McDermott was beside himself. How could the guy be in court without the arresting officers? he asked. The sergeant shook his head. "You didn't arrest him, son," he said. "Those plainclothes guys did."

"We arrested him!" McDermott screamed. "It's a murder case and we arrested him!"

That night, Frankie stopped by the house to tell my father the story. Coincidentally, my father happened to know the squad commander of that particular precinct, and the next morning he gave him a call. "What's going on?" my father asked. "The kids got gypped out of a collar, a nice collar. The least you could do is write up a 49." (A UF 49 is a letterlike interoffice memo form; to give you an indication of the bureaucracy of the police department, if you fill out only half the page, it's called a 49A.) My father asked the squad commander to send a UF 49 to the police commissioner's office, or at least to the precinct commander. The squad commander did neither, and the "gun," the award for best arrest, went to a recruit who foiled an armed robbery while he was off duty. A good arrest, but not a murder.

When the summer of 1967 folded into a chilly New York fall, Frankie thought he would finally be sent back to the Academy to finish his training. He wasn't. As the Christmas holidays neared, he was assigned to Traffic Safety Unit B (the descendant of Tom Skelly's traffic squad). Housed in the old 18th Precinct, by then called Midtown North, Safety Unit B was responsible for the traffic detail in the heart of Manhattan. With just a few months of police experience and no experience as a traffic cop, Frankie found himself in the middle of Herald Square, in front of R. H.

Macy's department store—at Christmastime—besieged by relentless traffic, hordes of package-laden pedestrians, and tourists asking directions to the Statue of Liberty. Though at first he wasn't that familiar with Manhattan, Frankie quickly learned the locations of subway entrances, bus routes, and landmarks. He bought and carried with him the *Red Book*, an information guide to New York. Within just a few days, he had all the material on Midtown memorized.

Just like any other unit of the police department, Traffic had its share of Runyonesque characters. One afternoon, a few days before Christmas, Frankie took his lunch break in the basement of the Horn and Hardart Automat on Thirty-fourth Street and Eighth Avenue. In police parlance, the basement was known as a "coop," a place to have lunch or sneak a cigarette break. That afternoon, while Frankie was eating a sandwich, a traffic cop named Kirby came in and sat at a nearby table. About the size of a city mailbox, but somewhat wider, with a flat, whiskey-burned face, Kirby had worked the corner of Thirty-fourth Street and Eighth Avenue for over twenty years. He knew just about everybody who worked near that busy intersection, and Christmastime was very lucrative for him. Frankie watched as he unbuttoned his choker—the old-time police blouse with a double row of buttons—and removed a handful of envelopes. Each of the envelopes contained a card or note wishing Kirby a happy holiday, and a five- or ten-dollar bill. Though a fair distance away, and pretending not to watch, Frankie could barely contain his laughter as the veteran traffic cop commenced a running commentary on each gift. For his part, Kirby didn't care who was watching, and became more animated with each envelope, until he finally opened one that had two one-dollar bills in it.

"Can you believe this?" he said incredulously, holding the bills between two stubby fingers like he was holding the tail of a dead mouse.

"A fuckin' deuce! The cheap bastard! Merry Christmas my ass, I ought to give it back, da prick."

Years later, when Frankie was working City-Wide Street Crime, he read that Kirby had retired after thirty years. The local businesspeople erected a plaque for him that still hangs on his corner of Eighth Avenue.

It was while working the Christmas traffic detail that Frankie made his first arrest. And with it, some of the veneer peeled off his new career.

The day following the arrest, looking haggard, he sat in the living room and told my father the story. He said it was the toughest fight he had ever been in. With a knowing smile, my father told Frankie that he had better get used to it: New York was filled with tough guys. Frankie took a sip of his beer, nodded, and said, "And some of those guys are women."

The arrest occurred two days before Christmas, while Frankie was assigned to Thirty-third Street and Seventh Avenue. About four o'clock that afternoon, the cars on the side block were stopped dead and backed up all the way to Sixth Avenue. When Frankie walked down Thirty-third Street to investigate, he saw a very large woman spread-eagled on the hood of a cab. At first he thought it was an accident. But as he drew closer, he realized that the woman was drunk. As he went to grab her hand and help her off the cab, she wheeled and whacked him across the side of the head with a nearly empty bottle of Four Roses whiskey, knocking his hat halfway across the street. Frankie was more stunned than hurt, but as he tried to pull the woman out of the street, she removed one of her shoes and with it began beating him on the head. Meanwhile, a crowd gathered around to watch the show.

Frankie said that it got to the point where he was going to have to do something. From his utility belt, he removed the little rubber club called a day stick, but it proved useless, he said, like trying to fight a grizzly bear with a hot dog.

As the woman continued to pummel him with her shoe and the fist of her free hand, the crowd swelled to Times-Square-on-New-Year's-Eve proportions. Blood streamed from Frankie's nose, and his face was red from the mortifying predicament. As the woman backed up, readying for another charge, he had had enough. My brother balled his left hand into a fist, and when she was nearly on him, he hauled off and punched her as hard as he could flush in the face. Wheeling backward, she slammed into a pillar of a building, the force of the collision knocking off her wig, exposing a completely bald head. Stunned by the sight of the hairless woman, Frankie tried to collect himself. But he had little time, in a moment she was up and coming at him again. Finally, a cop from a nearby post arrived and called in a 10-13, "Cop needs assistance." Ultimately it took a half-dozen cops to get the woman in cuffs and in the backseat of a patrol car.

Her name was Bernice Williams, he found out. As he filled out the arrest card in the back room of the station house, Bernice sat cuffed to a metal chair, a broomstick wedged underneath the arms of the chair, immobilizing her like the safety bar in a roller-coaster car. The veins in her bald head throbbed as she fought against her restraints. She let out wild, whooping screams and spat at anyone who passed. Across the room, a thin cop wearing glasses was filling out "alarms," forms on stolen cars. For a long while, the cop sat quietly going about his work as if oblivious to Bernice and her antics. Then, without warning, after one particularly eardrum-piercing scream, he stood, walked over to her, and put his hands on the back of her chair. With frightening speed, he drove her across the tile floor, ramming her headfirst into the cinder-block wall. The force of the impact, Frankie said, was so hard that Bernice's stockings exploded. Without saying a word, the cop went back to his desk, sat down, and continued his task, as Bernice slumped, semiconscious, in the chair.

The next day, at court, Bernice was sober and, incredibly, none the worse for wear. She pleaded guilty to the assault charge and, having a record of attacking policemen, was immediately remanded to jail for six months. On the way out of the courtroom she winked at Frankie.

The incident taught Frankie a lesson. Though he wasn't completely a wide-eyed innocent when he went into the police department, his intentions in becoming a cop were perhaps the purest of any of my relatives who joined the force—he really thought he would be helping people. For all Frankie's atomic anger, underneath he was something of a Boy Scout: He coached Mighty Midget football even though he didn't have a son playing for the team; in a family crisis he could be counted on as the first there and the last to leave. For him, the uniform of the police department was a perfect fit, the teams clearly defined—the good guys wore the blue shirts. But he quickly found out that the job had a way of crushing virtuous traits under the heel of a shined brogan. In the New York City police department, the lines between good and bad became blurred very quickly. Bernice Williams was his introduction to the ambiguity that would cloud many of his experiences as a cop.

For me, the wonder of Frankie's story was enhanced by the difference in the two worlds—the one in which he worked and the one that my father had moved us to. The sign on Veterans Parkway, the exit road off the Palisades toward town, read: "Welcome to Pearl River, the town of friendly people." But among the townfolk, our little hamlet was better known as "lily-white" Pearl River. The only thing I knew about black people was the stories I heard from my father, and with Bernice Williams, the stories contributed by my brother.

While I was growing up in Pearl River, I did know one black kid—not even a whole family; he was an exchange student of sorts who came from Georgia and lived with a family named Graf. I never knew the particulars of why Lionel Macon moved to Pearl River. He was a very dark-skinned child with a big, fast smile and close-cropped hair. We would play basketball in the driveway of the McKeons' house, and when one of the kids called him nigger or spade, Lionel would go into his "happy darkie" routine: His smile grew to his ears and he shuffled his feet.

It was surprising to me, of course, that he wasn't very good at basketball. I mean, he was okay, but just okay—he never did live up to his color on the court. When we all went to high school, with those racist preconceptions in place, the coaches made a spot for him on the junior varsity team. Once, I sat near Macon in the stands watching our varsity squad play against Mount Vernon, a predominantly black team from lower Westchester. During the warm-up, I watched Macon as he intently watched the Mount Vernon team: their lithe black bodies glistening, gracefully cutting through the air to the basket. No one dunked the basketball in those days, at least no one among the puny white players of Pearl River or the other white towns of Rockland County. Yet at least three of the Mount Vernon squad slammed the ball through the hoop, bringing waves of murmurs from the crowd. Mount Vernon won that day, by at least 50 points. With every basket they scored, Macon clapped and whistled. I was angry that he was rooting for the other team. Now, I realize that Pearl River was not, could never be, his team.

Even before Macon's arrival, there were signs that Pearl River was less than welcoming to black people. One of these signs was the controversy caused by a statue of St. Martin de Porres.

When I was about eleven or twelve, my best friend on the block was a boy with a wide, freckled face and bushy brown hair named Henry Reynolds. The two of us would ride our bikes and play softball with the other kids on the block in the parking lot of the Jewish camp at the end of McKinley Street. I always wanted to be on Henry's team. He could hit a softball farther than any of the other kids. He was the oldest of a family that numbered six or seven then, and seemed to add a new member every year. His house was filled with runny-nosed babies in drooping cloth diapers.

Henry's father was in the merchant marine, and not at home much (enough, I guess, to keep his wife always pregnant). Mrs. Reynolds was a gentle, temperate woman, with a soft Irish brogue and a baby permanently clasped to her breast. She was also very religious. Every morning she would load the passel of kids into a dark-green Pontiac station wagon and drive to Mass at St. Aedan's, the new parish church built just a few blocks from McKinley Street.

One late summer night, after dinner, I went down to visit Henry to see if he wanted to take a ride on our bikes. He was sitting on the front stoop of his house, his hands under his chin, his eyes cast down to the ground between his sneakers. He couldn't leave the house, he said, because his mother was at the hospital and he had to watch his brothers and sisters. I didn't ask what was wrong. Henry was not much of a talker.

For an hour or so we sat together in silence. Then Mrs. Reynolds pulled into the driveway. I could see her face was streaked with tears as she rushed by us and into the house without saying a word.

As Henry and I walked our bikes up Champ Avenue, nearing the top of the long, steep hill, he began to explain: His brother John was very sick, and had been rushed to Good Samaritan Hospital that afternoon. I can't recall exactly what the illness was, but I do remember clearly that John's condition was very severe. At first, doctors weren't sure whether he would live. There was talk of brain damage if he did.

I kept vigil with Henry those few days. His father, I think, was away at sea, and his mother spent the time at John's bedside or in St. Aedan's praying to Martin de Porres, patron saint of sick children.

For those not versed in Butler's *Lives of the Saints*, Martin de Porres was black. Though he was born in Peru, of a Peruvian father, his mother was a colored freedwoman from Panama, and Martin inherited his mother's complexion. He founded orphanages and foundling hospitals in Peru, where he lived all of his life. Unlike St. Anthony, my mother's favorite saint, whose statue I would find in every church I visited, and whose illustrated image I'd see in the pages of my religion books, St. Martin wasn't well known—I had no idea who he was or what he looked like. But Mrs. Reynolds knew of the saint. And if a miracle was needed to save her son, it was Martin de Porres who could perform it.

Within a few days, John's condition improved dramatically. And a week or so later, he was home, pale and thin, but heading towards full recovery. When John came home, Mrs. Reynolds was as happy as I can remember seeing her. Her eyes flickered like altar candles, her normally rigid countenance was replaced with the serene glow of an elderly nun on Easter Sunday. Her prayers had been answered.

About a month later, she pulled into her driveway with a box the size of a refrigerator in the back of the station wagon. It contained a four-foot-high statue of St. Martin, which she and Henry promptly positioned on the front lawn of her home. This was her way of showing her gratitude for the saintly intercession. But for the neighbors on McKinley Street, who reacted to it with absolute outrage, it was a threat to the very harmony of the block. No sooner was the statue of St. Martin on the lawn than neighborhood phone lines buzzed with the news.

The family that lived next to the Reynoldses was especially infuriated. One neighbor suggested that they glue a lantern to it so people would think it was a lawn jockey. A city cop who lived up the block said the only thing the statue was missing was handcuffs. One night someone, I never knew who, spray-painted part of the statue's face white.

Mrs. Reynolds answered the neighbors' desecration and snipes by having a brick grotto built around St. Martin and placing a spotlight on the lawn, shining it on the statue day and night. The Reynoldses also acquired an ill-tempered German shepherd who was given just enough leash to reach almost to the street. A stroll past their house would prompt Rommel, the dog, to fly from his lair under the bushes, his chain unraveling with the speed of an anchor chain on an ocean liner, until it snapped taut, yanking Rommel into midair while he bared a mouth filled with frightening teeth. The kids on the block were terrified of Rommel. Even Skipper, my dog, judiciously took the backyard route behind the houses across the street from the Reynolds home on his way to visit one of his paramours in the developments near St. Aedan's.

For a while, McKinley Street became sort of a tourist attraction. Our stickball and touch football games on the normally quiet street were constantly interrupted by curious townsfolk who would drive slowly past to gawk at the statue on their way to mass at St. Aedan's. As the months, then years, went by, the grumbling subsided somewhat. But, for as long as I lived on McKinley Street, St. Martin was never welcome there.

By April, Frankie was back in the Academy building. But again, his stay wouldn't last long. At 3:15 in the morning of April 5, 1968, Police Commissioner Howard R. Leary issued an emergency order that mobilized his entire 28,788-man police force into a thirteen-hour-a-day, six-day-a-week work schedule. The day before, on April 4, Martin Luther King, Jr., had been assassinated in Memphis. Frankie's class was once again assigned to the streets.

Though major rioting erupted in cities across the country—Washington, D.C., Chicago, Baltimore, and Pittsburgh—in New York there were only scattered episodes of violence and looting. The night after Dr. King was shot, a band of black teenagers swarmed through Times Square and Columbus Circle, breaking windows and engaging in fights, and looting occurred in Harlem and Bedford-Stuyvesant. The fear of violence, however, was much worse than the violence itself. Rumors of bombing and mass assaults flooded Manhattan. The paranoia reached such a pitch that on the Friday after Dr. King was assassinated, major corporations like Time, Inc., General Electric, and RCA closed early because of rumors that swarming black mobs were headed downtown.

Though racial tensions would remain extremely high through-out that summer, and indeed, for several years after, within a week after Dr. King's assassination New York was, relatively, back to normal.

During those weeks, the only swarming Frankie saw was of prostitutes around their prospective customers' cars. He was as-signed to a post on Thirty-first Street and Eighth Avenue, a few blocks south of the General Post Office building. That strip of Eighth Avenue was favored by hookers known as "tunnel host-esses," who serviced the Jersey trade that came through the Lin-coln Tunnel. One night, one of the prostitutes became especially infuriated about Frankie's presence, which had seriously affected her business. Brazenly, she went to the police call box and made a citizen's complaint, saying in an obviously slurred voice that Frankie was harassing her. Frankie took the phone from her hand and spoke to the lieutenant on the line. He explained that the woman was a prostitute and intoxicated. Instead of sending a pa-trol car to check the validity of the complaint, the lieutenant told him to put her back on the phone and completed the complaint form. Frankie learned another early career lesson that night: Do-ing your job does not necessarily mean you're not going to get in trouble. Indeed, he would find out, sometimes the harder you did your job, the greater the opportunity for it.

In May, Frankie finally graduated from the Academy. The cere-mony was held at the Armory, on Sixty-seventh Street and Lexington Avenue. This time, Frankie, and Jimmy McDermott, would be on time.

The day before the ceremony, my father waited anxiously for him to stop by the house. That week Frankie had filled out what was called a wish list, his top three choices of precincts. My father called Gus Harms, his old Rat Pack cohort, now a full inspector.

"He wants something close to home," my father said. "If there's anything you can do, I'd appreciate it."

With Harms' rank, it would only be a matter of a phone call. But just in case he didn't come through, my father also called the clerical sergeant at the Academy, who had once worked for him as a detective in the Four-One squad.

More and more, Frankie stopped by the house to speak to our father. I would watch how our father straightened in his chair and leaned toward his son when Frankie told a war story or asked a question. They had a way of talking to each other that seemed to exclude everyone else in the room. Frankie had finally found a way of scaling the wall around my father. And in some ways, this newfound closeness was even greater than the usual feeling between father and son. They both now belonged to an insular brotherhood. They were cops.

When Frankie arrived late that afternoon, my father handed him a yellow receipt—the credit slip for his service revolver, which he had turned in on his retirement. Frankie would take the slip to a gun store on Broome Street, near police headquarters. There he traded in the slip for his off-duty gun, a Colt Cobra. Though the event was about as ceremonious as a third beer, the torch was effectively passed that day.

With my father's help, in the middle of May Frankie was assigned to the 34th precinct. He'd been in his new command only a couple of days when he was sent with a detail to Columbia University. He and a dozen other rookie cops were secreted away in a university-owned building in Morningside Heights, one of many such squads housed in Columbia-owned buildings.

A few weeks before, while Frankie was still walking the Eighth Avenue beat, students at Columbia University had commandeered several buildings on campus and held three university officials hostage, including the acting dean, who was barricaded in his office for twenty-four hours. The siege began as a dual protest, against the construction of a university gymnasium on Morningside Park, which the protesters believed was a racist endeavor, meant to serve university students and not the poor residents of the neighborhood; and the university's association with the Institute for Defense Analysis, which the protesters believed aided the war in Vietnam and studied methods of controlling antiwar protests. The uprising was led by Mark Rudd, the campus president of Students for a Democratic Society (SDS) and was joined by members of the Congress of Racial Equality (CORE) and other black organizations. The seizure completely shut down the university. Classes and other school activities were canceled. It also focused the eyes of the entire nation on Columbia.

For several days, university officials wavered between requesting police action and resolving the dispute themselves. Even the faculty was divided on the issue, with an ad hoc group of professors siding with the demonstrators. But as the days drew on, and an outside mediator's efforts proved fruitless, the prospect of the conflict ending without police involvement became increasingly remote.

By 1968, anticop sentiment had reached perhaps the highest level in modern history, especially among two groups: college students protesting the war in Vietnam, who viewed police as representatives of the establishment; and parts of the black community, who saw cops as racist. For public relations–conscious police department officials, the Columbia riots were a potential nightmare. The last thing the police department needed then was to be drawn into a student protest rife with racial overtones. Still, on April 30, at 2:30 a.m (a time, as one police official quoted in *The New York Times* put it, "when Harlem was asleep"), at the university's request, a force of 1,000 New York City cops wearing riot gear swept onto the campus, removing and arresting the protesters. Although the police tactics that night were widely criticized, and there were several reported injuries to students (and policemen), the raid effectively brought an end to the occupation. But it did little to ease the tension.

Throughout that spring, the campus remained a tinder box. Rallies and protests were common. There were rumors of further occupations, and agitators with bullhorns stirred the already strained emotions. Columbia asked the police department to maintain a presence in case tensions erupted again. The school officials wanted the cops on the premises, but they also wanted them out of plain sight.

As the days went by, and the likelihood of another student takeover lessened, cops assigned to Columbia became lulled into a boring routine. Frankie and the others in his squad spent their time playing cards and eating hero sandwiches from a local deli. But one day, there were rumors that a planned protest had the possibility of turning violent. A speaker at a rally promoting the protest had announced: "We are taking the campus back."

The lieutenant in charge of Frankie's detail was a man named Dan Brady, who lived in Pearl River. When the phone rang in the cops' basement apartment, Brady picked it up. On the line was a deputy chief checking on manpower. Brady, in a field general's tone, told the boss that he had "a hundred men with hats and bats at the ready." Overhearing this, the dozen or so cops in the room, including Frankie, looked at each other, perplexed. A half-hour later, the deputy chief arrived. On seeing just Brady with the twelve officers—plus the decks of cards and the remnants of the sandwiches—the chief became incensed.

"You told me you had a hundred men here!" he shouted.

Brady shrugged. "How was I supposed to know you weren't the enemy?"

The next day, Brady's secret squad was reassigned, the rumors of trouble proved unfounded, and Frankie was placed at a post at the main gate to the university, at 116th and Broadway. Though he was well aware of the antipolice sentiment on the campus (and practically everywhere else, for that matter), he hadn't realized how deep it ran. Like a Buckingham Palace guard, he stood stone-faced as students passed calling him "pig" and giving him the finger. His orders were explicit: Do not engage the students for any reason. One student, a girl no more than nineteen, spat in his face as she walked by. Later that same night, Frankie stopped by the Commodore for a beer and relayed the story to another city cop.

"Right now," the cop said philosophically, "it's us against everybody else. It's time to circle the wagons."

Frankie was the first to come to the aid of a friend in trouble, but with cops, sometimes the distress signals aren't so clear. Such was the case with Jimmy McDermott. Frankie's close relationship with his first friend on the force lasted only through the term of the Academy. It goes that way in the police department. As my brother often said, you make intense friendships with partners, even fellow precinct or unit members, and then transfers jettison those people from your life.

On graduating from the Academy, McDermott was sent to the precinct in Central Park This was the cause of a great deal of good-natured ribbing by Frankie and others of their Academy class. McDermott had thought of himself as something of a "super-cop," one who would right all the wrongs in the city. In Central Park, he ended up policing nuts and squirrels.

Periodically, throughout their careers, my brother and Jimmy ran into each other at police rackets and functions. They even talked on the phone once in a while. McDermott eventually worked his way out of Central Park and into the 32nd Precinct in Harlem, the precinct my father had worked in his short tenure as a patrol sergeant. There McDermott built a reputation as a very good cop, and ultimately he was assigned to the Emergency Service Unit. For the most part, Emergency Service is made up of the true elite of the department. Some cops do gain entrance into Emergency Service by being "hooked up," police parlance for having good connections, but by and large those cops are the exceptions. According to my brother and others, Jimmy McDermott earned his way into Emergency Service.

As the years went by, my brother all but lost touch with his old Academy pal. He had heard through the grapevine that Jimmy had become involved in politics: first in the Bronx, where he lived, and later with American sympathizers of the struggles in Northern Ireland. Then one day my brother learned that Jimmy had died—by his own hand. At Jimmy's funeral, Frankie was told by other cops that Jimmy had some kind of trouble with one of his kids. But what was obvious to Frankie, and the rest of the cops gathered in the church that day, was that Jimmy McDermott's emotional problems ran much deeper than those caused by even the worst of family disputes. The night of the incident, he had had an argument with his kid on the steps of his home. At some point during the argument, he went inside his house and got his gun. He then returned to the front stoop, and right in front of his son, he shot himself in the head.

According to a recent survey by Columbia University, policemen are four to five times more likely to kill themselves than are regular citizens. There are obvious reasons for this, not the least of which is that they have guns. But the tragic ending of Jimmy McDermott's life demonstrates circumstances that no statistics can capture. Sometimes, cops who are heroic, devoted, and, like Jimmy, have a sparkling sense of humor live with inner demons so ferocious that even in a job fraught with as much peril as theirs, the most dangerous person such a cop will ever face is himself.

# 4

The apartment in Pearl River where Frankie and Pam first lived was in a Victorian house on Henry Street, one of the houses built during the 1920s, when industrial growth brought prosperity to the town. The windows in their living room looked down on the Esso station. They had a threadbare couch, a secondhand dining room set with unmatched chairs (all gifts from Pam's mother) and one of those old-fashioned, round-edged refrigerators that hummed like a mosquito zapper in a Texas roadside diner. Frankie was twenty-four, Pam just twenty-two.

When Pam gave birth to Laura, their first child, she was in labor for nearly twenty-four hours. In the waiting room of Nyack Hospital sat Eugene and Diane, Pam's mother, Ann, and Pam's brother, Clem. One of the nurses told Pam she had better hurry—because, the nurse said, her family was waiting on her.

Pam assured the nurse she was trying her hardest.

With the arrival of Laurie, the first order of business for the new parents was to find a bigger apartment—no easy feat in Pearl River, a town almost wholly made up of private houses. Buying a house was then well beyond their reach. After a few weeks of searching, they finally found an apartment slightly bigger than the one they had, near the center of the small business district on Franklin Avenue. It was a convenient location for Pam, who, without a car, could walk to the laundry with the baskets filled with dirty diapers, and to markets for groceries, baby clothes, and formula. But it was nearly impossible for a young family to exist in suburbia on Frankie's starting yearly salary of $7,022. Though Frankie worked "around-the-clock" tours, his schedule changing every week (day tours for five days, "four-to-twelves" for five days, midnights for four days), he managed to pick up some extra money working part-time for a construction company he had worked for in high school. Though moonlighting was still against regulations, the police department looked the other way as long as cops didn't work as bartenders or strikebreakers, or take any job that necessitated the carrying of a firearm. One side job he had was at a rail shipping company on Thirty-third Street and Twelfth Avenue. One day a week he'd work an 8 p.m–to–8 a.m. shift on a loading dock, guarding the "crib car," a railroad car loaded with such desirables as cameras, stereos, and other items with a propensity for growing legs. In the wintertime, it seemed the coldest place on the planet—an open loading dock next to the Hudson River. Frankie'd stuff newspaper in his shirt, constantly walk back and forth, once in a while sneak a few hundred yards down Twelfth Avenue to grab a little warmth from a trash can blaze, something the longshoreman called a Harlem heater.

With Frankie working an extra job, and Pam home nursing Laurie, they didn't exactly have a bustling social calendar. When they did try to have some fun, it mostly consisted of inviting friends over for a few beers and a pizza, or, once in a while, a dinner out at an inexpensive restaurant called Steak & Brew, which served unlimited pitchers of beer during the meal. Frankie had continued his friendships with some of the Brothers, who had then returned from Vietnam. Several of them—Bobby Myers, Willie Ahlmyer, and Bobby Stevenson—had joined the Orangetown Police Department. Frankie and Pam also struck up friendships with other New York City cop families in Rockland. One of the cops, Phil McAleer, a sergeant on the West Side of Manhattan, told Frankie he was wasting his money paying rent and should buy a house instead. Frankie told Phil that he'd love nothing better, but didn't have the money for a down payment. By the late 1960s, homes in Pearl River had already begun to climb in price; long gone were the $500 down payments of our father's day.

"Ask your dad to help you out," McAleer urged.

For Frankie, going to his father for advice—even to use his influence for assignments in the police department—was one thing, but going to him to borrow money was quite another. McAleer's suggestion, however, had planted an idea that would begin to consume Frankie's thoughts: He would get the money for a down payment somehow, even if he had to work three jobs.

After he was pulled from the Columbia University detail, in late May 1968, Frankie was brought back to the 34th Precinct and assigned to a foot post. He was finally a cop with a precinct.

Though there are cops who are happy to walk a beat (Christy Smith, a cop Frankie worked with in the 34th Precinct, was a foot patrolman the whole of his thirty-year career and was known as the mayor of Dyckman Street), Frankie had greater aspirations. The first step up the ladder for a beat cop is a "sector car." In one of their living room chats, Frankie asked my father the best way to go about getting assigned to one. "Get noticed," my father said, advising him to "build a batting average" and "make a lot of arrests." Frankie took the advice to heart and quickly learned the street.

In those early days on the beat, he arrested a number of purse snatchers—who preyed on elderly women walking home from church on St. Nicholas Avenue—and shoplifters near the stores on Broadway and 181st Street. One of the first tricks he learned was to look for the glassine envelopes that junkies would leave behind on the sidewalks in front of buildings where they got high. Quite often, on the rooftops of those buildings, he would catch an addict in the act of shooting up. One day he found a shooting gallery on 165th Street and in it saw dozens of handbags with broken straps. That address became a gold mine of arrests for him, as he would wait for junkies to return with a just-snatched purse, or from copping their drugs. He once foiled a confidence team that had convinced a woman they were bank examiners trying to catch a crooked teller. The con men had talked the woman into helping them—by making a withdrawal from her account. Frankie didn't make the arrest, turning the case over to the detective squad, but he bolstered his standing in the precinct.

For Frankie, the job was fun. He liked the way he looked in the uniform. He liked the authority it gave him. But most of all, he liked that he was good at the work. It was as though the whole of his prior existence had led him to his job: being the son (and grandson) of a cop; his childhood on the streets of the Bronx; the tough-guy persona of his football days and with the Brothers. His life experience, his bloodlines, had endowed him with an inherent knowledge of police work. Even all the disappointments of his school years, the nuns who had told him he would amount to nothing more than a hooligan, mattered little now. Or so he thought.

One night he was taken off his regular beat and assigned a post at a dance at Mother Cabrini High School. The nun in charge of the festivities came to Frankie and, in a frightening replay of his days in St. Margaret's, ordered him to move from his post to another position.

"Excuse me," Frankie said resentfully. "I don't think I work for you."

The nun's face went white with anger, a look Frankie was all too familiar with.

"We'll see about that," she said, as she turned and stormed away.

Fifteen minutes later, a radio car pulled up, the window rolled down about four inches, and a gravelly voice came from within.

"Did you speak to the nun?" the sergeant asked curtly.

Frankie admitted he had.

"Well, when she tells you to do something, you do it! And don't give her any more shit." The window went up and the radio car pulled away.

Frankie stood there for a moment or two, his jaw scraping his shoes. Given his history with nuns, the irony of the event left him with only unprintable words to express his feelings.

At the end of the dance the same nun approached Frankie and Billy Rutter, the other cop assigned to the school, and handed them each an envelope. Inside was a crisp $5 bill. Frankie's first exposure to police corruption was perpetrated by a nun.

Along with Jimmy McDermott, Billy Rutter was one of Frankie's first friends in the police department. They had been in the Academy together, and were both assigned to the 34th Precinct. Rutter also lived in Rockland County, and often they car-pooled to work. Frankie would kid Rutter about his patch-work Corvair, which he was always putting junkyard parts into. Rutter was an affable fellow with an easygoing sense of humor. He needed one. Not only did he take a ribbing about his car, he wore a bad toupee, which, after several Budweisers, would invariably slip to the side of his head, making him look like an accident victim.

One night, when Frankie was reporting for a night tour, the captain of the precinct, John Charles Daly, a dinosaur of a cop, well into his sixties, was walking down the steps of the precinct house. "Jump behind the wheel of that radio car, son," Daly ordered. "We're taking a little ride."

Two days before, *The New York Times* had printed a front-page exposé on cops cooping on duty. The story had rankled the brass at headquarters, and had even drawn Mayor Lindsay's attention, so orders were issued to precinct commanders to put an end to cops catching catnaps instead of bad guys. The best-known coop in the 34th Precinct was under the 207th Street Bridge, which was the exact location where Daly directed Frankie to drive.

Frankie knew that there was a real good chance of someone getting caught. But as a rookie cop, who had spoken all of six words to his captain ("*Good morning, captain,*" twice), he wasn't exactly in a position to try and talk Daly out of his plans. Sure enough, they pulled under the bridge, and there sat a sector car. But the worst was yet to come: As they rolled closer, their headlight illuminated the scene of a cop, in full uniform, taking a tire

off an abandoned Ford Fairlane. On a closer look, my brother realized that the cop was Billy Rutter. Holy shit, Frankie muttered,
holding his forehead in his hand. The captain stepped from the
car. Rutter, still holding the tire under one arm, addressed Daly
with a crisp salute. Meanwhile, Rutter's partner was sound asleep
in the radio car.

For weeks, Rutter thought Frankie had set him up. But finally, after buying him a few Budweisers, Frankie convinced him it was
none of his doing. With the two new openings in sector cars
(Rutter and his partner were demoted to foot posts), Frankie was
assigned Sector G, or George, and his new partner was a cop
named Paul Gibbons.

Lanky, with a wild head of straw-colored hair, Gibbons had a
reputation as an arrest machine. A seasoned cop, he taught Frankie
the nuances of radio car patrol. "Keep turning corners" was his
catch-phrase. Though simple, the tactic was brilliant. With Gibbons at the wheel, the green-black-and-white Dodge radio car
took on the characteristics of a panther, prowling the darkness of
the Washington Heights side streets. Each corner they turned
gave them the element of surprise. That first year together, Gibbons and Frankie led the precinct in arrests—and each arrest paid
a dividend.

"Collars for dollars" was a favorite saying of cops in those days.
With each arrest, overtime in court put Frankie one step closer to
a down payment on a house. Though money, and the prospect
of one day owning his own home, were important to Frankie,
he wasn't a mercenary. There was enough crime in Washington
Heights then that he and Gibbons didn't have to rely on collaring
drug users who boosted radios from cars and steaks from supermarkets to survive. Instead, they tried to focus on those who sold
them the heroin. And, information on dealers was easy to develop. A junkie facing a bust—and however many days in jail, with

the horrors of withdrawal—would inform on dealers without so much as a second thought.

For Frankie, just as the collars brought him closer to the down payment, they also brought him closer to his ultimate career goal—the gold shield of the Detective Division.

In his last years at the 41st Precinct, my father had worked for the man who then ran the Bronx Borough Detective Division and since then had become the chief of detectives. About this time, he arranged for Frankie to have a meeting with the man. During the short meeting at the chief's office, Frankie was promised that he would "get a call."

Though Frankie'd only been a cop for a few years then, using my father's influence to open the door to the Detective Division wasn't that big a favor. There were plenty of detectives with less time on the job than Frankie had whose entry into the division was secured by their fathers, who worked as bartenders on Fordham Road or in cop bosses' haunts in Manhattan, the contract having been sealed with the picking up of a small bar tab and a wink of the eye. Many a contract to the Detective Division was made after mass in the parking lot of St. Margaret's Church. In fact, the Catholic church itself often wielded its formidable influence to secure promotions and assignments in the police department. One contemporary of my father's, a detective who lived in Pearl River, had once studied to be a priest. He kept up friendships with his fellow seminarians, and one of them rose to become the personal secretary to New York's then archbishop, Francis Cardinal Spellman. While still laboring as a patrolman, the ex-seminarian called his priest friend and asked for a favor. Soon after, the chief of detectives received a call from Spellman, and a promotion to the Detective Division was arranged.

But Frankie once told me there is an old adage in the police department: "When you're in, you're the best; when you're out, you're a pest." My father was out, and Frankie never received the call he was promised.

\* \* \*

After a year together, Frankie and Gibbons were assigned to the "school car"—a promotion of sorts, patrolling one of the busiest sections of Washington Heights—George Washington High School and the immediate surrounding area. Because of increased violence in the schools, a result of severe overcrowding, extended school hours to make up time lost during teacher strikes, and the increase in juvenile illegal-drug use, a special unit was formed in December 1968 to patrol school grounds and the areas immediately around them. The overcrowding in George Washington High was so bad the school held three sessions a day. The crime problem around the school reached the point where shop owners would lock their doors—some even shutting down completely—during school recesses.

In June 1969, Frankie and Gibbons responded to a call about an unruly crowd assembled outside the high school. An agitator who billed himself as a Black Panther was preaching from the front steps. The principal demanded of Frankie and Gibbons that the man be removed. When Gibbons tried to grab the agitator's arm, the would-be Panther (it turned out he was not a member of the party) punched him in the jaw, knocking him sprawling down the steps. Frankie began to wrestle the man, trying to get his cuffs on him. Gibbons, dazed but back on his feet, went to Frankie's aid. Meanwhile, the crowd became hostile. They chanted for the man's release. Frankie called for backup as he and Gibbons dragged the agitator through the crowd, being pummeled and pulled. When they finally got into the radio car, Frankie sighed with relief. But the students surrounded the car and began rocking it. He was sure they were going to tip over—the car was at least up on two wheels. Just then he heard the sirens of the backup on the way. For Frankie and Gibbons, those sirens were like the bugle of the cavalry.

The backup teams were led by a tough veteran sergeant who had no qualms about using his nightstick, and the scene escalated into a riot. Finally, Frankie was able to move the radio car through the mass of students and cops. Safely away from the scene, the two partners looked at each other and shook their heads.

"That could have been really bad," Gibbons said, with typical understatement.

In the backseat, the agitator's attitude changed dramatically. He became polite and soft-spoken, no doubt sure that he was headed for a beating in the station house. He didn't receive one. Frankie and Gibbons were content to have escaped with their lives. Later, Gibbons complained about his jaw, which had taken the first blow. He had it checked at nearby Columbia Presbyterian Hospital and found it had been slightly fractured. From that day on, it clicked when he talked.

With each passing month of 1968, violence against police became more frequent and frightening. In August that year, two police officers responding to what turned out to be a false alarm walked into a trap and were shotgunned. Though they survived, both were badly wounded. In November, a bomb exploded outside a Harlem station house, close enough to shatter most of the windows. But cops weren't just victims: In September, off-duty police officers had attacked members of the Black Panther Party outside a Brooklyn courthouse where a Panther was on trial for assaulting a cop. Lines had been drawn. The sides were clearly delineated. Things, as Frankie would say, were heating up.

Frankie and Gibbons's next step up the precinct ladder was an assignment to the "narcotics car." What was ludicrous, the narcotics car was a regular patrol car, about as inconspicuous as an ice cream truck during a heat wave. By 1969, there was a nationwide explosion of drug abuse. In New York City, desperate narcotics addicts—and the business of supplying them drugs—became the number one cause of crime. Nowhere was this more in evidence than in the 34th Precinct.

Washington Heights was then a neighborhood in transition, with a high percentage of teenagers—the sons and daughters of a recent Hispanic infusion into the area. It was also easily accessible from New Jersey, just over the George Washington Bridge. This was the time when Washington Heights first became known as a drug bazaar, a marketplace for suburban as well as local users. The narcotics division of the NYPD then numbered only 800 full-time cops. By 1970, there were over 40,000 narcotics arrests, nearly 70 percent of those for heroin. Of the more than 100,000 felons arrested that year, nearly 20 percent admitted to being addicts. And it seems likely that the number who chose not to confess their addictions would boost that percentage significantly higher. These statistics also did not include dealers and suppliers of narcotics, a percentage of whom—at least the smart ones—were not addicts. Even at the most conservative estimates, the narcotics business was now responsible for fully half of felony crimes.

The brain trust at police headquarters worked full-time trying to stem the rising crime rates. Meanwhile, an inspector of the 5th Division decided to abolish the narcotics car and strip away the obvious indicators that marked cops in the street. In the precincts of the 5th Division, including the 34th, uniform cops assigned to the narcotics units would be put in plainclothes and unmarked cars. It was a radical move, but it worked. Soon after, Police Commissioner Patrick Murphy authorized the use of up to 5 percent of each precinct's uniform force for this innovative program. His edict was carried out despite two major roadblocks. One, department regulations forbade uniform cops to work in plainclothes (although a few special squads, such as gambling and vice, were exempt from this rule). Two, there were no funds available for unmarked cars. A waiver was obtained to override the plainclothes regulations, but finding the money for the cars was impossible, because New York City was entering a fiscal crisis that would last for a decade. In an unorthodox move, cops were authorized to use their personal cars as undercover vehicles. Some of the cops assigned to the narcotics units balked at the idea, but Frankie and Gibbons both decided to do it. Gibbons had little to lose, since he drove a green 1962 Volkswagen Beetle, but Frankie had just bought, with a few dollars down and a heavy monthly loan payment, a brand-new Plymouth Duster. The police department would pay for gas but not for repairs of any damage incurred in the line of duty.

For Frankie, if his new assignment meant a couple of dents in the Duster, so be it. The new unit was his chance to see real action—to "get noticed," as his father advised. Though undercover policing has its downside (in the heat of the chase it is hard to tell the good guys from the bad; undercover cops are regularly involved in scary near-misses with the uniform force. And, for drug dealers, the difference between an undercover bust and a stickup team looking to rip them off is nearly imperceptible), for Frankie, the rewards were well worth the risk. For him, Undercover was a field where gold shields grew like dandelions.

Though this makeshift approach to police work was irregular, to say the least, the unit was an immediate success. The arrest rate grew considerably, and with it, Frankie's reputation.

For the first time in his career, my brother did not wear a patrolman's uniform to work. Instead he donned jeans and a Jets football jersey, number 13 (belonging to Don Maynard, one of his favorite players). His hair was long, nearly shoulder-length, red near the ends, and it curled up in the back. To the seasoned observer he still looked like a cop, that was for sure. The Irish-ruddy complexion and his thin lips pressed in a tough-guy smirk remained even when the uniform came off. But he certainly didn't look like the other city cops, and he certainly fooled the bad guys often enough.

But being this new type of policeman brought with it a kind of split personality. In Pearl River, Frankie was struggling with all the typical problems of other young suburban marrieds: money and children, trying to plan and save for schools, doctors, Little League and soccer teams. In Washington Heights, he was a guerrilla fighting a battle on darkened city streets, in alleys and on rooftops. At home he was a father who put his whole heart into trying to build a home for his family. In the city, that heart was often covered with a bulletproof vest.

In 1970, Pam gave birth to their second daughter, Patrice. Now, with two babies in diapers, she had little time to worry about her husband, but she could not stave off the dread that accompanied each story Frankie told when he returned from work. She lived in a kind of suspended terror. Each time the phone rang late at night, a cold shiver ran through her. One night, the local TV news led with a story of an undercover cop killed in Washington Heights. The report did not give the name of the officer, pending notification of his family. Pam sat in front of the TV watching the on-the-scene report—the police cars with "34" emblazoned on their sides, the flashing lights, the dark street starkly illuminated by the TV lights—and felt her heart race.

As soon as he had the chance, Frankie called Pam to tell her he was all right, and that, because of the shooting, he would have to work late. Lying awake in their bed, she had answered the phone on the first ring, and, during the short conversation with her husband, pretended that she hadn't watched the news.

About the same time, there had been a rash of robberies and murders of taxi drivers in New York. Cabbies, concerned about their safety, refused to work the late-night shifts, causing a shortage of taxis on the streets. Those who did drive at night equated black people with crime and often refused to pick them up. They also sped away from fares with destinations in high-crime neighborhoods like Harlem and Bedford-Stuyvesant in Brooklyn. The city began discussions of allowing off-duty cops to work as cabbies on the night shifts, when most of the crimes occurred. It was not an original idea. In Philadelphia the program had been instituted some years earlier with great success. As in Philadelphia, the New York cops would carry their revolvers.

For Frankie, and other industrious cops, the program was a godsend. Once he obtained his taxi driver's license, he could just show up at night at any number of cab companies and be assured of work. And even though the moonlighting cops were mostly assigned cabs without a Plexiglas partition—this innovation came about in response to the wave of violent crimes—the money was good, even terrific. Cabbies in those days kept 49 percent of all they made, plus tips. On the average, Frankie was taking down $100 a night from his second job. With extra money like that coming in three, sometimes four nights a week, a down payment for a home was squarely in his sights.

Pam wasn't thrilled with the idea of spending so much time alone, not to mention that her husband was now working two of the most dangerous jobs in New York. But she, too, was excited by the prospect of a home of her own, and she tried not to worry.

Though it meant incredibly long workdays, sometimes stretching to seventeen or eighteen hours, Frankie enjoyed driving a cab. It gave him the opportunity to learn the city: the location of landmarks, of good restaurants and hotels. He learned the streets— knowledge that later on in his career would prove invaluable. He learned the fastest routes to the airports and knew his way around the maze of Greenwich Village. He even learned the outer boroughs, Brooklyn and Queens. Whether because of his desire to make as much money as he could, the swaggering confidence he had as a tough guy and a cop, or the revolver strapped in his ankle holster, he never refused a fare, no matter how dangerous the destination or what color the skin of the hand waving him down.

One night, after dropping a fare off in the theater district, he drove up Eighth Avenue, where a man flagged him down. He pulled over, and the man held the door open as two other men appeared from a doorway and jumped into the backseat. Something was wrong. He asked the destination and one of the men said only:

"Just drive uptown."

Frankie watched his three passengers in the rearview mirror. At one point his eyes met those of one of the men, and they held each other's gaze for some moments. Again, Frankie asked where they wanted to go, and again "Uptown," was the only answer. Frankie gently reached his hand down his leg and removed the revolver from his ankle holster, then slid it between his legs. Every fiber in his body, all the experience of his two years on the street, told him that this situation was not good. He kept watch in the rearview mirror as furtive glances were exchanged among his passengers. He decided he had to do something to put himself at the advantage. He casually removed the revolver from between his legs and held it against the steering wheel, then turned again to the backseat and in an overly friendly tone asked the destination once more.

"Right here," said the spokesman of the three. "You can leave us right here, man."

Between them, they barely had enough for the two-dollar fare, paid in nickels and dimes.

As often happens between partners, Gibbons and Frankie became good friends. On many occasions, Pam and Frankie went to the Gibbonses' home in Babylon, Long Island, to visit; a few times they stayed overnight. Gibbons later moved to Pearl River. But, as close as they became, sitting in a car with each other for at least eight hours a day, five days a week, going on three years, there were, as there are in the best of friendships, uncomfortable times. What bothered Frankie most about Gibbons was how much he liked to talk. He wasn't a braggart, which Frankie would not have put up with. What poured from Gibbons's mouth was just a constant babbling monologue about anything and everything. Over their years together, Frankie learned to tune his partner out, nodding and "mmmming" his way through the verbal barrage.

Gibbons thought himself a bit of a gourmand, and on dinner breaks, he would often stop at a local butcher shop and order a shell steak, then go to the Legion Diner and have the short-order cook broil it for him. Sometimes he would go to Yingie's Chinese restaurant and emerge with an amazing array of cartons of spare ribs, sweet-and-sour pork, fried dumplings, and other delicacies. Invariably, as Frankie and Gibbons sat eating behind the Isabella Nursing Home, their favorite meal-break coop, a call would come over the radio to which they would have to respond. Frankie would take his time and replace the covers on his food, but Gibbons would just toss it out of the window. If the call proved inconsequential, Gibbons would sit like a dog under a dinner table watching Frankie eat. "What? You're not going to give me none?" he'd ask.

Though at times Gibbons wore on his patience, Frankie's partner had an innocent quality that was quite endearing. One of his favorite hobbies was baking. The cop who for several years made the most arrests in the 34th Precinct also made holiday cookies and elaborately frosted cakes, which he would sometimes present to other cops in the precinct on their birthdays. Gibbons also had a reputation for the kind of frankness that made even the most jaded cop's jaw drop. Whether it was his vasectomy or any aspect of his sex life, no matter was too personal or sacrosanct for him to address, and rank was never an obstacle to disclosure. Often, Frankie would hold his head in his hand as his partner approached a commanding officer and began a discussion on the most intimate of subjects.

Another aspect of Gibbons's personality that wore on Frankie was his hypochondria. He was always complaining about his back, his kidneys, a twisted ankle, a cold he was sure was going to develop into pneumonia. He called in sick often, for the slightest of reasons. He did, however, have one malady that was not psychosomatic—asthma. Several times he collapsed during chases.

One day, when Frankie and Gibbons were still in the sector car, they had received a call to respond to the Dyckman Houses on Nagle Avenue. It was a medical emergency involving a baby, and an ambulance was also directed to the scene. But Gibbons and Frankie, just a block or two away, arrived first. In the lobby a table was set up and several tenants were collecting signatures for a petition to fix the elevators: They were out of order, and had been apparently for some time. The baby was on the twelfth floor. Both Frankie and Gibbons charged up the staircase. Frankie was nearly to the twelfth floor before he realized Gibbons was no longer behind him. There was no time, however, to locate his partner. The baby's mother stood in the open doorway of her apartment screaming hysterically.

Inside the dining room area, on a waist-high hutch, the baby lay in a plastic bathtub. She was so small, so completely motionless, that to Frankie the tiny girl looked like a doll. A blue doll, because the baby had ingested the bathwater and couldn't breathe. When Frankie was a child living in our Bronx apartment, a neighbor, Mrs. Farrell, banged on the door screaming that her baby was drowning in the bath. Frankie remembered my mother running into the Farrells' apartment, picking the baby up by his feet, and slapping him hard on the back. Emulating her, Frankie took the infant and gave her a whack. As though a thermos jug spigot had opened, a gush of water spilled from the baby's mouth, and she began to cry. Just then, the Emergency Service Unit and the ambulance workers came into the apartment. A sergeant arrived and asked what happened. When Frankie told him, he said: "Write this one up, it's a good one."

On the way down the stairs Frankie saw Gibbons sitting on a landing, an oxygen mask on his face.

"You okay, Paul?" he asked.

More embarrassed than anything else and in a voice muffled by the mask, Gibbons said: "Keep this to yourself."

After an examination at the hospital, the baby returned home that same night, and for months after, Frankie kidded his partner on his missed shot at being the hero. Although paradoxically long-winded and short on breath, Gibbons had one trait that Frankie completely admired: He was absolutely fearless.

On a hot early-fall day in 1970, Gibbons and Frankie sat in the Duster, stuck in traffic on 177th Street. Gibbons tugged uncomfortably at his red-raspberry summer shirt, regaling Frankie with several theories on how to solve New York City's traffic problem. In the middle of his rhetorical riff, a call came over the radio about a robbery in progress just two blocks away. Gibbons opened the door and jumped from the car. Frankie was about to follow, then realized he couldn't leave the Duster, with only a thousand or so miles on it, in the middle of the street. It took him maybe five minutes to snake his way through traffic to the building where the robbery was taking place. When he arrived, there was no sign of Gibbons. Then, as Frankie was about to enter the building, two shots rang out. A woman passing by began to scream, and pointed into an adjacent alley. There a body lay motionless. From where he stood, all Frankie could see was that the form was wearing a bright red shirt.

For a split second, he stood paralyzed in horror, believing his partner lay there dead. But just as quickly the fear evaporated: Gibbons's high-pitched shout for help came from the building. Frankie drew his service revolver and raced up the steps. A door to an apartment on the fifth floor was flung wide open. Inside, Gibbons and one of the robbers were on the floor, wrestling for Gibbons's gun, which lay just out of their reach. With a surge of adrenaline, Frankie flew into the apartment and in one graceful motion, as hard as he could, kicked Gibbons's opponent in the face. Reeling backward, the man slammed into the wall, then slumped unconscious back to the floor.

Gibbons thought he had shot the man who'd fallen to the alley. He hadn't intended to, he told Frankie in a quivering voice, but his gun discharged when the other robber jumped on him. But in fact Gibbons hadn't shot the guy. The man in the alley was trying to escape through the window, the same way the two suspects had entered the apartment. The technique was called a stepover: Burglars would go out a hallway window, then jump to an apartment window ledge to one side of the hall window. The man who lay in the alley had missed the hallway window ledge in his attempt to escape and fallen the five stories.

In several minutes, the apartment was filled with uniform cops who had responded to the second call of "shots fired." When the patrol sergeant arrived, having seen the one burglar lying in the alley, and the unconscious one in the apartment, he asked Frankie what had happened. Still confused by the rapid events, Frankie said he wasn't sure.

"Well, I'm taking a walk," the sergeant said. "When I come back have a story."

Whenever a cop shoots his gun, a detailed written report is filed, and the gun has to be tested by ballistics. Though Gibbons denied that he meant to fire his weapon, and even though he was undoubtedly within his right to shoot if he had intended to, the fact that his weapon had discharged meant a full investigation. And several aspects of the incident didn't fall in Gibbons's favor: Frankie had arrived on the scene after the fact, and there were no other corroborating witnesses; also, there was the physical condition of the two robbers—the man in the alley seriously hurt from the fall, and the man in the apartment with quite a dent in his head from Frankie's size 11 shoe.

Back at the station house, filling out the numerous reports (Gibbons, who had wrenched his back in the struggle, had been taken to the hospital for tests), Frankie was approached by a clerical sergeant. The sergeant, perhaps realizing that for him the case had all the characteristics of a nightmare of forms and reports, dropped an application for a newly formed unit in front of Frankie.

"Why don't you and your partner give it some thought," the sergeant said.

The application was for a unit called Anti-Crime, an experimental, undercover squad that would almost immediately become one of the most heralded crime-fighting tools in the history of the New York City police department.

# 5

On the night of May 21, 1971, as two New York city police officers lay clinging to life in New York Hospital, my brother Frankie and his fill-in partner, a cop named McQuaid (Gibbons had called in sick), were working Anti-Crime in the 34th Precinct. Two days before, Patrolmen Thomas Curry and Nicholas Binetti had been sitting in a patrol car stationed in front of Manhattan District Attorney Frank Hogan's home at 404 Riverside Drive, a quiet and fashionable street that winds along the Hudson River. Six days earlier, Hogan's prosecution of thirteen Black Panthers for conspiring to bomb police stations and kill police officers had resulted in a not-guilty verdict on all counts, a verdict that had left the police department vibrating from shock. During the trial, angry Panther demonstrations outside the courthouse erupted into near riots, and the home of the presiding judge, John M. Murtagh, had been firebombed. Racial tension in New York City was explosive.

Still, Curry and Binetti had every reason to believe that a long, boring night lay ahead of them. Why, given the verdict, would the black militant organization want revenge against Hogan now?

Just fifteen minutes into their night shift, which began at nine p.m., a dark maroon Buick slowly rolled by, going the wrong way down a one-way street. The cops wheeled their patrol car in pursuit, and, some six blocks south of Hogan's building, pulled up alongside the Buick. Just as they did, the residential street exploded with the crackle of a .45-caliber machine gun. Over twenty rounds were discharged. Curry and Binetti were shot in the face, body, and arms. Their patrol car slammed into a parked car. The Buick disappeared into the night.

On the twenty-first, *The New York Times* received the Buick's license plate, accompanied by a letter from an ultra-militant splinter group of the Black Panther Party. The last part of the letter read: "The domestic armed forces of racism and oppression will be confronted with the guns of the Black Liberation Army, who will mete out in the tradition of Malcolm and all true revolutionaries real justice. We are revolutionary justice. All power to the people."

That night, as Frankie and McQuaid cruised the streets of northern Manhattan in the Duster, the radio blared to life. The initial "10-13," "Cop needs assistance," was quickly followed by a "10-40," one of the most urgent of calls. With my brother at the wheel, the partners raced down the Harlem River Drive toward a housing project on 159th Street facing the Harlem River, where the Polo Grounds baseball stadium once stood. By the time they arrived, not more than a few minutes after the initial call, the small streets within the project were jammed with emergency vehicles, ambulances, and police cars with sirens blasting and lights flashing. It seemed every police officer in Manhattan, on duty or not, had responded to the call.

The information imparted over the radio during the first few minutes after the shootings was sketchy, even dead wrong. The first reports said that two housing patrolmen had been shot. In actuality, the victims were two regular patrol cops; their names,

Frankie would learn later, were Waverly Jones and Joseph Piagentini. The description of the shooters was vague at best: two
young black males, wearing dark clothing. Piagentini and Jones
had responded to a call for assistance, a woman who was superfi-
cially stabbed, but had refused help. The two cops were shot in
the back as they walked from the Colonial Park Houses, the official name of the Polo Grounds projects: Jones three times, once
in the back of the head, killing him instantly; Piagentini, thirteen
times. There were bullet wounds in Piagentini's hands. He had
lain dying on the ground and tried to cover his face as the last of
the bullets—fired from his own service revolver, which had been
taken from him—were pumped into him.

Frankie turned the Duster from the gridlock that lay before
him and raced to a location known as the hole. On the northern
edge of the projects, a steep block wall topped by a wire mesh
fence ran alongside the access road to the Harlem River Drive.
Beyond the access road lay Highbridge Park, a huge wooded tract
that rolled and rambled from the Polo Grounds projects to the
very northern border of the 34th Precinct. Anti-Crime cops from
the 34th knew this fence well—especially the torn-away portion
of it. Criminals who lived in the Polo Grounds projects and
feasted on the residential and business areas of Washington Heights
used the cover of Highbridge Park and the hole in the fence to
make good their escape. Frankie pulled to the shoulder of the access road, and he and McQuaid leaped from the car. The park lay
in front of them, a huge black ocean of woods. The only sound
was the leaves rustling in the light night breeze, and the distant
wail of police sirens. They knew a search of the woods would be
senseless—like trying to find someone in Central Park. Instead,
Frankie and McQuaid jumped back in the Duster and headed
back to the Three-Four, holding on to the hope that the killers
had the same idea.

Adrenaline, fueled by anger, pumped in Frankie's veins. Though his tour was supposed to end at midnight, he and McQuaid worked until the sun rose. They stopped and searched dozens of suspicious characters on the street. They tossed a bar on Amsterdam Avenue, one that McQuaid knew had a sordid clientele, searching every single patron, including the bartender, and came up with nothing—not so much as a nail file. Word of the dead cops had already reached the streets. It didn't matter to Frankie and McQuaid that they were performing illegal searches, and that nothing they would find would hold up in court. For them, and most every police officer in New York that night, there was only one objective: find the cop killers.

The consensus among investigators assigned to the case was that the shooters of Piagentini and Jones did escape the projects through the hole in the fence and most probably crossed the Harlem River into the Bronx by the High Bridge, a pedestrian span. But if in fact they had, they had done so in the minutes before Frankie and McQuaid arrived.

A few days later, the girlfriend of one of the shooters, who lived on Fox Street in my father's old precinct, told police she had overheard a conversation between her boyfriend and several other men, the very night of the shooting. She remembered one man saying that one of the cops was a "brother"—Waverly Jones, who was black. Another man in that apartment answered: "A pig is a pig."

Though most of the BLA members responsible for the cop killings were eventually brought to justice (one was killed in a shoot-out with cops in St. Louis, others apprehended as far away as San Francisco), the months and years of the BLA siege wrecked the city's nerves, further polarized the already strained relationship between the NYPD and the black community, and pushed cops into a wartime mentality.

In a twelve-month period during 1971 and 1972 alone, ten New York City police officers were killed in the line of duty; another dozen were maimed. I knew their names well. The city cops in Pearl River would repeat them like a mantra: Foster and Laurie, Piagentini and Jones, Curry and Binetti, Cardillo . . .

During that twelve-month period, Frankie went to at least half a dozen cop funerals. He stood among the sea of navy blue. He saluted with a sparkling-white-gloved hand while the single bagpiper hauntingly played "Amazing Grace" as the coffin was carried by sturdy blue shoulders into the church, and he would wipe the tears that had begun to form in the corners of his eyes while the piper played "Coming Home" and the coffin was carried to the hearse. Each time he would try not to look at the widow and family, but each time his eyes would be drawn to them. He knew—all cops knew—the routine the widow had been forced to endure. Soon after the cop had been shot, a phone call would have been made to the home of the dead officer. It would have been cryptic, the call, with not a lot of information imparted. Soon a police car would have arrived, to drive the worried wife to police headquarters, where a ranking officer would tell her that her children no longer had a father. . . . At each of these funerals, Frankie thought of Pam, watching late-night TV, waiting for him to come home from work. He thought of his two little girls, Laurie and Patrice, snuggled in their Little Red Riding Hood comforters in their bedroom. When he looked at a dead cop's widow, not even the white gloves could soak up the tears that would stream down his face.

The house Pam and Frankie had set their sights on was just off Forest Avenue in Pearl River, on a street covered in the spring and summer with a cooling canopy of trees, lined with modest split-level brick and wood homes with neatly kept lawns strewn with plastic toys and divided by tarred driveways on which were parked tricycles and Ford station wagons. On the top of Forest Avenue was a 7-Eleven, where preteen girls and boys would walk to buy Slurpies and grape-flavored bubble gum, and young teenagers would buy cigarettes and smoke them clandestinely behind the store.

And a few blocks down from the 7-Eleven, on Middletown Road—the AOH's St. Patrick's Day parade, held here on the Sunday after March 17, had grown to be one of the biggest in the country—was a tavern called the Grasshopper. The walls of the "Hopper" were dark-stained panel, hung with New York Jets schedules and cheesy Budweiser's mirror signs. The tables had checkered cloths, and toward the back, there were red Naugahyde booths. The bar, on the left as you walked in, ran the length of the place. There, seated on bar stools, on any night of the week, would be patrolmen, detectives, retired detectives, the rank and file, most of whom worked, or had once worked, in the precincts of the Bronx and Manhattan. Cops weren't the only ones to patronize the Hopper; there were firemen (so many Jack Ryans in the fire department lived in Rockland County that they were numbered. Jack Ryan Number 7 moonlighted as a bartender at the Hopper), local businessmen, and, on weekends, all of their wives. But for all intents and purposes, the Hopper was a New York City cops' bar, "Bronx North," as it was sometimes called, the mirror image of any number of bars across the street from Bronx precinct houses. By then, the wave of cops who had emigrated to Pearl River during the mid-fifties was neatly tucked into suburbia. The sons of cops and firemen, who became cops and firemen themselves, bought homes and staked their claim to a town that was now their birthright.

Though Frankie continued driving the taxi to save money for the down payment, and though he was still racking up the collars, the bills seemed to eat up every dime. Although every fiber in his body told him not to go to his father for money, ultimately he did just that. My father took a bank loan for $5,000 and solemnly handed the payment book to my brother. When Frankie took the payment book home, he noticed that the loan officer had made a mistake: What was supposed to be a three-year repayment plan instead was a two-year plan. With the loan my father gave them, and a few thousand that Frankie had saved, he and Pam closed on the house near Forest Avenue. But now they had two large monthly payments, the mortgage and the loan, and the financial strain was immense.

Pam suggested that she take a job. The neighbor across the street could watch the children during the day, she reasoned. "I'll find a way to make more money," Frankie answered. Perhaps the prospect of not being able to provide for his family was too great a blow to his pride. Other cops in Pearl River could afford homes, why couldn't he? But other cops weren't the only ones with whom Frankie compared himself. Eugene was well on his way to a meteoric rise in business—criss-crossing the country, with a promotion and a bigger, more impressive house with each transfer. Although the competition between Eugene and Frankie for their father's attention had waned with time, Frankie always felt an underlying jealousy of his older brother's success.

"I'll just work more nights in the cab," he promised Pam.

As the months went by, even with the extra work, the monthly nut seemed harder and harder to make. Several times Frankie had Pam choose between paying the mortgage and paying my father's loan. Each time, he paid the latter, and pretended, in conversations with my father, that he was doing just fine.

One day, Pam saw in the "help wanted" section of the *Journal News* an ad for a waitress in a local restaurant. Though she had been around restaurants most of her life, she'd never actually worked in one. How hard could it be? she wondered. The restaurant, Hoppin' John's, was located in Tappan, just a few miles from Pearl River. She called the number and was told to come down right away for an interview, which she did. With the help of a small lie, saying that she had experience, she was hired on the spot. Though Pam was worried about his reaction, her nervousness disappeared when Frankie walked through the door.

"I got a job," she said straightforwardly. "And don't start yelling, because we need the money."

Surprisingly, Frankie's reaction was subdued. The reality was, they desperately needed the money.

Frankie and Pam's financial problems coincided with the Knapp Commission. Like its predecessors, the Lexow Committee in my grandfather's day, the 1914 Curran Commission, which unseated Police Commissioner Waldo, and the Harry Gross case of 1949, when my father was a young detective, the 1970 Knapp Commission investigated police corruption, mostly centering on the plainclothes division and a newly formed narcotics investigation unit. One of the star witnesses for the Commission was Frank Serpico, a name that in my house was uttered as a curse. According to my father and brother, and therefore, the law in our family, the world was divided in half. You were either a "stand-up guy," sort of a Jimmy Cagney character going silently to the chair, or you were a rat. And Serpico, in my home, was the quintessential rat. Both my father and brother were honest cops. If nothing else, the financial struggles that plagued their lives were ample evidence of their refusal to take anything but their salaries. For Frankie, the Knapp Commission was just more fuel for the anti-cop fire that burned so brightly in the early 1970s, but even that Frankie had gotten used to. Being called a pig didn't bother him much anymore. But corruption was all around him, and though the Knapp Commission would not directly affect his life, Frankie watched, ringside, as the commission shattered the lives of cops close to him. One such cop worked with Frankie in Anti-Crime.

Within Dan Diggins's circle of friends, it was common knowledge that Matty Sirica, Diggins's brother-in-law, was a thief. The joke was that Matty could steal a hot stove. He worked as a maintenance mechanic at Kennedy Airport. With easy access to freight hangars, Matty had a veritable shopping mall at his disposal. Still, except for an occasional power tool or stereo speaker that "fell off the truck"—or in this case, off the plane—Diggins rarely took advantage of his brother-in-law's expertise. But on a clear October morning of 1971, a brand-new $800 transponder for a Cessna 150 sat wrapped in brown paper like a T-bone steak on his kitchen table—compliments of Matty.

It was a Saturday, and Diggins had been doing some jobs around the house—spreading grass seed and fertilizer, preparing the lawn for winter. He enjoyed keeping up his half-acre in the suburban Rockland County town of New City. With all the overtime he was putting in at Anti-Crime, he wanted to take advantage of this rare day off. His job in the new unit placed him in the highest-crime neighborhoods and had instilled in him a new-found appreciation for his home: the dirt in his flower garden turned over for its winter slumber, the garage swept and tidied, the house newly painted. That Saturday, Diggins would have been happy to spend the rest of the afternoon doing chores, but he had a contract; and a contract with a fellow cop always took precedence, always drew him away.

The promise had been made two weeks earlier, in a bar called Maruffi's on the corner of Baxter and Bayard Streets across from the back entrance of 100 Centre Street, the Manhattan Criminal Court building. Perhaps it was made at one of the tiny tables with checkered cloths, where Phillie the waiter presided, serving hero sandwiches that arrived from the basement kitchen by dumb-waiter. Or maybe it was at the long oaken bar, where Hawkie, so named because of his enormous hooked nose and tiny squinting eyes, swooped down, landing ice-cold beers before cops who laughed raucously at last night's fruitless chase of a perp. These same cops also talked in hushed confessional tones, lips moving in expressionless faces, and eyes, like those of a nun standing in front of a testing class, scanning the room assessing everyone. In those days, just prior to the Knapp Commission, there was a lot of assessing. Rumors of cops wearing wires circulated in station-house locker rooms and in places like Maruffi's. Like other cop bars—the Jesse James across from the Five-Oh precinct, French Charlie's in the Five-Two, the Melody Lounge in Washington Heights near the 34th, the Pub on Queens Boulevard, across from the Queens County Court house—Maruffi's was a church where the cop brotherhood congregated. Here the confidences that bound this fraternity were passed, asylum was found, the legendary blue wall of silence was transubstantiated into fake stucco.

If cop bars are churches, then Maruffi's was the cathedral. Cops from all over Manhattan waited there for arraignments across the street. The seasoned ones, the cops who could predict the wait by the court calendar or the day of the week, would know whether their appointments with the D.A. were hours or days away. Diggins had gone through the ritual of lodging a prisoner at 100 Centre, submitting prints at the Bureau of Criminal Identification at police headquarters, and then heading back to the Criminal Court Building to put his name on the waiting list at the complaint room. He figured his wait to be three or four hours. He went to Maruffi's to pass the time in quiet contemplation.

Huey Collins was at the end of the bar—a fixture, wearing his black raincoat over his uniform, as he always did, even when it was ninety-eight degrees. Cops and court officers filled the tables, Phillie the waiter yelled to the sandwich maker in the basement, and Hawkie cursed about this or that. As Diggins sat at the bar sipping a cold one, a cop from the 19th Precinct named Bill Phillips appeared at the door. Phillips had thin dark hair, combed back, and muttonchop sideburns. His eyes twinkled with the look of either a sinister practical joker or a conscienceless killer. He sidled up next to Diggins at the bar. Although they didn't work together, Diggins knew Phillips fairly well. The Anti-Crime cop was a flying buff, and Phillips owned the NYPD Flying School at MacArthur Airport on Long Island. The school wasn't sanctioned by the department; Phillips just used the name. But a number of cops had learned to fly, and obtained their private pilot's licenses, at Phillips's school. Diggins had taken a couple of lessons there himself, but his job in Anti-Crime, and the responsibilities of his new home, kept him from seriously working toward his license. He made a promise, however, to both Phillips and himself, to pursue it when he had the time.

The NYPD Flying School owned a couple of single-engine Cessnas, a Cherokee, and a $14,000 twin-engine Cardinal. How a patrolman got the money to underwrite such an enterprise was something known only to Phillips. And Diggins, even in the sanctity of Maruffi's, would never ask.

Phillips was, in my father's vernacular, a "bright lights" guy. He had a reputation for dressing in immaculate suits, doing up the singles bars on the East Side of Manhattan, and hanging around KGs—known gamblers—and other sordid types. Diggins also knew that Phillips had been "flopped" from the detective division, losing his gold shield for accepting drinks "on the arm" (for free), at one of his East Side haunts. The incident, though, gave Phillips almost martyr status among some cops, who viewed the bust in rank as unusually cruel punishment for something many had done. After a few beers, Phillips casually asked about Diggins's brother-in-law, Matty. He dropped a few not-so-subtle hints about one of his planes needing a transponder, a transmitter that sends pulse signals to air traffic control radar. Though Diggins was wary of Phillips, this was a favor that could be exchanged for flying lessons sometime in the future. He promised to see what he could do.

The following week, Phillips called Diggins at his house and asked about the transponder. The call bothered Diggins for two reasons. First, in the covenant between cops, a single promise is usually binding. Second—and more important—conversations like this one were never held over a phone. Though Diggins was a smart cop, highly regarded by Frankie and his other partners, he foolishly shrugged off his suspicions.

Early the next week, Matty, as usual, delivered on the order.

The transponder, shipped from the Cessna plant in Wichita, Kansas, was taken from the Flying Tigers freight warehouse at Kennedy. A few days later, when Diggins next ran into Phillips, again at Maruffi's, he told him that the package had arrived. Phillips asked if he would be able to bring it to him at the flight school the following Saturday in exchange for a quick hop out to Montauk, and Diggins agreed. That Saturday, as Diggins grabbed the plain brown package and headed for the door, the phone rang.

After agents assigned to Whitman Knapp's investigation, armed with a warrant, had searched his home, Diggins thought about the voice on the phone earlier that afternoon. He hadn't recognized it. There were only two words spoken—"Don't go"—then the click of the receiver, and the dial tone. The Knapp agents didn't find the transponder, which lay at the bottom of the pond on Merrick Road. Still, they didn't give up on Diggins, interrogating him for months afterward. Every day, the threat of prosecution hung over him. He was reassigned from Anti-Crime to the seclusion of a desk. Just a week after agents searched Diggins's home, Whitman Knapp announced that William Phillips would testify before his commission. And, for three days, he did. Though Frank Serpico was perhaps the most high-profile witness to testify (thanks to Peter Maas's best-selling book and Al Pacino's portrayal of him in the movie) most people familiar with the proceedings agree that Phillips's testimony was the most damaging to the police department. In a villainous star turn that put his face on the front page of every New York paper and in the lead story on every televised newscast, Phillips was nothing short of brilliant. His testimony seemed as frank as it was riveting. He was well spoken, well dressed, and handsome, but the story he told in front of the bank of microphones belied all of that. He was perhaps the most corrupt and evil cop in the modern history of the New York City police department. He shook down drug dealers for hundreds of thousands of dollars. He extorted protection money from mobsters and pimps.

Phillips had been caught by a sometime private detective and eavesdropping expert by the name of Teddy Ratnoff, who was hired by the Knapp Commission to bug the East Side apartment of Xaviera Hollander. Hollander, perhaps better known as the Happy Hooker (the title she gave her autobiography), ran a high-class whorehouse out of her apartment. Ratnoff, who had a dubious past himself, struck up a friendship with Hollander, greed being his primary motive. Ratnoff's initial association with the Knapp Commission was as a supplier of highly technical bugging devices, but he quickly sensed the possibility of making more money from the commission by offering to set up situations where dirty cops would be taped. A madam and whorehouse, he thought, would be the perfect bait. The trap for Phillips was set in P. J. Clarke's, a well-known saloon on the East Side. The Knapp Commission used several retired federal agents, whom Phillips knew casually, to help reel him in. At a back table at Clarke's, the agents told Phillips of a madam looking to go "on the pad," jargon for paying protection. That very night, and in several subsequent meetings, Phillips was taped, compliments of Teddy Ratnoff's expertise, arranging protection for Hollander.

As tough and slick as Phillips thought himself to be, when he was caught he immediately "turned," agreeing to wear a wire for the Knapp Commission. As a result of his testimony, scores of cops lost their jobs and some were jailed. At least one committed suicide. Because of death threats to Phillips, the NYPD provided protection for him during and after the hearings. He was moved to another city, where he received full pay and wrote a book (with Leonard Schechter) called *On the Pad* about his experiences as a crooked cop. For a while it looked as though he had escaped his own criminal career unscathed. The New York State district attorney's office, however, was preparing its own case against him. Phillips was ultimately convicted of murder. While still a policeman, he had killed a pimp and a prostitute on the East Side of

Manhattan. During the trial he was represented by F. Lee Bailey, on appeal by Henry Rothblatt. He lost, and was sent to prison.

When the investigation of Diggins subsided, he put in for a medical retirement on account of a leg injury sustained on duty years earlier. The NYPD fought the request, but eventually gave in to an avalanche of doctors' reports. The day Diggins turned in his badge and gun to the paymaster at police headquarters, he walked over to Maruffi's for the last time. As he looked around the barroom, filled with cops in secretive conversations, he wondered which one was the angel on the phone . . . and which, if any, of them were wearing a wire.

Less than a month after the Knapp Commission hearings began, Police Commissioner Patrick V. Murphy unveiled the innovative "City Wide Anti-Crime Section." The undercover units on the precinct level had been so successful that the commissioner decided to expand the concept and form a unit that would focus on high-crime areas throughout the city. The charter members of this new unit would be taken from the precinct Anti-Crime units and the Tactical Patrol Unit (an elite mobile unit used to respond to riots or protests, and to augment precincts during flare-ups in the crime rate); the whole of the Taxi-Truck Surveillance Unit, a squad formed as a result of an increase in truck hijackings and taxi crime, would also join.

The head of the Taxi-Truck unit was Terry McKeon, who lived in Pearl River. It was in his driveway where I played basketball with Lionel Macon. McKeon's brother, Francis, was the cop whose memorial plaque hung on the wall of the staircase at the old police headquarters.

Though my father called McKeon to put in a contract for Frankie, chances are he would have been picked for the squad without my father's help. Frankie and Gibbons's record in precinct Anti-Crime spoke for itself.

In the coming months, the Knapp Commission would maintain its choke hold over the Department, and because of the nature of the unit (undercover, and in high-crime neighborhoods, an arena rife with the possibility of corruption) applicants were put through a stringent series of background investigations. Police brass was not about to take any chances. Frankie's personal index was cross-checked with the Internal Affairs Division, the Civilian Complaint Review Board, the Disciplinary Records Unit, the Public Morals Division, and the newly formed Organized Crime Control Bureau, among other interdepartmental agencies. Though Frankie's record was clean, even exemplary, the background checks were only half of the admission process. The other and possibly more weighty half was the personal interview.

Interviews for the unit were held in a small office in the Queens Safety Division headquarters in Flushing Meadows Park, the site of the 1964 World's Fair. Frankie sat in a metal folding chair in front of two wooden desks behind which sat a lieutenant named Joe Bainer and the then chief of detectives, Joe Borelli. Borelli did most of the talking. He asked about Frankie's past assignments, arrests he had made, and why he wanted to join the unit. After about twenty minutes of this, Bainer, a gravel-voiced, lantern-jawed man, finally spoke:

"You ever been in the Legion Diner in the Three-Four?" he growled.

Frankie answered that he had.

"Did you ever get a cup of coffee for nothing?" Bainer asked, glaring at Frankie.

No, Frankie answered.

"You're full of shit," said Bainer.

On that note, the interview was over. Frankie was sure Bainer didn't want him, and the disappointment must have shown: When the obligatory photograph was taken, the chief of detectives, seeing the downcast expression on Frankie's face in the picture, turned to Bainer and said: "Boy, this guy don't like you."

But, in November 1971, both Frankie and Gibbons were among the charter members of the new unit.

# 6

The summer of 1972 my brother had a cookout—one of the first parties held at his new home. The redwood deck off the back of the house had not yet been built. Nor had the dormers been added for the kids' bedroom, or the extension, the "new room," where Frankie later held his annual Christmas Eve party. There was a patio, a patchwork of square slabs of slate, with weeds sprouting between them. He had a portable, round charcoal grill on which sizzled hot dogs and hamburgers. There was a Styrofoam cooler filled with Bud. Paul Gibbons came with his wife, Pat, and so did some of the other cops from Anti-Crime. Some of the Brothers came, Bobby Myers and Ahlmyer among them. Billy Rutter showed up late, wearing a T-shirt with "P.I.G." printed on it. Under the letters, the shirt read, "Pride, Integrity and Guts." We all laughed and clenched our fists in a show of solidarity.

The summer before, between my junior and senior years in Pearl River High School, I smoked my first joint in a fort in the woods behind some kid's house. A half-dozen of us sat cross-legged on the plywood floor, passing it back and forth. "Don't bogart it," someone said to me. We drank Boone's Farm apple wine. Though it was sickly-sweet, I guzzled it down. My head began to spin like the label of the Sly and the Family Stone record on the stereo, and I began to loudly sing along.

"Keep it down, man," I was warned. "You'll attract the pigs."

I laughed in response, what with the buzz in my head and the absurdity of the statement.

I was torn between the cop universe I had been born to and this tepid social rebellion left over from the 1960s. Only now, looking back, do I see the dichotomy of that situation. Watered-down as it was, that social rebellion was still an expression of peace and love, words of which I had little understanding. By then, in high school, I had plenty of friends who had grown up outside the insular cop society I had known as a child. Their fathers, like mine, had worked hard and built homes and futures for their families. But in their homes there was communication and love that were as alien to me as Latin. I can remember being at a friend's house watching, astonished, as his father kissed him good-bye on the cheek. My father's most outward display of emotion was a pat on the head, and even that was more of a slap. No fault lay at his door. Nor is it my intention to elicit sympathy. I know now the myriad of reasons why my father could not express his love: his job, his impoverished youth, his own father's alcoholism. Still, as a young man I felt that in his relations with me he acted more like a squad commander than a father, and my communication with him resembled that of a subordinate to a boss. Often he'd search my room, barreling through the cherished teenage boundaries. Once he found a stack of pornographic magazines. He removed them, and never said a word, sexuality being far too intimate an issue to be discussed in my home. In the world of an Irish Catholic cop's family, sex was shoved in the back of a drawer, like the metal box in my mother's bureau where my father locked his off-duty gun. Instead, a Catholic priest named Joyce provided sex education. With a slight Irish brogue, Father Joyce would lecture the class on male and female vessels and the damnation that awaited those who aroused themselves or others before the consecration of the sacrament of marriage. With all his talk of vessels, I was never quite sure if I was being lectured on maritime history or sex. As Father Joyce was an ex-seaman, perhaps it was the former. Another time, my father found a small bag of marijuana in my sock drawer. He left it on top of the dresser for me to find when I came home that afternoon. A whole day went by, a family dinner, then breakfast the following morning, eaten in stony silence. The wait was excruciating. Finally, he told me to take a ride with him in his car, his favorite venue for lecturing. I sat expressionless on the seat next to him. He rattled off his stock phrases—"not under my roof," and such. He told me he hadn't told my mother, because "It would break her heart." He said that if I were arrested it would shame the whole family. He reminded me that he had been a policeman for twenty-three years (as if I could have forgotten), and that my brother was now a policeman. "I've arrested people for what I found in your room," he said. "So has your brother."

I said nothing in response. It seemed that the only time I talked to my father was during these lectures. But silently I seethed. I didn't care about the shame or his law enforcement background. And I didn't need his cop words.

On the other hand, there was Frankie, and my enduring hero-worship of him. In the summer of 1972, after I graduated from Pearl River High School, I took the job I mentioned earlier as a bartender in Chuck's Pub, a small, dark tavern, the last store in a mini-mall on Middletown Road in Pearl River. The clientele was mostly college-age kids who went to Rockland Community, or were home from out-of-state schools. Sometimes Frankie would stop in with his cop friends—Paul Gibbons, Billy Rutter, and others. Once in a while, on my nights off, I would go out with them.

The world in which my brother and his friends worked—with its abandoned buildings, drug addicts, murders—was so alien to the suburban world where they lived and raised families, it was impossible to go from one to the other without some time in a decompression chamber. Although it didn't happen often, I loved being with Frankie and his cop friends during these times. They were like cowboys in town after a month-long cattle drive, tinning their way into sporting events and clubs where civilians had to wait on line, and out of speeding tickets with local cops.

On one of these nights, I sat in the backseat of Paul Gibbons's family car, a station wagon, the kind with the wood paneling on the sides. We were traveling so fast the tires squealed with each bend in the road. There were six of us—myself and Frankie, and four of his crazy cop friends—jammed into the car with beers between our legs and empties rolling around the back cargo area. We flew down Route 340 in Sparkill, deserted at this early morning hour, and passed St. Thomas Aquinas College, a future stop in my staccato pursuit of higher education. I pointed the campus out to Gibbons and he slammed the brakes, pulling the car to a screeching halt. A small cement pool with a fountain in the middle decorated the lawn of the convent adjacent to the school. A cop named Seely bolted from the car, ripping off his clothing like a crazed lover—first his shirt, then, hopping on one leg, his pants, next his underwear, and finally his ankle holster. He stood on the brick ledge that surrounded the pool, bent over, and spread the cheeks of his ass in a salute to us left behind in the car. The cops and I laughed wildly as we watched Seely's performance. He held his arms straight out from his sides, bent his knees, and did a perfect belly flop into the pool. The water was only a foot and a half deep. Seely rose from the blackness and turned to us, glistening and scraped, raising his fists and howling like a mad dog.

"He's a little fucking nuts, isn't he, Frankie?" I asked.

"He's a good cop." Frankie shrugged, as if that, measured against Seely's insanity, constituted a wash.

Yeah, I thought, the citizens of the Bronx must sleep soundly knowing Officer Seely has the watch.

As Seely stood howling, the others dashed from the car. Clothes were strewn across the lawn of the nunnery. One by one, the naked cops dove into the pool. Lights went on in the convent. Frankie and I leaned against the car, the only wallflowers, laughing and sipping our beers.

Down the winding path from the convent came the lights of a compact sedan. The night watchman stepped from the car with St. Thomas emblazoned on its side, his eyes wide as he took in the scene: the four naked men, the piles of clothing, and the guns lying on the grass. Frankie, the only cop clothed and remotely sober, approached the guard, reached into his back pocket, and pulled out his badge, flipping open the leather case to give the guard just a flash of his shield. "Fish and Wildlife," he said with the utmost sincerity. "We think there are goldfish missing from this pool."

The cops stepped from the pond and in single file casually walked past the befuddled guard, picked up their clothing and guns, and piled into the station wagon.

It was while watching such playfulness and unbridled emotion that I began to formulate the idea that joining the force didn't have to mean being straitjacketed in my feelings the way I thought my father was. It was seeing my brother and his friends so uninhibited that made me think that perhaps I, too, could become a cop.

By the summer of 1972, the City Wide Anti-Crime Sections, later renamed the Street Crime Unit (SCU), had become the kind of police work true crime authors and TV producers live for. Originally consisting of some two hundred cops divided into twenty ten-person squads, the unit was first housed in the Queens Safety Division headquarters, but as it grew, it moved to the Harbor Precinct Building, a kind of Bat Cave on Randalls Island, under the Triborough Bridge. The cavernous room was divided into sections partitioned by rows of lockers. Each team's section resembled backstage at a Broadway play, or Central Casting. In lockers and on hooks hung on the walls were costumes decoys would wear. They ranged from "streetwalker" garb to the black suit and white collar of a Catholic priest. (An early publicity shot of the unit was taken and appeared in the newspaper. The police commissioner immediately received a call from the archdiocese and decoys were forbidden to wear the priest outfit.) The squads were broken down into three-person teams, each consisting of one decoy and two backup cops. The decoy, dressed as a streetwalker, a lost tourist, or, in parts of Brooklyn, as a Hasidic Jew (there were no complaints from the Jewish sector), would attract muggers, drug dealers, and confidence men. When a crime was committed—and only when the crime was committed—the back-up team, alerted by a prearranged sign, would rush in and make the arrest.

Frankie's squad was assigned to high-crime areas in Brooklyn and the Bronx, but mostly to Times Square—in the early 1970s, a veritable Sam's Club crime store. Prostitution, drug dealing, and cons of every conceivable kind happened twenty-four hours a day, seven days a week. Just the criminals in and around the Port Authority Bus Terminal would have kept Frankie's squad in court most of the time. The work became so routine that Frankie's team made a game of it—"Pick the Perp." As they drove the streets of Times Square in taxicabs, the undercover vehicle of choice, they would keep a scorecard among themselves, each team member getting a chance to guess which street character would commit the next crime.

Because of his size and his unmistakable cop looks—only the dumbest of crooks would have tried to take him off—Frankie always worked as a backup. Several cops rotated as the team's decoys. Paddy Quinn played such a realistic drunk, he was mugged by the same guy twice in one week. After the first arrest, the mugger was whirled through New York's revolving-door justice and back onto the street. The second time, Quinn even tried to lose the mugger, to no avail. Ironically, in real life, Quinn didn't drink. Another decoy, Freddy Shroeder, played a character the team called Fenwick Babbitt, an upstate businessman looking for kicks. He wore a short-brimmed hat and a loud sports coat. Shroeder was so believable in his role that once, only moments after he stepped from the undercover cab, he was inundated by a posse of prostitutes. There were so many of them swarming around him, fighting over him, pulling him by his arms, he couldn't get his hands free to lift his hat to signal for backup. Frankie also worked with Mary Glatzle, known as Muggable Mary. During her career as a decoy, Glatzle was "mugged" some 500 times.

The new unit seemed perfectly suited to Frankie's personality. Never the conformist, he felt stifled by structure and chain of command. Compared to the rest of the department, the Street Crime Unit was assembled along less "military" lines, with sergeants and lieutenants working alongside their men—and women—in tight-knit undercover teams. It was an environment in which Frankie's police skills thrived. But, sometimes, felons stumbled right into him.

While Frankie was working as a backup along Forty-second Street west of Eighth Avenue, a strip lined with pornographic movie houses, two men walked out of the fire door of one of the theaters and, right in front of him, rifled through a wallet. Frankie signaled the team, and the men were apprehended. When my brother walked into the theater he asked the manager to turn on the lights so he could find the wallet's owner. The expression on the manager's face was of utter disbelief: "In this theater?" he said. "The lights haven't been on in this theater for thirty years."

As an image of the most graphic of sexual acts flashed on the screen behind him—and with the sound of zippers quickly being closed all around—Frankie announced to the startled audience the name found in the wallet. Reluctantly, the owner identified himself. As he stood, he realized his pants had been cut by a razor and most of his backside was sticking out.

For Frankie, however, there was one important ingredient the unit lacked. Though he made close friendships with his partners in his immediate team—Shroeder and Quinn—and with his sergeant, Buddy Ayers, who lived across town from Frankie in Pearl River, as a whole the unit lacked the camaraderie that he had experienced at the precinct level. SCU cops were treated like an invading army in the neighborhoods, and in the station houses, where they worked. Animosity arose within the ranks of precinct cops who viewed the unit as headline and glory grabbers, while they, roving targets in uniforms, were given little credit. The SCU was also far more competitive than precinct-level units. It seemed to Frankie that everyone in the SCU was trying to forward their careers—even if it meant stepping over their comrades on the way. The administration of the unit didn't help matters any; they encouraged competition by instituting a point system for arrests—a score card. Robbery arrests garnered 3 points, as did gun arrests; grand larceny on the person (taking money without physical force, like a pickpocket or a confidence scammer) earned 2 points; a stolen car earned 1. The incentive was promotion. The top fifty point holders would be promoted to detective. The system wasn't altogether fair. Decoys, for example, who took the greatest risks, made fewer arrests than did the backup team. And luck, being in the right place at the right time, was far too big a component. Some cops who led in point totals didn't deserve promotion, while other cops, lower on the list, did.

Although Frankie saw the unfairness of the system, he quickly realized that it *was* the system. He made up his mind to work as hard as he could, make every arrest that he could, and hope that luck was with him. It was. When the list for promotion to detective was posted, his name was on it. He had his gold shield. He had been a cop less than four years.

Just a few months later, it would be taken away from him.

# 7

The hearing for the incident in Spring Valley was postponed several times, so for a few months Frankie lived in limbo, not knowing whether he was going to retain his rank and stay a part of SCU. He had pleaded not guilty to the charges (and years later, when the case was reviewed at his request, he was exonerated). But at the time, he didn't want to take a "five-day rip," a suspension. In the argot of the police department, getting such a strike on your record is known as "picking up a nail," and it marks you—forever—as damaged goods.

Strange as it seems, the only time he didn't think about that night was when he was working. He put every ounce of his energy into policing. It was what he was good at, and the only source of relief. He had obtained his detective's gold shield even quicker than his father had. When he was away from the job, he was the classic dark, Irish figure, guilt-ridden and self-deprecating. I hated that he gave that voice so much power. One episode, one night, one mistake was all it took. And that one mistake outweighed thousands of days of hard work, years of sacrifice and struggle.

As far as the police department was concerned, Frankie's fate had already been sealed. From outside the hearing room in the newly built headquarters at One Police Plaza, Frankie called the "wheel," the clerical officer at SCU, to find out his assignment the day he entered his plea. He was told he had been transferred to the 50th Precinct. At first Frankie thought he meant the 50th Detective Squad. Several gold shield Street Crime cops had made the jump from his unit to squads. But the assignment officer told him that this transfer was back to uniform.

"Tell the boss I'm coming right up," Frankie said on the phone.

No punishment could have been worse—a transfer, a demotion, a nail, and what's more, to the quiet precinct of Riverdale. His thoughts went to the house. How could he afford it now? He was struggling as it was, at detective pay. Things were caving in, and he couldn't let that happen. He would talk to his C.O., Captain Flynn, he thought. There must have been a mistake, and Flynn was the one who could rectify it.

When he arrived, he found Flynn's office empty. The captain had left only the message "Tell him I'm gone for the day."

Frankie had some time coming, so he put in for vacation. He needed space and distance to think. He needed time to decide whether to go back into uniform or leave the job entirely.

A year before, Eugene had moved into a new home in St. Louis. By that summer, Diane was pregnant with their third child. Eugene had invited Frankie and Pam out several times to see the new place. Each time, Frankie put him off. But the day he found out he was being demoted, he called Eugene and took him up on the offer.

Although Eugene was completely unaware of the circumstances, he knew as soon as Frankie got off the plane that something was wrong. There was none of the usual brotherly razzing from Frankie. No jokes. Just a handshake and a subdued greeting. That first night in St. Louis, Eugene and Diane proudly gave Frankie and Pam a tour of the house, a four-bedroom colonial, built to their specifications. After the children were put to bed, the two couples played board games in the family room, paneled in rich, dark mahogany, with a natural-finished plank floor and a brick fireplace. Though the girls, Pam and Diane, drank wine, and the brothers polished off the better part of a bottle of Johnnie Walker Red, the conversation was awkward.

The next afternoon Eugene suggested that Frankie take a walk with him to see the neighborhood. They made small talk as Eugene steered through a just-built subdivision with saplings and sodded lawns, and up a hill to a section of larger homes. He pointed out where the quarterback of the St. Louis Cardinals, Jim Hart, lived. Finally, after a mile or so, Frankie could no longer hold back his emotions.

"They're trying to screw me," he said, and he began to tell Eugene the story he had assembled: While he was on duty, someone had spat at his partner, and Frankie had overreacted by grabbing the man and throwing him to the sidewalk. Because of the altercation, he had been brought in front of the Civilian Complaint Review Board. As a result of the complaint, he said, the department was taking his gold shield. Frankie then said something that made Eugene stop and glare at his brother in disbelief: "I think I'm going to quit."

Eugene had no way of knowing that his brother had altered the events. Nor did it matter much. Lies, and secrets kept, had always been the language of our home—the language of a cop home.

They walked together for some time in silence. Then Frankie began to remark about how nice the area was where Eugene now lived. "What are you going to do if you walk out now?" Eugene asked. This was the perfect place to raise a family, Frankie said, stalling. "What else do you want to do?" Eugene said. I'm sick and tired of New York, Frankie answered. "Have you given it much thought?" Eugene asked. I gave them my soul, Frankie said, shaking his head.

As they turned onto the block where Eugene lived, Frankie stopped. His eyes were red and filled with tears. "I don't know what I'm going to do," he said.

When Frankie returned from St. Louis, he did report to the 50th Precinct. Inside the station house, he approached the desk lieutenant and said he was newly assigned. At first, the lieutenant thought he was a detective or an Anti-Crime cop. But when Frankie asked for permission to leave so he could turn in his gold badge at police headquarters, the lieutenant suspiciously eyed the sight before him: the long, unkempt hair, the sour, defeated expression.

"I'm starting to get the picture," the lieutenant said.

As Frankie turned to leave, the lieutenant yelled after him with contempt: "And get a haircut."

My brother sat in his car in the parking lot of police headquarters and stared at the gold badge in his hand. He remembered when he had shown it to his father for the first time. It had linked them even more than the uniform, like a Cracker Jacks ring for members of a secret society. Certainly, at times, he felt as though the badge contained magical powers. Sometimes he would reach to his wallet just to feel its outline. And each time he did, it assured him of who and what he was.

The keeper of the shield room in headquarters, a civilian employee, was straight out of Dickens. Old, wrinkled, with purple veins popping from his face, he reached over the desk with bony fingers, snatched the badge, and, with an indifferent flip, tossed it into a box—a cardboard coffin for dead careers.

For me, that fall of 1972 was a schizophrenic time. On the one hand, I enrolled at Rockland Community College, where I spent more time in the lounge with the suburban student body, holding onto the longhaired remnants of the 1960s—playing card games like hearts and casino, smoking pot in the parking lot—than I did in class. But on the other hand, I nurtured a halfhearted desire to become a cop. My schooling was being paid by a federal grant under LEEP, the Law Enforcement Education Program. RCC had instituted a police science curriculum to accommodate Rockland County's many New York City police officers' sons and daughters who were now of college age and were interested in law enforcement careers. I didn't have to pay tuition, nor was I beholden to my father. Nor, for that matter, did I have to attend class to get a passing grade. Most of the instructors either had worked with my father or had been my brother's bosses. But this familiarity, and the grant, only made me take the whole thing less seriously, even though the grant came with the stipulation that the student become a police officer within two years of graduation. Otherwise, it would be considered a loan, and would have to be repaid. So cavalier was I about my college career, I cashed one of my $75 book allowance checks at a topless bar called Mel's.

At night, I worked at Chuck's Pub, the first of several bars where I worked in my late teens and early twenties (the legal drinking age in New York State then was eighteen); my days off were spent at the racetrack. My father hated my lifestyle, especially working behind the bar. "You're spinning your wheels," he said more than once. It wasn't, however, as though he was pressuring me to become a cop. Only six years had passed since he retired, and the disappointment of his police career still burned in his stomach. Anyhow, I'm sure he thought I didn't have what it takes to become a cop. At the time, he was working as a security manager for Eastern Airlines, and he once tried to get me into the baggage handlers' union. He even set up an interview for a ticket agent position. But I was supposed to learn rudimentary typing. I didn't bother, and didn't get the job. He extolled the virtues of the Transit Authority and the Sanitation Department—the twenty-year pension and the city paycheck; no doubt his high opinion of these was born of the dire financial situation he grew up in. But I was interested in neither. I'd work until three a.m., then go to friends' houses to party or to an after-hours place to play cards. I'd drive home, my eyes squinting against the morning sunlight, and pass bus stops filled with people hurrying to work or school, even friends on the way to RCC. In my youthful arrogance, driving a souped-up Pontiac LeMans and always walking around with a couple of hundred in my pocket, I thought of them as suckers. On several occasions, I walked into the house while my father sat at the kitchen table eating his breakfast of cornflakes and prune juice. He didn't even look at me as I half staggered up the stairs to my room.

I moved out of the house several times during this period, only to have to slink back when I lost a job or owed too much to the bookmakers. My moving out was always a melodramatic ritual: My mother cried as she stood on the front steps watching me go, while my father sat in the living room, his face hidden behind the *Journal News*, undoubtedly whispering "Good riddance" under his breath.

In 1974, I took a job in a place called the King's Arms, a restaurant and dance club in Tappan, New York. The crowd was mostly older (at least to me then) married couples and cheaters. One night my father—now, in my vernacular, "the old man"—stopped into the restaurant for a drink. It was a rarity for me to serve him over the bar. I felt awkward, and, for some reason, a little bit ashamed. A few days later he said, "You're working in a mob joint." I told him that the place was owned by a couple of

Englishmen. "I don't care who you think owns it," he said. "There's mob money behind it."

He came to this conclusion because of Joe DiMassio, the bartender who worked with me. A Dean Martin look-alike, DiMassio was one of the funniest people I've ever known. His dyed hair was as black as shoe polish. He drove a Godzilla-sized candy-apple-red Cadillac convertible, and had a bevy of ex-wives and current girlfriends, whom he would juggle as expertly as a Wallenda. Before the King's Arms, Joe had worked in a place called Connie's Cloud Room, near La Guardia Airport in Queens. At Connie's, he worked with a waitress by the name of Alice Crimmins, who became one of New York City's most infamous murderers. She strangled her two children. The Cloud Room was also notorious because its owner, Conrad, was gunned down one night as he walked from the restaurant. Because there was no robbery motive, police thought Conrad, a known gambler, must have just dealt with the wrong people. Right after Conrad was shot, Joe moved out of Queens and up to Rockland County. My old man knew of Joe's exotic past. "The guineas always put one of their own close to the operation," he said more than once. Though my father had spent many nights in places like the Bronx restaurant owned by Joe Valachi and other known mob hangouts, I didn't believe his statement about the King's Arms. When I told him he was wrong, he squinted and shook his head. It was bad enough his son was working for mobsters, his expression said, but that he didn't even know it was an inexcusable offense. I would later, however, work in a club where I wasn't so naive. And in my rebellion against my father, relish the thought of how he'd have reacted to my toy-gangster friends. Back then, I thought of myself as much more suited for a life on the periphery of the law than one upholding it. I spent a lot of my time at Aqueduct and Roosevelt racetracks, with gamblers who were known by descriptive middle names, and I knew bookmakers by their first names. I owed all of them money. If you wanted to get me by phone, you would have to know the code: one ring, hang up; two rings, hang up. (Once, perhaps by luck, an IRS agent broke the code.)

Still, for a while, during my time at the King's Arms, I half-heartedly tried to get my life in order. After dropping out of RCC, I enrolled in St. Thomas Aquinas College in Sparkill, again taking their version of a police science curriculum, reactivating my LEEP grant. I even studied for the police entrance exam. It was as though something on an unconscious level propelled me toward being a cop. Maybe this force was trying to move me closer to my father.

The day of the test, I waited on line with my friends John Murphy and Eric Schweitzer outside a high school in Washington Heights. Both Murphy and Schweitzer had studied police science with me at RCC, though neither came from a cop family. Murphy's father was a city bus mechanic, and Schweitzer's worked at the Lederle laboratory. I think they got their inclinations toward police careers from television shows. They seemed much more enthusiastic than I was. But, then again, they didn't have my intimate knowledge that being a policeman wasn't all *Kojak* or *Columbo*.

I was on line that day for the thinnest of reasons. Not to carry on the tradition of my family, that's for sure. Rather, I was there like someone invited to a party, and going because he has no other plans. Not only was I ambivalent, but also things had changed in the police department. Long gone were the days when it was a vehicle for Irish societal acceptance as it was when my grandfather was a cop. The Irish had been accepted for fifty years in New York, and had decided there were better places to be accepted, moving en masse to the suburbs. And the department no longer offered the security so sought after by the Depression-era cops of my father's day. The year I took the test, angry cops had circled City Hall demanding raises and the back pay they had given up to avoid more layoffs. Two thousand cops had lost their jobs the year before. Cop unions printed leaflets titled "Fear

City" and were handing them out to city visitors at bus depots and airports as a way of exerting financial pressure on the mayor. No, there was no security left.

I also saw no reason to follow Frankie's path. I knew how much he had loved being a cop, and I knew that the police department as an institution did not return or reward such love. The disappointment of my brother's demotion, my father's physical condition when he retired, the stories my mother told of her father's treatment at the hands of Tammany, all combined to form a picture in my mind of the NYPD as a trash compactor that squashed lives and spat its members out broken and defeated.

I don't remember much about the test itself—what questions were asked or even how I'd felt I had done. I do remember what I did afterward, though. With my friends Murphy and Schweitzer, I went back to Pearl River and stopped in the Grasshopper. In the dimly lit bar we sat among the usual crowd of New York City cops, drank Miller Lites, and pretended we, too, were "on the Job."

Months went by. There were stories in the newspapers nearly every day about the city's budget crisis, and the freeze on hiring cops. There were also stories about the soaring crime rate. I took a job in a club called the Talk of the Town in Hillsdale, New Jersey. It was that kind of hipster joint the late 1970s had spun out after the release of the movie *Saturday Night Fever*. The place was filled with white leisure suits and matching shoes. Even I, with a face plastered with an undeniable Irish heritage, owned a pair of ivory-colored loafers, though my leisure suit (bought out of the trunk of an Impala from a huckster who also sold throw rugs emblazoned with moose and felt paintings of dogs playing poker) was lime green.

Aside from the Tony Manero look-alikes, dancing to "Stayin' Alive" on the sound system, the club was frequented by a steady clientele of Mafioso wanna-bes. They went by names like Tony Lips, Johnny D., and Matty O. In reality, most of them owned delicatessens and sliced provolone for a living, but at night, dressed in their open collars and gold chains, they talked in gangster jargon of "families" and "business."

Johnny D. did have a bookmaking operation, and lent money at five points—$25 weekly interest on $100 borrowed. And Matty O. ran a floating card game, replete with expatriate Vegas dealers. Entranced by such things as the flash of a pinkie ring on a hand dropping a $50 bill on the bar, by a gleaming hearse-black Oldsmobile 98, I forgot all about the cop test—and my family's heritage—and enrolled in gangster school.

The first class was Driving 101. My job was to shuttle players who parked their late-model Eldorados in the lot of a diner on Kinderkamack Road to a card game held in rotating locations in Hillsdale and Woodcliff Lake. I sat in my "starter" gangster car, a 1972 Thunderbird (I had cracked the axle of my LeMans on a curb one rainy night), wearing an orange hunter's hat, the signal to the gamblers—and probably most of the cops in Bergen County—that I was the taxi to the game.

Once I proved myself a capable wheelman, Matty O. made me an offer that constituted a considerable financial windfall. For $100 a night, the house I shared with two other bartenders (it was on a quiet residential block, and one of the neighboring homes belonged to the police chief of Woodcliff Lake) would be turned into a casino. At nine o'clock each Thursday evening, Matty O. backed a white Ford van, which smelled of grated cheese, into my driveway and unloaded two green felt blackjack tables. By ten-thirty my house was filled with the odors of fat men wearing fruity cologne, the smoke of Macanudo cigars, and the sounds of Tally-Ho cards being expertly shuffled. My weekly take now was $175; I wasn't exactly a full-fledged racketeer, but my career was gaining momentum. On nights off I'd drive into Little Italy, sometimes with Patricia Leahy, an almost girlfriend who, although she didn't really look the part with her auburn hair and freckles, I envisioned as my gun moll. We'd have dinner at

Umberto's or Luna's, drink labelless bottles of red wine, and have Sambuca with espresso for dessert. Fuck being a cop, I thought. This was a much better way to live.

# 8

After his transfer, I often saw Frankie running along the tree-shaded streets of Pearl River and the surrounding towns, a solitary figure, head down, legs pumping. Sometimes, when I passed him, driving in my car, I'd beep the horn, and he'd raise his hand in the air, a gesture of acknowledgment and a signal to leave him alone. He was a pioneer at running. It had not, in 1974, in suburbia, caught fire the way it would in the coming years, when the streets were lined with would-be marathoners wearing $100 sneakers.

Rarely did I talk to him during those days. He hardly ever stopped over the house for one of his once-cherished cop-to-cop talks with my father. There was nothing for either of them to say. There certainly were no war stories for Frankie to tell. The 50th Precinct was then, and remains, the slowest in the Bronx. It encompasses a section called Riverdale, part of which is as affluent as any in neighboring Westchester County. The money there is as old as the elm and maple trees that shade the manicured lawns of the million-dollar homes. For Frankie, this assignment was like being exiled. Back in a radio car, with partners fresh from the Academy, the biggest excitement on a tour might be a "cat call," a pet stuck in a tree.

But this solitude enabled Frankie to experience a new clarity of purpose. Just as he had after being disciplined in the navy, he turned to books by enrolling in Rockland Community College. With the exception of the Class of 1,200 in those last years of the Depression, when Mayor La Guardia championed the cause of "professional policing," the New York City police department had historically been aligned against college education for its members. Civil Service schools like Delahanty's were the educational route endorsed by the department. In 1971, only 3 percent of the entire department had college degrees. That year, a black detective had been forced to resign because he had accepted a three-year scholarship to Harvard Law School. The acceptable leave of absence was only one year—without pay. Commissioner Patrick V. Murphy overturned the forced resignation and declared that any cop would be granted any term of leave for college or postgraduate studies. His decision changed more than policy, it changed the department's attitude toward education.

Frankie didn't need, nor could he afford, a leave of absence. In uniform, he was working steady tours, which gave him the opportunity to fit in a schedule of college classes. His schooling was paid for by a combination of the G.I. Bill and LEEP, which was also available to working policemen.

His first day at the Five-Oh was also the new commanding officer's first day. After about a week, Frankie was called into the captain's office. Aaron Rosenthal's reputation had preceded him. He was a rising star in the department, and known to not take any shit. He wasn't about to jeopardize his accession to a new command with any insubordination amongst his troops. Frankie didn't know what to expect from Rosenthal, but considering how his career had gone of late, he didn't think it would be good news.

In his office, Rosenthal held my brother's file in his hand, and Frankie felt a tinge of apprehension. Rosenthal's manner was cold and aloof. But the captain looked him directly in the eye as he began to speak, and this was both disarming and refreshingly different. Bosses never looked you in the eye, especially if they were about to dress you down.

"I just wanted you to know something," Rosenthal began as he dropped the yellow folder on his desk. "As far as I'm concerned, your career starts right here and right now."

For a moment, Frankie stood in front of the captain absent of words. It was the last thing he had expected to hear, and most likely the best thing Rosenthal could have said to him. For the first time in his career, perhaps in his entire life, Frankie had received a break from a figure of authority.

Rosenthal's issuance of a clean slate reenergized Frankie. Acceptance replaced resignation. Okay, he thought, this isn't the greatest situation, but I'll deal with it the best I can. And Rosenthal hadn't spouted empty words. The captain began to match Frankie, in sort of a tutor's role, with rookies who showed promise. Among these was a young cop named Slattery. One day they sat together in a radio car on Reservoir Avenue, taking their lunch break. As they wolfed down the hero sandwiches, Frankie looked in the rearview mirror and noticed a guy walking toward them. During his time in SCU, Frankie was the undisputed champion of Pick the Perp, and the guy approaching them set off every one of his alarms: the slightly forced casual gait, the way he held his hands in the pockets of his coat. Frankie deliberately wrapped the sandwich and placed it next to him on the seat. Slattery quizzically watched as Frankie dropped his gaze from the rearview to the side-view mirror. In a voice just louder than a whisper, my brother announced: "We're taking this guy."

Frankie leaped from the car and was on his suspect before Slattery had realized what was happening. Amid a barrage of denials—"What are you doing, man? I didn't do nothing"—Frankie put him against the radio car and began questioning him. As if on cue, just then the radio blared to life with a description of the man Frankie was cuffing, wanted for a burglary. As the two cops drove back to the station house, their collar cuffed in the backseat, Slattery sat slack-jawed, staring at Frankie. Finally the rookie spoke: "How did you know?"

"You get lucky," Frankie answered.

Sometime later, Rosenthal matched Frankie with a cop named Neal Sullivan, who was newly assigned to the precinct. When the captain introduced the new partners, Rosenthal said to Sullivan: "This guy I'm putting you with is the best cop I have. Don't bring him down." But Sullivan brought something of his own to the new partnership. He was born on the Lower West Side of Manhattan, an area known as Chelsea and now an upscale enclave; but in Sullivan's youth, it had been predominantly Irish-American, filled with longshoremen, local toughs, and other sordid characters. Sullivan's father ran a saloon there, but died when Neal was only eight. After his father's death, his mother moved the family back to her native Ireland, where Neal spent the rest of his childhood. In his early teens, he came back to the old neighborhood in New York to live with relatives. Now more Irish than American, he had difficulty fitting in: he wore knickers and Bournine sweaters, and talked with a slight brogue. Because of this, he became a target of the street-hardened neighborhood kids. One day, when he was walking home from school, several local bullies jumped him and beat him severely.

Over the next year or so, Neal spent most of his after-school hours in a local gym, strapping on gloves and learning to box, the vivid memory of the beating fueling his desire. When he was ready, he knocked on each of the bullies' doors, one by one, to settle the score, and one by one, he knocked each of the bullies cold. The story was passed around the neighborhood, and made him something of a legend in Chelsea. His interest in boxing continued up until his police career. As a club fighter, he billed himself as "Irish Neally Sullivan." Later, when he was Frankie's partner, he spent much of his off time with the Police Athletic League, teaching neighborhood kids the art of pugilism.

To his complete astonishment, Frankie found out that he actually liked college. At first, the whole process was uncomfortable. He was older than most of his fellow students, and had overwhelming feelings of scholastic inferiority. But as the days passed, as he sat in the front row of the classroom, as he did his assignments at night at home, or in the radio car on quiet shifts, a subtle trans-formation occurred. He realized that the same brainpower that made him a good cop could be used to make him a good student, even a great student. He was able to integrate his life experience, hard duty in the biggest classroom in the world, the streets of New York City, with what was being elaborated in his textbooks. Like an inmate blowing dust off the jacket of a crumbling old copy of *Treasure Island* in the far reaches of the jail's library racks, Frankie had found the way to escape the confinements in his life.

It was during this time he realized that, in many ways, the po-lice universe was a stagnant pool, festering with bias and narrow-mindedness passed on from generation to generation. In college, Frankie took his first step out of that swamp and found a whole dry world, in which he could not only survive but thrive. His list of priorities shifted, and with the change came a quiet confidence. Yes, being a good cop was still on the list, but it was no longer the most important thing in his life.

He also turned his attention to renovating his house. To cut costs, he and his friend Bobby Myers did all the work. The first job was putting dormers in the upstairs rooms, expanding them into spacious bedrooms for Laurie and Patrice. Whenever I stopped by, I'd see Frankie and Bobby hanging perilously from the roof, hammers instead of revolvers hooked on their belts. Though the furniture inside still looked like a collection from a yard sale—the dining set had wobbly legs and mismatched chairs, when you sat on the couch or one of the living room chairs you sank nearly to the floor, and other sections of the house were in obvious disrepair—these inadequacies took second place to bed-rooms for his children.

As Laurie and Patrice grew older, Frankie found time to volun-teer in still more organized activities, like the soccer and softball leagues. In Pearl River and the other neighboring towns, these coaching positions were almost exclusively filled by city cops. Once Frankie needed to find help in coaching a team because his

work schedule was such that he couldn't make a few of the practice days. He asked a man whose daughter played on the team.
But the man, who owned an auto body shop in town, and came to
just about every practice and game, declined, telling Frankie that
coaching kids' teams was a civil service duty, not for real citizens
like himself.

With work, school, renovations on the house, coaching and
finding time to get his runs in, there was no time left over for so-
cializing. He hardly ever stopped at the Grasshopper (couldn't afford it), nor did he gather with the cops he worked with at Jesse
James, the bar across from the 50th Precinct. And his family's financial burden was now heavier than it ever had been. Gone was
the overtime from all the arrests he made in SCU; gone, too, was
the yearly $2,500 pay increase that came with the gold shield. Out
of necessity, Pam began to work more and more shifts at the
restaurant. At first, Frankie had grudgingly gone along with Pam
working a few lunches. But now they relied on her contribution
to the family budget, and the more she could work, the better off
they were. When Hoppin' John's was sold, Pam stayed on with
the new owners and began to work weekends and nights. With
Frankie and Pam both working nights, they arranged for several
teenage girls on the block, daughters of city cops, to baby-sit.

In a way, Pam was lucky. The restaurant, now called the Steak
Pub, was an instant success, and at one point she was taking home
as much as her husband. But the job was exhausting. Sometimes
she'd work until two or three o'clock in the morning, all that time
on her feet, carrying heavy trays laden with dinner plates of
porterhouse steaks. Through it all, though, she never complained. As mercurial as Frankie was, Pam's personality was the
opposite: level-tempered, good-natured and, even at the roughest
financial points in her marriage, optimistic. Buried beneath the
burdens of the now full-time job at the restaurant and the responsibilities of motherhood was the flicker of a dream. Pam had al-

ways been interested in interior design. As a child, visiting her grandparents, who lived in a fashionable section of Park Slope, Brooklyn, Pam was taken by the opulence of the apartment: the huge living room adorned with oak furnishings, the roaring fireplace, the grand piano. One New Year's Eve, she saw her grandparents on a broadcast from the elegant Stork Club. Though the glimpse was fleeting, she had witnessed firsthand what it meant to have money. And some of that taste longed to be nourished. She greedily read *Architectural Digest*, but passed on *House & Garden*, in the racks at the checkout counter. She imagined, down to the colors, fabrics, and wood, what her house would look like, if she had the finances.

When Laurie and Patrice both reached school age, Frankie encouraged Pam to take a course at Parsons School of Design in Manhattan. She did, and immediately showed promise. Her instructor told her she had a natural flair. Pam was buoyed by the possibility of doing what she loved as a career, and for a while it looked as though she would.

By word of mouth, Pam got jobs decorating other cops' homes in Pearl River and surrounding towns. She took an ad in a local advertising letter called the *Welcome Wagon*, and received a number of responses. Charlie A, her boss at the Steak Pub, commissioned her to design a new bar and lounge for the restaurant. For a short time, she worked in a store called Nassau Decorators, in a shopping mall in Hackensack, New Jersey. But there business was slow, as the store was more of a tax write-off for the wealthy Armenian owner than anything else. When she left Nassau Decorators, she went to work for the wife of a city cop who lived in Spring Valley. But here too, things didn't quite work out (the woman had a habit of not paying Pam), and she decided to go back out on her own, where she steadily began to build a profitable business, earning over $37,000 one year. But running her own business was filled with pitfalls. People were slow in paying for her work; some didn't pay her at all. Pam cut out the middle-man by buying carpeting and drapes herself. Though this increased her profit margin considerably, it was also something of a gamble. If the customer backed out on the deal, she had to hope that the carpeting could be returned, or that she could sell it to someone else. But one time when this happened, she could do neither.

The job was for a friend with whom Pam had worked in the Steak Pub. The woman, a waitress in the restaurant, was getting married and moving to a new home in Virginia. She asked Pam to decorate the home and buy furniture, carpeting, and drapes, the cost of which was $13,000. Frankie and Pam agreed to take a huge gamble: They would apply for yet another loan to cover the cost. They went to my father to cosign it.

A few days later, the friend called Pam to say that her husband-to-be had decided to use another decorator. There was no written contract; the deal had been made with a minimal deposit and a handshake. To make matters worse, Pam received a call from the trucking company she had hired to ship the already paid-for—and uninsured—furniture. The furniture, they said, had been stolen out of the truck in Virginia.

At one point, Pam and Frankie came close to losing the house. I heard all of this secondhand, at the dinner table, my father calling the whole idea "stupid" and "their own fault."

At first, Frankie, too, was angry at Pam. But in a way, the venture's failure brought them closer together. Frankie realized that most of his brooding over life's knocks had been selfish. His wife, his family, had suffered just as much as he had. So what if things didn't go as planned? he thought. At least Pam had the guts to try. Throughout their marriage they had experienced a myriad of financial roadblocks, and had always survived. Though this was the biggest hurdle yet, Frankie knew they would get through it somehow. But the bitter experience extinguished the flame of Pam's dream and, again, she went back to waiting on tables.

\* \* \*

Though Frankie learned to live with his situation at work, he still yearned for action. It also became clear to him that he was being passed over for busier assignments. Patrolmen in the 50th were rotated to fill slots during the precinct Anti-Crime cops' vacations and sick leaves. Frankie watched as time and again younger cops were chosen over him for these assignments. One day, in a hallway in the station house, Frankie approached the roll call officer in charge of the Anti-Crime schedule and asked why he was never picked. The cop answered him curtly, saying he wasn't on the list, and offering no further explanation. Frankie hadn't even been aware there *was* a list. Just then, Captain Rosenthal walked down the hallway and stopped to talk to Frankie. Though, because of the distance in rank, their relationship couldn't be considered a friendship, they had developed a mutual respect. When the captain asked him how he was doing, Frankie seized the opportunity.

"For some reason, I'm not on the list for Anti-Crime fill-in," Frankie said.

Rosenthal leveled a stare at the roll-call cop and said: "You are now."

The Anti-Crime detail in the 50th Precinct was tame compared to the SCU, or to Anti-Crime in the 34th. But at least it was better than the "cat calls" Frankie was enduring in the radio car. The 50th Precinct wasn't fully made up of million-dollar homes. There was a section called the Hill where most of the precinct's crime occurred, and where most of the criminals—who once in a while were ballsy enough to break into a house in the fashionable sections—lived. There was also a strip along Reservoir Avenue that was a favorite hunting ground for out-of-precinct car thieves and drug addicts boosting radios and tape players. At night, especially in the winter, only cops and car thieves would be out along the quiet stretch of road. For Frankie, the apprehension of these thieves amounted to a elemental game of hide-and-seek.

My brother's prowess as an undercover cop did not go unnoticed, and one of the Anti-Crime cops who took note was the star of the unit, Artie Schwartz.

Frankie and Schwartz hit it off right away. An energetic insomniac, Schwartz seemed to go full-bore twenty-four hours a day. Like Jimmy McDermott, he had an engaging personality and would talk to anybody and everybody. Even a good portion of the criminals knew Schwartz by name and liked him—even when they were handcuffed in the back of his unmarked car. One night, after he and Frankie had arrested four car thieves, Schwartz told his handcuffed prisoners to "walk this way" into the station house, then affected a Groucho Marx–like crouch, with the willing prisoners falling into step. But Schwartz was also a "numbers man," consistently leading the Anti-Crime unit in arrests. His biggest supporter was Pat Malloy, the sergeant in charge of the unit. When Schwartz's primary partner was transferred, he went to see Malloy about who would fill the spot.

Working full-time again in Anti-Crime was bittersweet for Frankie. On the one hand, he was thrilled to be permanently assigned to the unit. But he knew that this time around, because of his demotion, he wasn't eligible for "Career Path," a system put in place to promote officers who had high arrest numbers and met other criteria. He felt as though he were still branded. Still, for the first time since his days in SCU, going to work became fun again.

Schwartz prided himself on his foot speed. In terrific physical condition, he often boasted that he never lost a race, be it just a challenge or running after a perp. If someone fled a crime scene, Frankie would fold his arms, say to his partner, "Go get 'em," and watch as Schwartz ran the guy down. In the 50th Precinct, there was a teenage gang led by the Jordan brothers, Joey and Cliff. Schwartz and Frankie knew them well, as the teens were constantly in some kind of trouble. One day on Mosholu Avenue, outside Joey Jordan's apartment, the sixteen-year-old challenged

Schwartz to a race. In front of the rest of his gang, Jordan lost by half the length of the block.

Soon after Schwartz and Frankie became partners, there was a rash of robberies in the row stores under the elevated subway train. The *Riverdale Press*, the local paper, had dubbed the perpetrators the Termite Gang, because of their method of breaking into one store, then burrowing through the walls into as many as five stores in the row. Stores on this strip had also frequently been robbed by a method called smash and dash. Thieves would wait until a train was rattling loudly overhead, then break the front windows of the stores and clean out the showcases.

The new partners decided to stake out the area from the rooftop of one of the row stores. That night, they arrested Joey Jordan breaking into the back of a hardware store (Jordan didn't try to run). Jordan told them he was only after "some spending money," and, bargaining for a lesser charge, he said that if they were interested in some information, his gang was planning a major heist the following evening.

The plan, Jordan said, was to break into a fruit stand in the middle of the block, then hammer through the walls into the adjacent stores. Captain Rosenthal, who was shouldering most of the ire of the local business community, agreed that a stake-out of the fruit stand was the right way to proceed. The owner went along, giving Schwartz and Frankie the keys to the store. Sure enough, a few hours into the stake-out, the skylight opened. One by one, the members of the gang climbed down into the store. One by one, Schwartz and Frankie cuffed them to pipes and to each other, in a back room. The lookout on the roof became impatient and called down into the store: "What's going on down there?"

Schwartz responded, in a husky whisper, "Come on down," which the lookout proceeded to do, and was promptly cuffed with his friends.

*  *  *

Even in the busiest precincts, a good portion of cop partners' time is spent away from stake-outs and chases. In the 50th Precinct, Frankie and Schwartz had more than their share of down time. During these uneventful hours, Schwartz's sense of humor was at its biting best. Sometimes, when there was a short-age of uniform cops, he and Frankie would be taken off Anti-Crime, put in uniform, and assigned to a radio car. On one of these occasions, at six on a rainy morning, the partners received a call about a man trying to break into a church on the Henry Hud-son Parkway in a tony section of Riverdale. As they rolled up to the church they saw the man, his hair matted from the rain, wear-ing a soaking-wet coat, standing in front of the church and pounding on the front doors. As the partners stepped from the ra-dio car, they heard the man screaming: "God, why have you for-saken me?" Schwartz asked the man what he thought he was doing. On seeing the uniform cop, the man tried, without much success, to make himself appear sober. Looking contrite, the man explained that he ran a men's religious retreat at the Paulist Fa-thers Mission House about a half-mile from the church. He said that after the evening meditation he had sneaked out to a local tavern, and had ended up closing the place. With his internal compass a bit askew from the night's festivities, he walked in the wrong direction. Then it started to rain, he explained, and as it did, he began to be flooded with guilt for his indiscretion. When he saw the church, he said, he became angry with God for his own human shortcomings. With an understanding expression, and his arm draped in comfort around the man's shoulder, Schwartz said that they would give him a lift back to the retreat. The man stiff-ened in horror. "Oh, you can't do that," he said. "What if some-one from the mission sees me get out of the police car?" Schwartz assured the rain-soaked man, now mumbling to himself, that they would drop him off down the block where no one would see him. Instead, he pulled up right in front of the mission house. Horri-fied, the man stumbled from the car and, in a crouch, began to run up the driveway. Schwartz turned on the lights and siren. Shades in the windows of the mission house popped up; the man tried to hide behind a sapling tree. Several retreat members, on their way to seven o'clock mass, stood and watched the scene in astonishment. As if that wasn't enough, Schwartz drove halfway down the block, turned, and pulled up in front of the mission and hit the lights and sirens again. Throughout, he didn't even crack a smile. My brother, however, was doubled over in laughter at the thought of his partner doing the work of God—instantly administering the man's penance.

In 1975, Frankie graduated with an associate's degree from Rockland Community College and enrolled in St. Thomas Aquinas College in Sparkill, where I'd gone to school, and next to the convent where Seely and the other cops had taken their naked midnight swim. Frankie's major was political science, but his favorite courses were in the social science curriculum. He enjoyed comparing the theories of a textbook on abnormal psychology with the real-life laboratory in which he worked each night. In school he'd engage in hypothetical discussions of the social complications and treatment of drug abuse; at night he'd have a whacked-out junkie in cuffs in the backseat of his unmarked car.

Frankie rocketed through school, graduating from St. Thomas in 1976. With absolutely no college credits to start with, he obtained his bachelor's degree in the traditional four years—this with a full-time job and family responsibilities. Now that he had the degree, his goal was to obtain his teaching certificate. When I first heard him talk about it, I laughed. Was this the same guy who was the scourge of the nuns at St. Margaret's?

When he received his teacher's certificate, he put his name into a pool of substitutes for the Pearl River school system. At first, he was picked infrequently, because full-time substitutes were given priority. But even though he only taught now and then, he came to love it more and more. Most of the teaching jobs were one-day stints and in the lower grades. One day, Frankie substituted for a gym teacher in the Franklin Elementary School in Pearl River. He organized a dodge-ball game, dividing the class into two teams. One of the kids was a terror, throwing the ball as hard as he could at kids who weren't looking in his direction. Frankie knew well who the little boy was. Shaking his head, Frankie thought of his old partner. The boy was Paulie Gibbons, Jr.

Even though he was happy substitute teaching, he began to miss going to class and began explore various master's programs. At the time, the Police Academy was renting out space to Long Island University. For the university, the deal offered a central location on the East Side of Manhattan. For the police department, the motivation was primarily financial. But it also proved convenient for cops like Frankie who were interested in postgraduate studies. He began studying for his master's in the same classrooms he had sat in, twelve years earlier, as a rookie cop.

Frankie and Schwartz primarily worked the midnight-to-eight shift. They both liked the tour because it not only put them on the street at the optimum hours for crime—especially grand larceny auto, the staple of the precinct's criminal element—but also left their days free. This schedule allowed Frankie to attend day classes in his master's studies.

But in the late 1970s, a new lieutenant took over the precinct's Anti-Crime unit and changed their schedule. Frankie's new hours, two in the afternoon until ten at night, not only interfered with his classes and substitute teaching, but affected his police performance. As in his early career with Gibbons, he and Schwartz consistently led the precinct in arrests. They had developed systems, street sources, and instincts that seemed to position them in the right place at the right time. They had become so accustomed to each other, it was as though they thought as one, as the new lieutenant was to find out.

Before Frankie became his partner, Schwartz had become

friendly with a man who owned a deli on 228th Street and Broadway. Paddy Balardi was famous for his over-stuffed sandwiches and gregarious personality. A young boy named Tommy Welsh worked for him. Tommy's home life wasn't the best, and Balardi would often let the kid stay with him. Schwartz took a liking to Tommy, and later so did Frankie. Often, when Tommy was closing up the deli around midnight, Schwartz and Frankie would cruise by to make sure he was okay, sometimes giving him a ride home or to the diner on 231st Street where Tommy would order the same meal, French toast and bacon, every time. Tommy was an avid bowler, and would pester Schwartz and Frankie into having a game with him. One slow evening, while on duty, they took Tommy up on his offer. Later that day, as they were cruising in their undercover car, a radio car pulled alongside. The uniform cops in the radio car told them that their new boss, Lieutenant Quigley, had put out a 10-2, "Return to station house," for them an hour ago, and that he was good and mad that they hadn't responded.

Without even formulating a cover plan, Schwartz and Frankie drove into the station house parking lot, where Lieutenant Quigley was waiting. The lieutenant ordered Schwartz inside and questioned Frankie in the parking lot:

"Where were you?" The lieutenant was bristling.

"We were out of the car, following some guys up Broadway," Frankie answered calmly.

"How come you didn't have your radio on?"

"We did, but we had it on channel two [a different frequency] so we could talk to each other."

"How many guys were there?" asked the lieutenant suspiciously.

"There was three of them," Frankie answered.

The lieutenant told Frankie to stay right where he was, and marched into the station house to talk to Schwartz.

"Where were you?" the lieutenant asked Schwartz.

"We were out of the car, following some guys up Broadway."

"How many were there?"

"Three," came Schwartz's answer.

"Where was your radio?"

"Channel two."

Frustrated, the lieutenant ordered them back to work. An hour later, they returned to the station house with a mugging collar. As he passed, Quigley, who was still upset, asked Frankie if he wanted to go for a beer after work.

"You guys are good," Quigley said as he sipped his brew. "You got your story down pretty good."

"We didn't have a story," Frankie said. "And if you want to know how we're doing our jobs, just look at our numbers. You don't have to supervise us, Lieutenant," he said without rancor. "We're not out there drinking, fooling around, or taking money. We're out there working."

Schwartz and Frankie assembled the same story simply because they were of the same ilk. They shared the same instincts, ones that made them good cops and partners, and ones that allowed them to survive in a job where the employer was inherently suspicious of its employees. The truth is, veteran cops always have a story, and good partners always have the same one.

The following week, Quigley put them back on midnights and left them pretty much alone. It wasn't as though Frankie didn't like Quigley. As time went by, and he got to know his commander, he respected him as both a cop and a boss. They even became friendly off-duty. Quigley lived in Pearl River and had a daughter Laurie's age. The girls played soccer together.

When they went back on midnight-to-eight's, Schwartz and Frankie decided not to put chases of stolen cars over the radio. There had been too much confusion with backup teams joining the chase. Once or twice, the apprehension of car thieves had escalated into a road rally, with Schwartz and Frankie, the thieves, and several patrol cars screaming through the streets of Riverdale. On more than one occasion, when the thieves were caught, uniform cops, filled with adrenaline from the chase, had beaten them. One time, two patrol cars slammed into each other. Although there were no injuries, there easily could have been.

One night, cruising in their undercover vehicle, my brother and his partner pulled next to a late-model Mercedes, in which were two young Hispanic men. The car's ignition mechanism had been yanked out. Car thieves then employed an auto body tool called a slapper or bam-bam. The tool was used in pulling dents out of fenders, but was equally efficient in breaking the housing off the steering column. With the housing removed, starting a car was just a matter of using a screwdriver as a key. The men in the Mercedes quickly made Schwartz and Frankie as cops, and a pursuit ensued. Several blocks away, the thieves abandoned the car and ran into a building. Moments later, Schwartz and Frankie arrived and followed. There were staircases on opposite ends of the lobby. Schwartz took one, Frankie the other. When Frankie reached the roof, he paused momentarily. The worst thing a cop could do, he knew, was to stumble out into the darkness before his eyes adjusted. From the far end of the roof, he heard rattling in a small entranceway to a back staircase, not the staircase his partner had climbed. With his gun in his hand, Frankie gingerly ran across the roof and pulled open the entranceway door. It was an uncharacteristic mistake, and one that almost cost him his life.

The small compartment exploded with a deafening sound and a flash of brilliant yellow-orange light. As Frankie let go of the handle, in the millisecond it took for the door to close with a smack on its spring hinge, he saw the blue uniform standing in the stairway. With his arms spread out from the sides of his body, his palms pointed upward like he was holding a pair of pizza pies, he looked down at his Kevlar vest, positive that he would see a smoldering hole. How could it have missed? His six-foot, two-hundred-pound frame filled the entire doorway. As the shock began to subside, and the realization that, by some miracle, he had not been hit, Frankie again opened the door. The uniform cop's face was the color of chalk, he was frozen in an unblinking, horrified stare. Riding in a patrol car, the cop had witnessed the pursuit of the stolen car, and had also followed the thieves into the building.

"Are you okay?" the cop finally managed.

"Yeah," Frankie answered, still eyeing the vest for a hole. "I don't know how, but yeah."

In the confusion, the thieves escaped and, to the uniform cop's relief, Frankie never reported the incident, not even the weapon discharging, knowing that if he had, the uniform cop would be subject to an investigation and possible discipline. My brother was just happy to be alive. The next day, in his locker in the station house he found a bottle of Johnnie Walker Black Label, compliments of the uniform cop.

By 1979, with twelve years on the job, Frankie became resigned to the notion that his police career would go no higher than where it was. Not that that was so bad. He liked working with Schwartz; he liked that he was building a future outside the police department. Still, a *what if* cloud followed him: Where would his career be now if Spring Valley had never happened? He also knew that some cops had it worse.

Each morning, when their tour was just about finished, Frankie and Schwartz would stop and buy some coffee and sit in a little spot on Kingsbridge Road near the Armory, to kill the last half-hour or so of their shift. On a few mornings, Frankie noticed the same man walk by, dressed in a work uniform and carrying one of those Ralph Kramden lunch boxes. There was something familiar about the guy, but Frankie just couldn't place him.

One morning, my brother stopped into a corner grocery store to buy some cigarettes. As he was walking out he found himself face to face with the man with the lunch pail. There, it came to him. The face was older now, lined and creased, the man's hair gray and receding. But the eyes were the same, and in them was a tempered glimmer of recognition.

When my brother was a rookie cop in Washington Heights, three new detectives had been assigned to the Three-Four squad. Frankie knew them only as a uniform cop would get to know a detective—casually. Detectives were known for talking down to uniform cops, treating them as subordinates. But one of the new detectives struck Frankie as being different. The first thing Frankie noticed was that he wore expensive suits. But more than that, when Frankie led a collar up to the squad room, this fellow, unlike most detectives, wouldn't seem annoyed at the bother of booking the criminal. And he never tried to steal a collar from Frankie, as some of the detectives did. When Frankie left the Three-Four for City Wide Anti-Crime sections, he lost touch with the detective. But less than a year later he read about him in the *Daily News*. Before coming to the squad, the detective had been a member of SIU, the narcotics division special investigation unit. A member of that unit, a cop named Bob Leuci, who would become better known as the Prince of the City, testified before the Knapp Commission. As a result of Leuci's testimony, the ex-detective, now carrying a lunch pail, was sent to jail. But compared to those of other cops involved in the scandal, his punishment was light. Two of the convicted cops killed themselves. One, a detective by the name of Cody, who had also been transferred in Frankie's early days to the Three-Four, shot himself in Van Cortland Park in the 50th Precinct, where his brother worked as a detective. As Frankie stood in the doorway, the ex-detective managed a crooked smile. "Still on the Job, huh," he said. Frankie nodded. Just out of jail, the ex-detective, once nearly rich from working in narcotics, was now a night watchman. Then, making Frankie think of his Academy days, and his father's advice, the man said: "Well, keep your nose clean."

By 1980, the Anti-Crime partners had their act, literally, down to a mathematical science. Artie Schwartz kept the statistics. He carried a logbook in which he kept track of arrests and pertinent information on criminal trends in the precinct. By his count, he and Frankie averaged sixty or seventy collars a year. In comparison with other, busier precincts, and certainly with Frankie's time in the SCU, these numbers are not overly dramatic. But considering that the 50th Precinct was the quietest in the entire Bronx, the numbers become astounding. Schwartz also carried what he called his bag of tricks. Although Frankie knew that in the bag Schwartz kept his logbook, an extra pair of handcuffs, and other items, he was never entirely sure of its contents. Even in partnerships as close as theirs, some territory was considered personal, and those boundaries were strictly respected. Schwartz's bag of tricks lay within those bounds.

One night, over the radio they heard a call about a robbery in progress. A man driving up the Deegan Expressway saw some kids breaking into a Mobil station and called 911. Though they mentally noted the call, it wasn't of any real interest to them because it would be answered by radio cars.

When the uniform cops responded to the call, the thieves fled the gas station into a swath of woods, about 500 yards wide, that separated the Deegan from the Mosholu Extension. Schwartz and Frankie listened to the radio as the initial responding cars called for backup to intercept the kids on the Mosholu. As those cars arrived, the kids doubled back toward the Deegan. The radio banter between the two groups of cops began to sound comical, as if the kids were playing the game of "running bases." Each time they headed up through the woods, the cops below would warn the cops above that the suspects were coming in their direction, and then vice versa. Though at first Schwartz and Frankie listened to the antics with a sort of amused detachment, as the situation lingered it began to become embarrassing.

"The whole sector is listening to this," Frankie grumbled.

Schwartz wheeled the car around and headed toward the scene. They approached the uniform sergeant and offered their assistance.

"What are you guys gonna do that we haven't?" the sergeant

asked sardonically. But, reluctantly, he agreed to give them a chance.

Schwartz grabbed his bag of tricks. Standing at the edge of the woods, he shouted: "Fuck this—get the shotgun, Frankie."

Frankie slammed the car door, then followed his partner into the woods. From his bag of tricks, Schwartz removed an M-80 firecracker. He lit the fuse and tossed it into the thicket. As the M-80 exploded, the kids appeared like grouse from the brush and began running down the hill. Frankie and Schwartz took off after them. This was Schwartz's element, and Frankie, in top shape from his daily runs, kept in step. Side by side, the partners high-stepped over fallen trees and stumps, holding their hands in front of their faces to push away the branches. For some reason, about a hundred yards into the race, Schwartz began to let out an Indian war whoop, and then Frankie did, too. A few hundred yards into the chase, they caught their suspects. Tackled, and now cowering on the ground, two of the three thieves looked up in astonishment as these men, whoever they were, danced around them like Apaches, pretending they had tomahawks.

A few weeks after the Indian chase, Lieutenant Quigley met Frankie in a hallway in the station house.

"You got a few minutes?" the lieutenant asked.

He told Frankie that headquarters had decided to bolster the Detective Division. They asked each precinct commander to recommend one or two cops, preferably from the Anti-Crime units. Getting his gold shield back was something Frankie never allowed himself to think about. Why be disappointed? Even as the words came from Quigley's mouth, he wasn't quite sure what the lieutenant was saying.

"Frankie. If you want the division, it's yours," Quigley said succinctly. "I'll give your name to the captain."

For a moment, Frankie stood there unable to formulate any words. His mind, however, was a rush of memories: the thought of those bony white fingers throwing his gold badge into the cardboard box, the look of disappointment on his father's face, the talk with his brother Eugene, and how close he had come to quitting. Then his thoughts went to his partner.

"What about Artie?" he asked.

"If he wants it, he goes too," Quigley answered.

# 9

A few years before Frankie got back his gold shield, a kid I had grown up with was released from jail. He had shocked Pearl River, filled with its commuting New York City cops, by robbing the Nanuet National Bank. A few years older than me, Eddie had always been in trouble at school—a teenage marijuana bust and numerous suspensions for fighting or stealing from lockers. But he was, to my knowledge, the first and only bank robber from Pearl River.

One night, after his release, he walked into the Talk of the Town. The adolescent face I remembered was now hardened by his three years behind bars; his body, once skinny, had taken on jailhouse proportions from hours of lifting weights. He swaggered, and he spoke in black jargon. As he glanced around the barroom, he liked what he saw: the girls, the steady stream of white jackets headed to the bathroom for a snort of cocaine, the undercurrent of illegal activity that he instinctively sought. A smirk cut across his face as if to say: This is home.

For all their bravado, Matty O. and the boys steered clear of Eddy. Making book or running a card game was one thing; walking into a bank with a loaded shotgun, something else. I, on the other hand, wasn't repelled by his infamy. We had known each other all our lives, and no matter how big and bad he had grown in jail, in some sense he was still the kid with whom I had ridden bicycles.

Eddie began to spend a lot of time at the house in Woodcliff

Lake. One night, I walked in as he was cutting lines of an amber-tinted white powder on the dining room table. He handed me a rolled-up $100 bill; his expression was cut in a sneer, daring me. If there was ever a moment in which I drove a stake through the heart of the idea of my becoming a cop, it was then. I don't remember if my father or brother came into my thoughts as I took the bill and bent over the table. But on some level I knew that this was the ultimate act of defiance against them. From my earliest memories, that childhood eavesdropping on my father's conversations, I knew that heroin was the enemy of cops, I knew that it had taken the Bronx from them, that it fueled the demonic army that had defeated them. My father never railed against the evils of heroin. Rather, when he talked about it he seemed to drift off, like a survivor remembering some unfathomable tragedy: "An elderly woman stabbed forty times for her Social Security check . . ." He would shake his head and mumble something about "those goddamned junkies."

As we sat at the table, both, to different degrees, high on his smack, my friend told stories of his time in jail, the "brothers" he was in with, and the crimes they had committed.

I fought a wave of nausea from the heroin that turned my stomach upside down, and told him in turn of a restaurant owner and entrepreneur who owed me a thousand dollars. I had worked for him briefly as a bartender and as a salesman in his big-screen TV business. Though, as the first of their kind, the TVs were terrible—their pictures snowy and constantly blurred—I was able to sell one to a sports bar near Giants Stadium, and another to a pizza restaurant in northern Bergen County. The TV business, however, quickly went bankrupt, and I was never paid my commissions. My friend listened with only passing interest. That is, until I told him that a skylight in the restaurant was easily jimmied open, and that the weekend take was kept in a beer cooler behind the bar. At five o'clock that morning, my sense of justification fortified by cognac and heroin, we drove in my Thunderbird to Englewood Cliffs, and within an hour, were back sitting at the dining room table dividing up $1,600 worth of $5, $10, and $20 bills.

As the effect of the heroin and booze began to wane, I was flooded with guilt. Sunlight poured through the kitchen window onto the table, giving the scene an unbearable cheery feel. I pushed myself back from the table, leaving the money there, went to my bedroom, and pulled the covers over my head.

When I awoke, hours later, I was happy to see that both Eddie and the money were gone, and had the sincere hope that I would not see either again. That day, I drove up to my parents' home. As I pulled in to the driveway, I noticed the ladder leaning against the side of the house. My father, dressed in a plaid flannel shirt, was on the roof, cleaning out the gutters and leaders. His hair, now just about all white, resembled a cloud against the pale after-noon sky. He gave me a curt nod as I stepped from the car. I asked if he needed help, and he shook his head no, without saying a word. I walked inside and picked up a pile of mail addressed to me. There in the stack was a letter from the New York City Civil Service Department. The list for appointments to the police de-partment had been frozen until further notice. The letter didn't say whether or not I had passed the test or made the list, just that appointments were, for now, not going to be made from it. I sat at the kitchen table, my head throbbing, my insides churning from the events of the night before, as my mother made me a ham sandwich. Her voice was soothing and happy. I wanted her to grab hold of me, the way she had so often when I was a child. I wanted the forbidding feeling within me to just go away, to not have happened. I felt as though I had betrayed something intrin-sic inside me. Something instilled from childbirth, taught by ex-ample from a father and, later, a brother, and reinforced by the community in which I grew up. The masses, the regular people in the middle, didn't matter. The world was made up of only two camps—cops and bad guys. I had crossed over to the enemy, and I wanted a do-over. I wanted another chance. As I sat there, my thoughts swirling, I held to the slightest of hopes that it was all just a bad dream, that from the kitchen, where I now sat, my mother would call up the stairs that I was late for school, and I would yawn and stretch and see the light tumbling through my bedroom window, the one with the geraniums in the flower box outside. It didn't happen. At least, not right away.

I never went back to the house in Woodcliff Lake, and I vowed to change. A month or so later, Eddie was arrested for armed robbery and sent to jail again, and I counted myself lucky that I didn't go along with him.

Some years later, in 1981, I moved out of the house in Pearl River for good. Twenty-six years old, the police test a distant memory, and just becoming an adult, I took a small apartment over a coffee shop on the East Side of Manhattan. Once a week I'd hop on a bus to the Talk of the Town in Hillsdale. There I would leave an envelope with a hundred dollars in it for a loan shark, every week until my debt was paid off. Then I'd continue on to my parents' house for a visit and a home-cooked meal.

During this period, my relationship with my father began to change. It didn't happen all at once. For months, even years, he sized me up with a suspicious glare when I walked into the house, wondering if I had reverted to my old ways. And it took at least as long for me to forgive him.

In Manhattan, I again worked in the restaurant business. But this time my aspirations did not lie with gangsterdom or the racetrack. Instead, I took acting lessons and even joined a small theater company. Frankie, and even my father, came to a couple of my performances. I also began to write, first just scenes and monologues for my acting class, then one-act plays and later, short stories. One day, when I visited my father in Pearl River, he presented me with a gift—an old-style Underwood typewriter. For fourteen years that typewriter had sat on his desk in the 41st Precinct squad room. It weighed a ton, and had several crooked keys. But as I sat in front of it, hunt and pecking my nascent prose, I felt as close to being a cop as I ever would.

On October 1, 1981, Frankie arrived at the 52nd Precinct Detective Squad, in the north-central section of the Bronx. He was assigned to a team of veteran detectives: John Borris, Tony Martin and Mike Kelly, all of whom had worked together for some time. For the first week or so, he didn't catch a case; he spent most of those days trying not to get in anyone's way. The squad was housed in a converted garage next to the station house. More than the physical separation of the squad room, there seemed to be a discernible rift between the uniform cops and the detectives. Or was this cool breeze only blowing his way? By nature, cops are suspicious toward new assignees, especially those assigned to detective squads. Most times, the initial reaction is: Someone must have put in a contract. "Who the fuck does he know?" is a favored line. This exclusion is not overt by any means. Its signals are subtle—conversations held as if you weren't present; eye contact kept to a minimum; official interaction handled in a slow, detached manner. Once or twice, Frankie felt the urge to scream: "Listen, I just spent a good part of the last fourteen years in uniform!" He didn't, though. And it was just as well. The police department's rumor mill would deliver his tale soon enough. And when it did, the cops would know that he had won this assignment with no one's help.

Precincts in New York City are classified by letters: A is the busiest, B, the second busiest, and so on. The alphabetical codification, however, is deceiving just to the south of the Five-Two. The 46th Precinct was an "A" house, but staffed by almost twice as many detectives as the 52nd, which was then a "B," with only fourteen detectives in its squad. What's more, the 52nd was huge. Just before Frankie arrived there, the city charter was amended to provide for something called co-terminality. Simply explained, precincts would share boundaries with community boards. Because of this, the 52nd Precinct annexed a half-dozen blocks from the 46th. These blocks, in the 1980s, were the highest-crime area in the Five-Two.

Once it started for Frankie, it never slowed down. Though part of his new precinct, on the west, bordered Frankie's old one, there was no comparison between the two. The 50th Precinct and its midnight car thieves seemed like suburbia next to the crime in the Five-Two. Frankie's partner, Tony Martin, a DeNabli cigar–smoking detective, often told him that the Five-Two had "good crime." What he meant was that their precinct did not have the depraved crack-addled crime that happened in the South Bronx or parts of Brooklyn, where crackheads killed their mothers for stealing their pipes. "Good crime," to Martin, meant a lot of it, and a lot of different kinds of it: real, professional burglars, stick-up men who lasted more than a week in their careers, and murders that were harder to solve than just following the bloody footprints to the apartment next door.

But Martin's statement didn't mean there wasn't a crack co-caine problem in the Five-Two. In my father's time, it took years for neighborhoods to deteriorate, but in the early 1980s crack destroyed them seemingly overnight. One of those shattered neighborhoods was Fordham: Sedgwick Avenue, Devoe Park, St. Nicholas of Tolentine, lay square in the middle of the 52nd Precinct. In his time there, Frankie would work countless murders, rapes, and robberies, and every other conceivable crime, on the same blocks where, as a kid, he played and walked to school.

One day, early in his time in the 52nd squad, Frankie's team caught a robbery case. A nun from St. Nicholas of Tolentine was mugged as she entered her building on University Avenue, just a few blocks from the church. All four detective team members—Frankie, John Borris, Tony Martin, and Mike Kelly—were assigned. The reason for the unusual manpower (usually only a pair of partners caught cases) was because the chief of the Bronx at the time, a man by the name of Ciccarelli, was a daily communicant and a personal friend of the cardinal. Any crime against the church got his complete attention, and therefore the attention of all his detectives. As the team arrived at the scene, uniform cops filled them in on the particulars. The detectives were told that the nun, who was shaken and bruised, but not badly hurt, had been knocked to the floor in the vestibule of the building, and that the thief made off with her bag. But, the uniform cops said, the mugger left something behind: his German shepherd. Apparently the suspect had been walking his dog and saw the opportunity but, in the struggle, lost hold of the leash, and the dog was trapped in the nun's building.

John Borris and Tony Martin conferred and came up with an idea. Their plan was to let the dog loose and follow it—a *Lassie Come Home* strategy. Because they were in the best shape of the team, Frankie and Martin were designated as the runners. With the uniform cops looking on with amused expressions, John Borris walked the dog out to the sidewalk, and Frankie and Martin took runner's stances. When Borris unhooked the leash, the dog shot down University Avenue and across busy Fordham Road, with Frankie and Martin in close pursuit. As the cars whizzing by just missed them, the two detectives raced up Kingsbridge Terrace after the German shepherd. Sure enough, about three quarters of the way up Kingsbridge Terrace, the dog ran into the open door of a building. From the vestibule, and over their loud gasps for breath, Frankie and Martin could hear the dog scratching on a door a couple of floors above. Up they went, and knocked on the door, which was opened by a small Hispanic woman. Do you live alone? the detectives asked. With my husband, she said. Is your husband home? She shook her head no. Do you mind if we come in? She shrugged. Just inside the apartment was a hall closet with the door open. On the floor of the closet was the nun's bag.

The woman in the apartment refused to cooperate. She told

Frankie and Martin that she did not know where her husband was. Days went by and she was brought to the station house and questioned several times, but she still would not give any information. The detective team did find out that the husband had relatives in the East Bronx, and Frankie and John Borris took trips there each day—and each day, Chief Ciccarelli checked on the progress of the case. But like the wife, the relatives wouldn't tell them the husband's whereabouts.

Days stretched into a couple of weeks, and the husband was still in the wind. One day, while Frankie and Borris were on the way to the East Bronx, a call came over the radio: a bank robbery in progress on Fordham Road, right nearby. The two detectives joined in canvassing for witnesses. My brother spotted two deliverymen standing near their straight-rig truck, which sat in front of Devoe Park.

"Yeah, I saw the whole thing," one of the deliverymen began. "There were four young kids in ski masks—they ran out of the bank and hopped into a car down here." Frankie asked the routine questions: What kind of car? Did you get a license plate? And so on. But the man said he didn't get that close a look.

While he was interviewing the witness, my brother's eyes were drawn to the man's partner. Emaciated, with sunken cheeks, red eyes, and a cigarette hanging from his lip, he looked to Frankie as though he'd been on the wrong end of a chase a couple of times himself.

You see anything? Frankie asked. The man let the cigarette drop to the ground. "See that guy over there?" he said. "The fat one in the army jacket, getting into his car? He was part of it. We tried to stop the kids and he ran over and got in our way."

For whatever reason—years of police experience, instinct, or just a hunch—Frankie gave credence to the skinny man's words. With Borris, he walked up to the man in the army jacket, and amid a flurry of protests, escorted him to their car.

When they arrived at the station house there was utter pandemonium. Because it was a bank robbery, the FBI was there; so were most of the bosses from the Bronx, including Chief Ciccarelli.

As Frankie escorted his suspect into the interrogation room, he was approached by a smallish man with heavy-lidded eyes and a few days' growth of beard. Politely, the man asked Frankie if he could talk with him. Just then word was received that four kids with ski masks, suspects in the bank robbery, had been caught in Queens. In the back of a patrol car on the way to the Bronx, the four kids gave up a description of the heist's mastermind: heavyset, wearing an army jacket.

Frankie turned to the little man and explained that he had no time to talk to him at that moment, but if he would be patient, and take a seat, he would get to him as soon as he had the chance. Although most of the bosses there were elated that Frankie and Borris had already apprehended the suspect, Ciccarelli chose that moment to ask Frankie about progress on the nun's case. Jesus, Frankie thought, what does this guy want from me? After an hour and a half of questioning the bank robbery suspect, Frankie, needing a break, walked out of the interrogation room, where he was again approached by the small man. "Please, sir," the man implored, "I have to talk to you." By this time, Frankie had almost had it. "Can't you see I'm busy right now?" he said, bristling. "But this is very important," the man pleaded, as he followed Frankie to a Coke machine. Finally, Frankie turned to the man and said: "What? What the hell is so important?"

"I'm the guy who lost the dog," the man said.

If there were any doubts in Frankie's mind about whether he was going to be accepted in his detective team they were dispelled that day. He and Borris got credit for collaring the bank robbery suspect, and the team was credited for breaking the nun case. Both suspects were ultimately convicted.

\* \* \*

As was the case with every aspect of police work Frankie was involved with, he quickly found out that he was inherently good at being a detective. By just his second year in the 52nd, Frankie was frequently taken off the schedule and assigned to important and high-profile cases. One of these was the investigation into an attempted murder of a policeman.

Mike Palladino worked as an Anti-Crime cop in the 52nd Precinct. At the time, he was dating a local girl who lived on Jerome Avenue. Very early one warm late-spring morning in 1982, as the couple sat in Palladino's Trans Am in front of the girlfriend's apartment, Palladino saw two men breaking into a car. The young cop jumped from the Trans Am, and after a short chase apprehended the men. Across the street from where Palladino stood with his two suspects was an Italian social club, in front of which sat several patrons. The club members knew Palladino from the neighborhood—they called him "Mikey the Cop." Without backup, Palladino enlisted the club members' aid to watch his suspects as he went to retrieve their burglar tools. When Palladino returned, the suspects were gone. Later, in front of a grand jury, one of the patrons of the social club explained: "We threw the guys a beating, then kicked them in the ass out of the neighborhood."

The very next afternoon, in his girlfriend's apartment, Palladino was told by a neighborhood kid that two carloads of teenagers were waiting for him out front. Palladino took his service revolver and slid it into the waist of his pants. Outside, one of the suspects from the night before—a guy who was missing most of his teeth—pointed to Palladino. The two cars rumbled to life, heading in opposite directions down Jerome Avenue. When they were separated by a few blocks, they turned and headed back toward where Palladino stood. From one of the cars, a teenager was held by his belt as he leaned out the window. In his hand was a nine-millimeter automatic. It was a warm afternoon, and along Jerome Avenue, a residential block, neighborhood people sat in lawn chairs. Later investigators recovered fourteen shell casings from the automatic and from a revolver fired from the other car. Miraculously, neither Palladino nor any of the neighbors was hit.

During the shooting, someone from the neighborhood copied down the license plate of one of the cars and reported it to the police. Although the plate turned out to be registered to a fake address, the plate number and a description of the car were issued to all boroughs. Two nights later a uniform cop, John Turino from the 34th Precinct, spotted the car in front of Junior's restaurant in Washington Heights. The driver of the car, who had also been the driver the night of the shooting, was arrested.

Afterward, Frankie and John Fox, the lead investigator on the case, began to assemble important information on the driver's cohorts. During this time, the early 1980s, crime in New York City's subway system was rampant. Muggings by teenage gangs were commonplace. Funded by an infusion of cash—the result of community outrage that put pressure on politicians—the transit police had formed special squads to investigate organized gang crime. One of the most infamous gangs of that day called themselves the Ball Busters. Their leader was one Oscar Fernandez. According to the driver, it was Fernandez who'd fired the nine-millimeter at Palladino.

Riding in a van with a small peephole in its side, Frankie and a team of five other detectives, dressed in bulletproof vests and carrying shotguns, cruised the streets of north Harlem as—looking through the peephole—the driver pointed out his fellow gang members, one by one. After just a few hours, seven of the eight members had been apprehended. Only Oscar Fernandez remained at large.

During interrogation, one of the gang gave up Fernandez's address, an apartment on West 148th Street. Four of the team of detectives entered the building and approached the suspect's apartment door. Frankie and a detective named Fuselli covered the alleyway in the back of the building. Just a few moments later, the back window of Fernandez's apartment slid open. Though the apartment was on the first floor, the window was some twenty feet above the dark alleyway. Fuselli had positioned himself at one end of the open corridor, with Frankie at the other. As Fernandez readied to jump from the window, both detectives raised their shotguns to their shoulders. When the suspect hit the ground, Frankie yelled, identifying himself as a police officer. Just then there was a popping sound and a flash of light, from a small handgun. Though Fernandez was only some fifteen feet from Frankie— and from the shotgun he held against his shoulder—my brother didn't fire. In the darkness of the alleyway, he couldn't be absolutely sure that the spray of the blast wouldn't hit Fuselli. Instead, he took off after the suspect, tackled him from behind, and wrestled a small derringer from him. The bullet from the gun was later pried out of the wall only a few feet from where Frankie had stood.

All eight members of the Ball Busters were arraigned on charges of attempted murder. Several of them, including Oscar Fernandez, made bail and fled to their native Dominican Republic. Several years later, Fernandez returned to the United States and killed two people during an armed robbery. This time, when he was arrested, he was held without bail, and was ultimately convicted of the murders and sent to prison for life.

In his other world—Pearl River—Frankie coached his daughters, Laurie and Patrice, in Little League softball. The teams were called the Phillies and the Chargers. The girls wore brightly colored sweatshirts and baseball caps pulled down to their ears. A good portion of the fathers who watched the games from the stands of Anderson Field were cops, and almost all of the coaches were New York City policemen.

Much like Eugene and Frankie, Laurie and Patrice were strikingly different. In Little League, Laurie, the classic overachiever, worked hard in practice and gave a hundred percent during the games. For Patrice, being good at sports was just a matter of showing up. With little effort, she was the pitcher and star of the Chargers, and was picked for the all-star team. As the years passed, Laurie grew tall and slender, with a natural beauty accented by dark chestnut hair and perfect features. Patrice was also pretty but, as though she didn't believe it, she covered her face with layers of makeup, and streaked and bleached her hair. At one game when Patrice was about twelve, she came on the field wearing makeup and earrings. Her first boyfriend was in the stands, and she wanted to look her best. Embarrassed by his daughter's garish appearance, Frankie banished her from the pitcher's mound to left field. Patrice gave her father a steely stare as she walked to the outfield.

From very early on, there was noticeable friction between Frankie and Patrice, perhaps because they were, in personality, so alike. While Laurie played the role of doting daughter, Patrice met her father head-on, as if to show him that she could be every bit as rebellious as he had been. Laurie was an A student; Patrice hated school with a passion equaled only by her father in his early life.

By the time Patrice went to high school, her rebellious streak really did rival her father's. But the temptations of high school in Patrice's day were far more dangerous than they'd been in the tame 1950s-greaser era of Frankie's youth. By the eighties, crack cocaine showed little respect for the distance city cops had moved from New York City. Where once the joke among the habitués of the Bronx Criminal Court was "Criminal justice? Yeah, *just us*," crack had changed the very complexion of crime. Streets like DeKalb Avenue in the far northern section of the 52nd Precinct—which, not too long before, had been a stable working-class neighborhood—became a kind of drive-through crack market for white suburban customers: lawyers and store managers and secretaries who drove Toyotas and Nissans. The market also served white high school students behind the wheel of Mom or Daddy's car. Some of them were cops' kids.

\* \* \*

In the summer of 1982, a detective named Kenny Dudonis, a fellow Little League coach, asked Frankie if he would like to teach his class at Rockland Community College. A year and some months earlier, on St. Patrick's Day, 1981, Dudonis, a member of the NYPD's Bomb Squad, had been severely burned when an incendiary device he was trying to disarm exploded. The bomb was located in front of the Youth International Headquarters on Bleecker Street. Doctors had to reconstruct his face and hand. Though he was not able to teach during his recuperation, he wanted to keep his position at Rockland while he counted the days until he was eligible to retire from the NYPD.

Not too many years earlier, Frankie had walked into that college without a single credit. Now he jumped at the chance to teach there. The course was in criminalistics, more commonly known as forensics, the scientific side of investigation. That summer, a few weeks before the semester was to begin, Frankie took the course textbook with him on vacation to the New Jersey shore. He read it twice, and, while lying on the beach, dreamt about leading stimulating class discussions. For three days before the first day of class, he wrote and rewrote his opening lecture several times, in the same black-and-white marbled composition books where he kept his case notes. He even practiced in front of the mirror. For the first day of class, he wore his best blue blazer and khaki pants, trying hard to look less like a cop and more like a college professor. When the class began he was so nervous he kept his hands in his pants pockets because they were sweating profusely. He forgot everything he'd memorized. His lecture lasted all of ten minutes, the longest ten minutes of his life. Flustered, he finally said to the class: "Why don't you just go buy your books?"

He took good-natured ribbing from the detectives in his squad. They called him professor, just to break his shoes. He didn't mind. He liked being called professor. And teaching the class made him a better detective: He learned more about crime labs than he could have in a career on the street. For his students, his enthusiasm brought excitement to the class. As the semester went on, he found he didn't have to spend time memorizing lessons; much of what he taught, he already knew. What he didn't know, he learned along with his students. He brought in guest lecturers: detectives, Anti-Crime cops, and forensics experts. He even brought an old squad commander in to speak to his class. My father was in top form with the built-in audience for his war stories.

During those days at Rockland Community College, Frankie found out there was a job he could do that was more fulfilling than running after bad guys, and that he could actually fit in with civilians in a normal lifestyle. But it was always only a matter of time before Frankie caught a case that would, again, make being a cop the most important thing in his life.

On August 12, 1985, a burning furnace of a summer evening, Briggs Avenue was filled with kids playing games in slow motion. The sidewalks around them, strewn with every imaginable color of broken glass, glinted in the setting sun. Men stood on the corner under red and white corrugated-metal awnings, drinking beer from cans clothed in brown paper bags. The night hummed with a high-pitched crackle, like a radio station not quite tuned in. The street reeked with the sour odor of poverty, the kind that squeezes your nasal passages deep below the bridge of your nose, like the smell of a rat dead in a wall for weeks—not unbearable, just always there.

On the television show *Missing Children*, Frankie stood with Terry Hodrick on the porch in front of her home on Briggs Avenue. Her golden-brown skin was moist with sweat. She wore a loose-fitting housedress, which draped her pregnant stomach. She listened to Frankie's words intently, but did not look at him. Her eyes were distant and worried as they stared out over the street that had swallowed her eight-year-old daughter whole.

Later on, in a close-up shot, Frankie's face filled the screen. "Probably half my working hours are spent on this case," he said in the interview. "A lot of my thoughts go into this case—a lot of all of our thoughts. But we have to deal with facts. And the facts are: Equilla ran down the block that night. Turned the corner. And hasn't been seen or heard from since."

What Frankie didn't say into the camera was that he thought of little else but Equilla Hodrick. From the day of her disappearance that August, to the day he retired as a policeman, and beyond, in every quiet moment, during every drive home in his car, each time he sat at his desk at work, even in his dreams, the picture of her bright, engaging smile, her disarming hazel eyes, her delicately smooth, brown skin haunted him. For Frankie, this was even more than a missing-child case, it was an obsession. And, in some ways an act of atonement.

I never really knew—didn't want to know—what my brother had said to those six black men in Spring Valley that foggy night. But any stain of bigotry on him disappears in light of the attention and care he lavished on Equilla Hodrick's case—and the love he had for the little girl he searched for for years, but never knew, never found.

Both as a uniform and as an undercover cop, Frankie entered people's lives like a car accident: lights, siren, and shouts; an arrest, or sometimes not; and on to the next collision. Now, as a detective, he dealt with emotions that weren't fueled by adrenaline. Instead of shouts there were whimpers; instead of chases, there were sighs. Instead of thinking of victims as crime statistics, he found that they were human beings with lives and families. He knew that Terry Hodrick wasn't an addict. She didn't sell her body or peddle drugs. She was a mother who tucked her daughter into bed each night and stroked her head. She prayed on her knees and hummed gospel hymns all the time. Frankie stopped by her house at least once a day, even though, as time wore on, he could offer little more than support and optimistic words. One night, several weeks after her daughter's disappearance, Terry hugged him. At first, as the pregnant black woman draped her arms around him, he held her woodenly. But as she laid her head on his shoulder, and as he could feel her moist sobs against his neck, his arms tightened around her and tears filled his own eyes. He held her that way for some time, as curious neighborhood people walked slowly by and looked at them.

With his partner, John Borris, Frankie conducted hundreds of interviews with neighbors, shop owners, family members, anyone who might offer even the smallest insight into Equilla's disappearance. For all intents and purposes, Borris and Frankie worked the case alone. Several years earlier, a young boy in Greenwich Village named Etan Patz disappeared, almost the way Equilla had. For Etan Patz, the NYPD mobilized an entire task force; a hundred detectives worked the case for months, years. But Equilla didn't live in Greenwich Village, nor did she have blond hair or white skin.

To be fair, in the days immediately after her disappearance, the police department did use helicopters and bloodhounds. One of the dogs picked up her scent and led police to a hole in a fence that ran along a Metro North train right-of-way. The tracks cut a canyon through this section of the Bronx, ferrying commuters back and forth from Westchester. Along the edges of the tracks, homeless people lived in a squatter's camp filled with cardboard-box homes, shopping carts, and junk. Frankie and Borris decided to conduct a thorough search of the canyon. It was about eleven a.m. on a Thursday when Frankie called Metro North. On the phone, he was told that an official would be sent to speak to him in person. During the months prior, Metro North had been under scrutiny by commuter groups and the city for inadequacies in service: shortages of trains and frequent equipment problems.

In a construction trailer beside the tracks, Frankie and his squad commander, Sergeant Malvey, met with the official from Metro North. The man nervously played with his beard and glasses as he told Frankie that a shutdown of the trains would be impossible.

"Do you know how many people you want to inconvenience?" he asked.

Though Frankie was inwardly seething at the man's valuing commuters' convenience over a young girl's life, his outward response was measured:

"This is an urgent police matter," Frankie said. "We're searching for a missing eight-year-old girl. We need your cooperation."

"I'm sorry," the man replied. "There's nothing I can do."

"Well, who can?" asked Malvey, glaring at the official, who was now sweating profusely.

By phone, Malvey was connected to a Metro North supervisor in Manhattan, and was given pretty much the same answer: no. Malvey then asked for the supervisor's boss. Finally, he heard a sympathetic voice. Although the Metro North vice president wouldn't go as far as stopping the trains, he did agree to slow them down to thirty miles per hour—a safe enough speed, he said, for the cops to search the sides of the track. Frankie and Borris, with a half-dozen uniform cops and the same number of Emergency Service officers, conducted the search. As they rooted through the debris, they could feel the suction from the trains zipping by.

The executive from Metro North had agreed to a half-hour search. But once the cops were in the tunnel, there was nothing the railroad could do to get them out. The search stretched to almost three hours. Meanwhile, the slowing of the trains began to have a domino effect on service. By the time rush hour arrived, there was total havoc in Grand Central Station, with hundreds of thousands of commuters stranded and delays of several hours.

The search of the tunnel produced a dozen homeless people, each of whom was interrogated exhaustively, and one possible lead: a man with obvious emotional problems, who had several children's dolls in his possession. But after several hours of questioning the man, it became clear that he was innocent, and he was released.

Disappointed, Frankie began making phone calls from his boss's office, checking on sightings. He had been in contact with several missing-children agencies, which were now distributing fliers and information about Equilla around New York and in several other cities. A hot line had been set up, and every lead, no matter how unlikely, had to be followed up.

As Frankie sat there behind the desk, phone cradled under his chin, a local TV reporter knocked on the door. As she did, TV lights behind her filled the squad room. The reporter thrust the microphone in Frankie's face and asked if he had made the decision to disrupt the commuter traffic.

"Nobody made that decision," he said. "We made the decision to search for a missing child."

When the reporter pressed for an answer, Frankie stopped her in mid-sentence.

"What is your story?" he asked contemptuously. "That an eight-year-old girl is missing? Or that a few assholes from Westchester came home to a cold dinner? I don't have anything more to say to you."

Over the coming weeks, with the aid of a couple of Emergency Service cops, Frankie searched nearly fifty abandoned buildings, storefronts, and apartments. Terry Hodrick insisted she come along on these searches. And for those weeks, Frankie sat next to her in the squad car, promising her he would find Equilla.

The people of the neighborhood around Briggs Avenue were very involved. The flier with the little girl's picture was in just about every shop window, and residents, most of whom knew Frankie was the detective in charge of the case, would stop him in the street to ask about any progress. One Saturday afternoon, a block party was held on 194th Street. Fernando Ferrer, then a congressman from the Bronx, stepped onto the bandstand to thank the neighborhood for its help in the Equilla Hodrick case and ask for continued assistance. From the bandstand, he introduced Frankie, who was standing in the crowd, and announced the phone number that anyone with information should call. As Frankie walked back to his car from the block party, he passed a shriveled old woman, rooting through a garbage can. As he did, he heard her say: "You're never gonna find that little girl alive—she is buried up in Yonkers." Frankie knew the woman as a "can gatherer" and a little bit of a nut. Her words didn't register until he was driving back to the squad room, and then he spun the car around and raced back. Frantically, he ran through the crowd, looking for her, asking people if they had seen her. Nobody had.

Yonkers. Terry Hodrick had a boyfriend who sometimes lived in a house right next to hers on Briggs Avenue. But the rest of the boyfriend's time was spent in an apartment in Yonkers. On the night of Equilla's disappearance, the boyfriend had been seen running, shirtless, on Hoe Avenue, just a few blocks from the Hodricks' home. Later that same night, witnesses placed him riding in a red car with another man. By interviewing at least a dozen people, Frankie was able to identify the other man. His address was the apartment Terry Hodrick's boyfriend lived in in Yonkers.

During the first months of the investigation, Frankie had brought the boyfriend in for interrogation half a dozen times. More. One night, alone with him in the 52nd squad room, Frankie asked him how he was going to live with himself. Every day, Frankie told him, Equilla's little face would appear in his thoughts, and would never let him forget. The boyfriend began to cry—deep, heaving sobs. Slowly, he lifted his head from his hands and turned to Frankie. His eyes were a watery red, with blood and tears. He began to speak, and Frankie was sure he was about to confess. But all the boyfriend said was "I didn't do nothing."

The interrogation of the boyfriend's Yonkers roommate proved as fruitless. For months, Frankie searched for the woman who had been rooting through the garbage. But she disappeared like an apparition. Indeed, several times Frankie even doubted her existence. Perhaps she had been admitted to a psychiatric ward and was now in the labyrinth of New York City's institutional system. Or maybe she had died. Her words, though, lived in his thoughts for the rest of the Equilla Hodrick investigation. How, he often wondered, did the old woman know about Yonkers?

Two years after her daughter disappeared, Frankie still talked to Terry Hodrick four or five times a week. Two years after Equilla had disappeared, Frankie still followed up every lead that came from the private sector's missing-persons network. Equilla's picture was on the back of milk cartons and tractor-trailers. Her story was on national television. Two years later, there were still plenty of leads coming in. None led anywhere.

By this time, Frankie was certain that Equilla was dead. During the investigation, he had come to know her like she was his own daughter. She was smart, with street smarts that inner-city kids learn the way country-club kids learn golf, by just being there. Frankie knew that she loved her mother, and in some ways took care of her. Terry Hodrick was not the brightest of people—she couldn't have been, to get mixed up with a junkie boyfriend. If Equilla was alive, she would have found a way to come home by then.

Yet, on some level, Frankie couldn't allow himself to believe the inescapable. The Equilla Hodrick case was the biggest disappointment of his career. More than almost anything, he wanted to solve it. More than that, he wanted to find her alive. Just a week before he retired, he took out the twenty-five-pound case folder and placed it on his desk. One last time, he looked through it, as if, magically, this time he would find the answer.

That afternoon, he went to see Terry Hodrick to tell her he was leaving the force and another detective would be assigned to the case. She slowly shook her head back and forth, her eyes were dull, as if there were no more tears left to shed. "Well, that's the end of it," she said simply, the words as empty as they were final. For a few moments they stood together on the porch in awkward silence. Then Frankie walked down the steps and out of Terry Hodrick's life. Eleven years later, Equilla is still listed as a missing child.

# 10

Built atop the Palisades, cliffs that drop hundreds of feet to the Hudson River, and through a forested tract of land bequeathed by the Rockefeller family, the Palisades Parkway is about as lovely a drive as any in the New York area. In spring, with the windows down, the cool rush of pine- and maple-scented air fills the nostrils; in fall, you're surrounded by explosions of reds, yellows, and maroons as the foliage changes. In the winter, when the leaves have fallen, you can see the Hudson River, and across to Riverdale and north to Westchester. So beautiful is the vista, there are lookouts along the parkway with binocular stands, like the kind you find on the observation deck of the Empire State Building.

It takes no longer than twenty minutes to drive the Palisades Parkway from the George Washington Bridge, through a corner of New Jersey, to the exit for Pearl River. There are only two lanes in each direction, there are no trucks, no tolls (except for the bridge), no billboards. For cops, the drive is like the first cold beer after a hot summer tour, when they can finally stop holding their breath.

There is a story that city cops in Pearl River tell. One of their brethren, who worked four-to-twelves, drove the Palisades home early each morning. Each time he did, he noticed a small, perfectly shaped pine on the side of the highway. One day, a few weeks before Christmas, as he left for work, he threw a shovel into the trunk of his car.

Coming home from work that night, he pulled his car off the highway and onto the winter-browned grass near the tree he admired. As he began to dig, he imagined how perfect the tree would look in front of his house, first wrapped with Christmas lights, and then, in the spring and summer, shading the new steps and walkway he had just put in that fall. When he had almost finished digging up the tree, a Palisades Parkway police car pulled off the highway behind him.

"What the hell do you think you're doing?" the Jersey cop sternly asked.

"Listen," his New York counterpart said, his mind in full engagement. "I'm a cop in the city. This tree is from my front yard, and I just put a walkway in. I didn't have the heart just to cut it down, so I dug it up and thought I'd plant it here, on my way home from work."

"You can't do that," said the Jersey cop. "You're going to have to get it out of here."

But for New York City cops who live in Rockland, the Palisades Parkway is more than a pleasant drive and a chance to unwind. It serves as the demilitarized zone, the buffer between their two worlds. No matter how far the crime stain of New York spread, they believed that it could never, ever reach Pearl River.

In denial, city cops wouldn't believe that Pearl River was not safe anymore from crack cocaine. It *had* to be, because if it wasn't, they had lost the crime war not only in New York City, but in their homeland, too. By the time Patrice was in Pearl River High School, the homeland was no longer safe.

I often wondered how my brother must have felt when the very agent he fought in his latter police career broached the moat of the Hudson River and crawled up the Palisades Parkway and past its reeling elms to his own backyard? As heroic as he was, battling drugs as a cop in the Bronx, did he think he had failed as a father in protecting his daughter from them in Pearl River?

In his defense, riding through the inner city in an unmarked police car, and watching your daughter climb the stairs to her bedroom after being at a high school party, are two distinctly different vantage points. And, at first, none of us had any clue. Patrice's personality bubbled over with a quick wit accentuated by smiling, clear, aqua eyes. She called me Uncle Brian, which made me feel so very adult around her, and she never missed a family get-together. We—my entire family—knew all of her close-knit group of friends. In fact, at family gatherings, visits from Patrice's friends were a high point. They were funny and harmlessly mischievous. One of her friends, Michael, even aspired to be a stand-up comic. A natural mimic, he had Frankie down pat.

But in Patrice's junior year in high school, it became clear that she had problems. Though certainly a bright kid, she was failing every subject. She just didn't go to class. She had been suspended from school on at least one occasion. Although the reason for the suspension was never discussed—at least not with me—it was known to have something to do with drugs. That year, my brother and Pam arranged for Patrice to live with Pam's brother Clem's ex-wife in Scottsdale, Arizona. Their thinking was to remove her from the bad influences in Pearl River. But the problem lay in Patrice, not in outside influences.

About a month after Patrice moved to Scottsdale, her aunt called Pam to say it wasn't working out. Patrice wasn't going to class in Arizona either, and the aunt was worried about her own daughter, who was Patrice's age, and who was now spending far too much time with her cousin. Pam flew to Scottsdale to talk to school officials. She was told that Patrice was doing just fine—but obviously the school didn't have its information correct. Pam rented a small apartment, planning to live with Patrice until the school year was over. But Patrice was already immersed in the illegal-drug culture of Scottsdale. She would borrow Pam's car to go for cigarettes and not return until the next day. One of these disappearances stretched to three days. Frantic, Pam called Frankie, and my brother booked the next available flight.

For the first couple of harrowing days, Frankie and Pam weren't really sure what had happened to Patrice. But when Patrice's cousin, also seventeen, turned up missing too, they knew the girls had gone somewhere together. Three days later, when the cousin returned home, she told Pam where Patrice was staying.

As Frankie packed a carry-on bag to go to Arizona, he looked at the gleaming Colt Cobra, his off-duty weapon, in the sock drawer. In some ways, at least symbolically, he had always reached for the gun as the answer when drug addiction was the issue. But, in this case, that symbol was the last thing he needed. Whether or not police guns work to stop illegal drugs on the streets of the Bronx is debatable. Whether a gun would help in rescuing his daughter was not. He closed the drawer with the Colt still in it.

For a moment, as he sat in his rental car in the parking lot of the run-down roadside motel, his thoughts again went to the gun. He didn't know what he would find in the motel room, but he feared the worst, and he felt almost naked without the Colt. So many times he had gone through the same motions in the Bronx, and the gun was always there to reassure him—the biscuit, he called it.

He pulled himself from the car and walked toward the door of the motel room. When he knocked, the door was opened a crack, but held by the chain. "I'm Patrice's father," he said to the squinting eyes that looked out at him. The eyes darted away, but before the door could be slammed, Frankie threw his shoulder into it, snapping it open. Inside, there were two men in their early twenties in the room, and another girl about Patrice's age. Patrice lay half asleep on the bed; her eyes had sunk into her skull, with dark circles underneath. She had lost a great deal of weight, and the sight of her shocked Frankie. It wasn't as though he hadn't seen the likes of what lay before him. The Port Authority bus terminal, the streets of Times Square, and sections of the Bronx were filled with such forlorn souls. But the skeleton he now looked at wore the just barely recognizable features of his own daughter. One of the men, who had a hardened face and greasy jet-black hair, began to yell: "Get the fuck out of my room!" From experience, I can easily imagine what Frankie looked like in that moment: the glaze descending over his eyes, the skin on the back of his neck crimson—the only tell-tale signs that beneath the otherwise placid exterior his blood raced fiery hot.

The other man silently leered at Frankie. My brother could see the outline of a handgun under his shirt. For a moment, my brother and the man held each other's eyes in a sizing-up stare, and in that moment my brother thought of the Colt he had left behind. Though Frankie didn't know this then, the young man knew he was a cop; Patrice had told him. Undoubtedly, he thought Frankie had a gun, too. A heavy silence engulfed the room. Then the young man slowly walked past Frankie, brushing up against him as he did. For a few seconds my brother's cop instincts took over. He listened intently to the man's footsteps climbing the stairs outside the door. In that moment, he imagined the man positioning himself for a clear shot. But as he looked again toward his daughter, cop worries were swept aside. Frankie walked to the bed, cradled Patrice in his arms, and carried her from the room to the car, glancing over his shoulder only once. The man with the gun was nowhere in sight.

Perhaps it was then that Frankie first realized that, for the whole of his daughters' lives, his priorities had been, at the very least, divided between being a good father and being a good cop. In some ways, you can't be both. The job not only steals cops' time from their families, it takes words from their mouths. Witnessing lives sliced apart, seeing horrors upon horrors, dulls cops' ability to express love.

With Patrice, Frankie was given another chance. Soon after he brought his daughter home, I sat in a room and watched as he told her how much he loved her. I saw his eyes flood with tears that began to drip down his tough cop face, as he told her how he didn't want her to die. I saw him hold her tenderly, like the best of fathers, and watched as she cried, too. In that moment, a police shield no longer covered his heart.

The day Frankie retired, he drove up the Palisades as a civilian for the first time in twenty years. Snow still swirled from the white-gray sky and clung to the bare branches of the trees. For the first time in twenty years there wasn't a badge on his person, there wasn't a service revolver in the glove compartment of his car. The thought came to him of how much space those articles had occupied, and he felt uneasy and vulnerable in their absence. He thought about the offer that had lured him away from the job that had defined him all his adult life. He hoped that, with time, his pension and his new salary would fill the longing. When he was out from under the weight of his debts and bills, leaving the job he loved wouldn't seem so painful.

By accepting the offer, he had completed the trifecta mirror image of his father's life: the navy, the police department, and now airline security—working for TWA. That snowy day, he pulled in to his father's driveway to tell one last war story, the events of Patrolman Michael Reidy's murder investigation.

Over the coming weeks and months, Frankie was by turns fascinated with his new career—in a world of white-collar criminals, of credit-card fraud and airline ticket forgery—and melancholy over his departure from the police department. At TWA, his first assignment was to investigate a lost-luggage claim—thirteen Halliburton aluminum suitcases belonging to a Hollywood producer. He flew to Orlando to interview ticket and rental-car agents. No longer a cop, he realized on his way to the first interview that these people didn't have to talk to him if they didn't want to. They did talk, though. The aura of authority from his twenty years on the force still draped Frankie like a uniform.

The claim turned out to be false. A retired detective, working as a security manager in a New York hotel, told Frankie that the hotel bellhop had records of the producer checking the Halliburton bags there—days after he had reported them lost or stolen in Florida.

When the *Daily News* or *New York Post* headlines blared another major crime story, Frankie couldn't help but think that he had made a mistake; he desperately missed the action of the street. Even the perks of the new job (with flying privileges, he and Pam once took a weekend in Rome) didn't quell the yearning for some squad-room banter and a greasy meatball hero. But as time went by, he slowly became acclimated to the corporate world, and even though the commute from Kennedy Airport to Pearl River was on some nights a two-hour push through bumper-to-bumper traffic, he liked being home each night for dinner and, for the first time in his life, having the normal hours of a working father.

About a year after he began the job at TWA, he started to teach again, part-time, for a university in New York City. Throughout his time at TWA, and later, when he went into academia full-time, Frankie's classes in police science were filled to capacity. Young, scrubbed faces of every hue looked toward him for guidance—and a grade—in the hope of fulfilling their dreams of careers in law enforcement. He began each first class of the semester with the same words: "A cop's life is not for everybody. But," he would add, "it was for me." He knew what he was talking about.

A few years ago, I met my brother in downtown Manhattan, in Foley Square, outside the federal courthouse. The college where he worked was just a few blocks away. I was there covering the trial of a drug dealer for a story I was writing freelance for *The New York Times*. We grabbed a couple of hot dogs from a vendor and sat on a green city bench. All gray now, with a St. Anthony bald spot on the crown of his head, his body thick around the middle, my brother began the conversation in his usual way: the joke of the week. The square was filled with those on both sides of the law rushing for a quick lunch before afternoon court sessions and work. It was a beautiful April day, and a young cop in shirtsleeves walked by. I watched my brother's eyes, their blue a match for the cop's shirt, as they followed the patrolman. It was as though he was looking into his own past.

"Being a policeman," he said wistfully, "was the only thing I ever wanted to do."

# 11

Some sixty years after my grandfather's death, over thirty years since my father retired, and now some twelve years since my brother left the job, we are still a family delineated by the badge and gun of the NYPD.

Each Christmas Eve, Frankie hosts a party at his home, which is now completely paid for. The festivity is held in the "new" room, an extension off the side of the house that Frankie and Paul Gibbons built. Thanks to Pam's expertise, the room looks like a picture out of *Architectural Digest*: cream-colored walls, recessed lighting, walnut shelves, forest-green couches and chairs. The shelf over the fireplace is lined with mementos of Frankie's police career: a plaque with a replica of his gold shield presented to him on his retirement by his old squad; a photograph of him as a rookie cop.

All of my family attends the party, even Eugene and Diane, who make the four-hour drive from an affluent Boston suburb where they now live. Patrice is always there too, with her boys, Mikey and Danny. Patrice and Frankie have worked hard at their relationship over the years. Family loyalty is strong—as is Frankie's

LITIGATION AND ADMINISTRATIVE
PRACTICE SERIES
Criminal Law and Urban Problems
Course Handbook Series
Number C-177

TAX LAW AND ESTATE PLANNING SERIES
Estate Planning and Administration
Course Handbook Series
Number D-255

# Child Custody

# and Support

## 1997

*Chair*
## Mona R. Millstein

To order this book, call (800) 260-4PLI  or fax us at (800) 321-0093.  Ask our
Customer Service Department, Dept.  BAV5.

Practising Law Institute
810 Seventh Avenue
New York, New York 10019

"This publication is designed to provide information in regard to the subject matter covered. It is sold with the understanding that the publisher is not engaged in rendering legal, accounting or other professional service. If legal advice or other expert assistance is required, the services of a competent professional person should be sought."
—from Declaration of Principles jointly adopted by Committee of American Bar Association and Committee of Publishers and Associations

# Foreword

This course handbook is one of about 150 published each year by the Practising Law Institute.

Its primary function is to serve as an educational supplement to each program. It may also be used as a reference manual by attorneys and related professionals unable to attend the sessions.

The method of reproduction utilized has been chosen to insure that registrants receive these materials as quickly as possible and in the most usable form practicable.

The Practising Law Institute wishes to acknowledge its debt and extend its sincere appreciation to the authors who have rendered this valuable service. They exemplify the finest tradition of our profession by sharing their expertise with their colleagues.

Prepared for distribution at the
CHILD CUSTODY AND SUPPORT
Program
July 1997

## CONTENTS:

1

# INTRODUCTION

Mona R. Millstein

Reprinted from the PLI Course Handbook,
Child Custody and Support 1996.
Order Number C4-4214

This course handbook is intended to supplement our program 'Child Custody and Support." Included within the handbook are certain of the relevant statutes, as well as articles, outlines, case lists, and forms concerning subjects of particular interest in the custody and child support area. Custody cases are uniquely fact intensive, and, therefore, the articles, outlines, and case lists provided in this handbook include are illustrative examples of particular determinations dependent upon particular facts. The faculty hopes that these materials, in conjunction with the program, will be helpful as a guideline and tool to attorneys in analyzing and handling their clients' custody and child support matters.

**NOTES**

2

# DOMESTIC RELATIONS LAWS

Reprinted from the PLI Course Handbook,
<u>Child Custody and Support 1996</u>.
Order Number C4-4214

## § 240. Custody and child support; orders of protection.

1. In any action or proceeding brought (1) to annul a marriage or to declare the nullity of a void marriage, or (2) for a separation, or (3) for a divorce, or (4) to obtain, by a writ of habeas corpus or by petition and order to show cause, the custody of or right to visitation with any child of a marriage, the court must give such direction, between the parties, for the custody and support of any child of the parties, as, in the court's discretion, justice requires, having regard to the circumstances of the case and of the respective parties and to the best interests of the child. In all cases there shall be no prima facie right to the custody of the child in either parent. Such direction shall make provision for child support out of the property of either or both parents. The court shall make its award for child support pursuant to subdivision one-b of this section. Such direction may provide for reasonable visitation rights to the maternal and/or paternal grandparents of any child of the parties. Such direction as it applies to rights of visitation with a child remanded or placed in the care of a person, official, agency or institution pursuant to article ten of the family court act, or pursuant to an instrument approved under section three hundred fifty-eight-a of the social services law, shall be enforceable pursuant to part eight of article ten of the family court act and sections three hundred fifty-eight-a and three hundred eighty-four-a of the social services law and other applicable provisions of law against any person having care and custody, or temporary care and custody, of the child. Notwithstanding any other provision of law, any written application or motion to the court for the establishment, modification or enforcement of a child support obligation for persons not in receipt of aid to dependent children must contain either a request for child support enforcement services which would authorize the collection of the support obligation by the immediate issuance of an income execution for support enforcement as provided for by this chapter, completed in the manner specified in section one hundred eleven-g of the social services law; or a statement that the applicant

has applied for or is in receipt of such services; or a statement that the applicant knows of the availability of such services, has declined them at this time and where support enforcement services pursuant to section one hundred eleven-g of the social services law have been declined that the applicant understands that an income deduction order may be issued pursuant to subdivision (c) of section five thousand two hundred forty-two of the civil practice law and rules without other child support enforcement services and that payment of an administrative fee may be required. The court shall provide a copy of any such request for child support enforcement services to the support collection unit of the appropriate social services district any time it directs payments to be made to such support collection unit. Additionally, the copy of any such request shall be accompanied by the name, address and social security number of the parties; the date and place of the parties' marriage; the name and date of birth of the child or children; and the name and address of the employers and income payors of the party from whom child support is sought or from the party ordered to pay child support to the other party. Such direction may require the payment of a sum or sums of money either directly to the custodial parent or to third persons for goods or services furnished for such child, or for both payments to the custodial parent and to such third persons; provided, however, that unless the party seeking or receiving child support has applied for or is receiving such services, the court shall not direct such payments to be made to the support collection unit, as established in section one hundred eleven-h of the social services law. Such direction shall require that if either parent has health insurance available through an employer or organization that may be extended to cover the child, that such parent exercise the option of additional coverage in favor of such child and execute and deliver any forms, notices, documents or instruments necessary to assure timely payment of any health insurance claims for such child. Where employer or organization subsidized health insurance coverage is available, the court shall order the legally responsible relative immediately to enroll the eligible dependents named in the order who are otherwise eligible for such coverage without regard to any seasonal enrollment restrictions. Such order shall further direct the legally responsible relative to maintain such coverage as long as it remains available to such relative. Upon a finding that a responsible relative wilfully failed to obtain such health insurance in violation of a court order, such relative will be presumptively liable for all medical expenses incurred on the behalf of such dependents from the first date such dependent was eligible to be enrolled in medical insurance coverage after the issuance of the order of support directing the acquisition of such coverage. In making an order for employer or organization provided health insurance pursuant to this section the court shall consider the availability of such insurance to all parties to the order and direct that either or both parties obtain such insurance and allocate the costs therefor consistent with obtaining comprehensive medical insurance for the child at reasonable cost to the parties. Such direction shall be effective as of the date of the application therefor, and any retroactive amount of child support due shall be support arrears/past due support and shall, except as provided for herein, be paid in one sum or periodic sums, as the court shall direct, taking into account any amount of temporary support which has been paid. In addition, such retroactive child support shall be enforceable in any manner provided by law including, but not limited to, an execution for support enforcement pursuant to subdivision (b) of section fifty-two hundred forty-one of the civil practice law and rules. When a child receiving support is a public assistance recipient, or the order of support is being enforced or is to be enforced pursuant to section one hundred eleven-g of the social services law, the court shall establish the amount

14

# DOMESTIC RELATIONS LAW

of retroactive child support and notify the parties that such amount shall be enforced by the support collection unit pursuant to an execution for support enforcement as provided for in subdivision (b) of section fifty-two hundred forty-one of the civil practice law and rules, or in such periodic payments as would have been authorized had such an execution been issued. In such case, the courts shall not direct the schedule of repayment of retroactive support. Where such direction is for child support and paternity has been established by a voluntary acknowledgement of paternity as defined in section forty-one hundred thirty-five-b of the public health law, the court shall inquire of the parties whether the acknowledgement has been duly filed, and unless satisfied that it has been so filed shall require the clerk of the court to file such acknowledgement with the appropriate registrar within five business days. Such direction may be made in the final judgment in such action or proceeding, or by one or more orders from time to time before or subsequent to final judgment, or by both such order or orders and the final judgment. Such direction may be made notwithstanding that the court for any reason whatsoever, other than lack of jurisdiction, refuses to grant the relief requested in the action or proceeding. Any order or judgment made as in this section provided may combine in one lump sum any amount payable to the custodial parent under this section with any amount payable to such parent under section two hundred thirty-six of this chapter. Upon the application of either parent, or of any other person or party having the care, custody and control of such child pursuant to such judgment or order, after such notice to the other party, parties or persons having such care, custody and control and given in such manner as the court shall direct, the court may annul or modify any such direction, whether made by order or final judgment, or in case no such direction shall have been made in the final judgment may, with respect to any judgment of annulment or declaring the nullity of a void marriage rendered on or after September first, nineteen hundred forty, or any judgment of separation or divorce whenever rendered, amend the judgment by inserting such direction. Subject to the provisions of section two hundred forty-four of this article, no such modification or annulment shall reduce or annul arrears accrued prior to the making of such application unless the defaulting party shows good cause for failure to make application for relief from the judgment or order directing such payment prior to the accrual of such arrears. Such modification may increase such child support nunc pro tunc as of the date of application based on newly discovered evidence. Any retroactive amount of child support due shall be support arrears/past due support and shall be paid in one lump sum or periodic sums, as the court shall direct, taking into account any amount of temporary child support which has been paid. In addition, such retroactive child support shall be enforceable in any manner provided by law including, but not limited to, an execution for support enforcement pursuant to subdivision (b) of section fifty-two hundred forty-one of the civil practice law and rules.

1-a. In any proceeding brought pursuant to this section to determine the custody or visitation of minors, a report made to the statewide central register of child abuse and maltreatment, pursuant to title six of article six of the social services law, or a portion thereof, which is otherwise admissible as a business record pursuant to rule forty-five hundred eighteen of the civil practice law and rules shall not be admissible in evidence, notwithstanding such rule, unless an investigation of such report conducted pursuant to title six of article six of the social services law has determined that there is some credible evidence of the alleged abuse or maltreatment and that the subject of the report has been notified that the report is indicated. If such report has been reviewed by the state commissioner of social services or his designee and has been expunged, it shall not be

15

admissible in evidence. If such report has been so reviewed and has been amended to delete any finding, each such deleted finding shall not be admissible. If the state commissioner of social services or his designee has amended the report to add any new finding, each such new finding, together with any portion of the original report not deleted by the commissioner or his designee, shall be admissible if it meets the other requirements of this subdivision and is otherwise admissible as a business record. If such a report, or portion thereof, is admissible in evidence but is uncorroborated, it shall not be sufficient to make a fact finding of abuse or maltreatment in such proceeding. Any other evidence tending to support the reliability of such report shall be sufficient corroboration.

1-b. (a) the court shall make its award for child support pursuant to the provisions of this subdivision. The court may vary from the amount of the basic child support obligation determined pursuant to paragraph (c) of this subdivision only in accordance with paragraph (f) of this subdivision.

(b) For purposes of this subdivision, the following definitions shall be used:

(1) "Basic child support obligation" shall mean the sum derived by adding the amounts determined by the application of subparagraphs two and three of paragraph (c) of this subdivision except as increased pursuant to subparagraphs four, five, six and seven of such paragraph.

(2) "Child support" shall mean a sum to be paid pursuant to court order or decree by either or both parents or pursuant to a valid agreement between the parties for care, maintenance and education of any unemancipated child under the age of twenty-one years.

(3) "Child support percentage" shall mean:

(i) seventeen percent of the combined parental income for one child;

(ii) twenty-five percent of the combined parental income for two children;

(iii) twenty-nine percent of the combined parental income for three children;

(iv) thirty-one percent of the combined parental income for four children; and

(v) no less than thirty-five percent of the combined parental income for five or more children.

(4) "Combined parental income" shall mean the sum of the income of both parents.

(5) "Income" shall mean, but shall not be limited to, the sum of the amounts determined by the application of clauses (i), (ii), (iii), (iv), (v) and (vi) of this subparagraph reduced by the amount determined by the application of clause (vii) of this subparagraph:

(i) gross (total) income as should have been or should be reported in the most recent federal income tax return. If an individual files his/her federal income tax return as a married person filing jointly, such person shall be required to prepare a form, sworn to under penalty of law, disclosing his/her gross income individually;

(ii) to the extent not already included in gross income in clause (i) of this subparagraph, investment income reduced by sums expended in connection with such investment;

(iii) to the extent not already included in gross income in clauses (i) and (ii) of this subparagraph, the amount of income or compensation voluntarily deferred and income received, if any, from the following sources:

(A) workers' compensation,

(B) disability benefits,

(C) unemployment insurance benefits,

(D) social security benefits,

(E) veterans benefits,

(F) pensions and retirement benefits,

(G) fellowships and stipends, and

(H) annuity payments;

(iv) at the discretion of the court, the court may attribute, or impute income from, such other resources as may be available to the parent, including, but not limited to:

(A) non-income producing assets,

(B) meals, lodging, memberships, automobiles or other perquisites that are provided as part of compensation for employment to the extent that such perquisites constitute expenditures for personal use, or which expenditures directly or indirectly confer personal economic benefits,

(C) fringe benefits provided as part of compensation for employment, and

(D) money, goods, or services provided by relatives and friends;

(v) an amount imputed as income based upon the parent's former resources or income, if the court determines that a parent has reduced resources or income in order to reduce or avoid the parent's obligation for child support;

(vi) to the extent not already included in gross income in clauses (i) and (ii) of this subparagraph, the following self-employment deductions attributable to self-employment carried on by the taxpayer:

(A) any depreciation deduction greater than depreciation calculated on a straight-line basis for the purpose of determining business income or investment credits, and

(B) entertainment and travel allowances deducted from business income to the extent said allowances reduce personal expenditures;

(vii) the following shall be deducted from income prior to applying the provisions of paragraph (c) of this subdivision:

(A) unreimbursed employee business expenses except to the extent said expenses reduce personal expenditures,

(B) alimony or maintenance actually paid to a spouse not a party to the instant action pursuant to court order or validly executed written agreement,

(C) alimony or maintenance actually paid or to be paid to a spouse that is a party to the instant action pursuant to an existing court order or contained in the order to be entered by the court, or pursuant to a validly executed written agreement, provided the order or agreement provides for a specific adjustment, in accordance with this subdivision, in the amount of child support payable upon the termination of alimony or maintenance to such spouse,

(D) child support actually paid pursuant to court order or written agreement on behalf of any child for whom the parent has a legal duty of support and who is not subject to the instant action,

(E) public assistance,

(F) supplemental security income,

(G) New York City or Yonkers income or earnings taxes actually paid, and

(H) Federal Insurance Contributions Act (FICA) taxes actually paid.

(6) "Self-support reserve" shall mean one hundred thirty-five percent of the poverty income guidelines amount for a single person as reported by the federal Department of Health and Human Services. For the calendar year nineteen hundred eighty-nine, the self-support reserve shall be eight thousand sixty-five dollars. On March first of each year, the self-support reserve shall be revised to reflect the annual updating of the poverty income guidelines as reported by the federal Department of Health and Human Services for a single person household.

(c) The amount of the basic child support obligation shall be determined in accordance with the provision of this paragraph:

(1) The court shall determine the combined parental income.

(2) The court shall multiply the combined parental income up to eighty thousand dollars by the appropriate child support percentage and such amount shall be prorated in the same proportion as each parent's income is to the combined parental income.

(3) Where the combined parental income exceeds the dollar amount set forth in subparagraph two of this paragraph, the court shall determine the amount of child support for the amount of the combined parental income in excess of such dollar amount through consideration of the factors set forth in paragraph (f) of this subdivision and/or the child support percentage.

(4) Where the custodial parent is working, or receiving elementary or secondary education, or higher education or vocational training which the court determines will lead to employment, and incurs child care expenses as a result thereof, the court shall determine reasonable child care expenses and such child care expenses, where incurred, shall be prorated in the same proportion as each parent's income is to the combined parental income. Each parent's pro rata share of the child care expenses shall be separately stated and added to the sum of subparagraphs two and three of this paragraph.

(5) The court shall prorate each parent's share of future reasonable health care expenses of the child not covered by insurance in the same proportion as each parent's income is to the combined parental income. The noncustodial parent's pro rata share of such health care expenses shall be paid in a manner determined by the court, including direct payment to the health care provider.

(6) Where the court determines that the custodial parent is seeking work and incurs child care expenses as a result thereof, the court may determine reasonable child care expenses and may apportion the same between the custodial and noncustodial parent. The noncustodial parent's share of such expenses shall be separately stated and paid in a manner determined by the court.

(7) Where the court determines, having regard for the circumstances of the case and of the respective parties and in the best interests of the child, and as justice requires, that the present or future provision of post-secondary, private, special, or enriched education for the child is appropriate, the court may award educational expenses. The noncustodial parent shall pay educational expenses, as awarded, in a manner determined by the court, including direct payment to the educational provider.

(d) Notwithstanding the provisions of paragraph (c) of this subdivision, where the annual amount of the basic child support obligation would reduce the noncustodial parent's income below the poverty income guidelines amount for a single person as reported by the federal department of health and human services, the basic child support obligation shall be twenty-five dollars per month or the difference between the noncustodial parent's income and the self-support reserve, whichever is greater.

Notwithstanding the provisions of paragraph (c) of this subdivision, where the annual amount of the basic child support obligation would reduce the noncustodial parent's income below the self-support reserve but not below the poverty income guidelines amount for a single person as reported by the federal department of health and human services, the basic child support obligation shall be fifty dollars per month or the difference between the noncustodial parent's income and the self-support reserve, whichever is greater.

(e) Where a parent is or may be entitled to receive nonrecurring payments from extraordinary sources not otherwise considered as income pursuant to this section, including but not limited to:

(1) Life insurance policies;

(2) Discharges of indebtedness;

(3) Recovery of bad debts and delinquency amounts;

(4) Gifts and inheritances; and

(5) Lottery winnings, the court, in accordance with paragraphs (c), (d) and (f) of this subdivision may allocate a proportion of the same to child support, and such amount shall be paid in a manner determined by the court.

(f) The court shall calculate the basic child support obligation, and the noncustodial parent's pro rata share of the basic child support obligation. Unless the court finds that the noncustodial parents's pro-rata share of the basic child support obligation is unjust or inappropriate, which finding shall be based upon consideration of the following factors:

(1) The financial resources of the custodial and noncustodial parent, and those of the child;

(2) The physical and emotional health of the child and his/her special needs and aptitudes;

(3) The standard of living the child would have enjoyed had the marriage or household not been dissolved;

(4) The tax consequences to the parties;

(5) The nonmonetary contributions that the parents will make toward the care and well-being of the child;

(6) The educational needs of either parent;

(7) A determination that the gross income of one parent is substantially less than the other parent's gross income;

(8) The needs of the children of the noncustodial parent for whom the noncustodial parent is providing support who are not subject to the instant action and whose support has not been deducted from income pursuant to subclause (d) of clause (vii) of subparagraph five of paragraph (b) of this subdivision, and the financial resources of any person obligated to support such children, provided, however, that this factor may apply only if the resources available to support such children are less than the resources available to support the children who are subject to the instant action;

(9) Provided that the child is not on public assistance (i) extraordinary expenses incurred by the noncustodial parent in exercising visitation, or (ii) expenses incurred by the noncustodial parent in extended visitation provided that the custodial parent's expenses are substantially reduced as a result thereof; and

(10) Any other factors the court determines are relevant in each case, the court shall order the noncustodial parent to pay his or her pro rata share of the basic child support

obligation, and may order the noncustodial parent to pay an amount pursuant to paragraph (e) of this subdivision.

(g) Where the court finds that the noncustodial parent's pro rata share of the basic child support obligation is unjust or inappropriate, the court shall order the noncustodial parent to pay such amount of child support as the court finds just and appropriate, and the court shall set forth, in a written order, the factors it considered; the amount of each party's pro rata share of the basic child support obligation; and the reasons that the court did not order the basic child support obligation. Such written order may not be waived by either party or counsel; provided, however, and notwithstanding any other provision of law, the court shall not find that the noncustodial parent's pro rata share of such obligation is unjust or inappropriate on the basis that such share exceeds the portion of a public assistance grant which is attributable to a child or children. In no instance shall the court order child support below twenty-five dollars per month. Where the noncustodial parent's income is less than or equal to the poverty income guidelines amount for a single person as reported by the federal department of health and human services, unpaid child support arrears in excess of five hundred dollars shall not accrue.

(h) A validly executed agreement or stipulation voluntarily entered into between the parties after the effective date of this subdivision presented to the court for incorporation in an order or judgment shall include a provision stating that the parties have been advised of the provisions of this subdivision, and that the basic child support obligation provided for therein would presumptively result in the correct amount of child support to be awarded. In the event that such agreement or stipulation deviates from the basic child support obligation, the agreement or stipulation must specify the amount that such basic child support obligation would have been and the reason or reasons that such agreement or stipulation does not provide for payment of that amount. Such provision may not be waived by either party or counsel. Nothing contained in this subdivision shall be construed to alter the rights of the parties to voluntarily enter into validly executed agreements or stipulations which deviate from the basic child support obligation provided such agreements or stipulations comply with the provisions of this paragraph. The court shall, however, retain discretion with respect to child support pursuant to this section. Any court order or judgment incorporating a validly executed agreement or stipulation which deviates from the basic child support obligation shall set forth the court's reasons for such deviation.

(i) Where either or both parties are unrepresented, the court shall not enter an order or judgment other than a temporary order pursuant to section two hundred thirty-seven of this article, that includes a provision for child support unless the unrepresented party or parties have received a copy of the child support standards chart promulgated by the commissioner of social services pursuant to subdivision two of section one hundred eleven-i of the social services law. Where either party is in receipt of child support enforcement services through the local social services district, the local social services district child support enforcement unit shall advise such party of the amount derived from application of the child support percentage and that such amount serves as a starting point for the determination of the child support award, and shall provide such party with a copy of the child support standards chart. In no instance shall the court approve any voluntary support agreement or compromise that includes an amount for child support less than twenty-five dollars per month.

(j) In addition to financial disclosure required in section two hundred thirty-six of this article, the court may require that the income and/or expenses of either party be verified with documentation including, but not limited to, past and present income tax returns, employer statements, pay stubs, corporate, business, or partnership books and records, corporate and business tax returns, and receipts for expenses or such other means of verification as the court determines appropriate. Nothing herein shall affect any party's right to pursue discovery pursuant to this chapter, the civil practice law and rules, or the family court act.

(k) When a party has defaulted and/or the court is otherwise presented with insufficient evidence to determine gross income, the court shall order child support based upon the needs or standard of living of the child, whichever is greater. Such order may be retroactively modified upward, without a showing of change in circumstances.

(l) In any action or proceeding for modification of an order of child support existing prior to the effective date of this paragraph, brought pursuant to this article, the child support standards set forth in this subdivision shall not constitute a change of circumstances warranting modification of such support order; provided, however, that where the circumstances warrant modification of such order, or where an adjustment of a child support order is sought by the support collection unit or either of the parties pursuant to subdivision twelve of section one hundred eleven-h of the social services law, or subdivision three of section four hundred thirteen of the family court act or subdivision four of section two hundred forty of the domestic relations law, such standards shall apply. In applying such standards, when the order to be modified incorporates by reference or merges with a validly executed separation agreement or stipulation of settlement, the court may consider, in addition to the factors set forth in paragraph (f) of this subdivision, the provisions of such agreement or stipulation concerning property distribution, distributive award and/or maintenance in determining whether the amount calculated by using the standards would be unjust or inappropriate.

2. a. An order directing payment of money for child support shall be enforceable pursuant to section fifty-two hundred forty-one or fifty-two hundred forty-two of the civil practice law and rules or in any other manner provided by law. Such orders or judgments for child support and maintenance shall also be enforceable pursuant to article fifty-two of the civil practice law and rules upon a debtor's default as such term is defined in paragraph seven of subdivision (a) of section fifty-two hundred forty-one of the civil practice law and rules. The establishment of a default shall be subject to the procedures established for the determination of a mistake of fact for income executions pursuant to subdivision (e) of section fifty-two hundred forty-one of the civil practice law and rules. For the purposes of enforcement of child support orders or combined spousal and child support orders pursuant to section five thousand two hundred forty-one of the civil practice law and rules, a "default" shall be deemed to include amounts arising from retroactive support.

b. (1) When a child receiving support is a public assistance recipient, or the order of support is being enforced or is to be enforced pursuant to section one hundred eleven-g of the social services law, the court shall direct that the child support payments be made to the support collection unit. Unless (i) the court finds and sets forth in writing the reasons that there is good cause not to require immediate income withholding; or (ii) when the child is not in receipt of public assistance, a written agreement providing for an alternative arrangement has been reached between the parties, the support collection unit shall issue an income execution immediately for child support or combined maintenance and child support, and may issue an execution for medical support enforcement in accordance with the provisions of the order of support. Such written agreement may include an oral stipulation made on the record resulting in a written order. For purposes of this paragraph, good cause shall mean substantial harm to the debtor. The absence of an arrearage or the mere issuance of an income execution shall not constitute good cause. When an immediate income execution or an execution for medical support enforcement is issued by the support collection unit, such income execution shall be issued pursuant to section five thousand two hundred forty-one of the civil practice law and rules, except that the provisions thereof relating to mistake of fact, default and any other provisions which are not relevant to the issuance of an income execution pursuant to this paragraph shall not apply; provided, however, that if the support collection unit makes an error in the issuance of an income execution pursuant to this paragraph, and such error is to the detriment of the debtor, the support collection unit shall have thirty days after notification by the debtor to correct the error. Where permitted under federal law and where the record of the proceedings contains such information, such order shall include on its face the social security number and the name and address of the employer, if any, of the person chargeable with support; provided, however, that failure to comply with this requirement shall not invalidate such order. When the court determines that there is good cause not to immediately issue an income execution or when the parties agree to an alternative arrangement as provided in this paragraph, the court shall provide expressly in the order of support that the support collection unit shall not issue an immediate income execution. Notwithstanding any such order, the support collection unit shall issue an income execution for support enforcement when the debtor defaults on the support obligation, as defined in section five thousand two hundred forty-one of the civil practice law and rules.

(2) When the court issues an order of child support or combined child and spousal support on behalf of persons other than those in receipt of public assistance or in receipt of services pursuant to section one hundred eleven-g of the social services law, the court shall issue an income deduction order pursuant to subdivision (c) of section five thousand two hundred forty-two of the civil practice law and rules at the same time it issues the order of support. The court shall enter the income deduction order unless the court finds and sets forth in writing (i) the reasons that there is good cause not to require immediate income withholding; or (ii) that an agreement providing for an alternative arrangement has been reached between the parties. Such agreement may include a written agreement or an oral stipulation, made on the record, that results in a written order. For purposes of this paragraph, good cause shall mean substantial harm to the debtor. The absence of an arrearage or the mere issuance of an income deduction order shall not constitute good cause. Where permitted under federal law and where the record of the proceedings contains such information, such order shall include on its face the social security number and the name and address of the employer, if any, of the person chargeable with support; provided, however, that failure to comply with this requirement shall not invalidate the order. When the court determines that there is good cause not to issue an income deduction order immediately or when the parties agree to an alternative arrangement as provided in this paragraph, the court shall provide expressly in the order of support the basis for its decision and shall not issue an income deduction order.

c. Any order of support issued on behalf of a child in receipt of public assistance or child support services pursuant to section one hundred eleven-g of the social services law shall be subject to review and adjustment by the support collection unit pursuant to subdivision twelve of section one hundred eleven-h of the social services law. Such review and adjustment shall be in addition to any other activities undertaken by the support collection unit relating to the establishment, modification, and enforcement of support orders payable to such unit.

3. Order of protection. The court may make an order of protection in assistance or as a condition of any other order made under this section. The order of protection may set forth reasonable conditions of behavior to be observed for a specified time by any party. Such an order may require any party:

(1) to stay away from the home of the child or any other party;

(2) to permit a parent to visit the child at stated periods;

(3) to abstain from offensive conduct against the child or against the other parent or against any person to whom custody of the child is awarded;

(4) to give proper attention to the care of the home;

(5) to refrain from acts of commission or omission that tend to make the home not a proper place for the child; or

(6) to pay the reasonable counsel fees and disbursements involved in obtaining or enforcing the order of the person who is protected by such order if such order is issued or enforced.

An order of protection entered pursuant to this subdivision shall bear in a conspicuous manner, on the front page of said order, the language "order of protection issued pursuant to section two hundred forty of the domestic relations law." The absence of such language shall not affect the validity of such order. The presentation of a copy of such an order to any peace officer acting pursuant to his or her special duties, or police officer, shall constitute authority, for that officer to arrest a person when that person has violated the terms of such an order, and bring such person before the court and, otherwise, so far as lies within the officer's power, to aid in securing the protection such order was intended to afford.

An order of protection entered pursuant to this subdivision may be made in the final judgment in any matrimonial action or in a proceeding to obtain custody of or visitation with any child under this section, or by one or more orders from time to time before or subsequent to final judgment, or by both such order or orders and the final judgment. The order of protection may remain in effect after entry of a final matrimonial judgment and during the minority of any child whose custody or visitation is the subject of a provision of a final judgment or any order. An order of protection may be entered notwithstanding that the court for any reason whatsoever, other than lack of jurisdiction, refuses to grant the relief requested in the action or proceeding.

4. Adjustment of child support orders. Any party to a child support order issued on the behalf of a child in receipt of public assistance or child support services pursuant to section one hundred eleven-g of the social services law may make application for an adjustment of such order once every thirty-six months from the date such order was issued or from the date of the last review. A hearing on the adjustment of such order shall be granted pursuant to the provisions of this section. A new support order shall be issued upon a showing that as of the date of the application for adjustment the correct amount of child support as calculated pursuant to the provisions of this section would deviate by at least ten percent from the child support ordered in the last permanent support order of the court. Additionally, a new support order shall be issued upon a showing that the last permanent support order does not provide for the health care needs of the child through insurance or otherwise. Eligibility of the child for medical assistance shall not relieve any obligation the parties otherwise have to provide for the health care needs

of the child. Application for adjustment of a child support order shall be made on notice to all parties to the last permanent child support order of the court. In any case where a child support order or modification thereto was issued subsequent to September fifteenth, nineteen hundred eighty-nine, where the percentages for establishing the presumptively correct basic child support obligation pursuant to this section were not applied due to a finding by the court that such application was unjust or inappropriate, the court and the support collection unit shall consider, in establishing such adjustment, whether the factors which gave rise to the rebuttal of the application of such percentages still exist to the extent that such factors are known. Nothing herein shall be deemed in any way to limit, restrict, expand or impair the rights of any party to file for a modification of a child support order as is otherwise provided by law.

(1) Parties eligible for adjustment of child support orders shall receive notice of the right to review of such orders as provided for herein:

(a) All applications or petitions by the support collection unit or applications or petitions seeking support enforcement services through the support collection unit for the establishment, enforcement, violation or adjustment of child support orders shall on their face in conspicuous type state: NOTE: (i) A COURT ORDER OF SUPPORT RESULTING FROM A PROCEEDING COMMENCED BY THIS APPLICATION (PETITION) SHALL BE REVIEWED BY THE SUPPORT COLLECTION UNIT FOR SUBSEQUENT COMPLIANCE WITH THE CHILD SUPPORT STANDARDS ACT THIRTY-SIX MONTHS AFTER SUCH ORDER IS ISSUED UPON THE REQUEST OF ANY PARTY TO THE ORDER. SUCH REVIEW SHALL BE ON NOTICE TO BOTH PARTIES WHO SHALL HAVE THE RIGHT TO BE HEARD BT THE COURT AND TO PRESENT EVIDENCE IN SUPPORT OF OR IN OPPOSITION TO THE ADJUSTMENT FINDING.

(ii) PARTIES SEEKING SUPPORT FOR CHILDREN WHO ARE RECIPIENTS OF PUBLIC ASSISTANCE SHALL HAVE CHILD SUPPORT ORDERS REVIEWED EVERY THREE YEARS BY THE SUPPORT COLLECTION UNIT FOR ADJUSTMENT PURPOSES WITHOUT FURTHER APPLICATION OF ANY PARTY. ALL PARTIES WILL RECEIVE NOTICE OF ADJUSTMENT FINDINGS.

(iii) UPON THE FAILURE OF A PARTY TO PROVIDE A COMPLETED NET WORTH AFFIDAVIT, THE MOST RECENT FEDERAL TAX RETURN AND REPRESENTATIVE PAY STUB TO THE SUPPORT COLLECTION UNIT, THE STATE DEPARTMENT OF SOCIAL SERVICES SHALL BE ENTITLED TO CERTAIN TAX INFORMATION FROM THE STATE COMMISSIONER OF TAXATION AND FINANCE PURSUANT TO SECTION ONE HUNDRED SEVENTY-ONE-g OF THE TAX LAW AND SECTION ONE HUNDRED ELEVEN-c OF THE SOCIAL SERVICES LAW, WHICH THE SUPPORT COLLECTION UNIT MAY REVIEW AND USE TO INITIATE PROCEEDINGS TO ADJUST THE CHILD SUPPORT ORDER.

(b) All court orders of support payable through a support collection unit shall on their face in conspicuous type state: NOTE: (i) THIS ORDER OF CHILD SUPPORT SHALL BE REVIEWED BY THE SUPPORT COLLECTION UNIT FOR SUBSEQUENT COMPLIANCE WITH THE CHILD SUPPORT STANDARDS ACT THIRTY-SIX MONTHS AFTER THIS ORDER IS ISSUED UPON THE REQUEST OF ANY PARTY TO THE ORDER. UPON THE FINDING BY THE SUPPORT COLLECTION UNIT OF A BASIS FOR UPWARD ADJUSTMENT OF THIS COURT ORDER OF CHILD SUPPORT, A NEW PROPOSED ORDER AND FINDINGS IN SUPPORT THEREOF SHALL BE SENT TO THE PARTIES WHO SHALL HAVE THIRTY (30) DAYS TO

OBJECT IN WRITING THERETO TO THE COURT INDICATED ON SUCH PRO-POSED ORDER. UPON RECEIPT OF SUCH WRITTEN OBJECTION THE COURT SHALL SCHEDULE A HEARING AT WHICH THE PARTIES MAY BE PRESENT TO OFFER EVIDENCE IN SUPPORT OF OR IN OPPOSITION TO ADJUSTMENT OF THE CHILD SUPPORT ORDER.

(ii) RECIPIENTS OF PUBLIC ASSISTANCE PAYMENTS SHALL HAVE CHILD SUPPORT ORDERS REVIEWED EVERY THREE YEARS FOR ADJUSTMENT PURPOSES WITHOUT FURTHER APPLICATION OF ANY PARTY. ALL PARTIES WILL RECEIVE NOTICE OF ADJUSTMENT FINDINGS.

(iii) WHERE ANY PARTY FAILS TO PROVIDE A COMPLETED NET WORTH AFFIDAVIT, THE MOST RECENT FEDERAL TAX RETURN AND REPRESENTA-TIVE PAY STUB TO THE SUPPORT COLLECTION UNIT, THE STATE DEPART-MENT OF SOCIAL SERVICES SHALL BE ENTITLED TO CERTAIN TAX INFOR-MATION FROM THE STATE COMMISSIONER OF TAXATION AND FINANCE PURSUANT TO SECTION ONE HUNDRED SEVENTY-ONE-G OF THE TAX LAW AND SECTION ONE HUNDRED ELEVEN-C OF THE SOCIAL SERVICES LAW, WHICH SHALL BE SUBMITTED TO THE COURT, AND THE COURT SHALL USE SUCH INFORMATION TO ADJUST THE CHILD SUPPORT ORDER. WHERE TAX RETURN INFORMATION IS NOT AVAILABLE BY VOLUNTARY DISCLOSURE OR AS PROVIDED FOR HEREIN, THE SUPPORT COLLECTION UNIT SHALL ISSUE A PROPOSED CHILD SUPPORT ORDER BASED UPON THE NEEDS OR STANDARD OF LIVING OF THE CHILD, WHICHEVER IS GREATER, WHICH SHALL BE SUBMITTED TO THE COURT.

(c) First class mail notice to the parties pursuant to section one hundred eleven-h of the social services law.

(2) Upon receipt of an adjustment finding and where appropriate a proposed order in conformity with such finding filed by either party or by the support collection unit, a party shall have thirty days to submit to the court identified thereon written objections to such finding and proposed order. If objections are submitted by either party or by the support collection unit, a hearing shall be scheduled by the court on notice to the parties and the support collection unit, who then shall have the right to be heard by the court and to offer evidence in support of or in opposition to adjustment of the support order. If the court receives no written objection to the support order within thirty-five days of the mailing of the proposed order the clerk of the court shall immediately enter the order without further review, modification, or other prior action by the court or any judge or hearing examiner thereof, and the clerk shall immediately transmit copies of the order of support to the parties and to the support collection unit.

(3) A motion to vacate an order of support adjusted pursuant to this section may be made no later than forty-five days after an adjusted support order is executed by the court where no written objection to the proposed order has been timely received by the court. Such motion shall be granted only upon a determination by the court issuing such order that personal jurisdiction was not timely obtained over the moving party.

Added by Laws 1962, Ch. 313, from former CPA §§ 1140, 1155, 1164, 1170, 1170-b; amended by Laws 1963, Ch. 685; Laws 1976, Ch. 133; Laws 1980, Ch. 281, 645, eff. July 19, 1980, Ch. 530, eff. Aug. 23, 1980; amended by Laws 1981, Ch. 695, eff. Oct. 19, 1981; amended by Laws 1981, Ch. 416, eff. Aug. 6, 1981, added subd. 2(6); amended by Laws 1983, Ch. 347, eff. Aug. 22, 1983; added by Laws 1985, Ch. 809, eff. Nov. 1, 1985; amended by Laws 1986, Ch. 849, eff. Aug. 2, 1986; **amended** by Laws 1986, Ch. 892, eff. Aug. 2, 1986; **amended** by Laws 1988, Ch. 452, § 1, eff. Aug. 1, 1988; amended by Laws 1988, Ch. 457, § 9, eff. Aug. 1, 1988; **amended** by Laws 1989, Ch. 164, eff. Oct. 15, 1989; **amended** by Laws 1989, Ch. 567, § 6, eff. Sept. 15, 1989; **amended** by Laws 1990, Ch. 818, §§ 7, 8, eff. July 25, 1990, and applicable to all pending petitions, motions and applications for child support; **amended** by Laws 1990, Ch. 818, § 6, eff. Sept. 30, 1990; **amended** by Laws 1990, Ch. 818, § 9, eff. Nov. 1, 1990, and applicable to all pending petitions, motions and applications for child support; **amended** by Laws 1992, Ch. 41, §§ 141, 145, 146, eff. Apr. 2, 1992; **amended** by Laws 1993, Ch. 59, §§ 3, 4, 10, 23, eff. July 1, 1993; **amended** by § 17, adding new subd. (4) to DRL § 240; **amended** by § 24, adding new para. (c) to DRL § 240(2); **amended** by Laws 1993, Ch. 354, § 1, eff. July 1, 1993; **amended** by Laws 1994, Ch. 170, §§ 361-362, eff. June 15, 1994, and § 363, eff. June 9, 1994.

## § 240-a. Judgment or decree; additional provision.

In any action or proceeding brought under the provisions of this chapter wherein all or part of the relief granted is divorce or annulment of a marriage any interlocutory or final judgment or decree shall contain, as a part thereof, a provision that each party may resume the use of his or her premarriage surname or any other former surname.

Added by Laws 1973 Ch. 642, eff. July 11, 1973; **amended** by Laws 1982, Ch. 668, eff. July 22, 1982; **amended** by Laws 1985, Ch. 583, eff. Sept. 1, 1985.

## § 241. Interference with or withholding of visitation rights; alimony or maintenance suspension.

When it appears to the satisfaction of the court that a custodial parent receiving alimony or maintenance pursuant to an order, judgment or decree of a court of competent jurisdiction has wrongfully interfered with or withheld visitation rights provided by such order, judgment or decree, the court in its discretion, may suspend such payments or cancel any arrears that may have accrued during the time that visitation rights have been or are being interfered with or withheld. Nothing in this section shall constitute a defense in any court to an application to enforce payment of child support or grounds for the cancellation of arrears for child support.

Added by Laws 1978, Ch. 232, eff. June 5, 1978; **amended** by Laws 1980, Ch. 281, eff. July 19, 1980; **amended** by Laws 1986, Ch. 892, eff. Aug. 5, 1986.

## § 242. Final judgment in action to annul a voidable marriage or for divorce.

*Repealed by Laws 1968, Ch. 645, eff. June 16, 1968.*

## § 243. Security for payments by defendant in action for divorce, separation or annulment; sequestration.

Where a judgment rendered or an order made in an action in this state for divorce, separation or annulment, or for a declaration of nullity of a void marriage, or a judgment rendered in another state for divorce upon any of the grounds provided in section one hundred seventy of this chapter, or for separation or separate support and maintenance for any of the causes specified in section two hundred, or for relief, however designated, granted upon grounds which in this state would be grounds for annulment of marriage

# ARTICLE 5–A

# UNIFORM CHILD CUSTODY JURISDICTION ACT

*(Article 5-A was added by Laws 1977, Ch. 493, eff. Sept. 1, 1978.)*

## SUMMARY OF ARTICLE

## § 75-a. Short title.

This article shall be known as the "Uniform Child Custody Jurisdiction Act."

## § 75-b. Purposes of article; construction of provisions.

1. The general purposes of this article are to:

(a) avoid jurisdictional competition and conflict with courts of other states in matters of child custody which have in the past resulted in the shifting of children from state to state with harmful effects on their well-being;

(b) promote cooperation with the courts of other states to the end that a custody decree is rendered in that state which can best decide the case in the interest of the child;

(c) assure that litigation concerning the custody of a child take place ordinarily in the state with which the child and his family have the closest connection and where significant evidence concerning his care, protection, training, and personal relationships is most readily available, and that courts of this state decline the exercise of jurisdiction when the child and his family have closer connection with another state;

(d) discourage continuing controversies over child custody in the interest of greater stability of home environment and of secure family relationships for the child;

(e) deter abductions and other unilateral removals of children undertaken to obtain custody awards;

(f) avoid re-litigation of custody decisions of other states in this state insofar as feasible;

(g) facilitate the enforcement of custody decrees of other states;

(h) promote and expand the exchange of information and other forms of mutual assistance between the courts of this state and those of other states concerned with the same child; and

(i) make uniform the law of those states which enact it.

2. This article shall be construed to promote the general purposes stated in this section.

## § 75-c.  Definitions.

As used in this article, the following terms have the following meanings:

1. "Contestant" means a person, including a parent, who claims a right to custody or visitation rights with respect to a child.

2. "Custody determination" means a court decision and court orders and instructions providing for the temporary or permanent custody of a child, including visitation rights.

3. "Custody proceeding" includes proceedings in which a custody determination is at issue or is one of several issues including any action or proceeding brought to annul a marriage or to declare the nullity of a void marriage, or for a separation, or for a divorce, but not including proceedings for adoption, child protective proceedings or proceedings for permanent termination of parental custody, or proceedings involving the guardianship and custody of neglected or dependent children, or proceedings initiated pursuant to section three hundred fifty-eight-a of the social services law.

4. "Decree" or "custody decree" means a custody determination contained in a judicial decree or order made in a custody proceeding, and includes an initial decree and a modification decree.

5. "Home state" means the state in which the child at the time of the commencement of the custody proceeding, has resided with his parents, a parent, or a person acting as parent, for at least six consecutive months. In the case of a child less than six months old at the time of the commencement of the proceeding, home state means the state in which the child has resided with any of such persons for a majority of the time since birth.

6. "Initial decree" means the first custody decree concerning a particular child.

7. "Modification decree" means a custody decree which modifies or replaces a prior decree, whether made by the court which rendered the prior decree or by another court.

8. "Physical custody" means actual possession and control of a child.

9. "Person acting as parent" means a person, other than a parent, who has physical custody of a child and who has either been awarded custody by a court or claims a right to custody.

10. "State" means any state, territory, or possession of the United States, the Commonwealth of Puerto Rico, and the District of Columbia.

## § 75-d. Jurisdiction to make child custody determinations.

1. A court of this state which is competent to decide child custody matters has jurisdiction to make a child custody determination by initial or modification decree only when:

(a) this state (i) is the home state of the child at the time of commencement of the custody proceeding, or (ii) had been the child's home state within six months before commencement of such proceeding and the child is absent from this state because of his removal or retention by a person claiming his custody or for other reasons, and a parent or person acting as parent continues to live in this state; or

(b) it is in the best interest of the child that a court of this state assume jurisdiction because (i) the child and his parents, or the child and at least one contestant, have a significant connection with this state, and (ii) there is within the jurisdiction of the court substantial evidence concerning the child's present or future care, protection, training, and personal relationships; or

(c) the child is physically present in this state and (i) the child has been abandoned or (ii) it is necessary in an emergency to protect the child; or

(d) (i) it appears that no other state would have jurisdiction under prerequisites substantially in accordance with paragraph (a), (b), or (c), or another state has declined to exercise jurisdiction on the ground that this state is the more appropriate forum to determine the custody of the child, and (ii) it is in the best interest of the child that this court assume jurisdiction.

2. Except under paragraphs (c) and (d) of subdivision one of this section, physical presence in this state of the child, or of the child and one of the contestants, is not alone sufficient to confer jurisdiction on a court of this state to make a child custody determination.

3. Physical presence of the child, while desirable, is not a prerequisite for jurisdiction to determine his custody.

## § 75-e. Notice and opportunity to be heard.

Before making a decree under this article, reasonable notice and opportunity to be heard shall be given to the contestants, any parent whose parental rights have not been previously terminated, and any person who has physical custody of the child. If any of these persons is outside the state, notice and opportunity to be heard shall be given pursuant to section seventy-five-f of this article. Any person who is given notice and an opportunity to be heard pursuant to this section shall be deemed a party to the proceeding for all purposes under this article.

## § 75-f. Notice to persons outside the state.

1. If a person cannot be personally served with notice within the state, the court shall require that such person be served in a manner reasonably calculated to give actual notice, as follows:

(a) by personal delivery outside the state in the manner prescribed in section three hundred thirteen of the civil practice law and rules;

(b) by any form of mail addressed to the person and requesting a receipt; or

(c) in such manner as the court, upon motion, directs, including publication, if service is impracticable under paragraph (a) or (b) of subdivision one of this section.

2. Notice under this section shall be served, mailed, delivered, or last published at least twenty days before any hearing in this state.

3. Proof of service outside the state shall be by affidavit of the individual who made the service, or in the manner prescribed by the order pursuant to which the service is made. If service is made by mail, proof may be a receipt signed by the addressee or other evidence of delivery to the addressee.

4. Notice is not required if a person submits to the jurisdiction of the court.

## § 75-g. Simultaneous proceedings in other states

1. A court of this state shall not exercise its jurisdiction under this article if at the time of filing the petition a proceeding concerning the custody of the child was pending in a court of another state exercising jurisdiction substantially in conformity with this article, unless the proceeding is stayed by the court of the other state because this state is a more appropriate forum or for other reasons.

2. Before hearing the petition in a custody proceeding the court shall examine the pleadings and other information supplied by the parties under section seventy-five-j of this article. If the court has reason to believe that proceedings may be pending in another state it shall direct an inquiry to the state court administrator or other appropriate official of the other state.

3. If the court is informed during the course of the proceeding that a proceeding concerning the custody of the child was pending in another state before the court assumed jurisdiction it shall stay the proceeding and communicate with the court in which the other proceeding is pending to the end that the issue may be litigated in the more appropriate forum and that information be exchanged in accordance with sections seventy-five-s through seventy-five-v of this article. If a court of this state has made a custody decree before being informed of a pending proceeding in a court of another state, it shall immediately inform that court of the fact. If the court is informed that a proceeding was commenced in another state after it assumed jurisdiction, it shall likewise inform the other court to the end that the issues may be litigated in the more appropriate forum.

## § 75-h. Inconvenient forum.

1. A court which has jurisdiction under this article to make an initial or modification decree may decline to exercise its jurisdiction any time before making a decree if it finds that it is an inconvenient forum to make a custody determination under the circumstances of the case and that a court of another state is a more appropriate forum.

2. A finding of inconvenient forum may be made upon the court's own motion or upon motion of a party or a guardian ad litem or other representative of the child.

3. In determining if it is an inconvenient forum, the court shall consider if it is in the interest of the child that another state assume jurisdiction. For this purpose it may take into account the following factors, among others, whether:

(a) another state is or recently was the child's home state;

(b) another state has a closer connection with the child and his family or with the child and one or more of the contestants;

(c) substantial evidence concerning the child's present or future care, protection, training, and personal relationships is more readily available in another state;

(d) the parties have agreed on another forum which is no less appropriate; and

(e) the exercise of jurisdiction by a court of this state would contravene any of the purposes stated in section seventy-five-b of this article.

4. Before determining whether to decline or retain jurisdiction the court may communicate with a court of another state and exchange information pertinent to the assumption of jurisdiction by either court with a view to assuring that jurisdiction will be exercised by the more appropriate court and that a forum will be available to the parties.

5. If the court finds that it is an inconvenient forum and that a court of another state is a more appropriate forum, it may dismiss the proceedings, or it may stay the proceedings upon condition that a custody proceeding be promptly commenced in another named state or upon any other conditions which may be just and proper, including the condition that a moving party stipulate his consent and submission to the jurisdiction of the other forum.

6. Where the court has jurisdiction of an action or proceeding brought to annul a marriage or to declare the nullity of a void marriage or for a separation or for a divorce, the court may decline to exercise jurisdiction of an application for a custody determination made therein while retaining jurisdiction of the matrimonial action.

7. If it appears to the court that it is clearly an inappropriate forum it may require the party who commenced the proceedings to pay, in addition to the costs of the proceedings in this state, necessary travel and other expenses, including attorneys' fees, incurred by other parties or their witnesses. Payment shall be made to the clerk of the court for remittance to the proper party.

8. Upon dismissal or stay of proceedings under this section the court shall inform the court found to be the more appropriate forum of such dismissal or stay, or if the court which would have jurisdiction in the other state is not certainly known, shall transmit the information to the court administrator or other appropriate official for forwarding to the appropriate court.

9. Any communication received from another state to the effect that its courts have made a finding of inconvenient forum because a court of this state is the more appropriate forum shall be filed with the clerk of the appropriate court. Upon assuming jurisdiction the court of this state shall inform the original court of this fact.

## § 75-i. Jurisdiction declined because of conduct.

1. If the petitioner for an initial decree has wrongfully taken the child from another state or has engaged in similar reprehensible conduct the court may decline to exercise jurisdiction if this is just and proper under the circumstances.

2. Unless required in the interest of the child, the court shall not exercise its jurisdiction to modify a custody decree of another state if the petitioner, without consent of the person entitled to custody, has improperly removed the child from the physical custody of the person entitled to custody or has improperly retained the child after a visit or other temporary relinquishment of physical custody. If the petitioner has violated any other provision of a custody decree of another state the court may decline to exercise its jurisdiction if this is just and proper under the circumstances.

3. In appropriate cases a court dismissing a petition under this section may charge the petitioner with necessary travel and other expenses, including attorneys' fees, incurred by other parties or their witnesses.

## § 75-j. Pleadings and affidavits; duty to inform court.

1. Except as provided in subdivisions four and five of this section, every party to a custody proceeding shall, in his or her first pleading or in an affidavit attached to that pleading, give information under oath as to the child's present address, the places where the child has lived within the' last five years, and the names and present addresses of the persons with whom the child has lived during that period. In this pleading or affidavit every party shall further declare under oath whether he or she:

(a) has participated as a party, witness, or in any other capacity in any other litigation concerning the custody of the same child in this or any other state;

(b) has information of any custody proceeding concerning the child pending in a court of this or any other state; and

(c) knows of any person not a party to the proceedings who has physical custody of the child or claims to have custody or visitation rights with respect to the child.

2. If the declaration as to any of the above items is in the affirmative the declarant shall give additional information under oath as required by the court. The court may examine the parties under oath as to details of the information furnished and as to other matters pertinent to the court's jurisdiction and the disposition of the case.

3. If, during the pendency of a custody proceeding, any party learns of another custody proceeding concerning the child in this or another state, he shall immediately inform the court of this fact.

4. In an action for divorce or separation, or to annul a marriage or declare the nullity of a void marriage, (a) where neither party is in default in appearance or pleading and the issue of custody is uncontested, the affidavit required by this section need not be submitted. In any other such action, such affidavit shall be submitted by the parties within twenty days after joinder of issue on the question of custody, or at the time application for a default judgment is made.

(b) Notwithstanding any other provision of law, if the party seeking custody of the child has resided or resides in special care home as defined in subdivision thirty-one of section two of the social services law, the present address of the child and the present address of the party seeking custody and the address of the special care home shall not be revealed.

(c) Notwithstanding any other provision of law, the court shall waive disclosure of the present and all prior addresses of the child or a party upon notice to the adverse party when such relief is necessary for the physical or emotional safety of a child or a party.

5. Notwithstanding any other provision of law, in any custody proceeding, the court shall waive disclosure of the present or a prior address of the child or a party when such relief is necessary for the physical or emotional safety of a child or a party. Application for an order waiving disclosure of the present or a prior address of the child or a party shall be on notice to all other parties, who shall have an opportunity to be heard. Provided, however, that in no case shall the address of a special care home, as defined in subdivision thirty-one of section two of the social services law, be disclosed.

Amended by Laws 1981, Ch. 416, eff. Aug. 6, 1981.

### § 75-k. Additional parties.

If the court learns from information furnished by the parties pursuant to section seventy-five-j of this article, or from other sources that a person not a party to the custody proceeding has physical custody of the child or claims to have custody or visitation rights with respect to the child, it shall order that person to be joined as a party and to be duly notified of the pendency of the proceeding and of his joinder as a party. If the person joined as a party is outside this state he shall be served with process or otherwise notified in accordance with section seventy-five-f of this article.

### § 75-l. Appearance of parties and the child.

1. The court may order any party to the proceeding who is in the state to appear personally before the court. If that party has physical custody of the child the court may order that he appear personally with the child.

2. If a party to the proceeding whose presence is desired by the court is outside the state with or without the child the court may order that the notice given under section seventy-five-f of this article include a statement directing that party to appear personally with or without the child and declaring that failure to appear may result in a decision adverse to that party.

3. If a party to the proceeding who is outside the state is directed to appear under subdivision two or desires to appear personally before the court with or without the child, the court may require another party to pay to the clerk of the court travel and other necessary expenses of the party so appearing and of the child if this is just and proper under the circumstances.

### § 75-m. Force and effect of custody decrees.

A custody decree rendered by a court of this state which had jurisdiction under section seventy-five-d of this article shall be binding upon all parties who have been personally served in this state or notified pursuant to section seventy-five-f of this article or who have submitted to the jurisdiction of the court, and who have been given an opportunity to be heard. As to these parties the custody decree is conclusive as to all issues of law and fact decided and as to the custody determination made unless and until that determination is modified pursuant to law, including the provisions of this article.

### § 75-n. Recognition of out-of-state custody decrees.

The courts of this state shall recognize and enforce an initial or modification decree of a court of another state which had assumed jurisdiction under statutory provisions substantially in accordance with this article or which was made under factual circumstances meeting the jurisdictional standards of this article, so long as the decree has not been modified in accordance with jurisdictional standards substantially similar to those of this article.

### § 75-o.  Modification of custody decree of another state.

1. If a court of another state has made a custody decree, a court of this state shall not modify that decree unless (1) it appears to the court of this state that the court which rendered the decree does not now have jurisdiction under jurisdictional prerequisites substantially in accordance with this article or has declined to assume jurisdiction to modify the decree and (2) the court of this state has jurisdiction.

2. If a court of this state is authorized under subdivision one of this section and section seventy-five-i of this article to modify a custody decree of another state, it shall give due consideration to the transcript of the record and other documents of all previous proceedings submitted to it in accordance with section seventy-five-v of this article.

### § 75-p.  Filing and enforcement of custody decree of another state.

1. A certified copy of a custody decree of another state may be filed in the office of the clerk of the supreme court or of the family court. The clerk shall treat the decree in the same manner as a custody decree of the supreme court or of the family court. A custody decree so filed has the same effect and shall be enforced in like manner as a custody decree rendered by a court of this state.

2. A person violating a custody decree of another state which makes it necessary to enforce the decree in this state may be required to pay necessary travel and other expenses, including attorneys' fees, incurred by the party entitled to the custody or his witnesses.

### § 75-q.  Certified copies of custody decrees.

The clerk of the supreme court or the family court, at the request of the court of another state or, upon payment of the appropriate fees, if any, at the request of a party to the custody proceeding, the attorney for a party or a representative of the child shall certify and forward a copy of the decree to that court or person.

### § 75-r.  Examination of witnesses outside the state.

In addition to other procedural devices available to a party, any party to the proceeding or a guardian ad litem or other representative of the child may examine witnesses, including parties and the child, in another state by deposition or otherwise in accordance with the applicable provisions of the civil practice law and rules.

### § 75-s.  Hearings and studies in another state; orders to appear.

1. A court of this state may request the appropriate court of another state to hold a hearing to adduce evidence, to order a party within its jurisdiction, to produce or give evidence under other procedures of that state, or to have social studies made with respect to the custody of a child involved in proceedings pending in the court of this state; and to forward to the court of this state certified copies of the transcript of the record of

the hearing, the evidence otherwise adduced, or any social studies prepared in compliance with the request. The cost of the services may be assessed against the parties.

2. A court of this state may request the appropriate court of another state to order a party to custody proceedings pending in the court of this state to appear in the proceedings, and if that party has physical custody of the child, to appear with the child. The request may state that travel and other necessary expenses of the party and of the child whose appearance is desired will be assessed against another party or will otherwise be paid.

### § 75-t.  Assistance to courts of other states.

1. Upon request of the court of another state the courts of this state which are competent to hear custody matters may order a party or witness in this state to appear at an examination to be conducted in the same manner as if such person were a party to or witness in an action pending in the supreme court. A certified copy of the deposition or the evidence otherwise adduced shall be forwarded by the clerk of the court to the court which requested it.

2. A person within the state may voluntarily give his testimony or statement for use in a custody proceeding outside this state.

3. Upon request of the court of another state a competent court of this state may order a person within the state to appear alone or with the child in a custody proceeding in another state. The court may condition compliance with the request upon assurance by the other state that travel and other necessary expenses will be advanced or reimbursed.

### § 75-u.  Preservation of evidence for use in other states.

In any custody proceeding in this state the court shall preserve the pleadings, orders and decrees, any record that has been made of its hearings, social studies, and other pertinent documents until the child reaches twenty-one years of age. Upon appropriate request of the court of another state the court shall forward to the other court certified copies of any or all of such documents.

### § 75-v.  Request for court records from another state.

If a custody decree has been rendered in another state concerning a child involved in a custody proceeding pending in a court of this state, the court of this state upon taking jurisdiction of the case shall request of the court of the other state a certified copy of the transcript of any court record and other documents mentioned in section seventy-five-u.

### § 75-w.  International application.

The general policies of this article extend to the international area. The provisions of this article relating to the recognition and enforcement of custody decrees of other states apply to custody decrees and decrees involving legal institutions similar in nature to custody institutions rendered by appropriate authorities of other nations if reasonable notice and opportunity to be heard were given to all affected persons.

## § 75-x.  Priority.

Upon the request of a party to a custody proceeding which raises a question of existence or exercise of jurisdiction under this article the case shall be given calendar priority and handled expeditiously.

## § 75-y.  Separability.

If any part of this article or the application thereof to any person or circumstance is adjudged invalid by a court of competent jurisdiction, such judgment shall not affect or impair the validity of the remainder of such article or the application thereof to other persons and circumstances.

## § 75-z.  Inconsistent provisions of other laws superseded.

Insofar as the provisions of this article are inconsistent with the provisions of any other law, general, special or local, the provisions of this article shall be controlling.

42 USC 1305
note.

SEC. 6. Sections 6 to 10 of this Act may be cited as the "Parental Kidnaping Prevention Act of 1980".

FINDINGS AND PURPOSES

28 USC 1738A
note.

SEC. 7. (a) The Congress finds that—

(1) there is a large and growing number of cases annually involving disputes between persons claiming rights of custody and visitation of children under the laws, and in the courts, of different States, the District of Columbia, the Commonwealth of Puerto Rico, and the territories and possessions of the United States;

(2) the laws and practices by which the courts of those jurisdictions determine their jurisdiction to decide such disputes, and the effect to be given the decisions of such disputes by the courts of other jurisdictions, are often inconsistent and conflicting;

(3) those characteristics of the law and practice in such cases, along with the limits imposed by a Federal system on the authority of each such jurisdiction to conduct investigations and

94 STAT. 3568

37

take other actions outside its own boundaries, contribute to a tendency of parties involved in such disputes to frequently resort to the seizure, restraint, concealment, and interstate transportation of children, the disregard of court orders, excessive relitigation of cases, obtaining of conflicting orders by the courts of various jurisdictions, and interstate travel and communication that is so·expensive and time consuming as to disrupt their occupations and commercial activities; and

(4) among the results of those conditions and activities are the failure of the courts of such jurisdictions to give full faith and credit to the judicial proceedings of the other jurisdictions, the deprivation of rights of liberty and property without due process of law, burdens on commerce among such jurisdictions and with foreign nations, and harm to the welfare of children and their parents and other custodians.

(b) For those reasons it is necessary to establish a national system for locating parents and children who travel from one such jurisdiction to another and are concealed in connection with such disputes, and to establish national standards under which the courts of such jurisdictions will determine their jurisdiction to decide such disputes and the effect to be given by each such jurisdiction to such decisions by the courts of other such jurisdictions. National system of locating parents, establishment.

(c) The general purposes of sections 6 to 10 of this Act are to—

(1) promote cooperation between State courts to the end that a determination of custody and visitation is rendered in the State which can best decide the case in the interest of the child;

(2) promote and expand the exchange of information and other forms of mutual assistance between States which are concerned with the same child;

(3) facilitate the enforcement of custody and visitation decrees of sister States;

(4) discourage continuing interstate controversies over child custody in the interest of greater stability of home environment and of secure family relationships for the child;

(5) avoid jurisdictional competition and conflict between State courts in matters of child custody and visitation which have in the past resulted in the shifting of children from State to State with harmful effects on their well-being; and

(6) deter interstate abductions and other unilateral removals of children undertaken to obtain custody and visitation awards.

FULL FAITH AND CREDIT GIVEN TO CHILD CUSTODY DETERMINATIONS

SEC. 8. (a) Chapter 115 of title 28, United States Code, is amended by adding immediately. after section 1738 the following new section: 28 USC 1731 *et seq.*

"§1738A. Full faith and credit given to child custody determinations 28 USC 1738A.

"(a) The appropriate authorities of every State shall enforce according to its terms, and shall not modify except as provided in subsection (f) of this section, any child custody determination made consistently with the provisions of this section by a court of another State.

"(b) As used in this section, the term— Definitions.

"(1) 'child' means a person under the age of eighteen;

"(2) 'contestant' means a person, including a parent, who claims a right to custody or visitation of a child;

"(3) 'custody determination' means a judgment, decree, or other order of a court providing for the custody or visitation of a child, and includes permanent and temporary orders, and initial orders and modifications;

"(4) 'home State' means the State in which, immediately preceding the time involved, the child lived with his parents, a parent, or a person acting as parent, for at least six consecutive months, and in the case of a child less than six months old, the State in which the child lived from birth with any of such persons. Periods of temporary absence of any of such persons are counted as part of the six-month or other period;

"(5) 'modification' and 'modify' refer to a custody determination which modifies, replaces, supersedes, or otherwise is made subsequent to, a prior custody determination concerning the same child, whether made by the same court or not;

"(6) 'person acting as a parent' means a person, other than a parent, who has physical custody of a child and who has either been awarded custody by a court or claims a right to custody;

"(7) 'physical custody' means actual possession and control of a child; and

"(8) 'State' means a State of the United States, the District of Columbia, the Commonwealth of Puerto Rico, or a territory or possession of the United States.

"(c) A child custody determination made by a court of a State is consistent with the provisions of this section only if—

"(1) such court has jurisdiction under the law of such State; and

"(2) one of the following conditions is met:

"(A) such State (i) is the home State of the child on the date of the commencement of the proceeding, or (ii) had been the child's home State within six months before the date of the commencement of the proceeding and the child is absent from such State because of his removal or retention by a contestant or for other reasons, and a contestant continues to live in such State;

"(B)(i) it appears that no other State would have jurisdiction under subparagraph (A), and (ii) it is in the best interest of the child that a court of such State assume jurisdiction because (I) the child and his parents, or the child and at least one contestant, have a significant connection with such State other than mere physical presence in such State, and (II) there is available in such State substantial evidence concerning the child's present or future care, protection, training, and personal relationships;

"(C) the child is physically present in such State and (i) the child has been abandoned, or (ii) it is necessary in an emergency to protect the child because he has been subjected to or threatened with mistreatment or abuse;

"(D)(i) it appears that no other State would have jurisdiction under subparagraph (A), (B), (C), or (E), or another State has declined to exercise jurisdiction on the ground that the State whose jurisdiction is in issue is the more appropriate forum to determine the custody of the child, and (ii) it is in the best interest of the child that such court assume jurisdiction; or

"(E) the court has continuing jurisdiction pursuant to subsection (d) of this section.

"(d) The jurisdiction of a court of a State which has made a child custody determination consistently with the provisions of this section continues as long as the requirement of subsection (c)(1) of this

94 STAT. 3570

section continues to be met and such State remains the residence of the child or of any contestant.

"(e) Before a child custody determination is made, reasonable notice and opportunity to be heard shall be given to the contestants, any parent whose parental rights have not been previously terminated and any person who has physical custody of a child.

"(f) A court of a State may modify a determination of the custody of the same child made by a court of another State, if—

"(1) it has jurisdiction to make such a child custody determination; and

"(2) the court of the other State no longer has jurisdiction, or it has declined to exercise such jurisdiction to modify such determination.

"(g) A court of a State shall not exercise jurisdiction in any proceeding for a custody determination commenced during the pendency of a proceeding in a court of another State where such court of that other State is exercising jurisdiction consistently with the provisions of this section to make a custody determination.".

(b) The table of sections at the beginning of chapter 115 of title 28, United States Code, is amended by inserting after the item relating to section 1738 the following new item:

*Ante,* p. 3569.

"1738A. Full faith and credit given to child custody determinations.".

(c) In furtherance of the purposes of section 1738A of title 28, United States Code, as added by subsection (a) of this section, State courts are encouraged to—

28 USC 1738A note.

(1) afford priority to proceedings for custody determinations; and

(2) award to the person entitled to custody or visitation pursuant to a custody determination which is consistent with the provisions of such section 1738A, necessary travel expenses, attorneys' fees, costs of private investigations, witness fees or expenses, and other expenses incurred in connection with such custody determination in any case in which—

*Ante,* p. 3569.

(A) a contestant has, without the consent of the person entitled to custody or visitation pursuant to a custody determination which is consistent with the provisions of such section 1738A, (i) wrongfully removed the child from the physical custody of such person, or (ii) wrongfully retained the child after a visit or other temporary relinquishment of physical custody; or

(B) the court determines it is appropriate.

USE OF FEDERAL PARENT LOCATOR SERVICE IN CONNECTION WITH THE ENFORCEMENT OR DETERMINATION OF CHILD CUSTODY AND IN CASES OF PARENTAL KIDNAPING OF A CHILD

SEC. 9. (a) Section 454 of the Social Security Act is amended—

42 USC 654.

(1) by striking out "and" at the end of paragraph (15);

(2) by striking out the period at the end of paragraph (16) and inserting in lieu thereof "; and"; and

(3) by inserting after paragraph (16) the following new paragraph:

"(17) in the case of a State which has in effect an agreement with the Secretary entered into pursuant to section 463 for the use of the Parent Locator Service established under section 453, to accept and transmit to the Secretary requests for information authorized under the provisions of the agreement to be furnished by such Service to authorized persons, and to impose and collect (in accordance with

*Post,* p. 3572.
42 USC 653.

take other actions outside its own boundaries, contribute to a tendency of parties involved in such disputes to frequently resort to the seizure, restraint, concealment, and interstate transportation of children, the disregard of court orders, excessive relitigation of cases, obtaining of conflicting orders by the courts of various jurisdictions, and interstate travel and communication that is so· expensive and time consuming as to disrupt their occupations and commercial activities; and

(4) among the results of those conditions and activities are the failure of the courts of such jurisdictions to give full faith and credit to the judicial proceedings of the other jurisdictions, the deprivation of rights of liberty and property without due process of law, burdens on commerce among such jurisdictions and with foreign nations, and harm to the welfare of children and their parents and other custodians.

(b) For those reasons it is necessary to establish a national system for locating parents and children who travel from one such jurisdiction to another and are concealed in connection with such disputes, and to establish national standards under which the courts of such jurisdictions will determine their jurisdiction to decide such disputes and the effect to be given by each such jurisdiction to such decisions by the courts of other such jurisdictions.

*National system of locating parents, establishment.*

(c) The general purposes of sections 6 to 10 of this Act are to—

(1) promote cooperation between State courts to the end that a determination of custody and visitation is rendered in the State which can best decide the case in the interest of the child;

(2) promote and expand the exchange of information and other forms of mutual assistance between States which are concerned with the same child;

(3) facilitate the enforcement of custody and visitation decrees of sister States;

(4) discourage continuing interstate controversies over child custody in the interest of greater stability of home environment and of secure family relationships for the child;

(5) avoid jurisdictional competition and conflict between State courts in matters of child custody and visitation which have in the past resulted in the shifting of children from State to State with harmful effects on their well-being; and

(6) deter interstate abductions and other unilateral removals of children undertaken to obtain custody and visitation awards.

FULL FAITH AND CREDIT GIVEN TO CHILD CUSTODY DETERMINATIONS

SEC. 8. (a) Chapter 115 of title 28, United States Code, is amended by adding immediately after section 1738 the following new section:

*28 USC 1731 et seq.*

"§1738A. Full faith and credit given to child custody determinations

*28 USC 1738A.*

"(a) The appropriate authorities of every State shall enforce according to its terms, and shall not modify except as provided in subsection (f) of this section, any child custody determination made consistently with the provisions of this section by a court of another State.

"(b) As used in this section, the term—

*Definitions.*

"(1) 'child' means a person under the age of eighteen;

"(2) 'contestant' means a person, including a parent, who claims a right to custody or visitation of a child;

"(3) 'custody determination' means a judgment, decree, or other order of a court providing for the custody or visitation of a

tion with respect to the unlawful taking or restraint of a child.".

(c) Section 455(a) of such Act is amended by adding after paragraph (3) the following: "except that no amount shall be paid to any State on account of amounts expended to carry out an agreement which it has entered into pursuant to section 463.". 42 USC 655.

(d) No agreement entered into under section 463 of the Social Security Act shall become effective before the date on which section 1738A of title 28, United States Code (as added by this title) becomes effective.

*Ante*, p. 3572.
Effective date.
42 USC 663 note.
*Ante*, p. 3569.

## PARENTAL KIDNAPING

SEC. 10. (a) In view of the findings of the Congress and the purposes of sections 6 to 10 of this Act set forth in section 302, the Congress hereby expressly declares its intent that section 1073 of title 18, United States Code, apply to cases involving parental kidnaping and interstate or international flight to avoid prosecution under applicable State felony statutes. 18 USC 1073 note. 42 USC 502.

(b) The Attorney General of the United States, not later than 120 days after the date of the enactment of this section (and once every 6 months during the 3-year period following such 120-day period), shall submit a report to the Congress with respect to steps taken to comply with the intent of the Congress set forth in subsection (a). Each such report shall include—

(1) data relating to the number of applications for complaints under section 1073 of title 18, United States Code, in cases involving parental kidnaping;

(2) data relating to the number of complaints issued in such cases; and

(3) such other information as may assist in describing the activities of the Department of Justice in conformance with such intent.

## TECHNICAL AMENDMENTS AND AMENDMENTS RELATING TO CHILD SUPPORT AUDITS

SEC. 11. (a)(1) Section 127(a)(1) of the Food Stamp Act Amendments of 1980 (Public Law 96–249), is amended by striking out "Subsection (i) of section 6103" and inserting in lieu thereof "Subsection (l) of section 6103". *Ante*, p. 365.

(2)(A) Section 408(a)(1) of the Social Security Disability Amendments of 1980 (Public Law 96–265), is amended by striking out (in the new paragraph added thereby to subsection (l) of section 6103 of the Internal Revenue Code of 1954) "(7) Disclosure" and inserting in lieu thereof "(8) Disclosure". *Ante*, p. 468.

(B) Section 408(a)(2) of the Social Security Disability Amendments of 1980 is amended—

(i) in subparagraph (A), by—

(I) striking out "(l)(1) or (4)(B) or (5)" and inserting in lieu thereof "(l)(1), (4)(B), (5), or (7)", and

(II) striking out "(l)(1), (4)(B), (5), or (7)" and inserting in lieu thereof "(l)(1), (4)(B), (5), (7), or (8)";

(ii) in subparagraph (B), by—

(I) striking out "(l) (3) or (6)" and inserting in lieu thereof "(l) (3), (6), or (7)", and

(II) striking out "(l) (3), (6), or (7)" and inserting in lieu thereof "(l) (3), (6), (7), or (8)";

(iii) in subparagraph (C), by—

## 94 STAT. 3573

**NOTES**

44

3

# VISITATION AND THE DEVELOPMENTAL RIGHTS OF YOUNG CHILDREN

Michelle Ascher Dunn, C.S.W.

# Visitation and the Developmental Rights of Young Children
by
Michelle Ascher Dunn, M.A., C.S.W.

When parents of young children separate, the essential features of normal development are immediately challenged. The complex sequence that culminates in the child's independent identity and healthy self esteem is called separation-individuation by developmental psychologists. Under non-divorced circumstances, separation-individuation generally unfolds gradually and therefore is not thrown into disorganization. To the eyes of a child psychologist, the child's development has the lawfulness and chronological intricacy of a space ship launch. The dissolution of a family shatters this natural sequence, especially if parents selfishly insist on legal rights that clash with the child's developmental needs. Parents, attorneys and judges need to be acutely attuned to the sequence of normal child development so that custody and visitation issues may be resolved against the backdrop of the child's psychological requirements.

The normal separation-individuation process can be understood by comparing it to the phenomena of cell division. The child begins psychologically and organically as one with the mother and gradually divides in such a way as to gain independent boundaries and a sense of self. This stable sense of identity is as important to a person's psychological health as the immune system is to their physical health. Sound early psychological development buffers the slings and arrows of absence, illness, toxic emotions and all manner of misfortune. It takes about five years for a child to become a person in his or her own right, endowed with a degree of psychological immunity against stress. During this time it is critical that well intentioned caretakers do not interfere with this process, since the child will have to rely on his or her psychological resources for a lifetime.

The process leading to a healthy identity is long and involves predictable interactions with both parents. Knowledge of separation-individuation will serve as an invaluable map to all in the legal community working towards the best interest of the child.

## Birth to Three Months

During the first 3 months of life, the infant is establishing sleeping and eating patterns and is getting ready for the deep contact relationship which has been called, symbiosis. Visitation with the non-custodial parents needs to be mostly on baby-time and in the baby's nursery in order to satisfy the babies needs. The baby is just beginning to map out the outlines of crib, day/night, breast/bottle, and so on. For the baby, the first three months of life may be compared to the beginning chapters of Genesis. During this time, the baby lays down the basic patterns of organization. Infants have an inborn defense to protect from excess stimulus, and they guard their inner peace at all costs since the psychological tasks with which they are grappling are so large..

The important developmental need of the baby is not to be traumatically over-stimulated. When the father comes into the nursery and suddenly removes the child he is unwittingly challenging the child's barrier against stimulation. I call this the "milk shake phenomena" because the child's patterns are shaken up and derailed from their newly formed tracks by a well intentioned father intent on quality time.

Visitation during this early period should generally be in the nursery and on the baby's schedule. The visiting parent can feed, rock, change, bathe and coo to the newborn. To be in synch with the developmental needs of the child, the visit should be scheduled during a time when the infant is characteristically awake and alert. Awakening the baby to make emotional contact satisfies the parent at the expense of the baby.

### Three months to Five months

The stimulus barrier recedes and the baby turns more to the outside world by about the third month. Children of this age smile when they see a friendly face. There is an increase in awareness of and tolerance for stimulation. Now the parents must provide the protective shield that was provided first by the womb and then by the infant's natural stimulus barrier. The baby lives in relative symbiotic fusion with the mothering person, so the visits with the non-custodial parent are potentially disruptive.

The optimal way to handle visitation at this age is comparable to the process of moving a soap bubble from the right hand to the left hand without breaking it. It requires that both hands be covered with bubble juice so that the bubble feels no friction during the transition. Visitations need to be as seamless as possible. The aim is to maintain continuity and not disrupt the child's homeostasis. What will later be viewed by the same child as exciting and enriching - the dramatic differences between mother and father- at this age is experienced by the child as "bubble breaking." The parent who visits must try as best as possible, in other words, to reproduce the environment in which the baby has found safety and comfort. Between 3 and 5 months, fluctuations in and between environments need to be kept at a minimum.

### Five to Ten Months

This is the time that the baby turns from attending almost exclusively to the mothering person and becomes curious about the world at large. This is the time of stranger anxiety, separation anxiety and the beginning of game playing. A child of this age begins to play peek-a-boo both with the parents and with any object in sight. Spoons unpredictably disappear at the dinner table.

The baby can now discriminate between the familiar mother/father unit and all other people. This means that the child can no longer be left willy-nilly with different baby sitters. It also results in the child's preoccupation with the location of the primary parent and the need to check back by making eye contact with the parent. The capacity to check back with the mothering pattern is an important- essential behavior because the child can move away from the mother and then return for docking and reorientation.

During long visitations away from the mothering person this process if often strained because the child can no longer re-find the absent, custodial parent. The child begins to live in two separate worlds and to view each as a home base. This may result in a sort of dual citizenship in which the child appears adapted in both "countries" before he/she has a firm identity. While child authorities differ, my own experience suggests that it is best if the child does not develop a double world so early. It is optimal that visitations be arranged so that the child can still check back and dock with the mothering parent on a regular basis, thus firming-up a primary identity.

Visitations during this phase best serve the child if they did not exceed four or five hours at a time and take place during daylight hours. Longer visitations are reasonable if the visiting parent folds into the schedule of the baby at home. Transitions need to be cheerful and low-keyed.

## Ten to Fifteen Months

The child of this age can now crawl and begins to walk away from the parent; to take a drunk delight in the world. Under non-divorced circumstances, the mother is the beacon of orientation and the child ventures away for only brief periods - coming back for emotional re-fueling as needed. Typically the child of this age becomes attached to a particular object - called a transitional object - which they cling to at points of separation. Father is no longer a secondary mothering person but primary in his own right.

Armed with his/her treasured transitional object (e.g. blanket, a teddy bear) the junior toddler can tolerate visitations of about six to eight hours. The child's capacity to self-soothe, to walk and begin to talk, equips this youngster with increasingly more complex and emotionally challenging needs for the non-custodial parent. Father's need to eat with, organize, discipline and play with their young toddlers in order to provide a meaningful depth to the developing relationship. This phase child needs the non-custodial parent to support separation and individuation by providing visitations which include the child's new ability to feed himself, to show oppositional behavior in an accepting environment, to talk and to be listened to.

## Fifteen to Twenty Two Months

This is a crucial phase; one in which some psychologists believe the child's identity is definitively formed. The mother's emotional availability become vitally important once again because the child's cognitive ability makes them painfully aware of their vulnerability. Because of the toddler's hyper-awareness of his/her separation, there is now a moment when the child's attempt to reunite with the mother alternates with urges to be independent. The result is a child who may at times be afraid to be alone and a moment later crave independence. This is the age of the "terrible twos ." It is a normal developmental crisis out of which the child may emerge ready for the triad of mother/father/child - or if the visitations are handled clumsily - may emerge regressed back into a dyad with the mother.

Visitation during this stage needs to be catered to the developmentally based separation fears. There may be a resurgence of stranger wariness, shyness, and anger when away from the mother. Father's are best advised to cut their visits short if the child is particularly temperamental during this difficult developmental way station.

### The Special Role of the Father From Fifteen to Twenty Two Months

During this phase visitation makes special and unique quantitative and qualitative demands on the father. All things being equal, he is a treasured love object and is viewed by the child as such. Because he helps the child fight the normal regressive pull back towards the mother, the father maintains a critical place for the young child to develop and define true autonomy.

Visitations come more and more to represent external reality. Father is and always has been outside of the bubble of mother-child unit. Now visitations include cycles of play, language, exchange, excitement, food, naps and baths which are not as fraught with separation anxiety as before. However, this same child may suddenly need mother in the middle of a visit, and is generally not yet developmentally ready for overnights.

If divorced or divorcing parents would tolerate it, this phase child thrives on the presence of both parents. Why? New identifications are emerging. As the love for two objects/parents deepen, the child begins to identify with the parent of the same sex. Gender identity is consolidated during this time and is best facilitated in the ongoing presence of both parents. The shift from dyad to triad helps to organize sexual identity. Visitation which facilitates triangulation during the transitions are well worth the trouble. Drop-offs and pick-ups which are oriented towards giving the child a timely dose of "3" may very well be preventive, that timely ounce of prevention could last a lifetime.

### Two Years to Four Years Olds: The Nursery School Years

Visitations and custody arrangements which are developmentally accountable to the child, include allowing the child normal access to a full cycle with the non custodial parent. However the full cycle should not include overnights until object constancy is attained at which point the child can retain and maintain the mental image of the mother when away from her. A full cycle includes the daily milestones which anchor the child within a familiar setting: meal time, baths, naps, play and play dates should now be included in the visitation in increasingly longer duration. As the child nears the 48th month some may even be able to tolerate being away from the primary caretaker overnight. It all depends upon the individual child's ability to retain in his or her mind's eye, a sustaining image of the primary caretaker with whom the child lives. Generally speaking, overnights are implemented before a child's identity is formed, then the child often regresses and exhibits more immature behavior at home and at school. Similarly, if overnights are unduly delayed, the child's development may be slowed.

50

When children this age exhibit readiness for overnights both parents will know. How? The child will slowly express yearning for and ask to telephone the non-custodial parent. When the child is on a visit, he or she will ask for and openly miss the custodial parent. In both instances, the child remembers, misses and can tolerate being separated from, the absent parent.

## Four and Five Year Olds

These are significant years - between nursery and kindergarten. Symbolic thinking, though still pre-logical, begins to organize the child's thoughts. The four or five year old has a sense of purpose, pride, determination, curiosity, orderliness, cooperativeness in play, imaginary companions, the capacity to complete tasks and to sustain friendships. The non custodial parent now has a distinct role and an identity and is usually valued and sought after as such. Overnights are more a probability than a developmental possibility and may in fact be requested by the secure child. Here we see how the patience of the non custodial parent may be rewarded by the secure child who has achieved object constancy and is developmentally ready to separate overnight from a mother. The non custodial parent should deliver the child before the late afternoon as a rule, since dusk and early evening invite sleepiness and regression.

## Six to Eight Year Olds

The myriad accomplishments of this age child include functioning in school away from both parents for many hours at a clip. After school the child engages in activities: play dates, lessons, doctor's appointments, homework. On top of all of this real world activity - most of which takes place in other than mommy/daddy world - the child has the developmental tasks of latency to negotiate. These include needing to spend more time with the same sex parent without hurting the feeling of the opposite sex parent. This is the time when the parents do their most important social role mentoring.

Visitations need to be sensitive to latency needs. Boys may request more time with father and mom needs to allow it. Girls may want to spend weekends with mother, instead of visiting father. Dad needs to be open to this.

Latency is a phase of life in which the need to be with the same sex parent will result in a child requesting more time with the same sex parent than the court may have ordered. In my judgment parents need to be flexible to this developmental need. To the parent who feels injured, I would only say, "This too shall pass." In handling visitation from a developmental perspective, rather than an exclusively legal perspective, the parent of children six seven and eight years old will be less burdened by anger and side-taking if they are mindful that in development first one parent and then the other is given center stage.

## Conclusion

Decisions about custody and visitation need to be organized around the present and future developmental status of each child, not around the child's parents and their perceived rights. It is in the nature of the human condition that a child whose developmental rights have been compromised has no "second chance." You only get one chance to be a child. Parents, on the other hand, can delay their wishes and needs to be satisfied at a later time, putting the temporarily preeminent developmental needs of their child first.

4

# CHECKLIST OF PRINCIPLE AREAS OF INQUIRY IN CUSTODY AND VISITATION MATTERS

Mona R. Millstein

Reprinted from the PLI Course Handbook,
Child Custody and Support 1996.
Order Number C4-4214

## Checklist of Principle Areas of
## Inquiry in Custody and Visitation Matters

### Basic Data of the Parties

1. Name and address of parties

2. Names and dates of birth of children

3. Age, health, education of all family members

4. Relevant history of the marriage

5. Occupation and place of employment

6. Existence of prior marriages and the disposition of those marriages

7. If there is a pending action, all information concerning status of that action

### Background of Child

1. History of the child's residence--with whom child resides, and has resided, where child resides, length of residences

2. Relationship of child to siblings

3. Relationship of child to relatives

4. Child's school history, names of teachers, and information concerning child's performance in school

5. Previous custodial arrangements and visitation arrangements

6. Any special medical or emotional issues

7. Religious history

8. Extracurricular activities, sports, organizations

9. History of financial support, including which party is responsible for support, amount of child support paid, etc.

10. Names and addresses of children's physicians, group leaders, or any persons rendering services or treatment to the child

11. Relationship of child to potential second spouse or stepchildren

## Historical Details

1. Details of the current and former custodial and/or caretaking arrangements for the child

2. Whether the caretaking-custodial arrangements were pursuant to an action, voluntary or formalized by any agreement

3. Acceptability to client and other party of the present arrangements and any issues or problems arising within the present arrangements

4. Child's preference as to custodial and visitation arrangements, including particulars of places and periods of visitation

5. Insight into child's character and willingness to be forthright as to true preference

6. Preference of parties as to custody and visitation

7. Factual circumstances of client which support award of custody

8. Factual circumstances of client which do not support award of custody

9. Factual circumstances of adversary client which support award of custody

10. Factual circumstances of adversary client which do not support award of custody

11. Relocation issues

12. Financial and emotional capability, and time accessibility, of each parent for child

13. Names and addresses of all potential witnesses in a custody case

14. Previous intervention of any mental health experts in the family's history

15. Lifestyle and lifestyle changes of parents and child

16. Childcare history, including third-party childcare throughout the child's life

17. Complete and detailed schedule of previous visitation

The above checklist is not exhaustive, but should serve as a
general guideline of the preliminary information necessary to be
elicited from a client in the beginning of a custody matter.   At
least the foregoing factual information should be obtained in order
to enable a practitioner to devise a strategy for going forward
and advising the client on the issues of custody and visitation.

# NOTES

5

*TROPEA V. TROPEA*
TROPEA AND ITS RECENT
AFTERMATH:
RELOCATION CASES DECIDED
AFTER TROPEA

Michele A. Katz

Reprinted from the PLI Course Handbook,
<u>Child Custody and Support 1996</u>.
Order Number C4-4214

# FAMILY LAW
## Request to Relocate by Custodial Parent

No. 1. In the Matter of Tammy Louise Tropea,
Respondent, v. John Peter Tropea, Appellant.

No. 2. In the Matter of Jacqueline Browner,
Respondent, v. Andrew Kenward, Appellant.

*Decided March 26, 1996*

*No. 1: Sigmund V. Mazur, for appellant.*
*J. Scott Porter, for respondent.*
*Marsha A. Hunt, law guardian.*

*No. 2: Brian D. Graifman, for appellant.*
*Theresa M. Daniele, law guardian.*
*Kathleen Donelli, for respondent.*

TITONE, J. — In each of these appeals, a divorced spouse who was previously granted custody of the couple's minor offspring seeks permission to move away from the area in which the noncustodial spouse resides. Both noncustodial spouses oppose the move, contending that it would significantly reduce the access to the children that they now enjoy. Their respective appeals from the Appellate Division order and the Family Court judgment authorizing the requested moves raise significant questions regarding the scope and nature of the inquiry that should be made in cases where a custodial parent proposes to relocate and seeks judicial approval of the relocation plan.

### ◆ I ◆

#### Tropea v. Tropea

The parties in this case were married in 1981 and have two children, one born in 1985 and the other in 1988. They were divorced in 1992 pursuant to a judgment that incorporated their previously executed separation agreement. Under that agreement, petitioner-mother, who had previously been the children's primary caregiver, was to have sole custody of the children and respondent-father was granted visitation on holidays and "at least three * * * days of each week." Additionally, the parties were barred from relocating outside of Onondaga County, where both resided, without prior judicial approval.

On June 4, 1993, petitioner brought this proceeding seeking changes in the visitation arrangements and permission to relocate with the children to the Schenectady area. Respondent opposed the requested relief and filed a cross-petition for a change of custody. At the ensuing hearing, petitioner testified that she wanted to move because of her plans to marry an architect who had an established firm in Schenectady. According to petitioner, she and her fiance had already purchased a home in the Schenectady area for themselves and the Tropea children and were now expecting a child of their own. Petitioner stated that she was willing to cooperate in a liberal visitation schedule that would afford respondent frequent and extended contact and that she was prepared to drive the children to and from their father's Syracuse home, which is about two and a half hours away from Schenectady. Nonetheless, as all parties recognized, the distance between the two homes made midweek visits during the school term impossible.

Respondent took the position that petitioner's "need" to move was really the product of her own life-style choice and that, consequently, he should not be the parent who is "punished" with the loss of proximity and weekday contact. Instead, respondent proposed that he be awarded custody of the children if petitioner chose to relocate. To support this proposal, respondent adduced evidence to show that he had maintained frequent and consistent contact with his children at least until June of 1993, when the instant proceeding was commenced. He had coached the children's football and baseball teams, participated in their religion classes and had become involved with his older son's academic education during the 1992-1993 school year. However, there was also evidence that respondent harbored a continuing bitterness toward petitioner which he had verbalized and demonstrated to the children in a number of inappropriate ways. Respondent admitted being bitter enough to have called petitioner "a tramp" and "a low-life" in the children's presence and, in fact, stated that he saw nothing wrong with this conduct, although he acknowledged that it had a negative effect on the children. Respondent's mother confirmed that he had spoken negatively about petitioner in the children's presence and that this behavior had not been helpful to the children.

Following the hearing, the presiding Judicial Hearing Officer denied petitioner's request for permission to relocate. Applying what he characterized as "a more restrictive view of relocation," the JHO opined that whenever a proposed move "unduly disrupts or substantially impairs the [noncustodial parent's] access rights to [the] children," the custodial spouse seeking judicial consent must bear the burden of demonstrating "exceptional circumstances" such as a "concrete economic necessity." Applying this principle to the evidence before it, the JHO found that petitioner's desire to obtain a "fresh start" with a new family was insufficient to justify a move that would "significantly impact upon" the close and consistent relationship with his chidren that respondent had previously enjoyed.

On petitioner's appeal, however, the Appellate Division reversed, holding that petitioner had made the necessary showing that the requested relocation would not deprive respondent of "regular and meaningful access to his children." Further, the court noted, petitioner's proposed visitation schedule afforded respondent the opportunity for frequent and extended contact with his children. Finally, the court found that the move would be in the best interests of the children. Accordingly, the court ruled that petitioner should be permitted to move to Schenectady and remitted the matter to Family Court for the establishment of an appropriate visitation schedule. The final Family Court judgment from which respondent appeals awards respondent substantial weekend, summer and vacation visitation in accordance with the Law Guardian's recommended schedule.[1]

*Browner v. Kenward*

The parties to this proceeding were married in August of 1983 and had a son three years later. After marital discord led the parties to separate, they executed a Stipulation of Settlement and Agreement in January of 1992 which gave petitioner-mother physical custody of the couple's child and gave respondent-father liberal visitation, including midweek overnight visits and alternating weekends. Under the Stipulation, respondent was to remain in the marital residence, which was located in White Plains, New York, and petitioner and the parties' son were to live with petitioner's parents in nearby Purchase. Petitioner was required to seek prior approval of the court if she intended to move more than 35 miles from respondent's residence. The Stipulation was incorporated but not merged in the parties' divorce judgment, which was entered in June of 1992.

In October of 1992, petitioner brought the present proceeding for permission to relocate with the couple's child to Pittsfield, Massachusetts, some 130 miles from respondent's Westchester County home. Petitioner requested this relief because her parents were moving to Pittsfield and she wished to go with them. Respondent opposed the application, contending that he was a committed and involved noncustodial parent and that the proposed move would deprive him of meaningful contact with his son.

A hearing was conducted over a period of several months. The hearing evidence disclosed that petitioner's parents had been considering moving for some time and had made the final decision to do so in September of 1992, coinciding fairly closely with the loss of petitioner's job. Petitioner testified that she had tried to find work in New York but was unable to do so. She further testified that her prospects of finding affordable housing in the Purchase area were bleak. She ultimately located a marketing job in Pittsfield that would give her enough income to rent a home of her own in that area. Petitioner had also investigated the facilities for children in Pittsfield and had found a suitable school and synagogue for her son.

An additional motivating factor for petitioner was the emotional support and child care that she received from her parents and that she expected to receive from her extended family in Pittsfield. According to the evidence, petitioner was somewhat dependent on her parents for financial and moral support, and petitioner's son had become especially close to his grandparents after his own parents had separated. Further, the boy had a long-standing close relationship with his Pittsfield cousins.

Respondent argued that permission for the move should be denied because it would significantly diminish the quantity and quality of his visits with his child. Respondent noted that the move would eliminate the midweek visits that h˙ had previously enjoyed as well as his opportunity to participate in the child's daily school, sports and religious activities. Accordingly, respondent argued, petitioner's proposed relocation to Pittsfield would deprive him of meaningful access to his child.

The Family Court found petitioner's argument that she was unable to secure employment and new housing within the Westchester area to be less than convincing. The court further found that respondent had been "vigilant" in visiting his son and was "sincerely interested in guiding and nurturing [the] child." Nonetheless, the court ruled in petitioner's favor and authorized the proposed move, granting respondent liberal visitation rights. In so ruling, the court noted that the move would not deprive respondent of meaningful contact with his son and that, in light of the psychological evidence that had been adduced, the move would be in the child's best interests. With respect to the best-interests question, the court stated that the parents' separation from each other would reduce the bickering that was causing the child difficulty and would enable the child to have the healthy peer relationships that he needed. Additionally, the emotional advantages that petitioner would realize from proximity to her parents would ultimately enhance the child's emotional well-being. On respondent's appeal, the Appellate Division affirmed, stating only that "the relocation did not deprive [respondent] of regular and meaningful access to the child" and, thus, petitioner was "not required to show exceptional circumstances to justify relocation." This Court subsequently granted respondent leave to appeal.

◆ II ◆

RELOCATION CASES such as the two before us present some of the knottiest and most disturbing problems that our courts are called upon to resolve. In these cases, the interests of a custodial parent who wishes to move away are pitted against those of a noncustodial parent who has a powerful desire to maintain frequent and regular contact with the child. Moreover, the court must weigh the paramount interests of the child, which may or may not be in irreconcilable conflict with those of one or both of the parents.

Because the resolution of relocation disputes is ordinarily a matter entrusted to the fact-finding and discretionary powers of the lower courts, our Court has not had frequent occasion to address the question. We discussed the issue in general terms in *Weiss v. Weiss* (52 NY2d 170, 174-175), in which we recognized the importance of continued regular and frequent visitation between the child and the noncustodial parent and stated that "absent exceptional circumstances * * * , appropriate provision for visitation or other access for the noncustodial parent follows almost as a matter of course" (citing *Strahl v. Strahl*, 66 AD2d 571, affd 49 NY2d 1036). We revisited the issue a year later in *Daghir v. Daghir* (56 NY2d 938), but the majority memorandum in that case merely commented on the trial court's failure to separately consider the child's best interests and did not otherwise elucidate the proper standard to be used in assessing requests by custodial parents for permission to relocate (see also, *Priebe v. Priebe*, 55 NY2d 997 [upholding Appellate Division's discretionary determination]).

Since our decisions in *Weiss* and *Daghir*, the lower courts have evolved a series of formulae and presumptions to aid them in making their decisions in these difficult relocation cases. The most commonly used formula involves a three-step analysis that looks first to whether the proposed relocation would deprive the noncustodial parent of "regular and meaningful access to the child" (e.g., *Lavane v. Lavane*, 201 AD2d 623; *Lake v. Lake*, 192 AD2d 751; *Radford v. Propper*, 190 AD2d 93; *Schaefer v. Brennan*, 170

AD2d 879; *Cassidy v. Kapur*, 164 AD2d 513; *Schouten v. Schouten*, 155 AD2d 461; *Blundell v. Blundel*, 150 AD2d 321; *Murphy v. Murphy*, 145 AD2d 857; *Zaleski v. Zaleski*, 128 AD2d 865; *Klein v. Klein*, 93 AD2d 807). Where a disruption of "regular and meaningful access" is not shown, the inquiry is truncated, and the courts generally will not go on to assess the merits and strength of the custodial parents' motive for moving (*see, e.g., Bennett v. Bennett*, 208 AD2d 1042; *Partridge v. Meyerson*, 162 AD2d 507; *Lake v. Lake*, supra). On the other hand, where such a disruption is established, a presumption that the move is not in the child's best interest is invoked and the custodial parent seeking to relocate must demonstrate "exceptional circumstances" to justify the move (e.g., *Lavelle v. Freeman*, 181 AD2d 977; *Rybicki v. Rybicki*, 176 AD2d 867; *Hathaway v. Hathaway*, 175 AD2d 336). Once that hurdle is overcome, the court will go on to consider the child's best interests.

The premise underlying this formula is that children can derive an abundance of benefits from "the mature guiding hand and love of a second parent" (*Weiss v. Weiss*, supra at 175; accord, *Radford v. Propper*, supra at 99) and that, consequently, geographic changes that significantly impair the quantity and quality of parent-child contacts are to be "disfavored" (*see, Farmer v. Deruay*, 174 AD2d 857, 858; *Matter of Pasco v. Nolen*, 154 AD2d 774, 776; *Matter of Towne v. Towne*, 154 AD2d 766, 767). While this premise has much merit as a tenet of human dynamics, the legal formula that it has spawned is problematic and, in many respects, unsatisfactory (see Miller, Hon. S., *Whatever Happened to the "Best Interests" Analysis in New York Relocation Cases?*, 15 Pace L Rev 339).

One problem with the three-tiered analysis is that it is difficult to apply.

The lower courts have not settled on a uniform method of defining "meaningful access" (*compare, Bennett v. Bennett, supra, at 1043* [ability to maintain "close and meaningful relationship with * * * children], *with Radford v. Propper*, supra at 99 ["frequent and regular access"]), and even the distance of the move has not been a reliable indicator of whether the "meaningful access" test has been satisfied (*compare, Rybicki v. Rybicki*, supra [disapproving 84-mile move] *with Schouten v. Schouten*, 155 AD2d 461 [approving 258-mile move]; *Murphy v. Murphy*, 145 AD2d 857 [approving 340-mile move]).

On a more fundamental level, the three-tiered test is unsatisfactory because it erects artificial barriers to the courts' consideration of all of the relevant factors. Most moves outside of the noncustodial parent's locale have some disruptive effect on that parent's relationship with the child. Yet, if the disruption does not rise to the level of a deprivation of "meaningful access," the three-tiered analysis would permit it without any further inquiry into such salient considerations as the custodial parent's motives, the reasons for the proposed move and the positive or negative impact of the change on the child. Similarly, where the noncustodial parent has managed to overcome the threshold "meaningful access" hurdle, the three-tiered approach requires courts to refuse consent if there are no "exceptional circumstances" to justify the change, again without necessarily considering whether the move would serve the child's best interests or whether the benefits to the children would outweigh the diminution in access by the noncustodial parent. The distorting effect of such a mechanical approach may be amplified where the courts require a showing of economic necessity or health-related compulsion to establish the requisite "exceptional circumstances" (*see, e.g., Lavelle v. Freeman*, supra; *Leslie v. Leslie*, 180 AD2d 620; *Goodwin v. Goodwin*, 173 AD2d 769; *Coniglio v. Coniglio*, 170 AD2d 477) or where the demands of a new marriage are summarily rejected as a sufficient basis for satisfying this test (e.g., *Rybicki v. Rybicki*, supra; *Richardson v. Howard*, 135 AD2d 1140).

In reality, cases in which a custodial parent's desire to relocate conflicts with the desire of a noncustodial parent to maximize visitation opportunity are simply too complex to be satisfactorily handled within any mechanical, tiered analysis that prevents or interferes with a simultaneous weighing and comparative analysis of all of the relevant facts and circumstances. Although we have recognized and continue to appreciate both the need of the child and the right of the noncustodial parent to have regular and meaningful contact (*see generally, Weiss v. Weiss*, supra), we also believe that no single factor should be treated as dispositive or given such disproportionate weight as to predetermine the outcome. There are undoubtedly circumstances in which the loss of mid-week or every-weekend visits necessitated by a distant move may be devastating to the relationship between the noncustodial parent and the child. However, there are undoubtedly also many cases where less frequent but more extended visits over summers and school vacations would be equally conducive, or perhaps even more conducive, to the maintenance of a close parent-child relationship, since such extended visits give the parties the opportunity to interact in a normalized domestic setting. In any event, given the variety of possible permutations, it is counterproductive to rely on presumptions whose only real value is to simplify what are necessarily extremely complicated inquiries.

Accordingly, rather than endorsing the three-step meaningful access-exceptional circumstance analysis that some of the lower courts have used in the past, we hold that each relocation request must be considered on its own merits with due consideration of all the relevant facts and circumstances and with predominant emphasis being placed on what outcome is most likely to serve the best interests of the child. While the respective rights of the custodial and noncustodial parents are unquestionably significant factors that must be considered (see *Strahl v. Strahl*, 66 AD2d 571, affd 49 NY2d 1036, supra), it is the rights and needs of the children that must be accorded the greatest weight, since they are innocent victims of their parents' decision to divorce and are the least equipped to handle the stresses of the changing family situation.

Of course, the impact of the move on the relationship between the child and the noncustodial parent will remain a central concern. Indeed, even where the move would leave the noncustodial parent with what may be considered "meaningful access," there is still a need to weigh the effect of the quantitative and qualitative losses that naturally will result against such other relevant factors as the custodial parent's reasons for wanting to relocate and the benefits that the child may enjoy or the harm that may ensue if the move is or is not permitted. Similarly, although economic necessity or a specific health-related concern may present a particularly persuasive ground for permitting the proposed move, other justifications, including the demands of a second marriage and the custodial parent's opportunity to improve his or her economic situation, may also be valid motives that should not be summarily rejected, at least where the overall impact on the child would be beneficial. While some courts have suggested that the custodial spouse's remarriage or wish for a "fresh start" can never suffice to justify a distant move (*see, e.g., Elkus v. Elkus*, 182 AD2d 445, 48; *Stec v. Levindofske*, 153 AD2d 310), such a rule overlooks the value for the children that strengthening and stabilizing the new, post-divorce family unit can have in a particular case.

In addition to the custodial parent's stated reasons for wanting to move and the noncustodial parent's loss of access, another factor that may well become important in a particular case is the noncustodial parent's interest in securing custody, as well as the feasibility and desirability of a change in custody. Obviously, where a child's ties to the noncustodial parent and to the community are so strong as to make a long-distance move undesirable, the availability of a transfer of custody as realistic alternative to forcing the custodial parent to remain may have a significant impact on the outcome. By the same token, where the custodial parent's reasons for moving are deemed valid and sound, the court in a proper case might consider the possibility and feasibility of a parallel move by an involved and committed noncustodial parent as an alternative to restricting a custodial parent's mobility.

Other considerations that may have a bearing in particular cases are the good faith of the parents in requesting or opposing the move, the child's respective attachments to the custodial and noncustodial parent, the possibility of devising a visitation schedule that will enable the noncustodial parent to maintain a meaningful parent-child relationship, the quality of the lifestyle that the child would have if the proposed move were permitted or denied, the negative impact, if any, from continued or exacerbated hostility between the custodial and noncustodial parents, and the effect that the move may have on any extended-family relationships. Of course, any other facts or circumstances that have a bearing on the parties' situation should be weighed with a view toward minimizing the parents' discomfort and maximizing the child's prospects of a stable, comfortable and happy life.

Like Humpty Dumpty, a family, once broken by divorce, cannot be put back together in precisely the same way. The relationship between the parents and the children is necessarily different after a divorce and, accordingly, it may be unrealistic in some cases to try to preserve the noncustodial parent's accustomed close involvement in the children's everyday life at the expense of the custodial parent's efforts to start a new life or to form a new family unit. In some cases, the child's interests might be better served by fashioning visitation plans that maximize the noncustodial parent's opportunity to maintain a positive nurturing relationship while enabling the custodial parent, who has the primary child-rearing responsibility, to go forward with his or her life. In any event, it serves neither the interests of the children nor the ends of justice to view relocation cases through the prisms of presumptions and threshold tests that artificially skew the analysis in favor of one outcome or another.

Rather, we hold that, in all cases, the courts should be free to consider and give appropriate weight to all of the factors that may be relevant to the determination. These factors include, but are certainly not limited to each parent's reasons for seeking or opposing the move, the quality of the relationships between the child and the custodial and noncustodial parents, the impact of the move on the quantity and quality of the child's future contact with the noncustodial parent, the degree to which the custodial parent's and child's life may be enhanced economically, emotionally and educationally by the move, and the feasibility of preserving the relationship between the noncustodial parent and child through suitable visitation arrangements. In the end, it is for the court to determine, based on all of the proof, whether it has been established by a preponderance of the evidence that a proposed relocation would serve the child's best interests.[2]

◆ III ◆

TURNING FINALLY to the cases before us, we conclude that the orders of the courts below, which approved each of the petitioners' requests to move, should be upheld. In *Tropea*, petitioner sought permission to relocate from Onondaga County to the Schenectady area so that she could settle into a new home with her fiance and raise her sons within a new family unit. The Appellate Division found that the move was in the children's best interest and that the visitation schedule that petitioner proposed would afford respondent frequent and extended visitation[3]. We find no reason derived from the record to upset the Appellate Division's determinations on these points (see *Daghir v. Daghir*, supra at 940). It is true that the court considered whether the relocation would deprive respondent of "meaningful access" to his children. However, it is apparent from the remainder of its writing that the court did not treat that factor as a threshold test barring further inquiry into the salient "best interests" question.

We note that respondent has offered no persuasive legal reason for disturbing the Appellate Division's finding that the proposed relocation would be in the children's best interest. Indeed, in this appeal, respondent's arguments are directed almost entirely to petitioner's purported "unclean hands" in developing a relationship with a person she met before the marriage was dissolved and in choosing to marry that individual after her divorce from respondent. As is evident from our earlier discussion, relocation determinations are not to be made as a means of castigating one party for what the other deems personal misconduct, nor are the courts to be used in this context as arbiters of the parties' respective "guilt" or "innocence." Children are not chattel, and custody and visitation decisions should be made with a view toward what best serves their interests, not what would reward or penalize a purportedly "innocent" or "blameworthy" parent.

Our analysis in *Browner v. Kenward* is somewhat different. The Appellate Division in *Browner* found that the proposed move did not deprive the noncustodial parent of regular and meaningful access to his child and that it was therefore not necessary to weigh the validity and strength of petitioner's reasons for moving against the significant change in the parent-child relationship that the move would entail. The court's methodology was thus at variance with the open-ended balancing analysis that the law requires. However, respondent's only argument in this Court is that the Appellate Division misapplied the three-tiered *Radford v. Propper* (supra) test to the particular facts of his case. Specifically, respondent argues that the 130-mile move from Westchester County to Pittsfield will eliminate his mid-week visitation opportunity, reduce his ability to participate in his son's religious worship and diminish the quality of the weekend visits he has with his son. While these losses are undoubtedly real and are certainly far from trivial, it cannot be said that they operated to deprive respondent of a meaningful opportunity to maintain a close relationship with his son. Hence, respondent was not entitled to an order reversing the outcome below and denying petitioner the permission to relocate that she sought. We note that the Family Court found that the proposed relocation in *Browner* was in the child's best interests and the Appellate Division did not disturb that finding.

Accordingly, in *Tropea v. Tropea*, the judgment of the Family Court and the prior nonfinal order of the Appellate Division brought up for review should be affirmed, with costs. In *Browner v. Kenward*, the order of the Appellate Division should be affirmed, with costs.

(1) This Court dismissed respondent's earlier motion leave to appeal from the prior Appellate Division order on the ground that order did not finally determine the proceeding within the meaning of the Constitution (85 NY2d 968).

(2) The separation agreements in both Tropea and Browner require only that the custodial parent apply for judicial approval before moving out a specified area without making any mention of criteria or standards. A geographical relocation restriction agreed to by the parties and included in their separation agreement might be an additional factor relevant to a court's best interests determination.

(3) Significantly, the Appellate Division's ruling in this regard did not represent a reversal of any contrary first-level factual finding by the nisi prius court. The Family Court JHO did not reach the best-interest question, since, in his view, petitioner's failure to show "exceptional circumstances" to justify the move obviated the need for further inquiry.

◆

No. 1: Judgment of Family Court appealed from and order of the Appellate Division brought up for review affirmed, with costs. Opinion by Judge Titone. Chief Judge Kaye and Judges Simons, Bellacosa, Smith, Levine and Ciparick concur.

No. 2: Order affirmed, with costs. Opinion by Judge Titone. Chief Judge Kaye and Judges Simons, Bellacosa, Smith, Levine and Ciparick concur.

1. Millay v. Millay, 226 A.D.2d 728, 641 N.Y.S.2d 699 (2d Dep't 1996).

2. Sandman v. Sandman, ___ A.D.2d ___, 643 N.Y.S.2d 755 (3d Dep't 1996)

3. Schindler v. Schindler, 227 A.D.2d 634, 643 N.Y.S.2d 196 (2d Dep't 1996)

4. Harder v. Yandoh, ___ A.D.2d ___, 644 N.Y.S.2d 83 (3d Dep't 1996)

5. King v. Mitchell, ___ A.D.2d ___, 645 N.Y.S.2d 570 (3d Dep't 1996)

6. Clark v. Williams, ___ A.D.2d ___, 645 N.Y.S.2d 160 (3d Dep't 1996)

7. Cate v. LaValley, ___ A.D.2d ___, 645 N.Y.S.2d 236 (4th Dep't 1996)

8. Malandro v. Lido, ___ A.D.2d ___, 645 N.Y.S.2d 845 (2d Dep't 1996)

9. Edgerly v. Moore, ___ A.D.2d ___, 647 N.Y.S.2d 773 (1st Dep't 1996)

10. Caputo-Desiderio v. Desiderio, ___ A.D.2d ___, 648 N.Y.S.2d 1005 (2d Dep't 1996).

11. Coryell P. v. Louis J.P., ___ A.D.2d ___, 648 N.Y.S.2d 122 (2d Dep't 1996)

12. Frayne v. Frayne, ___ A.D.2d ___, 651 N.Y.S.2d 583 (2d Dep't 1996)

13. DiMedio v. DiMedio, ___ A.D.2d ___, 650 N.Y.S.2d 746 (2d Dep't 1996)

14. Caganek v. Caganek, ___ A.D.3d ___, 650 N.Y.S. 365 (3d Dep't 1996)

15. Castler v. Castler, ___ A.D.3d ___, 650 N.Y.S.2d 351 (3d Dep't 1996)

16. Fehr v. Imm, ___ A.D.3d ___, 651 N.Y.S.2d 952 (3d Dep't 1996)

17. Caska v. Caska, N.Y.L.J., April 5, 1996, p. 35, col. 6 (Sup. Ct. Rockland Co., Weiner, J.)

18. Dukett v. Zoll, N.Y.L.J., Sept. 6, 1996, p. 26, col. 2 (Sup. Ct. Nassau Co., McCabe, J.)

19. K.H. v. P.H., N.Y.L.J., October 11, 1996, p. 28, col. 2 (Sup. Ct. N.Y. Co., Lobis, J.)

20. Stearns v. Baxter, N.Y.L.J., January 30, 1997, p. 33, col. 2 (Fam. Ct. Ulster Co., Traficanti, J.)

21. DeJesus v. DeJesus, N.Y.L.J., February 24, 1997, p. 31, col. 4 (Sup. Ct. Suffolk Co., Lifson, J.)

22. Blackburn v. Santiago, N.Y.L.J., April 1, 1997, p. 33, col. 2 (Fam. Ct. Queens Co., Elkins, J.)

# NOTES

6

## LAW GUARDIAN/GUARDIAN AD LITEM SELECTED CASES

Saul Edelstein

⟨/⟩

· PART ___5___
INDEX NO. __24525/87__.
CALENDAR NO. _____

ORDER

ETHAN P▉▉▉                    *Plaintiff*

PRESENT:     NOV 06 1992

  - *Against* -

CARLA P▉▉▉                    *Defendant*

HON.  WILLIAM RIGLER

The following papers numbered 1 to ___4___ used on this motion

| | PAPERS NUMBERED |
|---|---|
| No. _____ on Calendar of _10/28/92_ | |
| Notice of Motion - ~~Order to Show Cause - Affidavit~~ (s) | _1_ |
| Affirmation ~~(s), Petition, and Exhibits Annexed~~ | |
| Answering ~~Affidavit (s) and~~ Affirmation ~~(s)~~ | _2_ |
| ~~Reply Affidavit (s) and~~ Affirmation ~~(s)~~    w/Exhibit | _3_ |
| _Opposition_ ~~Affidavit (s) and~~ Affirmation ~~(s)~~ | _4_ |
| Other Papers _____ | |

**Upon the foregoing papers**

    In this ongoing matrimonial action, the court is now being asked to define the limits of a child's autonomy in directing who may represent him or her within a matrimonial action. Specifically, the question raised is whether an eleven year old child can dismiss a court appointed law guardian in favor of an attorney of his or her own choosing? The application is being brought on behalf of the child by the proposed new attorney.

    A review of the facts is essential before an adjudication of the question itself may be rendered. The action was commenced in 1987. Custody has always been a key factor in this case. Originally, in this case, the court was faced with the question of whether or not New York State was the proper forum to determine the issue of custody. This court determined that the case belonged in the New York State courts (Pavlo v. Pavlo, 137 Misc 2d 418).

71

Unfortunately, the action has not been easily resolved.
The parties have continued to litigate the matter. In February,
1992, the court appointed Goldah Magill, Esq. to act as
law guardian for the child pursuant to Judiciary §35. Compensation
for this law guardian was to be made pursuant to the Judiciary
Law and County Law §18b. It is important to note that plaintiff-
wife's counsel is appearing pro bono through the offices
of the Brooklyn Bar Association and defendant-husband is
appearing by retained counsel.

Ms. Magill interviewed the child on at least two occasions.
She also recommended that the parties and the child take
part in forensic evaluations. The court ordered the parties
to submit to such evaluations. The costs of these evaluations
were to be borne by the assigned law guardian panel. The
amount of compliance with this order is the subject of additional
litigation between the parties.

Sometime in September 1992 Ms. Magill received a letter
from her client purporting to dismiss her. Ms. Magill,
as an officer of the court, brought this letter to the court's
attention at the appropriate juncture. The parties' counsel
were also fully apprised of the letter. The court informed
Ms. Magill that she was counsel to the child until the court
ordered otherwise.

During this same period the child who is 11 years old
contacted Professor Martin Guggenheim of New York University
School of Law. The child clearly found Mr. Guggenheim with
the help of his father (the defendant). Mr. Guggenheim
was not aware of the father's involvement at that time.
During the first meeting with Mr. Guggenheim the child explained
to Mr. Guggenheim that he was not getting along with Ms.
Magill. The child expressed the desire to obtain counsel
of his choice and sought out Mr. Guggenheim for advice.
Mr. Guggenheim recommended several attorneys to the child.
The child did try to meet with some of the attorneys recommended
by Mr. Guggenheim. However, their schedules prevented an
immediate conference. A few days later the child requested
that Mr. Guggenheim represent him. Mr. Guggenheim agreed
to make an application seeking to have him substituted for
Ms. Magill.

On October 12, 1992 defendant-father entered into a
written retainer agreement with Mr. Guggenheim wherein the
father agreed not to take part in any representations of
the child by Mr. Guggenheim but agreed to pay an initial
retainer and be responsible for any additional fees. It
is also apparent that the father took the child to Mr.
Guggenheim's offices when necessary and has in fact met
Mr. Guggenheim on at least one occasion prior to the court
appearance in this application. Plaintiff-wife did not

take part in any of these actions. She was not truly informed of these events until the present motion was made (except for knowledge of the purported "firing" letter of September).

Mr. Guggenheim now makes this application which has two parts. First, is the question of whether or not Ms. Magill should be removed as law guardian for the child? The second question is whether or not it would be appropriate for Mr. Guggenheim to be permitted to act as the replacement?

Before the court starts the analysis it wants to make clear that it holds both Ms. Magill and Mr. Guggenheim in the highest esteem. Ms. Magill has appeared before the court on occasions too numerous to count, both as retained counsel and as court appointed law guardian. Absent attorneys like Ms. Magill this court could not function. Similarly, Mr. Guggenheim has appeared before this court on many occasions, albeit while this jurist sat in the Family Court. The court is well aware of the nationally respected program in the area of juvenile rights and family law that Mr. Guggenheim has built at the New York University School of Law. Furthermore, the court must start the analysis by clearly stating that it has not found that either attorney acted improperly in any fashion. The questions are simple: 1) is the relationship between the child and Ms. Magill such that it would be better to change counsel and 2) would it be appropriate for Mr. Guggenheim to be the new counsel?

The child has been interviewed in camera to determine his views on this matter. Additionally, Mr. Guggenheim as the proposed incoming attorney was questioned in front of counsel solely on the subject of how the child came to choose him.

<u>ANALYSIS</u>

There is no dispute that as a general concept a child whose parents are involved in a custody dispute may be represented by independent counsel of their choosing (See, Family Court Act §§241, 249, Subd (a)). As corollary to that concept, under the right circumstances a child can ask the court to replace a court appointed attorney with an attorney of the child's choosing (See, Mtr of Fargnoli v. Faber, 105 AD2d 523). However, there should be a showing that the relationship between the child and the court appointed counsel is in someway tainted before substitution is permitted (See, Fargnoli, 105 2nd at 525).

In the present case the child has indicated that he has had some differences of opinion with his appointed counsel. At this juncture it is clear that to continue the relationship between the child and Ms. Magill would not be fruitful. Thus, it would be appropriate for this court to excuse Ms. Magill from her appointment as law guardian for the child.

- The court, however, does not think it is appropriate
for Mr. Guggenheim to represent the child. The father brought
the child to see Mr. Guggenheim. Mr. Guggenheim was specifically
retained by the father. "Parents may not, however, retain
counsel for their children or become involved in the representation
of their children because of the appearance or possibility
of a conflict of interest or the likelihood that such interference
will prevent the children's representation from being truly
independent (See, Robert N. v. Carol W., NYLJ, September
30, 1983, p 15, col 6; Besharov, Practice Commentary, McKinney's
Cons Laws of NY, Book 29A, Family Ct Act, §249, p 202)."
(Mtr of Fargnoli v. Faber, 105 AD2d at 524.) In light of
how the services of Mr. Guggenheim were obtained there is
an appearance of a possible conflict of interest. Thus,
he should not represent the child.

The court must now secure counsel for the child. In
discussions with Mr. Guggenheim and the child it became
apparent that Mr. Guggenheim had recommended other counsel.
The child was unable to consummate a connection with one
particular firm recommended by Mr. Guggenheim. The firm
of Abbot, Duncan and Weiner has a fine reputation. In particular,
Ms. Nancy Duncan and Mr. Elliot Weiner appeared before this
jurist in their capacity as law guardians in Family Court
and in Supreme Court as counsel to litigants in divorce
proceedings. Since the firm was recommended initially by
Mr. Guggenheim in whom the child has confidence it is believed
that the child will transfer that confidence to these attorneys.
Thus, the court appoints Nancy Duncan, Esq. to act as counsel
to the child.

Since the father was already more than willing to compensate
outside counsel for the child he will be responsible for
the retainer and fees of Ms. Duncan, subject of course to
court review. In this way the new counsel will be shielded
from any outside influences.

The court is aware that psychological forensics were
ordered in this case. They should be put on hold until
Ms. Duncan has had a change to become familiar with the
case. She should then contact the court as to her recommendation
on the issue of forensics.

The court wants to stress that it does not believe
that either Ms. Magill or Mr. Guggenheim did anything inappropriate.
It is just that the court wants all the parties and the
child to be comfortable with their own representation as
well as secure that there are no appearances of conflict.

Finally, counsel have raised the issue that private
attorneys retained to represent a child in a custody dispute
are somehow different than court appointed counsel who are

called law guardians. This court does not see a distinction. All attorneys representing children must be guided by the same set of dictates; to represent their clients - the children. Furthermore, if an attorney represents a child in a custody case the attorney, whether court appointed or not, should be guided by the "Law Guardian Representation Standards, Volume II: Custody Cases" recently promulgated by the New York State Bar Association. In no other way can it be assured that all children in this state get equal representation.

Accordingly, it is ordered that:

1.  Ms. Magill is relieved as law guardian for the child.

2.  Mr. Guggenheim's application to be substituted for Ms. Magill is denied.

3.  Ms. Duncan is appointed as counsel to the child. Ms. Duncan's telephone number is (212) 619-3930. Compensation for Ms. Duncan shall be the responsibility of the plaintiff.

This constitutes the order of the court.

J.S.C.

Justice Harkavy

★ JURDAK v. JURDAK—Plaintiff-wife moves to relieve Saul Edelstein, Esq., as counsel for the children in the custody proceedings herein.

On or about March 20, 1995, plaintiff and defendant entered into a stipulation in Family Court, Kings County, providing, among other things, for joint custody of the children; and, that as of September 1995, the children will attend P.S. 60 in Richmond County, rather than St. Anselm School in Bay Ridge, which they had been attending up until then. Helen Jurdak, the paternal grandmother, was unhappy with the stipulation. As a result, she wanted to obtain a lawyer to intervene in the action for her, in order to protect her grandchildren, Adam Jurdak, born March 16, 1987 and Matthew Jurdak, born December 29, 1990. She felt her grandchildren's interests were not being protected by the consent agreement entered into in Family Court.

Helen Jurdak consulted with the Brooklyn Bar Association in order to obtain a recommendation for an attorney whom she could engage to espouse what she alleges to be the children's position. Through the Brooklyn Bar Association she ultimately found her way to Saul Edelstein's office. After discussing the matter with Helen Jurdak, Mr. Edelstein informed her that she would have no standing in this matter. However, he suggested that she rent, at a video store, the movie "The Client" and that she and the children watch the movie. It appears that Helen Jurdak did so and thereafter she and the two children came back to Mr. Edelstein's office. While Helen Jurdak sat in the anteroom, Mr. Edelstein interviewed the children, who then retained him by the payment of one dollar each to him. According to Mr. Edelstein, the children told him they were not happy with the situation. They said that they wanted to continue attending St. Anselm School; that they were unhappy with the long trip from their mother's house in Bulls Head, Staten Island to St. Anselm in Bay Ridge; and that they would be just as unhappy with the long trip from their father's house in Bay Ridge to P.S. 60 in Staten Island. After his conversation with the children, Saul Edelstein met with Helen Jurdak, who paid him a substantial retainer on behalf of the children. He then filed a notice of appearance and appeared in the action when it was on the calendar in the Family Court and/or the Supreme Court. Once the case was marked ready for trial the attorney for the plaintiff-mother, by order to show cause, asked the Court to relieve Mr. Edelstein as counsel for the children. Oral argument was held and the Court determines as set forth herein.

#### Law

Custody and visitation proceedings have as their objective the best interests of the child (Eschbach v. Eschbach, 56 NY2d 167; Matter of Jaeger v. Jaeger, 207 AD2d 448). A law guardian may be appointed by the Court to protect the interests of the child or the child may choose independent counsel. The Court may order the parties and the child to submit to forensic examina-

sel to represent children in custody cases and that no statutory authority is necessary to do so. However, there is statutory authority to appoint law guardians under Family Court Act §241, which provides that minors who are the subject of Family Court proceedings or appeals originating in the Family Court, should be represented by counsel of their own choosing or by law guardians.

Judiciary Law §35(7) provides in part that counsel will be compensated in accordance with its provisions, whenever the Supreme Court appoints counsel in a proceeding over which Family Court might have exercised jurisdiction if it had been commenced there or referred there, and the circumstances which, if the proceedings were pending in Family Court, the Court would have been authorized by Family Court Act §249 to appoint a law guardian.

Furthermore, the rules of the Chief Judge, §202.16(f) provides that the Court may appoint a law guardian for an infant. The rule also sets forth a procedure where the parties can recommend attorneys who may act as the law guardian.

Family Court Act §249 provides that in any proceeding in which it has jurisdiction, the Court may appoint a law guardian to represent a child, when in the opinion of the Family Court Judge, such representation will serve the purpose of the Family Court Act, and if independent legal counsel is not available to the child.

The Appellate Division, in Koppenhoefer v. Koppenhoefer, 159 AD2d 113 (2d Dept 1990) held that the role of a law guardian in disputed custody and visitation litigations has been to act as the champion of the child's best interests, as advocate for the child's preferences, as investigator seeking the truth on controverted issues or to recommend alternatives for the Court's considerations. The role of the law guardian appointed pursuant to the Family Court Act is the same role as that of independent counsel.

In the case of Anonymous v. Anonymous decided by Justice Jacqueline W. Silbermann on August 18, 1995 (NYLJ, September 8, 1995, page 27, column 3), we had a situation where the children were dissatisfied; with the guardian ad litem appointed by a prior judge. They contacted an attorney after seeing his name in a magazine. This attorney made an application on behalf of the children to be appointed as their law guardian. The Court granted the motion and appointed him as a law guardian. The Court ordered the father to pay the law guardian's fees in the first instance, with final determination as to a proper allocation of fees to be made by the trial Court.

The law guardian had asked for a retainer and the father opposed the motion on the grounds that the law guardian was not acting as a law guardian pursuant to the Family Court Act because he was not independently selected and since he is not acting as a neutral evaluator.

Justice Silbermann confirmed that the Court had the authority to appoint a law guardian and further stated that there is no distinction between the role of a law guardian and the role of an attorney individually selected by the children.

The Court has also reviewed the case of P v. P, (NYLJ November 10, 1992, page 29, column 3), where Justice Rigler removed the originally appointed law guardian appointed law guardian for the child, but denied the substitution of an attorney, a law professor at N.Y.U., chosen by the children who had requested to be substituted for the law guardian. Instead, Justice Rigler appointed

a member of the Academy of Matrimonial attorney. He is a member of the Academy of Matrimonial Lawyers and well versed in matrimonial law. Since Mr. Edelstein is a competent experienced attorney, the Court sees no reason why Mr. Edelstein could not be a law guardian, even though he's not on the official list of the Appellate Division for 18B law guardians. He is well suited to expound the views of the children and to protect them from the parents who are more interested in their dislike for each other, than the best interests of the children.

As far as this Court is concerned a law guardian or an independent counsel is the same in this case. The law guardian's role is what was stated by the Appellate Division.

It is as an independent counsel whose function is to champion the child's positions, advocate for the child's preferences as an investigator seeking truth in controverted issues, and/or to recommend alternatives to issues for the Court's consideration. The Court is of the opinion that Mr. Edelstein is well able to do this whether he's a law guardian or an independent counsel.

The Court further notes that there is a question as far as the legal fee is concerned. Except for the token dollar paid by each child, the actual legal fee was paid to Saul Edelstein by Helen Jurdak, the defendant's mother. The Court does see a problem in that. On the other hand, the Court does note that in every case somebody has to pay the legal fees. The Court will permit Helen Jurdak to pay Mr. Edelstein's fee in the first instance. A final determination as to a proper allocation of the fee is to be made by the trial Court after trial. The fact that Helen Jurdak is in the first instance paying the fee, does not necessarily mean that she will be responsible for these counsel fees at the end of the case.

#### Conclusion

The Court concludes that it is in the best interests of the children for Saul Edelstein to continue as the independent counsel for the children. In case there is any question, I am changing his title to "independent counsel/law guardian", to cover all bases. This constitutes the opinion, decision and order of this Court.

IN Koppenhoefer v Koppenh...
supra

②

SUPREME COURT OF THE STATE OF NEW YORK · NEW YORK COUNTY

PART 50L

PRESENT:

Hon.   Jacqueline W. Silbermann
_____ Justice.

*NYLJ 9/8/95, p. 27, col. 3*

ANONYMOUS.

Plaintiff,

— against —

ANONYMOUS,

Defendant.

INDEX NUMBER   65123/92

MOTION DATE _____

MOTION SEQ. NO.   22

TRIAL CAL. NO. _____

The following papers numbered 1 to ____ read on this motion to _____

| | PAPERS NUMBERED |
|---|---|
| Notice of Motion/Order to Show Cause - Affidavits - Exhibits | 1,2 |
| Answering Affidavits - Exhibits | 3 |
| Replying Affidavits | |

Upon the foregoing papers it is ordered that this motion  is decided in accordance

with the accompanying memorandum decision.

FILED

AUG 2 8 1995

COUNTY CLERK'S OFFICE
NEW YORK

Dated   August 18 , 1995

J.S.C.

79

SUPREME COURT OF THE STATE OF NEW YORK
COUNTY OF NEW YORK
----------------------------------------X
ANONYMOUS,

                    Plaintiff,

        -against-                    Index No.:  65123/92

ANONYMOUS,

                    Defendant.
----------------------------------------X
Jacqueline W. Silbermann,        J.:

     Robert Z. Dobrish, Esq., Law Guardian for the parties'
children moves for an order awarding him interim counsel fees in
the sum of $25,000, to be paid initially by the defendant with
leave to apply for additional fees if necessary. Defendant opposes
the motion.

     The parties' children contacted Mr. Dobrish after seeing his
name listed as a custody "specialist" in a New York magazine
article.  He subsequently made an application on behalf of the
children requesting that he be appointed as their law guardian
thereby replacing the guardian ad litem.  This court in an order
dated May 9, 1995, appointed Mr. Dobrish as the children's law
guardian and ordered that defendant pay Mr. Dobrish's fees in the
first instance with a final determination as to the proper
allocation of the fees to be made by the trial court.  The court
had, in effect, followed the decision of the prior Judge assigned
to this case who had appointed a guardian ad litem and directed

defendant to pay his fees in the first instance until a final
allocation was made.

Defendant opposes the instant motion asserting that Mr.
Dobrish is not acting as a law guardian pursuant to the Family
Court Act because he was not independently selected by the court
and since he is not acting as a neutral evaluator. Although
defendant claims that Mr. Dobrish is not a law guardian, he
contends that Mr. Dobrish should be paid at the statutory rate
designated for law guardians rather than the rate he is billing for
his services in this action.  He further claims that Mr. Dobrish is
not acting as a court appointed neutral expert; that he has not
submitted a detailed breakdown of his time spent on this matter;
and that he has duplicated some of the work of the guardian ad
litem.

The court finds defendant's reasoning somewhat flawed with
respect to his assertion as to Mr. Dobrish's status as a law
guardian.  First, while defendant firmly claims that Mr. Dobrish
may not be considered a law guardian based on the Family Court Act
§241, he also argues that Mr. Dobrish should be paid pursuant to
the statutory framework designated for law guardians.  These two
positions are inconsistent.  If one were to follow defendant's
claim that Mr. Dobrish is not a law guardian, then he would not be
subject to the statutory rate for any services that he rendered.

Second, the court finds the defendant's omission of the very next section of the Family Court Act extremely troubling. While §241 addresses the representation of minors "by counsel of their own choosing or by law guardian", §242 defines a law guardian as an "attorney admitted to practice law in the state of New York and designated under this part to represent minors pursuant to section two hundred and forty nine of this act." Thus, the Family Court Act, contrary to defendant's assertion, squarely supports the concept of the law guardian as attorney for a child.

Nor does the court find persuasive the cases submitted by defendant to support his position as to Mr. Dobrish's purported lack of law guardian status. In this connection defendant annexes as an exhibit to his opposition papers the case of Young v. Young, NYLJ 6/30/95, p. 25, col. 3. He contends that the Appellate Division, Second Department notes that the law guardian in that action made a recommendation to the court. However, nowhere does the court state that this is the sole province of a law guardian nor does the court set forth any specific criteria or factors which would define the role of a law guardian. As such, this court finds this decision to be inapposite to the current request before it.

Defendant further cites an Appellate Division, Fourth Department case which he claims follows the Second Department's "view." The court in Van Gorder v. Van Gorder, 188 A.D.2d 1049 (Fourth Department 1992), similarly does not state that the law guardian's role is to be neutral as opposed to an advocate for the children. Rather, the court specifically states ". . .Family Court should appoint a different Law Guardian who should take an active role in assisting the court to make a determination in [the child's] best interest."   Theoretically, it is every attorney's role when he or she appears before the court to assist the court in making it's determination.     This is accomplished by the introduction of evidence and the taking of testimony at trial and also through discussion at any pre-trial conferences which may be held before the court.   Thus, the court finds that the Van Gorder case is not instructive as to the present application nor does it support the defendant's position.

Similarly disturbing is defendant's reliance on the case P. v. P., NYLJ, 11/10/92 (Sup. Ct. Kings Cty.).   Defendant lists this case for the proposition, inter alia, that the court refused to select a lawyer as a law guardian with whom the child had spoken. According to defendant, Justice Rigler chose a lawyer with whom the court was familiar but who had not met the child or either of the parents.   Presumably, defendant's argument addresses the fact that his children had met with Mr. Dobrish prior to his selection as Law Guardian.

The court disagrees with defendant's interpretation of the P v. P. decision.    Justice Rigler's decision does not support

defendant's claim as to the significance of the children's contact
with the law guardian, but addresses a possible conflict in that
"[t]he father brought the child to see [the attorney]."  Indeed, in
P. v. P., supra, the court appointed a law guardian recommended by
the attorney whom the child had selected.  The court opined that
this would strengthen the confidence which the child felt in his or
her law guardian, a concept endorsed by Justice Rigler as it is by
this court.

It is clear after a review of the papers submitted in
connection with this motion, that it is necessary for this court to
set forth the authority from which it derives the ability to
appoint an attorney to represent a child or children in a custody
proceeding.  It is clear that there is a lack of understanding both
as to the court's ability to appoint and as to the role of the law
guardian upon his or her appointment.

Under 22 NYCRR §202.16(f), the matrimonial rules, the court
may appoint a law guardian for the infant children or have the
parties submit a list of names for possible selection.  Thus, the
matrimonial rules unequivocally permit a Supreme Court Justice to
select a law guardian for the children.  While the rules suggest
that this be done at the preliminary conference, this is not always
feasible.  Where as in this case, the court receives a case well
after it's commencement or where the issue of custody is not raised

and only subsequently becomes an issue, it is apparent by inference that the court would be similarly able to make an appointment albeit at a later stage of the proceedings.

While the matrimonial rules permit this court to make an appointment of a law guardian, the rules apply to cases commenced after November 30, 1993. This case was commenced prior to that date and as such this court must look toward a different source of authority to demonstrate its ability to appoint. Under the Family Court Act in combination with Judiciary Law §35, law guardians may also be appointed in Supreme (and Surrogate Court) in those case where the Family Court may have exercised jurisdiction. Thus, under Family Court Act §§241 and 249, it is within this court's discretion to appoint a law guardian for a child in an action involving custody. The Family Court Act also acknowledges the concept that a child whose parents are involved in a custody dispute may be represented by independent counsel of their own choosing. See Family Court Act §§241, 249 and P. v. P., supra.

While the court recognizes that defendant sees the role of a law guardian and an attorney selected by the children as different, it is clear that no such distinction is contemplated by the Family Court Act itself. As stated previously, the section of that statute omitted by defendant, §242, clearly defines the role of a law guardian as that of the child's advocate and as such demonstrates how that role is no different than that of an attorney selected individually by the children.

The courts have also addressed the role of the law guardian in custody actions.  In Koppenhoeffer v. Koppenhoeffer, 159 A.D.2d 113, 117 (2nd Dept. 1990), the Appellate Division, Second Department listed the "tasks" faced  by  the law guardian by stating:

> [t]he attorney may act as a champion of the child's best interest, as advocate for the child's preferences, as investigator seeking truth on controverted issues, or may serve to recommend alternatives for the court's consideration (citations ommitted)

Thus, neither the courts nor the Family Court Act perceives the role of the law guardian as neutral evaluator.  Although the children involved in this action may have approached Mr. Dobrish as to his representation of them thus prompting him to make a motion on their behalf to have the guardian ad litem previously appointed replaced, this in no way affected this court's appointment of Mr. Dobrish and his status based on that appointment.  Mr. Dobrish was appointed to represent the children to be their attorney.  Whether we call him a law guardian, or an attorney of choice, it is abundantly clear that this court did not appoint him as a neutral evaluator for the court.

While Mr. Dobrish may be asked to make recommendations to the court in the context of his representation of the children, this in no way diminishes his role as an advocate for his clients and should not impact on his ability to receive compensation for the services he renders. Although defendant asserts that Mr. Dobrish should be paid at the 18-B statutory rate, this court directed in the May 9, 1995 order that he be paid by the defendant for his services with a final apportionment to occur after a hearing is held in this matter. The statutory rate referred to by defendant has no bearing on Mr. Dobrish's fees as he was not appointed pursuant to the 18-B assigned counsel plan since it was clear that the parties were neither indigent nor incapable of affording private counsel fees at the time of the appointment.

Accordingly, Mr. Dobrish's motion is granted to the extent of directing defendant to pay $15,000 to Mr. Dobrish within thirty (30) days of the date of this decision. Should defendant fail to pay that amount, Mr. Dobrish will be entitled to a money judgment and the clerk is directed to enter that judgment upon written notice to defendant. This is without prejudice to any future applications to be made at the hearing or sooner if the need arises.

All matters not decided herein are hereby denied.

This constitutes the decision and order of the court.

Dated:   New York, New York
         August 18 , 1995

AUG 23 1995

COUNTY CLERK'S OFFICE
NEW YORK

J.S.C.

FAMILY COURT OF THE STATE OF NEW YORK
COUNTY OF KINGS
-----------------------------------------X
In the Matter of a Proceeding for Custody
under Article Six of the Family Court Act

GERALD C. ▮▮▮▮▮

                              Petitioner,
          -against-

JANICE M. J▮▮▮▮▮▮

                              Respondents
-----------------------------------------X

Docket No.
V06087/96

DECISION
on Motion for
Substitution of
Counsel

APPEARANCES:
Eli Yeger, Esq.
16 Court Street, suite 206
Brooklyn, N.Y. 11241
Attorney for Petitioner Father

Mannarino, Yagerman & Greenhaus, P.C.
By: Susan G. Mintz, Esq.
292 Madison Ave., 15th floor
New York, N.Y. 10017
Attorneys for Respondent Mother

Paul A. Crotty, Esq.
Corporation Counsel
By: Gerald Harris, Esq.
Janet Lam, Esq. of counsel
283 Adams Street, Room 342
Brooklyn, N.Y. 11201
Attorney for Commissioner of Social Services

Jane M. Spinak, Esq.
Robin Karasyk, of counsel
The Legal Aid Society
175 Remsen Street
Brooklyn, New York 11201
Law Guardian

Saul Edelstein, Esq.
Edelstein and Brown
26 Court Street
Brooklyn, N.Y. 11242
Movant

1

89

SARA P. SCHECHTER, J.

On February 26, 1997 a private attorney, Saul
Edelstein, Esq.,moved to be substituted as counsel for the
eight-year-old subject child in the pending custody
proceeding.  This proceeding is to be tried jointly with the
dispositional phase of a child abuse proceeding, pending for
months, in which the mother of the child was a respondent.
The child was injured when struck by a cousin who resided in
the home of the child.  The respondent mother, who also
resided in the home, admitted to improper supervision in
that she failed to protect the child from injury by the
cousin.  The father, who is the petitioner in the custody
case, was not a respondent in the child protective
proceeding.  The child has been paroled to him since April,
1996.  Throughout the pretrial and factfinding stages of the
abuse proceeding the child has been represented by a law
guardian from the Juvenile Rights Division of the Legal Aid
Society.
     The circumstances under which Mr. Edelstein became
involved in this matter, as stated in his memorandum, are as
follows:

          I have been advocating the traditionalist
     position for representing a child for many years
     and have established some type of reputation in
     that regard.  I have been on the lecture tour, I
     have received significant amount of publicity, and
     I have been involved substantially in some
     reasonably interesting cases dealing with that
     issue.  As a result of that reputation and
     publicity, Mr. Eli Yeger [the father's attorney]
     sought me out.  I know Mr. Yeger for many years
     and we have always had a friendly and warm
     relationship.  Indeed, when we meet either in the
     Family Court or the Supreme Court we are usually
     not adversaries and indeed have no legal or
     financial arrangement together, but merely enjoy
     each others's company at times in the hallways
     discussing various cases and problems....
     Recently, he sought my advice in regard to the
     instant case while waiting for an elevator in the
     Supreme Court.  He indicated that in his opinion,
     based upon the manner of representation that the
     child has had so far from the Legal Aid Society,
     he thought they were advocating a position
     contrary to the child's position.  He
     unequivocally stated to me that the child wished

2

90

to remain and live with the father but
nevertheless the law guardian was advocating a
position different than the child. He expressed
his concern on what my advice would be. My advice
was that the child should fire the law guardian,
if that be the case. He indicated that he was
representing the father and didn't have that
jurisdiction. I indicated to him that I would
like to see the child, and I would then act
accordingly.

Several months ago I saw the child, not in the
presence of the father and found him to be eight
going on fifteen. He was communicative,
intelligent, and seemed to understand what was
going on. He indicated to me the following:
"Daddy I love him very much. He's my favorite one.
While I was in the foster home [before the
decision in the 1028 hearing] I was always
thinking of him and want to live with him." I
really don't know if this was expressed to his
Legal Aid attorney, and I don't really know
whether the Legal Aid attorney was representing
his best interests or not, but under the
assumption that Mr. Yeger was correct, I decided
that I would represent the child. He came in with
a family friend, one Quentin Redden, and upon my
initial interview with the child I suggested that
Mr. Redden have the child watch a video that they
could rent ...called "The Client."... I then said
to him that he had to hire me, did he have any
money, he then smiled, took out a dollar bill,
handed it to me and said, "I want you to be my
lawyer." I had him sign a retainer agreement,
which he obviously did not read or understand but
I wished the formality to be continued, and I took
the dollar an proceeded to tell the family friend
that I would need the balance of my retainer in
the amount of Twenty Two Hundred ($2.2000.00)
Dollars. I had been previously given Three
Hundred ($300.00)Dollars as a consultation fee.
Mr. Redden indicated that would be forthcoming,
and I ultimately received a check from him [in
that amount.] The child is truly a client for the
fact that I have just been recently informed as I
am dictating this today, that the check has
bounced and that I should redeposit it. If that
is not a true lawyer/client relationship, I don't
know what is. My sole responsibility is to the

3

child, and I had been paid and I am not beholden
to Mr. Yeger's client, the father. I am beholden
to my client.

Both sections 241 and 249(a) of the Family Court
Act establish the right of the subject child to be
represented by counsel. While appointment of counsel for
the child is discretionary in custody proceedings, it is
mandatory in child protective proceedings. Section 249(a)
states:

> In a proceeding under article...ten...the family
> court shall appoint a law guardian to represent a
> minor who is the subject of the proceeding or who
> is sought to be placed in protective custody, if
> independent legal representation is not available
> to such minor.... In any other proceeding in which
> the court has jurisdiction, the court may appoint
> a law guardian to represent the child, when, in
> the opinion of the family court judge, such
> representation will serve the purposes of the act,
> if independent legal counsel is not available to
> the child.

Since the statute contemplates appointment of counsel
only when "independent legal representation is not
available," this court must decide whether the attorney who
seeks to be substituted in this case offers such
"independent representation," and, if so, whether the
preference for such representation is so strong as to
justify substitution of counsel at this late stage of the
case. As used in section 249(a), the term "independent
legal representation" has a double meaning. It is
apparently synonymous with "counsel of the child's own
choosing," as used in section 241, but the entire statutory
scheme for the appointment of law guardians points to the
conclusions that the child's attorney must also be
"independent" in the sense of being obligated only to the
child. Thus, the term addresses both the formation of the
attorney-client relationship and the unconflicted nature of
the advocacy that the child's attorney - whether appointed
or privately retained — will provide, that is, that the
child's interests must never be subordinated to those of the
adult litigants.
Mr. Edelstein contends that he was sought out because
the child's appointed law guardian was not representing the
child's expressed interests. All attorneys who represent
children struggle daily with their sometimes conflicting

4

dual obligation to represent both the best interests and the expressed interests of their minor clients. Mr. Edelstein, firmly in the "expressed interests" camp, argues that when an attorney seeks to represent the best interest of a child, the result is what Mr. Edelstein characterizes as "wink and nod" representation, in which the child's expressed wishes are given short shrift. Mr. Edelstein's contention that an attorney representing a child should advocate *only* for the child's expressed interests is unsupported by the Family Court Act and the controlling case law, however. According to the Family Court Act, attorneys representing children should both "help protect their interests" *and* "help them express their wishes to the court." FCA § 241. The Appellate Division, Second Department has stated, "The attorney [for the child] may act as champion of the child's best interest, as advocate for the child's preferences, as investigator seeking the truth on controverted issues, or may serve to recommend alternatives for the court's consideration." *Koppenhoefer v. Koppenhoefer*, 159 A.D.2d 113, 117. Precisely where the balance is to be struck depends on the age and maturity of the child and on the circumstances of the case. If the child in this case, who was not present in the courtroom during the proceedings, was led to believe, on the basis of information supplied by one of the adult parties or counsel, that his wishes had not been conveyed to the court, that information was erroneous. The Legal Aid Society law guardian has consistently conveyed the child's expressed wishes to the court.

The practical limitations on "pure" advocacy for a child of eight in a custody proceeding have previously been addressed by this court in *Matter of Scott L. v. Bruce N.*, 134 Misc.2d 240. An attorney-client relationship in which the attorney's multiple functions are at least implicitly acknowledged may be on a more candid footing than one in which an attorney leads a child to believe that the child's instructions will be followed to the letter. Consider the circumstances under which the subject child "retained" Mr. Edelstein: the child signed (in his nickname) a legal document, the retainer agreement, which he admittedly did not read or understand and which is of no legal effect. He then tendered a dollar, and believed he had retained an attorney. He left the office unaware that another individual, sent to escort him to the interview, had signed another retainer agreement (which is also of dubious legal effect, since this individual is neither custodian nor guardian of the child) and had tendered the true fee, exactly 2,500 times greater than that paid by the child. Is this not "wink and nod" representation?

Since section 241 specifies that appointed counsel is to be utilized only when the child does not have "counsel of his own choosing," however, the issue before the court is not whether a proper balance between "best interest" and "expressed interest" has been achieved in this case, but rather whether Mr. Edelstein is truly counsel of the child's own choosing. To decide this question, courts have looked to the circumstances surrounding the initiation of the new representation, payment of the attorney who seeks to be substituted, and the quality of the relationship between the child and the original attorney.

In this case, it is clear from Mr. Edelstein's account that the contact between Mr. Edelstein and the child came about as a result of contact by the father's attorney with Mr. Edelstein. Prior to Mr. Edelstein's February 26th appearance, no one had informed this court that the child was dissatisfied with his lawyer, although the father's attorney had mentioned in a conference with the court that he (the attorney) felt that she was not doing her job properly. Courts have consistently refused to permit counsel selected by one of the adult parties to act as law guardian for the subject child. See *Fargnoli v. Farber*, 105 A.D.2d 523; *P. v. P.*, 11/10/92 NYLJ 29, col.3 (Sup.Ct Kings County). The case at bar is in marked contrast to *Jurdak v. Jurdak*, 4/9/96 NYLJ 33, col. 6 (Sup.Ct. Kings County), in which the court refused to remove Mr. Edelstein as law guardian for children who had retained him with the help of their grandmother because the children believed their interests had not been fairly considered in a stipulation between the parents.

The payment of Mr. Edelstein's fee in the present case by a friend of the father also raises concerns. That Mr. Edelstein did not regard himself as retained by the child's payment of one dollar, but only when the full retainer was paid, is evidenced by the timing of his first appearance in this case. The retainer agreement signed by the child is dated November 21, 1996. The case was next before the court on December 18, 1996, at which time the trial schedule was finalized and provisions for the child's Christmas visitation with the mother were made. Mr. Edelstein neither appeared on that court date nor notified counsel nor this court that he had been "retained." The Legal Aid law guardian continued her representation in complete ignorance of any dissatisfaction on the part of her client. Mr. Edelstein's first appearance in this matter occurred on February 26, 1997, when the trial was scheduled to begin. The retainer agreement executed by Mr. Redden was also initially signed on November 21, 1996, but that date was

6

crossed out and the date February 24, 1997 written above the
original date.  February 24, 1997 is also the date of the
check for the balance of the retainer fee.  Surely the child
did not "instruct" his attorney to allow three months to
pass and wait to make the application for substitution when
the forensic evaluator was about to take the witness stand.

The disciplinary Rules of the Code of Professional
Responsibility specify that a lawyer shall not accept
compensation for legal services from one other than the
client except with the consent of the client after full
disclosure. 22 NYCRR 1200.26. Apparently no such disclosure
was made in this case, and in any event the child is not
legally competent to consent. Certainly, the law condones
situations in which attorneys are paid by an adverse party
and are nevertheless ethically bound to zealously advocate
for their clients. Attorneys representing birth parents are
often paid by the adoptive parents [SSL § 374(6)], for
example, and counsel fees for one spouse in a matrimonial
proceeding may be paid by the other party.  In those
situations, however, the parties are adults, presumed
capable of consenting to such payment and of selecting,
supervising and instructing their attorneys without the
intervention of the party paying the fee.  In some cases,
counsel fees for the law guardian representing a child who
is the subject of a custody proceeding also have been
apportioned between the parents in accordance with their
ability to pay.  See *Anonymous v. Anonymous,* 222 A.D.2d 295.
There is no indication in those cases that the apportionment
of payment was in any way entwined with the selection of the
attorney, however, nor should it be.  See *Jurdak v. Jurdak,*
*supra.*  The issue, thus, is not who ultimately pays the fee,
but what impact that payment has on the independence of the
representation.  In the circumstances of this case, where it
was clear from the outset that Mr. Edelstein would look to
the father for his fee, that independence appears to have
been compromised.

The quality of the relationship between the original
attorney and the child is the most crucial factor in the
decision whether to permit substitution.  Courts have
generally permitted substitution in situations where the
relationship has broken down. *Matter of Elianne M.,* 196
A.D.2d 439; *P. v. P., supra.*  Here, throughout the many
interviews the law guardian had with the child, even those
that took place after the child "retained" Mr. Edelstein,
the child never expressed any dissatisfaction with her
representation.  She has represented the child vigorously,
has procured the services of a social worker employed by the
Legal Aid Society, and has communicated the child's wishes

7

to the court.

Finally, even in situations where an adult seeks to substitute new counsel in the middle of a proceeding, substitution is permitted only upon a showing of good cause, such as irreconcilable conflict or conflict of interest. *People v. Rua*, 198 A.D.2d 311; *Matter of Ashley "JJ"*, 640 N.Y.S.2d 314. Here, although the custody hearing was set to begin at the moment the oral application for substitution was made, the related child protective proceeding has already gone through a 1028 hearing and factfinding. Substitution of counsel at this stage would cause a loss of continuity in representation of the child and may occasion further delay of the proceedings. The requisite showing of good cause to incur such risks has not been made.

For the reasons stated herein, the application for substitution of counsel for the subject child is denied. Notify counsel.

ENTER

*Tara P. Schechter*

Judge of the Family Court

DATED: Brooklyn, New York
      April 18, 1997

8

96

capped children without specified facility having received prior approval of State Commissioner of Education. Matter of Jeremy G., 1984, 105 A.D.2d 285, 482 N.Y.S.2d 872.

Section of Family Court Act providing that educational services for preschool-age, handicapped children, and all handicapped children during months of July and August, remains within jurisdiction of family court does not in any way limit family court to placing children, within its jurisdiction, in facilities which have received prior approval of the State Commissioner of Education. Matter of Jeremy G., 1984, 105 A.D.d 285, 482 N.Y.S.2d 872.

Authority to order the provision of educational services when public school is not in session rests with the Family Court, not with an impartial hearing officer. Matter of Handicapped Child, 1982, 21 Educ. Dept.Rep. 553.

**5. Preschool children**

Speech and physical therapy were "educational" rather than medical services, and thus, preschool handicapped child was entitled to receive those services free of cost pursuant to the Family Court Act, where

legislative intent was for early detection and treatment of preschool handicapped children in order to enhance their educational potential. Matter of David JJ, 1987, 129 A.D.2d 355, 517 N.Y.S.2d 606.

**7. Reimbursement, right to—Generally**

The issue of reimbursement for occupational therapy provided during the summer months is subject to a Family Court order under this section. Matter of Handicapped Child, 1982, 21 Educ.Dept. Rep. 553.

**16. —— Power of court in general**

Continual review of reimbursement of tuition expenses of handicapped child is necessary because handicapped child's condition may change substantially within course of single school year and school's facilities may also change. Schwartz v. Nassau County, 1985, 111 A.D.2d 242, 489 N.Y.S.2d 274.

Authority to order the provision of educational services when public school is not in session is vested in Family Court. Matter of the Board of Education of Floral Park-Bellerose Union Free School District, 1984, 24 Educ.Dept.Rep. 29.

## PART 4—LAW GUARDIANS

### Law Review Commentaries

The meaningful representation of children: An analysis of the State Bar Association Law Guardian Legislative Proposal. Merril Sobie. 64 N.Y.S.B.J. 52 (1992).

## § 241. Findings and purpose

This act declares that minors who are the subject of family court proceedings or appeals in proceedings originating in the family court should be represented by counsel of their own choosing or by law guardians. This declaration is based on a finding that counsel is often indispensable to a practical realization of due process of law and may be helpful in making reasoned determinations of fact and proper orders of disposition. This part establishes a system of law guardians for minors who often require the assistance of counsel to help protect their interests and to help them express their wishes to the court. Nothing in this act is intended to preclude any other interested person from appearing by counsel.

(As amended L.1988, c. 476, § 3.)

### Historical and Statutory Notes

**1988 Amendment.** L.1988, c. 476, § 3, eff. Jan. 1, 1989, inserted reference to appeals in proceedings originating in the family court.

34

## Supplementary Practice Commentaries.

*By Douglas J. Besharov*

### 1992

:ction 241 states that the law guardian system is established "for
ors who often require the assistance of counsel to help protect their
rests and to help them express their wishes to the court." It is hard to
how counsel can do either without speaking to the minor, assuming
. the minor is old enough for the contact to be meaningful. [*See, e.g.,*
*ter of Karl W.,* 168 A.D.2d 997, 564 N.Y.S.2d 940 (4th Dept., 1990),
:rsing a Family Court order that the law guardian "refrain from
tacting the children whom she represented" in an Article 10 proceed-
]

### 1991

tandard practice is to appoint one Law Guardian to represent all of the
dren in the family that is before the court. At times, however, a real
potential conflict of interest among the children requires the appoint-
nt of more than one Law Guardian. (*See* the original Practice Com-
ntary to this section, on p. 194 of the main volume.) The real or
ential conflict of interest among the children, however, must be palpa-
demonstrated on the basis of the specific circumstances of the case
l, of course, the burden of proof is on the moving party. [*See, e.g., In
Matter of Department of Social Services, on Behalf of Jennifer M.,*
)0, 148 Misc.2d 584, 561 N.Y.S.2d 347 (Fam. Ct., Ulster Co.), holding
ufficient the fact that the two children were not related by blood, with
: natural child desiring visitation with her father but the step-daughter
: wanting it.]

The records of child welfare and social service agencies are made
ifidential by various state and federal laws. In general, these laws
ike little or no provision for access to records by Law Guardians or
ier representatives of the children involved. (*But see* Fam.Ct.Act
1038.) This is more oversight than deliberate decision. After all, the
rpose of confidentiality is to protect the subject of the records and not to
event having a well-informed advocate. Thus, over the years, courts
ve rightly exercised their discretion to insure that the child's representa-
·e is given the maximum access to agency records that a liberal reading
the statutes will allow. [*See, e.g., In the Matter of Kimberly H.,* 1990,
.7 Misc.2d 711, 556 N.Y.S.2d 220, 221–22 (Fam. Ct. Westchester Co.),
lowing the Law Guardian to examine a child's social services file,
cluding adoption records, in order to prepare adequately for a foster care
atus review hearing. The court stated: "[t]he very nature of a 392 foster
re review places the agency's care of the child, and her status, in issue.
he case record represents the only history of the child while in foster
re. Social Services Law § 372(4) affords these case records the protec-
ve aegis of confidentiality. However, pursuant to section 372 and Family
ourt Act section 166, the decision whether to disclose these records is in
ie discretion of the court (*Matter of Carla L.,* 1974, 45 A.D.2d 375, 357
l.Y.S.2d 987)."]

### 1990

Early Practice Commentaries describe the controversy over the specific
ole that Law Guardians should play in various Family Court proceedings.
3y adding section 1075 to the Family Court Act in 1990, the Legislature
nay have inadvertently settled the dispute, at least at the post-disposition-
l stage of child protective proceedings. That new section requires Law
juardians to "apply to the court for appropriate relief" when they have
'reasonable cause to suspect that the child is at risk of further abuse or
ieglect or that there has been a substantive violation of a court order."
Since there is no mention of the child's wishes or desires, the Law

35

Guardian seems to have been transformed into an auxiliary child protective worker.

### 1988

Law Guardians are not neutral automatons. After an appropriate inquiry, it is entirely appropriate, indeed expected, that a Law Guardian form an opinion about what action, if any, would be in a child's best interest. The Law Guardian should act on that judgment—presenting evidence and argument to the court—unless the child is of sufficient maturity to instruct the Law Guardian on how to proceed.

The interests of a child can differ significantly from those of one or both parents. Hence, Law Guardians are not required to meet performance standards placed on them by counsel for any other party in the proceedings. So long as they promote the interests of the child and do not misuse confidential information, they cannot be removed for developing and communicating their opinions to the court. [*Stien v. Stien*, 130 Misc.2d 609, 496 N.Y.S.2d 902 (Fam.Ct., Westchester Co., 1985).]

### Practice Commentaries Cited

Matter of Brooke D. (4 Dept.1993) ___ A.D.2d ___, 598 N.Y.S.2d 633.
Matter of Department of Social Services, 1990, 148 Misc.2d 584, 561 N.Y.S.2d 347.
Stien v. Stien, 1985, 130 Misc.2d 609, 496 N.Y.S.2d 902.
Matter of Kimberly H., Fam.Ct., Westchester Co., N.Y., N.Y.Law J., June 7, 1990, p. 34.

### Law Review Commentaries

The representation of children: a summary and analysis of the bar association law guardian study. Sobie. 57 N.Y.S. B.J. 41 (February, 1985).

### Notes of Decisions

Generally  1
Conflicts of interest  3
Right to counsel  2

---

### 1. Generally

Guardians ad litem should not normally be appointed when minors are subject of proceedings in family court but law guardians or counsel of minors' own choice should represent them. Fargnoli v. Faber, 1984, 105 A.D.2d 523, 481 N.Y.S.2d 784, appeal dismissed 65 N.Y.2d 631, 491 N.Y.S.2d 158, 480 N.E.2d 746, motion to vacate denied 65 N.Y.2d 783, 492 N.Y.S.2d 948, 482 N.E.2d 566.

### 2. Right to counsel

Children are entitled to independent representation in family court proceedings since their interests are at stake and neither parents, parents' counsel, nor court can properly represent children's interests; children involved in family court proceedings can be represented by counsel of their own choosing. Fargnoli v. Faber, 1984, 105 A.D.2d 523, 481 N.Y.S.2d 784, appeal dismissed 65 N.Y.2d 631, 491 N.Y.S.2d 158, 480 N.E.2d 746, motion to vacate denied 65 N.Y.2d 783, 492 N.Y.S.2d 948, 482 N.E.2d 566.

Children subject of proceedings in family court may be represented by counsel to whom they are merely referred by a parent; however, parents may not retain counsel for their children or become involved in the representation of their children in proceedings involving them before family court because of the appearance or possibility of a conflict of interest or a likelihood that such interference will prevent the children's representation from being truly independent. Fargnoli v. Faber, 1984, 105 A.D.2d 523, 481 N.Y.S.2d 784, appeal dismissed 65 N.Y.2d 631, 491 N.Y.S.2d 158, 480 N.E.2d 746, motion to vacate denied 65 N.Y.2d 783, 492 N.Y.S.2d 948, 482 N.E.2d 566.

Mere fact that there is a proceeding in family court between parents which indirectly affects children does not give children right to participate or to be represented by counsel. Larisa F. v. Michael S., 1984, 122 Misc.2d 520, 470 N.Y.S.2d 999.

### 3. Conflicts of interest

It would have been impossible for law guardian to participate meaningfully in hearing on issue of sibling visitation, in proceeding concerning placement of children determined to be abused or neglec-

by their father, in absence of separate presentation of children with conflicting interests. Mattar of Brooke D. (4 Dept. 83) ___ A.D.2d ___ 598 N.Y.S.2d 633. In proceedings under Article 10 of Family Court Act in which it was alleged that ather sexually abused his 13-year-old stepdaughter in presence of father's four-year natural daughter, law guardian who represented both minors exercised independent professional judgment on behalf of each of her clients, such that appointment of additional law guardian was un-

necessary; law guardian balanced not only legal rights of natural daughter but also her general welfare in advocating that no visitation be permitted until court-ordered psychological evaluations be completed, and natural daughter, being of same household and exposed to same set of circumstances as older child, shared similar interest to older child whether related by blood or not. Matter of Department of Social Services, on Behalf of Jennifer M. 1990, 148 Misc.2d 584, 561 N.Y.S.2d 347.

## 243. Designation

(a) The office of court administration may enter into an agreement with a legal aid society for the society to provide law guardians for the family court or appeals in proceedings originating in the family court in a county having a legal aid society.

(b) The appellate division of the supreme court for the judicial department in which a county is located may enter into an agreement, subject to regulations as may be promulgated by the administrative board of the judicial conference, with any qualified attorney or attorneys to serve as law guardian or as law guardians for the family court or appeals in proceedings originating in the family court in that county.

(c) The appellate division of the supreme court for the judicial department in which a county is located may designate a panel of law guardians for the family court and appeals in proceedings originating in the family court in that county, subject to the approval of the administrative board of the judicial conference. For this purpose, it may invite a bar association to recommend qualified persons for consideration by the said appellate division in making its designation, subject to standards as may be promulgated by such administrative board.

(As amended L.1988, c. 476, § 4.)

### Historical and Statutory Notes

1988 Amendment. L.1988, c. 476, § 4, eff. Jan. 1, 1989, inserted references to appeals in proceedings originating in the family court wherever appearing.

## § 245. Compensation

*[See main volume for (a)]*

(b) If an appellate division proceeds pursuant to subdivision (b) or (c) of such section two hundred forty-three, law guardians shall be compensated and allowed expenses and disbursements in the same amounts established by subdivision three of section thirty-five of the judiciary law.

(As amended L.1986, c. 25, § 1.)

### Historical and Statutory Notes

1986 Amendment. Subd. (b). L.1986, c. 25, § 1, eff. Apr. 3, 1986, substituted "subdivision three of section thirty-five of the judiciary law" for "subdivision two of section thirty-five of the judiciary law".

## § 249. Appointment of law guardian

(a) In a proceeding under article seven, three or ten or where a revocation of an adoption consent is opposed under section one hundred fifteen-b of the

37

LAW OFFICES

**EDELSTEIN & BROWN**

PHIL BROWN

SAUL EDELSTEIN, P. C.

(718) 875-3550

26 Court Street, Brooklyn Heights, New York 11242

PAUL EDELSTEIN (1912-1968)

March 19, 1997

Hon. Sara P. Schechter
Family Court : State of New York
County of Kings
283 Adams Street
Brooklyn, New York 11201

      Re:  Elliot v. Jackson
           Docket No. V-6087/96

Dear Honorable Madam:

      Ralph Basso was kind enough to remit to me a copy
of the transcript of our initial appearance in court on February
26, 1997, a copy of which I assume you have.

      It is interesting to note that some of the
colloquy between the court and Ms. Karasyk supports my argument
in my post submission.

> **"Page 15...I have spoken, also, to Ms. Mintz,
> and Mr. Yeger to have their permission for
> her, Ms. Dietrich, to work both -- have
> permission to speak to the father, and to the
> mother, <u>and to interview Jeremy so that I
> could reevaluate my position</u>, and that I
> would submit, for the record, that I --<u>I have
> always said, all along, that Jeremy's
> position is that he wanted to live with his
> father, but I wasn't sure, exactly, if that
> was -- if I was supporting that</u>, but they
> have been aware of that, that my social
> worker has been working with Mr. Elliott, and
> -- and Ms. Deitrich met with Mr.  Elliott
> yesterday morning..."**

      The above emphasis was added by me.  Apparently
the child told his lawyer that he wanted to live with his father.
Ms. Karasyk, the child's lawyer, admits in court on the record
that she is not sure if she can support that position and must
speak with the Social Worker.  Frankly, that type of attitude
makes the hair upon my neck bristle and it brings in my opinion
discredit to our profession.

101

**WE ARE LAWYERS. WE ARE NOT TO SUBSTITUTE OUR** ✓
**JUDGMENT FOR THE JUDGMENT OF OUR CLIENTS. WE ARE NOT SOCIAL**
**WORKERS.**

        Imagine if the aforementioned was said to an adult
client. A grievance would immediately be sent to the Bar
Association and a suit for malpractice would be available.
Children, legally, should not be treated in a different manner,
especially non-impaired children. Under our code of professional
responsibility a lawyer can substitute his or her judgment for a
client who is impaired, but not for one who is *sui juris*. This
client is of sufficient age and maturity to have apparently
communicated to her lawyer what he wanted. How could she
possibly disregard it?

                            Respectfully submitted,

                            SAUL EDELSTEIN

SE/sc

cc: Eli Yeger, Esq.
    Susan G. Mintz, Esq.
    Robin Karasyk, Esq.

P.S. The new National, politically correct, American Bar
Association accepted terminology for infant clients are: impaired
and non-impaired children. It is suggested that a child of
sufficient age and maturity to direct his own fate is a non-
impaired child. An example of an impaired child would be an
infant age 0 months to who knows what.

PHIL BROWN                                            *26 Court Street, Brooklyn Heights, New York 11242*

SAUL EDELSTEIN, P. C.                                              PAUL EDELSTEIN (1912-1968)

*April 4, 1997*

Hon. Sara P. Schechter
Family Court : State of New York
County of Kings
283 Adams Street
Brooklyn, New York 11201

Re:    Elliot v. Jackson
        <u>Docket No. V-6087/96</u>

Dear Honorable Madam:

       Let me briefly share with you some thoughts in response to the reply affirmations of respective counsels.

       FIRST:    In response to Ms. Mintz's reply dated March 25, 1997, I concur with my colleague that an Article 10 proceeding should be severed from the custody trial although I believe it to be injudicious. However, they are two separate proceedings dealing with separate issues and should not be consolidated. Therefore they should be severed. Notwithstanding the aforementioned, I respect and will live with whatever Your Honor decides.

       SECOND:    How could the child ever express dissatisfaction with his representation when he didn't know that she might be selling him down the river in his "best interests". He thinks that "he's got a lawyer". He's been lead to believe that she would do whatever he wants. He doesn't know that his attorney has a Social Worker whispering in her ear after which she might act differently. That's my evidence and it is admitted by his attorney.

       THIRD:    Ms. Mintz got it wrong. I was never recommended to be the attorney in the P.v.P. case. I don't really care if I am the attorney or not. If you want to disqualify me,... be my guest. The check bounced anyway. I'm sure it will be made good and I'm sure that my reputation and integrity cannot be compromised by a few pennies that allegedly have been funneled to me through an intermediary.

1

*I WANT AN INDEPENDENT LAWYER FOR THIS CHILD... ONE* ✓
*WHO SERVES ONLY ONE MASTER,...HIS CLIENT.*

*I want to do it but if you want to pick someone else that's fine.   On page 5 of the Memorandum of Law. Ms. Karasyk stops just short of calling me a con-artist. The events that transpired on November 22, 1996 were meant too inspire confidence in the child.*

*FOURTH:    Don't question my integrity in some back handed matter. The retainer, the dollar and the client participated in the game playing to enlist the child's confidence on November 22, 1996.  I got a consultation fee in addition to a dollar on November 22, 1996. The check came in on February 24, 1997. A copy of which is enclosed. On December 18, 1996, I wasn't the attorney.*

*In regard to attorney Lamm's affirmation. I agree wherein she states "That a showing must be made that the relationship between child and court appointed attorney is someway tainted before substitution is permitted." I have made such a showing out of the mouth of the child's attorney who states that she might have to re-evaluate her position and didn't know if she could support her client's position to live with his father.  She further indicated that she would have to speak to the Social Worker. If that's not tainting... (See minutes dated February 26, 1997, Page 15)*

*I take umbrage with the fact that there is a possibility that I could be bought for $2,500.00 and therefore there is the possibility of a conflict of interest.  If it were $2,600.00, it might make a difference.*

*All kidding aside, I am a very successful attorney, practicing this type of law for over thirty-five (35) years and frankly am doing this instant case for this instant principal of law.*

*Counsel Karasyk's memorandum reveals that she is an extraordinarily good lawyer. I must apologize to her for her making her the scapegoat in this age old controversy.  She is doing exactly what one half of the law guardians in the State do with the imprimatur of the judicial system.  The other half of law guardians, usually in the Juvenile Criminal Division are purists like myself who state... Damn the social consequences and morality and what's right, fair and reasonable...Prove your case and if you can't,... my client walks.*

2

104

*Again with all due respect, change the name of the courthouse if we don't agree with the latter position because its <u>not</u> a courthouse but, in reality, a social agency. I don't wish to continue to participate in consumer fraud. Attorney Karasyk was hired as a lawyer not a Ms. goody two shoes.*

*If counsel Karasyk promises me and the court that she will represent her client and do exactly what he wants, even if its contrary to the A.C.S., and contrary to all the other agencies with initials,... I'll take a pass. I'm satisfied and she's a darn good lawyer, probably more experienced and effective than I am in the Family Court. She has to be able to beat up Dr. Grant on cross-examination because Dr. Grant is against her client. Can she handle that? Does she have a conflict?*

*During a brief discussion with attorney Karasyk I posed a hypothetical situation where a 13 year old, female child, in a custody case, wished to live or visit with her step-father with whom she was sexually involved. I inquired from attorney Karasyk could she represent the child and advocate the child's position in that case? She responded "Of course not."*

*It's a trick question. It shows that she can't be the zealous lawyer advocating even the foolishness of her client's position. She's substituting her judgment for the client's judgment and if her argument is foolish it is up to the Judge to make a determination not the attorney. As Harry Truman once said "If you can't stand the heat, stay out of the kitchen." By the way the above mentioned is an actual case out of Cook County in Illinois, in which their Appellate Division reversed and declared a mis-trial because the law guardian/attorney in that exact case advocated the position that it was in the "best interest" of the child to be with the mother, notwithstanding the child's wishes.*

*The Appellate Division admonished the law guardian that she had a duty to present her client's wishes and it was the duty of the court to throw it out.*

3

*In conclusion, win or lose, I want everyone to know that I hope once and for all a decision will be made that will answer this controversy dispositively and I hope that I had some part in bringing this problem to the forefront.*

*Respectfully submitted,*

*SAUL EDELSTEIN*

SE/sc

cc:   *Eli Yeger, Esq.*
      *Susan G. Mintz, Esq.*
      *Robin Karasyk, Esq.*

4

QUENTIN
BETTY
720 E. 32ND ST. APT. 7-E
BROOKLYN, NY 11210

0170

1-7803/2280
1359

Pay to the
order of   EDELsteiN & BrowN                          $ 2,200.00

Two Thousand Two hundred and 00/00 00 Dollars

2/24 19 97

M
MCU TO: Municipal
Credit Union
New York, New York

For Jeremy Jackson          Quentin Redden

Colorful Classic ® WDC                                              107

FAMILY COURT OF THE STATE OF NEW YORK
CITY OF NEW YORK : COUNTY OF KINGS PART XII
- - - - - - - - - - - - - - - - - - - X
GERALD C. ELLIOTT,

                 Petitioner,               Docket No.:
                                        V-06087/96

    -against-                            **MEMORANDUM**
                                        **OF LAW**

JANICE M. JACKSON & CSS

                 Respondent.

- - - - - - - - - - - - - - - - - - - X

## "YOU'RE WHO?"

### INTRODUCTION

    Any thinking lawyer who represents children has struggled with the question of what role to assume in that representation, a struggle that classically comes down to a choice between "best interest" and "expressed interest" representation. Most of us end up passionately committed to one model of representation or another and try to live out that model in practice. In my practice, I have assumed the expressed interest, or "traditional attorney" role and have sought to take direction from my clients about which objectives to pursue.

    During the many years that I have practiced both in the Family Court and the Supreme Court, I observed what I believed to be the confusion for lawyers of under-age clients, who have assumed the "best interest" approach. Unfortunately, I see children making false assumptions about their lawyers - assuming they have advocates for their expressed positions, ... when they do not. The children - clients assume that the information that they reveal to their lawyers will be kept secret and they assume that their lawyers are obligated to take action upon their request when unfortunately they are not. The role of the lawyer, unfortunately at times when he or she is called a law guardian, is at times both meaningless and at worst fraudulent. At times its the practice of the "wink & nod" between the attorneys and the court.

The lawyers representing children both in the Family Court and the Supreme Court certainly in custody cases generally are divided into two camps: those favoring a "traditional attorneys role" which I firmly believe, (representing what the child wants for the child's "expressed interest") and those favoring sort of a guardian ad litem role (GAL) representing what the lawyer has determined to be in the child's best interest.

What I have seen happen over the years is that many lawyers profess to take "a hybrid role" somehow representing both positions to the court. I don't believe that's possible, except possibly in the instance when the children-clients lack the maturity of judgment or the cognitive capacity for decision making necessary to access appropriately their own interest, particularly their long term interest. That is not the instant case.

110

As a traditionalist and purist in litigating and advocating a client's position in court it is my position that it is the <u>Judge</u> and not the child's lawyer who is responsible for determining the child's best interest. The court bases its decision on the evidence elicited through an adversarial process and the child has a right along with his parents, to have his position zealously advocated to the ✓ Judge. *(See generally, Martin Guggenheim "The Right To Be Represented But Not Heard: Reflections on Legal Representation For Children" 59 N.Y.U. Law Review, page 93-94 Note 4.*

The child in the instant case is age eight (8). Give him a voice in the process that will determine his fate. He is old enough to speak and he is old enough to engage in a rational decision making process, especially about himself. He should be able to direct his counsel, especially upon the issue as to with whom he would like to reside. In my view, there is no distinction between representing children from that of representing adults and that the ethical considerations of my chosen profession demand that I take the absolute position advocating this traditional attorney approach of zealous advocacy. That's what we lawyers have been trained to do and we lack the expertise and training to substitute our judgment for the judgment of either the <u>Court</u> or the <u>client</u>. We are not social workers. We are attorneys. We, who practice in the

Supreme Court, are at times representing children occasionally as law guardians, ancillary to a custody case within the divorce proceeding. We usually have no problem advocating the child's position without taking on the role of a quasi social legal worker. Anecdotally, I have been informed that the law guardians in delinquency proceedings before the Family Court, specifically the Legal Aid attorneys, also have no problem in regard to representing their client without facing any purported moral dilemma. The fourteen (14) year old, with the smoking gun in his hand, who just shot and robbed some people, was arrested by the police and was illegally searched and wasn't given his Miranda warnings, etc. etc., is routinely represented by Legal Aid who would support their client's Constitutional Rights to suppress the offended evidence. Their clients walk. They sleep well at night. They are not social workers. As Harry Truman once said, "If you can't stand the heat, get out of the kitchen."

I am old enough to remember the old Children's Court which the instant court is its direct decendant. The coming of this court initiated a new era in the legal systems focus on children. This court now takes a new albeit, paternalistic look at the interaction between children and the law. In a real sense, this court at times, could be considered, by purist like myself, (no offense intended) to be "anti-legal". This court's dependency on

non legal resources and focusing on the best interests or
welfare of the children, the "child savers" perceives no
duty to formulate legal regulations, thus effectively
"disenfranchising" children of their legal rights.  It would
seem to me lawyers under this scheme serve little purpose
other than to obstruct and delay.  I would hesitate to say
that if this trend continues this court is really not a
place for law, lawyers  or reporters but is instead a Social
Institution responsible for protecting children and families
by overseeing the child welfare system and holding them
accountable without operating with legal oversight.  If that
be the real case, then lets do it.  Let's not keep up with a
charade.

    In 1966 the United States Supreme Court intimated
in _Kent v. The United States_, *383 U.S. 541,* that children
have enforceable constitutional rights, including the right
to be represented by counsel in cases involving juvenile
delinquency.  In the following year the court rejected the
traditional doctrinal supremacy of *Parens patriae* in the
historic case of, In Re. Gault, 387 U.S. 1. The court held
that "neither the 14th Amendment nor the Bill of Rights are
for adults only."

    It is my position that the provision of separate
independent legal counsel is the only effective means for
securing legal rights in this country and independent
counsel should be required in any case where a child's

interests are being enunciated. *See, e.g. Hillary Rodham, Children Under the Law in the Rights of Children, 43 Harvard Educational Review 487, 509.*

It is commendable that on or about that time and subsequent to the aforementioned decisions, the Family Court Act, in 1970, was amended and Section 241 of the Family Court Act provided for the representation of minors who are the subject of Family Court proceedings and the act declares as follows: *Minors who are subject of Family Court proceedings should be represented by counsel of their own choosing or by law guardians, Family Court Act Section 241.* The act went further and stated that it was designed to *"help them express their wishes to the court"*. Who is doing that? Is it assigned counsel, Robin Karasyk, Esq., from the Juvenile Rights Division of the Legal Aid Society? I'm not sure and that is why I'm here.

I have been advocating the aforementioned traditionalist position for representing a child for many years and have established some type of reputation in that regard. I have been on the lecture tour, I have received significant amount of publicity, and I have been involved substantially in some reasonably interesting cases dealing with that issue. As a result of that reputation and publicity, Mr. Eli Yeger, sought me out. I know Mr. Yeger for many years and we have always had a friendly and warm relationship. Indeed when we meet either in the Family Court

114

or the Supreme Court we are usually not adversaries and indeed have no legal or financial arrangement together, but merely enjoy each others company at times in the hallway discussing various cases and problems. I would pick his brains and he would pick mine. Recently, he sought my advice in regard to the instant case while waiting for an elevator in the Supreme Court. He indicated that in his opinion, [1] based upon the manner of representation that the child has had so far from the Legal Aid Society, he thought they were advocating a position contrary to the child's position. He unequivocally stated to me that the child wished to remain and live with the father but nevertheless the law guardian was advocating a position different then the child. He expressed his concern on what my advice would be. My advice was that the child should fire the law guardian, if that be the case. He indicated that he was representing the father and didn't have that jurisdiction. I indicated to him that I would like to see the child and I would then act accordingly.

Several months ago I saw the child, not in the presence of the father, and found him to be eight (8) going on fifteen (15). He was communicative, intelligent, and seemed to understand what was going on. He indicated to me the following: "Daddy I love him very much." "He's my favorite one." "While I was in the foster home I was always

---

[1] He might be wrong, it's irrelevant.

thinking of him and want to live with him." I really don't
know if this was expressed to his Legal Aid attorney and I
don't really know whether the Legal Aid attorney was
representing his best interests or not but under the
assumption that Mr. Yeger was correct I decided that I would
represent the child. He came in with a family friend, one
Quentin Redden, and upon my initial interview with the child
I suggested that Mr. Redden have the child watch a video
that they could rent from Blockbuster called, "The Client".
That video suggests the role of a lawyer to a child in a
very cute and dramatic fashion and I wanted to see whether
the child would be able to perceive the role playing and
when I saw him a subsequent time as to whether he would
"hire his lawyer". He subsequently came back again with his
family friend, not his father, and when I inquired as to
whether he knew what a lawyer was he answered that he did.
He explained to me my role, I then said to him that he had
to hire me,... did he have any money,... he then smiled,
took out a dollar bill, handed it to me and said  "I want
you to be my lawyer." I had him sign a retainer agreement,
which he obviously did not read or understand but I wished
the formality to be continued, and I took the dollar and
proceeded to tell the family friend that I would need the
balance of my retainer in the amount of Twenty Two Hundred
($2,200.00) Dollars. I had been previously given Three
Hundred ($300.00) Dollars as a consultation fee. Mr. Redden

indicated that would be forth coming and I ultimately received a check from him in the amount of Twenty Two Hundred ($2,200.00) Dollars. The child is truly a client for the fact that I have just been recently informed as I am dictating this today, that the check has bounced and that I should redeposit it. If that is not a true lawyer/client relationship I don't know what is. My sole responsibility is to the child and I had been paid and I am not beholden to Mr, Yeger's client, the father. I am beholden to my client.

I have appeared in Court and I thank this court for permitting me to make this application on paper rather than orally, to substitute in place and in stead of the Legal Aid lawyer and to represent my client.

Parenthetically, it should be noted, that after my appearance in court, a discussion was held outside the courtroom in regard to the role of the respective attorneys. I inquired from the Law Guardian what her position was and she indicated that indeed her position might be exactly what mine is, which would be to represent the child and the child wishes to reside with the father. But, she was equivocal and wasn't 100% sure. If indeed, that is her position that she would zealously advocate the child's position, right or wrong and leave the best interests and welfare of the child to be determined by the court and not by her, I will withdraw graciously and proudly and let her continue to represent the child. The problem that I have is that she is always speaking to the social worker. Before acting, in advocating the child's position and her particular agenda she indicates that the social worker said this and the social worker said that and let me get my social worker. There is a philosophical problem here. It might be even an ethical dilemma here. When I am representing the child I will indicate to my adversary or to the court or to my client, let me speak to my investigators, ...not my social worker. When you are presenting a client in the court and before proceeding you indicate to the court that I must speak to and/or call my social worker to the stand, it is in my opinion that you are not a lawyer. You are a therapist. I put on the stand detectives and investigators. Not social scientists.

## CONCLUSION

The cases and precedents that support my position, photocopies of which I enclose, are as follows: *P v. P, NYLJ, November 10, 1992, P. 29, col. 3 and Anonymous v. Anonymous NYLJ, September 8, 1995 p. 27 col. 3, which was affirmed by the Appellate Division in its entirety and Jurdak v. Jurdak, NYLJ, April 9, 1996, P. 33, Col.6, Sup. Ct., Kings County.*

The Family Court Act section 249 states as follows: *"In any other proceedings in which the court has jurisdiction, the court may appoint a law guardian to represent the child, when, in the opinion of the Family*

*Court Judge, such representation will serve the purposes of this act, if independent legal counsel is not available to the child."*

Independent counsel is available to this child.

Most Respectfully submitted,

SAUL EDELSTEIN

FAMILY COURT OF THE STATE OF NEW YORK
COUNTY OF KINGS
----------------------------------------X

In the Matter of a Proceeding for    :    Docket No. ██████████
Custody under Article Six of the
Family Court Act                     :

      GERALD ████████,          :
              Petitioner

                       :

      -against-
                       :

    JANICE ████████ & C.S.S.,        :
             Respondents.          :

----------------------------------------X

## MEMORANDUM OF LAW

Respectfully, etc.

**JANE M. SPINAK, ESQ.**
**ROBIN KARASYK**, of Counsel
Attorney for Respondent
THE LEGAL AID SOCIETY
Juvenile Rights Division
175 Remsen Street, 10th Fl.
Brooklyn, New York  11201
(718) 237-3100

# I. STATEMENT OF FACTS

This custody case was filed by Gerald ███████ against Janice ██████ before the Honorable Cira A. Martinez on March 18, 1996. The neglect/abuse proceeding was filed on March 19, 1996, apparently as a result of an investigation by the Administration for Childrens' Services that had begun prior to the filing of the custody case. The abuse case was adjourned to March 25, 1996, for a hearing pursuant to Family Court Act (F.C.A.) Section 1028. The child was produced for and interviewed by the Law Guardian, Robin Karasyk, the first time on that date. Due to a death in the family of counsel for Respondent Mother, the hearing pursuant to F.C.A. §1028 was adjourned until March 27, 1996. At the close of the testimony that day, the non-Respondent Father requested release of the child to him. Respondent Mother objected and the application was denied. The §1028 hearing continued on March 28, April 3, April 8, April 10, and April 22, 1996. Ms. Karasyk interviewed the child again during this period. (The custody case was adjourned concurrently with the neglect/abuse case.) On April 22, 1996, the §1028 hearing concluded and the Court made a finding of imminent risk. The child was released to the non-Respondent Father and the Respondent Mother was granted visitation. (Although the older child is not the subject of this Memorandum of Law, it should be noted that he is and always has been throughout these proceedings paroled to the Respondent Mother. He is not the child of Gerald Elliott.)

1

Following the finding of imminent risk, the case was adjourned to June 12, 1996, then to July 18, 1996, and finally to August 8, 1996. Ms. Karasyk interviewed the child again during this period.

On August 8, 1996, the Respondents made admissions and findings of neglect were entered against them. The case was adjourned to November 1, 1996, for an Investigation and Report by the Administration for Childrens' Services (A.C.S.). This Investigation and Report, prepared by Ms. Katrina Canady, recommended release of the child to non-Respondent Father under A.C.S. supervision. It also recommended that both parents continue to attend a parenting skills program and that the parents and child continue in counseling. The case was adjourned to December 18, 1996 for disposition. Between November 1, 1996 and December 18, 1996, the Court and all counsel received the report of Dr. Swadesh Grant, a forensic psychologist mutually agreed upon and retained by the parties to produce a report for the Court. Dr. Grant's report recommended the return of the child to the Respondent Mother with liberal visitation for the Father and counseling for all parties. On December 18, 1996, the Court received an updated Investigation and Report. This second Investigation and Report recommended return of the child to Respondent Mother under supervision by the Administration for Childrens' Services. It also recommended that both parents continue in a parenting skills program and in counseling and that Respondent Mother not leave the child alone with Respondent Cousin.

2

The cases were adjourned for a dispositional hearing to February 26, 1997, and March 6, 1997.

The Legal Aid Society Law Guardian appointed to represent the child in these proceedings, Ms. Karasyk, has provided the child with independent counsel throughout her period of representation. Ms. Karasyk requested that a social worker be assigned to assist her in her representation. Molly Dieterich, an experienced social worker was assigned to the case.

Ms. Karasyk and Ms. Dieterich have reviewed all of the reports and documents generated in this case, including, but not limited to, the report of forensic psychologist Dr. Swadesh Grant, and the two Investigation and Reports submitted by the A.C.S. Additionally, they have obtained and reviewed court files from a prior case involving these parties. Ms. Karasyk has discussed Dr. Grant's forensic report with her at length and both Ms. Karasyk and Ms. Dieterich have discussed with Ms. Canady, the A.C.S. worker, the substance of her two reports and the basis for her change of position. Ms. Karasyk has met with both the attorney and the caseworker for the Administration for Childrens' Services on many occasions. Ms. Karasyk and Ms. Dieterich have met with Jeremy, separately or together, at least six times. During these meetings, they have discussed with Jeremy his wishes and have attempted to ascertain and address the child's needs and concerns. At the same time, they have strived to keep Jeremy apprised of the court proceedings and help him to understand them on his developmental level. Ms. Karasyk has spoken to both parents with counsel

3

124

present. Ms. Dieterich, after receiving appropriate permission, has met with each of the parties at their respective homes in order to interview them, review certain documents, including financial statements, and observe their interaction with Jeremy. Ms. Dieterich has spoken to the CBCC preventive services worker, Ms. Johnson, regarding the issues raised in this case. She has also spoken to the principal and the guidance counsel of Jeremy's school and his first, second and third grade teachers.

The work that Ms. Karasyk and Ms. Dieterich have done during the past year exemplifies the duties of an independent law guardian. Moreover, at no time during Ms. Karasyk's period of representation--not during any of the interviews by Ms. Karasyk or Ms. Dieterich,(the most recent of which took place the day prior to Mr. Edelstein's first appearance in court), not by way of phone call or writing, or through contact by a third party--did Jeremy ever convey that he was dissatisfied with the representation that he was receiving from Ms. Karasyk.

On February 26, 1997, Saul Edelstein, Esq., appeared in court and made an oral application that he be substituted for Ms. Karasyk as attorney for the child, Jeremy. Ms. Karasyk requested the opportunity to respond, memoranda of law were requested by the court and the case was adjourned.

## II. QUESTIONS PRESENTED

A.  A CHILD'S RIGHT TO COUNSEL IN A CUSTODY PROCEEDING BETWEEN PARENTS WILL BE VIOLATED BY REMOVING A LAW GUARDIAN WHO HAS INDEPENDENTLY REPRESENTED THE CHILD FOR A YEAR AND SUBSTITUTING COUNSEL SOLICITED BY A FRIEND OF THE FATHER'S.

4

125

B. NEW YORK LAW REQUIRES COUNSEL FOR A CHILD IN A CUSTODY PROCEEDING TO VIGOROUSLY ADVOCATE WISHES AND INTERESTS.

### III. LEGAL ARGUMENT

A. A CHILD'S RIGHT TO COUNSEL IN A CUSTODY PROCEEDING BETWEEN PARENTS WILL BE VIOLATED BY REMOVING A LAW GUARDIAN WHO HAS INDEPENDENTLY REPRESENTED THE CHILD FOR A YEAR AND SUBSTITUTING COUNSEL SOLICITED BY A FRIEND OF THE FATHER'S.

Children who are the subject of Family Court proceedings may be represented by "counsel of their own choosing or by law guardians." (See, Family Court Act §§241, 249, subd. (a)). Children are entitled to such representation because their interests are at stake and because neither the parents, the parents' counsel, nor the court can properly represent the children's interests. Fargnoli v. Faber, 105 A.D.2d 523, 481 N.Y.S.2d 784 (3rd Dept. 1984). Such representation, in order to be truly independent, must be free of outside influence by any of the parties as well as the appearance of such interference.

The cases cited by Mr. Edelstein are inapplicable in this case. In those cases, the child was dissatisfied with the original counsel and counsel received notice of the child's dissatisfaction prior to the application for substitution of counsel. In P v. P, NYLJ, Nov. 10, 1992, p.29, col.3, the court appointed attorney received a letter from her child client purporting to dismiss her and in Matter of Elianne M., 196 A.D.2d 439, 601 N.Y.S.2d 481 (1st Dept. 1993), both the Law Guardian and the teenage child had explicitly expressed their failure to communicate, and the child

5

had expressed her lack of trust in, fear of misrepresentation by and outside interference with the representation she was receiving from the Law Guardian. At no time in this proceeding has the child indicated dissatisfaction with the representation provided by Ms. Karasyk either to Ms. Karasyk or to the court. In Anonymous v. Anonymous[1], NYLJ, September 8, 1995, p.27, col.3, another case cited by Mr. Edelstein, the court focused on the standard of payment to a Law Guardian selected by the children in a custody proceeding. In the courts decision, it also discussed the role of the Law Guardian describing it as an advocate who assists the court in making a determination.

In Jurdak v. Jurdak, NYLJ, April 9, 1996, p.33, col.6), a case cited by Mr. Edelstein in support of his application, Justice Harkavy held that a Law Guardian approached and retained by the paternal grandmother could provide independent counsel. The grandmother was not aligned with either party in the custody action and obtained counsel for the children for the sole purpose of protecting their interests.

Jeremy's right to be represented by independent counsel would not be fulfilled by the substitution of Saul Edelstein as Law Guardian. It is clear from the sequence of events leading up to Jeremy allegedly retaining Mr. Edelstein, that he cannot provide independent representation of the child. In fact, the second

---

[1]Mr. Edelstein on page 10 of his Memorandum of Law states that this case was affirmed by the Appellate Division. The Law Guardian was unable to find this decision.

6

retainer agreement was signed by Mr. Redden, who has no legal relationship whatsoever with Jeremy.

In a case similar to the one before the court, P. v. P., NYLJ, November 10, 1992, p.29 col.3, a father involved in a custody dispute had brought his child to Martin Guggenheim, a lawyer prominent in the field of family law, and subsequently retained him. Justice Rigler held that it was inappropriate to substitute Mr. Guggenheim as Law Guardian specifically because the father had retained him to represent the child.

> "Parents may not, however, retain counsel for their children or become involved in the representation of their children because of the appearance or possibility of a conflict of interest or the likelihood that such interference will prevent the children's representation from being truly independent (See, Robert N. v. Carol W., NYLJ, September 30, 1983, p. 15, col 6: Besharov, Practice Commentary, McKinney's Cons. Laws of NY, Book 29A, Family Ct Act, §249, p 202)," Mtr of Fargnoli v. Faber, 105 A.D.2d at 524.)

As this Court stated:

> "What is of the utmost importance is that the child's representation, whether provided by a "law guardian" or a "guardian ad litem," be absolutely independent of any influence from either parent, from other family members or from persons who would seek to use the litigation to promote a cause." Matter of Scott L v. Bruce N., 134 Misc.2d 240, 509 N.Y.S.2d 971. (Schechter, J.) (Annexed hereto along with other cases cited.)

The fact that it was a friend of the father who signed the retainer agreement does not remove the appearance of a conflict of interest. Contrary to Mr. Edelstein's assertions, he is not in a position to act as independent counsel for the child. Should the

7

The applicable rules of professional responsibility take cognizance of the Lawyer's Code of Professional Responsibility.

> "The responsibilities of a lawyer may vary according to the intelligence, experience, mental condition or age of a client, the obligation of a public officer, or the nature of a particular proceeding." (EC 7-11).

> "Any mental or physical condition of a client that renders him incapable of making a considered judgment on his own behalf casts additional responsibilities upon his lawyer. Where an incompetent is acting through a guardian or other legal representative, a lawyer must look to such representative for those decisions which are normally the prerogative of the client to make. If a client under disability has no legal representative, his lawyer may be compelled in court proceedings to make decisions on behalf of the client. If the client is capable of understanding the matter in question or if contributing to the advancement of his interests, regardless of whether he is legally disqualified from performing certain acts, the lawyer should obtain from all possible aid." (EC 7-12).

Therefore, the child's rights and interests necessarily include the child's wishes, but may extend beyond them. The Law Guardian must work with the child in understanding "the nature of the proceeding, the child's rights, the role and responsibilities of the Law Guardian, the attorney-client privileges, the court process, the possible consequences of the legal action...."[2] The Law Guardian must interview all the parties and gather information and use that information in discussions with the child. The Law Guardian must also assist the child in understanding his own needs

---

[2]Law Guardian Representation Standards, Vol. II: Custody Cases, New York State Bar Association, January, 1994.

9

and wishes as separate from that of his parents and the possible and realistic options available.

Only through skillful and trained interviewing and assessment skills, can the child and the Law Guardian truly determine and understand the child's interests and wishes. Both Ms. Karasyk and Ms. Dieterich possess and have utilized their skills and knowledge in this case.

To say, as Mr. Edelstein does, that "there is no distinction between representing children from representing adults and that the ethical considerations of my chosen profession demand that I take the absolute position advocating this traditional attorney approach of zealous advocacy"[3] is to ignore the Code of Professional Responsibility and the relevant caselaw, Koppenhoeffer v. Koppenhoeffer, 159 A.D.2d 113 (2nd Dept. 1990), ("the attorney may act as a champion of the child's best interests, as advocate for the child's preferences, as investigator seeking truth on controverted issues, or may serve to recommend alternatives for the court's consideration.") The position as expressed by Mr. Edelstein is a gross oversimplification of a very complex and multilayered form of representation. As this Court stated in Scott L. v. Bruce N., 134 Misc.2d 240, 245, 509 N.Y.S.2d 971, 975, (1986):

> "There is nothing in the statutes nor in caselaw, however, which says that a law guardian in a custody proceeding should advocate for the child's wishes at the expense of his overall interests or at the expense of

---

[3]Edelstein Memorandum of Law, p. 3

a full presentation of the facts. The canons of ethics provide that where a client is under a disability, which all minors are to a greater or lesser extent, "the lawyer should consider all circumstances then prevailing and act with care to safeguard and advance the interests of his client." Lawyer's Code of Professional Responsibility, EC7-12. (App. Vol. 29 McKinney's 1975). Interpreted in this light the role of the child's representative, whether called 'law guardian' or 'guardian ad litem', is to bring a mature judgment to the situation and to provide or arrange for the provision of the manifold services required by a child who is the subject of a custody proceeding."

## IV. CONCLUSION

Ms. Karasyk has skillfully and carefully assisted Jeremy in identifying his wishes and interests and has, throughout this custody proceeding, advocated independently on his behalf, as the law demands. The substitution of Mr. Edelstein, following his own description of how Jeremy allegedly became his client, would undermine any notion of independent counsel for children in this state. Therefore, Mr. Edelstein's application should be denied.

11

by fellow officer!). In the instant case. the employer placed signs prohibiting smoking and requiring that automobile engines be turned off. It can hardly be said that the employer condoned the throwing of a lighted match into a can of gasoline or that there was "a continuity of practice — conduct which has gained acceptance —·that transforms an extra-employment caper into an incident of employment" (*Matter of Ognibene v Rochester Mfg Co.. supra. p 87*). This horseplay. although unfortunate. was "an obviously unauthorized and 'isolated incident of foolery'" (*Matter of Kotlarich v Incorporated Vil. of Greenwood Lake. supra*), and it was thus error for the Board to conclude that the injury arose out of and in the course of employment.

Decision reversed. and claim dismissed. without costs. Mahoney. P. J.. Casey. Weiss. Levine and Harvey. JJ., concur.

24  In the Matter of LINDA F. FARGNOLI. Respondent. v DONALD FABER. Respondent. TONNI FABER et al.. Appellants. — Appeal. by permission. from an order of the Family Court of Delaware County (Estes. J.). entered April 2. 1984. which. *inter alia.* denied the motion of the parties' minor children for substitution of counsel or. in the alternative. for the appointment of a guardian ad litem.

Movants are the two minor daughters of the parties to this proceeding. which was commenced by petitioner to resolve a bitter dispute over respondent's visitation rights. To protect the daughters' interests during the proceeding. a Law Guardian was appointed to represent them but. during the course of the proceeding. the daughters sought to substitute counsel of their own choosing, the Rural Legal Rights Foundation (the Foundation). for the Law Guardian. or, in the alternative, to have a staff attorney of the Foundation appointed as guardian ad litem for them. The Foundation further sought to disqualify respondent's attorney on the ground that he was previously involved in the merits of the case when he served as Family Court Judge of Delaware County.

In a well-drafted opinion, Family Court denied the motion to substitute the Foundation as the daughters' counsel because it appeared that petitioner had initiated and been involved in the Foundation's representation of the daughters, thereby interfering with the independent and impartial representation which must be afforded children in these situations. Family Court further refused to appoint the staff member as guardian ad litem because such an appointment was not appropriate in Family Court proceedings such as this. Family Court also, *inter alia*, removed the Law Guardian, appointed a substitute Law Guardian, and enjoined the Foundation and petitioner from interfering with the representation provided to the daughters by the substituted Law Guardian. From the order entered thereon, the daughters appeal.[*]

Initially, Family Court properly denied the alternative motion to appoint the staff attorney of the Foundation as guardian ad litem for the daughters. It is evident that guardians ad litem should not normally be appointed when minors are the subject of proceedings in Family Court, but that Law Guardians or counsel of their own choice should represent the minor (see Family Ct Act, §§ 241, 249, subd [a]; Besharov, Practice Commentary, McKinney' Cons Laws of NY, Book 29A, Family Ct Act, § 241, p 188; see, also, *Matter of Anonymous v Anonymous*, 70 Misc 2d 584, 585).

We further conclude that Family Court properly denied the daughters' motion to substitute counsel of their own choosing for the Law Guardian. Children are entitled to independent representation in Family Court proceedings because their interests are at stake and because neither the parents, the parents' counsel, nor the court can properly represent the children's interest (see Family Ct Act, §§ 241, 249, subd [a]; *Borkowski v Borkowski*, 90 Misc 2d 957, 959-961). Thus, children involved in Family Court proceedings can be represented by counsel of their own choosing (Family Ct Act, §§ 241, 249, subd [a]) and even by counsel to whom they are merely referred by a parent (see *Doe v Doe*, 92 Misc 2d 184, 190). Parents may not, however, retain counsel for their children or become involved in the representation of their children because of the appearance or possibility of a conflict of interest or the likelihood that such interference will prevent the children's representation from being truly independent (see *Robert N. v Carol W.*, NYLJ, Sept. 30, 1983, p 15, col 6; Besharov, Practice Commentary, McKinney's Cons Laws of NY, Book 29A, Family Ct Act, § 249, p 202).

In this case, there is sufficient evidence to cast doubt on whether the Foundation can provide truly independent representation of the daughters' interests. Petitioner signed an authorization for release of records and information which indicates that the staff attorneys for the Foundation were her attorneys for at least some period of time. Furthermore, in a letter from a staff attorney for the Foundation dated February 21, 1984, petitioner was notified by the Foundation whether to attend a particular counseling session. Although petitioner, her

---

[*] Respondent has not appealed from so much of the order as disqualified his attorney and, thus, we do not address this aspect of the order.

attorney and the Foundation deny that the Foundation represented petitioner and assert that the Foundation can provide independent representation to the daughters, the apparent contacts between petitioner and the Foundation, as enumerated above, demonstrate, at a minimum, the appearance of a possible conflict of interest, which may infringe upon the independent representation to which the daughters are entitled. Thus, regardless of the precise relationship between the Foundation and petitioner, if any, this appearance of a possible conflict of interest warranted the prudent decision to deny the motion permitting the Foundation to be substituted as the daughters' counsel.

We further agree that the removal of the former Law Guardian and replacement with a new attorney to act as Law Guardian was wise. By providing the daughters with new representation untainted by the accusations and innuendo which seem to have thus far characterized this proceeding, we are hopeful that this matter can proceed to a prompt resolution designed to promote the best interest of the daughters.

Finally, we are of the view that Family Court had authority and grounds to enjoin the Foundation and petitioner from certain disparaging and disruptive communications concerning the daughters' representation by the Law Guardian. There is evidence that petitioner acted in a manner that reflected adversely upon the former Law Guardian and might have undermined his representation of the daughters. There is further evidence, as discussed above, of the appearance of a possible conflict of interest on the part of the Foundation. Family Court was, thus, concerned that the daughters' right to independent representation in this proceeding might be affected by further communications from the Foundation and or petitioner. Accordingly, an injunction was permissible (see CPLR 6301). Inasmuch as the injunction is narrowly directed and proscribes only certain communications which would be improper in any event (see *Robert N. v Carol W.*, NYLJ, Sept. 30, 1983, p 15, col 6, supra; Code of Professional Responsibility, EC 7-37), we are satisfied that no First Amendment rights have been infringed.

Order affirmed, without costs. Kane, J. P., Main, Mikoll, Yesawich, Jr., and Harvey, JJ., concur.

25   In the Matter of PHYLLIS TRAINOSKY, Appellant, v NEW YORK STATE DEPARTMENT OF TAXATION AND FINANCE, Respondent. — Appeal from a judgment of the Supreme Court at Special Term (Conway, J.), entered September 14, 1983 in Albany County, which dismissed petitioner's application, on a proceeding pursuant to CPLR article 78, to annul a determination of the State Department of Taxation and Finance terminating her employment.

**People v Nails (Thomas)** [196 AD2d 439, 601 NYS2d 280]

The People of the State of New York, Respondent,  v. Thomas Nails, Appellant.

First Department,

(August 12, 1993)

Judgment, Supreme Court, New York County (Richard Lowe, III, J.), rendered September 17, 1991, convicting defendant, upon his plea of guilty, of attempted criminal possession of a controlled substance in the fifth degree, and sentencing him, as a second felony offender, to a term of 1 1/2 to 3 years, unanimously affirmed.

After pleading guilty, defendant was informed that the People would file a predicate felony statement.  Defendant informed the court that he would not challenge the predicate felony statement, and the court immediately proceeded to impose sentence.  There is no merit to defendant's argument that it is reversible error to impose sentence without awaiting the filing of a predicate felony statement.  The People's failure to file it is rendered harmless where "[t]he statutory purposes for filing a predicate statement (CPL 400.21) have been satisfied, to wit:  apprising the court of the prior conviction and providing defendant with reasonable notice and an opportunity to be heard" (People v Bouvea, 64 NY2d 1140, 1142).

Concur—Carro, J. P., Rosenberger, Wallach, Kupferman and Rubin, JJ.

**Matter of Elianne M.** [196 AD2d 439, 601 NYS2d 481]

In the Matter of Elianne M., Also Known as Elizabeth Ann M., Appellant, and Another, Children Alleged to be Neglected. Commissioner of Social Services of the City of <*pg.440> New York et al., Respondents.

First Department,

(August 12, 1993)

Order, Family Court, Bronx County (Cira Martinez, J.),

1

entered on or about February 8, 1993, which denied the application of the Law Guardian to be relieved and denied the application of the child Elianne M. to permit the law firm of Sullivan & Liapakis to be substituted as counsel, unanimously reversed, on the law, the Law Guardian's application to be relieved is granted and the law firm of Sullivan & Liapakis is substituted as counsel, and the matter is remitted to the Family Court for further proceedings, without costs.

The Family Court erred in denying the Law Guardian's motion to be relieved and the child's application for substitution of counsel. Family Court Act §§ 241 and 249 (a) specifically provide for representation of a child by counsel of his or her own choosing. Children are entitled to counsel of their choice because it is their interests that are at stake (see, Matter of Fargnoli v Faber, 105 AD2d 523, appeal dismissed 65 NY2d 631).

The Law Guardian's role is to provide assistance of counsel to help protect the interests of minors who are the subject of Family Court proceedings and "to help them express their wishes to the court" (Family Ct Act § 241; see also, Matter of Scott L. v Bruce N., 134 Misc 2d 240, 242). Where, as here, both the Law Guardian and the teenage child have explicitly expressed their failure to communicate, the child has indicated her lack of trust in her appointed representative, her fear that this representative will not effectively communicate her wishes to the court and her belief that the Law Guardian has been influenced by her adoptive mother, the proper course was to relieve the Law Guardian and permit substitution of counsel of the child's choosing.

Concur—Milonas, J. P., Rosenberger, Rubin and Nardelli, JJ.

2

:tation*              Found Document          Rank 1 of 1          Databas·
)9 N.Y.S.2d 971                                                   NY-CS
:ite as: 134 Misc.2d 240, 509 N.Y.S.2d 971)

In the Matter of SCOTT L, Petitioner,
v.
BRUCE N, Respondent.
Family Court, City of New York,
New York County.
Aug. 25, 1986.

Father in custody dispute moved, inter alia, for appointment of law guardian
for children. The Family Court, City of New York, Schechter, J., held that
children's need for representation was being adequately met by the Society for
Prevention of Cruelty to Children as guardian ad litem.
Application denied.
See also, 126 A.D.2d 157, 513 N.Y.S.2d 121.

INFANTS⌐ 77
:11k77
Father in custody dispute was not entitled to appointment of law guardian for
the children, where children's need for representation was being adequately met
by Society for Prevention of Cruelty to Children as guardian ad litem.
McKinney's Family Court Act § 249.

**971 Tarnow & Frank by Herman Tarnow, New York City, for petitioner.
**972 *240 Wallman & Kramer by David Pugh, New York City, for respondent.
Society for the Prevention of Cruelty to Children by Mary Clarke, New York
City, guardian ad litem for the children.
DECISION ON MOTION

SARA P. SCHECHTER, Judge:
Respondent father in this custody dispute moves inter alia *241 for appointmen:
of a law guardian for the children. At the initial court appearance the court
had assigned the New York Society for Prevention of Cruelty to Children,
hereinafter "SPCC", as guardian ad litem for the two children, ages seven and
nine, but did not assign a law guardian pursuant to Family Court Act section
249. Since the appointment of a law guardian in a custody proceeding is
discretionary with the court (F.C.A. § 249), the court must decide whether such
representation would add in any meaningful way to that already being provided b
SPCC.
A child who is the subject of a custody proceeding may require a variety of
services: investigation of the family's circumstances, mediation of the disput
when appropriate, communication of age-appropriate information concerning the
litigation, moral support and legal representation during the litigation. From
county to county these needs are addressed in various ways, depending on the
resources available in a particular locality. The probation department, the
Juvenile Rights Division of the Legal Aid Society, 18-B panel attorneys, social
services agencies and children's advocacy groups are often utilized in various
combinations.
In New York County, SPCC is often assigned by the court in custody proceedings

ecause the agency, which employs field investigators, court liaisons and
ttorneys, offers all the aforementioned services in a coordinated fashion and
s, moreover, a statutorily constituted child protective agency, with authority
ɔ file petitions pursuant to Article 10 of the Family Court Act, should the
nvestigation uncover evidence of child abuse or neglect.  (F.C.A. § 1032).
FN1]

> FN1. In New York City attorneys from the Juvenile Rights Division of the
> Legal Aid Society, who usually serve as law guardians in proceedings
> pursuant to articles three, seven and ten of the Family Court Act, prefer
> not to be assigned to routine custody cases because they are seriously
> overburdened by their caseload of mandated cases.  They do accept
> assignment in special circumstances, however, for example, where they have
> previously represented the subject child in prior proceedings.

Although New York statutes mandate neither a "guardian ad litem " nor a "law
uardian" in custody cases, recognition of the child as a person rather than
hattel, requires that the child's position be distinguished and asserted
ndependently of the battling adults.  O'Shea v. Brennan, 88 Misc.2d 233, 387
.Y.S.2d 212 (Sup.Ct., Queens Co., 1976);  Borkowski v. Borkowski, 90 Misc.2d
57, 396 N.Y.S.2d 962 (Sup.Ct., Steuben Co., 1977);  Matter of Marilyn H., 100
isc.2d 402, 420 N.Y.S.2d 445 (Fam.Ct., N.Y.Co., 1979);  Foster and *242 Freed,
hild Custody and the Adversary Process:  Forum Conveniens? Vol. XVII No. 2,
am.Law Q. 133 (1983);  Eitzen, A Child's Right to Independent Legal
epresentation in a Custody Dispute, 19 Fam.Law Q. 53 (1985).  The question is
ɒt whether, but rather, how to make the child's voice heard in the proceedings
Although in some cases the child's point of view will emerge sufficiently in
he investigations performed by court-appointed probation officers or
sychologists, in most cases it is preferable, often essential, to appoint a
epresentative for the child who can participate fully in all stages of the
itigation process. [FN2]  Among the various jurisdictions which have recognize
his need, **973 there is no consensus as to what to call the child's
epresentative, nor is there even agreement concerning which functions--
nvestigative, advocacy, etc.--go with which label.  (See Eitzer, Id., and
oster and Freed, Id., for a summary of the diverse statutes.)

> FN2. The question of whether the child who is the subject of a proceeding
> should be regarded as having full party status, which would bear upon the
> child's rights to discovery, to veto proposed settlements and to appeal, a
> well as to have legal representation, is not before the court in the
> present case, since neither of the adult parties is seeking to curtail
> rights which the child would enjoy as a party.

The term "guardian ad litem " is not statutorily defined in New York.
lassically a guardian ad litem for one under a disability functions as the
itigant would function were it not for the disability.  Where the disability i
nfancy, therefore, the guardian ad litem does what the child would presumably

do if she were an adult--select, retain and supervise counsel, gather factual information, and generally assist counsel in the preparation of the case. (See I. Horowitz and H. Davidson, Legal Rights of Children § 3.03 (Family Law Series, 1984)). In custody cases, there has traditionally been an association of the investigative function with the role of guardian ad litem. (See Braiman v. Braiman, 44 N.Y.2d 584, 591, 407 N.Y.S.2d 449, 378 N.E.2d 1019 (1979) where the court recommends appointment of a guardian ad litem "who would be charged with the responsibility of close investigation and exploration of the truth....") The term "law guardian" is defined only as "an attorney admitted to practice law in the State of New York." (F.C.A. § 242). The law guardian's functions are to provide assistance of counsel to help protect the "interests" of minors who are the subject of family court proceedings and "to help them express their wishes to the court." (F.C.A. § 241). *243 That the fulfillment of this role often requires some factual investigation is obvious. It is equally obvious that when the child subject of the proceeding is very young, the function of the law guardian can differ little from that of the guardian ad litem: "In some cases involving children incapable of considered judgment, the lawyer must facilitate full presentation of adequate and reliable evidence, essentially remaining neutral as to the outcome, but filling critical gaps in the case as portrayed by petitioner and respondent so that the court can make a more informed judgment." Practice Note: In the Matter of Jennifer G., Vol. 11 No. 3 J.R.D. Newsletter 5, 18 (March 1985). Where the case involves a young child, therefore, and where the law guardian has access to investigative services, or where, as here, the guardian ad litem can readily provide an attorney, the service rendered to the child by either will be essentially the same.

The question remains whether there is a significant distinction in the type of legal representation provided by the two types of representatives in a custody case involving older children. SPCC contends that it is the proper function of the guardian ad litem to advocate for the child's best interests, whereas the law guardian is said to be ethically bound to assert the child's wishes, even when they may be at variance with the best interests. [FN3]

> FN3. A discrepancy between the child's wishes and best interests may also
> occur in cases other than custody proceedings. A New Hampshire court, for
> example, has found that guardians ad litem should be appointed in addition
> to appointed defense counsel in certain children in need of services
> (CHINS) cases. In re Lisa G., 127 N.H. 585, 504 A.2d 1 (1986).

The Juvenile Rights Division of the Legal Aid Society does take the position that the "best interests" of the child are properly left to the determination of the court, while the "interests" which the law guardian is charged by F.C.A. § 241 to protect "may be quite distinct from what the court ultimately adjudges to be in the child's best interest." Id. at 16. That a law guardian may properly form and assert a position wholly divergent from that ultimately articulated by the trial court or an appellate court is a proposition which this court heartily endorses. It does not follow, however, that the child-client should dictate what that position will be.

The extent to which the child's wishes should influence the formulation of the
position must vary according to the maturity, intelligence and emotional
stability of the child in question.  *244 Where the child is a **974 teenager of
reasonably sound judgment, either a law guardian or a guardian ad litem would be
very likely to advocate for the outcome the child prefers, and properly so,
since the wishes of a mature youngster also carry greater weight with the court
than those of a younger child.  Eschbach v. Eschbach, 56 N.Y.2d 167, 451
N.Y.S.2d 658, 436 N.E.2d 1260 (1982).  Although the law guardian might see this
course as arising out of the attorney-client relationship, whereas the guardian
ad litem would see it in terms of a diminution of the disability of infancy, the
effect on the case would be the same.

The problem arises with regard to children, like the seven and nine-year-old
subjects of the instant proceeding, who are of borderline maturity.  SPCC as the
guardian ad litem " will make an assessment of the child's best interests and
assert that position in the litigation and urge it upon the court as a
recommendation, although obviously not with the expectation of substituting its
judgment for that of the court.  Although a "law guardian" would make a similar
assessment, the law guardian might arguably feel obligated to assert the
position in the case which the child desires, and asserting a position in a
litigation involves much more than merely expressing the child's wishes to the
court.  Indeed, it is obvious that a primary duty of a guardian ad litem is to
make the child's wishes known to the court, since a major component of the
disability of infancy is the inability of a child to express himself adequately
in words.  Thus, through either a guardian ad litem or law guardian the child's
wishes should be communicated to the court.

The posture of the child's representative--neutral, pro-petitioner or pro-
respondent--affects his handling of the case at every stage, however, from
settlement negotiations to closing statements and possible appeal.  If it were
to be assumed that the proper function of a "law guardian" is to advocate for
the wishes of any child old enough to express them, then a "guardian ad litem "
would be a preferable representative for a child of borderline maturity in a
custody proceeding.  The classically "pure" advocacy that a law guardian would
provide in a delinquency proceeding, for example, is simply not possible in a
situation where the client is not possessed of all the facts, is not present in
the courtroom and where, moreover, it might be emotionally damaging for the
child to learn the entire truth about the parents.

An endless number of situations come to mind when flexibility would benefit the
child more than would rigid adherance *245 to his wishes.  For example, the
child's representative may ascertain that the child's position in a particular
case has such a slight chance of prevailing after trial that it would be
preferable to agree to a settlement which displeases the child, but which
includes concessions (such as timing of change of custody, visitation,
continuation in same school or therapy) which could only be obtained through
negotiations.

There is also the troubling question of whether in a custody case a "law
guardian," in the effort to have a particular position prevail, should attempt,
albeit by perfectly legal means, to suppress or withhold information which could

e relevant to the court's determination of the child's best interests, when
uch evidence runs contrary to the result the child desires.  Although we would
ot anticipate that any law guardian would fail to put before the court evidence
f neglect or abuse which would be cognizable under article 10 of the Family
ourt Act, [FN4] there is much else which the court would want to know which
ight be unknown to the adult parties or which they might both choose to
ithhold for their own reasons. X To uncover and **975 offer such evidence is an
mportant part of the role of the child's representative in a custody
roceeding.  Borkowski v. Borkowski, supra.  Zealous advocacy should never be
ermitted to interfere with this crucial function.

> FN4. According to the Practice Commentary, "most observers agree that the
> Law Guardian has the 'duty to disclose' information concerning the abuse o:
> neglect of his or her young client." N.Y.Fam.Ct.Act, Practice Commentary,
> p. 194, 195 (McKinney's 1983).

There is nothing in the statutes nor in caselaw, however, which says that a la
guardian in a custody proceeding should advocate for the child's wishes at the
expense of his overall interests or at the expense of a full presentation of th
acts.  The canons of ethics provide that where a client is under a disability,
which all minors are to a greater or lesser extent, "the lawyer should conside:
all circumstances then prevailing and act with care to safeguard and advance th
interests of his client."  Lawyer's Code of Professional Responsibility, EC 7-1:
(App.Vol. 29 McKinney's 1975).  Interpreted in this light the role of the child'
representative, whether called "law guardian" or "guardian ad litem ", is to
oring a mature judgment to the situation and to provide or arrange for the
orovision of the manifold services required by a child who is the subject of a
custody proceeding.  (See Anonymous v. Anonymous, 70 Misc.*246 2d 584, 333
N.Y.S.2d 897 (Rockland Co., 1972) holding that the duties of a law guardian are
coterminous with those of a guardian ad litem in representing a minor who is a
respondent in a paternity proceeding.) & What is of the utmost importance is tha
the child's representation, whether provided by a "law guardian" or "guardian a:
litem," be absolutely independent of any influence from either parent, from
other family members or from persons who would seek to use the litigation to
oromote a cause.  Fargnoli v. Faber, 105 A.D.2d 523, 481 N.Y.S.2d 784 (3rd
Dept.1984);  Robert N. v. Carol W., N.Y.L.J. 9/30/83 p. 15 col. 6; Matter of
Roxanne F., 79 A.D.2d 505, 433 N.Y.S.2d 762 (1st Dept.1980).
For the reasons stated herein, we find that the children's need for
representation is being adequately met by SPCC as guardian ad litem, and the
application for the appointment of a law guardian is, therefore, denied.
END OF DOCUMENT

SHARON FRIEDERWITZER, Appellant, v ELLIOT FRIEDERWITZER, Respondent.

Argued January 4, 1982; decided February 16, 1982

### SUMMARY

APPEAL from an order of the Appellate Division of the Supreme Court in the Second Judicial Department, entered April 13, 1981, which, by a divided court, (1) modified, and, as modified, affirmed an order of the Supreme Court at Special Term (VINCENT R. BALLETTA, J.), entered in Nassau County, modifying the judgment of divorce by inserting directions that defendant shall have custody and control of the infant issue of the marriage and that plaintiff shall have visitation rights, and (2) remitted the matter to the Supreme Court to determine the visitation rights of the plaintiff. The modification consisted of deleting so much of the order as specified the visiting rights of the plaintiff.

An uncontested divorce was awarded plaintiff wife by judgment dated July 24, 1979. The separation agreement entered into by them provided that as to the two children of the marriage the husband and wife would have joint custody with the children residing with the wife and reasonable visitation rights to the husband. It provided further that the terms of the agreement would survive a judgment of divorce "without merging, other than child support which shall merge in said decree." The judgment of divorce provided that the parties have joint custody of the children, the father to have visitation as provided in the separation agreement, and that the agreement should survive and not merge in the judgment. It also contained a retention of jurisdiction provision required by Appellate Division rule. Less than a year after the original judgment, the father moved for modification of the judgment of divorce so as to award him sole custody of the children. The Trial Judge found that the mother, while not unfit, was less fit to have custody than the father because her own best interests and social life appeared to be of "paramount concern to her, to the total exclusion of the best interests of her children". He predicated that conclusion on the mother having frequently left her then 11- and 8-year-old girls alone in the apartment until late at night when she went out for the evening even though the children informed her that they were afraid to stay alone, and on the mother's profession of raising the children in the tenets of Orthodox Judaism while at the same time flagrantly violating those tenets.

The Court of Appeals affirmed the order of the Appellate Division, holding, in an opinion by Judge MEYER, that extraordinary circumstances are not a *sine qua non* of a change in parental custody of a child, whether the original award of custody is made after plenary trial or by adoption of the agreement of the parties, and the standard ultimately to be applied remains the best interests of the children.

*Friederwitzer v Friederwitzer*, 81 AD2d 605, affirmed.

### HEADNOTE

**Parent and Child — Custody — Modification of Custody Award**

Extraordinary circumstances are not a *sine qua non* of a change in parental custody of a child, whether the original award of custody is made after plenary trial or by adoption of the agreement of the parties; this is also true with respect to a judgment governed by an Appellate Division rule containing a retention of jurisdiction provision. No agreement of the parties can bind the court to a disposition other than that which a weighing of all the factors involved shows to be in the child's best interest, and the standard ultimately to be applied remains the best interests of the child when all of the applicable factors are considered, not whether there exists one or more circumstances that can be denominated extraordinary; accordingly, where the separation agreement, which survived and did not merge in the judgment of divorce, provided that the parents would have joint custody and the father moved, less than a year after the original judgment, for modification so as to award him sole custody, it was not error to award sole custody to the father, inasmuch as it was found that the mother, while not unfit, was less fit to have custody than the father because her own best interests and social life appeared to be of paramount concern to her, to the total exclusion of the best interests of her children.

### POINTS OF COUNSEL

*Carl D. Bernstein* for appellant. I. There were no extraordinary changes in circumstances which justified a switch in custody to the father. (*Matter of Nehra v Uhlar*, 43 NY2d 242; *Corradino v Corradino*, 48 NY2d 894; *La Veglia v La Veglia*, 54 AD2d 727; *Matter of Austin v Austin*, 65 AD2d 903; *Matter of Heller v Bartman*, 65 AD2d 876; *McLaughlin v McLaughlin*, 71 AD2d 738; *Martin v Martin*, 74 AD2d 419.) II. The wishes of an 11-year-old child are of little weight in determining custody. (*Matter of Calder v Woolverton*, 50 AD2d 587, 39 NY2d 1042; *Pino v Pino*, 57 AD2d 919.) III. There has been no showing that the mother was in any sense unfit or that the father was more fit.

*Stanley Lehrer* for respondent. I. The court found sufficient grounds to justify transferring custody from the
mother to the father. (*Matter of Barkley v Barkley*, 60 AD2d
954, 45 NY2d 936; *Braiman v Braiman*, 44 NY2d 584.) II.
The totality of the circumstances justified the custodial
change. (*Matter of Nehra v Uhlar*, 43 NY2d 242; *Corradino
v Corradino*, 48 NY2d 894; *Matter of Nierenberg v Nierenberg*, 36 NY2d 850; *Opferbeck v Opferbeck*, 57 AD2d 1074;
*Papernik v Papernik*, 55 AD2d 846; *Mantell v Mantell*, 45
AD2d 918; *Matter of D'Alessandro v Parisi*, 60 AD2d 897.)
III. The wishes of Lisa Friederwitzer, 11 years and 9
months old at the time of the trial, should be accorded
consideration. (*Martin v Martin*, 308 NY 136; *Pact v Pact*,
70 Misc 2d 100; *Matter of Barry v Glynn*, 59 Misc 2d 75.) IV.
The trial court was in the best position to fully evaluate the
facts. The best interests of the children will not now be
served by another uprooting. (*Matter of Gloria S. v Richard
B.*, 80 AD2d 72.)

OPINION OF THE COURT

MEYER, J.

Extraordinary circumstances are not a *sine qua non* of a
change in parental custody of a child, whether the original
award of custody is made after plenary trial or by adoption
of the agreement of the parties, without contest, and without merging the agreement in the judgment. The more
particularly is this so with respect to a judgment governed
as is the judgment in this case by rule 699.9 of the Appellate Division, Second Department (22 NYCRR 699.9), pursuant to which the trial court expressly "retains jurisdiction * * * for the purpose" to the extent permitted by law,
"of making such further decree with respect to * * *
custody * * * as it finds appropriate under the circumstances existing at the time application for that purpose is
made to it" (22 NYCRR 699.9 [b], Approved Forms For
Matrimonial Judgments, J13). The order of the Appellate
Division affirming Special Term's order changing custody
to the father should, therefore, be affirmed, without costs.

The parties were married in 1968. An uncontested divorce was awarded plaintiff wife after inquest, by judgment dated July 24, 1979. The separation agreement en-

tered into by them provided that as to the two children of
the marriage, Lisa and Nicole, the husband and wife would
have joint custody* with the children residing with the wife
and reasonable visitation rights to the husband. It provided further that the terms of the agreement would survive a judgment of divorce "without merging, other than
child support which shall merge in said decree." The judgment of divorce provided that the parties have joint custody of the children, the father to have visitation as provided in the separation agreement, and that the agreement
should survive and not merge in the judgment. It also
contained the retention of jurisdiction provision (Approved
Forms, J13) required by Appellate Division rule.

In September, 1979, the mother, who had been living
with the children on Long Island close to the residence of
the father, moved with the children to an apartment on
East 93rd Street in Manhattan. Both parties and the
children have been reared as Orthodox Jews, strictly observing both the Sabbath and the dietary laws. The children, who had attended a yeshiva on Long Island, were
transferred to a yeshiva in Manhattan. Less than a year
after the original judgment, in April, 1980, the father
moved for modification of the judgment of divorce so as to
award him sole custody of his daughters. The mother cross-
moved for sole custody. After a trial during which the
mother, father and both children testified, the Trial Judge
found the father to be "a loving and caring person * * *
well qualified as a fit parent." He found that the mother,
while not unfit, was less fit to have custody than the father
because her own best interests and social life appeared to
be of "paramount concern to her, to the total exclusion of
the best interests of her children." He predicated that
conclusion on the mother having frequently left her then
11- and 8-year-old girls alone in the apartment until late at
night when she went out for the evening even though the
children informed her that they were afraid to stay alone,
and on the mother's profession of raising the children in
the tenets of Orthodox Judaism while at the same time
flagrantly violating those tenets by permitting a male

---

* While physical custody was not to be shared under the agreement, it required
consultation between the parties on all matters pertaining to the health, welfare,
education and upbringing of the children.

friend to stay in the apartment and share her bed to the
knowledge of the children, by failing, except rarely, to take
the children to Sabbath services, and by permitting the
male friend to violate the Sabbath by turning on the
television, all of which confused the children and was
contrary to their religious beliefs and detrimental to their
religious feeling. Noting the older daughter's strong desire
to live with her father and the younger child's wish to
continue living with her mother but not to be separated
from her sister, the Trial Judge acknowledged that the
wishes of the children was an element to be considered, but
held it controlled in this instance by the overriding considerations above detailed. He therefore modified the judgment to award custody of both children to the father.

The Appellate Division by a divided court modified in a
respect not material to our determination and affirmed
Special Term's order. The majority found the Trial Judge's
conclusion that custody in defendant would serve the best
interests of the children to be supported by the evidence.
The dissenter, interpreting our decisions in *Corradino v
Corradino* (48 NY2d 894) and *Matter of Nehra v Uhlar* (43
NY2d 242) as holding that custody "pursuant to an agreement should not be transferred absent extraordinary circumstances" (81 AD2d, p 606) of which he found no evidence in the record, voted to reverse and deny the father's
motion. The mother's appeal to us presents the question of
law whether extraordinary circumstances are required as
the dissent suggested. We affirm.

The only absolute in the law governing custody of children is that there are no absolutes. The Legislature has so
declared in directing that custody be determined by the
circumstances of the case and of the parties and the best
interests of the child, but then adding "In all cases there
shall be no prima facie right to the custody of the child in
either parent" (Domestic Relations Law, § 240; see, also,
§ 70). Because the section speaks to modification as well as
to an original matrimonial judgment, "all cases" must be
read as including both. That, of course, does not mean that
custody may be changed without regard to the circumstances considered by the court when the earlier award
was made but rather that no one factor, including the

149

existence of the earlier decree or agreement, is determinative of whether there should, in the exercise of sound
judicial discretion, be a change in custody.

Indeed, in *Matter of Nehra v Uhlar* (43 NY2d 242, *supra*),
we were at pains to point out many of the factors to be
considered and the order of their priority. Thus, we noted
that "Paramount in child custody cases, of course, is the
ultimate best interest of the child" (p 248), that stability is
important but the disruption of change is not necessarily
determinative (pp 248, 250), that the desires of the child
are to be considered, but can be manipulated and may not
be in the child's best interests (p 249), that self-help
through abduction by the noncustodial parent must be
deterred but even that "must, when necessary, be sub-
merged to the paramount concern in all custody matters:
the best interest of the child" (p 250), that the relative
fitness of the respective parents as well as length of time
the present custody had continued are also to be considered
(pp 250-251), that "Priority, not as an absolute but as a
weighty factor, should, in the absence of extraordinary
circumstances, be accorded to the first custody awarded in
litigation or by voluntary agreement" (p 251), whereas of
lesser priority will be the abduction, elopement or other
defiance of legal process as well as the preferences of the
child (*id.*).

The priority which is accorded the first award of custody,
whether contained in court order or voluntary agreement,
results not from the policy considerations involved in *res
judicata* (which permits change in custody decrees when
warranted by the circumstances, *Kunker v Kunker*, 230
App Div 641, 645; cf. *Matter of Bachman v Mejias*, 1 NY2d
575, 581; *Goldman v Goldman*, 282 NY 296, 304; see
Restatement, Judgments 2d [Tent Draft No. 3], § 74, Comment *d;* and [Tent Draft No. 5], § 61, Comment *f,* illustra-
tion 11), so much as from the conceptions that stability in a
child's life is in the child's best interests and that the prior
determination reflects a considered and experienced judgment concerning all of the factors involved (*Martin v
Martin*, 74 AD2d 419, 427). But the weight to be given the
prior award necessarily depends upon whether it results
from the Trial Judge's judgment after consideration of all

relevant evidence introduced during a plenary trial or, as here, finds its way into the judgment through agreement of the parties proven as part of a proceeding in which custody was not contested and no evidence contradictory of the agreement's custody provision has been presented. No agreement of the parties can bind the court to a disposition other than that which a weighing of all of the factors involved shows to be in the child's best interest (*People ex rel. Wasserberger v Wasserberger,* 42 AD2d 93, 95, affd on opn below 34 NY2d 660). Nor is an agreement so contradictory of considered judgment as to determine custody solely upon the basis of the wishes of the young children involved a " 'weighty factor' " for consideration (*Martin v Martin,* 74 AD2d 419, 426, *supra*). Thus, *Nehra's* phrase "absence of extraordinary circumstances" is to be read as "absence of countervailing circumstances on consideration of the totality of circumstances," not that some particular, sudden or unusual event has occurred since the prior award. The standard ultimately to be applied remains the best interests of the child when all of the applicable factors are considered, not whether there exists one or more circumstances that can be denominated extraordinary.

An additional reason for so holding in the instant case exists in rule 699.9 of the Appellate Division, Second Department, to which the decree in the instant case is subject. Custody decrees remain subject to modification because the governing statute so provides (*Goldman v Goldman,* 282 NY 296, 304, *supra;* Domestic Relations Law, § 240; Siegel, 1964 Practice Commentary, McKinney's Cons Laws of NY, Book 14, Domestic Relations Law, § 240, 1981-1982 Pocket Part, p 165; Ann., 73 ALR2d 1444). Rule 699.9 expressly states that "as to support, custody and visitation, no such [separation] agreement or stipulation is binding" (22 NYCRR 699.9 [f] [4]) and requires, as earlier noted, that the judgment contain the provision (*id.,* Approved Forms, J13) that the court retains jurisdiction for the purpose of making such further custody decree "as it finds appropriate under the circumstances existing *at the time application for that purpose is made to it*" (italics supplied). Such a modification is, as already noted, permitted by law when authorized by the totality of

circumstances, including the existence of the prior decre
Moreover, the language of the rule makes indelibly clea
that it is the circumstances existing at the time of th
application for change that governs whether a chang
should be made, whether or not any of them can be charac
terized as extraordinary. This, of course, does not mear
that a matrimonial court in the Second Department has
the authority to change custody simply because change is
requested, but that it has the discretion to do so when the
totality of circumstances, including the existence of the
prior award, warrants its doing so in the best interests of
the child.

It thus appears that the standard applied by the courts
below was not legally incorrect. Moreover, the record supports the determination of the courts below that the change
of custody was warranted by the lesser concern of the
mother for the emotional well-being of her children than
for her own life style demonstrated after the original
award was made, particularly in light of the short period of
time it had been in existence when the application for
modification was made and the fact that the custody provisions of the divorce judgment were based on the agreement
of the parties rather than plenary consideration by the
trial court.

For the foregoing reasons, the order of the Appellate
Division should be affirmed, without costs.

Chief Judge COOKE and Judges JASEN, GABRIELLI,
WACHTLER and FUCHSBERG concur; Judge JONES taking no
part.

Order affirmed.

---

DONALD ESCHBACH, Appellant, v RITA ESCHBACH, Respondent.

Argued March 29. 1982: decided May 13. 1982

SUMMARY

APPEAL from so much of an order of the Appellate Division of the Supreme Court in the Second Judicial Department, entered August 10, 1981, as modified, on the law and the facts, and, as modified, affirmed a judgment of the Supreme Court at Special Term (MORRIE SLIFKIN, J.). entered in Westchester County, awarding custody of the parties' three infant children to plaintiff. The modification consisted of substituting a provision granting exclusive custody only of the parties' two older children to plaintiff.

Plaintiff father sought custody of his three daughters. who resided with defendant mother pursuant to the terms of a stipulation between the parties. which was incorporated in their judgment of divorce. The relationship between the two older girls and their mother has deteriorated since the time of the parties' divorce and the older girls expressed a strong desire to live with their father. Although the youngest child. Laura. did not express such a preference in favor of one parent, she did express a strong desire to remain with her sisters. The trial court made no specific finding that defendant was an unfit mother for Laura, but it implicitly found that defendant is the less fit parent. The court awarded custody of the three girls to plaintiff. The Appellate Division agreed that the antagonistic relationship of the older children with their mother and their preference for living with their father required a change in custody for the older girls. However. with respect to Laura. the Appellate Division modified the Supreme Court judgment and ordered that she remain with her mother. On this appeal, the question is limited to which parent should have custody of Laura. defendant not having appealed from that part of the Appellate Division order affirming the award of custody of the older children to plaintiff.

The Court of Appeals reversed the Appellate Division order and reinstated the Supreme Court judgment, holding, in an opinion by Judge JASEN, that the trial court

properly found that under the totality of the circumstances, Laura's best interests required changing custody
of the child from her mother to her father.

*Eschbach v Eschbach*, 83 AD2d 845, reversed.

### HEADNOTE

**Parent and Child — Custody — Placement with Siblings**

The trial court's determination that, under the totality of the circumstances, it is in
the best interests of the youngest child of the parties to change the custody of the child
from defendant mother to plaintiff father, along with her two older sisters, conforms
with the weight of the evidence and, accordingly, said judgment is reinstated: although
the youngest child did not express the definite preference for living with her father that
the older girls did, she expressed a strong desire to remain with her sisters, and, while
the trial court made no specific finding that defendant was an unfit mother for the child,
a finding that defendant is the less fit parent is implicit in its order to change custody
and is supported by the record.

### POINTS OF COUNSEL

*Herbert J. Malach* and *Robert G. Schneider* for appellant.
I. The trial court had sufficient evidence to transfer custody of Laura to the father and that finding should not
have been disturbed. (*Matter of Darlene T.*, 28 NY2d 391;
*Matter of Ray A. M.*, 37 NY2d 619; *Matter of Jewish Child
Care Assn. of N. Y.*, 5 NY2d 222; *People ex rel. Portnoy v
Strasser*, 303 NY 539; *Bunim v Bunim*, 298 NY 391; *Matter
of Ebert v Ebert*, 38 NY2d 700; *Matter of Irene O.*, 38 NY2d
776; *Bistany v Bistany*, 66 AD2d 1026; *Kesseler v Kesseler*,
10 NY2d 445; *Aberbach v Aberbach*, 33 NY2d 592.) II. It
was error for the court below to separate Laura from her
two sisters and this was clearly not in Laura's best interests. (*Matter of Ebert v Ebert*, 38 NY2d 700; *Obey v Degling*,
37 NY2d 768; *Bistany v Bistany*, 66 AD2d 1026; *Aberbach v
Aberbach*, 33 NY2d 592; *Lucey v Lucey*, 60 AD2d 757.) III.
The decision of the trial court specifically found the mother
to be unfit and less fit than the father which would warrant
a change of custody of Laura. (*People ex rel. Sibley v
Sheppard*, 54 NY2d 320; *Aberbach v Aberbach*, 33 NY2d
592; *Martin v Martin*, 74 AD2d 419; *Kuleszo v Kuleszo*, 59
AD2d 1059; *Matter of Goho v Goho*, 59 AD2d 1045.)

*Edward D. Loughman, Jr.*, for respondent. I. In contrast
to appellant's distortion of the record, not a shred of evidence shows respondent to be an unfit mother of Laura.
(*Matter of Henson*, 77 Misc 2d 694; *Sandman v Sandman*,

64 AD2d 698; *Porges v Porges,* 63 AD2d 712; *People ex rel. Repetti v Repetti,* 50 AD2d 913; *Matter of Darlene T.,* 28 NY2d 391; *Bunim v Bunim,* 298 NY 391; *Matter of Ray A. M.,* 37 NY2d 619; *Matter of Susanne U. NN v Rudolf OO,* 57 AD2d 653, affd *sub nom. Matter of Nehra v Uhlar,* 43 NY2d 242.) II., Appellant's failure to prove Mrs. Eschbach an unfit mother of Laura required continuation of custody in her mother. (*Matter of Nehra v Uhlar,* 43 NY2d 242; *Corradino v Corradino,* 48 NY2d 894; *Sandman v Sandman,* 64 AD2d 698; *Porges v Porges,* 63 AD2d 712; *Mullins v Mullins,* 76 AD2d 914; *Bistany v Bistany,* 66 AD2d 1026; *People ex rl. Selbert v Selbert,* 60 AD2d 692; *People ex rel. Repetti v Repetti,* 50 AD2d 913; *Obey v Degling,* 37 NY2d 768.)

## OPINION OF THE COURT

JASEN, J.

The question to be resolved on this appeal is whether custody of the youngest child of the parties herein should be changed, along with that of her two older sisters, from her mother to her father.

Plaintiff, Donald Eschbach, and defendant, Rita Eschbach, were married on November 23, 1963. Donald Eschbach was granted a divorce on May 28, 1979 on the basis of the couple having lived separate and apart pursuant to a separation agreement for one year. (Domestic Relations Law, § 170, subd [5].) Custody of the three daughters of the marriage was granted to their mother pursuant to an oral stipulation of the parties entered in the minutes of the court at the inquest hearing held on January 16, 1979. The stipulation, which also provided visitation rights for the children's father, was incorporated but not merged in the judgment of divorce.

Events over the course of the next year indicated a progressive deterioration in the mother's relationship with her daughters. On several occasions, the two older girls, Karen and Ellen, ran away from defendant's home, either to their father's residence or to friends' homes. The record also reveals that the mother refused to allow the girls to participate in extracurricular activities at school and imposed severe limitations on what activities they could participate in and with whom they were allowed to associate. Concerned that the children were being raised in an unhealthy atmosphere which was affecting their emotional and psychological development. the father commenced this action seeking a modification of the judgment of divorce to the extent of awarding him custody of his three daughters.

The trial court took testimony from both parents, representatives of the school, and the two older daughters. Although the youngest daughter, Laura, did not testify, she was interviewed by the court *in camera,* and a transcript of that proceeding is included in the record before us. Additionally. a report was prepared for the court by a probation officer who had interviewed the parties.

The trial court found that the mother's unreasonable demands and restrictions were jeopardizing the older daughters' emotional and intellectual development and that there was a total breakdown of communication between the older children and their mother. Furthermore. the court found that the strong prefrence to live with their father expressed by these children. who were age 16 and 14 at the time of the hearing. should be given consideration.

Although Laura, who was 10 at the time of the hearing, had not expressed a similarly strong preference to live with her father rather than her mother. the court recognized her strong desire to remain with her sisters. After considering all the factors presented, the court found that her best interests would be served by continuing her close relationship with her sisters and that a change of custody to her father was necessary under these circumstances.

On appeal. the Appellate Division agreed that "the antagonism [of the older] children * * * toward defendant and their strong preference to live with plaintiff" (83 AD2d 845. 846) required a change in custody for Karen and Ellen. That court, however, modified the judgment and ordered that Laura's custody remain with the mother because there was "nothing to suggest that defendant has been anything but a fit parent toward her." (*Id.*)

On this appeal, the father seeks custody of Laura. The mother has not sought a further appeal from that part of the order which affirmed the judgment awarding custody of Karen and Ellen to the plaintiff. The question on this appeal is thus limited to which parent should have custody of Laura. We agree with the trial court that Laura's best interests require a change in her custody from her mother to her father.

Any court in considering questions of child custody must make every effort to determine "what is for the best interest of the child, and what will best promote its welfare and happiness". (Domestic Relations Law, § 70; *Matter of Ebert v Ebert*, 38 NY2d 700, 702; *Obey v Degling*, 37 NY2d 768, 769; *Matter of Lincoln v Lincoln*, 24 NY2d 270; *Bistany v Bistany*, 66 AD2d 1026; *Sandman v Sandman*, 64 AD2d 698, mot for lv to app den 46 NY2d 705; *Matter of Saunders v Saunders*, 60 AD2d 701.) As we have recently stated, there are no absolutes in making these determinations; rather, there are policies designed not to bind the courts, but to guide them in determining what is in the best interests of the child. (*Friederwitzer v Friederwitzer*, 55 NY2d 89, 93-95.)

Where the parties have entered into an agreement as to which parent should have custody, we have stated that "[p]riority, not as an absolute but as a weighty factor, should, in the absence of extraordinary circumstances, be accorded" to that agreement. (*Matter of Nehra v Uhlar*, 43 NY2d 242, 251.) This priority is afforded the first determination of custody in the belief the stability this policy will assure in the child's life is in the child's best interests. (*Friederwitzer v Friederwitzer*, *supra*, at p 94; *Corradino v Corradino*, 48 NY2d 894; *Matter of Nehra v Uhlar, supra; Obey v Degling, supra; Dintruff v McGreevy*, 34 NY2d 887; *Aberbach v Aberbach*, 33 NY2d 592; *People ex rel. Selbert v Selbert*, 60 AD2d 692.) But as this court noted in *Friederwitzer*, "[n]o agreement of the parties can bind the court to a disposition other than that which a weighing of all the factors involved shows to be in the child's best interests (*People ex rel. Wasserberger v Wasserberger*, 42 AD2d 93, 95, affd on opn below 34 NY2d 660)." (*Friederwitzer v Friederwitzer, supra*, at p 95.) Thus, an agreement between the parties is but one factor to be weighed by the court in deciding whether a change of custody is warranted.

The weight to be given the existence of a prior agreement depends on whether the prior disposition resulted from a full hearing by a trial court or was merely incorporated in the court's judgment pursuant to an uncontested stipulation. (*Friederwitzer v Friederwitzer, supra,* at pp 94-95.) This is particularly true where, as in this case, the rules of the court require that the decree specify that "as to support, custody and visitation, no such agreement or stipulation is binding" (22 NYCRR 699.9 [f] [4]) and that the court retains jurisdiction for the purpose of making such further custody decree "as it finds appropriate under the circumstances existing at the time application for that purpose is made to it". (22 NYCRR 699.9. Approved Forms, J13.) Since the court was not bound by the existence of the prior agreement, it has the discretion to order custody changed "when the totality of circumstances, including the existence of the prior award. warrants its doing so in the best interests of the child." (*Friederwitzer v Friederwitzer, supra,* at p 96.)

Primary among those circumstances to be considered is the quality of the home environment and the parental guidance the custodial parent provides for the child. (*Matter of Ebert v Ebert,* 38 NY2d 700, 702, *supra; Bistany v Bistany,* 66 AD2d 1026, *supra: Sandman v Sandman.* 64 AD2d 698, mot for lv to app den 46 NY2d 705. *supra; Matter of Saunders v Saunders,* 60 AD2d 701. *supra.*) While concerns such as the financial status and the ability of each parent to provide for the child should not be overlooked by the court. an equally valid concern is the ability of each parent to provide for the child's emotional and intellectual development. (*Sandman v Sandman. supra: Porges v Porges,* 63 AD2d 712; *Matter of Saunders v Saunders. supra.*)

In determining whether the custodial parent can continue to provide for the child's various needs, the court must be cognizant of the individual needs of each child. It is, of course, entirely possible that a circumstance such as a total breakdown in communication between a parent and child that would require a change in custody would be applicable only as to the best interests of one of several children. (*Bistany v Bistany. supra: Sandman v Sandman, supra; Porges v Porges, supra.*) To this end, it is important for the court to consider the desires of each child. But again, this is but one factor to be considered, as with the other factors, the child's desires should not be considered determinative. (*Matter of Ebert v Ebert, supra,* at p 702; *Obey v Degling,* 37 NY2d 768, 770, *supra; Dintruff v McGreevy,* 34 NY2d 887, 888, *supra; Sandman v Sandman, supra.*) While not determinative, the child's expressed preference is some indication of what is in the child's best interests. Of course, in weighing this factor, the court must consider the age and maturity of the child and the potential for influence having been exerted on the child! (See, e.g., *Obey v Degling, supra,* at p 770; *Dintruff v McGreevy, supra,* at p 888.)

Finally, this court has long recognized that it is often in the child's best interests to continue to live with his siblings. While this, too, is not an absolute, the stability and companionship to be gained from keeping the children together is an important factor for the court to consider. "Close familial relationships are much to be encouraged." (*Matter of Ebert v Ebert, supra,* at p 704.) "Young brothers and sisters need each other's strengths and association in their everyday and often common experiences, and to separate them, unnecessarily, is likely to be traumatic and harmful." (*Obey v Degling, supra,* at p 771; *Matter of Gunderud v Gunderud,* 75 AD2d 691; *Bistany v Bistany, supra.*)

The weighing of these various factors requires an evaluation of the testimony, character and sincerity of all the parties involved in this type of dispute. Generally, such an evaluation can best be made by the trial court which has direct access to the parties and can supplement that information with whatever professionally prepared reports are necessary. "In matters of this character 'the findings of the nisi prius court must be accorded the greatest respect' (*Matter of Irene O.,* 38 NY2d 776, 777)" (*Matter of Ebert v Ebert, supra,* at p 703; *Bistany v Bistany, supra*). Appellate courts should be reluctant to substitute their own evaluation of these subjective factors for that of the nisi prius court (*People ex rel. Portnoy v Strasser,* 303 NY 539, 542; *Bistany v Bistany, supra*), and if they do, should articulate the reasons for so doing. Similarly, the existence or absence of any one factor cannot be determinative on appellate review since the court is to consider the totality of the circumstances. (*Friederwitzer v Friederwitzer,* 55 NY2d 89, *supra.*)

Turning then to the facts of this case, we hold that the determination of the trial court that the totality of the circumstances warrants awarding custody of Laura to her father conforms to the weight of the evidence. The record indicates that although the mother is not an unfit parent for Laura. she is. under all the circumstances present here, the less fit parent. Thus, the trial court was not bound by the stipulation of the parties, but was free to, and indeed required to, review the totality of the circumstances to determine what would be in Laura's best interests. In doing so, the Trial Judge weighed the testimony of all the parties, including Laura, and considered the testimony of school officials and reports from a probation officer appointed by the court. The court made no specific finding that defendant was an unfit mother for Laura, but a finding that the mother was the less fit parent is implicit in its order to change custody and is supported by the record. Additionally, the trial court, while noting Laura's ambivalence as to which parent she would prefer to live with. gave significant weight to her strong desire to remain with her older sisters. The record indicates that all relevant factors. including the mother's ability to cope with raising children as they approach maturity and the father's desire to provide a fuller and more enriched environment for his daughters were considered. It is abundantly clear from the record that the trial court. in this case. made a careful and studied review of all the relevant factors. As the determination of the nisi prius court. we believe this holding should be accorded great deference on review.

Accordingly, the order of the Appellate Division should be reversed, without costs, and the judgment of Supreme Court. Westchester County, reinstated.

Chief Judge COOKE and Judges GABRIELLI, JONES. WACHTLER, FUCHSBERG and MEYER concur.

Order reversed, etc.

DELANA L. KOPPENHOEFER, Respondent, v PETER KOPPENHOE-
FER, Appellant.

Second Department, July 18, 1990

SUMMARY

APPEAL from so much of an order of the Family Court,
Orange County (Andrew P. Bivona, J.), entered November 1,
1989, as restricted the visitation rights of respondent father
and denied his application for a transfer of custody.

### HEADNOTE

Parent and Child — Custody — Visitation — Sound Basis for Best
Interests Determination

In order to form a sound and substantial basis for a determination of
custody and visitation rights founded upon the best interests of the children,
a court should seek the expertise of other professionals and should ascertain
the wishes of the children; moreover, in disputed custody/visitation litigation, the appointment of a Law Guardian is appropriate and helpful to the
court. Accordingly, in a proceeding to determine visitation and custody of
the parties' children, aged 15 and 13, an order of the Family Court, which
restricted the visitation rights of the father and denied his application for a
transfer of custody, is reversed, insofar as appealed from, as lacking a sound
and substantial basis pursuant to law. The court failed to refer to earlier
forensic or other reports and evaluations, to order updated evaluations, or
even to elicit information and recommendations from the children's current
treating therapist. In addition, the children, though sufficiently mature to
articulate their needs and preferences to the court, were not provided an
opportunity to communicate with the court. Moreover, no Law Guardian
spoke for the children in these proceedings.

### TOTAL CLIENT-SERVICE LIBRARY® REFERENCES

By the Publisher's Editorial Staff

AM JUR 2d, Divorce and Separation, §§ 974-980, 999-1001.
NY JUR 2d, Domestic Relations, §§ 344-353, 363-365.

### ANNOTATION REFERENCE

See Index to Annotations under Custody and Support of
Children; Expert and Opinion Evidence; Visits and Visitation.

### APPEARANCES OF COUNSEL

*Sheila Callahan O'Donnell* for appellant.

*Martin R. Goldberg* for respondent.

OPINION OF THE COURT

MILLER, J.

The two children born to the parties, Hans, age 16 and Alicia, age 13, have been the subjects of embattled visitation disputes since their parents divorced in 1977. Pursuant to a separation agreement incorporated into the divorce judgment, the parties determined that custody of the children remain with the mother while the father was accorded liberal visitation. The liberal but unstructured visitation presented problems from the beginning, each parent complaining of deprivation.

By order dated March 24, 1982, the Family Court (in the first of three Family Court visitation orders), modified the liberal visitation provisions of the separation agreement. The order set forth specific hours for alternate weekend visitation (from Friday 5:30 P.M. "to Monday morning in time for school") and for midweek visitation (every Wednesday "from 5:00 P.M. to Thursday morning in time for school"), unspecified holidays were to be alternated, the father was entitled to four weeks every year, one in August, one at Christmas, and the remainder in separate days on 72 hours' notice.

Interwoven with the ongoing controversy surrounding visitation was the issue of support (a phenomenon so common to ongoing custody/visitation disputes as to raise the question of whether the primary motivation of the parties is economic rather than their interests in the child). The order dated March 24, 1982, also terminated alimony and increased child support for the children from $50 per week to $105 per week. However, child support payments were subsequently contested, with the father at times unilaterally deducting from the support checks certain extra expenses he paid for the children.

Visitation remained troubled. The parties never entirely followed the 1982 schedule. Each year the father mailed the mother a schedule of claimed holidays and weeks, which the parties followed without much alternation, the father always taking, for example, the weeks of Christmas, Easter, and the Thanksgiving holiday. The father returned the children directly to school Monday and Thursday mornings sometimes with and sometimes without their belongings, creating further confusion and disagreement.

Early in 1988, the mother petitioned for an increase in child support and modification of the visitation schedule, followed by the father's cross petition for custody, or in the alternative, for direct payment of the children's expenses rather than to the mother. The issue of support was determined separately by a Hearing Examiner in April 1989, who increased the father's obligation to $150 per week plus $25 per week arrears.

The issues of visitation and custody raised by the 1988 petition and cross petition were heard by a second Family Court Judge, who appropriately assigned a Law Guardian and ordered psychiatric evaluations of both parties and the children. The professionals recommended retention of custody by the mother, with the result that the parties reached a stipulation of settlement, continuing the visitation and custody arrangements that had failed to work previously. In an order dated October 31, 1988, the court, pursuant to that stipulation, directed that the custody and visitation arrangements previously in effect remain unchanged. While the court did not alter the visitation arrangements, it solicited the father to recognize the children's needs. It is unclear whether the court ever interviewed Hans and Alicia, who were then 14 and 12 years old, respectively. The transcript of the hearing and the order make no reference to a consultation. Less than one year later, in further court proceedings, the parties' attorneys could not agree whether the Judge had interviewed the children in 1988.

In September 1989 the parties were back in court before a third Family Court Judge. The mother sought to modify the visitation schedule with regard to holidays and weekends, claiming she was deprived of certain holidays with the children, and that Mondays presented a special problem for the children requiring them to retrieve their belongings from the father's home after school, or carry them to school Monday morning. She further sought to forbid the father from making therapy arrangements for the children additional to those recently made by her. She had engaged a therapist for the children and herself only to find the father insisted on taking the children to a therapist of his choice.

In response the father once again cross-petitioned for custody. After two days of testimony from only the father and mother, the court, in the order appealed from, substantially revised the children's visitation schedule, *inter alia*, by shortening their weekend visitation with their father, ending it on Sunday at 7:00 P.M. rather than Monday morning, dividing their Christmas holiday between both parents, and requiring them to spend four weeks of summer recess with their father, rather than distributing the father's four weeks throughout the year as previously. The children were not heard from directly, or through a Law Guardian. Whether or not the children found the original weekend visitation that ended on Monday unduly burdensome was never ascertained from them, although they were the obvious direct source of such information. The sacrifice to their academic, athletic, and social opportunities that may have resulted from the altered schedule remained unexplored from the children's viewpoint. The emotional, harmful impact on the children of ignoring their needs and preferences in such circumstances has been repeatedly documented (Wallerstein, Impact of Division on Children, 3 Psychiatric Clinics of North America, at 455-468 [Dec. 1980]; Loeb, *Fathers and Sons—Some Effects of Prolonged Custody Litigation,* 14 [No. 2] Bull Am Acad Psychiatric Law 177). The father appealed, contending that the order was improperly based. We agree.

In adjudicating custody and visitation rights, the most important factor to be considered is the best interests of the children *(Friederwitzer v Friederwitzer,* 55 NY2d 89, 93-95). "[I]n a custody proceeding arising out of a dispute between divorced parents, the first concern of the court is and must be the welfare and the interests of the children (Domestic Relations Law, § 70). Their interests are paramount. The rights of their parents must, in case of conflict, yield to that superior demand" *(Matter of Lincoln v Lincoln,* 24 NY2d 270, 271-272). The hearing court's determination will not be set aside or modified unless it lacks a sound and substantial basis *(see, Alfano v Alfano,* 151 AD2d 530; *Corsell v Corsell,* 101 AD2d 766). However, in order that more than lip service be accorded the vague and amorphous concept of best interests, the court must inquire into the emotional, intellectual, physical, and social needs of the children, as well as the children's preferences if the children are capable of verbalizing them.

It is well settled that to formulate a sound basis the court should seek the expertise of other professionals *(see, Hughes v Hughes,* 37 AD2d 606, 607; *Anonymous v Anonymous,* 34 AD2d 942, 943; *see also, Eschbach v Eschbach,* 56 NY2d 167, 171; Family Ct Act §§ 241, 249, 251, 252). In the case at bar, the court failed to refer to earlier forensic or other reports and evaluations, to order updated evaluations, or even to elicit information and recommendations from the children's current treating therapist.

The court should also ascertain the wishes of the children, particularly when, as here, the children are of a sufficient age to articulate their needs and preferences to the court (see, *Eschbach v Eschbach, supra; Dintruff v McGreevy,* 34 NY2d 887; *Feldman v Feldman,* 58 AD2d 882; *Hughes v Hughes, supra.* While the express wishes of children are not controlling, they are entitled to great weight, particularly where their age and maturity would make their input particularly meaningful *(Hughes v Hughes, supra; cf., Eschbach v Eschbach, supra).* This court has held that the preference of a 15 year old was "entitled to great weight" *(Bergson v Bergson,* 68 AD2d 931, 932). Further, this court has cited the failure of the trial court to ascertain the wishes of a 16 year old as the basis for reversal of a custody determination (see, *Feldman v Feldman, supra;* see also, *Spain v Spain,* 130 AD2d 806, 809). In this case, the children who form the subject of this appeal were 14 and 12 years old, respectively, at the time of trial and concededly mature. Their input would have been highly relevant.

The preferred practice in a custody/visitation case in order to determine best interests, is to have an in camera interview with child on the record in the presence of the Law Guardian *(see, e.g., Hasan Abu Romi v Hazieem Hamdan,* 70 AD2d 934; *Matter of Ehrlich v Ressner,* 55 AD2d 953; *Matter of Fleishman v Walters,* 40 AD2d 622, 623; see also, *Eschbach v Eschbach,* 56 NY2d 167, supra; *Matter of Lincoln v Lincoln,* 24 NY2d 270, 272, supra; Family Ct Act § 664; CPLR 4019). The record in this case fails to indicate that Hans and Alicia, the subject of four separate visitation orders, have had the opportunity to communicate with the court.

Furthermore, in disputed custody/visitation litigation, the appointment of a Law Guardian has been recognized as appropriate and helpful to the court. The attorney may act as champion of the child's best interest, as advocate for the child's preferences, as investigator seeking the truth on controverted issues, or may serve to recommend alternatives for the court's consideration (see, Family Ct Act § 249; CPLR 1202; Judiciary Law § 35 [7]; *Braiman v Braiman,* 44 NY2d 584; *Borkowski v Borkowski,* 90 Misc 2d 957). This court has held that the failure of the court-appointed Law Guardian to take an active role in the proceedings is grounds for vacatur of an order based on an insufficient record (see, *Matter of Elizabeth R. [Catherine S.],* 155 AD2d 666). No Law Guardian spoke for the children in these proceedings.

We therefore find that the order appealed from lacked a sound and substantial basis pursuant to law. In determining custody and visitation proceedings in the children's best interest, the court's primary focus must be upon the children, not the parents. The court's obligation as *parens patriae* of children requires that the children's days and years be shared by the parents in accordance with the court's considered assessment of the children's needs and preferences rather than distributed and divided between the embattled parents as the spoils of matrimonial warfare.

Accordingly, the order is reversed insofar as appealed from, on the law, without costs or disbursements, and the matter is remitted to the Family Court for a hearing and determination de novo on the issues of visitation in accordance herewith. Pending the hearing and determination, the present visitation schedule, set forth in the order appealed from, shall remain in effect so as not to disrupt the family further.

THOMPSON, J. P., RUBIN and ROSENBLATT, JJ., concur.

Ordered that the order is reversed insofar as appealed from, on the law, without costs or disbursements, and the matter is remitted to the Family Court, Orange County, for a hearing and determination de novo on the issues of visitation in accordance herewith. Pending the hearing and determination, the present visitation schedule, set forth in the order appealed from, shall remain in effect. [*See*, ___ AD2d ___, Nov. 19, 1990.]

FAMILY COURT OF THE STATE OF NEW YORK
CITY OF NEW YORK, COUNTY OF KINGS, PART 12
- - - - - - - - - - - - - - - - - - - x

In The Matter of:

Docket #

GERALD ███████ ──

              Petitioner,

      - against -

JANICE ███████

              Respondent.

JEREMY ███████: Subject Child.

- - - - - - - - - - - - - - - - - - x

In the Matter of:

CHRISTOPHER ███████ and JEREMY ███████,
children under the age of eighteen
years, alleged to have been neglected/
abused.

           Subject Children.

JANICE ███████: Respondent.

- - - - - - - - - - - - - - - - - - x

              283 Adams Street
              Brooklyn, New York
              February 26, 1997

B E F O R E :

        HONORABLE SARA P. SCHECHTER, Judge

RALPH A. BASSO, SR.,
Official Court Reporter

Appearances: (Cont'd.)

JANET LAM, ESQ.,
Special Assistant Corporation Counsel,
appearing for the Commissioner of
Social Services on the neglect/
abuse docket.


MANARINO, YEGERMAN & GREENHAUS, ESQS.,
Appearing on behalf of the Respondent on both
dockets, Janice ███████
BY:  SUSAN MINTZ, ESQ.,
                    of Counsel


SAUL EDELSTEIN, ESQ.,
Appearing as retained counsel on behalf of
the subject child, Jeremy ████████ on
both dockets.
        26 Court Street
        Brooklyn, N. Y.  11242


JANE SPINAK, ESQ.,
Office of the Legal Aid Society
BY:  ROBYN KARASYK, ESQ.,
        Law Guardian for the subject children,
        Jeremy and Christopher ████████ on the
        neglect/abuse docket


            *       *       *       *

1

2       COURT OFFICER:  Your Honor, matter of Jackson.

3       Counsel, note your appearances for the record,

4       please.

5       MS. LAM:  Special Assistant Corporation

6       Counsel by Janet Lam, for the Commissioner of

7       Social Services.

8       MS. MINTZ:  Manarino, Yegerman & Greenhaus,

9       by Susan Mintz, for the respondent, Janice ▬▬▬.

10      THE COURT:  Is your client the

11      respondent/mother?

12      MS. MINTZ:  Sorry?

13      THE COURT:  You are representing the

14      respondent, Ms. Jackson?

15      MS. MINTZ:  Yes, your Honor.  I'm appearing

16      for the respondent mother, Janice ▬▬▬.

17      MR. EDELSTEIN:  Saul Edelstein, 26 Court

18      Street, Brooklyn, New York, with the permission of

19      the Court, privately retained counsel for the

20      child, Jeremy ▬▬▬.

21      THE COURT:  You are appearing for whom?  There

22      is a law guardian already assigned.

23      MR. EDELSTEIN:  Yes, your Honor.  I am about

24      to formally make application to ask this Court to

25      substitute myself for the law guardian as private

counsel for the child, Jeremy.  I would like to be

heard on this issue, your Honor.

THE COURT:  No, no, no.  I'm -- I think that

we have to find Ms. Karasyk.

MR. EDELSTEIN:  Sorry, your Honor.

THE COURT:  I can't do this now without Ms.

Karasyk.  As it turns out -- where did she go?

COURT OFFICER:  To Part 1, and she is not

there now.  She didn't know that this attorney was

here.  He wasn't here when I went to the office

to get her.

THE COURT:  Ms. Mintz is always here, and she

is also private counsel.

COURT OFFICER:  That's true, your Honor.

We don't know where Ms. Karasyk is, your Honor.

THE COURT:  We'll just wait a few minutes.

(Whereupon, at this time, there was a brief

pause in the proceedings, for the purpose

indicated, after which time the following

occurred.)

COURT OFFICER:  Your Honor, should I get the

rest of the appearances while the other officer

goes and looks for Ms. Karasyk, again?

THE COURT:  Call her at the Legal Aid office

and see if she is over there.

       THE CLERK:  Call the supervisor.

       COURT OFFICER:  We just did, your Honor, and it's busy.  I just tried calling them.

       THE COURT:  All right, we'll need to get the appearances.

       COURT OFFICER:  Your name, title and agency?

       MS. CANADY:  Deana (phonetic) Canady, A.C.S. caseworker.

       COURT OFFICER:  Your appearance, please?

       MS. KARASYK:  The Legal Aid Society by Robyn Karasyk, on behalf of the children.

       COURT OFFICER:  All right, your name and relationship to the children?

       THE RESPONDENT:  Janice ████, the mother.

       THE COURT:  The appearances in the back, I need the names and relationships of those people.

       A VOICE NUMBER 1:  I am Gerard, Elliott's father.

       MS. S. JACKSON:  Sabrina ████.

       MS. B. JACKSON:  Brenda ████.

       We're the aunts.

       THE COURT:  Get her appearance, get the doctor's appearance.

COURT OFFICER: Your name, please?

DR. GRANT: Swadesh (phonetic) S. Grant,
Psychologist.

THE COURT: Let's pick up where we left off.

MR. EDELSTEIN: May I, your Honor?

THE COURT: All right.

MR. EDELSTEIN: Thank you, your Honor.

If your Honor pleases, the child, Jeremy
████████, has contacted and has sought my advice
and counsel. I have interviewed the child and he
has retained our firm to represent him in this
matter. He has -- after I spoke with him, I
spoke with him in the presence of his uncle,
Mr. Quinton, or he is some relative, or purports
to be a relative by the name of Quinton Redding
(phonetic). They got my name, to be very candid
with the Court, from Mr. Yeger, who indicated
that if the child was dissatisfied with,
apparently, the Court appointed law guardian, who
is his counsel, that they should seek other
counsel. Mr. Yeger is familiar with a case that I,
apparently, had here in New York City that seemed
to get a great deal of attention with regard to
children having private counsel, and he attended,

172

I believe, some lectures that I had been doing with
regard to this, and indicated that there seemed to
be a lawyer that is knowledgeable with regard to
this, and to see him. That's the last
communication with Mr. Yeger, other than my asking
him to give me the case history. Since then, there
has been no more communications with Mr. Yeger, so
that I could keep my ethical responsibilities
appropriate to this matter.

Your Honor, I spoke to the child in the
presence of Mr. Redding, and then asked Mr. Redding
to step outside. The child is vocal and articulate
and seemed to know what he wants. He seemed to
know what he is doing, and, unfortunately, he
indicated to me that he did not feel, and this is
in his own language, that he was being properly
represented by counsel, the law guardian, not in a
technical sense, but, and I am paraphrasing, that
what the child basically said to me.

I asked the child, "Do you know who I am?"

And the child said, "Yes, you are an
attorney.

"Do you know what I do?"

And the child seemed to describe it just fine.

Then, I indicated to him, "Go home, and I want
you to see, and I want your uncle, Mr. Redding, to
get out a video called 'The Client,' and I want you
to see that video." And he did.  He came back, and
he came back with a dollar, and your Honor might
remember that --

THE COURT:  Yes, I do.

MR. EDELSTEIN:  And he hired me for a dollar,
and he signed a piece of paper that said, "You are
my lawyer," and gave me the dollar, and seemed to
understand what is going on.

I spoke with him, and then I asked the
relative outside, now, can you come up with
twenty-five hundred dollars -- I'm being very
candid with the Court, and I want to be exactly
candid with this Court, and I indicated that,
indeed, I have been paid by the relative to
represent the child.

Your Honor, needless to say, I am not doing
it for a dollar, unless they make a movie about it.

THE COURT:  Of course.

MR. EDELSTEIN:  I have reviewed the matter and
I believe that I have to ask your Honor's
permission.

174

THE COURT: Whatever it is, it is a

substitution of counsel. It will have to be with

the permission of the Court.

MR. EDELSTEIN: So, I would ask your Honor,

under the authority that I seem to have established

in Pavlow against Pavlow (phonetic), reported only

in the New York Law Journal, a copy that I have,

that seems to have a lot of notoriety -- and your

Honor, the child does have the right, "to fire a

law guardian," and that's exactly the case on all

"4's," and to hire a new counsel.

In addition, it has been supported by -- just

recently, which is shocking -- by Judge Jackie

Silverman in the Supreme Court, New York, in the

case called "Anonymous."

THE COURT: Yes.

MR. EDELSTEIN: In which it was decided that

the kid could hire a lawyer, in the same aspect,

and then to come in and say that I am the lawyer,

I am the lawyer for the child, and then said that

I want the husband, the father of this particular

child to pay $50,000 worth of counsel fees.

THE COURT: That's been affirmed on appeal.

MR. EDELSTEIN: Yes, your Honor -- I don't

have to go further. That was affirmed in articles
written, and it seemed that I have the authority,
and I would ask permission of this court to
substitute as private counsel.

THE COURT: Now, Ms. Karasyk, I gather you
want to have something to say about this?

MS. KARASYK: Of course, your Honor.

THE COURT: Do you need, first of all, do you
need time to confer with a supervisor; I mean, I
understand your policy and also -- do you now want
to answer on papers?

MS. KARASYK: Yes, your Honor.

THE COURT: All right, in the meantime we have
a doctor here today that we are paying to sit
here to, apparently, do nothing. If we had known
this would happen, we would have not brought the
doctor in.

MS. MINTZ: Well, your Honor, that's my --

MR. EDELSTEIN: That's true -- on my part, and
I didn't anticipate that I would -- your Honor,
Mr. Yeger, apparently, didn't inform me, the last
time it was adjourned, what it was on for, and he
said that we are on, and that it might go to trial.
I was not informed of the fact that there was a

2          doctor on call.

3                  THE COURT:  There she is (indicating).

4                  MR. EDELSTEIN:  I know Dr. Grant from past

5          experience and I apologize.  I wasn't told that she

6          would be here today and ready to go.

7                  THE COURT:  Okay.

8                  MS. VINCE:  I'm going to ask that Mr.

9          Edelstein and Mr. Yeger pay for the time that the

10         doctor, Dr. Grant, is in court today.  My client

11         had to pay for the last time, but has not yet paid

12         Dr. Grant for coming to court.  This case was last

13         on in December, I believe -- December 18th, and it

14         is now February 26th.  There is absolutely no

15         reason that the motion can't be made on papers --

16         it should have been, and why no other counsel were

17         notified that Mr. Edelstein was going to appear

18         today.

19                 Obviously, Mr. Yeger knew that Mr. Edelstein

20         was going to appear, but no other attorneys knew

21         that Mr. Edelstein was going to appear.  There has

22         been almost a three month adjournment --

23                 THE COURT:  Do you want to note your

24         appearance?

25                 MR. YEGER:  Yes, your Honor.

Eli Yeger, 16 Court Street, appearing for

Gerard Elliott.  Sorry, your Honor.

MR. EDELSTEIN:  More importantly, I have to

take blame for that.  Possibly, I should have made

an application on papers.  I thought that it was

redundant.  I didn't think that the matter --

THE COURT:  You know, this is not exactly

routine.

MR. EDELSTEIN:  Well noted.  But, I thought

today would be routine.  I was unaware of the fact

that there is a doctor on call, but I apologize.

I'm not usually rude to fellow counsel and judges.

THE COURT:  I know, that's very true.

MR. EDELSTEIN:  I apologize, your Honor.

THE COURT:  All right, now --

MS. KARASYK:  Judge, may I?

THE COURT:  That leaves the matter of payment.

He hasn't paid his portion of the examination that

was already performed; is that correct?

MS. MINTZ:  No, your Honor.  What Dr. Grant

did -- Dr. Grant had asked that they pay for her

time today, in court.

THE COURT:  In the same proportion?

MS. VINCE:  Correct, exactly.

Colloquy                        13

THE COURT:  And he paid his portion?

MR. YEGER:  If I may be heard on that.

If the doctor is being called as Ms. Jackson's

witness, it is incumbent upon her to pay for the

fees, if it is her witness.

THE COURT:  Normally, that's true, but under

the circumstances, to only put him in for his

portion -- I think we're being quite generous,

concerning the circumstances.

MS. MINTZ:  It wasn't my intention to call her

as my witness, your Honor.  Your Honor asked me to

have her available to testify on this date.  She

was appointed by the Court in this matter.

THE COURT:  No, no -- someone is going to pay,

and the one who is going to pay will be the one who

questions her, and it is her witness.

MR. YEGER:  I don't intend to call her as my

witness.

THE COURT:  Get this straight -- so we won't

bring her back if no one will call her.

MS. KARASYK:  Can I?

THE COURT:  How is this going to go; is

someone going to call this witness or not?

MS. MINTZ:  Well, your Honor -- I will ask

that the disposition go first, because Dr. Grant is

really not on the disposition.  I would ask to go

forward on the disposition today.

MS. KARASYK:  On the custody?

MS. MINTZ:  On the neglect, because Mr.

Edelstein is not retained for the neglect case, as

far as I understand, he is only retained for the

custody and visitation case.

THE COURT:  Then we have to do it all over

again.  I won't do that portion of that all over

again.  It'll be done once and for all.  Whatever

evidence is relevant to those aspects of the case,

I'm going to consider on both the custody and the

neglect.  I won't hear it all over again.

MS. KARASYK:  Can I add to the mix, that Mr.

Yeger was fully aware, as was Mr. Elliott, that --

MR. EDELSTEIN:  Mr. Edelstein --

MS. KARASYK:  I'm sorry.  Mr. Yeger and Mr.

Edelstein were fully aware that I have, and had a

social worker, Ms. Molly Dietrich, who has yet to

make an appearance, because she ran in after I did,

and Molly Dietrich is a social worker with the

Juvenile Services Unit of our office, and that she

was working on this case.

I had spoken, also, to Ms. Mintz, and Mr.
Yeger to have their permission for her, Ms.
Dietrich, to work both -- have permission to speak
to the father, and to the mother, and to interview
Jeremy so that I could reevaluate my position, and
that I would submit, for the record, that I -- I
have always said, all along, that Jeremy's position
is that he wanted to live with his father, but I
wasn't sure, exactly, if that was -- if I was
supporting that, but they have been aware of that,
that my social worker has been working with Mr.
Elliott, and -- and Ms. Dietrich met with Mr.
Elliott yesterday and today.

I don't believe -- I mean -- they may all have
an inkling as to what position I will be taking,
but I'm not sure that Mr. Edelstein, at this point,
knows what my position is today, or is aware of all
the work that we have put into the Juvenile
Services Unit up to today, and Mr. Edelstein has
represented to me that -- I don't know why they
didn't say that they were substituting counsel, and
that I didn't need all this --

THE COURT:  This is a major inconvenience all
around, and I understand all the work that you have

done, but one of the issues that you'll address

in your opposition papers, if you decide to oppose

it, and I don't want to, at this point, further

delay it for a formal written motion, but I would

like you to write down the cites that you are

relying upon.

MR. EDELSTEIN:  I'll send you a memo.

THE COURT:  Thank you.

MS. KARASYK:  And I'll need time to respond,

then.

MR. EDELSTEIN:  Yes.

MS. KARASYK:  After I get the memo.

MR. EDELSTEIN:  Sure.

THE COURT:  That's fine.

MR. EDELSTEIN:  When would you like the

memorandum?

Will next week be okay?

THE COURT:  All right, then, you have your

papers in, in another week.

MS. MINTZ:  Your Honor, I also wish to

respond.

THE COURT:  Give your memorandum to everyone.

MR. EDELSTEIN:  As long as I could have their

respective cards.

1

2      THE COURT:  All the opposition papers will

3  come in a week later.  So, let's fix an adjourned

4  date.

5      Do we need Dr. Grant here, or don't we?

6      MR. EDELSTEIN:  Your Honor, may I respectfully

7  -- may I submit that until your Honor makes a

8  determination of this motion, we don't need Dr.

9  Grant for the next date.

10      THE COURT:  If nobody will plan to call her,

11  it is a definite no.

12      MS. KARASYK:  Except, if there are reports put

13  in by someone.

14      THE COURT:  If there are reports put in --

15  this is also a custody case.  So, the doctor,

16  herself, will have to be available, and I want to

17  know if anybody will call her or try to put that

18  report in.

19      MS. LAM:  Yes, your Honor.

20      MS. MINTZ:  Yes, and I want the report in.

21      THE COURT:  Have Dr. Grant on call for the

22  next adjourned date which may, or may not be --

23  actually, I'm going to fix two days, and I'll fix

24  a date to decide on the substitution of counsel

25  issue, and another date for trial, and then we'll

1

2     do the trial date around Dr. Grant's schedule, as

3     well.

4          MS. LAM: We have an additional trial date set

5     for March 6th.

6          MR. YEGER: We'll have to vacate that.

7          THE COURT: It's too close for comfort.

8     That's not possible now.

9          Okay -- we'll vacate March 6th.

10         Thank you, Ms. Lam.

11         MS. MINTZ: Judge, I have to note my objection

12    to the disposition on the neglect case not going

13    forward today. This is, obviously, the way for the

14    father to have his child not returned to my client.

15    The reports are in and everyone knows what their

16    positions are. The goal has always been to return

17    the children to the mother, and again, this case

18    keeps getting put off, and put off.

19         THE COURT: Ms. Karasyk, I'll give you -- I'm

20    sorry, Mr. Edelstein -- I'm going to give you until

21    March 6th to get your memorandum to everyone.

22         MR. EDELSTEIN: May I have to Monday, March

23    10th, so that I could, probably, do it over the

24    weekend and it will go out on March 10th.

25         MS. MINTZ: Judge, again, note my objection.

It's only across the street, and he could deliver

it.

I would like to know when Mr. Edelstein was

retained.

MR. EDELSTEIN: Okay.

THE COURT: It doesn't matter. We have to be

realistic.

Okay, March 10th.

MR. EDELSTEIN: Thank you, Judge.

THE COURT: Then we'll give the rest of the

crew until March 19th to get their answers in, in

whatever form they choose, memorandum or opposition

papers, or whatever.

MR. EDELSTEIN: If necessary, may I have two

days to reply?

THE COURT: Okay, that -- that takes us out

to Monday, the 24th, and I'm going to need sometime

to work on it after that.

MS. KARASYK: Judge, I'm going to ask -- I

don't want to delay this. In all honesty, Mr.

Edelstein is, apparently, very familiar with this

issue, which I assume will be from his previous

involvements. But, with all due respect, our

calendar -- to give us full time to respond to

something that he pretty much already has written,

to some extent -- and the time between receiving

these memorandum and the date that we have to do it

-- there is really hardly any time for me to look

into the issue.

MR. EDELSTEIN: Frankly, I don't have to

submit the memorandum, if your Honor pleases, I'll

just give you --

THE COURT: I would like to have it, to tell

you the truth.

What date do you want?

MS. KARASYK: I could ask for a few more days

-- a few days after the 19th, being realistic, I'm

going to need the time.

THE COURT: How about the 24th, the 24th --

that's the 24th, okay?

Now, so then I can give you April 10th or the

11th for the ruling on the substitution of counsel

issue, and then I'm going to now send you out with

my court attorney to set the trial dates, taking

into consideration, Dr. Grant's schedule.

MR. EDELSTEIN: Is it possible to have a

2:00 o'clock call on the 11th?

THE COURT: Yes.

MS. MINTZ: April 10th or 11th.

THE COURT: He is asking for the 11th.

MR. EDELSTEIN: Yes, the 11th, at 2:00 o'clock, if that's all right with everyone.

THE COURT: Yes -- so that's it. We have an adjourned date, and then we'll set up the trial schedule again -- all right, outside.

MS. MINTZ: Your Honor, I would just ask for a modified visitation schedule, as this delay has nothing to do with my client, and I would ask that my client be given every weekend, and the full Easter recess with the child.

MR. YEGER: Your Honor --

MS. MINTZ: I don't think that that's unreasonable at this point.

MR. YEGER: Your Honor, this is unreasonable, as in any custody case, where there is two parents that want to have custody of the child, and where each is entitled to enjoy equal time with the child. My client works, as does the mother of the child, and my client -- I believe, is entitled to have weekends with the child, as the mother is entitled to have weekends with the child.

THE COURT: All right, keep the alternating

187

weekends and give her the -- give her the whole

school break.

    MS. MINTZ:  That's only three weekends.

    MR. YEGER:  She has more than every other

weekend.

    THE COURT:  Keep the same three, and give her

the whole school break.

    MR. YEGER:  Can my client have vacation time

with the child?

    THE COURT:  No.

    MS. KARASYK:  I don't -- I'm not sure if I

represent my client or not, at this point?

    THE COURT:  You do until you are relieved.

    MS. KARASYK:  Then I believe that my client

wants to have half of this school break with his

father.

    THE COURT:  Counsel, please --

    MR. EDELSTEIN:  I'm sorry, your Honor.

    Please, go ahead -- I'm sorry.

    MS. MINTZ:  You should be ashamed of yourself.

    MR. EDELSTEIN:  Please.

    MS. KARASYK:  Your Honor -- this is precisely

the issue.  I don't want to be in --

    THE COURT:  We'll split the school break.

188

MS. MINTZ:  This is not fair.

THE COURT:  I won't be in opposition of the law guardian's suggestion to split the time.

MS. MINTZ:  Your Honor --

MR. YEGER:  That's okay with us.

MS. MINTZ:  Let the law guardian speak to the child before there is a definite ruling.

MS. KARASYK:  Excuse me, but my social worker has had extensive meetings with the child, and I have been working with the child, and now Mr. Yeger, Mr. Elliott and Mr. Edelstein come in now and asking for something without knowing what my present position is, and I just can't --

THE COURT:  Step out, please.

COURT OFFICER:  Thank you, everyone please step out.

            *       *       *       *

        The above is certified to be a true and
accurate transcription of the proceedings in
the above entitled action.

                _____
                RALPH A. BASSO, SR.
                Official Court Reporter

189

# DRAFT

Guidelines for Guardians *ad item* for Children

I.  Qualifications

A.  A guardian *ad litem* must be a person who:

1.  is able to make independent, mature decisions on issues involved in the case.

2.  employs impartiality, open-mindedness, and fairness in determining what is in best interest of the child

3.  is aware and accepting of cultural, ethnic and class distinctions.

4.  has not represented a person or party in pending or past litigation involving the child

5.  has not been convicted of any crime listed in Chapter 3 of Title 16; Offenses Against the Person; in Chapter 15 of Title 16, Offenses Against Morality and Decency, in Article 3 of Chapter 53 of Title 44, Narcotics and Controlled Substances, or for the crime of contributing to the delinquency of a minor, provided for in Section 16-17-490

6.  has obtained appropriate training

II.  Training

A.  Appropriate training of the guardian *ad litem* includes instruction in these subjects:

1.  the court process including mediation
2.  interviewing techniques including witnesses and children
3.  report writing and drafting
4.  record keeping
5.  investigation skills
6.  attorney/guardian *ad litem* roles and duties including ethical issues
7.  negotiation skills
8.  impact of the litigation on the child
9.  social, emotional, physical, developmental, educational, vocational, and psychological stages and needs of children; impact on children
10. services and benefits available for children, i.e. school related issues such as special education, expulsion or suspension; health care issues for example Medicaid, Early Periodic Screening Diagnosis and

Treatment, and government benefits such as social security, and Youakim benefits.

11. role and process of relevant agencies

B. The appointing judge may waive the training requirements if it is determined that the person being appointed has:

    1. equivalent experience, or
    2. it would be in the best interest of the child

## III. Role

A. A guardian *ad litem* for a minor child is a special guardian appointed by the court in particular litigation. The guardian *ad litem* is lawfully invested with the power and charged with the duty of protecting the child's interests in the litigation.

B. A child becomes a party by virtue of the appointment of the guardian *ad litem*. The guardian *ad litem* is subject to all the rules of the court and shall receive all pleadings, notices, discovery, correspondence relating to the child, orders, and notices of appeal.

## IV. Process and duties

A. A guardian *ad litem* should conduct an independent investigation to determine what is in the best interests of the child.

B. A guardian *ad litem* should interview the parties, parents and caretakers of the child, unless it would be contrary to the child's interests or otherwise inappropriate under the circumstances. Consent of the parents' attorneys, if any, should be obtained by the guardian *ad litem* before communicating with the parents. Unless the parents' interests conflict with those of the child, the guardian *ad litem* should give deference to their wishes, absent a good reason to do otherwise.

C. A guardian *ad litem* should communicate with the child, as appropriate in light of the child's age and maturity. The guardian *ad litem* should explain the role which he or she will play in the particular litigation and the nature of the relationship the child should expect to have with the guardian *ad litem*. The guardian *ad litem* should be careful not to raise false hopes or unreasonable expectations, and keeping in mind the temporary nature of the relationship should not facilitate overdependence. A guardian *ad litem* should keep the child informed about the status of the litigation and the child's interests that may be affected by the litigation. A guardian *ad litem* should explain what he or she thinks is best for the child, even it it conflicts with the child's wishes.

192

D. A guardian *ad litem* should strive to protect confidential communications with the child and should help the child understand that anything that the child tells the guardian *ad litem* may be revealed. It will be up to the guardian *ad litem* to determine whether disclosing the confidential information is in the best interest of the child. A guardian *ad litem* should carefully explain to a child under what circumstances he or she is allowed, or may be compelled, to disclose the child's confidences. Prior to disclosure, the guardian *ad litem* should discuss with the child any intention to disclose a confidential communication and the reasons for doing so, if appropriate under the circumstances and to the extent possible in light of the child's age, development, and maturity. A guardian *ad litem* should give deference to the wishes of the child in deciding whether to disclose a confidential communication, absent an appropriate reason for doing otherwise.

E. A guardian *ad litem* should consult with the child and make decisions with the child about the outcome of the proceedings affecting the child, commensurate with the child's age, experience, maturity and judgment. A guardian *ad litem* should recognize that children have varying degrees of competence and, to the extent a child is able to articulate an opinion about the ultimate outcome of the proceeding, the child's opinion is entitled to weight. In any case in which the guardian *ad litem* must make important decisions on behalf of the child, the guardian *ad litem* should consider all the surrounding circumstances and act with care to safeguard and advance the best interests of the child.

F. When circumstances suggest the need for independent legal representation of the child, for example when a child of sufficient age and maturity disagrees with the position of the guardian *ad litem* regarding the proceedings, the guardian *ad litem* should move for a hearing on the issue. If the court finds that the child is capable of mature and independent decisions, the guardian *ad litem* should be dismissed and an attorney appointed for the child. In child protection cases, the guardian *ad litem* shall continue in addition to the child's attorney.

G. A guardian *ad litem* should inform the court of the relevant wishes of the child, irrespective of the child's age and if the child does not have his or her own attorney, should assist the child in conveying these wishes to the court through appropriate means, such as testimony or the introduction of evidence. This is a responsibility of the guardian *ad litem* regardless of whether the child's expressed wishes coincide with those of the guardian *ad litem*'s opinions of the best interests of the child.

H. A guardian *ad litem* should perform assigned duties competently and should be sufficiently prompt, diligent, and attentive to details to

193

assure that the matter undertaken is completed without avoidable harm to the child's best interests.

I.    A guardian ad litem should recognize areas of expertise beyond his or her competence and make efforts to obtain sufficient information, training, or assistance in those areas.

J.    A guardian ad litem should try to resolve all issues in a manner that lessens potential damage to the child or the child's family.

K.    If an attorney is appointed or hired to represent the guardian ad litem, the guardian ad litem is the client and is owed the same duties and has the same rights as any other client, including the right to determine the objectives of the litigation, receive legal advice and counseling, and direct the efforts of the attorney. It is the responsibility of the guardian ad litem to request the appointment of an attorney.

L.    In judicial proceedings involving issues affecting a child's interests, a guardian ad litem should through counsel (unless the guardian ad litem is an attorney) introduce evidence, examine, and cross-examine witnesses, and present the child's positions to the court, and the guardian ad litem should otherwise participate in the proceedings to the degree necessary to protect the child's interests. If the guardian ad litem becomes aware of benefits and services to which the child is entitled, the guardian ad litem should bring these issues to the attention of the court.

M.    A guardian ad litem may advocate a position in court on any issue concerning the interests of the child. Any recommendation to the court must be based on evidence in the record. A guardian ad litem may submit briefs, memoranda, affidavits, or other documents on behalf of the child the same as any other party. A guardian ad litem may not submit reports or other documents to the court which make recommendations or provide statements of fact, except to the extent that other parties are permitted to do so.

N.    In child protection cases written reports including recommendations should be submitted to the court pursuant to §20-7-122 (5). In other types of cases, a guardian ad litem should submit a report only when required to do so by the court or by statute.

O.    A guardian ad litem appointed by the court and paid by public funds shall be paid in accordance with law or SC Family Court Rules 12 and 41, and shall not seek or receive any additional payment from any party. A guardian ad litem appointed by the court shall be paid the amount assessed by the court. Ability to pay should be taken into account when assessing fees. A guardian ad litem shall submit itemized statements. At the earliest possible time the guardian ad litem should notify the parties of the proposed fee schedule. Nothing in this section precludes a private agreement among parties.

P. In dealing with an unrepresented party, the guardian *ad litem* should take steps to assure that the party understands the guardian *ad litem*'s purpose and that he or she is not serving as an attorney for any party. A guardian *ad litem* should not give advice to unrepresented parties but may answer questions about resources and procedures for obtaining an attorney. If the guardian *ad litem* believes that an unrepresented party may be incompetent he or she should bring this to the attention of the court.

Q. The duties of the guardian *ad litem* continue until relieved by the court or upon conclusion of the litigation. The guardian *ad litem* should be mindful that the litigation may not be concluded until all appeals are final. In cases involving a series of related actions (e.g. TPR, adoption), a guardian *ad litem* in one action should not be relieved until another is appointed in the subsequent matter.

# NOTES

7

## CASSANO V. CASSANO

85 N.Y.2D 651, 628 N.Y.S. 2d 11
(N.Y. 1995)

Reprinted from the PLI Course Handbook,
Child Custody and Support 1996.
Order Number C4-4214

------------------------ Page 628 N.Y.S.2d 10 follows ------------------------

85 N.Y.2d 649, 651 N.E.2d 878

In the Matter of Maryann CASSANO, Respondent,
v.
Dominick CASSANO, Appellant.

Court of Appeals of New York.
May 9, 1995.

In proceeding to modify child support, the Family Court, Queens County,
Marchetti, H.E., and Friedman J., directed former husband to pay portion of
son's private school tuition and all unreimbursed health expenses and upwardly
modified child support. Appeal was taken. The Supreme Court, Appellate
Division, 203 A.D.2d 563, 612 N.Y.S.2d 160, affirmed as modified, holding that
Family Court was required to state reasons for award of child support on
combined parental income over $80,000 but found that requirement satisfied by
hearing examiner's in-depth consideration of parties' circumstances. Father
appealed. The Court of Appeals, Kaye, C.J., held that: (1) under Child Support
Standards Act, trial court must articulate reason for its award of child support
on parental income exceeding $80,000 when it chooses simply to apply statutory
percentage, and (2) applying statutory percentage was not an abuse of
discretion.

Affirmed.


1.   PARENT AND CHILD k3.3(1)
        285    ----
        285k3    Support and Education of Child
        285k3.3    Actions to Compel Support or Payment for Necessaries
        285k3.3(1)    In general.

N.Y. 1995.
    Child Support Standards Act sought to create greater uniformity,
predictability, and equity in fixing child support awards, while at same time
maintaining degree of judicial discretion necessary to address unique
circumstances. McKinney's Family Court Act Sec. 413; McKinney's DRL Sec.
240.


2.   PARENT AND CHILD k3.3(6)
        285    ----
        285k3    Support and Education of Child
        285k3.3    Actions to Compel Support or Payment for Necessaries
        285k3.3(6)    Trial; findings.

N.Y. 1995.
    Under Child Support Standards Act, trial court must articulate reason for its
award of child support on parental income exceeding $80,000 when it chooses
simply to apply statutory percentage; given that trial court is vested with
discretion to apply factors listed in Act, to apply statutory percentage, or to

apply both in fixing basic child support obligation, and that exercise of discretion is subject to review for abuse, some record articulation of reasons for trial court's choice to apply percentage is necessary to facilitate that review. McKinney's Family Court Act Sec. 413; McKinney's DRL Sec. 240.

3.   PARENT AND CHILD k3.1(5)
        285   ----
        285k3      Support and Education of Child
        285k3.1     Right, Duties and Liabilities in General
        285k3.1(5)   Circumstances affecting duty to support in general.

        [See headnote text below]

3.   PARENT AND CHILD k3.3(7)
        285   ----
        285k3      Support and Education of Child
        285k3.3     Actions to Compel Support or Payment for Necessaries
        285k3.3(7)   Amount of award.


N.Y. 1995.
   Under Child Support Standards Act, as to combined parental income over $80,000, provision stating that court may apply factors set forth in Act "and/or the child support percentage" affords trial court discretion to apply factors, or to apply statutory percentage, or to apply both in fixing basic child support obligation. McKinney's Family Court Act Sec. 413, subd. 1(c)(3), (f).

See publication Words and Phrases for other judicial constructions and definitions.


4.   PARENT AND CHILD k3.3(6)
        285   ----
        285k3      Support and Education of Child
        285k3.3     Actions to Compel Support or Payment for Necessaries
        285k3.3(6)   Trial; findings.


N.Y. 1995.
   Trial court's stated basis for its exercise of discretion to apply Child Support Standards Act's statutory percentage when awarding child support on parental income exceeding $80,000 should, in sum and substance, reflect both that court has carefully considered parties' circumstances and that it had found no reason why there should be departure from prescribed percentage. McKinney's Family Court Act Sec. 413; McKinney's DRL Sec. 240.


5.   DIVORCE k308
        134   ----
        134VI     Custody and Support of Children
        134k308    Order, judgment, or decree as to support.


N.Y. 1995.
Copyright (c) West Publishing Co. 1995  No claim to original U.S. Govt. works.

Application of Child Support Standards Act's statutory percentage when
awarding child support on parental income exceeding $80,000 was not an abuse of
discretion;  hearing examiner conducted two-day inquiry into parties'
circumstances, set forth her findings in detail, and record indicated that no
extraordinary circumstances were present.  McKinney's Family Court Act Sec.
413;  McKinney's DRL Sec. 240.


------------------------ Page 628 N.Y.S.2d 11 follows ------------------------
[85 N.Y.2d 650] Schapiro & Reich, Lindenhurst (Perry S. Reich, of counsel),
for appellant.

Dikman, Dikman & Botter, Jamaica (Michael Dikman and Donna Dubinsky, of
counsel), for respondent.

[85 N.Y.2d 651] OPINION OF THE COURT

KAYE, Chief Judge.

The focus of this appeal is the Child Support Standards Act (Family Ct.Act
Sec. 413;  Domestic Relations Law Sec. 240), which includes a numeric formula
for calculating the award of child support, prescribing criteria as to combined
parental income under $80,000 and criteria as to income above that amount.  We
are asked to review an award determined by application of the statutory formula
to combined parental income exceeding $80,000.  We conclude that the award was
proper and affirm the Appellate Division order so holding.

The parties here were divorced in 1986, with two children, one of whom is now
emancipated.  Plaintiff mother was awarded custody of the children and defendant
father
------------------------ Page 628 N.Y.S.2d 12 follows ------------------------
was ordered to pay $125 per week in child support.  In 1989 plaintiff petitioned
for an upward modification of the support award for the nonemancipated child
pursuant to the newly enacted child support statute, and defendant
cross-petitioned for a downward modification.

After taking evidence in a two-day hearing relating to the family's income
and expenses, the Hearing Examiner found a substantial increase in the parties'
financial circumstances warranting increased child support.  On combined
parental income of $99,944 (64.4% of it attributable to the father), the Hearing
Examiner ordered defendant to pay $218 per week.  That amount was determined by
multiplying the parents' total income by the statutory percentage (17%) and then
allocating 64.4% of that amount to the father.  The Hearing Examiner further
ordered defendant to pay his pro rata share of the child's private school costs
(FN1) and unreimbursed medical expenses.

Before Family Court, the father contended that the Hearing [85 N.Y.2d 652]
Examiner erred in applying the statutory percentage to income over $80,000
without setting forth reasons for that particular award.  Family Court concluded
that the statute permitted that and, absent good cause, refused to interfere
with the Hearing Examiner's exercise of discretion to apply the percentage.  The
Appellate Division agreed with the father that Family Court was required to
state reasons for the award of child support on combined parental income over
$80,000 but found that requirement satisfied by the Hearing Examiner's in-depth
consideration of the parties' circumstances.  The Appellate Division
Copyright (c) West Publishing Co. 1995  No claim to original U.S. Govt. works.

additionally affirmed the award of unreimbursed medical expenses.  We now
affirm.

The Child Support Standards Act, effective September 15, 1989, replaced a
needs-based discretionary system with a precisely articulated, three-step method
for determining child support.  Enactment of this statute after long efforts
signalled a new era in calculating child support awards (see generally, Reichler
and Lefcourt, The New Child Support Standards Act, N.Y. St BJ 36 [Feb. 1990];
Note, The Child Support Standards Act and the New York Judiciary:  Fortifying
the 17 Percent Solution, 56 Brook L Rev 1299).

The Act had among its objectives the assurance that both parents would
contribute to the support of the children, and that the children would not
"unfairly bear the economic burden of parental separation" (Governor's Program
Bill Mem, Bill Jacket, L 1989, ch 567, at 1).  Emphasis was to shift "from a
balancing of the expressed needs of the child and the income available to the
parents after expenses to the total income available to the parents and the
standard of living that should be shared with the child" (Reichler and Lefcourt,
N.Y. St BJ, op. cit., at 44;  see also, Governor's Approval Mem, 1989 NY Legis
Ann, at 250 ["children will share in the economic status of both their
parents"].

[1] Further, the Legislature perceived that the existing system produced
inconsistent, unpredictable and often seemingly arbitrary results, which
undermined the parties' confidence in the fairness of the process (see, 1989
N.Y. Legis Ann, at 248, citing Rep of NY Commn on Child Support, at 69).
Consequently, the new statute sought to create greater uniformity,
predictability and equity in fixing child support awards, while at the same time
maintaining the degree of judicial discretion necessary to address unique
circumstances (Letter of Assembly Sponsor Helene E. Weinstein to Governor Mario
Cuomo, June 30, [85 N.Y.2d 653] 1989, Bill Jacket, L 1989, ch 567;  Governor's
Program Bill Mem, Bill Jacket, L 1989, ch 567, at 5).

As the statute directs, step one of the three-step method is the court's
calculation of "combined parental income" in accordance with Family Court Act
Sec. 413(1)(b)(4)-(5) (see, Domestic Relations Law Sec. 240 for analogous
provisions).  Second, the court multiplies that figure, up to $80,000, by a
specified percentage (FN2) based upon the number of children
---------------------- Page 628 N.Y.S.2d 13 follows ------------------------
in the household--17% for one child--and then allocates that amount between the
parents according to their share of the total income (Family Ct.Act Sec.
413[1][b][3];   [c].

Third, where combined parental income exceeds $80,000--the situation at issue
in this case--the statute provides that "the court shall determine the amount of
child support for the amount of the combined parental income in excess of such
dollar amount through consideration of the factors set forth in paragraph (f) of
this subdivision and/or the child support percentage" (Family Ct.Act Sec.
413[1][c][3].  The "paragraph (f)" factors include the financial resources of
the parents and child, the health of the child and any special needs, the
standard of living the child would have had if the marriage had not ended, tax
consequences, nonmonetary contributions of the parents toward the child, the
educational needs of the parents, the disparity in the parents' incomes, the
needs of other nonparty children receiving support from one of the parents,
extraordinary expenses incurred in exercising visitation and any other factors
Copyright (c) West Publishing Co. 1995  No claim to original U.S. Govt. works.

the court determines are relevant (Family Ct.Act Sec. 413[1][f].

Whenever the basic child support obligation derived by application of the
formula would be "unjust or inappropriate," the court must consider the
"paragraph (f)" factors.  That is so whether parental income is above or below
$80,000 (Family Ct.Act Sec. 413[1][b][1];  [c][2], [3].  If the formula is
rejected, the statute directs that the court "set forth, in a written order, the
factors it considered"--an unbending requirement that [85 N.Y.2d 654] cannot be
waived by either party or counsel (Family Ct.Act Sec. 413[1][g].

[2] The question now before us is whether the court must articulate a reason
for its award of child support on parental income exceeding $80,000 when it
chooses simply to apply the statutory percentage.  Defendant urges not only that
there must be a stated reason but also that the stated reason must relate to the
needs of the child, much as under prior law.

That question has generated uncertainty.  Some courts have calculated child
support awards simply by applying the statutory percentages to parental income
over $80,000 (see, e.g., De Bernardo v. De Bernardo, 180 A.D.2d 500, 502-503,
580 N.Y.S.2d 27;  Rosen v. Rosen, NYLJ, Oct. 9, 1990, at 31, col 5;  Brown v.
Brown, NYLJ, July 16, 1990, at 30, col 2;  Steel v. Steel, 152 Misc.2d 880,
884, 579 N.Y.S.2d 531).   Others have rejected a "blind application" of the
child support percentage to income over $80,000, requiring express findings as
to the child's actual needs (Harmon v. Harmon, 173 A.D.2d 98, 111, 578 N.Y.S.2d
897 ["a child is not a partner in the marital relationship, entitled to a 'piece
of the action' "];  see also, Chasin v. Chasin, 182 A.D.2d 862, 863, 582
N.Y.S.2d 512;  Colley v. Colley, 200 A.D.2d 839, 841, 606 N.Y.S.2d 796;
Panossian v. Panossian, 201 A.D.2d 983, 607 N.Y.S.2d 840;  Slankard v.
Chahinian, 204 A.D.2d 529, 531, 611 N.Y.S.2d 300 [all reversing trial court as
to child support].   The case law has even been read to limit the application of
the percentages to income below $80,000 (see, Florescue, Relocation of Custodial
Parent, NYLJ, June 14, 1993, at 4, col 6).

Obviously, determining what the Child Support Standards Act requires begins
with the statute itself.

Where combined parental income is less than $80,000 the statute plainly
directs that the court apply the formula percentages (Family Ct.Act Sec.
413[1][c][2]--thus implementing the objectives of uniformity and predictability.
Only where that amount would be "unjust or inappropriate" does the Act require
the court to set forth reasons.

[3] As to combined parental income over $80,000, the statute explicitly
affords an option:  the court may apply the factors set forth in section
413(1)(f) "and/or the child support percentage" (Family Ct.Act Sec.
413[1][c][3];  see also, 1 Tippins, New York
---------------------- Page 628 N.Y.S.2d 14. follows ------------------------
Matrimonial Law and Practice Sec. 5A:20;  Reichler and Lefcourt, N.Y. St BJ, op.
cit., at 40).  Pertinent as well to income above $80,000 is the provision that
the court may disregard the formula if "unjust or inappropriate" but in that
event, must give its reasons in. a formal written order, which cannot be waived
by either party (Family Ct.Act Sec. 413[1][g].

[85 N.Y.2d 655] The parties' arguments for and against requiring an
elaboration of reasons where the statutory percentage is applied to income

exceeding $80,000 center on the term "and/or"--a term that has long irked
grammarians (see, e.g., Fowler, A Dictionary of Modern English Usage 29 [2d ed].
In that legislative purpose, not linguistic perfection, guides our
determination, we must seek to give meaning to the term "and/or," in the context
of the statute's over-all objective.  Defendant's insistence on an elaboration
of needs-based reasons reads the word "or" out of the section and rolls back the
calendar to pre-1989 law.  In our view, "and/or" should be read to afford courts
the discretion to apply the "paragraph (f)" factors, or to apply the statutory
percentages, or to apply both in fixing the basic child support obligation on
parental income over $80,000.  That interpretation is consistent with the
language of the section and with the objectives of the Child Support Standards
Act.

[4] That conclusion does not, however, end our analysis.  Given that the
statute explicitly vests discretion in the court and that the exercise of
discretion is subject to review for abuse, some record articulation of the
reasons for the court's choice to apply the percentage is necessary to
facilitate that review (see, CPLR 4213[b];  Siegel, Practice Commentaries,
McKinney's Cons.Laws of N.Y., Book 7B, CPLR 4213:2, at 336 [meaningful review is
futile if court does not state facts upon which its decision rests];  see also,
4 Weinstein-Korn-Miller, N.Y. Civ Prac p 4213.07 [court must provide the
ultimate facts which support its conclusions of law "in order to enlighten the
parties and to make more effective the review of judgments on appeal"].  The
stated basis for an exercise of discretion to apply the formula to income over
$80,000 should, in sum and substance, reflect both that the court has carefully
considered the parties' circumstances and that it has found no reason why there
should be a departure from the prescribed percentage.

[5] In the present case, the Hearing Examiner conducted a two-day inquiry
into the parties' circumstances and set forth her findings in detail.  The
Appellate Division was satisfied, as are we, that there was sufficient record
indication that no extraordinary circumstances were present, and application of
the statutory 17% to the $19,214 income above $80,000 was therefore justified
and not an abuse of discretion.

Finally, we affirm as well the Appellate Division's conclusion that the
father is required to pay his pro rata share of [85 N.Y.2d 656] the child's
unreimbursed medical expenses.  The statute specifies that the court "shall
prorate each parent's share of future reasonable health care expenses of the
child not covered by insurance" (Family Ct.Act Sec. 413[1][c][5].  Defendant's
insistence that this order constitutes an impermissible open-ended obligation,
as the Second Department earlier held (see, e.g., Chirls v. Chirls, 170 A.D.2d
641, 566 N.Y.S.2d 931) is meritless in light of the Act.

Accordingly, the order of the Appellate Division, insofar as appealed from,
should be affirmed, with costs.

SIMONS, TITONE, BELLACOSA, SMITH, LEVINE and CIPARICK, JJ., concur.

Order, insofar as appealed from, affirmed, with costs.
FN1. The propriety of the award of private school costs was before Family Court
and the Appellate Division, but is not before us on this appeal.

FN2. The theory underlying the percentage-of-parental-income approach (rather
than allocating the cost of providing for the child's needs) is that expenses

of children tend to vary according to parents' income (see, 2 New York Practice Guide, Domestic Relations Sec. 31.03[3][a][ii] [Sovronsky & Jorgensen ed 1995]. The actual percentages can be traced to a study of the typical portion of household income generally devoted to the child (see, Note, 56 Brook L Rev, op. cit., at 1316-1319, citing Van der Gaag, On Measuring the Costs of Children, in III Child Support: Technical Papers [Institute for Research on Poverty, Special Rep Series No. SR32C].

New York Supp.2d, Vols 556-630     630 N.Y.S.2d 156, Martusewicz v. Martusewicz, (N.Y.A.D. 4 Dept. 1995)

------------------------ Page 630 N.Y.S.2d 156 follows ------------------------

Kim H. MARTUSEWICZ, Appellant,
v.
Tina MARTUSEWICZ, Respondent.

Supreme Court, Appellate Division,
Fourth Department.

July 14, 1995.

In divorce proceeding, the Supreme Court, Jefferson County, Gilbert, J., ordered equitable distribution, and father appealed. The Supreme Court, Appellate Division, held that: (1) lower court erred in reducing husband's visitation from parties' preexisting visitation agreement; (2) lower court erred in imputing annual income to husband of $60,000 per year in determining his child support obligation; (3) lower court erred in computing parties' basic child support obligation; and (4) lower court erred in failing to grant husband credit for payments he made on mortgage and tax associated with marital residence.

Modified and remitted.

1.   DIVORCE k297
        134   ----
        134VI     Custody and Support of Children
        134k297      Stipulations and agreements of parties.

     [See headnote text below]

1.   DIVORCE k299
        134   ----
        134VI     Custody and Support of Children
        134k299      Access to child by parent deprived of custody.

N.Y.A.D. 4 Dept. 1995.
     In its child custody determination, trial court gave appropriate consideration to custody agreement entered into by parties prior to trial, but erred in reducing father's visitation from parties' agreement, which allowed father alternating biweekly visitation with children during summer and school recess.

# NOTES

8

# CHILD SUPPORT - RECENT CASE LAW

Mona R. Millstein

## APPLICATION OF CSSA
## TO COMBINED INCOME OVER $80,000

Pauk v. Pauk, 648 NYS2d 134 (2d Dept. 1996)

Hunter v. Hunter, 650 NYS2d 710 (1st Dept. 1996)

Manno v. Manno, 637 NYS2d 743 (2d Dept. 1996)

Zaremba v. Zaremba, 654 NYS2d 176 (2d Dept. 1997)

Jones v. Reese, 642 NYS2d 378 (3d Dept. 1996)

Main v. Main, NYLJ Aug. 14, 1996, p. 25 col. 6 (Sup. Ct. Nassau Ct.)

Dona G. V. Thomas P., NYLJ, March 28, 1997 (Sup. Ct. Bronx Co.)


## CSSA APPLIED TO MODIFICATION

Collins v. Collins, 635 NYS2d 655 (2d Dept. 1995) (College)

Otero v. Otero, 636 NYS2d 22 (1st Dept. 1996) (College)

Commissioner of Social Services o/b/o Selena S. v. Conrad R.W., 635 NYS2d 653 (2d Dept. 1995) (Change of Circumstances)

Dona G. V. Thomas P., NYLJ, March 28, 1997, p. 33 (Change of Circumstances)

**APPLICATION OF CSSA TO IMPUTED**
**INCOME AND DEDUCTIONS FROM INCOME**

Orlando v. Orlando, 635 NYS2d 752 (3d Dept. 1995) (Imputed Income)

Zaremba v. Zaremba, 654 NYS2d 176 (2d Dept. 1997) (Imputed Income)

Polychronopoulos v. Polychronopoulos, 640 NYS2d 256 (2d Dept. 1996) (Mortgage Payments)

Hart v. Hart, 641 NYS2d 459 (3d Dept. 1996) (Mortgage Payments)

Baldino v. Baldino, NYLJ, Oct. 11, 1996, p. 33 (2d Dept.) (Maintenance Payments)

Marino v. Marino, 645 NYS2d 252 (4th Dept. 1996) (Maintenance Payments)

Commissioner of Social Services o/b/o Acuria v. Nieves, NYLJ July 15, 1996 (1st Dept.) (Support for Other Family)

Mary V.G. v. James X.S., 641 NYS2d 711 (2d Dept. 1996) (Support for Other Family)

**NOTES**

# 9

# CHILD SUPPORT WORKSHEETS AND CHILD SUPPORT STANDARDS CHART

Reprinted from the PLI Course Handbook,
Child Custody and Support 1996.
Order Number C4-4214

COURT

COUNTY OF                                                    Index/Docket No.

| | |
|---|---|
| against | Plaintiff, Petitioner |
| | Defendant, Respondent |

## CHILD SUPPORT
## WORKSHEETS

*References are to DRL §240(1-b)
and FCA §413(1)*

Prepared by ...........................................................................................................................

Submitted by ☐ Plaintiff ☐ Defendant ☐ Petitioner ☐ Respondent

*(All numbers used in these worksheets are YEARLY figures. Convert weekly or monthly figures to annualized numbers.)*

**STEP 1**   MANDATORY PARENTAL INCOME *(b)(5)*                          FATHER       MOTHER

1. Gross (total) income (as reported on most recent Federal tax return, or as computed in accordance with Internal Revenue Code and regulations): *(b)(5)(i)*..............

*The following items MUST be added if not already included in Line 1:*

2.  Investment income: *(b)(5)(ii)*...........................................
3. Workers' compensation: *(b)(5)(iii)(A)*....................................
4. Disability benefits: *(b)(5)(iii)(B)*......................................
5. Unemployment insurance benefits: *(b)(5)(iii)(C)*..........................
6. Social Security benefits: *(b)(5)(iii)(D)*.................................
7. Veterans benefits: *(b)(5)(iii)(E)*.......................................
8. Pension retirement income: *(b)(5)(iii)(F)*...............................
9. Fellowships and stipends: *(b)(5)(iii)(G)* ...............................
10. Annuity payments: *(b)(5)(iii)(H)*.......................................
11. If self-empoyed, depreciation greater than straight-line depreciation used in determining business income or investment credit: *(b)(5)(vi)(A)* ....................
12. If self-employed, entertainment and travel allowances deducted from business income to the extent the allowances reduce personal expenditures: *(b)(5)(vi)(B)* ....
13. Former income voluntarily reduced to avoid child support: *(b)(5)(v)* ...............
14. Income voluntarily deferred: *(b)(5)(iii)* ...............................

A. TOTAL MANDATORY INCOME: ...................................................

**STEP 2**   NON—MANDATORY PARENTAL INCOME

These items must be disclosed here. Their inclusion in the final calculations, however, is discretionary. In contested cases, the Court determines whether or not they are included. In uncontested cases, the parents and their attorneys or mediators must determine which should be included.

15. Income attributable to non-income producing assets: *(b)(5)(iv)(A)* ...................
16. Employment benefits that confer personal economic benefits: *(b)(5)(iv)(B)* (Such as meals, lodging, memberships, automobiles, other) .......................

17. Fringe benefits of employment: *(b)(5)(iv)(C)* ...........................
18. Money, goods and services provided by relatives and friends: *(b)(5)(iv)(D)* .........

B. TOTAL NON-MANDATORY INCOME: ..............................................

C. TOTAL INCOME *(add Line A + Line B)* ............................................

215

## STEP 3  DEDUCTIONS

19. Expenses of investment income listed on line 2: (b)(5)(ii) .......................... ............... ...............
20. Unreimbursed business expenses that do not reduce personal expenditures:
    (b)(5)(vii)(A) ........................................................................... ............... ...............
21. Alimony or maintenance actually paid to a former spouse: (b)(5)(vii)(B)............. ...............
22. Alimony or maintenance paid to the other parent but only if child support will
    increase when alimony stops: (b)(5)(vii)(C) ......................................... ...............
23. Child support actually paid to other children the parent is legally obligated to
    support: (b)(5)(vii)(D) ................................................................ ...............
24. Public assistance: (b)(5)(vii)(E)....................................................... ...............
25. Supplemental security income: (b)(5)(vii)(F)........................................... ...............
26. New York City or Yonkers income or earnings taxes actually paid: (b)(5)(vii)(G) ... ...............
27. Social Security taxes (FICA) actually paid: (b)(5)(vii)(H)........................... ...............

D. TOTAL DEDUCTIONS:................................................................. _____  _____

E. FATHER'S INCOME (Line C minus Line D) ....................................... $_____

F. MOTHER'S INCOME (Line C minus Line D)...................................................... $_____

## STEP 4  (b)(4)   G. COMBINED PARENTAL INCOME: *(Line E plus Line F)* ........................ $_____

## STEP 5  (b)(3) and (c)(2)

MULTIPLY Line G (up to $80,000) by the proper percentage *(insert in Line H)*:
For 1 child ...................... 17%   For 3 children ................. 29%   For 5 or more children ........ 35% (minimum)
For 2 children .................. 25%   For 4 children ................. 31%

H. COMBINED CHILD SUPPORT: .......................................................... _____

## STEP 6  (c)(2)

DIVIDE the non-custodial parent's amount on Line E or Line F............................... ...............
by the amount of Line G .......................................................................... ...............
to obtain the percentage allocated
I. to the non-custodial parent: ..................................................................... ............... %

## STEP 7  (c)(2)   J. MULTIPLY line H by Line I: ...............

## STEP 8  (c)(3)

K. DECIDE the amount of child support to be paid on any combined parental income exceeding $80,000 per
year using the percentages in Step 5 or the factors in Step 11-C or both: ................................... ...............

L. ADD Line J and Line K.......................................................................... _____
    This is the amount of child support to be paid by the non-custodial parent to the custodial parent for all costs of the children.
except for child care expenses, health care expenses, and college, post-secondary, private, special or enriched education.

## STEP 9  SPECIAL NUMERICAL FACTORS

CHILD CARE EXPENSES

M. Cost of child care resulting from custodial parent's
    ☐ seeking work *(c)(6)* [*discretionary*]   ☐ working   ☐ attending elementary education
    ☐ attending secondary education   ☐ attending higher education
    ☐ attending vocational training leading to employment: *(c)(4)*.......................................... ...............

N. MULTIPLY Line M by Line I: ..................................................................... _____
    This is the amount the non-custodial parent must contribute to the custodial parent for child care.

216

HEALTH EXPENSES *(c)(5)*

**O. Reasonable future health care expenses not covered by insurance:** .......................................... ..............................

**P. MULTIPLY Line O by Line I:** ............................................................................. ..............................
    This is the amount the non-custodial parent must contribute to the custodial parent for health care or pay directly to the health care provider.

**Q. EDUCATIONAL EXPENSE, if appropriate, see Step 11 (b)** *(c)(7)* ...................................... ..............................

## STEP 10   LOW INCOME EXEMPTIONS *(d)*

**R. Insert amount of non-custodial parent's income from Line E or Line F:** ................................. ..............................

**S. Add amounts on Line L, Line N, Line P and Line Q (This total is "basic child support"):** ................ _____

**T. SUBTRACT Line S from Line R:** ...................................................................... _____

    If Line T is more than $8,065*, then the low income exemptions do not apply and child support remains as determined in Steps 8 and 9. If so, go to Step 11.

    If Line T is less than $5,980†, then

**U. Insert amount of non custodial parent's income from Line E or Line F:** ................................ ..............................

**V. Self-support reserve:** .................................................................................. ___($8,065)*___

**W. Subtract Line V from Line U:** ........................................................................ _____

        If Line W is more than $300 per year, then Line W is the amount of basic child support. If Line
        W is less than $300 per year, then basic child support must be a minimum of $300 per year.

    If Line T is less than $8,065* but more than $5,980†, then

**X. Insert amount of non-custodial parent's income from Line E or Line F:** ............................... ..............................

**Y. Self-support reserve:** .................................................................................. ___($8,065)*___

**Z. SUBTRACT Line Y from Line X :** ...................................................................... _____

        If Line Z is more than $600 per year, then Line Z is the amount of basic child support. If Line
        Z is less than $600 per year, then basic child support must be a minimum of $600 per year.

## STEP 11   NON-NUMERICAL FACTORS

### (a) NON-RECURRING INCOME *(e)*

    A portion of non-recurring income, such as life insurance proceeds, gifts and inheritances or lottery winnings, may be allocated to child support. The law does not mention a specific percentage for such non-recurring income. Such support is not modified by the low income exemptions.

### (b) EDUCATIONAL EXPENSES *(c)(7)*

    New York's child support law does not contain a specific percentage method to determine how parents should share the cost of education of their children. Traditionally, the courts have considered both parents' complete financial circumstances in deciding who pays how much. The most important elements of financial circumstances are income, reasonable expenses, and financial resources such as savings and investments.

---

* $8,065 is the 1989 self-support reserve. In future years, use the current self-support reserve which is 135% of the official Federal poverty level for a single person household as promulgated by the U.S. Department of Health and Human Services.
† $5,980 is the 1989 Federal poverty level. In future years, use the current Federal poverty level for a single person household as promulgated by the U.S. Department of Health and Human Services.

### (c) ADDITIONAL FACTORS (f)

The child support guidelines law lists 10 factors that should be considered in deciding on the amount of child support for
- combined incomes of more than $80,000 per year or
- to vary the numerical result of these steps because the result is "unjust or inappropriate."

These factors are:
1. The financial resources of the parents and the child.
2. The physical and emotional health of the child and his/her special needs and aptitudes
3. The standard of living the child would have enjoyed if the marriage or household was not dissolved.
4. The tax consequences to the parents.
5. The non-monetary contributions the parents will make toward the care and well-being of the child.
6. The educational needs of the parents.
7. The fact that the gross income of one parent is substantially less than the gross income of the other parent.
8. The needs of the other children of the non-custodial parent for whom the non-custodial parent is providing support, but only (a) if Line 23 is not deducted; (b) after considering the financial resources of any other person obligated to support the other children; and (c) if the resources available to support the other children are less then the resources available to support the children involved in this matter.
9. If a child is not on public assistance, the amount of extraordinary costs of visitation (such as out-of-state travel) or extended visits (other than the usual two to four week summer visits), but only if the custodial parent's expenses are substantially reduced by the visitation involved.
10. Any other factor the court decides is relevant.

### NON JUDICIAL DETERMINATION OF CHILD SUPPORT (h)

Outside of court, parents are free to agree to any amount of support, so long as they sign a statement that they have been advised of the provisions of the child support guidelines law. However, the court cannot approve agreements of less than $300 per year. This minimum is not per child, meaning that the minimum for 3 children is $300 per year, not $900 per year. In addition, the courts retain discretion over child support.

**Verification** (b)(5)(i)   *Required if married person files joint income tax return.*

STATE OF NEW YORK, COUNTY OF                                      ss.:

being duly sworn, deposes and says: I am the
in this case; I have read
these Child Support Worksheets and I know their contents; they are true to my own knowledge, except as to the matters stated to be on information and belief, and as to those I believe it to be true.

Sworn to before me on

..............................................................................................
*The name signed must be printed beneath.*

218

# CHILD SUPPORT STANDARDS CHART
## PREPARED BY NEW YORK STATE
## DEPARTMENT OF SOCIAL SERVICES
## OFFICE OF CHILD SUPPORT ENFORCEMENT

1989

The tables provided as part of the Child Support Standards Chart should be used to determine the annual child support obligation pursuant to the provisions of Chapter 567 of the Laws of New York of 1989. The current poverty income guidelines amount for a person as reported by the United States Department of Health and Human Services is $5,980, and the self-support reserve for $8,065.

How to use the Chart:

1. Locate the "Income Range" you are looking for in the upper right hand corner of each page.
2. Locate the row labeled "Annual Income" on one of the tables of this page.
3. Go across the top of the table to the column corresponding to the "Number of Children" for whom support is sought.
4. The dollar amount listed where the "Annual Income" row and the "Number of Children" column meet is the amount of the child support obligation, where additional amounts are not applicable for the child care, health care and education f children for whom support is sought.
5. Where additional amounts for child care, health care and educational expenses are appropriate, see the worksheet on page

INCOME
0-

## Child Support Percentages

| | | ANNUAL INCOME | NUMBER OF CHILDREN | | | |
|---|---|---|---|---|---|---|
| | | | 1 | 2 | 3 | 4 |
| | | | ANNUAL OBLIGATION AMOUNT | | | |
| One Child | 17% of combined parental income | 8,000 -8,099 | 600 | 600 | 300 | 300 |
| Two Children | 25% of combined parental income | 8,100 -8,199 | 600 | 600 | 300 | 300 |
| Three Children | 29% of combined parental income | 8,200 -8,299 | 600 | 600 | 300 | 300 |
| Four Children | 31% of combined parental income | 8,300 -8,399 | 600 | 600 | 300 | 300 |
| Five Children | no less than 35% of combined parental income | 8,400 -8,499 | 600 | 600 | 335 | 335 |
| | | 8,500 -8,599 | 600 | 600 | 600 | 435 |
| | | 8,600 -8,699 | 600 | 600 | 600 | 535 |
| | | 8,700 -8,799 | 635 | 635 | 635 | 635 |
| | | 8,800 -8,899 | 735 | 735 | 735 | 735 |
| | | 8,900 -8,999 | 835 | 835 | 835 | 835 |

| ANNUAL INCOME | NUMBER OF CHILDREN | | | | | ANNUAL INCOME | NUMBER OF CHILDREN | | | |
|---|---|---|---|---|---|---|---|---|---|---|
| | 1 | 2 | 3 | 4 | 5+ | | 1 | 2 | 3 | 4 |
| | ANNUAL OBLIGATION AMOUNT | | | | | | ANNUAL OBLIGATION AMOUNT | | | |
| 0 -7,299 | 300 | 300 | 300 | 300 | 300 | 9,000 -9,099 | 935 | 935 | 935 | 935 |
| 7,300 -7,399 | 600 | 300 | 300 | 300 | 300 | 9,100 -9,199 | 1,035 | 1,035 | 1,035 | 1,035 |
| 7,400 -7,499 | 600 | 300 | 300 | 300 | 300 | 9,200 -9,299 | 1,135 | 1,135 | 1,135 | 1,135 |
| 7,500 -7,599 | 600 | 300 | 300 | 300 | 300 | 9,300 -9,399 | 1,235 | 1,235 | 1,235 | 1,235 |
| 7,600 -7,699 | 600 | 300 | 300 | 300 | 300 | 9,400 -9,499 | 1,335 | 1,335 | 1,335 | 1,335 |
| 7,700 -7,799 | 600 | 300 | 300 | 300 | 300 | 9,500 -9,599 | 1,435 | 1,435 | 1,435 | 1,435 |
| 7,800 -7,899 | 600 | 300 | 300 | 300 | 300 | 9,600 -9,699 | 1,535 | 1,535 | 1,535 | 1,535 |
| 7,900 -7,999 | 600 | 300 | 300 | 300 | 300 | 9,700 -9,799 | 1,635 | 1,635 | 1,635 | 1,635 |
| | | | | | | 9,800 -9,899 | 1,666 | 1,735 | 1,735 | 1,735 |
| | | | | | | 9,900 -9,999 | 1,683 | 1,835 | 1,835 | 1,835 |

| ANNUAL INCOME | NUMBER OF CHILDREN | | | | |
|---|---|---|---|---|---|
| | 1 | 2 | 3 | 4 | 5+ |
| | ANNUAL OBLIGATION AMOUNT | | | | |
| 10,000 -10,099 | 1,700 | 1,935 | 1,935 | 1,935 | 1,935 |
| 10,100 -10,199 | 1,717 | 2,035 | 2,035 | 2,035 | 2,035 |
| 10,200 -10,299 | 1,734 | 2,135 | 2,135 | 2,135 | 2,135 |
| 10,300 -10,399 | 1,751 | 2,235 | 2,235 | 2,235 | 2,235 |
| 10,400 -10,499 | 1,768 | 2,335 | 2,335 | 2,335 | 2,335 |
| 10,500 -10,599 | 1,785 | 2,435 | 2,435 | 2,435 | 2,435 |
| 10,600 -10,699 | 1,802 | 2,535 | 2,535 | 2,535 | 2,535 |
| 10,700 -10,799 | 1,819 | 2,635 | 2,635 | 2,635 | 2,635 |
| 10,800 -10,899 | 1,836 | 2,700 | 2,735 | 2,735 | 2,735 |
| 10,900 -10,999 | 1,853 | 2,725 | 2,833 | 2,833 | 2,833 |

| ANNUAL INCOME | NUMBER OF CHILDREN | | | | |
|---|---|---|---|---|---|
| | 1 | 2 | 3 | 4 | 5+ |
| | ANNUAL OBLIGATION AMOUNT | | | | |
| 11,000 -11,099 | 1,870 | 2,750 | 2,935 | 2,935 | 2,935 |
| 11,100 -11,199 | 1,887 | 2,775 | 3,035 | 3,035 | 3,035 |
| 11,200 -11,299 | 1,904 | 2,800 | 3,135 | 3,135 | 3,135 |
| 11,300 -11,399 | 1,921 | 2,825 | 3,235 | 3,235 | 3,235 |
| 11,400 -11,499 | 1,938 | 2,850 | 3,306 | 3,335 | 3,335 |
| 11,500 -11,599 | 1,955 | 2,875 | 3,335 | 3,435 | 3,435 |
| 11,600 -11,699 | 1,972 | 2,900 | 3,364 | 3,535 | 3,535 |
| 11,700 -11,799 | 1,989 | 2,925 | 3,393 | 3,427 | 3,433 |
| 11,800 -11,899 | 2,006 | 2,950 | 3,422 | 3,458 | 3,735 |
| 11,900 -11,999 | 2,023 | 2,975 | 3,451 | 3,689 | 3,835 |

| ANNUAL INCOME | NUMBER OF CHILDREN | | | | |
|---|---|---|---|---|---|
| | 1 | 2 | 3 | 4 | 5+ |
| | ANNUAL OBLIGATION AMOUNT | | | | |
| 12,000 -12,099 | 2,040 | 3,000 | 3,480 | 3,720 | 3,935 |
| 12,100 -12,199 | 2,057 | 3,025 | 3,509 | 3,751 | 4,035 |
| 12,200 -12,299 | 2,074 | 3,050 | 3,538 | 3,782 | 4,135 |
| 12,300 -12,399 | 2,091 | 3,075 | 3,567 | 3,813 | 4,235 |
| 12,400 -12,499 | 2,108 | 3,100 | 3,596 | 3,844 | 4,335 |
| 12,500 -12,599 | 2,125 | 3,125 | 3,625 | 3,875 | 4,375 |
| 12,600 -12,699 | 2,142 | 3,150 | 3,654 | 3,906 | 4,410 |
| 12,700 -12,799 | 2,159 | 3,175 | 3,683 | 3,937 | 4,445 |
| 12,800 -12,899 | 2,176 | 3,200 | 3,712 | 3,968 | 4,480 |
| 12,900 -12,999 | 2,193 | 3,225 | 3,741 | 3,999 | 4,515 |

| ANNUAL INCOME | NUMBER OF CHILDREN | | | | |
|---|---|---|---|---|---|
| | 1 | 2 | 3 | 4 | 5+ |
| | ANNUAL OBLIGATION AMOUNT | | | | |
| 13,000 -13,099 | 2,210 | 3,250 | 3,770 | 4,030 | 4,550 |
| 13,100 -13,199 | 2,227 | 3,275 | 3,799 | 4,061 | 4,585 |
| 13,200 -13,299 | 2,244 | 3,300 | 3,828 | 4,092 | 4,620 |
| 13,300 -13,399 | 2,261 | 3,325 | 3,857 | 4,123 | 4,655 |
| 13,400 -13,499 | 2,278 | 3,350 | 3,886 | 4,154 | 4,690 |
| 13,500 -13,599 | 2,295 | 3,375 | 3,915 | 4,185 | 4,725 |
| 13,600 -13,699 | 2,312 | 3,400 | 3,944 | 4,214 | 4,760 |
| 13,700 -13,799 | 2,329 | 3,425 | 3,973 | 4,247 | 4,795 |
| 13,800 -13,899 | 2,346 | 3,450 | 4,002 | 4,278 | 4,830 |
| 13,900 -13,999 | 2,363 | 3,475 | 4,031 | 4,309 | 4,865 |

| ANNUAL INCOME | NUMBER OF CHILDREN | | | | |
|---|---|---|---|---|---|
| | 1 | 2 | 3 | 4 | 5+ |
| | ANNUAL OBLIGATION AMOUNT | | | | |
| 14,000 -14,099 | 2,380 | 3,500 | 4,060 | 4,340 | 4,900 |
| 14,100 -14,199 | 2,397 | 3,525 | 4,089 | 4,371 | 4,935 |
| 14,200 -14,299 | 2,414 | 3,550 | 4,118 | 4,402 | 4,970 |
| 14,300 -14,399 | 2,431 | 3,575 | 4,147 | 4,433 | 5,005 |
| 14,400 -14,499 | 2,448 | 3,600 | 4,176 | 4,444 | 5,040 |
| 14,500 -14,599 | 2,465 | 3,625 | 4,205 | 4,495 | 5,075 |
| 14,600 -14,699 | 2,482 | 3,650 | 4,234 | 4,526 | 5,110 |
| 14,700 -14,799 | 2,499 | 3,675 | 4,263 | 4,557 | 5,145 |
| 14,800 -14,899 | 2,516 | 3,700 | 4,292 | 4,588 | 5,180 |
| 14,900 -14,999 | 2,533 | 3,725 | 4,321 | 4,619 | 5,215 |

| ANNUAL INCOME | NUMBER OF CHILDREN | | | | |
|---|---|---|---|---|---|
| | 1 | 2 | 3 | 4 | 5+ |
| | ANNUAL OBLIGATION AMOUNT | | | | |
| 15,000 -15,099 | 2,550 | 3,750 | 4,350 | 4,650 | 5,250 |
| 15,100 -15,199 | 2,567 | 3,775 | 4,379 | 4,681 | 5,285 |
| 15,200 -15,299 | 2,584 | 3,800 | 4,408 | 4,712 | 5,320 |
| 15,300 -15,399 | 2,601 | 3,825 | 4,437 | 4,743 | 5,355 |
| 15,400 -15,499 | 2,618 | 3,850 | 4,466 | 4,774 | 5,390 |
| 15,500 -15,599 | 2,635 | 3,875 | 4,495 | 4,805 | 5,425 |
| 15,600 -15,699 | 2,652 | 3,900 | 4,524 | 4,836 | 5,460 |
| 15,700 -15,799 | 2,669 | 3,925 | 4,553 | 4,867 | 5,495 |
| 15,800 -15,899 | 2,686 | 3,950 | 4,582 | 4,898 | 5,530 |
| 15,900 -15,999 | 2,703 | 3,975 | 4,611 | 4,929 | 5,565 |

| ANNUAL INCOME | NUMBER OF CHILDREN | | | | |
|---|---|---|---|---|---|
| | 1 | 2 | 3 | 4 | 5+ |
| | ANNUAL OBLIGATION AMOUNT | | | | |
| 16,000 -16,099 | 2,720 | 4,000 | 4,640 | 4,960 | 5,600 |
| 16,100 -16,199 | 2,737 | 4,025 | 4,669 | 4,991 | 5,635 |
| 16,200 -16,299 | 2,754 | 4,050 | 4,698 | 5,022 | 5,670 |
| 16,300 -16,399 | 2,771 | 4,075 | 4,727 | 5,053 | 5,705 |
| 16,400 -16,499 | 2,788 | 4,100 | 4,756 | 5,084 | 5,740 |
| 16,500 -16,599 | 2,805 | 4,125 | 4,785 | 5,115 | 5,775 |
| 16,600 -16,699 | 2,822 | 4,150 | 4,814 | 5,146 | 5,810 |
| 16,700 -16,799 | 2,839 | 4,175 | 4,843 | 5,177 | 5,845 |
| 16,800 -16,899 | 2,856 | 4,200 | 4,872 | 5,208 | 5,880 |
| 16,900 -16,999 | 2,873 | 4,225 | 4,901 | 5,239 | 5,915 |

| ANNUAL INCOME | NUMBER OF CHILDREN | | | | |
|---|---|---|---|---|---|
| | 1 | 2 | 3 | 4 | 5+ |
| | ANNUAL OBLIGATION AMOUNT | | | | |
| 17,000 -17,099 | 2,890 | 4,250 | 4,930 | 5,270 | 5,950 |
| 17,100 -17,199 | 2,907 | 4,275 | 4,959 | 5,301 | 5,985 |
| 17,200 -17,299 | 2,924 | 4,300 | 4,988 | 5,332 | 6,020 |
| 17,300 -17,399 | 2,941 | 4,325 | 5,017 | 5,363 | 6,055 |
| 17,400 -17,499 | 2,958 | 4,350 | 5,046 | 5,394 | 6,090 |
| 17,500 -17,599 | 2,975 | 4,375 | 5,075 | 5,425 | 6,125 |
| 17,600 -17,699 | 2,992 | 4,400 | 5,104 | 5,456 | 6,160 |
| 17,700 -17,799 | 3,009 | 4,425 | 5,133 | 5,487 | 6,195 |
| 17,800 -17,899 | 3,026 | 4,450 | 5,162 | 5,518 | 6,230 |
| 17,900 -17,999 | 3,043 | 4,475 | 5,191 | 5,549 | 6,265 |

| ANNUAL INCOME | NUMBER OF CHILDREN | | | | |
|---|---|---|---|---|---|
| | 1 | 2 | 3 | 4 | 5+ |
| | ANNUAL OBLIGATION AMOUNT | | | | |
| 18,000 -18,099 | 3,060 | 4,500 | 5,220 | 5,580 | 6,300 |
| 18,100 -18,199 | 3,077 | 4,525 | 5,249 | 5,611 | 6,335 |
| 18,200 -18,299 | 3,094 | 4,550 | 5,278 | 5,642 | 6,370 |
| 18,300 -18,399 | 3,111 | 4,575 | 5,307 | 5,673 | 6,405 |
| 18,400 -18,499 | 3,128 | 4,600 | 5,336 | 5,704 | 6,440 |
| 18,500 -18,599 | 3,145 | 4,625 | 5,365 | 5,735 | 6,475 |
| 18,600 -18,699 | 3,162 | 4,650 | 5,394 | 5,766 | 6,510 |
| 18,700 -18,799 | 3,179 | 4,675 | 5,423 | 5,797 | 6,545 |
| 18,800 -18,899 | 3,196 | 4,700 | 5,452 | 5,828 | 6,580 |
| 18,900 -18,999 | 3,213 | 4,725 | 5,481 | 5,859 | 6,615 |

| ANNUAL INCOME | NUMBER OF CHILDREN | | | | |
|---|---|---|---|---|---|
| | 1 | 2 | 3 | 4 | 5+ |
| | ANNUAL OBLIGATION AMOUNT | | | | |
| 19,000 -19,099 | 3,230 | 4,750 | 5,510 | 5,890 | 6,650 |
| 19,100 -19,199 | 3,247 | 4,775 | 5,539 | 5,921 | 6,685 |
| 19,200 -19,299 | 3,264 | 4,800 | 5,568 | 5,952 | 6,720 |
| 19,300 -19,399 | 3,281 | 4,825 | 5,597 | 5,983 | 6,755 |
| 19,400 -19,499 | 3,298 | 4,850 | 5,626 | 6,014 | 6,790 |
| 19,500 -19,599 | 3,315 | 4,875 | 5,655 | 6,045 | 6,825 |
| 19,600 -19,699 | 3,332 | 4,900 | 5,684 | 6,076 | 6,860 |
| 19,700 -19,799 | 3,349 | 4,925 | 5,713 | 6,107 | 6,895 |
| 19,800 -19,899 | 3,366 | 4,950 | 5,742 | 6,138 | 6,930 |
| 19,900 -19,999 | 3,383 | 4,975 | 5,771 | 6,169 | 6,965 |

2

| ANNUAL INCOME | NUMBER OF CHILDREN 1 | 2 | 3 | 4 | 5+ |
|---|---|---|---|---|---|
| | ANNUAL OBLIGATION AMOUNT | | | | |
| 20,000 -20,099 | 3,400 | 5,000 | 5,800 | 6,200 | 7,000 |
| 20,100 -20,199 | 3,417 | 5,025 | 5,829 | 6,231 | 7,035 |
| 20,200 -20,299 | 3,434 | 5,050 | 5,858 | 6,262 | 7,070 |
| 20,300 -20,399 | 3,451 | 5,075 | 5,887 | 6,293 | 7,105 |
| 20,400 -20,499 | 3,468 | 5,100 | 5,916 | 6,324 | 7,140 |
| 20,500 -20,599 | 3,485 | 5,125 | 5,945 | 6,355 | 7,175 |
| 20,600 -20,699 | 3,502 | 5,150 | 5,974 | 6,386 | 7,210 |
| 20,700 -20,799 | 3,519 | 5,175 | 6,003 | 6,417 | 7,245 |
| 20,800 -20,899 | 3,536 | 5,200 | 6,032 | 6,448 | 7,280 |
| 20,900 -20,999 | 3,553 | 5,225 | 6,061 | 6,479 | 7,315 |

| ANNUAL INCOME | NUMBER OF CHILDREN 1 | 2 | 3 | 4 | 5+ |
|---|---|---|---|---|---|
| | ANNUAL OBLIGATION AMOUNT | | | | |
| 25,000 -25,099 | 4,250 | 6,250 | 7,250 | 7,750 | 8,750 |
| 25,100 -25,199 | 4,267 | 6,275 | 7,279 | 7,781 | 8,785 |
| 25,200 -25,299 | 4,284 | 6,300 | 7,308 | 7,812 | 8,820 |
| 25,300 -25,399 | 4,301 | 6,325 | 7,337 | 7,843 | 8,855 |
| 25,400 -25,499 | 4,318 | 6,350 | 7,366 | 7,874 | 8,890 |
| 25,500 -25,599 | 4,335 | 6,375 | 7,395 | 7,905 | 8,925 |
| 25,600 -25,699 | 4,352 | 6,400 | 7,424 | 7,936 | 8,960 |
| 25,700 -25,799 | 4,369 | 6,425 | 7,453 | 7,967 | 8,995 |
| 25,800 -25,899 | 4,386 | 6,450 | 7,482 | 7,998 | 9,030 |
| 25,900 -25,999 | 4,403 | 6,475 | 7,511 | 8,029 | 9,065 |

| ANNUAL INCOME | NUMBER OF CHILDREN 1 | 2 | 3 | 4 | 5+ |
|---|---|---|---|---|---|
| | ANNUAL OBLIGATION AMOUNT | | | | |
| 21,000 -21,099 | 3,570 | 5,250 | 6,090 | 6,510 | 7,350 |
| 21,100 -21,199 | 3,587 | 5,275 | 6,119 | 6,541 | 7,385 |
| 21,200 -21,299 | 3,604 | 5,300 | 6,148 | 6,572 | 7,420 |
| 21,300 -21,399 | 3,621 | 5,325 | 6,177 | 6,603 | 7,455 |
| 21,400 -21,499 | 3,638 | 5,350 | 6,206 | 6,634 | 7,490 |
| 21,500 -21,599 | 3,655 | 5,375 | 6,235 | 6,665 | 7,525 |
| 21,600 -21,699 | 3,672 | 5,400 | 6,264 | 6,696 | 7,560 |
| 21,700 -21,799 | 3,689 | 5,425 | 6,293 | 6,727 | 7,595 |
| 21,800 -21,899 | 3,706 | 5,450 | 6,322 | 6,758 | 7,630 |
| 21,900 -21,999 | 3,723 | 5,475 | 6,351 | 6,789 | 7,665 |

| ANNUAL INCOME | NUMBER OF CHILDREN 1 | 2 | 3 | 4 | 5+ |
|---|---|---|---|---|---|
| | ANNUAL OBLIGATION AMOUNT | | | | |
| 26,000 -26,099 | 4,420 | 6,500 | 7,540 | 8,060 | 9,100 |
| 26,100 -26,199 | 4,437 | 6,525 | 7,569 | 8,091 | 9,135 |
| 26,200 -26,299 | 4,454 | 6,550 | 7,598 | 8,122 | 9,170 |
| 26,300 -26,399 | 4,471 | 6,575 | 7,627 | 8,153 | 9,205 |
| 26,400 -26,499 | 4,488 | 6,600 | 7,656 | 8,184 | 9,240 |
| 26,500 -26,599 | 4,505 | 6,625 | 7,685 | 8,215 | 9,275 |
| 26,600 -26,699 | 4,522 | 6,650 | 7,714 | 8,246 | 9,310 |
| 26,700 -26,799 | 4,539 | 6,675 | 7,743 | 8,277 | 9,345 |
| 26,800 -26,899 | 4,556 | 6,700 | 7,772 | 8,308 | 9,380 |
| 26,900 -26,999 | 4,573 | 6,725 | 7,801 | 8,339 | 9,415 |

| ANNUAL INCOME | NUMBER OF CHILDREN 1 | 2 | 3 | 4 | 5+ |
|---|---|---|---|---|---|
| | ANNUAL OBLIGATION AMOUNT | | | | |
| 22,000 -22,099 | 3,740 | 5,500 | 6,380 | 6,820 | 7,700 |
| 22,100 -22,199 | 3,757 | 5,525 | 6,409 | 6,851 | 7,735 |
| 22,200 -22,299 | 3,774 | 5,550 | 6,438 | 6,882 | 7,770 |
| 22,300 -22,399 | 3,791 | 5,575 | 6,467 | 6,913 | 7,805 |
| 22,400 -22,499 | 3,808 | 5,600 | 6,496 | 6,944 | 7,840 |
| 22,500 -22,599 | 3,825 | 5,625 | 6,525 | 6,975 | 7,875 |
| 22,600 -22,699 | 3,842 | 5,650 | 6,554 | 7,006 | 7,910 |
| 22,700 -22,799 | 3,859 | 5,675 | 6,583 | 7,037 | 7,945 |
| 22,800 -22,899 | 3,876 | 5,700 | 6,612 | 7,068 | 7,980 |
| 22,900 -22,999 | 3,893 | 5,725 | 6,641 | 7,099 | 8,015 |

| ANNUAL INCOME | NUMBER OF CHILDREN 1 | 2 | 3 | 4 | 5+ |
|---|---|---|---|---|---|
| | ANNUAL OBLIGATION AMOUNT | | | | |
| 27,000 -27,099 | 4,590 | 6,750 | 7,830 | 8,370 | 9,450 |
| 27,100 -27,199 | 4,607 | 6,775 | 7,859 | 8,401 | 9,485 |
| 27,200 -27,299 | 4,624 | 6,800 | 7,888 | 8,432 | 9,520 |
| 27,300 -27,399 | 4,641 | 6,825 | 7,917 | 8,463 | 9,555 |
| 27,400 -27,499 | 4,658 | 6,850 | 7,946 | 8,494 | 9,590 |
| 27,500 -27,599 | 4,675 | 6,875 | 7,975 | 8,525 | 9,625 |
| 27,600 -27,699 | 4,692 | 6,900 | 8,004 | 8,556 | 9,660 |
| 27,700 -27,799 | 4,709 | 6,925 | 8,033 | 8,587 | 9,695 |
| 27,800 -27,899 | 4,726 | 6,950 | 8,062 | 8,618 | 9,730 |
| 27,900 -27,999 | 4,743 | 6,975 | 8,091 | 8,649 | 9,765 |

| ANNUAL INCOME | NUMBER OF CHILDREN 1 | 2 | 3 | 4 | 5+ |
|---|---|---|---|---|---|
| | ANNUAL OBLIGATION AMOUNT | | | | |
| 23,000 -23,099 | 3,910 | 5,750 | 6,670 | 7,130 | 8,050 |
| 23,100 -23,199 | 3,927 | 5,775 | 6,699 | 7,161 | 8,085 |
| 23,200 -23,299 | 3,944 | 5,800 | 6,728 | 7,192 | 8,120 |
| 23,300 -23,399 | 3,961 | 5,825 | 6,757 | 7,223 | 8,155 |
| 23,400 -23,499 | 3,978 | 5,850 | 6,786 | 7,254 | 8,190 |
| 23,500 -23,599 | 3,995 | 5,875 | 6,815 | 7,285 | 8,225 |
| 23,600 -23,699 | 4,012 | 5,900 | 6,844 | 7,316 | 8,260 |
| 23,700 -23,799 | 4,029 | 5,925 | 6,873 | 7,347 | 8,295 |
| 23,800 -23,899 | 4,046 | 5,950 | 6,902 | 7,378 | 8,330 |
| 23,900 -23,999 | 4,063 | 5,975 | 6,931 | 7,409 | 8,365 |

| ANNUAL INCOME | NUMBER OF CHILDREN 1 | 2 | 3 | 4 | 5+ |
|---|---|---|---|---|---|
| | ANNUAL OBLIGATION AMOUNT | | | | |
| 28,000 -28,099 | 4,760 | 7,000 | 8,120 | 8,680 | 9,800 |
| 28,100 -28,199 | 4,777 | 7,025 | 8,149 | 8,711 | 9,835 |
| 28,200 -28,299 | 4,794 | 7,050 | 8,178 | 8,742 | 9,870 |
| 28,300 -28,399 | 4,811 | 7,075 | 8,207 | 8,773 | 9,905 |
| 28,400 -28,499 | 4,828 | 7,100 | 8,236 | 8,804 | 9,940 |
| 28,500 -28,599 | 4,845 | 7,125 | 8,265 | 8,833 | 9,975 |
| 28,600 -28,699 | 4,862 | 7,150 | 8,294 | 8,866 | 10,010 |
| 28,700 -28,799 | 4,879 | 7,175 | 8,323 | 8,897 | 10,045 |
| 28,800 -28,899 | 4,896 | 7,200 | 8,352 | 8,928 | 10,080 |
| 28,900 -28,999 | 4,913 | 7,225 | 8,381 | 8,959 | 10,115 |

| ANNUAL INCOME | NUMBER OF CHILDREN 1 | 2 | 3 | 4 | 5+ |
|---|---|---|---|---|---|
| | ANNUAL OBLIGATION AMOUNT | | | | |
| 24,000 -24,099 | 4,080 | 6,000 | 6,960 | 7,440 | 8,400 |
| 24,100 -24,199 | 4,097 | 6,025 | 6,989 | 7,471 | 8,435 |
| 24,200 -24,299 | 4,114 | 6,050 | 7,018 | 7,502 | 8,470 |
| 24,300 -24,399 | 4,131 | 6,075 | 7,047 | 7,533 | 8,505 |
| 24,400 -24,499 | 4,148 | 6,100 | 7,076 | 7,564 | 8,540 |
| 24,500 -24,599 | 4,165 | 6,125 | 7,105 | 7,595 | 8,575 |
| 24,600 -24,699 | 4,182 | 6,150 | 7,134 | 7,626 | 8,610 |
| 24,700 -24,799 | 4,199 | 6,175 | 7,163 | 7,657 | 8,645 |
| 24,800 -24,899 | 4,216 | 6,200 | 7,192 | 7,688 | 8,680 |
| 24,900 -24,999 | 4,233 | 6,225 | 7,221 | 7,719 | 8,715 |

| ANNUAL INCOME | NUMBER OF CHILDREN 1 | 2 | 3 | 4 | 5+ |
|---|---|---|---|---|---|
| | ANNUAL OBLIGATION AMOUNT | | | | |
| 29,000 -29,099 | 4,930 | 7,250 | 8,410 | 8,990 | 10,150 |
| 29,100 -29,199 | 4,947 | 7,275 | 8,439 | 9,021 | 10,185 |
| 29,200 -29,299 | 4,964 | 7,300 | 8,468 | 9,052 | 10,220 |
| 29,300 -29,399 | 4,981 | 7,325 | 8,497 | 9,083 | 10,255 |
| 29,400 -29,499 | 4,998 | 7,350 | 8,526 | 9,114 | 10,290 |
| 29,500 -29,599 | 5,015 | 7,375 | 8,555 | 9,145 | 10,325 |
| 29,600 -29,699 | 5,032 | 7,400 | 8,584 | 9,176 | 10,360 |
| 29,700 -29,799 | 5,049 | 7,425 | 8,613 | 9,207 | 10,395 |
| 29,800 -29,899 | 5,066 | 7,450 | 8,642 | 9,238 | 10,430 |
| 29,900 -29,999 | 5,083 | 7,475 | 8,671 | 9,269 | 10,445 |

3

| ANNUAL INCOME | 1 | NUMBER OF CHILDREN 2 | 3 | 4 | 5+ |
|---|---|---|---|---|---|
| | | ANNUAL OBLIGATION AMOUNT | | | |
| 30,000 -30,099 | 5,100 | 7,500 | 8,700 | 9,300 | 10,500 |
| 30,100 -30,199 | 5,117 | 7,525 | 8,729 | 9,331 | 10,535 |
| 30,200 -30,299 | 5,134 | 7,550 | 8,758 | 9,342 | 10,570 |
| 30,300 -30,399 | 5,151 | 7,575 | 8,787 | 9,393 | 10,605 |
| 30,400 -30,499 | 5,168 | 7,600 | 8,816 | 9,424 | 10,640 |
| 30,500 -30,599 | 5,185 | 7,625 | 8,845 | 9,455 | 10,675 |
| 30,600 -30,699 | 5,202 | 7,650 | 8,874 | 9,486 | 10,710 |
| 30,700 -30,799 | 5,219 | 7,675 | 8,903 | 9,517 | 10,745 |
| 30,800 -30,899 | 5,236 | 7,700 | 8,932 | 9,548 | 10,780 |
| 30,900 -30,999 | 5,253 | 7,725 | 8,961 | 9,579 | 10,815 |

| ANNUAL INCOME | 1 | NUMBER OF CHILDREN 2 | 3 | 4 | 5+ |
|---|---|---|---|---|---|
| | | ANNUAL OBLIGATION AMOUNT | | | |
| 31,000 -31,099 | 5,270 | 7,750 | 8,990 | 9,610 | 10,850 |
| 31,100 -31,199 | 5,287 | 7,775 | 9,019 | 9,641 | 10,885 |
| 31,200 -31,299 | 5,304 | 7,800 | 9,048 | 9,672 | 10,920 |
| 31,300 -31,399 | 5,321 | 7,825 | 9,077 | 9,703 | 10,955 |
| 31,400 -31,499 | 5,338 | 7,850 | 9,106 | 9,734 | 10,990 |
| 31,500 -31,599 | 5,355 | 7,875 | 9,135 | 9,765 | 11,025 |
| 31,600 -31,699 | 5,372 | 7,900 | 9,164 | 9,796 | 11,060 |
| 31,700 -31,799 | 5,389 | 7,925 | 9,193 | 9,827 | 11,095 |
| 31,800 -31,899 | 5,406 | 7,950 | 9,222 | 9,858 | 11,130 |
| 31,900 -31,999 | 5,423 | 7,975 | 9,251 | 9,889 | 11,165 |

| ANNUAL INCOME | 1 | NUMBER OF CHILDREN 2 | 3 | 4 | 5+ |
|---|---|---|---|---|---|
| | | ANNUAL OBLIGATION AMOUNT | | | |
| 32,000 -32,099 | 5,440 | 8,000 | 9,280 | 9,920 | 11,200 |
| 32,100 -32,199 | 5,457 | 8,025 | 9,309 | 9,951 | 11,235 |
| 32,200 -32,299 | 5,474 | 8,050 | 9,338 | 9,982 | 11,270 |
| 32,300 -32,399 | 5,491 | 8,075 | 9,367 | 10,013 | 11,305 |
| 32,400 -32,499 | 5,508 | 8,100 | 9,396 | 10,044 | 11,340 |
| 32,500 -32,599 | 5,525 | 8,125 | 9,425 | 10,075 | 11,375 |
| 32,600 -32,699 | 5,542 | 8,150 | 9,454 | 10,106 | 11,410 |
| 32,700 -32,799 | 5,559 | 8,175 | 9,483 | 10,137 | 11,445 |
| 32,800 -32,899 | 5,576 | 8,200 | 9,512 | 10,168 | 11,480 |
| 32,900 -32,999 | 5,593 | 8,225 | 9,541 | 10,199 | 11,515 |

| ANNUAL INCOME | 1 | NUMBER OF CHILDREN 2 | 3 | 4 | 5+ |
|---|---|---|---|---|---|
| | | ANNUAL OBLIGATION AMOUNT | | | |
| 33,000 -33,099 | 5,610 | 8,250 | 9,570 | 10,230 | 11,530 |
| 33,100 -33,199 | 5,627 | 8,275 | 9,599 | 10,261 | 11,585 |
| 33,200 -33,299 | 5,644 | 8,300 | 9,628 | 10,292 | 11,620 |
| 33,300 -33,399 | 5,661 | 8,325 | 9,657 | 10,323 | 11,655 |
| 33,400 -33,499 | 5,678 | 8,350 | 9,686 | 10,354 | 11,690 |
| 33,500 -33,599 | 5,695 | 8,375 | 9,715 | 10,385 | 11,725 |
| 33,600 -33,699 | 5,712 | 8,400 | 9,744 | 10,416 | 11,760 |
| 33,700 -33,799 | 5,729 | 8,425 | 9,773 | 10,447 | 11,795 |
| 33,800 -33,899 | 5,746 | 8,450 | 9,802 | 10,478 | 11,830 |
| 33,900 -33,999 | 5,763 | 8,475 | 9,831 | 10,509 | 11,865 |

| ANNUAL INCOME | 1 | NUMBER OF CHILDREN 2 | 3 | 4 | 5+ |
|---|---|---|---|---|---|
| | | ANNUAL OBLIGATION AMOUNT | | | |
| 34,000 -34,099 | 5,780 | 8,500 | 9,860 | 10,540 | 11,900 |
| 34,100 -34,199 | 5,797 | 8,525 | 9,889 | 10,571 | 11,935 |
| 34,200 -34,299 | 5,814 | 8,550 | 9,918 | 10,602 | 11,970 |
| 34,300 -34,399 | 5,831 | 8,575 | 9,947 | 10,633 | 12,005 |
| 34,400 -34,499 | 5,848 | 8,600 | 9,974 | 10,664 | 12,040 |
| 34,500 -34,599 | 5,865 | 8,625 | 10,005 | 10,695 | 12,075 |
| 34,600 -34,699 | 5,882 | 8,650 | 10,034 | 10,726 | 12,110 |
| 34,700 -34,799 | 5,899 | 8,675 | 10,063 | 10,757 | 12,145 |
| 34,800 -34,899 | 5,916 | 8,700 | 10,092 | 10,788 | 12,180 |
| 34,900 -34,999 | 5,933 | 8,725 | 10,121 | 10,819 | 12,215 |

| ANNUAL INCOME | 1 | NUMBER OF CHILDREN 2 | 3 | 4 | 5+ |
|---|---|---|---|---|---|
| | | ANNUAL OBLIGATION AMOUNT | | | |
| 35,000 -35,099 | 5,950 | 8,750 | 10,150 | 10,850 | 12,250 |
| 35,100 -35,199 | 5,967 | 8,775 | 10,179 | 10,881 | 12,285 |
| 35,200 -35,299 | 5,984 | 8,800 | 10,208 | 10,912 | 12,320 |
| 35,300 -35,399 | 6,001 | 8,825 | 10,237 | 10,943 | 12,355 |
| 35,400 -35,499 | 6,018 | 8,850 | 10,266 | 10,974 | 12,390 |
| 35,500 -35,599 | 6,035 | 8,875 | 10,295 | 11,005 | 12,425 |
| 35,600 -35,699 | 6,052 | 8,900 | 10,324 | 11,036 | 12,460 |
| 35,700 -35,799 | 6,069 | 8,925 | 10,353 | 11,067 | 12,495 |
| 35,800 -35,899 | 6,086 | 8,950 | 10,382 | 11,098 | 12,530 |
| 35,900 -35,999 | 6,103 | 8,975 | 10,411 | 11,129 | 12,565 |

| ANNUAL INCOME | 1 | NUMBER OF CHILDREN 2 | 3 | 4 | 5+ |
|---|---|---|---|---|---|
| | | ANNUAL OBLIGATION AMOUNT | | | |
| 36,000 -36,099 | 6,120 | 9,000 | 10,440 | 11,160 | 12,600 |
| 36,100 -36,199 | 6,137 | 9,025 | 10,469 | 11,191 | 12,635 |
| 36,200 -36,299 | 6,154 | 9,050 | 10,498 | 11,222 | 12,670 |
| 36,300 -36,399 | 6,171 | 9,075 | 10,527 | 11,253 | 12,705 |
| 36,400 -36,499 | 6,188 | 9,100 | 10,556 | 11,284 | 12,740 |
| 36,500 -36,599 | 6,205 | 9,125 | 10,585 | 11,315 | 12,775 |
| 36,600 -36,699 | 6,222 | 9,150 | 10,614 | 11,346 | 12,810 |
| 36,700 -36,799 | 6,239 | 9,175 | 10,643 | 11,377 | 12,845 |
| 36,800 -36,899 | 6,256 | 9,200 | 10,672 | 11,408 | 12,880 |
| 36,900 -36,999 | 6,273 | 9,225 | 10,701 | 11,439 | 12,915 |

| ANNUAL INCOME | 1 | NUMBER OF CHILDREN 2 | 3 | 4 | 5+ |
|---|---|---|---|---|---|
| | | ANNUAL OBLIGATION AMOUNT | | | |
| 37,000 -37,099 | 6,290 | 9,250 | 10,730 | 11,470 | 12,? |
| 37,100 -37,199 | 6,307 | 9,275 | 10,759 | 11,501 | 12, |
| 37,200 -37,299 | 6,324 | 9,300 | 10,788 | 11,532 | 13,020 |
| 37,300 -37,399 | 6,341 | 9,325 | 10,817 | 11,563 | 13,055 |
| 37,400 -37,499 | 6,358 | 9,350 | 10,846 | 11,594 | 13,090 |
| 37,500 -37,599 | 6,375 | 9,375 | 10,875 | 11,625 | 13,125 |
| 37,600 -37,699 | 6,392 | 9,400 | 10,904 | 11,656 | 13,160 |
| 37,700 -37,799 | 6,409 | 9,425 | 10,933 | 11,687 | 13,195 |
| 37,800 -37,899 | 6,426 | 9,450 | 10,962 | 11,718 | 13,230 |
| 37,900 -37,999 | 6,443 | 9,475 | 10,991 | 11,749 | 13,265 |

| ANNUAL INCOME | 1 | NUMBER OF CHILDREN 2 | 3 | 4 | 5+ |
|---|---|---|---|---|---|
| | | ANNUAL OBLIGATION AMOUNT | | | |
| 38,000 -38,099 | 6,460 | 9,500 | 11,020 | 11,780 | 13,300 |
| 38,100 -38,199 | 6,477 | 9,525 | 11,049 | 11,811 | 13,335 |
| 38,200 -38,299 | 6,494 | 9,550 | 11,078 | 11,842 | 13,370 |
| 38,300 -38,399 | 6,511 | 9,575 | 11,107 | 11,873 | 13,405 |
| 38,400 -38,499 | 6,528 | 9,600 | 11,136 | 11,904 | 13,440 |
| 38,500 -38,599 | 6,545 | 9,625 | 11,165 | 11,935 | 13,475 |
| 38,600 -38,699 | 6,562 | 9,650 | 11,194 | 11,966 | 13,510 |
| 38,700 -38,799 | 6,579 | 9,675 | 11,223 | 11,997 | 13,545 |
| 38,800 -38,899 | 6,596 | 9,700 | 11,252 | 12,028 | 13,580 |
| 38,900 -38,999 | 6,613 | 9,725 | 11,281 | 12,059 | 13,615 |

| ANNUAL INCOME | 1 | NUMBER OF CHILDREN 2 | 3 | 4 | 5+ |
|---|---|---|---|---|---|
| | | ANNUAL OBLIGATION AMOUNT | | | |
| 39,000 -39,099 | 6,630 | 9,750 | 11,310 | 12,090 | 13,650 |
| 39,100 -39,199 | 6,647 | 9,775 | 11,339 | 12,121 | 13,685 |
| 39,200 -39,299 | 6,664 | 9,800 | 11,368 | 12,152 | 13,720 |
| 39,300 -39,399 | 6,681 | 9,825 | 11,397 | 12,183 | 13,755 |
| 39,400 -39,499 | 6,698 | 9,850 | 11,426 | 12,214 | 13,790 |
| 39,500 -39,599 | 6,715 | 9,875 | 11,455 | 12,245 | 13,825 |
| 39,600 -39,699 | 6,732 | 9,900 | 11,484 | 12,276 | 13,860 |
| 39,700 -39,799 | 6,749 | 9,925 | 11,513 | 12,307 | 13,895 |
| 39,800 -39,899 | 6,766 | 9,950 | 11,542 | 12,338 | 13,930 |
| 39,900 -39,999 | 6,783 | 9,975 | 11,571 | 12,369 | 13,945 |

4

| ANNUAL INCOME | 1 | 2 | 3 | 4 | 5+ |
|---|---|---|---|---|---|
| | | ANNUAL OBLIGATION AMOUNT | | | |
| 40,000 -40,099 | 6,800 | 10,000 | 11,600 | 12,600 | 14,000 |
| 40,100 -40,199 | 6,817 | 10,025 | 11,629 | 12,431 | 14,035 |
| 40,200 -40,299 | 6,834 | 10,050 | 11,658 | 12,462 | 14,070 |
| 40,300 -40,399 | 6,851 | 10,075 | 11,687 | 12,493 | 14,105 |
| 40,400 -40,499 | 6,868 | 10,100 | 11,716 | 12,524 | 14,140 |
| 40,500 -40,599 | 6,885 | 10,125 | 11,745 | 12,555 | 14,175 |
| 40,600 -40,699 | 6,902 | 10,150 | 11,774 | 12,586 | 14,210 |
| 40,700 -40,799 | 6,919 | 10,175 | 11,803 | 12,617 | 14,245 |
| 40,800 -40,899 | 6,936 | 10,200 | 11,832 | 12,648 | 14,280 |
| 40,900 -40,999 | 6,953 | 10,225 | 11,861 | 12,679 | 14,315 |

| ANNUAL INCOME | 1 | 2 | 3 | 4 | 5+ |
|---|---|---|---|---|---|
| | | ANNUAL OBLIGATION AMOUNT | | | |
| 41,000 -41,099 | 6,970 | 10,250 | 11,890 | 12,710 | 14,350 |
| 41,100 -41,199 | 6,987 | 10,275 | 11,919 | 12,741 | 14,385 |
| 41,200 -41,299 | 7,004 | 10,300 | 11,948 | 12,772 | 14,420 |
| 41,300 -41,399 | 7,021 | 10,325 | 11,977 | 12,803 | 14,455 |
| 41,400 -41,499 | 7,038 | 10,350 | 12,006 | 12,834 | 14,490 |
| 41,500 -41,599 | 7,055 | 10,375 | 12,035 | 12,865 | 14,525 |
| 41,600 -41,699 | 7,072 | 10,400 | 12,064 | 12,896 | 14,560 |
| 41,700 -41,799 | 7,089 | 10,425 | 12,093 | 12,927 | 14,595 |
| 41,800 -41,899 | 7,106 | 10,450 | 12,122 | 12,958 | 14,630 |
| 41,900 -41,999 | 7,123 | 10,475 | 12,151 | 12,989 | 14,665 |

| ANNUAL INCOME | 1 | 2 | 3 | 4 | 5+ |
|---|---|---|---|---|---|
| | | ANNUAL OBLIGATION AMOUNT | | | |
| 42,000 -42,099 | 7,140 | 10,500 | 12,180 | 13,020 | 14,700 |
| 42,100 -42,199 | 7,157 | 10,525 | 12,209 | 13,051 | 14,735 |
| 42,200 -42,299 | 7,174 | 10,550 | 12,238 | 13,082 | 14,770 |
| 42,300 -42,399 | 7,191 | 10,575 | 12,267 | 13,113 | 14,805 |
| 42,400 -42,499 | 7,208 | 10,600 | 12,296 | 13,144 | 14,840 |
| 42,500 -42,599 | 7,225 | 10,625 | 12,325 | 13,175 | 14,875 |
| 42,600 -42,699 | 7,242 | 10,650 | 12,354 | 13,206 | 14,910 |
| 42,700 -42,799 | 7,259 | 10,675 | 12,383 | 13,237 | 14,945 |
| 42,800 -42,899 | 7,276 | 10,700 | 12,412 | 13,268 | 14,980 |
| 42,900 -42,999 | 7,293 | 10,725 | 12,441 | 13,299 | 15,015 |

| ANNUAL INCOME | 1 | 2 | 3 | 4 | 5+ |
|---|---|---|---|---|---|
| | | ANNUAL OBLIGATION AMOUNT | | | |
| 43,000 -43,099 | 7,310 | 10,750 | 12,470 | 13,330 | 15,050 |
| 43,100 -43,199 | 7,327 | 10,775 | 12,499 | 13,361 | 15,085 |
| 43,200 -43,299 | 7,344 | 10,800 | 12,528 | 13,392 | 15,120 |
| 43,300 -43,399 | 7,361 | 10,825 | 12,557 | 13,423 | 15,155 |
| 43,400 -43,499 | 7,378 | 10,850 | 12,586 | 13,454 | 15,190 |
| 43,500 -43,599 | 7,395 | 10,875 | 12,615 | 13,485 | 15,225 |
| 43,600 -43,699 | 7,412 | 10,900 | 12,644 | 13,516 | 15,260 |
| 43,700 -43,799 | 7,429 | 10,925 | 12,673 | 13,547 | 15,295 |
| 43,800 -43,899 | 7,446 | 10,950 | 12,702 | 13,578 | 15,330 |
| 43,900 -43,999 | 7,443 | 10,975 | 12,731 | 13,609 | 15,345 |

| ANNUAL INCOME | 1 | 2 | 3 | 4 | 5+ |
|---|---|---|---|---|---|
| | | ANNUAL OBLIGATION AMOUNT | | | |
| 44,000 -44,099 | 7,480 | 11,000 | 12,760 | 13,640 | 15,400 |
| 44,100 -44,199 | 7,497 | 11,025 | 12,789 | 13,671 | 15,435 |
| 44,200 -44,299 | 7,514 | 11,050 | 12,818 | 13,702 | 15,470 |
| 44,300 -44,399 | 7,531 | 11,075 | 12,847 | 13,733 | 15,505 |
| 44,400 -44,499 | 7,548 | 11,100 | 12,876 | 13,764 | 15,540 |
| 44,500 -44,599 | 7,565 | 11,125 | 12,905 | 13,795 | 15,575 |
| 44,600 -44,699 | 7,582 | 11,150 | 12,934 | 13,826 | 15,610 |
| 44,700 -44,799 | 7,599 | 11,175 | 12,963 | 13,857 | 15,645 |
| 44,800 -44,899 | 7,616 | 11,200 | 12,992 | 13,888 | 15,680 |
| 44,900 -44,999 | 7,633 | 11,225 | 13,021 | 13,919 | 15,715 |

| ANNUAL INCOME | 1 | 2 | 3 | 4 | 5+ |
|---|---|---|---|---|---|
| | | ANNUAL OBLIGATION AMOUNT | | | |
| 45,000 -45,099 | 7,650 | 11,250 | 13,050 | 13,950 | 15,750 |
| 45,100 -45,199 | 7,647 | 11,275 | 13,079 | 13,981 | 15,785 |
| 45,200 -45,299 | 7,684 | 11,300 | 13,108 | 14,012 | 15,820 |
| 45,300 -45,399 | 7,701 | 11,325 | 13,137 | 14,043 | 15,855 |
| 45,400 -45,499 | 7,718 | 11,350 | 13,166 | 14,074 | 15,890 |
| 45,500 -45,599 | 7,735 | 11,375 | 13,195 | 14,105 | 15,925 |
| 45,600 -45,699 | 7,752 | 11,400 | 13,224 | 14,136 | 15,960 |
| 45,700 -45,799 | 7,769 | 11,425 | 13,253 | 14,167 | 15,995 |
| 45,800 -45,899 | 7,786 | 11,450 | 13,282 | 14,198 | 16,030 |
| 45,900 -45,999 | 7,803 | 11,475 | 13,311 | 14,229 | 16,065 |

| ANNUAL INCOME | 1 | 2 | 3 | 4 | 5+ |
|---|---|---|---|---|---|
| | | ANNUAL OBLIGATION AMOUNT | | | |
| 46,000 -46,099 | 7,820 | 11,500 | 13,340 | 14,260 | 16,100 |
| 46,100 -46,199 | 7,837 | 11,525 | 13,369 | 14,291 | 16,135 |
| 46,200 -46,299 | 7,854 | 11,550 | 13,398 | 14,322 | 16,170 |
| 46,300 -46,399 | 7,871 | 11,575 | 13,427 | 14,353 | 16,205 |
| 46,400 -46,499 | 7,888 | 11,600 | 13,456 | 14,384 | 16,240 |
| 46,500 -46,599 | 7,905 | 11,625 | 13,485 | 14,415 | 16,275 |
| 46,600 -46,699 | 7,922 | 11,650 | 13,514 | 14,446 | 16,310 |
| 46,700 -46,799 | 7,939 | 11,675 | 13,543 | 14,477 | 16,345 |
| 46,800 -46,899 | 7,956 | 11,700 | 13,572 | 14,508 | 16,380 |
| 46,900 -46,999 | 7,973 | 11,725 | 13,601 | 14,539 | 16,415 |

| ANNUAL INCOME | 1 | 2 | 3 | 4 | 5+ |
|---|---|---|---|---|---|
| | | ANNUAL OBLIGATION AMOUNT | | | |
| 47,000 -47,099 | 7,990 | 11,750 | 13,630 | 14,570 | 16,450 |
| 47,100 -47,199 | 8,007 | 11,775 | 13,659 | 14,601 | 16,485 |
| 47,200 -47,299 | 8,024 | 11,800 | 13,688 | 14,632 | 16,520 |
| 47,300 -47,399 | 8,041 | 11,825 | 13,717 | 14,663 | 16,555 |
| 47,400 -47,499 | 8,058 | 11,850 | 13,746 | 14,694 | 16,590 |
| 47,500 -47,599 | 8,075 | 11,875 | 13,775 | 14,725 | 16,625 |
| 47,600 -47,699 | 8,092 | 11,900 | 13,804 | 14,756 | 16,660 |
| 47,700 -47,799 | 8,109 | 11,925 | 13,833 | 14,787 | 16,695 |
| 47,800 -47,899 | 8,126 | 11,950 | 13,862 | 14,818 | 16,730 |
| 47,900 -47,999 | 8,143 | 11,975 | 13,891 | 14,849 | 16,765 |

| ANNUAL INCOME | 1 | 2 | 3 | 4 | 5+ |
|---|---|---|---|---|---|
| | | ANNUAL OBLIGATION AMOUNT | | | |
| 48,000 -48,099 | 8,160 | 12,000 | 13,920 | 14,880 | 16,800 |
| 48,100 -48,199 | 8,177 | 12,025 | 13,949 | 14,911 | 16,835 |
| 48,200 -48,299 | 8,194 | 12,050 | 13,978 | 14,942 | 16,870 |
| 48,300 -48,399 | 8,211 | 12,075 | 14,007 | 14,973 | 16,905 |
| 48,400 -48,499 | 8,228 | 12,100 | 14,036 | 15,004 | 16,940 |
| 48,500 -48,599 | 8,245 | 12,125 | 14,065 | 15,035 | 16,975 |
| 48,600 -48,699 | 8,262 | 12,150 | 14,094 | 15,066 | 17,010 |
| 48,700 -48,799 | 8,279 | 12,175 | 14,123 | 15,097 | 17,045 |
| 48,800 -48,899 | 8,296 | 12,200 | 14,152 | 15,128 | 17,080 |
| 48,900 -48,999 | 8,313 | 12,225 | 14,181 | 15,159 | 17,115 |

| ANNUAL INCOME | 1 | 2 | 3 | 4 | 5+ |
|---|---|---|---|---|---|
| | | ANNUAL OBLIGATION AMOUNT | | | |
| 49,000 -49,099 | 8,330 | 12,250 | 14,210 | 15,190 | 17,150 |
| 49,100 -49,199 | 8,347 | 12,275 | 14,239 | 15,221 | 17,185 |
| 49,200 -49,299 | 8,364 | 12,300 | 14,268 | 15,252 | 17,220 |
| 49,300 -49,399 | 8,381 | 12,325 | 14,297 | 15,283 | 17,255 |
| 49,400 -49,499 | 8,398 | 12,350 | 14,326 | 15,314 | 17,290 |
| 49,500 -49,599 | 8,415 | 12,375 | 14,355 | 15,345 | 17,325 |
| 49,600 -49,699 | 8,432 | 12,400 | 14,384 | 15,376 | 17,360 |
| 49,700 -49,799 | 8,449 | 12,425 | 14,413 | 15,407 | 17,395 |
| 49,800 -49,899 | 8,466 | 12,450 | 14,442 | 15,438 | 17,430 |
| 49,900 -49,999 | 8,483 | 12,475 | 14,471 | 15,469 | 17,465 |

5

| ANNUAL INCOME | NUMBER OF CHILDREN | | | | |
|---|---|---|---|---|---|
| | 1 | 2 | 3 | 4 | 5+ |
| | ANNUAL OBLIGATION AMOUNT | | | | |
| 50,000 -50,099 | 8,500 | 12,500 | 14,500 | 15,500 | 17,500 |
| 50,100 -50,199 | 8,517 | 12,525 | 14,529 | 15,531 | 17,535 |
| 50,200 -50,299 | 8,534 | 12,550 | 14,558 | 15,562 | 17,570 |
| 50,300 -50,399 | 8,551 | 12,575 | 14,587 | 15,593 | 17,605 |
| 50,400 -50,499 | 8,568 | 12,600 | 14,616 | 15,624 | 17,640 |
| 50,500 -50,599 | 8,585 | 12,625 | 14,645 | 15,655 | 17,675 |
| 50,600 -50,699 | 8,602 | 12,650 | 14,674 | 15,686 | 17,710 |
| 50,700 -50,799 | 8,619 | 12,675 | 14,703 | 15,717 | 17,745 |
| 50,800 -50,899 | 8,636 | 12,700 | 14,732 | 15,748 | 17,780 |
| 50,900 -50,999 | 8,653 | 12,725 | 14,761 | 15,779 | 17,815 |

| ANNUAL INCOME | NUMBER OF CHILDREN | | | | |
|---|---|---|---|---|---|
| | 1 | 2 | 3 | 4 | 5+ |
| | ANNUAL OBLIGATION AMOUNT | | | | |
| 55,000 -55,099 | 9,350 | 13,750 | 15,950 | 17,050 | 19,250 |
| 55,100 -55,199 | 9,367 | 13,775 | 15,979 | 17,081 | 19,285 |
| 55,200 -55,299 | 9,384 | 13,800 | 16,008 | 17,112 | 19,320 |
| 55,300 -55,399 | 9,401 | 13,825 | 16,037 | 17,143 | 19,355 |
| 55,400 -55,499 | 9,418 | 13,850 | 16,066 | 17,174 | 19,390 |
| 55,500 -55,599 | 9,435 | 13,875 | 16,095 | 17,205 | 19,425 |
| 55,600 -55,699 | 9,452 | 13,900 | 16,124 | 17,236 | 19,460 |
| 55,700 -55,799 | 9,469 | 13,925 | 16,153 | 17,267 | 19,495 |
| 55,800 -55,899 | 9,486 | 13,950 | 16,182 | 17,298 | 19,530 |
| 55,900 -55,999 | 9,503 | 13,975 | 16,211 | 17,329 | 19,565 |

| ANNUAL INCOME | NUMBER OF CHILDREN | | | | |
|---|---|---|---|---|---|
| | 1 | 2 | 3 | 4 | 5+ |
| | ANNUAL OBLIGATION AMOUNT | | | | |
| 51,000 -51,099 | 8,670 | 12,750 | 14,790 | 15,810 | 17,850 |
| 51,100 -51,199 | 8,687 | 12,775 | 14,819 | 15,841 | 17,885 |
| 51,200 -51,299 | 8,704 | 12,800 | 14,848 | 15,872 | 17,920 |
| 51,300 -51,399 | 8,721 | 12,825 | 14,877 | 15,903 | 17,955 |
| 51,400 -51,499 | 8,738 | 12,850 | 14,906 | 15,934 | 17,990 |
| 51,500 -51,599 | 8,755 | 12,875 | 14,935 | 15,965 | 18,025 |
| 51,600 -51,699 | 8,772 | 12,900 | 14,964 | 15,996 | 18,060 |
| 700 -51,799 | 8,789 | 12,925 | 14,993 | 16,027 | 18,095 |
| 800 -51,899 | 8,806 | 12,950 | 15,022 | 16,058 | 18,130 |
| 51,900 -51,999 | 8,823 | 12,975 | 15,051 | 16,089 | 18,165 |

| ANNUAL INCOME | NUMBER OF CHILDREN | | | | |
|---|---|---|---|---|---|
| | 1 | 2 | 3 | 4 | 5+ |
| | ANNUAL OBLIGATION AMOUNT | | | | |
| 56,000 -56,099 | 9,520 | 14,000 | 16,240 | 17,360 | 19,600 |
| 56,100 -56,199 | 9,537 | 14,025 | 16,269 | 17,391 | 19,635 |
| 56,200 -56,299 | 9,554 | 14,050 | 16,298 | 17,422 | 19,670 |
| 56,300 -56,399 | 9,571 | 14,075 | 16,327 | 17,453 | 19,705 |
| 56,400 -56,499 | 9,588 | 14,100 | 16,356 | 17,484 | 19,740 |
| 56,500 -56,599 | 9,605 | 14,125 | 16,385 | 17,515 | 19,775 |
| 56,600 -56,699 | 9,622 | 14,150 | 16,414 | 17,546 | 19,810 |
| 56,700 -56,799 | 9,639 | 14,175 | 16,443 | 17,577 | 19,845 |
| 56,800 -56,899 | 9,656 | 14,200 | 16,472 | 17,608 | 19,880 |
| 56,900 -56,999 | 9,673 | 14,225 | 16,501 | 17,639 | 19,915 |

| ANNUAL INCOME | NUMBER OF CHILDREN | | | | |
|---|---|---|---|---|---|
| | 1 | 2 | 3 | 4 | 5+ |
| | ANNUAL OBLIGATION AMOUNT | | | | |
| 52,000 -52,099 | 8,840 | 13,000 | 15,080 | 16,120 | 18,200 |
| 52,100 -52,199 | 8,857 | 13,025 | 15,109 | 16,151 | 18,235 |
| 52,200 -52,299 | 8,874 | 13,050 | 15,138 | 16,182 | 18,270 |
| 52,300 -52,399 | 8,891 | 13,075 | 15,167 | 16,213 | 18,305 |
| 52,400 -52,499 | 8,908 | 13,100 | 15,196 | 16,244 | 18,340 |
| 52,500 -52,599 | 8,925 | 13,125 | 15,225 | 16,275 | 18,375 |
| 52,600 -52,699 | 8,942 | 13,150 | 15,254 | 16,306 | 18,410 |
| 52,700 -52,799 | 8,959 | 13,175 | 15,283 | 16,337 | 18,445 |
| 52,800 -52,899 | 8,976 | 13,200 | 15,312 | 16,368 | 18,480 |
| 52,900 -52,999 | 8,993 | 13,225 | 15,341 | 16,399 | 18,515 |

| ANNUAL INCOME | NUMBER OF CHILDREN | | | | |
|---|---|---|---|---|---|
| | 1 | 2 | 3 | 4 | 5+ |
| | ANNUAL OBLIGATION AMOUNT | | | | |
| 57,000 -57,099 | 9,690 | 14,250 | 16,530 | 17,670 | 19,95^ |
| 57,100 -57,199 | 9,707 | 14,275 | 16,559 | 17,701 | 19,9 |
| 57,200 -57,299 | 9,724 | 14,300 | 16,588 | 17,732 | 20,0. |
| 57,300 -57,399 | 9,741 | 14,325 | 16,617 | 17,763 | 20,055 |
| 57,400 -57,499 | 9,758 | 14,350 | 16,646 | 17,794 | 20,090 |
| 57,500 -57,599 | 9,775 | 14,375 | 16,675 | 17,825 | 20,125 |
| 57,600 -57,699 | 9,792 | 14,400 | 16,704 | 17,856 | 20,160 |
| 57,700 -57,799 | 9,809 | 14,425 | 16,733 | 17,887 | 20,195 |
| 57,800 -57,899 | 9,826 | 14,450 | 16,762 | 17,918 | 20,230 |
| 57,900 -57,999 | 9,843 | 14,475 | 16,791 | 17,949 | 20,265 |

| ANNUAL INCOME | NUMBER OF CHILDREN | | | | |
|---|---|---|---|---|---|
| | 1 | 2 | 3 | 4 | 5+ |
| | ANNUAL OBLIGATION AMOUNT | | | | |
| 53,000 -53,099 | 9,010 | 13,250 | 15,370 | 16,430 | 18,550 |
| 53,100 -53,199 | 9,027 | 13,275 | 15,399 | 16,461 | 18,585 |
| 53,200 -53,299 | 9,044 | 13,300 | 15,428 | 16,492 | 18,620 |
| 53,300 -53,399 | 9,061 | 13,325 | 15,457 | 16,523 | 18,655 |
| 53,400 -53,499 | 9,078 | 13,350 | 15,486 | 16,554 | 18,690 |
| 53,500 -53,599 | 9,095 | 13,375 | 15,515 | 16,585 | 18,725 |
| 53,600 -53,699 | 9,112 | 13,400 | 15,544 | 16,616 | 18,760 |
| 53,700 -53,799 | 9,129 | 13,425 | 15,573 | 16,647 | 18,795 |
| 53,800 -53,899 | 9,146 | 13,450 | 15,602 | 16,678 | 18,830 |
| 53,900 -53,999 | 9,163 | 13,475 | 15,631 | 16,709 | 18,865 |

| ANNUAL INCOME | NUMBER OF CHILDREN | | | | |
|---|---|---|---|---|---|
| | 1 | 2 | 3 | 4 | 5+ |
| | ANNUAL OBLIGATION AMOUNT | | | | |
| 58,000 -58,099 | 9,860 | 14,500 | 16,820 | 17,980 | 20,300 |
| 58,100 -58,199 | 9,877 | 14,525 | 16,849 | 18,011 | 20,335 |
| 58,200 -58,299 | 9,894 | 14,550 | 16,878 | 18,042 | 20,370 |
| 58,300 -58,399 | 9,911 | 14,575 | 16,907 | 18,073 | 20,405 |
| 58,400 -58,499 | 9,928 | 14,600 | 16,936 | 18,104 | 20,440 |
| 58,500 -58,599 | 9,945 | 14,625 | 16,965 | 18,135 | 20,475 |
| 58,600 -58,699 | 9,962 | 14,650 | 16,994 | 18,166 | 20,510 |
| 58,700 -58,799 | 9,979 | 14,675 | 17,023 | 18,197 | 20,545 |
| 58,800 -58,899 | 9,996 | 14,700 | 17,052 | 18,228 | 20,580 |
| 58,900 -58,999 | 10,013 | 14,725 | 17,081 | 18,259 | 20,615 |

| ANNUAL INCOME | NUMBER OF CHILDREN | | | | |
|---|---|---|---|---|---|
| | 1 | 2 | 3 | 4 | 5+ |
| | ANNUAL OBLIGATION AMOUNT | | | | |
| 54,000 -54,099 | 9,180 | 13,500 | 15,460 | 16,740 | 18,900 |
| 54,100 -54,199 | 9,197 | 13,525 | 15,489 | 16,771 | 18,935 |
| 54,200 -54,299 | 9,214 | 13,550 | 15,718 | 16,802 | 18,970 |
| 54,300 -54,399 | 9,231 | 13,575 | 15,747 | 16,833 | 19,005 |
| 54,400 -54,499 | 9,248 | 13,600 | 15,776 | 16,864 | 19,040 |
| 54,500 -54,599 | 9,265 | 13,625 | 15,805 | 16,895 | 19,075 |
| 54,600 -54,699 | 9,282 | 13,650 | 15,834 | 16,926 | 19,110 |
| 54,700 -54,799 | 9,299 | 13,675 | 15,863 | 16,957 | 19,145 |
| 54,800 -54,899 | 9,316 | 13,700 | 15,892 | 16,988 | 19,180 |
| 54,900 -54,999 | 9,333 | 13,725 | 15,921 | 17,019 | 19,215 |

| ANNUAL INCOME | NUMBER OF CHILDREN | | | | |
|---|---|---|---|---|---|
| | 1 | 2 | 3 | 4 | 5+ |
| | ANNUAL OBLIGATION AMOUNT | | | | |
| 59,000 -59,099 | 10,030 | 14,750 | 17,110 | 18,290 | 20,650 |
| 59,100 -59,199 | 10,047 | 14,775 | 17,139 | 18,321 | 20,685 |
| 59,200 -59,299 | 10,064 | 14,800 | 17,168 | 18,352 | 20,720 |
| 59,300 -59,399 | 10,081 | 14,825 | 17,197 | 18,383 | 20,755 |
| 59,400 -59,499 | 10,098 | 14,850 | 17,226 | 18,414 | 20,790 |
| 59,500 -59,599 | 10,115 | 14,875 | 17,259 | 18,445 | 20,82 |
| 59,600 -59,699 | 10,132 | 14,900 | 17,284 | 18,476 | 20,8. |
| 59,700 -59,799 | 10,149 | 14,925 | 17,313 | 18,507 | 20,89 |
| 59,800 -59,899 | 10,166 | 14,950 | 17,342 | 18,538 | 20,930 |
| 59,900 -59,999 | 10,183 | 14,975 | 17,371 | 18,569 | 20,965 |

THE CHILD SUPPORT STANDARDS CHART

| ANNUAL INCOME | 1 | 2 | 3 | 4 | 5+ |
|---|---|---|---|---|---|
| | | ANNUAL OBLIGATION AMOUNT | | | |
| 60,000 -60,099 | 10,200 | 15,000 | 17,400 | 18,600 | 21,000 |
| 60,100 -60,199 | 10,217 | 15,025 | 17,429 | 18,631 | 21,035 |
| 60,200 -60,299 | 10,234 | 15,050 | 17,458 | 18,662 | 21,070 |
| 60,300 -60,399 | 10,251 | 15,075 | 17,487 | 18,693 | 21,105 |
| 60,400 -60,499 | 10,268 | 15,100 | 17,516 | 18,724 | 21,140 |
| 60,500 -60,599 | 10,285 | 15,125 | 17,545 | 18,755 | 21,175 |
| 60,600 -60,699 | 10,302 | 15,150 | 17,574 | 18,786 | 21,210 |
| 60,700 -60,799 | 10,319 | 15,175 | 17,603 | 18,817 | 21,243 |
| 60,800 -60,899 | 10,336 | 15,200 | 17,632 | 18,848 | 21,280 |
| 60,900 -60,999 | 10,353 | 15,225 | 17,661 | 18,879 | 21,315 |

| ANNUAL INCOME | 1 | 2 | 3 | 4 | 5+ |
|---|---|---|---|---|---|
| | | ANNUAL OBLIGATION AMOUNT | | | |
| 61,000 -61,099 | 10,370 | 15,250 | 17,690 | 18,910 | 21,330 |
| 61,100 -61,199 | 10,387 | 15,275 | 17,719 | 18,941 | 21,385 |
| 61,200 -61,299 | 10,404 | 15,300 | 17,748 | 18,972 | 21,420 |
| 61,300 -61,399 | 10,421 | 15,325 | 17,777 | 19,003 | 21,455 |
| 61,400 -61,499 | 10,438 | 15,350 | 17,806 | 19,034 | 21,490 |
| 61,500 -61,599 | 10,455 | 15,375 | 17,835 | 19,065 | 21,525 |
| 61,600 -61,699 | 10,472 | 15,400 | 17,864 | 19,096 | 21,560 |
| 61,700 -61,799 | 10,489 | 15,425 | 17,893 | 19,127 | 21,595 |
| 61,800 -61,899 | 10,506 | 15,450 | 17,922 | 19,158 | 21,630 |
| 61,900 -61,999 | 10,523 | 15,475 | 17,951 | 19,189 | 21,665 |

| ANNUAL INCOME | 1 | 2 | 3 | 4 | 5+ |
|---|---|---|---|---|---|
| | | ANNUAL OBLIGATION AMOUNT | | | |
| 62,000 -62,099 | 10,540 | 15,500 | 17,980 | 19,220 | 21,700 |
| 62,100 -62,199 | 10,557 | 15,525 | 18,009 | 19,251 | 21,735 |
| 62,200 -62,299 | 10,574 | 15,550 | 18,038 | 19,282 | 21,770 |
| 62,300 -62,399 | 10,591 | 15,575 | 18,067 | 19,313 | 21,805 |
| 62,400 -62,499 | 10,608 | 15,600 | 18,096 | 19,344 | 21,840 |
| 62,500 -62,599 | 10,625 | 15,625 | 18,125 | 19,375 | 21,875 |
| 62,600 -62,699 | 10,642 | 15,650 | 18,154 | 19,406 | 21,910 |
| 62,700 -62,799 | 10,659 | 15,675 | 18,183 | 19,437 | 21,945 |
| 62,800 -62,899 | 10,676 | 15,700 | 18,212 | 19,448 | 21,980 |
| 62,900 -62,999 | 10,693 | 15,725 | 18,241 | 19,499 | 22,015 |

| ANNUAL INCOME | 1 | 2 | 3 | 4 | 5+ |
|---|---|---|---|---|---|
| | | ANNUAL OBLIGATION AMOUNT | | | |
| 63,000 -63,099 | 10,710 | 15,750 | 18,270 | 19,530 | 22,050 |
| 63,100 -63,199 | 10,727 | 15,775 | 18,299 | 19,561 | 22,085 |
| 63,200 -63,299 | 10,744 | 15,800 | 18,328 | 19,592 | 22,120 |
| 63,300 -63,399 | 10,761 | 15,825 | 18,357 | 19,623 | 22,155 |
| 63,400 -63,499 | 10,778 | 15,850 | 18,386 | 19,654 | 22,190 |
| 63,500 -63,599 | 10,795 | 15,875 | 18,415 | 19,685 | 22,225 |
| 63,600 -63,699 | 10,812 | 15,900 | 18,444 | 19,716 | 22,260 |
| 63,700 -63,799 | 10,829 | 15,925 | 18,473 | 19,747 | 22,295 |
| 63,800 -63,899 | 10,846 | 15,950 | 18,502 | 19,778 | 22,330 |
| 63,900 -63,999 | 10,863 | 15,975 | 18,531 | 19,809 | 22,345 |

| ANNUAL INCOME | 1 | 2 | 3 | 4 | 5+ |
|---|---|---|---|---|---|
| | | ANNUAL OBLIGATION AMOUNT | | | |
| 64,000 -64,099 | 10,880 | 16,000 | 18,560 | 19,840 | 22,400 |
| 64,100 -64,199 | 10,897 | 16,025 | 18,589 | 19,871 | 22,435 |
| 64,200 -64,299 | 10,914 | 16,050 | 18,618 | 19,902 | 22,470 |
| 64,400 -64,399 | 10,931 | 16,075 | 18,647 | 19,933 | 22,505 |
| 64,400 -64,499 | 10,948 | 16,100 | 18,676 | 19,964 | 22,540 |
| 64,500 -64,599 | 10,965 | 16,125 | 18,705 | 19,995 | 22,575 |
| 64,600 -64,699 | 10,982 | 16,150 | 18,734 | 20,026 | 22,610 |
| 64,700 -64,799 | 10,999 | 16,175 | 18,763 | 20,057 | 22,645 |
| 64,800 -64,899 | 11,016 | 16,200 | 18,792 | 20,088 | 22,680 |
| 64,900 -64,999 | 11,033 | 16,225 | 18,821 | 20,119 | 22,715 |

| ANNUAL INCOME | 1 | 2 | 3 | 4 | 5+ |
|---|---|---|---|---|---|
| | | ANNUAL OBLIGATION AMOUNT | | | |
| 65,000 -65,099 | 11,050 | 16,250 | 18,850 | 20,150 | 22,750 |
| 65,100 -65,199 | 11,067 | 16,275 | 18,879 | 20,181 | 22,785 |
| 65,200 -65,299 | 11,084 | 16,300 | 18,908 | 20,212 | 22,820 |
| 65,300 -65,399 | 11,101 | 16,325 | 18,937 | 20,243 | 22,855 |
| 65,400 -65,499 | 11,118 | 16,350 | 18,966 | 20,274 | 22,890 |
| 65,500 -65,599 | 11,135 | 16,375 | 18,995 | 20,305 | 22,925 |
| 65,600 -65,699 | 11,152 | 16,400 | 19,024 | 20,336 | 22,960 |
| 65,700 -65,799 | 11,169 | 16,425 | 19,053 | 20,367 | 22,995 |
| 65,800 -65,899 | 11,186 | 16,450 | 19,082 | 20,398 | 23,030 |
| 65,900 -65,999 | 11,203 | 16,475 | 19,111 | 20,429 | 23,065 |

| ANNUAL INCOME | 1 | 2 | 3 | 4 | 5+ |
|---|---|---|---|---|---|
| | | ANNUAL OBLIGATION AMOUNT | | | |
| 66,000 -66,099 | 11,220 | 16,500 | 19,140 | 20,460 | 23,100 |
| 66,100 -66,199 | 11,237 | 16,525 | 19,169 | 20,491 | 23,135 |
| 66,200 -66,299 | 11,254 | 16,550 | 19,198 | 20,522 | 23,170 |
| 66,300 -66,399 | 11,271 | 16,575 | 19,227 | 20,553 | 23,205 |
| 66,400 -66,499 | 11,288 | 16,600 | 19,256 | 20,584 | 23,240 |
| 66,500 -66,599 | 11,305 | 16,625 | 19,285 | 20,615 | 23,275 |
| 66,600 -66,699 | 11,322 | 16,650 | 19,314 | 20,646 | 23,310 |
| 66,700 -66,799 | 11,339 | 16,675 | 19,343 | 20,677 | 23,345 |
| 66,800 -66,899 | 11,356 | 16,700 | 19,372 | 20,708 | 23,320 |
| 66,900 -66,999 | 11,373 | 16,725 | 19,401 | 20,739 | 23,415 |

| ANNUAL INCOME | 1 | 2 | 3 | 4 | 5+ |
|---|---|---|---|---|---|
| | | ANNUAL OBLIGATION AMOUNT | | | |
| 67,000 -67,099 | 11,390 | 16,750 | 19,430 | 20,770 | 23,450 |
| 67,100 -67,199 | 11,407 | 16,775 | 19,459 | 20,801 | 23,485 |
| 67,200 -67,299 | 11,424 | 16,800 | 19,488 | 20,832 | 23,520 |
| 67,300 -67,399 | 11,441 | 16,825 | 19,517 | 20,863 | 23,555 |
| 67,400 -67,499 | 11,458 | 16,850 | 19,546 | 20,894 | 23,590 |
| 67,500 -67,599 | 11,475 | 16,875 | 19,575 | 20,925 | 23,625 |
| 67,600 -67,699 | 11,492 | 16,900 | 19,604 | 20,956 | 23,660 |
| 67,700 -67,799 | 11,509 | 16,925 | 19,633 | 20,987 | 23,695 |
| 67,800 -67,899 | 11,526 | 16,950 | 19,662 | 21,018 | 23,730 |
| 67,900 -67,999 | 11,543 | 16,975 | 19,691 | 21,049 | 23,765 |

| ANNUAL INCOME | 1 | 2 | 3 | 4 | 5+ |
|---|---|---|---|---|---|
| | | ANNUAL OBLIGATION AMOUNT | | | |
| 68,000 -68,099 | 11,560 | 17,000 | 19,720 | 21,080 | 23,800 |
| 68,100 -68,199 | 11,577 | 17,025 | 19,749 | 21,111 | 23,835 |
| 68,200 -68,299 | 11,594 | 17,050 | 19,778 | 21,142 | 23,870 |
| 68,300 -68,399 | 11,611 | 17,075 | 19,807 | 21,173 | 23,905 |
| 68,400 -68,499 | 11,628 | 17,100 | 19,836 | 21,204 | 23,940 |
| 68,500 -68,599 | 11,645 | 17,125 | 19,865 | 21,235 | 23,975 |
| 68,600 -68,699 | 11,662 | 17,150 | 19,894 | 21,266 | 24,010 |
| 68,700 -68,799 | 11,679 | 17,175 | 19,923 | 21,297 | 24,045 |
| 68,800 -68,899 | 11,696 | 17,200 | 19,952 | 21,328 | 24,080 |
| 68,900 -68,999 | 11,713 | 17,225 | 19,981 | 21,359 | 24,115 |

| ANNUAL INCOME | 1 | 2 | 3 | 4 | 5+ |
|---|---|---|---|---|---|
| | | ANNUAL OBLIGATION AMOUNT | | | |
| 69,000 -69,099 | 11,730 | 17,250 | 20,010 | 21,390 | 24,150 |
| 69,100 -69,199 | 11,747 | 17,275 | 20,039 | 21,421 | 24,185 |
| 69,200 -69,299 | 11,764 | 17,300 | 20,068 | 21,452 | 24,220 |
| 69,300 -69,399 | 11,781 | 17,325 | 20,097 | 21,483 | 24,255 |
| 69,400 -69,499 | 11,798 | 17,350 | 20,126 | 21,514 | 24,290 |
| 69,500 -69,599 | 11,815 | 17,375 | 20,155 | 21,545 | 24,325 |
| 69,600 -69,699 | 11,832 | 17,400 | 20,184 | 21,576 | 24,360 |
| 69,700 -69,799 | 11,849 | 17,425 | 20,213 | 21,607 | 24,395 |
| 69,800 -69,899 | 11,866 | 17,450 | 20,242 | 21,638 | 24,43: |
| 69,900 -69,999 | 11,883 | 17,475 | 20,271 | 21,669 | 24,44 |

7

| ANNUAL INCOME | 1 | NUMBER OF CHILDREN 2 | 3 | 4 | 5+ |
|---|---|---|---|---|---|
| | | ANNUAL OBLIGATION AMOUNT | | | |
| 70,000 -70,099 | 11,900 | 17,500 | 20,300 | 21,700 | 24,500 |
| 70,100 -70,199 | 11,917 | 17,525 | 20,329 | 21,731 | 24,535 |
| 70,200 -70,299 | 11,934 | 17,550 | 20,358 | 21,762 | 24,570 |
| 70,300 -70,399 | 11,951 | 17,575 | 20,387 | 21,793 | 24,605 |
| 70,400 -70,499 | 11,968 | 17,600 | 20,416 | 21,824 | 24,640 |
| 70,500 -70,599 | 11,985 | 17,625 | 20,445 | 21,855 | 24,675 |
| 70,600 -70,699 | 12,002 | 17,650 | 20,474 | 21,886 | 24,710 |
| 70,700 -70,799 | 12,019 | 17,675 | 20,503 | 21,917 | 24,745 |
| 70,800 -70,899 | 12,036 | 17,700 | 20,532 | 21,948 | 24,780 |
| 70,900 -70,999 | 12,053 | 17,725 | 20,561 | 21,979 | 24,815 |

| ANNUAL INCOME | 1 | NUMBER OF CHILDREN 2 | 3 | 4 | 5+ |
|---|---|---|---|---|---|
| | | ANNUAL OBLIGATION AMOUNT | | | |
| 71,000 -71,099 | 12,070 | 17,750 | 20,590 | 22,010 | 24,850 |
| 71,100 -71,199 | 12,087 | 17,775 | 20,619 | 22,041 | 24,885 |
| 71,200 -71,299 | 12,104 | 17,800 | 20,648 | 22,072 | 24,920 |
| 71,300 -71,399 | 12,121 | 17,825 | 20,677 | 22,103 | 24,955 |
| 71,400 -71,499 | 12,138 | 17,850 | 20,706 | 22,134 | 24,990 |
| 71,500 -71,599 | 12,155 | 17,875 | 20,735 | 22,165 | 25,025 |
| 1,600 -71,699 | 12,172 | 17,900 | 20,764 | 22,196 | 25,060 |
| 71,700 -71,799 | 12,189 | 17,925 | 20,793 | 22,227 | 25,095 |
| 71,800 -71,899 | 12,206 | 17,950 | 20,822 | 22,258 | 25,130 |
| 71,900 -71,999 | 12,223 | 17,975 | 20,851 | 22,289 | 25,165 |

| ANNUAL INCOME | 1 | NUMBER OF CHILDREN 2 | 3 | 4 | 5+ |
|---|---|---|---|---|---|
| | | ANNUAL OBLIGATION AMOUNT | | | |
| 72,000 -72,099 | 12,240 | 18,000 | 20,880 | 22,320 | 25,200 |
| 72,100 -72,199 | 12,257 | 18,025 | 20,909 | 22,351 | 25,235 |
| 72,200 -72,299 | 12,274 | 18,050 | 20,938 | 22,382 | 25,270 |
| 72,300 -72,399 | 12,291 | 18,075 | 20,967 | 22,413 | 25,305 |
| 72,400 -72,499 | 12,308 | 18,100 | 20,996 | 22,444 | 25,340 |
| 72,500 -72,599 | 12,325 | 18,125 | 21,025 | 22,475 | 25,375 |
| 72,600 -72,699 | 12,342 | 18,150 | 21,054 | 22,506 | 25,410 |
| 72,700 -72,799 | 12,359 | 18,175 | 21,083 | 22,537 | 25,445 |
| 72,800 -72,899 | 12,376 | 18,200 | 21,112 | 22,568 | 25,480 |
| 72,900 -72,999 | 12,393 | 18,225 | 21,141 | 22,599 | 25,515 |

| ANNUAL INCOME | 1 | NUMBER OF CHILDREN 2 | 3 | 4 | 5+ |
|---|---|---|---|---|---|
| | | ANNUAL OBLIGATION AMOUNT | | | |
| 73,000 -73,099 | 12,410 | 18,250 | 21,170 | 22,630 | 25,550 |
| 73,100 -73,199 | 12,427 | 18,275 | 21,199 | 22,661 | 25,585 |
| 73,200 -73,299 | 12,444 | 18,300 | 21,228 | 22,692 | 25,620 |
| 73,300 -73,399 | 12,461 | 18,325 | 21,257 | 22,723 | 25,655 |
| 73,400 -73,499 | 12,478 | 18,350 | 21,286 | 22,754 | 25,690 |
| 73,500 -73,599 | 12,495 | 18,375 | 21,315 | 22,785 | 25,725 |
| 73,600 -73,699 | 12,512 | 18,400 | 21,344 | 22,816 | 25,760 |
| 73,700 -73,799 | 12,529 | 18,425 | 21,373 | 22,847 | 25,795 |
| 73,800 -73,899 | 12,546 | 18,450 | 21,402 | 22,878 | 25,830 |
| 73,900 -73,999 | 12,563 | 18,475 | 21,431 | 22,909 | 25,865 |

| ANNUAL INCOME | 1 | NUMBER OF CHILDREN 2 | 3 | 4 | 5+ |
|---|---|---|---|---|---|
| | | ANNUAL OBLIGATION AMOUNT | | | |
| 74,000 -74,099 | 12,580 | 18,500 | 21,460 | 22,940 | 25,900 |
| 74,100 -74,199 | 12,597 | 18,525 | 21,489 | 22,971 | 25,935 |
| 74,200 -74,299 | 12,614 | 18,550 | 21,518 | 23,002 | 25,970 |
| 74,300 -74,399 | 12,631 | 18,575 | 21,547 | 23,033 | 26,005 |
| 74,400 -74,499 | 12,648 | 18,600 | 21,576 | 23,064 | 26,040 |
| 74,500 -74,599 | 12,665 | 18,625 | 21,605 | 23,095 | 26,075 |
| 74,600 -74,699 | 12,682 | 18,650 | 21,634 | 23,126 | 26,110 |
| 74,700 -74,799 | 12,699 | 18,675 | 21,663 | 23,157 | 26,145 |
| 74,800 -74,899 | 12,716 | 18,700 | 21,692 | 23,188 | 26,180 |
| 74,900 -74,999 | 12,733 | 18,725 | 21,721 | 23,219 | 26,215 |

| ANNUAL INCOME | 1 | NUMBER OF CHILDREN 2 | 3 | 4 | 5+ |
|---|---|---|---|---|---|
| | | ANNUAL OBLIGATION AMOUNT | | | |
| 75,000 -75,099 | 12,750 | 18,750 | 21,750 | 23,250 | 26,250 |
| 75,100 -75,199 | 12,767 | 18,775 | 21,779 | 23,281 | 26,285 |
| 75,200 -75,299 | 12,784 | 18,800 | 21,808 | 23,312 | 26,320 |
| 75,300 -75,399 | 12,801 | 18,825 | 21,837 | 23,343 | 26,355 |
| 75,400 -75,499 | 12,818 | 18,850 | 21,866 | 23,374 | 26,390 |
| 75,500 -75,599 | 12,835 | 18,875 | 21,895 | 23,405 | 26,425 |
| 75,600 -75,699 | 12,852 | 18,900 | 21,924 | 23,436 | 26,460 |
| 75,700 -75,799 | 12,869 | 18,925 | 21,953 | 23,467 | 26,495 |
| 75,800 -75,899 | 12,886 | 18,950 | 21,982 | 23,498 | 26,530 |
| 75,900 -75,999 | 12,903 | 18,975 | 22,011 | 23,529 | 26,565 |

| ANNUAL INCOME | 1 | NUMBER OF CHILDREN 2 | 3 | 4 | 5+ |
|---|---|---|---|---|---|
| | | ANNUAL OBLIGATION AMOUNT | | | |
| 76,000 -76,099 | 12,920 | 19,000 | 22,040 | 23,560 | 26,600 |
| 76,100 -76,199 | 12,937 | 19,025 | 22,069 | 23,591 | 26,635 |
| 76,200 -76,299 | 12,954 | 19,050 | 22,098 | 23,622 | 26,670 |
| 76,300 -76,399 | 12,971 | 19,075 | 22,127 | 23,653 | 26,705 |
| 76,400 -76,499 | 12,988 | 19,100 | 22,156 | 23,684 | 26,740 |
| 76,500 -76,599 | 13,005 | 19,125 | 22,185 | 23,715 | 26,775 |
| 76,600 -76,699 | 13,022 | 19,150 | 22,214 | 23,746 | 26,810 |
| 76,700 -76,799 | 13,039 | 19,175 | 22,243 | 23,777 | 26,845 |
| 76,800 -76,899 | 13,056 | 19,200 | 22,272 | 23,808 | 26,880 |
| 76,900 -76,999 | 13,073 | 19,225 | 22,301 | 23,839 | 26,915 |

| ANNUAL INCOME | 1 | NUMBER OF CHILDREN 2 | 3 | 4 | 5+ |
|---|---|---|---|---|---|
| | | ANNUAL OBLIGATION AMOUNT | | | |
| 77,000 -77,099 | 13,090 | 19,250 | 22,330 | 23,870 | 2... |
| 77,100 -77,199 | 13,107 | 19,275 | 22,359 | 23,901 | 26,... |
| 77,200 -77,299 | 13,124 | 19,300 | 22,388 | 23,932 | 27,020 |
| 77,300 -77,399 | 13,141 | 19,325 | 22,417 | 23,963 | 27,055 |
| 77,400 -77,499 | 13,158 | 19,350 | 22,446 | 23,994 | 27,090 |
| 77,500 -77,599 | 13,175 | 19,375 | 22,475 | 24,025 | 27,125 |
| 77,600 -77,699 | 13,192 | 19,400 | 22,504 | 24,056 | 27,160 |
| 77,700 -77,799 | 13,209 | 19,425 | 22,533 | 24,087 | 27,195 |
| 77,800 -77,899 | 13,226 | 19,450 | 22,562 | 24,118 | 27,230 |
| 77,900 -77,999 | 13,243 | 19,475 | 22,591 | 24,149 | 27,265 |

| ANNUAL INCOME | 1 | NUMBER OF CHILDREN 2 | 3 | 4 | 5+ |
|---|---|---|---|---|---|
| | | ANNUAL OBLIGATION AMOUNT | | | |
| 78,000 -78,099 | 13,260 | 19,500 | 22,620 | 24,180 | 27,300 |
| 78,100 -78,199 | 13,277 | 19,525 | 22,649 | 24,211 | 27,335 |
| 78,200 -78,299 | 13,294 | 19,550 | 22,678 | 24,242 | 27,370 |
| 78,300 -78,399 | 13,311 | 19,575 | 22,707 | 24,273 | 27,405 |
| 78,400 -78,499 | 13,328 | 19,600 | 22,736 | 24,304 | 27,440 |
| 78,500 -78,599 | 13,345 | 19,625 | 22,765 | 24,335 | 27,475 |
| 78,600 -78,699 | 13,362 | 19,650 | 22,794 | 24,366 | 27,510 |
| 78,700 -78,799 | 13,379 | 19,675 | 22,823 | 24,397 | 27,545 |
| 78,800 -78,899 | 13,396 | 19,700 | 22,852 | 24,428 | 27,580 |
| 78,900 -78,999 | 13,413 | 19,725 | 22,881 | 24,459 | 27,615 |

| ANNUAL INCOME | 1 | NUMBER OF CHILDREN 2 | 3 | 4 | 5+ |
|---|---|---|---|---|---|
| | | ANNUAL OBLIGATION AMOUNT | | | |
| 79,000 -79,099 | 13,430 | 19,750 | 22,910 | 24,490 | 27,650 |
| 79,100 -79,199 | 13,447 | 19,775 | 22,939 | 24,521 | 27,685 |
| 79,200 -79,299 | 13,464 | 19,800 | 22,948 | 24,552 | 27,720 |
| 79,300 -79,399 | 13,481 | 19,825 | 22,997 | 24,583 | 27,755 |
| 79,400 -79,499 | 13,498 | 19,850 | 23,026 | 24,614 | 27,... |
| 79,500 -79,599 | 13,515 | 19,875 | 23,055 | 24,645 | 27,... |
| 79,600 -79,699 | 13,532 | 19,900 | 23,084 | 24,676 | 27,... |
| 79,700 -79,799 | 13,549 | 19,925 | 23,113 | 24,707 | 27,895 |
| 79,800 -79,899 | 13,566 | 19,950 | 23,142 | 24,738 | 27,930 |
| 79,900 -79,999 | 13,583 | 19,975 | 23,171 | 24,769 | 27,965 |

8

228

| ANNUAL INCOME | 1 | 2 | 3 | 4 | 5+ |
|---|---|---|---|---|---|
| | | ANNUAL | OBLIGATION | AMOUNT | |
| 80,000 -80,099 | 13,600 | 20,000 | 23,200 | 24,800 | 28,000 |
| 80,100 -80,199 | 13,617 | 20,025 | 23,229 | 24,831 | 28,035 |
| 80,200 -80,299 | 13,634 | 20,050 | 23,254 | 24,862 | 28,070 |
| 80,300 -80,399 | 13,651 | 20,075 | 23,287 | 24,893 | 28,105 |
| 80,400 -80,499 | 13,668 | 20,100 | 23,316 | 24,926 | 28,140 |
| 80,500 -80,599 | 13,685 | 20,125 | 23,345 | 24,955 | 28,175 |
| 80,600 -80,699 | 13,702 | 20,150 | 23,374 | 24,986 | 28,210 |
| 80,700 -80,799 | 13,719 | 20,175 | 23,403 | 25,017 | 28,245 |
| 80,800 -80,899 | 13,736 | 20,200 | 23,432 | 25,048 | 28,280 |
| 80,900 -80,999 | 13,753 | 20,225 | 23,461 | 25,079 | 28,315 |

| ANNUAL INCOME | 1 | 2 | 3 | 4 | 5+ |
|---|---|---|---|---|---|
| | | ANNUAL | OBLIGATION | AMOUNT | |
| 81,000 -81,099 | 13,770 | 20,250 | 23,490 | 25,110 | 28,350 |
| 81,100 -81,199 | 13,787 | 20,275 | 23,519 | 25,141 | 28,385 |
| 81,200 -81,299 | 13,804 | 20,300 | 23,548 | 25,172 | 28,420 |
| 81,300 -81,399 | 13,821 | 20,325 | 23,577 | 25,203 | 28,455 |
| 81,400 -81,499 | 13,838 | 20,350 | 23,606 | 25,234 | 28,490 |
| 41,500 -81,599 | 13,855 | 20,375 | 23,635 | 25,265 | 28,525 |
| 1,600 -81,699 | 13,872 | 20,400 | 23,644 | 25,296 | 28,540 |
| ,1,700 -81,799 | 13,889 | 20,425 | 23,693 | 25,327 | 28,595 |
| 81,800 -81,899 | 13,906 | 20,450 | 23,722 | 25,358 | 28,630 |
| 81,900 -81,999 | 13,923 | 20,475 | 23,751 | 25,389 | 28,665 |

| ANNUAL INCOME | 1 | 2 | 3 | 4 | 5+ |
|---|---|---|---|---|---|
| | | ANNUAL | OBLIGATION | AMOUNT | |
| 82,000 -82,099 | 13,940 | 20,500 | 23,780 | 25,420 | 28,700 |
| 82,100 -82,199 | 13,957 | 20,525 | 23,809 | 25,451 | 28,735 |
| 2,200 -82,299 | 13,974 | 20,550 | 23,838 | 25,482 | 28,770 |
| 82,300 -82,399 | 13,991 | 20,575 | 23,867 | 25,513 | 28,805 |
| 82,400 -82,499 | 14,008 | 20,600 | 23,896 | 25,544 | 28,840 |
| 82,500 -82,599 | 14,025 | 20,625 | 23,925 | 25,575 | 28,875 |
| 82,600 -82,699 | 14,042 | 20,650 | 23,954 | 25,606 | 28,910 |
| 82,700 -82,799 | 14,059 | 20,675 | 23,983 | 25,637 | 28,945 |
| 82,800 -82,899 | 14,076 | 20,700 | 24,012 | 25,668 | 28,980 |
| 82,900 -82,999 | 14,093 | 20,725 | 24,041 | 25,699 | 29,015 |

| ANNUAL INCOME | 1 | 2 | 3 | 4 | 5+ |
|---|---|---|---|---|---|
| | | ANNUAL | OBLIGATION | AMOUNT | |
| 83,000 -83,099 | 14,110 | 20,750 | 24,070 | 25,730 | 29,050 |
| 83,100 -83,199 | 14,127 | 20,775 | 24,099 | 25,761 | 29,085 |
| 83,200 -83,299 | 14,144 | 20,800 | 24,128 | 25,792 | 29,120 |
| 83,300 -83,399 | 14,161 | 20,825 | 24,157 | 25,823 | 29,155 |
| 83,400 -83,499 | 14,178 | 20,850 | 24,186 | 25,854 | 29,190 |
| 83,500 -83,599 | 14,195 | 20,875 | 24,215 | 25,885 | 29,225 |
| 83,600 -83,699 | 14,212 | 20,900 | 24,244 | 25,916 | 29,260 |
| 83,700 -83,799 | 14,229 | 20,925 | 24,273 | 25,947 | 29,295 |
| 83,800 -83,899 | 14,246 | 20,950 | 24,302 | 25,978 | 29,330 |
| 83,900 -83,999 | 14,263 | 20,975 | 24,331 | 26,009 | 29,365 |

| ANNUAL INCOME | 1 | 2 | 3 | 4 | 5+ |
|---|---|---|---|---|---|
| | | ANNUAL | OBLIGATION | AMOUNT | |
| 84,000 -84,099 | 14,280 | 21,000 | 24,360 | 26,040 | 29,400 |
| 84,100 -84,199 | 14,297 | 21,025 | 24,389 | 26,071 | 29,435 |
| 84,200 -84,299 | 14,314 | 21,050 | 24,418 | 26,102 | 29,470 |
| 84,300 -84,399 | 14,331 | 21,075 | 24,447 | 26,133 | 29,505 |
| 84,400 -84,499 | 14,348 | 21,100 | 24,476 | 26,164 | 29,540 |
| 84,500 -84,599 | 14,365 | 21,125 | 24,505 | 26,195 | 29,575 |
| 74,600 -84,699 | 14,382 | 21,150 | 24,534 | 26,226 | 29,610 |
| ,700 -84,799 | 14,399 | 21,175 | 24,543 | 26,257 | 29,645 |
| 84,800 -84,899 | 14,416 | 21,200 | 24,592 | 26,288 | 29,680 |
| 84,900 -84,999 | 14,433 | 21,225 | 24,621 | 26,319 | 29,715 |

| ANNUAL INCOME | 1 | 2 | 3 | 4 | 5+ |
|---|---|---|---|---|---|
| | | ANNUAL | OBLIGATION | AMOUNT | |
| 85,000 -85,099 | 14,450 | 21,250 | 24,650 | 26,350 | 29,750 |
| 85,100 -85,199 | 14,467 | 21,275 | 24,679 | 26,381 | 29,785 |
| 85,200 -85,299 | 14,484 | 21,300 | 24,708 | 26,412 | 29,820 |
| 85,300 -85,399 | 14,501 | 21,325 | 24,737 | 26,443 | 29,855 |
| 85,400 -85,499 | 14,518 | 21,350 | 24,766 | 26,474 | 29,890 |
| 85,500 -85,599 | 14,535 | 21,375 | 24,795 | 26,505 | 29,925 |
| 85,600 -85,699 | 14,552 | 21,400 | 24,824 | 26,536 | 29,960 |
| 85,700 -85,799 | 14,569 | 21,425 | 24,853 | 26,567 | 29,995 |
| 85,800 -85,899 | 14,586 | 21,450 | 24,882 | 26,598 | 30,030 |
| 85,900 -85,999 | 14,603 | 21,475 | 24,911 | 26,629 | 30,065 |

| ANNUAL INCOME | 1 | 2 | 3 | 4 | 5+ |
|---|---|---|---|---|---|
| | | ANNUAL | OBLIGATION | AMOUNT | |
| 86,000 -86,099 | 14,620 | 21,500 | 24,940 | 26,660 | 30,100 |
| 86,100 -86,199 | 14,637 | 21,525 | 24,969 | 26,691 | 30,135 |
| 86,200 -86,299 | 14,654 | 21,550 | 24,998 | 26,722 | 30,170 |
| 86,300 -86,399 | 14,671 | 21,575 | 25,027 | 26,753 | 30,205 |
| 86,400 -86,499 | 14,688 | 21,600 | 25,056 | 26,784 | 30,240 |
| 86,500 -86,599 | 14,705 | 21,625 | 25,085 | 26,815 | 30,275 |
| 86,600 -86,699 | 14,722 | 21,650 | 25,114 | 26,846 | 30,310 |
| 86,700 -86,799 | 14,739 | 21,675 | 25,143 | 26,877 | 30,345 |
| 86,800 -86,899 | 14,756 | 21,700 | 25,172 | 26,908 | 30,380 |
| 86,900 -86,999 | 14,773 | 21,725 | 25,201 | 26,939 | 30,415 |

| ANNUAL INCOME | 1 | 2 | 3 | 4 | 5+ |
|---|---|---|---|---|---|
| | | ANNUAL | OBLIGATION | AMOUNT | |
| 87,000 -87,099 | 14,790 | 21,750 | 25,230 | 26,970 | 30,450 |
| 87,100 -87,199 | 14,807 | 21,775 | 25,259 | 27,001 | 30,485 |
| 87,200 -87,299 | 14,824 | 21,800 | 25,288 | 27,032 | 30,520 |
| 87,300 -87,399 | 14,841 | 21,825 | 25,317 | 27,063 | 30,555 |
| 87,400 -87,499 | 14,858 | 21,850 | 25,346 | 27,094 | 30,590 |
| 87,500 -87,599 | 14,875 | 21,875 | 25,375 | 27,125 | 30,625 |
| 87,600 -87,699 | 14,892 | 21,900 | 25,404 | 27,156 | 30,660 |
| 87,700 -87,799 | 14,909 | 21,925 | 25,433 | 27,187 | 30,695 |
| 87,800 -87,899 | 14,926 | 21,950 | 25,462 | 27,218 | 30,730 |
| 87,900 -87,999 | 14,943 | 21,975 | 25,491 | 27,249 | 30,765 |

| ANNUAL INCOME | 1 | 2 | 3 | 4 | 5+ |
|---|---|---|---|---|---|
| | | ANNUAL | OBLIGATION | AMOUNT | |
| 88,000 -88,099 | 14,960 | 22,000 | 25,520 | 27,280 | 30,800 |
| 88,100 -88,199 | 14,977 | 22,025 | 25,549 | 27,311 | 30,835 |
| 88,200 -88,299 | 14,994 | 22,050 | 25,578 | 27,342 | 30,870 |
| 88,300 -88,399 | 15,011 | 22,075 | 25,607 | 27,373 | 30,905 |
| 88,400 -88,499 | 15,028 | 22,100 | 25,636 | 27,404 | 30,940 |
| 88,500 -88,599 | 15,045 | 22,125 | 25,665 | 27,435 | 30,975 |
| 88,600 -88,699 | 15,062 | 22,150 | 25,694 | 27,466 | 31,010 |
| 88,700 -88,799 | 15,079 | 22,175 | 25,723 | 27,497 | 31,045 |
| 88,800 -88,899 | 15,096 | 22,200 | 25,752 | 27,528 | 31,080 |
| 88,900 -88,999 | 15,113 | 22,225 | 25,781 | 27,559 | 31,115 |

| ANNUAL INCOME | 1 | 2 | 3 | 4 | 5+ |
|---|---|---|---|---|---|
| | | ANNUAL | OBLIGATION | AMOUNT | |
| 89,000 -89,099 | 15,130 | 22,250 | 25,810 | 27,590 | 31,150 |
| 89,100 -89,199 | 15,147 | 22,275 | 25,839 | 27,621 | 31,185 |
| 89,200 -89,299 | 15,164 | 22,300 | 25,868 | 27,652 | 31,220 |
| 89,300 -89,399 | 15,181 | 22,325 | 25,897 | 27,683 | 31,255 |
| 89,400 -89,499 | 15,198 | 22,350 | 25,926 | 27,714 | 31,290 |
| 89,500 -89,599 | 15,215 | 22,375 | 25,955 | 27,745 | 31,325 |
| 89,600 -89,699 | 15,232 | 22,400 | 25,984 | 27,776 | 31,360 |
| 89,700 -89,799 | 15,249 | 22,425 | 26,013 | 27,807 | 31,395 |
| 89,800 -89,899 | 15,264 | 22,450 | 26,042 | 27,838 | 31,430 |
| 89,900 -89,999 | 15,283 | 22,475 | 26,071 | 27,869 | 31,465 |

INCOME RANGE
90,000 -99,999

| ANNUAL INCOME | 1 | NUMBER OF CHILDREN 2 | 3 | 4 | 5+ |
|---|---|---|---|---|---|
| | | ANNUAL OBLIGATION AMOUNT | | | |
| 90,000 -90,099 | 15,300 | 22,500 | 26,100 | 27,900 | 31,500 |
| 90,100 -90,199 | 15,317 | 22,525 | 26,129 | 27,931 | 31,533 |
| 90,200 -90,299 | 15,334 | 22,550 | 26,158 | 27,962 | 31,570 |
| 90,300 -90,399 | 15,351 | 22,575 | 26,187 | 27,993 | 31,605 |
| 90,400 -90,499 | 15,368 | 22,600 | 26,216 | 28,024 | 31,640 |
| 90,500 -90,599 | 15,385 | 22,625 | 26,245 | 28,055 | 31,675 |
| 90,600 -90,699 | 15,402 | 22,650 | 26,274 | 28,086 | 31,710 |
| 90,700 -90,799 | 15,419 | 22,675 | 26,303 | 28,117 | 31,745 |
| 90,800 -90,899 | 15,436 | 22,700 | 26,332 | 28,148 | 31,780 |
| 90,900 -90,999 | 15,453 | 22,725 | 26,361 | 28,179 | 31,815 |

| ANNUAL INCOME | 1 | NUMBER OF CHILDREN 2 | 3 | 4 | 5+ |
|---|---|---|---|---|---|
| | | ANNUAL OBLIGATION AMOUNT | | | |
| 91,000 -91,099 | 15,470 | 22,750 | 26,390 | 28,210 | 31,850 |
| 91,100 -91,199 | 15,487 | 22,775 | 26,419 | 28,241 | 31,885 |
| 91,200 -91,299 | 15,504 | 22,800 | 26,448 | 28,272 | 31,920 |
| 91,300 -91,399 | 15,521 | 22,825 | 26,477 | 28,303 | 31,955 |
| 91,400 -91,499 | 15,538 | 22,850 | 26,506 | 28,334 | 31,990 |
| 91,500 -91,599 | 15,555 | 22,875 | 26,535 | 28,345 | 31,990 |
| 91,600 -91,699 | 15,572 | 22,900 | 26,564 | 28,396 | 32,060 |
| 91,700 -91,799 | 15,589 | 22,925 | 26,593 | 28,427 | 32,095 |
| 91,800 -91,899 | 15,606 | 22,950 | 26,622 | 28,458 | 32,130 |
| 91,900 -91,999 | 15,623 | 22,975 | 26,651 | 28,489 | 32,165 |

| ANNUAL INCOME | 1 | NUMBER OF CHILDREN 2 | 3 | 4 | 5+ |
|---|---|---|---|---|---|
| | | ANNUAL OBLIGATION AMOUNT | | | |
| 92,000 -92,099 | 15,640 | 23,000 | 26,680 | 28,520 | 32,200 |
| 92,100 -92,199 | 15,657 | 23,025 | 26,709 | 28,551 | 32,235 |
| 92,200 -92,299 | 15,674 | 23,050 | 26,738 | 28,582 | 32,270 |
| 92,300 -92,399 | 15,691 | 23,075 | 26,767 | 28,613 | 32,305 |
| 92,400 -92,499 | 15,708 | 23,100 | 26,796 | 28,644 | 32,340 |
| 92,500 -92,599 | 15,725 | 23,125 | 26,825 | 28,675 | 32,375 |
| 92,600 -92,699 | 15,742 | 23,150 | 26,854 | 28,706 | 32,410 |
| 92,700 -92,799 | 15,759 | 23,175 | 26,883 | 28,737 | 32,445 |
| 92,800 -92,899 | 15,776 | 23,200 | 26,912 | 28,768 | 32,480 |
| 92,900 -92,999 | 15,793 | 23,225 | 26,941 | 28,799 | 32,515 |

| ANNUAL INCOME | 1 | NUMBER OF CHILDREN 2 | 3 | 4 | 5+ |
|---|---|---|---|---|---|
| | | ANNUAL OBLIGATION AMOUNT | | | |
| 93,000 -93,099 | 15,810 | 23,250 | 26,970 | 28,830 | 32,550 |
| 93,100 -93,199 | 15,827 | 23,275 | 26,999 | 28,861 | 32,585 |
| 93,200 -93,299 | 15,844 | 23,300 | 27,028 | 28,897 | 32,620 |
| 93,300 -93,399 | 15,861 | 23,325 | 27,057 | 28,923 | 32,655 |
| 93,400 -93,499 | 15,878 | 23,350 | 27,086 | 28,954 | 32,690 |
| 93,500 -93,599 | 15,895 | 23,375 | 27,115 | 28,985 | 32,725 |
| 93,600 -93,699 | 15,912 | 23,400 | 27,144 | 29,016 | 32,760 |
| 93,700 -93,799 | 15,929 | 23,425 | 27,173 | 29,047 | 32,795 |
| 93,800 -93,899 | 15,946 | 23,450 | 27,202 | 29,078 | 32,830 |
| 93,900 -93,999 | 15,963 | 23,475 | 27,231 | 29,109 | 32,865 |

| ANNUAL INCOME | 1 | NUMBER OF CHILDREN 2 | 3 | 4 | 5+ |
|---|---|---|---|---|---|
| | | ANNUAL OBLIGATION AMOUNT | | | |
| 94,000 -94,099 | 15,980 | 23,500 | 27,260 | 29,140 | 32,900 |
| 94,100 -94,199 | 15,997 | 23,525 | 27,289 | 29,171 | 32,935 |
| 94,200 -94,299 | 16,014 | 23,550 | 27,318 | 29,202 | 32,970 |
| 94,300 -94,399 | 16,031 | 23,575 | 27,347 | 29,233 | 33,005 |
| 94,400 -94,499 | 16,048 | 23,600 | 27,376 | 29,264 | 33,040 |
| 94,500 -94,599 | 16,065 | 23,625 | 27,405 | 29,295 | 33,075 |
| 94,600 -94,699 | 16,082 | 23,650 | 27,434 | 29,326 | 33,110 |
| 94,700 -94,799 | 16,099 | 23,675 | 27,443 | 29,357 | 33,145 |
| 94,800 -94,899 | 16,116 | 23,700 | 27,492 | 29,388 | 33,180 |
| 94,900 -94,999 | 16,133 | 23,725 | 27,321 | 29,419 | 33,215 |

| ANNUAL INCOME | 1 | NUMBER OF CHILDREN 2 | 3 | 4 | 5+ |
|---|---|---|---|---|---|
| | | ANNUAL OBLIGATION AMOUNT | | | |
| 95,000 -95,099 | 16,150 | 23,750 | 27,550 | 29,450 | 33,250 |
| 95,100 -95,199 | 16,167 | 23,775 | 27,579 | 29,481 | 33,285 |
| 95,200 -95,299 | 16,184 | 23,800 | 27,608 | 29,512 | 33,320 |
| 95,300 -95,399 | 16,201 | 23,825 | 27,637 | 29,543 | 33,355 |
| 95,400 -95,499 | 16,218 | 23,850 | 27,666 | 29,574 | 33,390 |
| 95,500 -95,599 | 16,235 | 23,875 | 27,695 | 29,605 | 33,425 |
| 95,600 -95,699 | 16,252 | 23,900 | 27,724 | 29,636 | 33,460 |
| 95,700 -95,799 | 16,269 | 23,925 | 27,753 | 29,667 | 33,495 |
| 95,800 -95,899 | 16,286 | 23,950 | 27,782 | 29,698 | 33,530 |
| 95,900 -95,999 | 16,303 | 23,975 | 27,811 | 29,729 | 33,545 |

| ANNUAL INCOME | 1 | NUMBER OF CHILDREN 2 | 3 | 4 | 5+ |
|---|---|---|---|---|---|
| | | ANNUAL OBLIGATION AMOUNT | | | |
| 96,000 -96,099 | 16,320 | 24,000 | 27,840 | 29,760 | 33,600 |
| 96,100 -96,199 | 16,337 | 24,025 | 27,869 | 29,791 | 33,635 |
| 96,200 -96,299 | 16,354 | 24,050 | 27,898 | 29,822 | 33,670 |
| 96,300 -96,399 | 16,371 | 24,075 | 27,927 | 29,853 | 33,705 |
| 96,400 -96,499 | 16,388 | 24,100 | 27,956 | 29,884 | 33,740 |
| 96,500 -96,599 | 16,405 | 24,125 | 27,985 | 29,915 | 33,775 |
| 96,600 -96,699 | 16,422 | 24,150 | 28,014 | 29,946 | 33,810 |
| 96,700 -96,799 | 16,439 | 24,175 | 28,043 | 29,977 | 33,845 |
| 96,800 -96,899 | 16,456 | 24,200 | 28,072 | 30,008 | 33,880 |
| 96,900 -96,999 | 16,473 | 24,225 | 28,101 | 30,039 | 33,915 |

| ANNUAL INCOME | 1 | NUMBER OF CHILDREN 2 | 3 | 4 | 5+ |
|---|---|---|---|---|---|
| | | ANNUAL OBLIGATION AMOUNT | | | |
| 97,000 -97,099 | 16,490 | 24,250 | 28,130 | 30,070 | 33,950 |
| 97,100 -97,199 | 16,507 | 24,275 | 28,159 | 30,101 | 33,985 |
| 97,200 -97,299 | 16,524 | 24,300 | 28,188 | 30,132 | 34,020 |
| 97,300 -97,399 | 16,541 | 24,325 | 28,217 | 30,163 | 34,055 |
| 97,400 -97,499 | 16,558 | 24,350 | 28,246 | 30,194 | 34,090 |
| 97,500 -97,599 | 16,575 | 24,375 | 28,275 | 30,225 | 34,125 |
| 97,600 -97,699 | 16,592 | 24,400 | 28,304 | 30,256 | 34,160 |
| 97,700 -97,799 | 16,609 | 24,425 | 28,333 | 30,287 | 34,195 |
| 97,800 -97,899 | 16,626 | 24,450 | 28,362 | 30,318 | 34,230 |
| 97,900 -97,999 | 16,643 | 24,475 | 28,391 | 30,349 | 34,265 |

| ANNUAL INCOME | 1 | NUMBER OF CHILDREN 2 | 3 | 4 | 5+ |
|---|---|---|---|---|---|
| | | ANNUAL OBLIGATION AMOUNT | | | |
| 98,000 -98,099 | 16,660 | 24,500 | 28,420 | 30,380 | 34,300 |
| 98,100 -98,199 | 16,677 | 24,525 | 28,449 | 30,411 | 34,335 |
| 98,200 -98,299 | 16,694 | 24,550 | 28,478 | 30,442 | 34,370 |
| 98,300 -98,399 | 16,711 | 24,575 | 28,507 | 30,473 | 34,405 |
| 98,400 -98,499 | 16,728 | 24,600 | 28,536 | 30,504 | 34,440 |
| 98,500 -98,599 | 16,745 | 24,625 | 28,565 | 30,535 | 34,475 |
| 98,600 -98,699 | 16,762 | 24,650 | 28,594 | 30,566 | 34,510 |
| 98,700 -98,799 | 16,779 | 24,675 | 28,623 | 30,597 | 34,545 |
| 98,800 -98,899 | 16,796 | 24,700 | 28,652 | 30,628 | 34,580 |
| 98,900 -98,999 | 16,813 | 24,725 | 28,681 | 30,659 | 34,615 |

| ANNUAL INCOME | 1 | NUMBER OF CHILDREN 2 | 3 | 4 | 5+ |
|---|---|---|---|---|---|
| | | ANNUAL OBLIGATION AMOUNT | | | |
| 99,000 -99,099 | 16,830 | 24,750 | 28,710 | 30,690 | 34,650 |
| 99,100 -99,199 | 16,847 | 24,775 | 28,739 | 30,721 | 34,685 |
| 99,200 -99,299 | 16,864 | 24,800 | 28,768 | 30,752 | 34,720 |
| 99,300 -99,399 | 16,881 | 24,825 | 28,797 | 30,783 | 34,755 |
| 99,400 -99,499 | 16,898 | 24,850 | 28,826 | 30,783 | 34,755 |
| 99,500 -99,599 | 16,915 | 24,875 | 28,853 | 30,845 | 34,825 |
| 99,600 -99,699 | 16,932 | 24,900 | 28,884 | 30,876 | 34,825 |
| 99,700 -99,799 | 16,949 | 24,925 | 28,913 | 30,907 | 34,1 |
| 99,800 -99,899 | 16,966 | 24,950 | 28,942 | 30,938 | 34,930 |
| 99,900 -99,999 | 16,983 | 24,975 | 28,971 | 30,949 | 34,965 |

10

### NUMBER OF CHILDREN — ANNUAL OBLIGATION AMOUNT

| ANNUAL INCOME | 1 | 2 | 3 | 4 | 5+ |
|---|---|---|---|---|---|
| 100,000 -100,099 | 17,000 | 25,000 | 29,000 | 31,000 | 33,000 |
| 100,100 -100,199 | 17,017 | 25,025 | 29,029 | 31,031 | 33,035 |
| 100,200 -100,299 | 17,034 | 25,050 | 29,058 | 31,062 | 33,070 |
| 100,300 -100,399 | 17,051 | 25,075 | 29,087 | 31,093 | 33,105 |
| 100,400 -100,499 | 17,068 | 25,100 | 29,116 | 31,124 | 33,140 |
| 100,500 -100,599 | 17,085 | 25,125 | 29,145 | 31,155 | 33,175 |
| 100,600 -100,699 | 17,102 | 25,150 | 29,174 | 31,186 | 33,210 |
| 100,700 -100,799 | 17,119 | 25,175 | 29,203 | 31,217 | 33,245 |
| 100,800 -100,899 | 17,136 | 25,200 | 29,232 | 31,248 | 33,280 |
| 100,900 -100,999 | 17,153 | 25,225 | 29,261 | 31,279 | 33,315 |

| ANNUAL INCOME | 1 | 2 | 3 | 4 | 5+ |
|---|---|---|---|---|---|
| 101,000 -101,099 | 17,170 | 25,250 | 29,290 | 31,310 | 33,350 |
| 101,100 -101,199 | 17,187 | 25,275 | 29,319 | 31,341 | 33,385 |
| 101,200 -101,299 | 17,204 | 25,300 | 29,348 | 31,372 | 33,420 |
| 101,300 -101,399 | 17,221 | 25,325 | 29,377 | 31,403 | 33,455 |
| 101,400 -101,499 | 17,238 | 25,350 | 29,406 | 31,434 | 33,490 |
| 101,500 -101,599 | 17,255 | 25,375 | 29,435 | 31,465 | 33,525 |
| 101,600 -101,699 | 17,272 | 25,400 | 29,464 | 31,496 | 33,560 |
| 101,700 -101,799 | 17,289 | 25,425 | 29,493 | 31,527 | 33,595 |
| 101,800 -101,899 | 17,306 | 25,450 | 29,522 | 31,558 | 33,630 |
| 101,900 -101,999 | 17,323 | 25,475 | 29,551 | 31,589 | 33,665 |

| ANNUAL INCOME | 1 | 2 | 3 | 4 | 5+ |
|---|---|---|---|---|---|
| 102,000 -102,099 | 17,340 | 25,500 | 29,580 | 31,620 | 33,700 |
| 102,100 -102,199 | 17,357 | 25,525 | 29,609 | 31,651 | 33,735 |
| 102,200 -102,299 | 17,374 | 25,550 | 29,638 | 31,682 | 33,770 |
| 102,300 -102,399 | 17,391 | 25,575 | 29,667 | 31,713 | 33,805 |
| 102,400 -102,499 | 17,408 | 25,600 | 29,696 | 31,744 | 33,840 |
| 102,500 -102,599 | 17,425 | 25,625 | 29,725 | 31,775 | 33,875 |
| 102,600 -102,699 | 17,442 | 25,650 | 29,754 | 31,806 | 33,910 |
| 102,700 -102,799 | 17,459 | 25,675 | 29,783 | 31,837 | 33,945 |
| 102,800 -102,899 | 17,476 | 25,700 | 29,812 | 31,868 | 33,980 |
| 102,900 -102,999 | 17,493 | 25,725 | 29,841 | 31,899 | 34,015 |

| ANNUAL INCOME | 1 | 2 | 3 | 4 | 5+ |
|---|---|---|---|---|---|
| 103,000 -103,099 | 17,510 | 25,750 | 29,870 | 31,930 | 34,050 |
| 103,100 -103,199 | 17,527 | 25,775 | 29,899 | 31,961 | 34,085 |
| 103,200 -103,299 | 17,544 | 25,800 | 29,928 | 31,992 | 34,120 |
| 103,300 -103,399 | 17,561 | 25,825 | 29,957 | 32,023 | 34,155 |
| 103,400 -103,499 | 17,578 | 25,850 | 29,986 | 32,054 | 34,190 |
| 103,500 -103,599 | 17,595 | 25,875 | 30,015 | 32,085 | 34,225 |
| 103,600 -103,699 | 17,612 | 25,900 | 30,044 | 32,116 | 34,260 |
| 103,700 -103,799 | 17,629 | 25,925 | 30,073 | 32,147 | 34,295 |
| 103,800 -103,899 | 17,646 | 25,950 | 30,102 | 32,178 | 34,330 |
| 103,900 -103,999 | 17,663 | 25,975 | 30,131 | 32,209 | 34,365 |

| ANNUAL INCOME | 1 | 2 | 3 | 4 | 5+ |
|---|---|---|---|---|---|
| 104,000 -104,099 | 17,680 | 26,000 | 30,160 | 32,240 | 34,400 |
| 104,100 -104,199 | 17,697 | 26,025 | 30,189 | 32,271 | 34,435 |
| 104,200 -104,299 | 17,714 | 26,050 | 30,218 | 32,302 | 34,470 |
| 104,300 -104,399 | 17,731 | 26,075 | 30,247 | 32,333 | 34,505 |
| 104,400 -104,499 | 17,748 | 26,100 | 30,276 | 32,364 | 34,540 |
| 104,500 -104,599 | 17,765 | 26,125 | 30,305 | 32,395 | 34,575 |
| 104,600 -104,699 | 17,782 | 26,150 | 30,334 | 32,426 | 34,610 |
| 104,700 -104,799 | 17,799 | 26,175 | 30,363 | 32,457 | 34,645 |
| 104,800 -104,899 | 17,816 | 26,200 | 30,392 | 32,488 | 34,680 |
| 104,900 -104,999 | 17,833 | 26,225 | 30,421 | 32,519 | 34,715 |

| ANNUAL INCOME | 1 | 2 | 3 | 4 | 5+ |
|---|---|---|---|---|---|
| 105,000 -105,099 | 17,850 | 26,250 | 30,450 | 32,550 | 34,750 |
| 105,100 -105,199 | 17,867 | 26,275 | 30,479 | 32,581 | 34,785 |
| 105,200 -105,299 | 17,884 | 26,300 | 30,508 | 32,612 | 34,820 |
| 105,300 -105,399 | 17,901 | 26,325 | 30,537 | 32,643 | 34,855 |
| 105,400 -105,499 | 17,918 | 26,350 | 30,566 | 32,674 | 34,890 |
| 105,500 -105,599 | 17,935 | 26,375 | 30,595 | 32,705 | 34,925 |
| 105,600 -105,699 | 17,952 | 26,400 | 30,624 | 32,736 | 34,960 |
| 105,700 -105,799 | 17,969 | 26,425 | 30,653 | 32,767 | 34,995 |
| 105,800 -105,899 | 17,986 | 26,450 | 30,682 | 32,798 | 35,030 |
| 105,900 -105,999 | 18,003 | 26,475 | 30,711 | 32,829 | 35,065 |

| ANNUAL INCOME | 1 | 2 | 3 | 4 | 5+ |
|---|---|---|---|---|---|
| 106,000 -106,099 | 18,020 | 26,500 | 30,740 | 32,860 | 35,100 |
| 106,100 -106,199 | 18,037 | 26,525 | 30,769 | 32,891 | 35,135 |
| 106,200 -106,299 | 18,054 | 26,550 | 30,798 | 32,922 | 35,170 |
| 106,300 -106,399 | 18,071 | 26,575 | 30,827 | 32,953 | 35,205 |
| 106,400 -106,499 | 18,088 | 26,600 | 30,856 | 32,984 | 35,240 |
| 106,500 -106,599 | 18,105 | 26,625 | 30,885 | 33,015 | 35,275 |
| 106,600 -106,699 | 18,122 | 26,650 | 30,914 | 33,046 | 35,310 |
| 106,700 -106,799 | 18,139 | 26,675 | 30,943 | 33,077 | 35,345 |
| 106,800 -106,899 | 18,156 | 26,700 | 30,972 | 33,108 | 35,380 |
| 106,900 -106,999 | 18,173 | 26,725 | 31,001 | 33,139 | 35,415 |

| ANNUAL INCOME | 1 | 2 | 3 | 4 | 5+ |
|---|---|---|---|---|---|
| 107,000 -107,099 | 18,190 | 26,750 | 31,030 | 33,170 | 35,450 |
| 107,100 -107,199 | 18,207 | 26,775 | 31,059 | 33,201 | 35,485 |
| 107,200 -107,299 | 18,224 | 26,800 | 31,088 | 33,232 | 35,520 |
| 107,300 -107,399 | 18,241 | 26,825 | 31,117 | 33,263 | 35,555 |
| 107,400 -107,499 | 18,258 | 26,850 | 31,146 | 33,294 | 35,590 |
| 107,500 -107,599 | 18,275 | 26,875 | 31,175 | 33,325 | 35,625 |
| 107,600 -107,699 | 18,292 | 26,900 | 31,204 | 33,356 | 35,660 |
| 107,700 -107,799 | 18,309 | 26,925 | 31,233 | 33,387 | 35,695 |
| 107,800 -107,899 | 18,326 | 26,950 | 31,262 | 33,418 | 35,730 |
| 107,900 -107,999 | 18,343 | 26,975 | 31,291 | 33,449 | 35,765 |

| ANNUAL INCOME | 1 | 2 | 3 | 4 | 5+ |
|---|---|---|---|---|---|
| 108,000 -108,099 | 18,360 | 27,000 | 31,320 | 33,480 | 35,800 |
| 108,100 -108,199 | 18,377 | 27,025 | 31,349 | 33,511 | 35,835 |
| 108,200 -108,299 | 18,394 | 27,050 | 31,378 | 33,542 | 35,870 |
| 108,300 -108,399 | 18,411 | 27,075 | 31,407 | 33,573 | 35,905 |
| 108,400 -108,499 | 18,428 | 27,100 | 31,436 | 33,604 | 35,940 |
| 108,500 -108,599 | 18,445 | 27,125 | 31,465 | 33,635 | 35,975 |
| 108,600 -108,699 | 18,462 | 27,150 | 31,494 | 33,666 | 36,010 |
| 108,700 -108,799 | 18,479 | 27,175 | 31,523 | 33,697 | 36,045 |
| 108,800 -108,899 | 18,496 | 27,200 | 31,552 | 33,728 | 36,080 |
| 108,900 -108,999 | 18,513 | 27,225 | 31,581 | 33,759 | 36,115 |

| ANNUAL INCOME | 1 | 2 | 3 | 4 | 5+ |
|---|---|---|---|---|---|
| 109,000 -109,099 | 18,530 | 27,250 | 31,610 | 33,790 | 36,150 |
| 109,100 -109,199 | 18,547 | 27,275 | 31,639 | 33,821 | 36,185 |
| 109,200 -109,299 | 18,564 | 27,300 | 31,668 | 33,852 | 36,220 |
| 109,300 -109,399 | 18,581 | 27,325 | 31,697 | 33,883 | 36,255 |
| 109,400 -109,499 | 18,598 | 27,350 | 31,726 | 33,914 | 36,290 |
| 109,500 -109,599 | 18,615 | 27,375 | 31,755 | 33,945 | 36,325 |
| 109,600 -109,699 | 18,632 | 27,400 | 31,784 | 33,976 | 36,360 |
| 109,700 -109,799 | 18,649 | 27,425 | 31,813 | 34,007 | 36,395 |
| 109,800 -109,899 | 18,666 | 27,450 | 31,842 | 34,038 | 36,430 |
| 109,900 -109,999 | 18,683 | 27,475 | 31,871 | 34,069 | 36,465 |

11

| ANNUAL INCOME | 1 | NUMBER OF CHILDREN 2 | 3 | 4 | 5+ |
|---|---|---|---|---|---|
| | | ANNUAL OBLIGATION AMOUNT | | | |
| 110,000 -110,099 | 18,700 | 27,500 | 31,900 | 34,100 | 38,500 |
| 110,100 -110,199 | 18,717 | 27,525 | 31,929 | 34,131 | 38,535 |
| 110,200 -110,299 | 18,734 | 27,550 | 31,958 | 34,162 | 38,570 |
| 110,300 -110,399 | 18,751 | 27,575 | 31,987 | 34,193 | 38,605 |
| 110,400 -110,499 | 18,768 | 27,600 | 32,016 | 34,224 | 38,640 |
| 110,500 -110,599 | 18,785 | 27,625 | 32,045 | 34,255 | 38,675 |
| 110,600 -110,699 | 18,802 | 27,650 | 32,074 | 34,286 | 38,710 |
| 110,700 -110,799 | 18,819 | 27,675 | 32,103 | 34,317 | 38,745 |
| 110,800 -110,899 | 18,836 | 27,700 | 32,132 | 34,348 | 38,780 |
| 110,900 -110,999 | 18,853 | 27,725 | 32,161 | 34,379 | 38,815 |

| ANNUAL INCOME | 1 | NUMBER OF CHILDREN 2 | 3 | 4 | 5+ |
|---|---|---|---|---|---|
| | | ANNUAL OBLIGATION AMOUNT | | | |
| 115,000 -115,099 | 19,550 | 28,750 | 33,350 | 35,650 | 40,250 |
| 115,100 -115,199 | 19,567 | 28,775 | 33,379 | 35,681 | 40,285 |
| 115,200 -115,299 | 19,584 | 28,800 | 33,408 | 35,712 | 40,320 |
| 115,300 -115,399 | 19,601 | 28,825 | 33,437 | 35,743 | 40,355 |
| 115,400 -115,499 | 19,618 | 28,850 | 33,466 | 35,774 | 40,390 |
| 115,500 -115,599 | 19,635 | 28,875 | 33,495 | 35,805 | 40,425 |
| 115,600 -115,699 | 19,652 | 28,900 | 33,524 | 35,836 | 40,460 |
| 115,700 -115,799 | 19,669 | 28,925 | 33,553 | 35,867 | 40,495 |
| 115,800 -115,899 | 19,686 | 28,950 | 33,582 | 35,898 | 40,530 |
| 115,900 -115,999 | 19,703 | 28,975 | 33,611 | 35,929 | 40,545 |

| ANNUAL INCOME | 1 | NUMBER OF CHILDREN 2 | 3 | 4 | 5+ |
|---|---|---|---|---|---|
| | | ANNUAL OBLIGATION AMOUNT | | | |
| 111,000 -111,099 | 18,870 | 27,750 | 32,190 | 34,410 | 38,850 |
| 111,100 -111,199 | 18,887 | 27,775 | 32,219 | 34,441 | 38,885 |
| 111,200 -111,299 | 18,904 | 27,800 | 32,248 | 34,472 | 38,920 |
| 111,300 -111,399 | 18,921 | 27,825 | 32,277 | 34,503 | 38,955 |
| 111,400 -111,499 | 18,938 | 27,850 | 32,306 | 34,534 | 38,990 |
| 111,500 -111,599 | 18,955 | 27,875 | 32,335 | 34,565 | 39,025 |
| 111,600 -111,699 | 18,972 | 27,900 | 32,364 | 34,596 | 39,060 |
| 111,700 -111,799 | 18,989 | 27,925 | 32,393 | 34,627 | 39,095 |
| 111,800 -111,899 | 19,006 | 27,950 | 32,422 | 34,658 | 39,130 |
| 111,900 -111,999 | 19,023 | 27,975 | 32,451 | 34,689 | 39,145 |

| ANNUAL INCOME | 1 | NUMBER OF CHILDREN 2 | 3 | 4 | 5+ |
|---|---|---|---|---|---|
| | | ANNUAL OBLIGATION AMOUNT | | | |
| 116,000 -116,099 | 19,720 | 29,000 | 33,640 | 35,960 | 40,600 |
| 116,100 -116,199 | 19,737 | 29,025 | 33,669 | 35,991 | 40,635 |
| 116,200 -116,299 | 19,754 | 29,050 | 33,698 | 36,022 | 40,670 |
| 116,300 -116,399 | 19,771 | 29,075 | 33,727 | 36,053 | 40,705 |
| 116,400 -116,499 | 19,788 | 29,100 | 33,756 | 36,084 | 40,740 |
| 116,500 -116,599 | 19,805 | 29,125 | 33,785 | 36,115 | 40,775 |
| 116,600 -116,699 | 19,822 | 29,150 | 33,814 | 36,144 | 40,810 |
| 116,700 -116,799 | 19,839 | 29,175 | 33,843 | 36,177 | 40,845 |
| 116,800 -116,899 | 19,856 | 29,200 | 33,872 | 36,208 | 40,880 |
| 116,900 -116,999 | 19,873 | 29,225 | 33,901 | 34,239 | 40,915 |

| ANNUAL INCOME | 1 | NUMBER OF CHILDREN 2 | 3 | 4 | 5+ |
|---|---|---|---|---|---|
| | | ANNUAL OBLIGATION AMOUNT | | | |
| 112,000 -112,099 | 19,040 | 28,000 | 32,480 | 34,720 | 39,200 |
| 112,100 -112,199 | 19,057 | 28,025 | 32,509 | 34,751 | 39,235 |
| 112,200 -112,299 | 19,074 | 28,050 | 32,538 | 34,782 | 39,270 |
| 112,300 -112,399 | 19,091 | 28,075 | 32,567 | 34,813 | 39,305 |
| 112,400 -112,499 | 19,108 | 28,100 | 32,596 | 34,844 | 39,340 |
| 112,500 -112,599 | 19,125 | 28,125 | 32,625 | 34,875 | 39,375 |
| 112,600 -112,699 | 19,142 | 28,150 | 32,654 | 34,906 | 39,410 |
| 112,700 -112,799 | 19,159 | 28,175 | 32,683 | 34,937 | 39,445 |
| 112,800 -112,899 | 19,176 | 28,200 | 32,712 | 34,968 | 39,480 |
| 112,900 -112,999 | 19,193 | 28,225 | 32,741 | 34,999 | 39,515 |

| ANNUAL INCOME | 1 | NUMBER OF CHILDREN 2 | 3 | 4 | 5+ |
|---|---|---|---|---|---|
| | | ANNUAL OBLIGATION AMOUNT | | | |
| 117,000 -117,099 | 19,890 | 29,250 | 33,930 | 34,270 | 40,950 |
| 117,100 -117,199 | 19,907 | 29,275 | 33,959 | 34,301 | 40 |
| 117,200 -117,299 | 19,924 | 29,300 | 33,988 | 34,332 | 41 |
| 117,300 -117,399 | 19,941 | 29,325 | 34,017 | 34,343 | 41,025 |
| 117,400 -117,499 | 19,958 | 29,350 | 34,046 | 36,394 | 41,090 |
| 117,500 -117,599 | 19,975 | 29,375 | 34,075 | 36,425 | 41,125 |
| 117,600 -117,699 | 19,992 | 29,400 | 34,104 | 36,456 | 41,160 |
| 117,700 -117,799 | 20,009 | 29,425 | 34,133 | 36,487 | 41,195 |
| 117,800 -117,899 | 20,026 | 29,450 | 34,162 | 36,518 | 41,230 |
| 117,900 -117,999 | 20,043 | 29,475 | 34,191 | 36,549 | 41,265 |

| ANNUAL INCOME | 1 | NUMBER OF CHILDREN 2 | 3 | 4 | 5+ |
|---|---|---|---|---|---|
| | | ANNUAL OBLIGATION AMOUNT | | | |
| 113,000 -113,099 | 19,210 | 28,250 | 32,770 | 35,030 | 39,550 |
| 113,100 -113,199 | 19,227 | 28,275 | 32,799 | 35,061 | 39,585 |
| 113,200 -113,299 | 19,244 | 28,300 | 32,828 | 35,092 | 39,620 |
| 113,300 -113,399 | 19,261 | 28,325 | 32,857 | 35,123 | 39,655 |
| 113,400 -113,499 | 19,278 | 28,350 | 32,886 | 35,154 | 39,690 |
| 113,500 -113,599 | 19,295 | 28,375 | 32,915 | 35,185 | 39,725 |
| 113,600 -113,699 | 19,312 | 28,400 | 32,944 | 35,216 | 39,760 |
| 113,700 -113,799 | 19,329 | 28,425 | 32,973 | 35,247 | 39,795 |
| 113,800 -113,899 | 19,346 | 28,450 | 33,002 | 35,278 | 39,830 |
| 113,900 -113,999 | 19,363 | 28,475 | 33,031 | 35,309 | 39,865 |

| ANNUAL INCOME | 1 | NUMBER OF CHILDREN 2 | 3 | 4 | 5+ |
|---|---|---|---|---|---|
| | | ANNUAL OBLIGATION AMOUNT | | | |
| 118,000 -118,099 | 20,060 | 29,500 | 34,220 | 36,580 | 41,300 |
| 118,100 -118,199 | 20,077 | 29,525 | 34,249 | 36,611 | 41,335 |
| 118,200 -118,299 | 20,094 | 29,550 | 34,278 | 36,642 | 41,370 |
| 118,300 -118,399 | 20,111 | 29,575 | 34,307 | 36,673 | 41,405 |
| 118,400 -118,499 | 20,128 | 29,600 | 34,336 | 36,704 | 41,440 |
| 118,500 -118,599 | 20,145 | 29,625 | 34,365 | 36,735 | 41,475 |
| 118,600 -118,699 | 20,162 | 29,650 | 34,394 | 36,766 | 41,510 |
| 118,700 -118,799 | 20,179 | 29,675 | 34,423 | 36,797 | 41,545 |
| 118,800 -118,899 | 20,196 | 29,700 | 34,452 | 36,828 | 41,580 |
| 118,900 -118,999 | 20,213 | 29,725 | 34,481 | 36,859 | 41,615 |

| ANNUAL INCOME | 1 | NUMBER OF CHILDREN 2 | 3 | 4 | 5+ |
|---|---|---|---|---|---|
| | | ANNUAL OBLIGATION AMOUNT | | | |
| 114,000 -114,099 | 19,380 | 28,500 | 33,060 | 35,340 | 39,900 |
| 114,100 -114,199 | 19,397 | 28,525 | 33,089 | 35,371 | 39,935 |
| 114,200 -114,299 | 19,414 | 28,550 | 33,118 | 35,402 | 39,970 |
| 114,300 -114,399 | 19,431 | 28,575 | 33,147 | 35,433 | 40,005 |
| 114,400 -114,499 | 19,448 | 28,600 | 33,176 | 35,464 | 40,040 |
| 114,500 -114,599 | 19,465 | 28,625 | 33,205 | 35,495 | 40,075 |
| 114,600 -114,699 | 19,482 | 28,650 | 33,234 | 35,526 | 40,110 |
| 114,700 -114,799 | 19,499 | 28,675 | 33,263 | 35,557 | 40,145 |
| 114,800 -114,899 | 19,516 | 28,700 | 33,292 | 35,588 | 40,180 |
| 114,900 -114,999 | 19,533 | 28,725 | 33,321 | 35,619 | 40,215 |

| ANNUAL INCOME | 1 | NUMBER OF CHILDREN 2 | 3 | 4 | 5+ |
|---|---|---|---|---|---|
| | | ANNUAL OBLIGATION AMOUNT | | | |
| 119,000 -119,099 | 20,230 | 29,750 | 34,510 | 36,890 | 41,650 |
| 119,100 -119,199 | 20,247 | 29,775 | 34,539 | 36,921 | 41,685 |
| 119,200 -119,299 | 20,264 | 29,800 | 34,568 | 36,952 | 41,720 |
| 119,300 -119,399 | 20,281 | 29,825 | 34,597 | 36,983 | 41,755 |
| 119,400 -119,499 | 20,298 | 29,850 | 34,626 | 37,014 | 41,790 |
| 119,500 -119,599 | 20,315 | 29,875 | 34,655 | 37,045 | 41,825 |
| 119,600 -119,699 | 20,332 | 29,900 | 34,684 | 37,076 | 41 |
| 119,700 -119,799 | 20,349 | 29,925 | 34,713 | 37,107 | 41 |
| 119,800 -119,899 | 20,366 | 29,950 | 34,742 | 37,138 | 41,930 |
| 119,900 -119,999 | 20,383 | 29,975 | 34,771 | 37,169 | 41,965 |

12

| ANNUAL INCOME | 1 | NUMBER OF CHILDREN 2 | 3 | 4 | 5+ |
|---|---|---|---|---|---|
| | | ANNUAL OBLIGATION AMOUNT | | | |
| 120,000 -120,099 | 20,400 | 30,000 | 34,800 | 37,200 | 42,000 |
| 120,100 -120,199 | 20,417 | 30,025 | 34,829 | 37,231 | 42,035 |
| 120,200 -120,299 | 20,434 | 30,050 | 34,858 | 37,262 | 42,070 |
| 120,300 -120,399 | 20,451 | 30,075 | 34,887 | 37,293 | 42,105 |
| 120,400 -120,499 | 20,468 | 30,100 | 34,916 | 37,324 | 42,140 |
| 120,500 -120,599 | 20,485 | 30,125 | 34,945 | 37,355 | 42,175 |
| 120,600 -120,699 | 20,502 | 30,150 | 34,974 | 37,386 | 42,210 |
| 120,700 -120,799 | 20,519 | 30,175 | 35,003 | 37,417 | 42,245 |
| 120,800 -120,899 | 20,536 | 30,200 | 35,032 | 37,448 | 42,280 |
| 120,900 -120,999 | 20,553 | 30,225 | 35,061 | 37,479 | 42,315 |

| ANNUAL INCOME | 1 | NUMBER OF CHILDREN 2 | 3 | 4 | 5+ |
|---|---|---|---|---|---|
| | | ANNUAL OBLIGATION AMOUNT | | | |
| 121,000 -121,099 | 20,570 | 30,250 | 35,090 | 37,510 | 42,350 |
| 121,100 -121,199 | 20,587 | 30,275 | 35,119 | 37,541 | 42,385 |
| 121,200 -121,299 | 20,604 | 30,300 | 35,148 | 37,572 | 42,420 |
| 121,300 -121,399 | 20,621 | 30,325 | 35,177 | 37,603 | 42,455 |
| 121,400 -121,499 | 20,638 | 30,350 | 35,206 | 37,634 | 42,490 |
| 121,500 -121,599 | 20,655 | 30,375 | 35,235 | 37,665 | 42,525 |
| 121,600 -121,699 | 20,672 | 30,400 | 35,264 | 37,696 | 42,560 |
| 121,700 -121,799 | 20,689 | 30,425 | 35,293 | 37,727 | 42,595 |
| 121,800 -121,899 | 20,706 | 30,450 | 35,322 | 37,758 | 42,630 |
| 121,900 -121,999 | 20,723 | 30,475 | 35,351 | 37,789 | 42,665 |

| ANNUAL INCOME | 1 | NUMBER OF CHILDREN 2 | 3 | 4 | 5+ |
|---|---|---|---|---|---|
| | | ANNUAL OBLIGATION AMOUNT | | | |
| 122,000 -122,099 | 20,740 | 30,500 | 35,380 | 37,820 | 42,700 |
| 122,100 -122,199 | 20,757 | 30,525 | 35,409 | 37,851 | 42,735 |
| 122,200 -122,299 | 20,774 | 30,550 | 35,438 | 37,882 | 42,770 |
| 122,300 -122,399 | 20,791 | 30,575 | 35,467 | 37,913 | 42,805 |
| 122,400 -122,499 | 20,808 | 30,600 | 35,496 | 37,944 | 42,840 |
| 122,500 -122,599 | 20,825 | 30,625 | 35,525 | 37,975 | 42,875 |
| 122,600 -122,699 | 20,842 | 30,650 | 35,554 | 38,006 | 42,910 |
| 122,700 -122,799 | 20,859 | 30,675 | 35,583 | 38,037 | 42,945 |
| 122,800 -122,899 | 20,876 | 30,700 | 35,612 | 38,068 | 42,980 |
| 122,900 -122,999 | 20,893 | 30,725 | 35,641 | 38,099 | 43,015 |

| ANNUAL INCOME | 1 | NUMBER OF CHILDREN 2 | 3 | 4 | 5+ |
|---|---|---|---|---|---|
| | | ANNUAL OBLIGATION AMOUNT | | | |
| 123,000 -123,099 | 20,910 | 30,750 | 35,670 | 38,130 | 43,050 |
| 123,100 -123,199 | 20,927 | 30,775 | 35,699 | 38,161 | 43,085 |
| 123,200 -123,299 | 20,944 | 30,800 | 35,728 | 38,192 | 43,120 |
| 123,300 -123,399 | 20,961 | 30,825 | 35,757 | 38,223 | 43,155 |
| 123,400 -123,499 | 20,978 | 30,850 | 35,786 | 38,254 | 43,190 |
| 123,500 -123,599 | 20,995 | 30,875 | 35,815 | 38,285 | 43,225 |
| 123,600 -123,699 | 21,012 | 30,900 | 35,844 | 38,316 | 43,260 |
| 123,700 -123,799 | 21,029 | 30,925 | 35,873 | 38,347 | 43,295 |
| 123,800 -123,899 | 21,046 | 30,950 | 35,902 | 38,378 | 43,330 |
| 123,900 -123,999 | 21,063 | 30,975 | 35,931 | 38,409 | 43,365 |

| ANNUAL INCOME | 1 | NUMBER OF CHILDREN 2 | 3 | 4 | 5+ |
|---|---|---|---|---|---|
| | | ANNUAL OBLIGATION AMOUNT | | | |
| 124,000 -124,099 | 21,080 | 31,000 | 35,960 | 38,440 | 43,400 |
| 124,100 -124,199 | 21,097 | 31,025 | 35,989 | 38,471 | 43,435 |
| 124,200 -124,299 | 21,114 | 31,050 | 36,018 | 38,502 | 43,470 |
| 124,300 -124,399 | 21,131 | 31,075 | 36,047 | 38,533 | 43,505 |
| 124,400 -124,499 | 21,148 | 31,100 | 36,076 | 38,564 | 43,540 |
| 124,500 -124,599 | 21,165 | 31,125 | 36,105 | 38,595 | 43,575 |
| 124,600 -124,699 | 21,182 | 31,150 | 36,134 | 38,626 | 43,610 |
| 124,700 -124,799 | 21,199 | 31,175 | 36,163 | 38,657 | 43,645 |
| 124,800 -124,899 | 21,216 | 31,200 | 36,192 | 38,688 | 43,680 |
| 124,900 -124,999 | 21,233 | 31,225 | 36,221 | 38,719 | 43,715 |

| ANNUAL INCOME | 1 | NUMBER OF CHILDREN 2 | 3 | 4 | 5+ |
|---|---|---|---|---|---|
| | | ANNUAL OBLIGATION AMOUNT | | | |
| 125,000 -125,099 | 21,250 | 31,250 | 36,250 | 38,750 | 43,750 |
| 125,100 -125,199 | 21,267 | 31,275 | 36,279 | 38,781 | 43,785 |
| 125,200 -125,299 | 21,284 | 31,300 | 36,308 | 38,812 | 43,820 |
| 125,300 -125,399 | 21,301 | 31,325 | 36,337 | 38,843 | 43,855 |
| 125,400 -125,499 | 21,318 | 31,350 | 36,366 | 38,874 | 43,890 |
| 125,500 -125,599 | 21,335 | 31,375 | 36,395 | 38,905 | 43,925 |
| 125,600 -125,699 | 21,352 | 31,400 | 36,424 | 38,936 | 43,960 |
| 125,700 -125,799 | 21,369 | 31,425 | 36,453 | 38,967 | 43,995 |
| 125,800 -125,899 | 21,386 | 31,450 | 36,482 | 38,998 | 44,030 |
| 125,900 -125,999 | 21,403 | 31,475 | 36,511 | 39,029 | 44,065 |

| ANNUAL INCOME | 1 | NUMBER OF CHILDREN 2 | 3 | 4 | 5+ |
|---|---|---|---|---|---|
| | | ANNUAL OBLIGATION AMOUNT | | | |
| 126,000 -126,099 | 21,420 | 31,500 | 36,540 | 39,060 | 44,100 |
| 126,100 -126,199 | 21,437 | 31,525 | 36,569 | 39,091 | 44,135 |
| 126,200 -126,299 | 21,454 | 31,550 | 36,598 | 39,122 | 44,170 |
| 126,300 -126,399 | 21,471 | 31,575 | 36,627 | 39,153 | 44,205 |
| 126,400 -126,499 | 21,488 | 31,600 | 36,656 | 39,184 | 44,240 |
| 126,500 -126,599 | 21,505 | 31,625 | 36,685 | 39,215 | 44,275 |
| 126,600 -126,699 | 21,522 | 31,650 | 36,714 | 39,246 | 44,310 |
| 126,700 -126,799 | 21,539 | 31,675 | 36,743 | 39,277 | 44,345 |
| 126,800 -126,899 | 21,556 | 31,700 | 36,772 | 39,308 | 44,380 |
| 126,900 -126,999 | 21,573 | 31,725 | 36,801 | 39,339 | 44,415 |

| ANNUAL INCOME | 1 | NUMBER OF CHILDREN 2 | 3 | 4 | 5+ |
|---|---|---|---|---|---|
| | | ANNUAL OBLIGATION AMOUNT | | | |
| 127,000 -127,099 | 21,590 | 31,750 | 36,830 | 39,370 | 44,450 |
| 127,100 -127,199 | 21,607 | 31,775 | 36,859 | 39,401 | 44,485 |
| 127,200 -127,299 | 21,624 | 31,800 | 36,888 | 39,432 | 44,520 |
| 127,300 -127,399 | 21,641 | 31,825 | 36,917 | 39,463 | 44,555 |
| 127,400 -127,499 | 21,658 | 31,850 | 36,946 | 39,494 | 44,590 |
| 127,500 -127,599 | 21,675 | 31,875 | 36,975 | 39,525 | 44,625 |
| 127,600 -127,699 | 21,692 | 31,900 | 37,004 | 39,556 | 44,660 |
| 127,700 -127,799 | 21,709 | 31,925 | 37,033 | 39,587 | 44,695 |
| 127,800 -127,899 | 21,726 | 31,950 | 37,062 | 39,618 | 44,730 |
| 127,900 -127,999 | 21,743 | 31,975 | 37,091 | 39,649 | 44,765 |

| ANNUAL INCOME | 1 | NUMBER OF CHILDREN 2 | 3 | 4 | 5+ |
|---|---|---|---|---|---|
| | | ANNUAL OBLIGATION AMOUNT | | | |
| 128,000 -128,099 | 21,760 | 32,000 | 37,120 | 39,680 | 44,800 |
| 128,100 -128,199 | 21,777 | 32,025 | 37,149 | 39,711 | 44,835 |
| 128,200 -128,299 | 21,794 | 32,050 | 37,178 | 39,742 | 44,870 |
| 128,300 -128,399 | 21,811 | 32,075 | 37,207 | 39,773 | 44,905 |
| 128,400 -128,499 | 21,828 | 32,100 | 37,236 | 39,804 | 44,940 |
| 128,500 -128,599 | 21,845 | 32,125 | 37,265 | 39,835 | 44,975 |
| 128,600 -128,699 | 21,862 | 32,150 | 37,294 | 39,866 | 45,010 |
| 128,700 -128,799 | 21,879 | 32,175 | 37,323 | 39,897 | 45,045 |
| 128,800 -128,899 | 21,896 | 32,200 | 37,352 | 39,928 | 45,080 |
| 128,900 -128,999 | 21,913 | 32,225 | 37,381 | 39,959 | 45,115 |

| ANNUAL INCOME | 1 | NUMBER OF CHILDREN 2 | 3 | 4 | 5+ |
|---|---|---|---|---|---|
| | | ANNUAL OBLIGATION AMOUNT | | | |
| 129,000 -129,099 | 21,930 | 32,250 | 37,410 | 39,990 | 45,150 |
| 129,100 -129,199 | 21,947 | 32,275 | 37,439 | 40,021 | 45,185 |
| 129,200 -129,299 | 21,964 | 32,300 | 37,468 | 40,052 | 45,220 |
| 129,300 -129,399 | 21,981 | 32,325 | 37,497 | 40,083 | 45,255 |
| 129,400 -129,499 | 21,998 | 32,350 | 37,526 | 40,114 | 45,290 |
| 129,500 -129,599 | 22,015 | 32,375 | 37,555 | 40,145 | 45,325 |
| 129,600 -129,699 | 22,032 | 32,400 | 37,584 | 40,176 | 45,360 |
| 129,700 -129,799 | 22,049 | 32,425 | 37,613 | 40,207 | 45,395 |
| 129,800 -129,899 | 22,066 | 32,450 | 37,642 | 40,238 | 45,430 |
| 129,900 -129,999 | 22,083 | 32,475 | 37,671 | 40,269 | 45,445 |

13

| ANNUAL INCOME | 1 | 2 | 3 | 4 | 5+ |
|---|---|---|---|---|---|
| | | ANNUAL | OBLIGATION | AMOUNT | |
| 130,000 -130,099 | 22,100 | 32,500 | 37,700 | 40,300 | 45,500 |
| 130,100 -130,199 | 22,117 | 32,525 | 37,729 | 40,331 | 45,535 |
| 130,200 -130,299 | 22,134 | 32,550 | 37,758 | 40,362 | 45,570 |
| 130,300 -130,399 | 22,151 | 32,575 | 37,787 | 40,393 | 45,605 |
| 130,400 -130,499 | 22,168 | 32,600 | 37,816 | 40,424 | 45,640 |
| 130,500 -130,599 | 22,185 | 32,625 | 37,845 | 40,455 | 45,675 |
| 130,600 -130,699 | 22,202 | 32,650 | 37,874 | 40,486 | 45,710 |
| 130,700 -130,799 | 22,219 | 32,675 | 37,903 | 40,517 | 45,745 |
| 130,800 -130,899 | 22,236 | 32,700 | 37,932 | 40,548 | 45,780 |
| 130,900 -130,999 | 22,253 | 32,725 | 37,961 | 40,579 | 45,815 |

| ANNUAL INCOME | 1 | 2 | 3 | 4 | 5+ |
|---|---|---|---|---|---|
| | | ANNUAL | OBLIGATION | AMOUNT | |
| 131,000 -131,099 | 22,270 | 32,750 | 37,990 | 40,610 | 45,850 |
| 131,100 -131,199 | 22,287 | 32,775 | 38,019 | 40,641 | 45,885 |
| 131,200 -131,299 | 22,304 | 32,800 | 38,048 | 40,672 | 45,920 |
| 131,300 -131,399 | 22,321 | 32,825 | 38,077 | 40,703 | 45,955 |
| 131,400 -131,499 | 22,338 | 32,850 | 38,106 | 40,734 | 45,990 |
| 131,500 -131,599 | 22,355 | 32,875 | 38,135 | 40,765 | 46,025 |
| 131,600 -131,699 | 22,372 | 32,900 | 38,164 | 40,796 | 46,060 |
| 131,700 -131,799 | 22,389 | 32,925 | 38,193 | 40,827 | 46,095 |
| 1,800 -131,899 | 22,406 | 32,950 | 38,222 | 40,858 | 46,130 |
| 1,900 -131,999 | 22,423 | 32,975 | 38,251 | 40,889 | 46,165 |

| ANNUAL INCOME | 1 | 2 | 3 | 4 | 5+ |
|---|---|---|---|---|---|
| | | ANNUAL | OBLIGATION | AMOUNT | |
| 132,000 -132,099 | 22,440 | 33,000 | 38,280 | 40,920 | 46,200 |
| 132,100 -132,199 | 22,457 | 33,025 | 38,309 | 40,951 | 46,235 |
| 132,200 -132,299 | 22,474 | 33,050 | 38,338 | 40,982 | 46,270 |
| 132,300 -132,399 | 22,491 | 33,075 | 38,367 | 41,013 | 46,305 |
| 132,400 -132,499 | 22,508 | 33,100 | 38,396 | 41,044 | 46,340 |
| 132,500 -132,599 | 22,525 | 33,125 | 38,425 | 41,075 | 46,375 |
| 132,600 -132,699 | 22,542 | 33,150 | 38,454 | 41,106 | 46,410 |
| 132,700 -132,799 | 22,559 | 33,175 | 38,483 | 41,137 | 46,445 |
| 132,800 -132,899 | 22,576 | 33,200 | 38,512 | 41,168 | 46,480 |
| 132,900 -132,999 | 22,593 | 33,225 | 38,541 | 41,199 | 46,515 |

| ANNUAL INCOME | 1 | 2 | 3 | 4 | 5+ |
|---|---|---|---|---|---|
| | | ANNUAL | OBLIGATION | AMOUNT | |
| 133,000 -133,099 | 22,610 | 33,250 | 38,570 | 41,230 | 46,550 |
| ,100 -133,199 | 22,627 | 33,275 | 38,599 | 41,261 | 46,585 |
| 3,200 -133,299 | 22,644 | 33,300 | 38,628 | 41,292 | 46,620 |
| 133,300 -133,399 | 22,661 | 33,325 | 38,657 | 41,323 | 46,655 |
| 133,400 -133,499 | 22,678 | 33,350 | 38,686 | 41,354 | 46,690 |
| 133,500 -133,599 | 22,695 | 33,375 | 38,715 | 41,385 | 46,725 |
| 133,600 -133,699 | 22,712 | 33,400 | 38,744 | 41,416 | 46,760 |
| 133,700 -133,799 | 22,729 | 33,425 | 38,773 | 41,447 | 46,795 |
| 133,800 -133,899 | 22,746 | 33,450 | 38,802 | 41,478 | 46,830 |
| 133,900 -133,999 | 22,763 | 33,475 | 38,831 | 41,509 | 46,865 |

| ANNUAL INCOME | 1 | 2 | 3 | 4 | 5+ |
|---|---|---|---|---|---|
| | | ANNUAL | OBLIGATION | AMOUNT | |
| 134,000 -134,099 | 22,780 | 33,500 | 38,860 | 41,540 | 46,900 |
| 134,100 -134,199 | 22,797 | 33,525 | 38,889 | 41,571 | 46,935 |
| 134,200 -134,299 | 22,814 | 33,550 | 38,918 | 41,602 | 46,970 |
| 134,300 -134,399 | 22,831 | 33,575 | 38,947 | 41,633 | 47,005 |
| 134,400 -134,499 | 22,848 | 33,600 | 38,976 | 41,664 | 47,040 |
| 134,500 -134,599 | 22,865 | 33,625 | 39,005 | 41,695 | 47,075 |
| 134,600 -134,699 | 22,882 | 33,650 | 39,034 | 41,726 | 47,110 |
| 134,700 -134,799 | 22,899 | 33,675 | 39,063 | 41,757 | 47,145 |
| 134,800 -134,899 | 22,916 | 33,700 | 39,092 | 41,788 | 47,180 |
| 134,900 -134,999 | 22,933 | 33,725 | 39,121 | 41,819 | 47,215 |

| ANNUAL INCOME | 1 | 2 | 3 | 4 | 5 |
|---|---|---|---|---|---|
| | | ANNUAL | OBLIGATION | AMOUNT | |
| 135,000 -135,099 | 22,950 | 33,750 | 39,150 | 41,850 | 47,250 |
| 135,100 -135,199 | 22,967 | 33,775 | 39,179 | 41,881 | 47,285 |
| 135,200 -135,299 | 22,984 | 33,800 | 39,208 | 41,912 | 47,320 |
| 135,300 -135,399 | 23,001 | 33,825 | 39,237 | 41,943 | 47,355 |
| 135,400 -135,499 | 23,018 | 33,850 | 39,266 | 41,974 | 47,390 |
| 135,500 -135,599 | 23,035 | 33,875 | 39,295 | 42,005 | 47,425 |
| 135,600 -135,699 | 23,052 | 33,900 | 39,324 | 42,036 | 47,460 |
| 135,700 -135,799 | 23,069 | 33,925 | 39,353 | 42,067 | 47,495 |
| 135,800 -135,899 | 23,086 | 33,950 | 39,382 | 42,098 | 47,530 |
| 135,900 -135,999 | 23,103 | 33,975 | 39,411 | 42,129 | 47,565 |

| ANNUAL INCOME | 1 | 2 | 3 | 4 | 5+ |
|---|---|---|---|---|---|
| | | ANNUAL | OBLIGATION | AMOUNT | |
| 136,000 -136,099 | 23,120 | 34,000 | 39,440 | 42,160 | 47,600 |
| 136,100 -136,199 | 23,137 | 34,025 | 39,469 | 42,191 | 47,635 |
| 136,200 -136,299 | 23,154 | 34,050 | 39,498 | 42,222 | 47,670 |
| 136,300 -136,399 | 23,171 | 34,075 | 39,527 | 42,253 | 47,705 |
| 136,400 -136,499 | 23,188 | 34,100 | 39,556 | 42,284 | 47,740 |
| 136,500 -136,599 | 23,205 | 34,125 | 39,585 | 42,315 | 47,775 |
| 136,600 -136,699 | 23,222 | 34,150 | 39,614 | 42,346 | 47,810 |
| 136,700 -136,799 | 23,239 | 34,175 | 39,643 | 42,377 | 47,845 |
| 136,800 -136,899 | 23,256 | 34,200 | 39,672 | 42,408 | 47,880 |
| 136,900 -136,999 | 23,273 | 34,225 | 39,701 | 42,439 | 47,915 |

| ANNUAL INCOME | 1 | 2 | 3 | 4 | 5+ |
|---|---|---|---|---|---|
| | | ANNUAL | OBLIGATION | AMOUNT | |
| 137,000 -137,099 | 23,290 | 34,250 | 39,730 | 42,470 | 47,9-- |
| 137,100 -137,199 | 23,307 | 34,275 | 39,759 | 42,501 | 47,-- |
| 137,200 -137,299 | 23,324 | 34,300 | 39,788 | 42,532 | 48,-- |
| 137,300 -137,399 | 23,341 | 34,325 | 39,817 | 42,563 | 48,055 |
| 137,400 -137,499 | 23,358 | 34,350 | 39,846 | 42,594 | 48,090 |
| 137,500 -137,599 | 23,375 | 34,375 | 39,875 | 42,625 | 48,125 |
| 137,600 -137,699 | 23,392 | 34,400 | 39,904 | 42,656 | 48,160 |
| 137,700 -137,799 | 23,409 | 34,425 | 39,933 | 42,687 | 48,195 |
| 137,800 -137,899 | 23,426 | 34,450 | 39,962 | 42,718 | 48,230 |
| 137,900 -137,999 | 23,443 | 34,475 | 39,991 | 42,749 | 48,265 |

| ANNUAL INCOME | 1 | 2 | 3 | 4 | 5+ |
|---|---|---|---|---|---|
| | | ANNUAL | OBLIGATION | AMOUNT | |
| 138,000 -138,099 | 23,460 | 34,500 | 40,020 | 42,780 | 48,300 |
| 138,100 -138,199 | 23,477 | 34,525 | 40,049 | 42,811 | 48,335 |
| 138,200 -138,299 | 23,494 | 34,550 | 40,078 | 42,842 | 48,370 |
| 138,300 -138,399 | 23,511 | 34,575 | 40,107 | 42,873 | 48,405 |
| 138,400 -138,499 | 23,528 | 34,600 | 40,136 | 42,904 | 48,440 |
| 138,500 -138,599 | 23,545 | 34,625 | 40,165 | 42,935 | 48,475 |
| 138,600 -138,699 | 23,562 | 34,650 | 40,194 | 42,966 | 48,510 |
| 138,700 -138,799 | 23,579 | 34,675 | 40,223 | 42,997 | 48,545 |
| 138,800 -138,899 | 23,594 | 34,700 | 40,252 | 43,028 | 48,580 |
| 138,900 -138,999 | 23,613 | 34,725 | 40,281 | 43,059 | 48,615 |

| ANNUAL INCOME | 1 | 2 | 3 | 4 | 5+ |
|---|---|---|---|---|---|
| | | ANNUAL | OBLIGATION | AMOUNT | |
| 139,000 -139,099 | 23,630 | 34,750 | 40,310 | 43,090 | 48,650 |
| 139,100 -139,199 | 23,647 | 34,775 | 40,339 | 43,121 | 48,685 |
| 139,200 -139,299 | 23,664 | 34,800 | 40,368 | 43,152 | 48,720 |
| 139,300 -139,399 | 23,681 | 34,825 | 40,397 | 43,183 | 48,755 |
| 139,400 -139,499 | 23,698 | 34,850 | 40,426 | 43,214 | 48,790 |
| 139,500 -139,599 | 23,715 | 34,875 | 40,455 | 43,245 | 48,-- |
| 139,600 -139,699 | 23,732 | 34,900 | 40,484 | 43,276 | 48,-- |
| 139,700 -139,799 | 23,749 | 34,925 | 40,513 | 43,307 | 48,895 |
| 139,800 -139,899 | 23,766 | 34,950 | 40,542 | 43,338 | 48,930 |
| 139,900 -139,999 | 23,783 | 34,975 | 40,371 | 43,369 | 48,965 |

14

| ANNUAL INCOME | 1 | 2 | 3 | 4 | 5+ |
|---|---|---|---|---|---|
| | | ANNUAL OBLIGATION AMOUNT | | | |
| 140,000 -140,099 | 23,800 | 35,000 | 40,600 | 43,400 | 49,000 |
| 140,100 -140,199 | 23,817 | 35,025 | 40,629 | 43,431 | 49,035 |
| 140,200 -140,299 | 23,834 | 35,050 | 40,658 | 43,462 | 49,070 |
| 140,300 -140,399 | 23,851 | 35,075 | 40,687 | 43,493 | 49,105 |
| 140,400 -140,499 | 23,868 | 35,100 | 40,716 | 43,524 | 49,140 |
| 140,500 -140,599 | 23,885 | 35,125 | 40,745 | 43,555 | 49,175 |
| 140,600 -140,699 | 23,902 | 35,150 | 40,774 | 43,586 | 49,210 |
| 140,700 -140,799 | 23,919 | 35,175 | 40,803 | 43,617 | 49,245 |
| 140,800 -140,899 | 23,936 | 35,200 | 40,832 | 43,648 | 49,280 |
| 140,900 -140,999 | 23,953 | 35,225 | 40,861 | 43,679 | 49,315 |

| ANNUAL INCOME | 1 | 2 | 3 | 4 | 5+ |
|---|---|---|---|---|---|
| | | ANNUAL OBLIGATION AMOUNT | | | |
| 141,000 -141,099 | 23,970 | 35,250 | 40,890 | 43,710 | 49,350 |
| 141,100 -141,199 | 23,987 | 35,275 | 40,919 | 43,741 | 49,385 |
| 141,200 -141,299 | 24,004 | 35,300 | 40,948 | 43,772 | 49,420 |
| 141,300 -141,399 | 24,021 | 35,325 | 40,977 | 43,803 | 49,455 |
| 141,400 -141,499 | 24,038 | 35,350 | 41,006 | 43,834 | 49,490 |
| 141,500 -141,599 | 24,055 | 35,375 | 41,035 | 43,865 | 49,525 |
| 141,600 -141,699 | 24,072 | 35,400 | 41,064 | 43,896 | 49,560 |
| 141,700 -141,799 | 24,089 | 35,425 | 41,093 | 43,927 | 49,595 |
| 141,800 -141,899 | 24,106 | 35,450 | 41,122 | 43,958 | 49,630 |
| 141,900 -141,999 | 24,123 | 35,475 | 41,151 | 43,989 | 49,665 |

| ANNUAL INCOME | 1 | 2 | 3 | 4 | 5+ |
|---|---|---|---|---|---|
| | | ANNUAL OBLIGATION AMOUNT | | | |
| 142,000 -142,099 | 24,140 | 35,500 | 41,180 | 44,020 | 49,700 |
| 142,100 -142,199 | 24,157 | 35,525 | 41,209 | 44,051 | 49,735 |
| 142,200 -142,299 | 24,174 | 35,550 | 41,238 | 44,082 | 49,770 |
| 142,300 -142,399 | 24,191 | 35,575 | 41,267 | 44,113 | 49,805 |
| 142,400 -142,499 | 24,208 | 35,600 | 41,296 | 44,144 | 49,840 |
| 142,500 -142,599 | 24,225 | 35,625 | 41,325 | 44,175 | 49,875 |
| 142,600 -142,699 | 24,242 | 35,650 | 41,354 | 44,206 | 49,910 |
| 142,700 -142,799 | 24,259 | 35,675 | 41,383 | 44,237 | 49,945 |
| 142,800 -142,899 | 24,276 | 35,700 | 41,412 | 44,268 | 49,980 |
| 142,900 -142,999 | 24,293 | 35,725 | 41,441 | 44,299 | 50,015 |

| ANNUAL INCOME | 1 | 2 | 3 | 4 | 5+ |
|---|---|---|---|---|---|
| | | ANNUAL OBLIGATION AMOUNT | | | |
| 143,000 -143,099 | 24,310 | 35,750 | 41,470 | 44,330 | 50,050 |
| 143,100 -143,199 | 24,327 | 35,775 | 41,499 | 44,361 | 50,085 |
| 143,200 -143,299 | 24,344 | 35,800 | 41,528 | 44,392 | 50,120 |
| 143,300 -143,399 | 24,361 | 35,825 | 41,557 | 44,423 | 50,155 |
| 143,400 -143,499 | 24,378 | 35,850 | 41,586 | 44,454 | 50,190 |
| 143,500 -143,599 | 24,395 | 35,875 | 41,615 | 44,485 | 50,225 |
| 143,600 -143,699 | 24,412 | 35,900 | 41,644 | 44,516 | 50,260 |
| 143,700 -143,799 | 24,429 | 35,925 | 41,673 | 44,547 | 50,295 |
| 143,800 -143,899 | 24,446 | 35,950 | 41,702 | 44,578 | 50,330 |
| 143,900 -143,999 | 24,463 | 35,975 | 41,731 | 44,609 | 50,345 |

| ANNUAL INCOME | 1 | 2 | 3 | 4 | 5+ |
|---|---|---|---|---|---|
| | | ANNUAL OBLIGATION AMOUNT | | | |
| 144,000 -144,099 | 24,480 | 36,000 | 41,760 | 44,640 | 50,400 |
| 144,100 -144,199 | 24,497 | 36,025 | 41,789 | 44,671 | 50,435 |
| 144,200 -144,299 | 24,514 | 36,050 | 41,818 | 44,702 | 50,470 |
| 144,300 -144,399 | 24,531 | 36,075 | 41,847 | 44,733 | 50,505 |
| 144,400 -144,499 | 24,548 | 36,100 | 41,876 | 44,764 | 50,540 |
| 144,500 -144,599 | 24,565 | 36,125 | 41,905 | 44,795 | 50,575 |
| 144,600 -144,699 | 24,582 | 36,150 | 41,934 | 44,826 | 50,610 |
| 144,700 -144,799 | 24,599 | 36,175 | 41,943 | 44,857 | 50,645 |
| 144,800 -144,899 | 24,616 | 36,200 | 41,992 | 44,888 | 50,680 |
| 144,900 -144,999 | 24,633 | 36,225 | 42,021 | 44,919 | 50,715 |

| ANNUAL INCOME | 1 | 2 | 3 | 4 | 5+ |
|---|---|---|---|---|---|
| | | ANNUAL OBLIGATION AMOUNT | | | |
| 145,000 -145,099 | 24,650 | 36,250 | 42,050 | 44,950 | 50,750 |
| 145,100 -145,199 | 24,667 | 36,275 | 42,079 | 44,981 | 50,785 |
| 145,200 -145,299 | 24,684 | 36,300 | 42,108 | 45,012 | 50,820 |
| 145,300 -145,399 | 24,701 | 36,325 | 42,137 | 45,043 | 50,855 |
| 145,400 -145,499 | 24,718 | 36,350 | 42,166 | 45,074 | 50,890 |
| 145,500 -145,599 | 24,735 | 36,375 | 42,195 | 45,105 | 50,925 |
| 145,600 -145,699 | 24,752 | 36,400 | 42,224 | 45,136 | 50,960 |
| 145,700 -145,799 | 24,769 | 36,425 | 42,253 | 45,167 | 50,995 |
| 145,800 -145,899 | 24,786 | 36,450 | 42,282 | 45,198 | 51,030 |
| 145,900 -145,999 | 24,803 | 36,475 | 42,311 | 45,229 | 51,065 |

| ANNUAL INCOME | 1 | 2 | 3 | 4 | 5+ |
|---|---|---|---|---|---|
| | | ANNUAL OBLIGATION AMOUNT | | | |
| 146,000 -146,099 | 24,820 | 36,500 | 42,340 | 45,260 | 51,100 |
| 146,100 -146,199 | 24,837 | 36,525 | 42,369 | 45,291 | 51,135 |
| 146,200 -146,299 | 24,854 | 36,550 | 42,398 | 45,322 | 51,170 |
| 146,300 -146,399 | 24,871 | 36,575 | 42,427 | 45,353 | 51,205 |
| 146,400 -146,499 | 24,888 | 36,600 | 42,456 | 45,384 | 51,240 |
| 146,500 -146,599 | 24,905 | 36,625 | 42,485 | 45,415 | 51,275 |
| 146,600 -146,699 | 24,922 | 36,650 | 42,514 | 45,446 | 51,310 |
| 146,700 -146,799 | 24,939 | 36,675 | 42,543 | 45,477 | 51,345 |
| 146,800 -146,899 | 24,956 | 36,700 | 42,572 | 45,508 | 51,380 |
| 146,900 -146,999 | 24,973 | 36,725 | 42,601 | 45,539 | 51,415 |

| ANNUAL INCOME | 1 | 2 | 3 | 4 | 5+ |
|---|---|---|---|---|---|
| | | ANNUAL OBLIGATION AMOUNT | | | |
| 147,000 -147,099 | 24,990 | 36,750 | 42,630 | 45,570 | 51,450 |
| 147,100 -147,199 | 25,007 | 36,775 | 42,659 | 45,601 | 51,485 |
| 147,200 -147,299 | 25,024 | 36,800 | 42,688 | 45,632 | 51,520 |
| 147,300 -147,399 | 25,041 | 36,825 | 42,717 | 45,663 | 51,555 |
| 147,400 -147,499 | 25,058 | 36,850 | 42,746 | 45,694 | 51,590 |
| 147,500 -147,599 | 25,075 | 36,875 | 42,775 | 45,725 | 51,625 |
| 147,600 -147,699 | 25,092 | 36,900 | 42,804 | 45,756 | 51,660 |
| 147,700 -147,799 | 25,109 | 36,925 | 42,833 | 45,787 | 51,695 |
| 147,800 -147,899 | 25,126 | 36,950 | 42,862 | 45,818 | 51,730 |
| 147,900 -147,999 | 25,143 | 36,975 | 42,891 | 45,849 | 51,765 |

| ANNUAL INCOME | 1 | 2 | 3 | 4 | 5+ |
|---|---|---|---|---|---|
| | | ANNUAL OBLIGATION AMOUNT | | | |
| 148,000 -148,099 | 25,160 | 37,000 | 42,920 | 45,880 | 51,800 |
| 148,100 -148,199 | 25,177 | 37,025 | 42,949 | 45,911 | 51,835 |
| 148,200 -148,299 | 25,194 | 37,050 | 42,978 | 45,942 | 51,870 |
| 148,300 -148,399 | 25,211 | 37,075 | 43,007 | 45,973 | 51,905 |
| 148,400 -148,499 | 25,228 | 37,100 | 43,036 | 46,004 | 51,940 |
| 148,500 -148,599 | 25,245 | 37,125 | 43,065 | 46,035 | 51,975 |
| 148,600 -148,699 | 25,262 | 37,150 | 43,094 | 46,066 | 52,010 |
| 148,700 -148,799 | 25,279 | 37,175 | 43,123 | 46,097 | 52,045 |
| 148,800 -148,899 | 25,296 | 37,200 | 43,152 | 46,128 | 52,080 |
| 148,900 -148,999 | 25,313 | 37,225 | 43,181 | 46,159 | 52,115 |

| ANNUAL INCOME | 1 | 2 | 3 | 4 | 5+ |
|---|---|---|---|---|---|
| | | ANNUAL OBLIGATION AMOUNT | | | |
| 149,000 -149,099 | 25,330 | 37,250 | 43,210 | 46,190 | 52,150 |
| 149,100 -149,199 | 25,347 | 37,275 | 43,239 | 46,221 | 52,185 |
| 149,200 -149,299 | 25,364 | 37,300 | 43,268 | 46,252 | 52,220 |
| 149,300 -149,399 | 25,381 | 37,325 | 43,297 | 46,283 | 52,255 |
| 149,400 -149,499 | 25,398 | 37,350 | 43,326 | 46,314 | 52,290 |
| 149,500 -149,599 | 25,415 | 37,375 | 43,355 | 46,345 | 52,325 |
| 149,600 -149,699 | 25,432 | 37,400 | 43,384 | 46,376 | 52,360 |
| 149,700 -149,799 | 25,449 | 37,425 | 43,413 | 46,407 | 52,395 |
| 149,800 -149,899 | 25,466 | 37,450 | 43,442 | 46,438 | 52,430 |
| 149,900 -149,999 | 25,483 | 37,475 | 43,471 | 46,469 | 52,465 |

15

| ANNUAL INCOME | 1 | 2 | 3 | 4 | 5+ |
|---|---|---|---|---|---|
| | | ANNUAL OBLIGATION AMOUNT | | | |
| 150,000 -150,099 | 25,500 | 37,500 | 43,500 | 44,500 | 52,500 |
| 150,100 -150,199 | 25,317 | 37,525 | 43,529 | 44,531 | 52,535 |
| 150,200 -150,299 | 25,334 | 37,550 | 43,558 | 44,562 | 52,570 |
| 150,300 -150,399 | 25,551 | 37,575 | 43,587 | 44,593 | 52,605 |
| 150,400 -150,499 | 25,568 | 37,600 | 43,616 | 44,624 | 52,640 |
| 150,500 -150,599 | 25,585 | 37,625 | 43,645 | 44,655 | 52,675 |
| 150,600 -150,699 | 25,602 | 37,650 | 43,674 | 44,686 | 52,710 |
| 150,700 -150,799 | 25,619 | 37,675 | 43,703 | 44,717 | 52,745 |
| 150,800 -150,899 | 25,636 | 37,700 | 43,732 | 44,748 | 52,780 |
| 150,900 -150,999 | 25,653 | 37,725 | 43,761 | 44,779 | 52,815 |

| ANNUAL INCOME | 1 | 2 | 3 | 4 | 5+ |
|---|---|---|---|---|---|
| | | ANNUAL OBLIGATION AMOUNT | | | |
| 155,000 -155,099 | 26,350 | 38,750 | 44,950 | 48,050 | 54,250 |
| 155,100 -155,199 | 26,367 | 38,775 | 44,979 | 48,081 | 54,285 |
| 155,200 -155,299 | 26,384 | 38,800 | 45,008 | 48,112 | 54,320 |
| 155,300 -155,399 | 26,401 | 38,825 | 45,037 | 48,143 | 54,355 |
| 155,400 -155,499 | 26,418 | 38,850 | 45,066 | 48,174 | 54,390 |
| 155,500 -155,599 | 26,435 | 38,875 | 45,095 | 48,205 | 54,425 |
| 155,600 -155,699 | 26,452 | 38,900 | 45,124 | 48,236 | 54,460 |
| 155,700 -155,799 | 26,469 | 38,925 | 45,153 | 48,267 | 54,495 |
| 155,800 -155,899 | 26,486 | 38,950 | 45,182 | 48,298 | 54,530 |
| 155,900 -155,999 | 26,503 | 38,975 | 45,211 | 48,329 | 54,565 |

| ANNUAL INCOME | 1 | 2 | 3 | 4 | 5+ |
|---|---|---|---|---|---|
| | | ANNUAL OBLIGATION AMOUNT | | | |
| 151,000 -151,099 | 25,670 | 37,750 | 43,790 | 44,810 | 52,850 |
| 151,100 -151,199 | 25,687 | 37,775 | 43,819 | 44,841 | 52,885 |
| 151,200 -151,299 | 25,704 | 37,800 | 43,848 | 44,872 | 52,920 |
| 151,300 -151,399 | 25,721 | 37,825 | 43,877 | 44,903 | 52,955 |
| 151,400 -151,499 | 25,738 | 37,850 | 43,906 | 44,934 | 52,990 |
| 151,500 -151,599 | 25,755 | 37,875 | 43,935 | 44,965 | 53,025 |
| 51,600 -151,699 | 25,772 | 37,900 | 43,964 | 44,996 | 53,060 |
| 51,700 -151,799 | 25,789 | 37,925 | 43,993 | 47,027 | 53,095 |
| 151,800 -151,899 | 25,806 | 37,950 | 44,022 | 47,058 | 53,130 |
| 151,900 -151,999 | 25,823 | 37,975 | 44,051 | 47,089 | 53,165 |

| ANNUAL INCOME | 1 | 2 | 3 | 4 | 5+ |
|---|---|---|---|---|---|
| | | ANNUAL OBLIGATION AMOUNT | | | |
| 156,000 -156,099 | 26,520 | 39,000 | 45,240 | 48,360 | 54,600 |
| 156,100 -156,199 | 26,537 | 39,025 | 45,269 | 48,391 | 54,635 |
| 156,200 -156,299 | 26,554 | 39,050 | 45,298 | 48,422 | 54,670 |
| 156,300 -156,399 | 26,571 | 39,075 | 45,327 | 48,453 | 54,705 |
| 156,400 -156,499 | 26,588 | 39,100 | 45,356 | 48,484 | 54,740 |
| 156,500 -156,599 | 26,605 | 39,125 | 45,385 | 48,515 | 54,775 |
| 156,600 -156,699 | 26,622 | 39,150 | 45,414 | 48,546 | 54,810 |
| 156,700 -156,799 | 26,639 | 39,175 | 45,443 | 48,577 | 54,845 |
| 156,800 -156,899 | 26,656 | 39,200 | 45,472 | 48,608 | 54,880 |
| 156,900 -156,999 | 26,673 | 39,225 | 45,501 | 48,639 | 54,915 |

| ANNUAL INCOME | 1 | 2 | 3 | 4 | 5+ |
|---|---|---|---|---|---|
| | | ANNUAL OBLIGATION AMOUNT | | | |
| 152,000 -152,099 | 25,840 | 38,000 | 44,080 | 47,120 | 53,200 |
| 152,100 -152,199 | 25,857 | 38,025 | 44,109 | 47,151 | 53,235 |
| 152,200 -152,299 | 25,874 | 38,050 | 44,138 | 47,182 | 53,270 |
| 152,300 -152,399 | 25,891 | 38,075 | 44,167 | 47,213 | 53,305 |
| 152,400 -152,499 | 25,908 | 38,100 | 44,196 | 47,244 | 53,340 |
| 152,500 -152,599 | 25,925 | 38,125 | 44,225 | 47,275 | 53,375 |
| 152,600 -152,699 | 25,942 | 38,150 | 44,254 | 47,306 | 53,410 |
| 152,700 -152,799 | 25,959 | 38,175 | 44,283 | 47,337 | 53,445 |
| 152,800 -152,899 | 25,976 | 38,200 | 44,312 | 47,368 | 53,480 |
| 152,900 -152,999 | 25,993 | 38,225 | 44,341 | 47,399 | 53,515 |

| ANNUAL INCOME | 1 | 2 | 3 | 4 | 5+ |
|---|---|---|---|---|---|
| | | ANNUAL OBLIGATION AMOUNT | | | |
| 157,000 -157,099 | 26,690 | 39,250 | 45,530 | 48,670 | 54,950 |
| 157,100 -157,199 | 26,707 | 39,275 | 45,559 | 48,701 | 54,985 |
| 157,200 -157,299 | 26,724 | 39,300 | 45,588 | 48,732 | 55,020 |
| 157,300 -157,399 | 26,741 | 39,325 | 45,617 | 48,763 | 55,055 |
| 157,400 -157,499 | 26,758 | 39,350 | 45,646 | 48,794 | 55,090 |
| 157,500 -157,599 | 26,775 | 39,375 | 45,675 | 48,825 | 55,125 |
| 157,600 -157,699 | 26,792 | 39,400 | 45,704 | 48,856 | 55,160 |
| 157,700 -157,799 | 26,809 | 39,425 | 45,733 | 48,887 | 55,195 |
| 157,800 -157,899 | 26,826 | 39,450 | 45,762 | 48,918 | 55,230 |
| 157,900 -157,999 | 26,843 | 39,475 | 45,791 | 48,949 | 55,265 |

| ANNUAL INCOME | 1 | 2 | 3 | 4 | 5+ |
|---|---|---|---|---|---|
| | | ANNUAL OBLIGATION AMOUNT | | | |
| 153,000 -153,099 | 26,010 | 38,250 | 44,370 | 47,430 | 53,350 |
| 153,100 -153,199 | 26,027 | 38,275 | 44,399 | 47,461 | 53,585 |
| 153,200 -153,299 | 26,044 | 38,300 | 44,428 | 47,492 | 53,620 |
| 153,300 -153,399 | 26,061 | 38,325 | 44,457 | 47,523 | 53,655 |
| 153,400 -153,499 | 26,078 | 38,350 | 44,486 | 47,554 | 53,690 |
| 153,500 -153,599 | 26,095 | 38,375 | 44,515 | 47,585 | 53,725 |
| 153,600 -153,699 | 26,112 | 38,400 | 44,544 | 47,616 | 53,760 |
| 153,700 -153,799 | 26,129 | 38,425 | 44,573 | 47,647 | 53,795 |
| 153,800 -153,899 | 26,144 | 38,450 | 44,602 | 47,678 | 53,830 |
| 153,900 -153,999 | 26,163 | 38,475 | 44,631 | 47,709 | 53,865 |

| ANNUAL INCOME | 1 | 2 | 3 | 4 | 5+ |
|---|---|---|---|---|---|
| | | ANNUAL OBLIGATION AMOUNT | | | |
| 158,000 -158,099 | 26,860 | 39,500 | 45,820 | 48,980 | 55,300 |
| 158,100 -158,199 | 26,877 | 39,525 | 45,849 | 49,011 | 55,335 |
| 158,200 -158,299 | 26,894 | 39,550 | 45,878 | 49,042 | 55,370 |
| 158,300 -158,399 | 26,911 | 39,575 | 45,907 | 49,073 | 55,405 |
| 158,400 -158,499 | 26,928 | 39,600 | 45,936 | 49,104 | 55,440 |
| 158,500 -158,599 | 26,945 | 39,625 | 45,965 | 49,135 | 55,475 |
| 158,600 -158,699 | 26,962 | 39,650 | 45,994 | 49,166 | 55,510 |
| 158,700 -158,799 | 26,979 | 39,675 | 46,023 | 49,197 | 55,545 |
| 158,800 -158,899 | 26,996 | 39,700 | 46,052 | 49,228 | 55,580 |
| 158,900 -158,999 | 27,013 | 39,725 | 46,081 | 49,259 | 55,615 |

| ANNUAL INCOME | 1 | 2 | 3 | 4 | 5+ |
|---|---|---|---|---|---|
| | | ANNUAL OBLIGATION AMOUNT | | | |
| 154,000 -154,099 | 26,180 | 38,500 | 44,660 | 47,740 | 53,900 |
| 154,100 -154,199 | 26,197 | 38,525 | 44,689 | 47,771 | 53,935 |
| 154,200 -154,299 | 26,214 | 38,550 | 44,718 | 47,802 | 53,970 |
| 154,300 -154,399 | 26,231 | 38,575 | 44,747 | 47,833 | 54,005 |
| 154,400 -154,499 | 26,248 | 38,600 | 44,776 | 47,864 | 54,040 |
| 154,500 -154,599 | 26,265 | 38,625 | 44,805 | 47,895 | 54,075 |
| 154,600 -154,699 | 26,282 | 38,650 | 44,834 | 47,926 | 54,110 |
| 154,700 -154,799 | 26,299 | 38,675 | 44,863 | 47,957 | 54,145 |
| 154,800 -154,899 | 26,316 | 38,700 | 44,892 | 47,988 | 54,180 |
| 154,900 -154,999 | 26,333 | 38,725 | 44,921 | 48,019 | 54,215 |

| ANNUAL INCOME | 1 | 2 | 3 | 4 | 5+ |
|---|---|---|---|---|---|
| | | ANNUAL OBLIGATION AMOUNT | | | |
| 159,000 -159,099 | 27,030 | 39,750 | 46,110 | 49,290 | 55,650 |
| 159,100 -159,199 | 27,047 | 39,775 | 46,139 | 49,321 | 55,685 |
| 159,200 -159,299 | 27,064 | 39,800 | 46,168 | 49,352 | 55,720 |
| 159,300 -159,399 | 27,081 | 39,825 | 46,197 | 49,383 | 55,755 |
| 159,400 -159,499 | 27,098 | 39,850 | 46,226 | 49,414 | 55,790 |
| 159,500 -159,599 | 27,115 | 39,875 | 46,255 | 49,445 | 55 |
| 159,600 -159,699 | 27,132 | 39,900 | 46,284 | 49,476 | 55 |
| 159,700 -159,799 | 27,149 | 39,925 | 46,313 | 49,507 | 55,8.. |
| 159,800 -159,899 | 27,166 | 39,950 | 46,342 | 49,538 | 55,930 |
| 159,900 -159,999 | 27,183 | 39,975 | 46,371 | 49,569 | 55,965 |

16

236

| ANNUAL INCOME | NUMBER OF CHILDREN 1 | 2 | 3 | 4 | 5+ |
|---|---|---|---|---|---|
| | | ANNUAL OBLIGATION AMOUNT | | | |
| 160,000 -160,099 | 27,200 | 40,000 | 46,400 | 49,600 | 56,000 |
| 160,100 -160,199 | 27,217 | 40,025 | 46,429 | 49,631 | 56,035 |
| 160,200 -160,299 | 27,234 | 40,050 | 46,458 | 49,662 | 56,070 |
| 160,300 -160,399 | 27,251 | 40,075 | 46,487 | 49,693 | 56,105 |
| 160,400 -160,499 | 27,268 | 40,100 | 46,516 | 49,724 | 56,140 |
| 160,500 -160,599 | 27,285 | 40,125 | 46,545 | 49,755 | 56,175 |
| 160,600 -160,699 | 27,302 | 40,150 | 46,574 | 49,786 | 56,210 |
| 160,700 -160,799 | 27,319 | 40,175 | 46,603 | 49,817 | 56,245 |
| 160,800 -160,899 | 27,336 | 40,200 | 46,632 | 49,848 | 56,280 |
| 160,900 -160,999 | 27,353 | 40,225 | 46,661 | 49,879 | 56,315 |

| ANNUAL INCOME | NUMBER OF CHILDREN 1 | 2 | 3 | 4 | 5+ |
|---|---|---|---|---|---|
| | | ANNUAL OBLIGATION AMOUNT | | | |
| 161,000 -161,099 | 27,370 | 40,250 | 46,690 | 49,910 | 56,350 |
| 161,100 -161,199 | 27,387 | 40,275 | 46,719 | 49,941 | 56,385 |
| 161,200 -161,299 | 27,404 | 40,300 | 46,748 | 49,972 | 56,420 |
| 161,300 -161,399 | 27,421 | 40,325 | 46,777 | 50,003 | 56,455 |
| 161,400 -161,499 | 27,438 | 40,350 | 46,806 | 50,034 | 56,490 |
| 161,500 -161,599 | 27,455 | 40,375 | 46,835 | 50,065 | 56,525 |
| 161,600 -161,699 | 27,472 | 40,400 | 46,864 | 50,096 | 56,560 |
| 161,700 -161,799 | 27,489 | 40,425 | 46,893 | 50,127 | 56,595 |
| 161,800 -161,899 | 27,506 | 40,450 | 46,922 | 50,158 | 56,630 |
| 161,900 -161,999 | 27,523 | 40,475 | 46,951 | 50,189 | 56,665 |

| ANNUAL INCOME | NUMBER OF CHILDREN 1 | 2 | 3 | 4 | 5+ |
|---|---|---|---|---|---|
| | | ANNUAL OBLIGATION AMOUNT | | | |
| 162,000 -162,099 | 27,540 | 40,500 | 46,980 | 50,220 | 56,700 |
| 162,100 -162,199 | 27,557 | 40,525 | 47,009 | 50,251 | 56,735 |
| 162,200 -162,299 | 27,574 | 40,550 | 47,038 | 50,282 | 56,770 |
| 162,300 -162,399 | 27,591 | 40,575 | 47,067 | 50,313 | 56,805 |
| 162,400 -162,499 | 27,608 | 40,600 | 47,096 | 50,344 | 56,840 |
| 162,500 -162,599 | 27,625 | 40,625 | 47,125 | 50,375 | 56,875 |
| 162,600 -162,699 | 27,642 | 40,650 | 47,154 | 50,406 | 56,910 |
| 162,700 -162,799 | 27,659 | 40,675 | 47,183 | 50,437 | 56,945 |
| 162,800 -162,899 | 27,676 | 40,700 | 47,212 | 50,468 | 56,980 |
| 162,900 -162,999 | 27,693 | 40,725 | 47,241 | 50,499 | 57,015 |

| ANNUAL INCOME | NUMBER OF CHILDREN 1 | 2 | 3 | 4 | 5+ |
|---|---|---|---|---|---|
| | | ANNUAL OBLIGATION AMOUNT | | | |
| 163,000 -163,099 | 27,710 | 40,750 | 47,270 | 50,530 | 57,050 |
| 163,100 -163,199 | 27,727 | 40,775 | 47,299 | 50,561 | 57,085 |
| 163,200 -163,299 | 27,744 | 40,800 | 47,328 | 50,592 | 57,120 |
| 163,300 -163,399 | 27,761 | 40,825 | 47,357 | 50,623 | 57,155 |
| 163,400 -163,499 | 27,778 | 40,850 | 47,386 | 50,654 | 57,190 |
| 163,500 -163,599 | 27,795 | 40,875 | 47,415 | 50,685 | 57,225 |
| 163,600 -163,699 | 27,812 | 40,900 | 47,444 | 50,716 | 57,260 |
| 163,700 -163,799 | 27,829 | 40,925 | 47,473 | 50,747 | 57,295 |
| 163,800 -163,899 | 27,846 | 40,950 | 47,502 | 50,778 | 57,330 |
| 163,900 -163,999 | 27,863 | 40,975 | 47,531 | 50,809 | 57,365 |

| ANNUAL INCOME | NUMBER OF CHILDREN 1 | 2 | 3 | 4 | 5+ |
|---|---|---|---|---|---|
| | | ANNUAL OBLIGATION AMOUNT | | | |
| 164,000 -164,099 | 27,880 | 41,000 | 47,560 | 50,840 | 57,400 |
| 164,100 -164,199 | 27,897 | 41,025 | 47,589 | 50,871 | 57,435 |
| 164,200 -164,299 | 27,914 | 41,050 | 47,618 | 50,902 | 57,470 |
| 164,300 -164,399 | 27,931 | 41,075 | 47,647 | 50,933 | 57,505 |
| 164,400 -164,499 | 27,948 | 41,100 | 47,676 | 50,964 | 57,540 |
| 164,500 -164,599 | 27,965 | 41,125 | 47,705 | 50,995 | 57,575 |
| 164,600 -164,699 | 27,982 | 41,150 | 47,734 | 51,026 | 57,610 |
| 164,700 -164,799 | 27,999 | 41,175 | 47,763 | 51,057 | 57,645 |
| 164,800 -164,899 | 28,016 | 41,200 | 47,792 | 51,088 | 57,680 |
| 164,900 -164,999 | 28,033 | 41,225 | 47,821 | 51,119 | 57,715 |

| ANNUAL INCOME | NUMBER OF CHILDREN 1 | 2 | 3 | 4 | 5+ |
|---|---|---|---|---|---|
| | | ANNUAL OBLIGATION AMOUNT | | | |
| 165,000 -165,099 | 28,050 | 41,250 | 47,850 | 51,150 | 57,750 |
| 165,100 -165,199 | 28,067 | 41,275 | 47,879 | 51,181 | 57,785 |
| 165,200 -165,299 | 28,084 | 41,300 | 47,908 | 51,212 | 57,820 |
| 165,300 -165,399 | 28,101 | 41,325 | 47,937 | 51,243 | 57,855 |
| 165,400 -165,499 | 28,118 | 41,350 | 47,966 | 51,274 | 57,890 |
| 165,500 -165,599 | 28,135 | 41,375 | 47,995 | 51,305 | 57,925 |
| 165,600 -165,699 | 28,152 | 41,400 | 48,024 | 51,336 | 57,960 |
| 165,700 -165,799 | 28,169 | 41,425 | 48,053 | 51,367 | 57,995 |
| 165,800 -165,899 | 28,186 | 41,450 | 48,082 | 51,398 | 58,030 |
| 165,900 -165,999 | 28,203 | 41,475 | 48,111 | 51,429 | 58,065 |

| ANNUAL INCOME | NUMBER OF CHILDREN 1 | 2 | 3 | 4 | 5+ |
|---|---|---|---|---|---|
| | | ANNUAL OBLIGATION AMOUNT | | | |
| 166,000 -166,099 | 28,220 | 41,500 | 48,140 | 51,460 | 58,100 |
| 166,100 -166,199 | 28,237 | 41,525 | 48,169 | 51,491 | 58,135 |
| 166,200 -166,299 | 28,254 | 41,550 | 48,198 | 51,522 | 58,170 |
| 166,300 -166,399 | 28,271 | 41,575 | 48,227 | 51,553 | 58,205 |
| 166,400 -166,499 | 28,288 | 41,600 | 48,256 | 51,584 | 58,240 |
| 166,500 -166,599 | 28,305 | 41,625 | 48,285 | 51,615 | 58,275 |
| 166,600 -166,699 | 28,322 | 41,650 | 48,314 | 51,646 | 58,310 |
| 166,700 -166,799 | 28,339 | 41,675 | 48,343 | 51,677 | 58,345 |
| 166,800 -166,899 | 28,356 | 41,700 | 48,372 | 51,708 | 58,380 |
| 166,900 -166,999 | 28,373 | 41,725 | 48,401 | 51,739 | 58,415 |

| ANNUAL INCOME | NUMBER OF CHILDREN 1 | 2 | 3 | 4 | 5+ |
|---|---|---|---|---|---|
| | | ANNUAL OBLIGATION AMOUNT | | | |
| 167,000 -167,099 | 28,390 | 41,750 | 48,430 | 51,770 | 58,450 |
| 167,100 -167,199 | 28,407 | 41,775 | 48,459 | 51,801 | 58,485 |
| 167,200 -167,299 | 28,424 | 41,800 | 48,488 | 51,832 | 58,520 |
| 167,300 -167,399 | 28,441 | 41,825 | 48,517 | 51,863 | 58,555 |
| 167,400 -167,499 | 28,458 | 41,850 | 48,546 | 51,894 | 58,590 |
| 167,500 -167,599 | 28,475 | 41,875 | 48,575 | 51,925 | 58,625 |
| 167,600 -167,699 | 28,492 | 41,900 | 48,604 | 51,956 | 58,660 |
| 167,700 -167,799 | 28,509 | 41,925 | 48,633 | 51,987 | 58,695 |
| 167,800 -167,899 | 28,526 | 41,950 | 48,662 | 52,018 | 58,730 |
| 167,900 -167,999 | 28,543 | 41,975 | 48,691 | 52,049 | 58,765 |

| ANNUAL INCOME | NUMBER OF CHILDREN 1 | 2 | 3 | 4 | 5+ |
|---|---|---|---|---|---|
| | | ANNUAL OBLIGATION AMOUNT | | | |
| 168,000 -168,099 | 28,560 | 42,000 | 48,720 | 52,080 | 58,800 |
| 168,100 -168,199 | 28,577 | 42,025 | 48,749 | 52,111 | 58,835 |
| 168,200 -168,299 | 28,594 | 42,050 | 48,778 | 52,142 | 58,870 |
| 168,300 -168,399 | 28,611 | 42,075 | 48,807 | 52,173 | 58,905 |
| 168,400 -168,499 | 28,628 | 42,100 | 48,836 | 52,204 | 58,940 |
| 168,500 -168,599 | 28,645 | 42,125 | 48,865 | 52,235 | 58,975 |
| 168,600 -168,699 | 28,662 | 42,150 | 48,894 | 52,266 | 59,010 |
| 168,700 -168,799 | 28,679 | 42,175 | 48,923 | 52,297 | 59,045 |
| 168,800 -168,899 | 28,696 | 42,200 | 48,952 | 52,328 | 59,080 |
| 168,900 -168,999 | 28,713 | 42,225 | 48,981 | 52,359 | 59,115 |

| ANNUAL INCOME | NUMBER OF CHILDREN 1 | 2 | 3 | 4 | 5+ |
|---|---|---|---|---|---|
| | | ANNUAL OBLIGATION AMOUNT | | | |
| 169,000 -169,099 | 28,730 | 42,250 | 49,010 | 52,390 | 59,150 |
| 169,100 -169,199 | 28,747 | 42,275 | 49,039 | 52,421 | 59,185 |
| 169,200 -169,299 | 28,764 | 42,300 | 49,068 | 52,452 | 59,220 |
| 169,300 -169,399 | 28,781 | 42,325 | 49,097 | 52,483 | 59,255 |
| 169,400 -169,499 | 28,798 | 42,350 | 49,126 | 52,514 | 59,290 |
| 169,500 -169,599 | 28,815 | 42,375 | 49,155 | 52,545 | 59,325 |
| 169,600 -169,699 | 28,832 | 42,400 | 49,184 | 52,576 | 59,360 |
| 169,700 -169,799 | 28,849 | 42,425 | 49,213 | 52,607 | 59,395 |
| 169,800 -169,899 | 28,866 | 42,450 | 49,242 | 52,638 | 59,430 |
| 169,900 -169,999 | 28,883 | 42,475 | 49,271 | 52,669 | 59,465 |

17

| ANNUAL INCOME | 1 | NUMBER OF CHILDREN 2 | 3 | 4 | 5+ |
|---|---|---|---|---|---|
| | | ANNUAL OBLIGATION AMOUNT | | | |
| 170,000 -170,099 | 28,900 | 42,500 | 49,300 | 52,700 | 59,500 |
| 170,100 -170,199 | 28,917 | 42,525 | 49,329 | 52,731 | 59,535 |
| 170,200 -170,299 | 28,934 | 42,550 | 49,358 | 52,762 | 59,570 |
| 170,300 -170,399 | 28,951 | 42,575 | 49,387 | 52,793 | 59,605 |
| 170,400 -170,499 | 28,968 | 42,600 | 49,416 | 52,824 | 59,640 |
| 170,500 -170,599 | 28,985 | 42,625 | 49,445 | 52,855 | 59,675 |
| 170,600 -170,699 | 29,002 | 42,650 | 49,474 | 52,886 | 59,710 |
| 170,700 -170,799 | 29,019 | 42,675 | 49,503 | 52,917 | 59,745 |
| 170,800 -170,899 | 29,036 | 42,700 | 49,532 | 52,948 | 59,780 |
| 170,900 -170,999 | 29,053 | 42,725 | 49,561 | 52,979 | 59,815 |

| ANNUAL INCOME | 1 | NUMBER OF CHILDREN 2 | 3 | 4 | 5+ |
|---|---|---|---|---|---|
| | | ANNUAL OBLIGATION AMOUNT | | | |
| 171,000 -171,099 | 29,070 | 42,750 | 49,590 | 53,010 | 59,850 |
| 171,100 -171,199 | 29,087 | 42,775 | 49,619 | 53,041 | 59,885 |
| 171,200 -171,299 | 29,104 | 42,800 | 49,648 | 53,072 | 59,920 |
| 171,300 -171,399 | 29,121 | 42,825 | 49,677 | 53,103 | 59,955 |
| 171,400 -171,499 | 29,138 | 42,850 | 49,706 | 53,134 | 59,990 |
| 171,500 -171,599 | 29,155 | 42,875 | 49,735 | 53,165 | 60,025 |
| 171,600 -171,699 | 29,172 | 42,900 | 49,764 | 53,196 | 60,060 |
| 1,700 -171,799 | 29,189 | 42,925 | 49,793 | 53,227 | 60,095 |
| 1,800 -171,899 | 29,206 | 42,950 | 49,822 | 53,258 | 60,130 |
| 171,900 -171,999 | 29,223 | 42,975 | 49,851 | 53,289 | 60,165 |

| ANNUAL INCOME | 1 | NUMBER OF CHILDREN 2 | 3 | 4 | 5+ |
|---|---|---|---|---|---|
| | | ANNUAL OBLIGATION AMOUNT | | | |
| 172,000 -172,099 | 29,240 | 43,000 | 49,880 | 53,320 | 60,200 |
| 172,100 -172,199 | 29,257 | 43,025 | 49,909 | 53,351 | 60,235 |
| 172,200 -172,299 | 29,274 | 43,050 | 49,938 | 53,382 | 60,270 |
| 172,300 -172,399 | 29,291 | 43,075 | 49,967 | 53,413 | 60,305 |
| 172,400 -172,499 | 29,308 | 43,100 | 49,996 | 53,444 | 60,340 |
| 172,500 -172,599 | 29,325 | 43,125 | 50,025 | 53,475 | 60,375 |
| 172,600 -172,699 | 29,342 | 43,150 | 50,054 | 53,506 | 60,410 |
| 172,700 -172,799 | 29,359 | 43,175 | 50,083 | 53,537 | 60,445 |
| 172,800 -172,899 | 29,376 | 43,200 | 50,112 | 53,568 | 60,480 |
| 172,900 -172,999 | 29,393 | 43,225 | 50,141 | 53,599 | 60,515 |

| ANNUAL INCOME | 1 | NUMBER OF CHILDREN 2 | 3 | 4 | 5+ |
|---|---|---|---|---|---|
| | | ANNUAL OBLIGATION AMOUNT | | | |
| 73,000 -173,099 | 29,410 | 43,250 | 50,170 | 53,630 | 60,550 |
| 173,100 -173,199 | 29,427 | 43,275 | 50,199 | 53,661 | 60,585 |
| 173,200 -173,299 | 29,444 | 43,300 | 50,228 | 53,692 | 60,620 |
| 173,300 -173,399 | 29,461 | 43,325 | 50,257 | 53,723 | 60,655 |
| 173,400 -173,499 | 29,478 | 43,350 | 50,286 | 53,754 | 60,690 |
| 173,500 -173,599 | 29,495 | 43,375 | 50,315 | 53,785 | 60,725 |
| 173,600 -173,699 | 29,512 | 43,400 | 50,344 | 53,816 | 60,760 |
| 173,700 -173,799 | 29,529 | 43,425 | 50,373 | 53,847 | 60,795 |
| 173,800 -173,899 | 29,544 | 43,450 | 50,402 | 53,878 | 60,830 |
| 173,900 -173,999 | 29,543 | 43,475 | 50,431 | 53,909 | 60,865 |

| ANNUAL INCOME | 1 | NUMBER OF CHILDREN 2 | 3 | 4 | 5+ |
|---|---|---|---|---|---|
| | | ANNUAL OBLIGATION AMOUNT | | | |
| 174,000 -174,099 | 29,580 | 43,500 | 50,440 | 53,940 | 60,900 |
| 174,100 -174,199 | 29,597 | 43,525 | 50,489 | 53,971 | 60,935 |
| 174,200 -174,299 | 29,614 | 43,550 | 50,518 | 54,002 | 60,970 |
| 174,300 -174,399 | 29,631 | 43,575 | 50,547 | 54,033 | 61,005 |
| 174,400 -174,499 | 29,648 | 43,600 | 50,576 | 54,064 | 61,040 |
| 174,500 -174,599 | 29,665 | 43,625 | 50,605 | 54,095 | 61,075 |
| 174,600 -174,699 | 29,682 | 43,650 | 50,634 | 54,126 | 61,110 |
| 174,700 -174,799 | 29,699 | 43,675 | 50,663 | 54,157 | 61,145 |
| 174,800 -174,899 | 29,716 | 43,700 | 50,692 | 54,188 | 61,180 |
| 174,900 -174,999 | 29,733 | 43,725 | 50,721 | 54,219 | 61,215 |

| ANNUAL INCOME | 1 | NUMBER OF CHILDREN 2 | 3 | 4 | 5+ |
|---|---|---|---|---|---|
| | | ANNUAL OBLIGATION AMOUNT | | | |
| 175,000 -175,099 | 29,750 | 43,750 | 50,750 | 54,250 | 61,250 |
| 175,100 -175,199 | 29,767 | 43,775 | 50,779 | 54,281 | 61,285 |
| 175,200 -175,299 | 29,784 | 43,800 | 50,808 | 54,312 | 61,320 |
| 175,300 -175,399 | 29,801 | 43,825 | 50,837 | 54,343 | 61,355 |
| 175,400 -175,499 | 29,818 | 43,850 | 50,866 | 54,374 | 61,390 |
| 175,500 -175,599 | 29,835 | 43,875 | 50,895 | 54,405 | 61,425 |
| 175,600 -175,699 | 29,852 | 43,900 | 50,924 | 54,436 | 61,460 |
| 175,700 -175,799 | 29,869 | 43,925 | 50,953 | 54,467 | 61,495 |
| 175,800 -175,899 | 29,886 | 43,950 | 50,982 | 54,498 | 61,530 |
| 175,900 -175,999 | 29,903 | 43,975 | 51,011 | 54,529 | 61,565 |

| ANNUAL INCOME | 1 | NUMBER OF CHILDREN 2 | 3 | 4 | 5+ |
|---|---|---|---|---|---|
| | | ANNUAL OBLIGATION AMOUNT | | | |
| 176,000 -176,099 | 29,920 | 44,000 | 51,040 | 54,560 | 61,600 |
| 176,100 -176,199 | 29,937 | 44,025 | 51,069 | 54,591 | 61,635 |
| 176,200 -176,299 | 29,954 | 44,050 | 51,098 | 54,622 | 61,670 |
| 176,300 -176,399 | 29,971 | 44,075 | 51,127 | 54,653 | 61,705 |
| 176,400 -176,499 | 29,988 | 44,100 | 51,156 | 54,684 | 61,740 |
| 176,500 -176,599 | 30,005 | 44,125 | 51,185 | 54,715 | 61,775 |
| 176,600 -176,699 | 30,022 | 44,150 | 51,214 | 54,746 | 61,810 |
| 176,700 -176,799 | 30,039 | 44,175 | 51,243 | 54,777 | 61,845 |
| 176,800 -176,899 | 30,056 | 44,200 | 51,272 | 54,808 | 61,880 |
| 176,900 -176,999 | 30,073 | 44,225 | 51,301 | 54,839 | 61,915 |

| ANNUAL INCOME | 1 | NUMBER OF CHILDREN 2 | 3 | 4 | 5+ |
|---|---|---|---|---|---|
| | | ANNUAL OBLIGATION AMOUNT | | | |
| 177,000 -177,099 | 30,090 | 44,250 | 51,330 | 54,870 | 61,950 |
| 177,100 -177,199 | 30,107 | 44,275 | 51,359 | 54,901 | 61,985 |
| 177,200 -177,299 | 30,124 | 44,300 | 51,388 | 54,932 | 62,020 |
| 177,300 -177,399 | 30,141 | 44,325 | 51,417 | 54,963 | 62,L |
| 177,400 -177,499 | 30,158 | 44,350 | 51,446 | 54,994 | 62,090 |
| 177,500 -177,599 | 30,175 | 44,375 | 51,475 | 55,025 | 62,125 |
| 177,600 -177,699 | 30,192 | 44,400 | 51,504 | 55,056 | 62,160 |
| 177,700 -177,799 | 30,209 | 44,425 | 51,533 | 55,087 | 62,195 |
| 177,800 -177,899 | 30,226 | 44,450 | 51,562 | 55,118 | 62,230 |
| 177,900 -177,999 | 30,243 | 44,475 | 51,591 | 55,149 | 62,265 |

| ANNUAL INCOME | 1 | NUMBER OF CHILDREN 2 | 3 | 4 | 5+ |
|---|---|---|---|---|---|
| | | ANNUAL OBLIGATION AMOUNT | | | |
| 178,000 -178,099 | 30,260 | 44,500 | 51,620 | 55,180 | 62,300 |
| 178,100 -178,199 | 30,277 | 44,525 | 51,649 | 55,211 | 62,335 |
| 178,200 -178,299 | 30,294 | 44,550 | 51,678 | 55,242 | 62,370 |
| 178,300 -178,399 | 30,311 | 44,575 | 51,707 | 55,273 | 62,405 |
| 178,400 -178,499 | 30,328 | 44,600 | 51,736 | 55,304 | 62,440 |
| 178,500 -178,599 | 30,345 | 44,625 | 51,765 | 55,335 | 62,475 |
| 178,600 -178,699 | 30,362 | 44,650 | 51,794 | 55,366 | 62,510 |
| 178,700 -178,799 | 30,379 | 44,675 | 51,823 | 55,397 | 62,545 |
| 178,800 -178,899 | 30,396 | 44,700 | 51,852 | 55,428 | 62,580 |
| 178,900 -178,999 | 30,413 | 44,725 | 51,881 | 55,459 | 62,615 |

| ANNUAL INCOME | 1 | NUMBER OF CHILDREN 2 | 3 | 4 | 5+ |
|---|---|---|---|---|---|
| | | ANNUAL OBLIGATION AMOUNT | | | |
| 179,000 -179,099 | 30,430 | 44,750 | 51,910 | 55,490 | 62,650 |
| 179,100 -179,199 | 30,447 | 44,775 | 51,939 | 55,521 | 62,685 |
| 179,200 -179,299 | 30,464 | 44,800 | 51,968 | 55,552 | 62,720 |
| 179,300 -179,399 | 30,481 | 44,825 | 51,997 | 55,583 | 62,755 |
| 179,400 -179,499 | 30,498 | 44,850 | 52,026 | 55,614 | 62,790 |
| 179,500 -179,599 | 30,515 | 44,875 | 52,055 | 55,645 | 62,825 |
| 179,600 -179,699 | 30,532 | 44,900 | 52,084 | 55,676 | 62,8.. |
| 179,700 -179,799 | 30,549 | 44,925 | 52,113 | 55,707 | 62,? |
| 179,800 -179,899 | 30,566 | 44,950 | 52,142 | 55,738 | 62,9.. |
| 179,900 -179,999 | 30,583 | 44,975 | 52,171 | 55,769 | 62,945 |

18

### NUMBER OF CHILDREN

| ANNUAL INCOME | 1 | 2 | 3 | 4 | 5+ |
|---|---|---|---|---|---|
| 180,000 -180,099 | 30,600 | 45,000 | 52,200 | 55,800 | 63,000 |
| 180,100 -180,199 | 30,617 | 45,025 | 52,229 | 55,831 | 63,035 |
| 180,200 -180,299 | 30,634 | 45,050 | 52,258 | 55,862 | 63,070 |
| 180,300 -180,399 | 30,651 | 45,075 | 52,287 | 55,893 | 63,105 |
| 180,400 -180,499 | 30,668 | 45,100 | 52,316 | 55,924 | 63,140 |
| 180,500 -180,599 | 30,685 | 45,125 | 52,345 | 55,955 | 63,175 |
| 180,600 -180,699 | 30,702 | 45,150 | 52,374 | 55,986 | 63,210 |
| 180,700 -180,799 | 30,719 | 45,175 | 52,403 | 56,017 | 63,245 |
| 180,800 -180,899 | 30,736 | 45,200 | 52,432 | 56,048 | 63,280 |
| 180,900 -180,999 | 30,753 | 45,225 | 52,461 | 56,079 | 63,315 |

| ANNUAL INCOME | 1 | 2 | 3 | 4 | 5+ |
|---|---|---|---|---|---|
| 181,000 -181,099 | 30,770 | 45,250 | 52,490 | 56,110 | 63,350 |
| 181,100 -181,199 | 30,787 | 45,275 | 52,519 | 56,141 | 63,385 |
| 181,200 -181,299 | 30,804 | 45,300 | 52,548 | 56,172 | 63,420 |
| 181,300 -181,399 | 30,821 | 45,325 | 52,577 | 56,203 | 63,455 |
| 181,400 -181,499 | 30,838 | 45,350 | 52,606 | 56,234 | 63,490 |
| 181,500 -181,599 | 30,855 | 45,375 | 52,635 | 56,265 | 63,525 |
| 181,600 -181,699 | 30,872 | 45,400 | 52,664 | 56,296 | 63,560 |
| 181,700 -181,799 | 30,889 | 45,425 | 52,693 | 56,327 | 63,595 |
| 181,800 -181,899 | 30,906 | 45,450 | 52,722 | 56,358 | 63,630 |
| 181,900 -181,999 | 30,923 | 45,475 | 52,751 | 56,389 | 63,665 |

| ANNUAL INCOME | 1 | 2 | 3 | 4 | 5+ |
|---|---|---|---|---|---|
| 182,000 -182,099 | 30,940 | 45,500 | 52,780 | 56,420 | 63,700 |
| 182,100 -182,199 | 30,957 | 45,525 | 52,809 | 56,451 | 63,735 |
| 182,200 -182,299 | 30,974 | 45,550 | 52,838 | 56,482 | 63,770 |
| 182,300 -182,399 | 30,991 | 45,575 | 52,867 | 56,513 | 63,805 |
| 182,400 -182,499 | 31,008 | 45,600 | 52,896 | 56,544 | 63,840 |
| 182,500 -182,599 | 31,025 | 45,625 | 52,925 | 56,575 | 63,875 |
| 182,600 -182,699 | 31,042 | 45,650 | 52,954 | 56,606 | 63,910 |
| 182,700 -182,799 | 31,059 | 45,675 | 52,983 | 56,637 | 63,945 |
| 182,800 -182,899 | 31,076 | 45,700 | 53,012 | 56,668 | 63,980 |
| 182,900 -182,999 | 31,093 | 45,725 | 53,041 | 56,699 | 64,015 |

| ANNUAL INCOME | 1 | 2 | 3 | 4 | 5+ |
|---|---|---|---|---|---|
| 183,000 -183,099 | 31,110 | 45,750 | 53,070 | 56,730 | 64,050 |
| 183,100 -183,199 | 31,127 | 45,775 | 53,099 | 56,761 | 64,085 |
| 183,200 -183,299 | 31,144 | 45,800 | 53,128 | 56,792 | 64,120 |
| 183,300 -183,399 | 31,161 | 45,825 | 53,157 | 56,823 | 64,155 |
| 183,400 -183,499 | 31,178 | 45,850 | 53,186 | 56,854 | 64,190 |
| 183,500 -183,599 | 31,195 | 45,875 | 53,215 | 56,885 | 64,225 |
| 183,600 -183,699 | 31,212 | 45,900 | 53,244 | 56,916 | 64,260 |
| 183,700 -183,799 | 31,229 | 45,925 | 53,273 | 56,947 | 64,295 |
| 183,800 -183,899 | 31,246 | 45,950 | 53,302 | 56,978 | 64,330 |
| 183,900 -183,999 | 31,263 | 45,975 | 53,331 | 57,009 | 64,365 |

| ANNUAL INCOME | 1 | 2 | 3 | 4 | 5+ |
|---|---|---|---|---|---|
| 184,000 -184,099 | 31,280 | 46,000 | 53,360 | 57,040 | 64,400 |
| 184,100 -184,199 | 31,297 | 46,025 | 53,389 | 57,071 | 64,435 |
| 184,200 -184,299 | 31,314 | 46,050 | 53,418 | 57,102 | 64,470 |
| 184,300 -184,399 | 31,331 | 46,075 | 53,447 | 57,133 | 64,505 |
| 184,400 -184,499 | 31,348 | 46,100 | 53,476 | 57,164 | 64,540 |
| 184,500 -184,599 | 31,365 | 46,125 | 53,505 | 57,195 | 64,575 |
| 184,600 -184,699 | 31,382 | 46,150 | 53,534 | 57,226 | 64,610 |
| 184,700 -184,799 | 31,399 | 46,175 | 53,563 | 57,257 | 64,645 |
| 184,800 -184,899 | 31,416 | 46,200 | 53,592 | 57,288 | 64,680 |
| 184,900 -184,999 | 31,433 | 46,225 | 53,621 | 57,319 | 64,715 |

### NUMBER OF CHILDREN

| ANNUAL INCOME | 1 | 2 | 3 | 4 | 5+ |
|---|---|---|---|---|---|
| 185,000 -185,099 | 31,430 | 46,250 | 53,450 | 57,350 | 64,750 |
| 185,100 -185,199 | 31,447 | 46,275 | 53,679 | 57,381 | 64,785 |
| 185,200 -185,299 | 31,484 | 46,300 | 53,708 | 57,412 | 64,820 |
| 185,300 -185,399 | 31,501 | 46,325 | 53,737 | 57,443 | 64,855 |
| 185,400 -185,499 | 31,518 | 46,350 | 53,766 | 57,474 | 64,890 |
| 185,500 -185,599 | 31,535 | 46,375 | 53,795 | 57,505 | 64,925 |
| 185,600 -185,699 | 31,552 | 46,400 | 53,824 | 57,536 | 64,960 |
| 185,700 -185,799 | 31,569 | 46,425 | 53,853 | 57,567 | 64,995 |
| 185,800 -185,899 | 31,586 | 46,450 | 53,882 | 57,598 | 65,030 |
| 185,900 -185,999 | 31,603 | 46,475 | 53,911 | 57,629 | 65,065 |

| ANNUAL INCOME | 1 | 2 | 3 | 4 | 5+ |
|---|---|---|---|---|---|
| 186,000 -186,099 | 31,620 | 46,500 | 53,940 | 57,660 | 65,100 |
| 186,100 -186,199 | 31,637 | 46,525 | 53,969 | 57,691 | 65,135 |
| 186,200 -186,299 | 31,654 | 46,550 | 53,998 | 57,722 | 65,170 |
| 186,300 -186,399 | 31,671 | 46,575 | 54,027 | 57,753 | 65,205 |
| 186,400 -186,499 | 31,688 | 46,600 | 54,056 | 57,784 | 65,240 |
| 186,500 -186,599 | 31,705 | 46,625 | 54,085 | 57,815 | 65,275 |
| 186,600 -186,699 | 31,722 | 46,650 | 54,114 | 57,846 | 65,310 |
| 186,700 -186,799 | 31,739 | 46,675 | 54,143 | 57,877 | 65,345 |
| 186,800 -186,899 | 31,756 | 46,700 | 54,172 | 57,908 | 65,380 |
| 186,900 -186,999 | 31,773 | 46,725 | 54,201 | 57,939 | 65,415 |

| ANNUAL INCOME | 1 | 2 | 3 | 4 | 5+ |
|---|---|---|---|---|---|
| 187,000 -187,099 | 31,790 | 46,750 | 54,230 | 57,970 | 65,450 |
| 187,100 -187,199 | 31,807 | 46,775 | 54,259 | 58,001 | 65,485 |
| 187,200 -187,299 | 31,824 | 46,800 | 54,288 | 58,032 | 65,520 |
| 187,300 -187,399 | 31,841 | 46,825 | 54,317 | 58,063 | 65,555 |
| 187,400 -187,499 | 31,858 | 46,850 | 54,346 | 58,094 | 65,590 |
| 187,500 -187,599 | 31,875 | 46,875 | 54,375 | 58,125 | 65,625 |
| 187,600 -187,699 | 31,892 | 46,900 | 54,404 | 58,156 | 65,660 |
| 187,700 -187,799 | 31,909 | 46,925 | 54,433 | 58,187 | 65,695 |
| 187,800 -187,899 | 31,926 | 46,950 | 54,462 | 58,218 | 65,730 |
| 187,900 -187,999 | 31,943 | 46,975 | 54,491 | 58,249 | 65,765 |

| ANNUAL INCOME | 1 | 2 | 3 | 4 | 5+ |
|---|---|---|---|---|---|
| 188,000 -188,099 | 31,960 | 47,000 | 54,520 | 58,280 | 65,800 |
| 188,100 -188,199 | 31,977 | 47,025 | 54,549 | 58,311 | 65,835 |
| 188,200 -188,299 | 31,994 | 47,050 | 54,578 | 58,342 | 65,870 |
| 188,300 -188,399 | 32,011 | 47,075 | 54,607 | 58,373 | 65,905 |
| 188,400 -188,499 | 32,028 | 47,100 | 54,636 | 58,404 | 65,940 |
| 188,500 -188,599 | 32,045 | 47,125 | 54,665 | 58,435 | 65,975 |
| 188,600 -188,699 | 32,062 | 47,150 | 54,694 | 58,466 | 66,010 |
| 188,700 -188,799 | 32,079 | 47,175 | 54,723 | 58,497 | 66,045 |
| 188,800 -188,899 | 32,096 | 47,200 | 54,752 | 58,528 | 66,080 |
| 188,900 -188,999 | 32,113 | 47,225 | 54,781 | 58,559 | 66,115 |

| ANNUAL INCOME | 1 | 2 | 3 | 4 | 5+ |
|---|---|---|---|---|---|
| 189,000 -189,099 | 32,130 | 47,250 | 54,810 | 58,590 | 66,150 |
| 189,100 -189,199 | 32,147 | 47,275 | 54,839 | 58,621 | 66,185 |
| 189,200 -189,299 | 32,164 | 47,300 | 54,868 | 58,652 | 66,220 |
| 189,300 -189,399 | 32,181 | 47,325 | 54,897 | 58,683 | 66,255 |
| 189,400 -189,499 | 32,198 | 47,350 | 54,926 | 58,714 | 66,290 |
| 189,500 -189,599 | 32,215 | 47,375 | 54,955 | 58,745 | 66,325 |
| 189,600 -189,699 | 32,232 | 47,400 | 54,984 | 58,776 | 66,360 |
| 189,700 -189,799 | 32,249 | 47,425 | 55,013 | 58,807 | 66,395 |
| 189,800 -189,899 | 32,266 | 47,450 | 55,042 | 58,838 | 66,430 |
| 189,900 -189,999 | 32,283 | 47,475 | 55,071 | 58,869 | 66,465 |

19

| ANNUAL INCOME | 1 | 2 | 3 | 4 | 5+ |
|---|---|---|---|---|---|
| | | NUMBER OF CHILDREN | | | |
| | | ANNUAL OBLIGATION AMOUNT | | | |
| 190,000 -190,099 | 32,300 | 47,300 | 55,100 | 58,900 | 66,500 |
| 190,100 -190,199 | 32,317 | 47,325 | 55,129 | 58,931 | 66,535 |
| 190,200 -190,299 | 32,334 | 47,350 | 55,158 | 58,962 | 66,570 |
| 190,300 -190,399 | 32,351 | 47,375 | 55,187 | 58,993 | 66,605 |
| 190,400 -190,499 | 32,368 | 47,400 | 55,216 | 59,024 | 66,640 |
| 190,500 -190,599 | 32,385 | 47,425 | 55,245 | 59,055 | 66,675 |
| 190,600 -190,699 | 32,402 | 47,450 | 55,274 | 59,086 | 66,710 |
| 190,700 -190,799 | 32,419 | 47,475 | 55,303 | 59,117 | 66,745 |
| 190,800 -190,899 | 32,436 | 47,500 | 55,332 | 59,148 | 66,780 |
| 190,900 -190,999 | 32,453 | 47,525 | 55,361 | 59,179 | 66,815 |

| ANNUAL INCOME | 1 | 2 | 3 | 4 | 5+ |
|---|---|---|---|---|---|
| | | NUMBER OF CHILDREN | | | |
| | | ANNUAL OBLIGATION AMOUNT | | | |
| 191,000 -191,099 | 32,470 | 47,750 | 55,390 | 59,210 | 66,850 |
| 191,100 -191,199 | 32,487 | 47,775 | 55,419 | 59,241 | 66,885 |
| 191,200 -191,299 | 32,504 | 47,800 | 55,448 | 59,272 | 66,920 |
| 191,300 -191,399 | 32,521 | 47,825 | 55,477 | 59,303 | 66,955 |
| 191,400 -191,499 | 32,538 | 47,850 | 55,506 | 59,334 | 66,990 |
| 191,500 -191,599 | 32,555 | 47,875 | 55,535 | 59,365 | 67,025 |
| 191,600 -191,699 | 32,572 | 47,900 | 55,564 | 59,396 | 67,060 |
| 191,700 -191,799 | 32,589 | 47,925 | 55,593 | 59,427 | 67,095 |
| 191,800 -191,899 | 32,606 | 47,950 | 55,622 | 59,458 | 67,130 |
| 191,900 -191,999 | 32,623 | 47,975 | 55,651 | 59,489 | 67,165 |

| ANNUAL INCOME | 1 | 2 | 3 | 4 | 5+ |
|---|---|---|---|---|---|
| | | NUMBER OF CHILDREN | | | |
| | | ANNUAL OBLIGATION AMOUNT | | | |
| 192,000 -192,099 | 32,640 | 48,000 | 55,680 | 59,520 | 67,200 |
| 192,100 -192,199 | 32,657 | 48,025 | 55,709 | 59,551 | 67,235 |
| 192,200 -192,299 | 32,674 | 48,050 | 55,738 | 59,582 | 67,270 |
| 192,300 -192,399 | 32,691 | 48,075 | 55,767 | 59,613 | 67,305 |
| 192,400 -192,499 | 32,708 | 48,100 | 55,796 | 59,644 | 67,340 |
| 192,500 -192,599 | 32,725 | 48,125 | 55,825 | 59,675 | 67,375 |
| 192,600 -192,699 | 32,742 | 48,150 | 55,854 | 59,706 | 67,410 |
| 192,700 -192,799 | 32,759 | 48,175 | 55,883 | 59,737 | 67,445 |
| 192,800 -192,899 | 32,776 | 48,200 | 55,912 | 59,768 | 67,480 |
| 192,900 -192,999 | 32,793 | 48,225 | 55,941 | 59,799 | 67,515 |

| ANNUAL INCOME | 1 | 2 | 3 | 4 | 5+ |
|---|---|---|---|---|---|
| | | NUMBER OF CHILDREN | | | |
| | | ANNUAL OBLIGATION AMOUNT | | | |
| 193,000 -193,099 | 32,810 | 48,250 | 55,970 | 59,830 | 67,550 |
| 193,100 -193,199 | 32,827 | 48,275 | 55,999 | 59,861 | 67,585 |
| 193,200 -193,299 | 32,844 | 48,300 | 56,028 | 59,892 | 67,620 |
| 193,300 -193,399 | 32,861 | 48,325 | 56,057 | 59,923 | 67,655 |
| 193,400 -193,499 | 32,878 | 48,350 | 56,086 | 59,954 | 67,690 |
| 193,500 -193,599 | 32,895 | 48,375 | 56,115 | 59,985 | 67,725 |
| 193,600 -193,699 | 32,912 | 48,400 | 56,144 | 60,016 | 67,760 |
| 193,700 -193,799 | 32,929 | 48,425 | 56,173 | 60,047 | 67,795 |
| 193,800 -193,899 | 32,946 | 48,450 | 56,202 | 60,078 | 67,830 |
| 193,900 -193,999 | 32,963 | 48,475 | 56,231 | 60,109 | 67,865 |

| ANNUAL INCOME | 1 | 2 | 3 | 4 | 5+ |
|---|---|---|---|---|---|
| | | NUMBER OF CHILDREN | | | |
| | | ANNUAL OBLIGATION AMOUNT | | | |
| 194,000 -194,099 | 32,980 | 48,500 | 56,260 | 60,140 | 67,900 |
| 194,100 -194,199 | 32,997 | 48,525 | 56,289 | 60,171 | 67,935 |
| 194,200 -194,299 | 33,014 | 48,550 | 56,318 | 60,202 | 67,970 |
| 194,300 -194,399 | 33,031 | 48,575 | 56,347 | 60,233 | 68,005 |
| 194,400 -194,499 | 33,048 | 48,600 | 56,376 | 60,264 | 68,040 |
| 194,500 -194,599 | 33,065 | 48,625 | 56,405 | 60,295 | 68,075 |
| 194,600 -194,699 | 33,082 | 48,650 | 56,434 | 60,326 | 68,110 |
| 194,700 -194,799 | 33,099 | 48,675 | 56,463 | 60,357 | 68,145 |
| 194,800 -194,899 | 33,116 | 48,700 | 56,492 | 60,388 | 68,180 |
| 194,900 -194,999 | 33,133 | 48,725 | 56,521 | 60,419 | 68,215 |

| ANNUAL INCOME | 1 | 2 | 3 | 4 | 5 |
|---|---|---|---|---|---|
| | | NUMBER OF CHILDREN | | | |
| | | ANNUAL OBLIGATION AMOUNT | | | |
| 195,000 -195,099 | 33,150 | 48,750 | 56,550 | 60,450 | 68,250 |
| 195,100 -195,199 | 33,167 | 48,775 | 56,579 | 60,481 | 68,285 |
| 195,200 -195,299 | 33,184 | 48,800 | 56,608 | 60,512 | 68,320 |
| 195,300 -195,399 | 33,201 | 48,825 | 56,637 | 60,543 | 68,355 |
| 195,400 -195,499 | 33,218 | 48,850 | 56,666 | 60,574 | 68,390 |
| 195,500 -195,599 | 33,235 | 48,875 | 56,695 | 60,605 | 68,425 |
| 195,600 -195,699 | 33,252 | 48,900 | 56,724 | 60,636 | 68,460 |
| 195,700 -195,799 | 33,269 | 48,925 | 56,753 | 60,667 | 68,495 |
| 195,800 -195,899 | 33,286 | 48,950 | 56,782 | 60,698 | 68,530 |
| 195,900 -195,999 | 33,303 | 48,975 | 56,811 | 60,729 | 68,565 |

| ANNUAL INCOME | 1 | 2 | 3 | 4 | 5+ |
|---|---|---|---|---|---|
| | | NUMBER OF CHILDREN | | | |
| | | ANNUAL OBLIGATION AMOUNT | | | |
| 196,000 -196,099 | 33,320 | 49,000 | 56,840 | 60,760 | 68,600 |
| 196,100 -196,199 | 33,337 | 49,025 | 56,869 | 60,791 | 68,635 |
| 196,200 -196,299 | 33,354 | 49,050 | 56,898 | 60,822 | 68,670 |
| 196,300 -196,399 | 33,371 | 49,075 | 56,927 | 60,853 | 68,705 |
| 196,400 -196,499 | 33,388 | 49,100 | 56,956 | 60,884 | 68,740 |
| 196,500 -196,599 | 33,405 | 49,125 | 56,985 | 60,915 | 68,775 |
| 196,600 -196,699 | 33,422 | 49,150 | 57,014 | 60,946 | 68,810 |
| 196,700 -196,799 | 33,439 | 49,175 | 57,043 | 60,977 | 68,845 |
| 196,800 -196,899 | 33,456 | 49,200 | 57,072 | 61,008 | 68,880 |
| 196,900 -196,999 | 33,473 | 49,225 | 57,101 | 61,039 | 68,915 |

| ANNUAL INCOME | 1 | 2 | 3 | 4 | 5+ |
|---|---|---|---|---|---|
| | | NUMBER OF CHILDREN | | | |
| | | ANNUAL OBLIGATION AMOUNT | | | |
| 197,000 -197,099 | 33,490 | 49,250 | 57,130 | 61,070 | 68,950 |
| 197,100 -197,199 | 33,507 | 49,275 | 57,159 | 61,101 | 68,985 |
| 197,200 -197,299 | 33,524 | 49,300 | 57,188 | 61,132 | 69,020 |
| 197,300 -197,399 | 33,541 | 49,325 | 57,217 | 61,163 | 69,055 |
| 197,400 -197,499 | 33,558 | 49,350 | 57,246 | 61,194 | 69,090 |
| 197,500 -197,599 | 33,575 | 49,375 | 57,275 | 61,225 | 69,125 |
| 197,600 -197,699 | 33,592 | 49,400 | 57,304 | 61,256 | 69,160 |
| 197,700 -197,799 | 33,609 | 49,425 | 57,333 | 61,287 | 69,195 |
| 197,800 -197,899 | 33,626 | 49,450 | 57,362 | 61,318 | 69,230 |
| 197,900 -197,999 | 33,643 | 49,475 | 57,391 | 61,349 | 69,265 |

| ANNUAL INCOME | 1 | 2 | 3 | 4 | 5+ |
|---|---|---|---|---|---|
| | | NUMBER OF CHILDREN | | | |
| | | ANNUAL OBLIGATION AMOUNT | | | |
| 198,000 -198,099 | 33,660 | 49,500 | 57,420 | 61,380 | 69,300 |
| 198,100 -198,199 | 33,677 | 49,525 | 57,449 | 61,411 | 69,335 |
| 198,200 -198,299 | 33,694 | 49,550 | 57,478 | 61,442 | 69,370 |
| 198,300 -198,399 | 33,711 | 49,575 | 57,507 | 61,473 | 69,405 |
| 198,400 -198,499 | 33,728 | 49,600 | 57,536 | 61,504 | 69,440 |
| 198,500 -198,599 | 33,745 | 49,625 | 57,565 | 61,535 | 69,475 |
| 198,600 -198,699 | 33,762 | 49,650 | 57,594 | 61,566 | 69,510 |
| 198,700 -198,799 | 33,779 | 49,675 | 57,623 | 61,597 | 69,545 |
| 198,800 -198,899 | 33,796 | 49,700 | 57,652 | 61,628 | 69,580 |
| 198,900 -198,999 | 33,813 | 49,725 | 57,681 | 61,659 | 69,615 |

| ANNUAL INCOME | 1 | 2 | 3 | 4 | 5+ |
|---|---|---|---|---|---|
| | | NUMBER OF CHILDREN | | | |
| | | ANNUAL OBLIGATION AMOUNT | | | |
| 199,000 -199,099 | 33,830 | 49,750 | 57,710 | 61,690 | 69,650 |
| 199,100 -199,199 | 33,847 | 49,775 | 57,739 | 61,721 | 69,685 |
| 199,200 -199,299 | 33,864 | 49,800 | 57,768 | 61,752 | 69,720 |
| 199,300 -199,399 | 33,881 | 49,825 | 57,797 | 61,783 | 69,755 |
| 199,400 -199,499 | 33,898 | 49,850 | 57,826 | 61,814 | 69,790 |
| 199,500 -199,599 | 33,915 | 49,875 | 57,855 | 61,845 | 69,825 |
| 199,600 -199,699 | 33,932 | 49,900 | 57,884 | 61,876 | 69,860 |
| 199,700 -199,799 | 33,949 | 49,925 | 57,913 | 61,907 | 69,895 |
| 199,800 -199,899 | 33,966 | 49,950 | 57,942 | 61,938 | 69,930 |
| 199,900 -199,999 | 33,983 | 49,975 | 57,971 | 61,969 | 69,965 |

# NOTES

# Program Schedule
# and
# Faculty

**Faculty**
**Chair:**
**Mona R. Millstein**
Law Offices of Mona R. Millstein, New York City

**Saul Edelstein**
Edelstein & Brown
Brooklyn, New York

**Iris M. Darvin**
Attorney at Law
New York City

**Michele A. Katz**
Morrison Cohen Singer & Weinstein
New York City

**Michelle Ascher Dunn, C.S.W.**
Co Director, Parent Infant Program
  New York Freudian Society
Assistant Clinical Professor
Child and Adolescent Psychiatry
  New York Medical College
Instructor
  Institute for Child Adolescent and Family Studies
Member of Interdisciplinary Study Forum on Mental  Health and Family Law
New York City

**Program Attorney:**
**Tina G. Coco**

# Program Schedule
## *for*
## Child Custody and Support

Morning Session: 9:30 a.m. - 12:30 p.m.

*9:30*
**Introduction**

*9:45*
**Factors and Criteria Used in Custody Determinations**
Ethical considerations

*10:15*
**The Role of Psychological Experts**

*11:00 Break*

*11:15*
**Sole/Joint Custody, Visitation and Children's Rights**
*Michele Ascher Dunn*

*12:10*
**Questions and Answers**
*Mona R. Millstein and Iris M. Darvin*

Afternoon Session: 2:00 p.m. - 5:00 p.m.

*2:00*
**Relocation and Jurisdiction for Custody/Uniform Child Custody Jurisdiction Act and Parental Kidnapping Prevention Act**

*3:00 Break*

*3:15*
**Child Support Under Child Support Standards Act, Recent Case Law**

*4:15*
**Panel Discussion Questions and Answers**
*Michele A. Katz and Saul Edelstein*

"Willard artfully blends the details of an absorbing individual story with a vivid panorama of gut-wrenching combat scenes. Another admirable, action-packed addition to a compelling multigenerational series that catalogs the incredibly heroic, and often overlooked, contributions of black soldiers to the history of the American military."
— *Booklist* on *Wings of Honor*

"The wonderfully exciting air battles bear comparison with James Wylie's 1977 Faulknerian classic, *The Homestead Grays*. . . . No dimming of the solid style Willard favors."
— *Kirkus Reviews* on *Wings of Honor*

"Well-written, with strong characterization, loads of historical information and a high level of entertainment value."
— *Charleston Post and Courier* on *Wings of Honor*

"Willard, a Vietnam veteran, has a remarkable skill for rendering of trench warfare, and his depiction of black military family life is true and natural. Altogether, this is an exciting historical novel about black soldiers who conspicuously honored their nation abroad while the Ku Klux Klan and kindred spirits conspicuously shamed it at home."
— *Publishers Weekly* on *The Sable Doughboys*

"The poorly understood record of the black cavalry is what makes Tom Willard's *Buffalo Soldiers* an important publication. . . . A solidly written, no-wasted-words story that will excite anybody wanting to know more about this important chapter of American black and Western history."
— *The Washington Times*

"Tom Willard delivers an engrossing story. . . . No previous work . . . has achieved the blend of historical accuracy, suspenseful action and rich characterization contained in *Buffalo Soldiers*. . . . Much historical research informs this novel, but truth does not detract from the fertile imagination of Tom Willard."
— *Fort Worth Star-Telegram*

# Books by Tom Willard

*The Dolomite Memorandum*
*Strike Fighters*
*Bold Forager*
*Sudden Fury*
*Red Dancer*
*Desert Star*
*Blood River*
*Golden Triangle*
*War Chariot*
*Death Squad*
*Afrikorps*
*Iron Horse*
*White Rhino*
*Sea Stallion*
*Lion Mountain*
*Cobra Curse*

THE BLACK SABRE CHRONICLES
*Buffalo Soldiers*
*The Sable Doughboys*
*Wings of Honor*
*The Stone Ponies*

# THE STONE PONIES

★

Book Four of the
Black Sabre Chronicles

## TOM WILLARD

A TOM DOHERTY ASSOCIATES BOOK
NEW YORK

This is a work of fiction. All the characters and events portrayed in this book are either products of the author's imagination or are used fictitiously.

THE STONE PONIES

Map and ornament by Ellisa H. Mitchell

A Forge Book
Published by Tom Doherty Associates, LLC
175 Fifth Avenue
New York, NY 10010

www.tor.com

Forge® is a registered trademark of Tom Doherty Associates, LLC.

ISBN: 0-812-56478-2
Library of Congress Catalog Card Number: 00-028805

First edition: August 2000
First mass market edition: July 2001

Printed in the United States of America

0  9  8  7  6  5  4  3  2  1

To:

Sergeant First Class John Franklin Hughes (Ret.)
Colonel David H. Hackworth (Ret.)
Command Sergeant Major Leo B. Smith (Ret.)
Warrant Officer Four Charlie Mussellwhite (Ret.)
Lieutenant Colonel Dennis Foley (Ret.)
Sergeant First Class Chuck Knowlan (Ret.)
Specialist Four Earl Wilson (Memphis, Tennessee)
Specialist Four Gaines Wilson (Fort Lauderdale, Florida)
Sergeant Jeffrey Letson Kockritz (KIA)
Master Sergeant Phillip Chassion (KIA)
Brigadier General John D. Howard (Ret.)
Sergeant Sheffield (KIA)
Specialist Four Eddie Carreon (San Antonio, Texas)
Specialist Four Willie Murrel (Gary, Indiana)
Specialist Five Jessie Copeland (Oklahoma City)
Specialist Five Juan Ybanaez (KIA)
Brigadier General George Shevlin (Ret.)
Colonel Ted Crozier (Ret.)
Command Sergeant Major Russ MacDonald (Ret.)
First Lieutenant James Alton Gardner (KIA), Posthumous
   Recipient, Medal of Honor

And all the many others . . .

I lie in my tent
Thanking God for free rent
While outside the rain pours
And inside my buddy snores
Muddy floors and a wet cot
But still thanking God a lot.
Got hot chow every day
Rain or shine, come what may,
Got a dog 'bout two weeks old
Eats C-rations hot or cold.
Special Forces all around
Keeping safe this hallowed ground.
1st Cav in the air
Landing, fighting here and there.
Ain't got much but could be worse
Just ask the men in the 101st.

—"Ode to the Infantryman in RVN,"
by an anonymous Signal Corpsman in Nha Trang,
Republic of Vietnam
(from the *Vietnam Reporter,* October 1965)

You see, a private had no right to know anything, and that is why generals did all the fighting, and that is today why generals and colonels and captains are great men. They fought the battles of our country. The privates did not. The generals risked their reputation, the private soldier his life. No one ever saw a private in battle. His history would never be written. It was the general that everybody saw charge such and such, with drawn sabre, his eyes flashing fire, his nostrils dilated, and his clarion voice ringing above the din of battle. . . .
—Private Sam Watkins, Maury Grays,
  First Tennessee Regiment,
   veteran of Shiloh, Perryville, Chattanooga, Chickamauga, Murfreesboro, Missionary Ridge, and Atlanta

This piece was provided to the author by a great friend and soldier, Colonel John D. Rosenberger, 11th Armored Cavalry Regiment (OPFOR), 58th Colonel of the Regiment, Commanding.

Ever go to the park? See the statue of a great general sitting on his horse, sabre extended, riding to glory?

The general got all the glory, but it was the "grunt" . . . that "stone pony" he's riding on . . . that carried him to glory.

—Anonymous

# Foreword

In the history of the United States, there has never been a more important time of personal decision for the African-American soldier fighting for his country than the war in Vietnam. In 1965, many aspects of the United States were segregated, schools as well as bathrooms, restaurants, and motels. People of color couldn't share the same drinking fountain with white people. But they could share their blood on the same battlefield.

Employment was not based on equality, rather on the color of a man's skin. The American economy was flourishing while a great void existed between the white and black races.

But changes came about, though slowly and often subtly. The Korean War was the first major foreign conflict utilizing integrated military forces. In Vietnam, for the first time, Negro officers led white soldiers into battle.

Yet racial disparity continued in the United States, where a white soldier and black soldier from Mississippi could fight and die alongside each other on foreign soil, sip from the same canteens, but couldn't drink from the same water fountain in Hattiesburg. The white and black soldiers could hold each other in the frightful moments of war, while in the streets of America whites and blacks fought each other over equality.

From Vietnam arose two distinctive factions: the men and women wearing the uniform and those opposed to the war. At war's end, both sides claimed victory. Both sides moved forward with their lives.

But the Vietnam soldier continued to harbor a resentment, to both the government and the people who turned their backs on them. The Vietnam soldier didn't want a parade or a welcome home party. A simple "Thank you" would have sufficed.

America sent its children to war and turned its back on them on both the battlefield and the home front. Unlike the Desert Stormers—offspring of the Vietnam soldier—who received well-deserved support and praise, the Vietnam veteran was left with the task of sorting out his place in history on an individual or collective basis.

This is a story of the *grunt*. That down-in-the-dirt, too-often-unappreciated reminder of war that society seems to want to avoid, except on Veterans Day.

The soldier who would follow a great leader through the gates of hell, put out the Devil's flames, and fight his way back up to good ground even if his hair was on fire.

# PROLOGUE

★

Franklin LeBaron Sharps's journey to war would begin the same way as his father's and grandfather's: standing on the railroad platform at Willcox, Arizona. Franklin's great-great-grandfather, the sergeant major, who served with the 10th Cavalry, joined the army at eighteen on the frozen plains of Kansas in 1868. He had heard the old stories, knew of the glory days of his great-grandfather riding to victory with the Buffalo Soldiers; his grandfather charging across no-man's-land in the Meuse-Argonne with the Sable Doughboys; his father screaming through the skies in a fighter plane, sleek and shining. He knew about their valor, lived with their legend.

Now it was his turn.

He had learned to overcome fear; one must confront fear. To understand fear, one must survive fear. To know fear, one must only be in a fearful place.

He was twenty, a high school dropout and, to some extent, an embarrassment to his father, Brigadier General

Samuel Sharps, one of the original "Tuskegee Airmen" fighter pilots.

Franklin was a paratrooper, tall and lean like his father, and lighter-skinned, which he attributed to his mother's partial Cherokee blood.

He had been given his two weeks' leave, like the other 5,500 troopers in the First Brigade, 101st Airborne Division. Now it was time to get back to Fort Campbell, Kentucky, and prepare for another journey.

"You'll be fine. Just fine," his mother said. Shania ran her hand across his forehead and kissed him lightly on the cheek. "Just don't go and try to be a hero."

He smiled that boyish smile she adored. "I won't. One's enough in the family."

Her face saddened. "You know your father would be here if he could."

He nodded. "Maybe we'll run into each other in Vietnam."

"Don't fill your heart with anger, baby. It'll only make things worse for you."

"How can you say that about him? After what he did to you. To our family!"

She had not forgotten the betrayal. "That's between your father and me. You and Kevin are both grown men, starting your own lives. Don't let his mistake destroy a lifetime of love and respect."

"Respect? He was carrying on with another woman! His secretary, for Chrissakes! He betrayed us all. And him, always talking about honor. I despise him."

She began to cry and reached into her purse and handed him a miniature replica of a cavalry sabre. "All Sharps men go to war carrying a sabre. Your daddy has your grandfather's. This one is for you."

He recognized it. It was the same sabre that had been returned with his brother Adrian's personal effects six months ago. After he was killed in Vietnam. A West Point graduate, Adrian had been killed by the Vietcong at an overrun Special Forces camp in the Central Highlands.

He slipped the sabre into his pocket. He gave no thought to the possibility it might bring him bad luck. He felt the kinship bleed through the blade and into his soul.

He would look at it later, on the train, and remember those moments that bring so much pain to the healing heart. He would remember.

And God help the sonsabitches who killed his brother. He was going to balance the books!


Two weeks later, Franklin studied the miniature sabre as he lay on his bunk, gear packed, trying to remember *not to remember*. He had been told not to think about yesterday—it's forgotten—or today, for it's uncertain; or tomorrow, for it doesn't exist.

From outside, near the barracks, at the beer garden Bastogne Club, the music and words of "You've Lost That Lovin' Feelin'" and the pristine voices of the Righteous Brothers cut through the still of the night with agonizing reminders of where he was and where he was going.

Intermingled was the nervous laughter of men and women spending their last night with soldiers stationed at the fort.

But for most of the young paratroopers, like the words of the song, there was a strong sense of being alone. Especially in the medical platoon of the First Brigade's Headquarters Company, First Battalion, 327th Airborne Infantry, where no one could sleep. And everyone listened.

They all knew two things: The song would end, and tomorrow they were going to war.

"You asleep, man?" PFC Tommie Wilkes, one of his fellow medics, asked softly. Like Franklin, he lay dressed in fatigues, his Corcoran jump boots unlaced. All the troopers were sleeping in similar fashion, waiting for the sudden thunder of First Sergeant Leo B. Smith's voice.

Franklin had heard Smith's voice on many occasions.

The most memorable was on the day he went searching
for his job as medic for the recon platoon. Breaking the
chain of command, he went directly to Master Sergeant
Phil Chassion, a Korean veteran, and applied for the position . . . which was not allocated in an Airborne infantry
unit.

"Recon don't have medics," Chassion snapped.

"It could, Sergeant," Franklin said.

Chassion eyed him warily, then asked in his gritty, low
voice, "Why do you want to be in recon?"

Franklin didn't flinch; he had prepared his answer.
"Medics carry forty-five pistols, Sergeant. If I'm going to
war, I want to carry an M-sixteen rifle. As your medic I
can carry an M-sixteen rifle. I'm infantry-trained and fired
expert on the range. It'll give you another source of firepower."

Chassion jumped directly into Franklin's face. "Have
you discussed this with your platoon leader and platoon
sergeant?"

Franklin shook his head. "No, Sergeant."

That was the beginning of a long line of ass-chewings
that would include his platoon leader and platoon sergeant, first sergeant, and, finally, company commander,
Captain George Shevlin.

By the end of that day Franklin would have little ass
left; however, he was given the position, along with an
M-16 rifle. He was also allowed to keep his .45 pistol.
And for the first time in its illustrious history, the 101st
Airborne Division assigned a permanent medic to a recon
platoon.


Franklin sat up and looked along the long bay. Every
bunk gave off some sign of wakefulness. "Naw. Who can
sleep?" he said to Wilkes. The glow of a match touching
a cigarette across the bay caught his attention. "Damn. I
wish we was on the move."

"What's the matter, Sharps? Can't wait to kill somebody?" a voice asked from the bunk where the cigarette glowed.

Franklin had started to reply when the barracks filled with light; then a voice boomed, and there was the thundering of a garbage can ricocheting off the floor.

"On your feet!" the voice of First Sergeant Smith roared. A short, muscular man, a combat veteran of the 187th Regimental Combat Team of Korea fame, Smith marched through the bay jabbing his fingers at each soldier, ordering them to their feet. Behind him walked several other noncommissioned officers, all wearing grizzled faces with eyes peering hard and relentless. "What are you!" Smith's voice again bellowed.

The troopers, now standing ramrod straight at attention in front of their bunks, responded in a chorus, "Airborne!"

"How far!" Smith barked.

"All the way! First Ser-geant!"

Sergeant First Class Bill Trout, new in the unit from the unit from the 173rd Airborne Brigade, walked behind Smith, staring for a single sharp moment at his troopers. He said nothing; his presence spoke for itself. He had broken his collarbone a week before and, now wearing a cast, he refused to be medically relieved from the shipment to Nam. A tough, no-nonsense soldier from Hershey, Pennsylvania, he had personally built the medic platoon, throwing out the shirkers and slackers with the ease of a butcher trimming fat from a slab of beef.

"The chow hall is open for thirty minutes," Smith blared. "Get yourselves fed, gear up, and report in formation in front of headquarters. Don't leave any of your gear behind. If you do . . . you'll go to war without it. Is that clear?"

"Yes, First Sergeant!" the troopers shouted.

Smith looked at Trout, nodded, then marched sharply away. Franklin watched as the platoon sergeant scanned the bay, his face tightened by the pain of his injury. "Any questions?" he asked.

There were none.

"Move out!"

The bay shook from the heavy paratrooper boots slamming against the floor until there was silence and the barracks was empty except for Trout, who checked the stacked duffel bags, helmets, weapons, medical aid kits, and assault packs of each man.

The OPORD—Operational Order—the method by which the brigade would be moved to Vietnam, was the written masterpiece of Major David H. Hackworth, Captain Hank Lunde, and Sergeant Major Grady Jones, and was nearly a foot thick when finished. The plan called for a combined use of commercial air travel for the troops and railway transportation for the massive amount of equipment required for an Airborne brigade. All were designed to reach the shipping point at the same time, which they did. In Oakland, California, the USS *General Eltinge* lay gray in sunlight and darkness. Franklin stared in awe at the huge transport ship and, like the other paratroopers, was still in shock from the rapid deployment from Fort Campbell, which had taken less than a day. The troopers boarded in long lines, carrying their duffel bags, with packs on, weapons shouldered. Used to jumping from planes in flight, they would now ride the waves of the Pacific, standing at the rails, sleeping in bunks of canvas, all likely longing for hard, even cold ground, rather than enclosed spaces.

The brigade arrived in Cam Ranh Bay, Republic of South Vietnam, on a hot July day in 1965. There to greet them was General William Childs Westmoreland, who had once been division commander of the "Screaming Eagles." As a special tribute to "Westy," officers and NCOs who had served with Westmoreland in the 187th Regimental Combat Team in Korea, his first general command, formed a special detail to greet their former commander of the

"Rakkassans," all wearing their combat patches of the "Angels from Hell."

Hackworth, a decorated battle veteran of World War II and Korea, watched the brigade assemble and listened to the words of Westmoreland, who, along with Ambassador Maxwell Taylor, also a former division commander of the 101st—his son an officer in the brigade—gave stirring speeches of the necessity of American forces to serve in Vietnam.

Hackworth, referred to as "Hack," always the realist, listened to the speeches and, when finished, muttered softly, "Ready or not . . . here we are!"


PFC Franklin Sharps, sweating profusely in the hot sun and out of range of Hack, muttered, "Here we are. . . . I hope we're ready!"

# PART 1

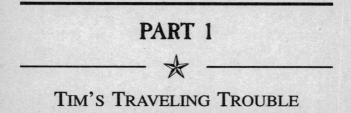

## TIM'S TRAVELING TROUBLE

# 1

\* \* \*

The thump and beat of the helicopter rotors made the air inside the Huey vibrate, giving Franklin the sensation that the chopper was alive and he was feeling its pulse. He sat on his helmet, as he and the others had learned to do in order to protect their private parts from enemy ground fire.

Gone were the heavy Corcoran jump boots, all of which had rotted from the troopers' feet within weeks of arriving at Cam Ranh Bay. Moisture and humidity had eaten the leather soles away, forcing the Americans to use tape, even communications wire, to bind the boots together until they were finally replaced by the new Vietnam jungle boots. Gone were the heavy fatigues, designed for cold weather, replaced by the looser-fitting and more practical poplin jungle fatigues.

And, as would be expected, gone was their innocence of war, and the short-lived bravado that began fading the first night in the bush. In less than six weeks, the brigade had been battled, blooded, and baptized by fire from an enemy they barely saw and could rarely catch in an open fight.

The brigade had became known as "Tim's Traveling Trouble" in honor of brigade commander Colonel James S. Timothy. A West Point officer and decorated veteran of World War II and Korea, Timothy was widely known as a "no bullshit commander," whose philosophy regarding the enemy was simple: Find them. Fix them. Then kill them.

Certainly bullshitless.

His troopers rolled out in the morning, on choppers gilded with guns spitting the hellfire of death.

His troopers took hills known to only the enemy.

His troopers pressed on.


Casualties had started early upon their arrival, ranging from gunshot to fragmentation wounds, malaria, intestinal disorders, and punctures from the punji stakes, dipped in human excrement, concealed in pits that lay on silent trails or a step over a log in the path.

Charlie knew the American better than the American knew himself.

Most American soldiers had run track.

Run the hurdles.

Charlie knew that . . . Americans go over . . . they don't go around.

Even the MACV—Military Advisory Command Vietnam—"rules of engagement," requiring American troops to carry unloaded weapons until fired upon, were rescinded. Due, no doubt, to the fact that Charlie would jump out, spray soldiers with automatic fire, then disappear. By the time survivors were loaded up, there were only the dead and wounded.

The brigade had traveled from Cam Ranh to the mountains of the Central Highlands, where their current mission was to clear Route 19 for the arrival of the First Air Cav-

alry Division. Patrol operations were under the most brutal of physical conditions, exacting from the troopers
every ounce of their courage and stamina. Rugged terrain,
monsoon rain, mosquitoes, leeches, even wild tigers in the
jungle added to the danger. But the elusive Charlie was
their greatest frustration, living in holes and popping up
at night to harass units and patrols. The fight was becoming one that required the Americans to get down into the
dirt and dig Charlie out of his underground sanctuaries.

The sudden yaw of the chopper snapped Franklin back to
reality. The weather was lousy and they were flying
through mountains above the rugged central highland
plains west of An Khe.

He glanced at the door gunner, who leaned against his
M-60 machine gun, his eyes scanning the terrain below.
It was black as night and raining like hell, and all the
recon team members were soaked to the bone as the rain
whipped through the open doors, stinging their faces,
numbing their bodies.

All wore a common expression on their camouflaged
faces: They'd rather be somewhere else!

"Get ready!" shouted the door gunner.

Franklin and the others slipped condoms over the muz-
zles of their M-16s to prevent mud and water from getting
into the barrels, adjusted their harnesses, locked and
loaded their rifles, and swung their legs outside, planting
their feet on the skids. A recon "insert" was quick and
risky, forcing the men to drop from as high as ten feet
from the moving helicopter. The trick was to hit the
ground running and not break any bones or become mired
to the knees in mud. Both would make the trooper a sitting target for the enemy.

Franklin braced his feet, felt the chopper's nose rise,
then heard the gunner shout, "Go!"

They slammed onto the wet, slimy, and deadly sharp

elephant grass, dropped to a prone position, and lay still until the chopper roared away.

Then they rose and, bent low, started toward a village that was the first stop on their ten-day long-range patrol.

# 2

\* \* \*

The recon team slipped through the dense foliage like ghosts moving through walls, touching nothing as they worked their way carefully toward a large opening where a small village was seen. The monsoon rain fell in windswept slants, nearly obscuring the tiny ville, nothing more than mud huts with thatch roofs, dividing the village into two sections, with a community gathering place between the two.

That was what recently promoted Spec Four Franklin Sharps was studying through his binoculars. What he saw wasn't pretty, twisting his face into a mask of fury. Although still officially a medic, he had become a valuable member of Recon Platoon, which was now a fast-moving, hard-hitting, "take back the night" commando force. He not only carried his rucksack and aid kit; he also carried greater responsibility.

Private John Dawes eased to his side and whispered, "What's the plan?"

Franklin whispered, "You take Kirkwood and Burkett

and cover the back door. I'll take Marion and Elliott and we'll go in and scope out the ville."

Dawes nodded and turned to Private Burkett, whose white face was a myriad of camouflage paint. He motioned with one finger toward thick jungle near the south end of the village. Then they disappeared without making a sound.

Three more scouts appeared wearing tiger-stripe fatigues, carrying rucksacks laden with explosives, ammunition, and other equipment vital to a long-range recon patrol team.

The night suddenly turned gray as a loud crash of thunder succeeded a finger of lightning, highlighting the three scouts as they moved from the jungle. When Franklin reached the first hut he looked right, then left, removed his bayonet, and showed it to the other two. He carefully locked the bayonet on the muzzle stud, then switched off the safety on his M-16 rifle.

Franklin slid along the edge of the hut, his heart pounding. He peered into the hut and found it empty. A small cook fire was smoldering, with only a slight wisp of smoke, telling him the owners had been gone for some time.

As he started toward the second hut there was a loud "squeal!" as a frightened pig shot past him. His heart was now racing, so he knelt and tried to calm his nerves by breathing in long, deep breaths. When he had settled down, he continued his sweep.

He quickly checked the second hut and found it empty. As was the third. One by one each hut was checked.

The three joined up on the far side of the first section and started forward. Franklin held up his fist and pointed. Marion and Elliott squinted and through the rain saw the hooch. He motioned them forward, raising his weapon, at the ready to fire.

Ten yards away, beneath the poncho hooch, four Vietcong soldiers slept in hammocks, their Kalashnikov AK-

47s lying across their chests. On the ground lay several empty bottles of Bamiba beer.

Franklin took aim, as did Marion and Elliott, then shouted, "Let's rock-and-roll!"

A startled Vietcong awoke just as Franklin opened fire with his M-16 fusillade. The jungle then came alive with the thunderous roar of the weapons as the hammocks swung wildly, bullets tearing bits of tissue and body.

Within seconds the four VC were dead, their blood running onto the wet ground, forming rivulets of red that ran onto the jungle boots of the LRRP (Long-Range Reconnaissance Patrol) soldiers. Smoke drifted lazily upward, then flattened as the humidity and rain seemed to want to deny it to the sky.

Marion stepped forward and kicked one of the dead soldiers in his hammock. "Sleep on that, sucker!"

Franklin pulled his knife from his harness and cut the rope attached to one end of the hammock of a dead Vietcong. The VC's body spilled onto the ground, his face in a pool of his blood. "That's for my dead brother Adrian, you son of a bitch!"

He stood there breathing heavy, smelling the gunpowder, the death, and loving every moment, as he had each time before when he avenged the death of his brother. Then he knelt heavily and said to Marion, "Check them out for papers. Money. Anything. You've got two minutes; then we move. We'll hook up with the others at the back door."

Franklin looked around, knowing there was still one piece of work left. He walked off, reloading a fresh magazine, as Marion and Elliott began searching the bodies. "Wire the bastards!" he said.

Marion checked the first body, found nothing, then took a hand grenade, pulled the pin, and placed it in the VC's armpit, rolling him carefully onto that side. If he was turned over by other Vietcong, a loud surprise would be waiting!

• • •

When Franklin reached the open area he felt sick at the sight before him. Dawes, Burkett, and Kirkwood stood looking at two Vietnamese children. "Are they still alive?" he asked Dawes.

Dawes tossed a cigarette onto the ground. "Barely."

Franklin looked at the two children suffering before him. "Charlie sure gets pissed when the locals step out of line."

The two small children appeared to be standing but weren't, their small feet dangling inches from the ground. Their tiny bodies were held by bamboo poles planted in the ground and shoved up their rectums. The little girl squirmed pitifully, then closed her eyes. Blood and excrement slowly oozed down the pole.

"How you want to do this?" asked Franklin.

"Can you do anything for them?" asked Dawes.

"Yeah, but you ain't going to like it. Only trouble, there ain't enough morphine to do the job right." He hawked and spit with disgust. "Otherwise, they're going to suffer. Can't get a chopper in with this weather. Besides, it wouldn't matter. Neither one's got a snowball's chance in hell. They're just living on minutes."

Franklin looked at their faces, then lifted the girl from the pole as Dawes lifted the boy from his stake. They laid the children on the ground, side by side. Franklin knelt and ran his hand along her face, pushing back her matted hair. He was surprised to see a brief moment of gratitude, as though she knew what he would do to relieve her torturous misery.

Franklin stood, as did Dawes, and lowered his M-16 to her head. Dawes did the same to the boy.

Both pulled their triggers at the same moment the earth shook with thunder and lightning forked through the sky.

# 3

✱ ✱ ✱

Franklin thought constantly of those wily little bastards called "Charlie." After six days there were plenty of signs of the VC, but no Charlie to be found. Roads had been rendered impassable by deep trenches cut diagonally, preventing farmers from transporting their crops to market. Whole villages had been forced to become staging areas and sanctuaries, even training and recreational sites. Charlie was smart. From the moment Americans arrived "in-country," he hid in the mountains and lowlands, watching, always watching, learning everything he could about American tactics and deployment. He even learned their eating habits and turned their garbage into a weapon.

Empty C-ration cans were turned into booby traps. Grenades found on the battlefield were planted near American areas to be discovered, the fuses shortened to nearly nothing, becoming instant death for soldiers who pulled the pin and released the safety spoon. Claymore mines were reversed, aiming their deadly ball-bearing swath of explosive at the soldier firing the device. And there were other psychological mind benders used by Sir Charles: Coca-Cola sold with ground glass in the bottles, baby carriages rigged with blocks of C-Four explosives, left to detonate near restaurants and bars in major cities. Even mousetraps became instruments of death: bullets were imbedded in doors, over which a mousetrap was placed, the spring loaded arm cocked above a nail pressed lightly against the percussion cap. When the door was opened—"boom"—another body bag bound for the "world."

Tough. Smart. Rice balls and bamboo rats their diet. When they did fight they fought on their terms, hugging the Americans' belt, fighting close in, denying effective use of tactical air and artillery support, grating on the emotional strength of the American soldier.

The Americans had learned that Charlie had more tricks than a monkey on a hundred yards of grapevine!

The team had patrolled all day, cutting through the thick entanglement beneath the canopy of trees flourishing on the highland terrain. Finally, they reached a road, which was nothing more than a narrow path winding through the brutal bush. Each man's eyes carefully studied the road from the thick foliage off the gravelly trail. Smiles filled their camo-covered faces as they looked at the edge of the trail, then above.

Poles had been driven into the ground on each side; at the top, another pole ran across the trail, joined to another. Latticed across the framework were thick branches, forming a crude tunnel, providing cover from air observation. This was a feed-off of the trail and less sophisticated than that which snaked toward the north, becoming more sophisticated with each mile.

Construction on the Ho Chi Minh Trail began in 1959, near the 17th parallel of North Vietnam. A guerrilla society, the North Vietnamese required a covert means of delivering supplies and personnel to the south while avoiding detection and attack. The trail ran more than fifteen hundred miles, winding from North Vietnam, through Laos and Cambodia, and into South Vietnam, a wondrous engineering feat. Hundreds of thousands of workers toiled and lived along the trail, constructing the supply route with every means imaginable from humans to trucks, carts, elephants. Where rivers or gorges appeared, make-shift bridges were constructed; bombings by the South Vietnamese or American forces were only minor incon-veniences, as work crews would hurry to the damaged area and quickly make repairs.

The Ho Chi Minh Trail was more than a supply route; it was a society within itself, complete with small cities, rest and recreational areas, hospitals staffed with doctors and nurses. Newspapers were printed along the route, sending word north and south of the status of the war. The trail was defended with antiaircraft gun emplace-ments, artillery, and tanks secreted into the caves and deep trenches covered with camouflage. The Vietnamese grew crops at various locations, manufactured ammunition and combat clothing, built schools and day-care centers for the children of the worker/soldiers, all underground in laby-rinths of sophisticated tunnel systems or beneath thick jungle canopy impenetrable to the human eye from air-borne platforms.

The trail was also a military training facility, although on the move, taking young Vietnamese men and women with no military experience and honing them into soldiers as they made the six-month journey from the north to the south. By the time a soldier had reached the sector of the south where his unit would be deployed, they had been trained in the rudiments of guerrilla warfare, which often included ground-to-air antiaircraft fire and artillery bom-bardment along the way. Overcoming the hardships of nature, including malaria, dysentery, poisonous snake-bites, even attacks by tigers, the NVA were hard as nails and eager to fight once they reached the Vietcong unit of assignment.

The Americans knew this, especially the Special Forces

teams living in outposts along the trail. The problem was the Vietnamese and American governments, who refused to believe such a sophisticated supply line actually existed. That was the job of the recon elements: to probe the trail, find its weak spots, harass the enemy, disrupt supply and communication lines. To get in close to Charlie, find where he slept, and turn the night or day into a fiery hell.

In August 1965, the mission of the First Brigade was to clear the An Khe area for the arrival of the 20,000-man First Air Cavalry Division's arrival and hit Charlie along the trail, cutting it wherever possible.

MACV in Saigon had ordered that every ounce of rice, bullets, and soldiers coming down the trail would be paid for by the North Vietnamese and Vietcong with their blood.

"I think we've found something," Marion whispered to the team. He motioned Franklin onto the trail.

Franklin crawled onto the trail and lay beneath the canopy. His eyes slowly scanned the dirt, which was still wet from the heavy rain. A grin suddenly filled his face. He reached and ran his fingers onto what appeared to be a small, narrow tire tread embedded in the dirt. It was no secret Charlie wore what were called "Ho Chi Minh sandals," crudely made footwear from discarded automobile tires. Carefully Franklin eased back into the protective concealment of the bush and crawled beside Marion.

"We got beaucoup troop movement on this baby," he whispered. "Plus deep grooves. Looks like bicycles. I think we've found a supply route."

Marion took out his map and, after confirming their position, reported to headquarters on the PRC-25 radio. The squelch was turned all the way down, eliminating the scratchy static from the radio. His words were low, no more than a whisper. "Tiger Base, this is Tiger One. Over."

There was a pause; then a voice replied, "State position and sit rep. Over."

Marion gave their position, then a situation report. "Have found heavy-duty signs of enemy troop and supply travel on canopied trail. Over."

There was a long pause; then the voice of platoon leader Lieutenant James Gardner was heard from the recon platoon base at battalion headquarters. "Roger, on the find. Continue recon from your position. Maintain radio contact. Do not—repeat—do not make contact with Charlie. Sit rep every fifteen minutes. Do you copy?"

"Roger. Copy five-by-five. Out."

Marion said, "Let's grab some chow while we can. It might get active here tonight. Check your socks, strap your shit down tight, and dust off your weapons."

Like the others, Franklin reached into his pack and pulled out several cans of C-rations, all bound together by tape or commo wire. This was done in order to keep the cans from clanging together, a dead giveaway in the bush, where sound traveled like lightning and could be a dead giveaway of their position.

He opened a can of turkey loaf with his P-38 can opener and dipped his mess spoon into the chow. He ate slowly, listening while chewing, his ears pricked for the sound of unexpected company.

Marion eased beside him, his face a mass of scratches from the prickly "wait-a-minute" vines they had fought through since leaving the village for the dense bush. He pointed down the right of the trail. "I'm going to put Burkett twenty meters to the right on this side of the trail. You go twenty meters to the left on the other side of the trail. That'll give us both enfiladed and cross fire if the balloon goes up. Set up claymores with angles on the center of the trail in front of my position."

Franklin shook his head, his face equally as scratched. "Your ass will be in the hurt locker if we have to use the claymores."

Marion grinned. "I'll keep my head down. If we have

to fight it out, move straight back from your position and to this point, five clicks to the south. That's extract Bandit. We'll hook up at dawn and call in a chopper." He tapped a spot on his map that was circled in red, a relatively low area five kilometers from their location where an extract helicopter could land to remove the team. Or what was left of them.

Franklin didn't like the situation, knowing there was more combined firepower in numbers if the team stayed together. But if the shit did hit the fan, there might be a chance for some of them to escape if they weren't in one concentrated group.

"OK. See you in the morning." They shook hands and Marion crawled toward the others to lay out the plan. Franklin reached into his pack and pulled out two squares of tire tread the size of the soles of his boots. With string he tied the squares on, giving him a portable set of Ho Chi Minh sandals. He checked the trail in both directions, then hurried across the trail in a diagonal path. When Charlie's point man came along the trail, even using flashlights at night, he would see only tire tread prints, not the distinctive sole print of American jungle boots.

Reaching the spot Marion had designated, Franklin took a claymore from his pack and braced the deadly device against a tree to give added blast force, connected the detonator wires, then moved to a position that would give him protection from the blast of the mine and good observation of the trail. He laid out his equipment for ready use: two grenades with the pins straightened for quick use, his M-79 grenade launcher beside his pack, loaded and ready to rock-and-roll, and his "quickie" magazine unit, three magazines taped top-and-bottom to give him fast reloading capability without reaching for another magazine. He turned on his radio, which was set to the same frequency as headquarters and the other men, making sure the squelch was off, and covered everything, including himself, with loose foliage.

The cover gave him a sense of security, like when he

was a child, lying beneath a blanket during a thunderstorm, hiding from the darkness within a suit of armor made of cloth that brought warmth and security. Hiding from the darkness inside another darkness.

Around him he could hear the trees breathe with each slight breeze at the tops, the only point where the trees could be touched. Beneath, the air was stifling, the heat sucking the bark and pulp dry.

He felt a bug crawl onto his face but didn't slap at the insect. Movement was critical now. He had learned to lie motionless and endure the agonies of the jungle and rice paddies.

Leeches. Mosquitoes. Snakes. Each had their particular form of deadliness in the war, brought about by movement. Pull at a leech while lying in a rice paddy and the water rippled or gave off a slight splashing that could alert a nearby Charlie. Slap at a mosquito and the sound could travel through the night as though he had fired his weapon. Snakes were different. A snake has its own personal death delivery system—with a snake he had learned to lie motionless, let the reptile slither over his body and disappear toward another place. He felt secure beneath the cover, he did what all soldiers in a combat area hated the most: He waited.

# 4

\* \* \*

**B**eneath the triple canopy of tall trees, smaller trees, and high brush, the cascading foliage made starlight impenetrable. So dark, Franklin thought he could see the veins in his eyes as he stared into the nothingness.

Most important in an ambush was sound. The enemy would not arrive with an orchestra playing; nor with talk, laughter, or the clanging of equipment. Charles would slip along the trail with the silence of a single drop of rain sliding down a leaf and dropping quietly onto the heavy ground cover. His rubber sandals would not kick up the dirt as he walked, nor his feet drag listlessly; each step would be an exercise in stealth and subtlety, as he was carefully trained to become one with the ground over which he traveled. There would be no glow of a lit cigarette, nor metal-to-metal contact between weapon and harness.

When Sir Charles entered the arena, it would be with no more warning than a bolt of lightning. Only there would be no brilliant flash of light, nor clap of thunder.

But even Charlie couldn't see in the dark. He might be good in the shadows, but he was neither bat nor owl, although as quick and wily.

An hour after darkness fell, Franklin saw what he had hoped and prayed for: A small, reddish light danced along the trail, coming in his direction. He knew the VC point man would carry a flashlight with a red filter and over that a piece of cloth to further cut down the glowing signature.

The point man was moving slow, the light low to the ground, as though he were searching for something lost. Franklin knew a second VC was close behind, within touching distance, only his back to the point man, his flashlight serving as a beacon for those who followed, like a lighthouse on a darkened shore.

Franklin heard the soft patter of the point man's feet as he passed, followed by the second, and carefully reached to his radio. He keyed the transmitter button—"breaking squelch"—for a long three-second count, a signal back to headquarters that Charlie had arrived. Slowly, the caravan began to appear, and only sound, though barely audible, now served as the recon squad's eyes. And it became something of a quessing game, trying to calculate how many soldiers and bicycles or carts were passing. He listened so hard his brain ached as he tried to judge the count. For every ten men, break squelch once on the transmitter. For every bicycle or cart, two clicks. Electronic Braille.

Not a perfect science, but the best they had under the circumstances.

From time to time there would be a soft cough or a scuffle of sandals on the dirt, but rarely. He lay there in his sweat, his finger on the button, his ears tuned to the mystery of what traveled through the night only a few feet away.

He felt a presence, froze. He nearly panicked as he realized one of the VC had stepped off the trail. A foot stepped onto his hand. He lay motionless. Then, he felt the warm stream of piss, smelled the ammonia.

The VC stood above him, one foot on his hand; Franklin fought to lay motionless as the piss splashed off the side of his face, flooded his ear, his mouth. Then, he felt the vibration as the VC shook himself and stepped from Franklin's hand and slipped quietly back onto the trail.

Franklin lay there, his heart pounding, his stomach rising into his throat. He felt the wetness in his crotch and realized that aside from the darkness, the war, and the danger that lurked, he and the VC shared another common denominator: Both had taken a piss together.

# 5

**H**ours after the caravan had passed, Franklin remained in place, whispering to Marion over the PRC-25. It was agreed that all would remain in their position in case of further activity. Near dawn, thin shafts of light filtered through the canopy, slowly illuminating the trail, then the dense wooded floor. When he heard Marion's voice over the radio calling him and Burkett to his position, he crossed the trail diagonally, still wearing the treads strapped to his boots.

The team sat in an area of thick brush, only discussing what had happened. Franklin gave his report, leaving out the pissing incident: Even in war, some things remained personal.

Marion spoke the obvious. "This is definitely an active trail and it has to lead to somewhere. We've been ordered to follow it and see where those supplies and troops were headed. We report back, then head for the extract point and call for the chopper."

Before anyone could respond, the team heard a strange

creaking sound, followed by a hellish bellowing. The
team snapped to the edge of the trail, their weapons at the
ready. When the subject of the commotion came into
sight, the troopers stared incredulously. Franklin, like the
others, could only watch and wonder. An old man was
driving a cart filled with cut branches. It rolled on a pair
of rickety wooden wheels, pulled by a single water buffalo.

Franklin looked at Marion. "You thinking what I'm
thinking?"

Marion nodded and the team stepped simultaneously
onto the trail, where the terrified old man drew the buffalo
to a stop.

"Hey, Papa-san. What you got in the cart?" Marion
said.

The man, short and squat, his arms thin, face emaciated
from age and hardship, shook his head and bowed politely.

Burkett walked around to the rear of the cart and began
sifting through the branches. Franklin ran his hand along
the buffalo's brisket. His hand came away wet and slimy
with white, frothy sweat.

"This animal's been pushed mighty hard."

The old man was now sweating himself, jabbering
away in a language the Americans had not yet mastered.
But they all understood fear. And the old man radiated
it—his eyes went quickly to Burkett, just as the trooper
said, "Look what I found."

Franklin took the old man by the wrist and led him to
the rear. Burkett removed some branches. They all whistled in chorus. All eyes moved to the trembling old man.

Beneath the branches lay an unexploded American artillery round. The troopers knew that Charlie was a master
at turning unexploded ordnance into deadly mines and
booby traps, even detonating entire rounds in populated
areas.

Marion radioed headquarters. "The lieutenant thinks the
old man can help lead us to Charlie's base camp."

"We can't understand a word he says," Franklin said, his eyes staring coldly and hatefully at the Vietnamese. His brother had been killed when his jeep hit a land mine fabricated from an American artillery round. "Besides, if he does talk it'll be nothing but lies. Probably lead us into an ambush."

Marion had a demonic grin on his face. "That's not what the lieutenant has in mind."

"What then?"

"The lieutenant wants us to make some noise. Charlie will come and investigate."

"Then we follow them back to their base camp," Franklin said.

"Roger that, Brother Franklin. Makes our job quick and easy. Then we catch the bird out of this shithole and report back to headquarters."

"What about Charlie? Won't he know we're in the area?" Dawes wondered.

Franklin grinned. "What will they find? Shard. A hole in the road. And nothing but blood, meat, and bone. Probably figured he hit a bump and the round detonated."

"What about this bastard?" Burkett angrily snapped.

"He stays with the artillery round. He'll be remembered as a hero of the Revolution."

The troopers laughed; the old man shook like a leaf in a gale.

"Tie his ass onto the cart," Marion ordered.

While the old man was gagged and tied, Burkett took a block of C-Four explosives, shaped it to the nose of the artillery round, and inserted a blasting cap attached with three feet of detonation cord.

The fuse was lit and the six troopers raced to the underbrush, where they found cover behind trees and in ditches carved into the landscape by the heavy rains.

The explosion tore a gap in the road and overhead canopy, shaking hundreds of branches from the surrounding trees, showering the troopers with branches and leaves.

Again it was time to play the waiting game.

• • •

An hour later the troopers, now lying in a concealed "star" defensive perimeter two hundred yards from the road, saw a Vietcong soldier appear suddenly near the demolition site. He looked around, then motioned to his left, and three more VC came into sight.

"Just a scout patrol," Franklin whispered to Marion as he watched the enemy through his binoculars. "I only see four."

Marion was doing the same. "Roger, on the four Charlies. Now, let's see what they do."

They watched in silence as the VC picked their way onto the trail and walked about, inspecting the remaining debris of cart, animal, and human. Two of the Cong stood guard while the other two took entrenching tools and began filling in the hole in the road.

"It's working," Franklin whispered. "They bought it."

When the hole was filled and smoothed over, the two enemy soldiers cleared the debris from the road and slipped back into the trees, in clear enough view of the troopers for them to see which direction to follow.

All the VC withdrew, except one, who sat watching the area, a silent rear guard. After ten minutes he followed in his comrades' path.

"Let's go," Marion whispered. "Keep five and stay low and quiet."

The "keep five" order was obeyed, each man maintaining five yards' distance from the other to avoid a burst of automatic weapon fire hitting them all at once. The troopers moved with the same pace as the single VC, who never looked back and never knew he was followed. The troopers, however, maintained constant situational awareness, being careful not to be detected by either the rear guard or the forward element.

The rear VC met up with the other three, who moved out again, allowing him a breather. Franklin eyed the soldier through his binoculars, wishing he could fire, knowing how much he wanted to kill the little bastard. But not now. Now was the time to play Charlie's game, hug close to his belt, find his camp, then bring in the artillery and tactical air support. Then would come the extract and the flight to their base camp.

The leapfrog advance and pursuit continued for about an hour, with the VC still unaware they were being trailed. Finally, the flat terrain began to descend into a small valley.

And there the four Vietcong disappeared!

"Shit!" Marion cursed. All were studying the valley through binoculars, their vision made unclear by their rapid pulses' causing their field glasses to move erratically in their hands.

"I got nothing," Burkett whispered.

"Nothing here," Franklin whispered.

The others checked in with the same report.

"Watch for any sign of movement," Franklin whispered. Then he saw something, slight movement. "There're the little bastards. Ten o'clock. At the base of the slope."

All binoculars swung slightly to the left, where the four appeared in an open clearing. They dashed across the clearing, and their formation was a sign to the veteran recon troopers.

"They're bunched up; they're getting close to the front door," Franklin said.

"Or the back door," Marion suggested.

The recon team watched as the VC scampered toward an outcropping of boulders covered by brush. Then the brush moved, revealing an opening between the boulders no larger than a man's body, and bushes closed over the opening.

They stared at the silent valley below, knowing that the enemy lay hidden beneath the ground in a labyrinth of tunnels concealing them from air reconnaissance.

"Not this time, Sir Charles," Franklin said aloud. "We know where you live now."

Marion pressed the transmitter button on the radio, sent in his report, checked his map, and relayed the coordinates to headquarters. He looked at the others. "Tomorrow morning, Battalion's going to launch a combined air and artillery strike. We're to remain at this position and direct the fire." He pointed to the map. "ABU Company is going to be helicoptered into this point." His finger tapped the north end of the valley. "Cobra Company will be deployed to the east, west, and south. ABU Company will push from their landing zone, Cobra Company sets up an ambush. All we got to do right now is keep giving them a sit rep every fifteen minutes and keep low."

The troopers knew the extract would not happen; it didn't matter. They were finally going to get Charlie in a box and wear his ass out.

An hour later their worst nightmare began to unfold as they held their position above the small valley that was Charlie's base camp.

It began to rain and the afternoon sky turned black and ominous.

"Damn," Franklin cursed. "The weather's going against us."

Marion studied the sky. For five hours the rain poured, the wind whipped and roared through the valley, lightning cracked, and the thunder rolled like a mad drumroll. He contacted headquarters with the weather report. Radio contact ended with the same order: "Sit tight. Sit rep every fifteen minutes."

Night came and the recon troopers knew there would be no battle. Mother Nature had given the Vietcong another day to avoid the fight the First Brigade had dreamed of having. That was confirmed around 2100 when hundreds of flashes of lightning provided enough illumination for the troopers to see the Vietcong begin to slip from their underground labyrinth and deploy in every direction on the compass, carrying on their backs what appeared to be their entire base camp.

"They're skying out!" Marion snapped throatily into the radio, his anger uncontrollable. "They're skying out! Goddammit! The little bastards know something's going on!"

Watching through his binoculars, Franklin could see the Vietcong during the intermittent flashes. The valley was peppered with the elusive enemy popping from the ground from "spider holes," appearing for a moment, then gone the next, like fireflies on a hot summer night.

"They know," Franklin said angrily.

"The bastards always know," Burkett said.

One of the frustrations the brigade had suffered in getting Charlie to come out and fight was his uncanny ability to know where and when American forces would strike their camps. Having spies and agents near large American units, especially helicopter squadrons, often determined when an operation was about to be mounted. The recon troopers watched helplessly.

"How many you make?" Marion asked Franklin.

"Can't tell, but there's beaucoup," Franklin replied. "But right now we got other problems. Some of them are going to be coming our way."

"Find a tree and climb as high as you can," Marion said. "We don't want the shit coming down on our head. Spread out and stay off anything that looks like a trail."

The men climbed quickly into the trees and hugged the thick trunks, hoping the height and the darkness would give them ample cover. Franklin stood on a thick branch, his weapon at the ready, and knew that, unlike the night before, Charlie's approach would not be so subtle.

The Vietcong's approach was signaled by the clatter of weapons banging off harnesses, grunting, heavy breathing, and the snapping of branches. The recon men hugged the wet trunks and branches as the wind whipped at their bodies, while clutching the swaying trees, making it nearly impossible to keep a tight grip on the wet bark.

Suddenly the enemy seemed to be everywhere, streaking through the bush like deer scattering in the forest. Lightning flashed and Franklin saw a group of three VC running directly toward his tree, but they didn't stop or look up. They ran headlong past his position and disappeared as quickly as they had arrived. Another group passed seconds later, and Franklin nearly laughed: They were carrying bicycles.

Although the exfiltration by the Vietcong past the Americans took only minutes, the time seemed interminable. Finally the forest returned to its pristine quiet, except for the rumble of thunder. An hour later, the troopers heard Marion's soft voice ordering them to regroup. Franklin climbed down, his muscles cramped from squatting on the branch, and joined the others.

Marion had that unique look of being calm and said, "We ride out the night in a tight defensive perimeter. Every other man awake for two hours."

That was the procedure: Keep the surveillance; get some sleep while the others covered your ass.

"Set out claymores?" Franklin asked.

Marion shook his head, his eyes steady. "No claymores. If there's stragglers, let them through. We don't want to make contact."

Contact. What they all longed for but not could have, at least not in strong force. That was the greatest source of frustration about being in recon. Contact was forbidden.

The troopers formed a six-man star, their weapons at the ready, every other man awake.

Franklin took the first watch, with Dawes and Burkett. They lay beneath the darkened triple canopy, seething that they had not had a chance to draw first blood.

# 6

The recon team moved from their position at first light, quickly covering the distance to the rim overlooking the valley, and reported to headquarters. Rain continued to fall, but not in the torrent of a few hours earlier. The small valley appeared quiet and empty. Marion listened to the platoon leader's orders and briefed the others on their next move.

"We're going to recon the area, but first there's going to be an artillery strike at zero-seven-hundred. If everything is cool, we move to the extract point." He grinned. "At least we get to make a little noise."

The men took cover in an outcropping of rocks overlooking the valley and, though maintaining vigilant watch for the enemy, found time to relax for the first time in days. Franklin removed his harness and sipped from his canteen as the first signal of incoming artillery whistled through the air.

A terrific explosion erupted two hundred meters south of the opening in which they had seen the VC disappear, then another, only closer, as the rolling barrage crept toward the base camp. Marion gave elevation adjustments until the rounds were hitting square in the center of the camp. "Fire for effect," Marion called on the radio.

Giant plumes of black-gray smoke rose as rounds began to saturate the area. Marion continued to guide the attack, moving carefully to the flanks, back to the center, then forward, slowly sweeping the enemy area until there was nothing but twisted trees, shattered rock, and potholes rapidly filling with the rain.

"Wow!" Burkett laughed. "Fourth of July!"

"Out of sight!" Dawes chimed in.

Franklin watched the massive destructive force of the 155 howitzers pound the valley into fodder, wishing there were Vietcong on the receiving end of the artillery. He watched through his binoculars and saw a round strike, caving in what appeared to be a tunnel system, which now, with the upper level blown away, looked like a long open trench, a deep, ugly scar where once there had been lush green natural beauty.

But Charlie was nowhere to be seen.

The troopers watched, eating C-rations like children licking cotton candy at a fireworks display, only not cheering aloud as they had as youngsters. It was a strange sight for all; none had ever had a front-row seat to such devastation. They had only heard it from a distance and were awed at the horrific destructive power of modern warfare. Theirs had been a silent world for the most part. Calling in mortar strikes and throwing grenades paled in light of what they now watched as the air shrieked with the telltale whistles; the ground shook, and huge masses of rock and dirt spewed from the earth as though it was being spit to the surface by some mammoth unseen subterranean force.

"It's beautiful," Franklin said softly. "Man, I don't want none of that shit to ever come down on me."

Suddenly quiet settled over the valley. Smoke clung to the ground, drifting along the shattered earth in eerie fingers of gray, ghostly and spooky, creeping into the trenches as though seeking the souls of the dead. All wondered if the enemy were dead.

The troopers could only watch, and all felt a chill, knowing that soon they would be in those trenches and wondering what they would find.

For a split second, Franklin found admiration for Charlie, who was willing to endure such massive destruction and deprivation to fight for his cause.

Then Marion ordered, "Let's move out. Two-by-two spread. Franklin and Dawes on the point. Elliot on me at the center. Burkett and Kirkwood bring up the rear. Each team keep ten from the other. Move out."

The recon teams employed a standard operational procedure when advancing across unknown ground: In pairs, one watched the ground for trip wires and punji pits while the other watched the trees for snipers. Charlie loved the game of mind-fuck; he had a Ph.D. in psy-war ops. But the Americans were fast-learning students, unlike when they first arrived and did "their Sunday afternoon walk in the park with their heads up their asses."

Progeny of the saviors of the world in World War II, reminded by uncles who had been at "Frozen Chosin" and parachuted onto "Munsenei" in Korea, the American soldiers in Vietnam felt an invincibility that required nothing more to survive combat than a good weapon, dry socks, and a piece of local pussy for an occasional reward for studious work.

In reality, class was just beginning.

Sir Charles was a great teacher, with a body bag and flag-draped coffin as a diploma for each of the Americans who failed to negotiate his course.


Signs abounded of the Vietcong's hasty withdrawal: sandal tracks, broken or twisted branches, pieces of black pajama clinging to the saw teeth of the wait-a-minute bushes, and a few bandoliers. Franklin even found an AK-

47, dropped by a frightened VC he figured must have been a recruit. No veteran Cong would lose his Kalashnikov. He'd die first. Franklin examined the weapon, which was filthy, but he knew it would fire, even if rusted. Unlike the M-16, the AK could take any kind of abuse. Americans were not allowed to carry recovered AKs, for if they were fired in combat, their distinctive "*clatter*" might give their own people the mistaken notion they were Cong and draw friendly fire. It had happened many times, with deadly results.

Where the wall of the ridge met the flatter terrain of the valley the earth looked as though huge fingers had clawed through the ground, leaving indelible etchings they recognized as collapsed tunnels. "Man," Franklin said to Dawes, "Mr. Charlie must be part gopher." The extent of the tunnel system was mind-boggling. No more than two feet wide and three deep, the maze wove from outer entry points to a central location that was much larger in dimension. Splintered support beams jutted from the floor; some lay twisted inside the opening.

Franklin's eyes narrowed, and the stench stung his nose. Though it was covered with dirt and debris, he realized what he had found.

*This is not my fault,* Franklin reminded himself as he stood staring into a deep crater. *I didn't start this war. But you killed my brother and I owe you no sympathy!*

"Must have been the infirmary," Dawes said. He pointed his rifle at the twisted remains of enemy bodies lying mangled and dismembered on the floor of the crater. "I count seven. Most of them bandaged."

"Yeah. Charlie skyed so quick, he had to leave behind the wounded." Franklin dropped into the infirmary and knelt beside a body. "She looks no older than ten years." A young girl, her head bandaged, lay twisted, the dressing black with dried blood. Clutched in her small hand was a wooden doll.

Odd, he thought. Children the world over have their specific needs. Little girls have their dolls. Like when he was a boy, only his toy was a cap gun. Charlie probably grew up playing with a cap gun. And like him, now the guns they played with were real.

And deadly.

"Look here." Dawes pointed to another body. "An old mama-san. Must have been a nurse or something. I suppose she stayed behind to comfort the wounded." The upper torso of an old woman, her long gray hair in a ponytail, lay in the center. "Wonder where the other half is?" Her intestines hung from her sunken belly, turning black as the air sucked at the tissue and the blood drained onto the ground. Flies would dwell on her soon, breeding maggots that would wind into the cavity, devour all that was flesh. Leaving only the bones. Symbolic of war. When it's over, there's nothing left but the bones. Everything else belongs to whoever stakes the first claim.

Franklin shook his head and turned, raised his fist, and pumped his arm, signaling the others to follow.

The team regrouped and were delighted to hear Marion say, "We'll be extracted from this point. The chopper's inbound." That was good news. Tired from the long patrol, the men looked forward to a hot shower and a long sleep, even if it would be on hard ground.

Franklin looked again into the crater and for a moment felt pity for the child and old woman. Then he spit and said acidly, "Don't mean nothing!"

That had become the "phrase" of the American soldier. To mean something, there has to be value. In Vietnam, life had become an equation that meant nothing.

Then, the greatest sound they had heard in nearly two weeks: the rotor slap from an incoming helicopter.

The chopper flew the team away, all knowing the Vietcong would return.

So would the Americans.

# PART 2

⋆

## Hugging the Belt

# 7

## ★ ★ ★

Brigadier General Samuel Sharps was tall and sapling lean, his physique strong and durable, like that of a long-distance runner. He wore his hair shaved two inches above the ears and close-cropped on top and allowed himself a narrow mustache, highlighting full lips. He wore a light blue jumpsuit as he sat at the large ormulu desk commanding his office at MACV headquarters in Saigon, where he served as liaison officer between the U.S. Air Force and South Vietnamese Air Force.

He glanced to the mahogany wall, slowly swiveling his leather chair as he studied a panorama of family photographs, awards, and decorations earned during a military career that spanned nearly three decades. When one particular frame caught his attention, he felt a sense of pride, followed by sadness, as he always felt when remembering the most painful day of his life.

The photograph was of his son Adrian, taken the day of his graduation from West Point. The next frame held the photograph of Adrian's wife, Darlene, proudly holding their daughter, Argonne, a daughter he never lived to see. She had been born while he was in Vietnam. Beside the picture was another, a photograph of son Franklin, taken the day he graduated from airborne school at Fort Benning. General Sharps's emotions were in conflict between the two young men. Adrian was the disciplined, methodical son, always ambitious and dependable; Franklin had always been a mustang, wild and undisciplined.

A sudden knock on Samuel's office door broke him from his reverie.

His secretary, Jessica Kovar, entered, carrying a cardboard box. "I have these for you, General, just as you ordered."

He forgot about all else and looked into the box, containing five smaller cartons, each in its original wrapping. "Outstanding!" he said to Kovar. "You have the addresses?"

"Of course." She reached into the box, removed one of the cartons, and laid it on the desk. "But this one is for you. I'll get the others in the overnight mail bag immediately."

He removed the cellophane wrapping. The tape recorder was just what he needed, the others what his family needed. Separated by so many miles—and differences— he yearned to begin bringing his family back together again. The sting of shame struck him, reminding him of past mistakes, particularly his betrayal of the ones he loved the most in the world.

After leaving his office at MACV headquarters, Samuel strolled along the wide boulevard. The air was muggy, thick with the moisture, nearly to the point of rain, that dogged the Vietnamese people hurrying about their business, past outdoor vendors selling the Vietnamese version of hamburgers and fries: slices of beef in French bread with thick fried potatoes in their crinkly peels. He enjoyed being among the people, even though his height made him stand out like an oak tree in a cornfield. Perhaps due to his race, the Vietnamese treated him friendlier than they did white Americans, whom they called "long noses," a throwback name to French colonialism.

As he reached the building where he and other high-ranking officers were billeted, there was a thunderous explosion. Fire belched from the building; then a second explosion followed, sending chunks of plaster and mortar in every direction.

Samuel felt a smothering blast of heat, then an impact and blinding, searing pain and blackness.

# 8

\* \* \*

The mission of the First Brigade, as defined by Colonel James Timothy, was to serve as "a reserve reaction force capable of airmobile or parachute assault anywhere in the theater." The troopers of the First Brigade learned that quickly. Crack assault troops, such as Airborne or Marines, were being used for operations that were designed for infantry units. Instead, these elite assets were deployed as "search-and-destroy" units.

Only the recon element was acting in its traditional role: searching for the enemy and providing constant intelligence. That meant long-range patrols and isolation, which sat well with the 1/327 Recon Platoon.

By the end of August, the clearing of the An Khe Pass had become one of drudgery and disappointment. *Where was Charlie?* was the question on everybody's mind. He was out there. That was certain, but where?

There were some certainties. The young paratroopers were receiving fine-tuning points of soldiering from seasoned combat veterans of Korea, many of whom had also fought in World War II and pulled a tour in Vietnam before assignment to the Screaming Eagles, the boldest, most courageous fighting unit in American military history. One of the finest—who took keen interest in the training of the young soldiers—was Major David Hackworth. He knew there was more to educating soldiers than a rough commanding voice and telling war stories.

" 'What's a soldier?' " Hack—as he was called—would ask. Rarely did he get a good answer. Hackworth would explain: "A soldier is a trooper who can fire a three-round burst at a charging enemy and hit three targets." Hack hated weapons fired on full automatic. "If you fire full automatic you'll generally miss everything. It's a waste of ammunition, and more important . . . it tells the enemy you're scared and inexperienced."

Combat was the true classroom for Vietnam. Hackworth always reminded his troopers, "You'll be fighting an enemy who feels his country has been invaded by you. On his terrain, which he knows better than you. And the population is more on his side than yours. Don't think of this enemy as bowlegged slopeheads who can't soldier. They've known war all their lives. They defeated the Japanese and the French. They were born in this country. Not New York City, or Dallas, or Los Angeles, where there are no trees or rice paddies or mountains. This is their ground. They'll choose the time and place to fight."

The brigade had learned fast that in a firefight a soldier never saw the totality of what was happening. There was too much foliage, places for the enemy to hide, too much smoke, and too much noise gnawing at the senses. Noise. God, was there noise. Gunfire. Grenade and artillery explosions. Mortar rounds crashing to the earth, ripping apart trees and chewing up the ground in large chunks. Helicopters screaming low over the ground. Bombs and napalm exploding, searing the blue from the sky, turning it charcoal. Radios crackling. And the most unforgettable, the screams of the wounded and dying.

The only silence came from the dead.

"Hugging the belt" was a terrible tactic. It meant getting close, trying to tear at the will of Charlie, to drive him back and into the open, then brutalize him as he scurried for his village sanctuaries or underground bunkers.

It had become Charlie's greatest strategy. Hackworth convinced the brass it was time the Americans "took back the night."

The tactic was employed at night with good effect. Instead of Charlie harassing the brigade, the troopers sent out ambush patrols, sat in the night along trails worn smooth, like ruts from wagon wheels. An M-60 machine gun commanded the trail; claymore mines were posted to provide a sudden deadly swatch of hellish steel.

The brigade was learning how to take the fight to Charlie, and it was paying off, but with a price higher than expected.

There were other new tactics evolving, and not all of them to the liking of the troopers. Especially to Franklin Sharps, whose next patrol included a Vietnamese soldier leading a German shepherd that looked as scrawny as his master. The Americans called him a Kit Carson scout— one of hundreds of former Vietcong who had come over to the Americans. And not necessarily for patriotic reasons as much as the fact that they were tired of being hounded in the bush, bombed by airplanes, or shelled by mortar and artillery. Most Americans thought it was the better food and the odds-on bet that they would live longer fighting against their former comrades than fighting the Americans.

But these men knew the habits of the Vietcong, and the dog was trained in tracking the Vietnamese by the distinctive odor of *Nuk Bam*, a foul-smelling cooking oil derived from fish drying in the sun, seeping into the oil during decomposition. Most Americans thought the oil smelled like liquid manure and tasted worse. The only drawback for the Kit Carsons was that they were allowed to eat only American chow; otherwise their smell might throw off the dog's ability to pick up Charlie's scent.

Franklin looked at the man, pockmarked face, high cheekbones, and flat, dead eyes. He thought more highly of the Vietcong than the Kit Carsons, who most Americans viewed as traitors. And, he thought, *he might be the motherfucker that killed my brother!*

Major Hackworth gave the briefing as platoon leader Lieutenant James Gardner looked on. The major pointed to a map, an area marked in black. "Intelligence reports from popular forces indicate the Vietcong are using this area as a staging point. They are stockpiling weapons, ammunition, rice, medical supplies . . . all the good shit Charlie needs for an offensive. We need you to get in there and sniff out the bastards. There'll be recon units from Second Brigade operating ten clicks from you." He tapped the map and warned, "Don't fire on each other, goddammit."

A week before, a soldier had fired an M-79 grenade launcher onto his comrades' position and wounded eleven troopers.

"Charlie's in there. Be assured of that. I want good eyes on all of you. Get sloppy . . . and you'll sleep in a body bag." He paused, grinned, and gave his classic final words of farewell: "And remember . . . always keep five!"

Hackworth glanced at Staff Sergeant John "Dynamite" Hughes and added, "Sergeant Hughes, you know the drill. Keep your squad tight." Hughes was a professional soldier; small, but strong as an ox, he could carry more weaponry and ammunition than any other man in the unit. He had acquired his nickname Dynamite from that very characteristic. It was a common joke that should he ever take a direct hit he would detonate like an atomic bomb.

"Yes, sir." Hughes looked at the men and gave his standard piece of advice: "We do our job. No heroes . . . and everybody comes home!"

The briefing over, the soldiers had started to leave when Captain George Shevlin, the headquarters company commander, motioned for Franklin Sharps. Shevlin, a stocky, robust man, who was considered one of the finest officers in the brigade, took a sheet of paper from his blouse pocket. He handed it to Franklin. "This communiqué came in from Saigon." He paused, then added, "I didn't know your father was a general."

"It's not something I discuss, sir. It's not the sort of thing that makes a guy popular among the troops."

Shevlin understood. He added, "Read the message. If there's anything I can do, I'll help."

Franklin read the message. His father had been wounded in a bomb explosion in Saigon.

"Do you want to go to Saigon?" Shevlin said.

"No, sir. I'm going out on a mission. Anything else, sir?"

"No. Good luck on the mission."

Franklin and the others climbed into waiting jeeps for the short ride to the chopper pad. The team began loading under the glaring eye of the door gunner, who stared curiously at the dog, then shook his head and said nothing. The dog was hoisted inside by the Kit Carson and the aircraft lifted off and raced toward the landing zone west of Pleiku.

# 9

## ★ ★ ★

The beauty of the landscape was mesmerizing: a quilt work of rice paddies, framed by green forests, that sat surrounded by towering mountains that formed the Central Highlands. Like a black widow, thought Franklin, so beautiful, and filled with the deadly poison of a hidden enemy. Sprinkling the rice paddies were Vietnamese, bent over, pulling at rice shoots, a water buffalo in each square section to carry the harvest. But the Americans knew that lurking beneath many of those baskets were AK-47s, RPG-7 rocket launchers, and hand grenades. Charlie was prepared to go down only after putting up one hell of a fight.

The sudden *stammer* of the door gunner's M-60 cut the air, getting everyone's attention except the dog's.

"Got you, motherfucker!" The gunner was blazing away at the paddies, where Franklin saw the peasants breaking frantically for cover. Another burst left the air tasting of gunpowder, and he saw a water buffalo twisting and jerking in the paddy.

"Yeah! Have that for supper, you little bastards!" The gunner was in a near state of grace as he continued his staccato of death aimed at the peasants.

Another burst rippled, and the gunner looked at Hughes, saying, "Have to clear my gun."

Hughes just looked at him with contempt. In the two months the brigade had been in the bush, they had seen it all. Nothing surprised any of the troopers anymore. Except for maybe the presence of the dog.

The chopper raced along the paddies, then banked toward a tree line in the distance. Passing over the leading edge of the tall trees, the Huey slowed up and began settling in an open area covered with elephant grass. Hughes's eyes narrowed; then he called to the pilot, "Get out of here! Charlie has this spot bracketed!"

The pilot throttled up, eased the nose forward. Hughes pointed at the opening. "Look at the elephant grass. It's been cut short. Each blade is like a sharp stake, and there's no cover from Charlie." He looked at the door gunner. "Cut loose on the tree line."

The gunner grinned and began firing; red tracers marked the deadly fusillade's path.

But Charlie wasn't to be denied his moment. The trees suddenly came alive with gunfire and the Americans instinctively ducked, as though that might save them. The door gunner screamed and fell over the skid into empty air, his fall cut short by the safety harness secured to the floor. Franklin and Hughes reached, grabbed the strap, and began pulling the heavy body into the fuselage. He had been hit in the throat; blood poured from his neck. His eyes were rolled back, face ashen, and Franklin knew he was dead.

Hughes hurried to the pilot. "Put us down at the far end of the tree line!" He was pointing at an area that was nearly a mile from where Charlie had opened fire.

The pilot nodded and looked at the gunner. "What's his status?"

Hughes shook his head. "He's bought the farm."

Hughes and the others perched on the skids, ready for a "hot insert." "Keep low and move out quick," Hughes ordered. "Charlie's in there." He looked at the Kit Carson and yelled, "Carry your dog. We ain't waiting!"

The Kit understood. The dog would be in water over his head, forced to swim, becoming a juicy target.

The Huey dropped low over the water but near the tree line when the troopers unassed the chopper and hit the water on the dead run, charging toward the security of the trees. Franklin looked back and saw the Kit Carson, dog in arms, both of their eyes filled with fear.

They crashed through the edge of the trees and spread out, forming a horseshoe defensive perimeter. No one spoke; all eyes were searching, ears tuned for the slightest sound. But they saw nothing and the only sounds were the labored breathing of the Kit and dog and the fading rotor slap of the Huey.

Hughes gave a hand signal, and the seven Americans and Kit began moving out in pairs, one watching the trees for snipers, the other watching the ground for booby traps. They moved quick, careful, and silent, threading through the thick trees like shadows, saying nothing, unseen— they hoped—knowing that Charlie was in the area.

An hour later they stopped for a break. While Hughes checked his map, Franklin slipped around to each of the men. He always carried two extra canteens with a heavy salt concentration in each. Loss of body salt in the extreme heat took nearly as high a toll as malaria and booby traps.

When the Kit Carson grunted, pointing at the canteen, Franklin gave him a look the Kit immediately understood. Hughes, watching the exchange, knelt by Franklin. "The dog could use some of your saltwater mixture."

"I ain't no goddamned veterinarian, Sarge. Let the dink look after his dog."

Hughes's lips tightened. "You unload your hatred on the Cong, young man. On a patrol you're the medic for everyone along ... including the Kit Carson and his dog. Do I make myself clear?"

Franklin tossed his canteen to the Kit and sat against a tree watching the Vietnamese pour the water into the dog's mouth, then wet a bandanna and wash the dog's face. For a moment, Franklin almost felt sorry for the two creatures. All they had in the world was each other, and to Franklin's way of seeing things, that meant neither had much.

"Let's move out," Hughes ordered.

Tired and sweat-soaked, the troopers got to their feet, hoisted their heavy packs onto their backs, and started forward. The Kit led out with the dog walking to the front. The others on the team followed, with Hughes at the center. Franklin took up his usual position at the rear.

PFC Jesus Marquez was a tall, muscular Hispanic from Fort Worth, Texas, and had the dubious role of carrying the M-60 machine gun, the largest weapon in the American infantry arsenal. Size was important where this weapon was concerned. Humping hills and paddies with the '60 was a backbreaking job, even for the strong. Strands of ammunition were wound around his upper torso, adding to the burden and giving him the appearance of wearing brass armor, gleaming in the sunlight.

PFC Miles Walker carried the PRC-25 radio behind Hughes. From Macon, Georgia, Walker was tall, rawboned, and tough. He loved the bush and moved through the thick foliage with the ease of water moving over hard ground.

Spec Four Boyd Graves was a black kid from Chicago with large hands and feet, giving his short frame an awkward appearance.

PFC George Has No Horses was a full-blooded Sioux from Wounded Knee, South Dakota. Square-faced and wiry, his eyes dark, brooding, a grandson of Sitting Bull, nephew of One Bull, George was born to the lance and smell of battle.

Spec Four Jessie Stark was black and the "cherry," the new member in the platoon.

With the exception of Hughes and Franklin, they were all still teenagers, kids playing for keeps in a deadly adult world.

After nearly an hour, Hughes stopped the patrol to check his map, then reported their position over the radio. They moved out, following a trail that would take them to a village tucked deep in the bush, which the Vietcong preferred, as compared to the rice paddies with their openness. Thick, razor-sharp vines tangled their bodies, stinging the skin and impeding their advance. Mosquitoes buzzed, adding to the aggravation. The misery.

From the rear, Franklin watched the Kit and dog, both appearing to flow through the tangle of foliage. The Kit's eyes were trained on the ground when his hand shot upward. He squatted and took out his machete. Hughes eased up to his side, where the Vietnamese had run the blade beneath a clump of branches. Carefully the clump was removed, revealing a hole in the earth.

"Punji pit," Hughes whispered to Marquez, who passed the word along to the others. Sharp stakes hardened with fire at the tips and dipped in human excrement lay planted in the hole, a painful welcome mat to the Vietnamese village.

"Move off the trail," Hughes whispered. "Move abreast and keep ten."

The going became more than a physical challenge; it was equally demanding on the mind. The bush was thicker, visibility nearly zero, where seeing a few feet ahead was nearly impossible. Monkeys scurried about in the treetops, chattering and swinging from the branches, adding to the intensity. And the nervousness. Sweat poured from the men's faces, each knowing that any moment contact could be made with a concealed enemy.

There would be little cover. The Vietcong would be in bunkers covered with logs, and there would be the mines: Bouncing Betties that exploded at the ground, rose five feet, then detonated a second explosion; and the Chinese "button mines," plastic devils the size of a silver dollar but capable of blowing off a foot or leg.

Booby traps were Charlie's forte. The psychological effect was as important as the physical destruction. Fear and apprehension gnawing at the mind caused mistakes, which took a toll on others if a trip wire was triggered.

Franklin was on the left wing of the advance when the explosion ripped through the thick brush. The heavy thunder of the M-60 roared through the dense vines; a scream echoed from his right, and he recognized the voice of Has No Horses. Automatic weapons fire filled the air; there was the deep "crump" of a grenade exploding from Franklin's right front, followed by the cry he knew he would hear: "Med-ic!"

He charged head-down, his weapon poised to the front, ignoring the thorns and pain; the sweat burned his eyes, and he could barely see. Hackworth had been right: "You don't see war. . . . You hear it!"

He followed the sound, the distinct chatter of AK-47s firing from the front. The sound of bullets passing over his head cracked sharply in the stifling air, then more shouts and another report from an exploding grenade.

Franklin reached Has No Horses, who lay cradled in Hughes's arms. Hughes was talking slow and calm into the radio headset, ordering an artillery fire mission. He looked up at Franklin and nodded at the wounded Has No Horses. There was a look in his eyes that chilled Franklin to the bone.

While Walker kept his weapon leveled toward the sound of the firefight, Hughes kept talking on the radio and Franklin knelt beside his wounded comrade. Both legs were gone at the knees. Blood gushed from the stumps, soaking the loam ground a dark brown where he lay. His legs were nowhere in sight.

Franklin removed his pack and took a Syrette of morphine, pushed the plunger in, releasing the medication, then injected Has No Horses in the neck. He slowly squeezed the Syrette until it was empty, then took two tourniquets from his aid pack. Has No Horses stared emptily at Franklin.

Around him, the clatter of M-16s and exploding grenades stunned the ground, the air, and the senses within its touch.

Stark suddenly appeared; his eyes wide as he looked at Has No Horses, turned away for a moment, seized his composure, then said, "There's a Charlie bunker twenty meters to the front."

"Just one?" Hughes snapped.

"That's all that's opened up for now. Could be more. What do we do, Sarge?"

Hughes took the handset and spoke quickly. "We're too close for arty. Negative on the fire mission." He tossed the handset to Walker and told Stark, "We move straight on the bunker. You from the right flank with Graves. I'll take Walker and Marquez and go up the middle and keep them busy." He looked at Franklin and said, "You and the Kit hit them from the left flank."

Franklin nodded and looked at Has No Horses. "I can't do any more for him. We need to get a chopper in here."

Hughes looked up. "No way in hell a chopper can land in here. Right now we got to take out that bunker." Hughes looked at the wounded man. "When you hear Marquez open up with the sixty, start moving in."

Franklin understood. He finished wrapping the second dressing on Has No Horses's bloody stumps, then stood and motioned for the Kit to follow him. The Vietnamese tied his dog to a tree and followed.

The men broke away and moved quickly toward their positions. Franklin let the Kit take the lead, following in his footprints and maintaining a separation in case of more mines. They moved swift and steady, bent low, their weapons at the ready, until the Kit stopped and pointed to his right.

Franklin's eyes strained to see what the man was pointing at. Then he saw a slight movement at ground level no more than ten meters away. The barrel of a rifle. He watched the Kit take a grenade, pull the pin, and point toward the bunker. Franklin did the same and waited.

Suddenly the loud stutter of the M-60 erupted; bullets struck in the ground in front of the bunker, kicking up dust and keeping the enemy occupied. When the Kit's arm swung back, Franklin did the same, and both men threw their grenades and dived for cover.

At the moment the grenades exploded, Franklin caught movement from his left. No more than a flash of black.

He saw a Vietcong racing through the trees, snapped to his feet, and charged after the soldier. He fired a short burst, then another, and suddenly reached an opening that revealed a slight ravine. Franklin could see the VC wasn't armed with an AK-47. He fired another burst that hit the VC in the legs, dropping him instantly.

Behind him was more gunfire from the M-60 and the M-16s, telling Franklin the others must have taken out the bunker. But now he had a wounded enemy soldier, and even wounded, he was still deadly. Franklin walked slowly toward the man, then stopped suddenly. It was a boy of no more than twelve. He was on his stomach, trying to crawl away.

Franklin wasn't sure what had caught his attention, whether it was the movement of the boy's hand or the slight metallic ring, but his instincts told him to dive for cover. He had started to dive, his finger on the trigger, firing toward the boy, when he saw the grenade fall from the VC's hand and roll only inches from his body.

The explosion tore the boy to shreds, showering Franklin with dirt, debris, and bits of metal that stung at his arm. The concussion thundered in his ears, setting off a ringing in his brain unlike any he had ever known. He felt himself still rolling, as most of the shrapnel mushroomed over his body and ripped at the trees. Had he been closer the concussion would have killed him; any farther away and the deadly metal fragments would have torn his body to pieces.

Then it grew quiet and he saw the Kit suddenly appear at his side. He looked into the man's eyes; they appeared saddened, not heartless and cold. Franklin tried to rise up, but the Kit gently forced him to lay back down, then removed his canteen and poured water over Franklin's face. Franklin rolled up his sleeve and checked his wounds. He was fortunate. The wounds were small punctures he could easily clean and dress with Band-Aids.

Both turned suddenly at the sound of movement and pointed their rifles. The dog appeared and ran straight for his master. Franklin figured the dog had pulled himself loose during the ruckus and followed the Kit's scent. The dog licked at the Vietnamese's face, and while only moments before there had been the fury of war all around, now there was no other sound except for the heavy breathing of the two soldiers and the dog.

# 10

* * *

When Franklin and the Kit reached the rest of the team at the bunker, Sergeant Hughes was examining what remained. The grenades had torn holes in the ground, and two mangled bodies lay off to the side. There was only one weapon, a Chinese machine gun that had suffered as poorly in the grenade explosions as the Vietcong.

"This must have been a listening post. By now the ville will be empty." Hughes looked at Franklin and asked, "Did you make contact?"

"Scratch one VC. But not much of one. He was just a kid with a grenade."

"Yeah, and the will to use it. Deadly combination." He pointed at Franklin's bloody sleeve. "You square?"

"Just a scratch. No problem."

Hughes took off his helmet and poured water over his head, then pointed at Has No Horses. "Better get him ready for a medevac." He looked up at the tall trees. "If we can get him out of here."

Franklin went to George Has No Horses, who lay nearly lifeless. He was unconscious, and that was a blessing, thought Franklin. He injected Has No Horses with another Syrette of morphine and started an intravenous drip of saline solution. There was nothing more he could do, and he felt helpless. He knew that Has No Horses had been a rodeo rider before volunteering for the army. His eyes went to the blood-soaked bandages covering the stumps and he said softly, "Guess you won't be needing any horses, George."

From behind him Hughes's voice could be heard giving a situation report and calling for a helicopter evacuation.

One of the main purposes of the helicopter was for medical evacuation of the wounded and a quick trip to a waiting team of surgeons at a field hospital. The dust-off, as it was termed, was a psychological ace in the hole for the American soldiers in Vietnam. Long trips over difficult roads in frontline ambulances were passé; the chopper was the modern angel of mercy. However, terrain played a major role in making the extraction of the wounded often as deadly as the enemy. Charlie knew it was far better to wound an opponent than to kill him because the wounded required extraction, which demanded manpower, putting other personnel and assets at risk.

Charlie knew that where an American soldier lay wounded a big, conspicuous helicopter would arrive.

Hughes knew that if he didn't get a medevac for the Indian damned quick, the man would die. It was decided to deploy the team and set up a defense perimeter to protect the chopper, which would hover over the site and lower a harness through the trees. Franklin and Hughes would connect the wounded recce soldier, and then a winch would raise him to the Huey.

Franklin knew of this extract procedure only in theory. He had never done it before. Though risky, it was the only available option to save the man's life.

Franklin and Hughes stayed with Has No Horses and waited for the Huey while the others set up the perimeter.

Franklin had given Has No Horses several more injections of morphine sulfate, rendering him totally unconscious. The tourniquets were stanching the flow of blood, and by the time the chopper arrived he was resting easy. Hughes tossed a purple smoke grenade, marking their position, and stood staring through the trees until he saw the helo suddenly appear at the tops of the towering forest.

Hughes had kept the PRC-25 and radioed the pilot to lower the harness. The lifesaving apparatus came down, and despite becoming entangled in a tree, it was freed when the pilot lifted the chopper slightly, then lowered the nose, allowing the tether to drop to the waiting Hughes.

Franklin and Hughes moved quickly, harnessed the wounded soldier, then signaled the crew chief, who sat in the open door, to begin winching the wounded man up.

The wounded paratrooper, Has No Horses, rose straight up, slowly, oblivious to what was happening. Franklin had taped the intravenous saline bottle to the harness. The continual flow would sustain the wounded soldier until he was received by the waiting surgical team.

Franklin and Hughes stood watching as the wounded man neared the tops of the trees. Then, without warning, they saw Has No Horses fall from the harness and plummet toward earth.

"Run, goddammit!" Hughes shouted.

Franklin stood frozen, heard Hughes shout again.

A huge cloud of dust rose from where the trooper impacted on the hard ground.

Franklin walked to the body, knowing there was no hope.

PFC George Has No Horses had landed flush on the stumps and died instantly, his mind unaware, narcotized by the morphine. He stared emptily into the trees above through dead eyes, as one might look on a sunshine-filled beach, buried to his waist in sand.

Hughes walked over, put his hand on the neck and felt

for a pulse, stepped away, and said to Franklin, "Tag him . . . and bag him."

Minutes later a body bag was lowered, and Franklin "tagged and bagged" his comrade. Hughes tied the bag to the harness, securing it with rope he carried for just this purpose.

Franklin watched in silence as Has No Horses's body rose again toward the opening in the top of the trees. Seconds afterward, the chopper peeled off and disappeared.

Hughes's voice thundered, "All right, let's saddle up. We've got a ville to recon."

# 11

* * *

The team reached the edge of the hamlet and found the ville empty. This was typical of the highland villages most sparsely populated, except for the Montegnards—the "mountain people"—who lived farther to the west. The mere existence of the village was evidence enough for most military leaders to suspect it was Vietcong. The National Liberation Front—the Vietcong—built small villages in isolated areas for one specific purpose: to serve as supply dumps for the guerrilla units operating in the region. The VC used these supply depots, well concealed and appearing harmless, to store supplies brought south from North Vietnam. The tiny hamlets would suddenly appear to serve as a momentary base of operations, then would be abandoned, the guerrillas moving to another area.

Hughes scanned through his binoculars and saw no movement. "I was right about the bunker. Not a soul."

"What now, Sarge?" Marquez said.

"Let's go in from three points. Nice and easy. We've

already lost one of our men. I don't want to lose any more."

They moved toward the hamlet from the tree line in the same groups as the assault on the bunker. There was not a sound coming from the ville, which was no more than a half-dozen mud huts.

The team moved from hut to hut, staying outside, until they were convinced there was no one to be found. Then they gathered up and took the next step. Each man took a grenade and tossed it through the crude glassless windows. The demolition took only seconds, with each explosion destroying the hut and any booby trap that might be planted inside. The Screaming Eagles had learned the hard lessons of the past few months: Take no chances.

Hughes ordered the Kit to turn loose the dog. "Let's see if that son of a bitch has a Tennessee coon hound's hunting nose," he muttered.

The paratroopers stood watching as the shepherd sniffed and pranced about the debris, appearing more playful than serious. He rooted beneath the thick blocks of mud that formed the huts, pawed at splintered wood, avoided spots where fires still burned.

"Nothing," Hughes mumbled. He was about to call off the dog when the shepherd stopped, stood motionless, then lay on the earth, on his side, his ear against the ground as though he were going to sleep.

When the dog barked, the troopers jerked alert, and the Kit smiled, walked over to Hughes, and pointed to the smooth ground. "VC," he said excitedly, pointing at the ground. "VC here."

Franklin stepped forward and looked at the dog. "I think the dog is dumber than the Kit."

Hughes shook his head. "Give me your ET."

Franklin took the entrenching tool from his rucksack and handed it to Hughes, who began digging into the ground until he had dug no more than a foot and an opening appeared through the ground. It was common among Vietnamese villagers to build shelters beneath their huts to provide a quick and accessible shelter from bombs and artillery or to use as storage areas for supplies.

"Underground shelter," Hughes said. He spaded around the edge until the hole was the size of a sewer cover, then lay down and peered inside. The sunlight filtered into the hole; beyond the light provided by the sun he saw nothing. "Probably a bomb shelter." He looked at Franklin. "Drop a Willie Peter in there, kid."

Franklin took a white phosphorus grenade from his harness and released the spoon. At the moment he tossed the grenade, he saw movement in the hole and the shepherd leaped forward, soared through the air, and disappeared into the ground.

The Kit shouted and started forward. Hughes grabbed him by his harness and threw him back. Franklin was mesmerized by what he saw in the floor of the shelter: two brown eyes stared helplessly at him from within.

"Move, dammit!" Hughes shouted.

Franklin stood frozen, his eyes joined to the child's in the shelter.

"Get down!" Hughes grabbed Franklin's harness and with all his strength jerked the young trooper away from the hole. The earth shook as the grenade exploded, collapsing the shelter, creating an even larger crater. White phosphorus smoke spewed from the crater, acrid and billowing, forming a volcanic cloud that rose, flattened, and descended to where it spread ghostlike across the ground.

The silence that followed was broken only by the whimpering of the Kit, who sat staring helplessly at the empty crater.

Hughes screamed in Franklin's face, "What the fuck's wrong with you, boy!"

Franklin said nothing. He walked to the edge of the crater and looked down. "The shelter wasn't empty."

Hughes looked and saw several arms and legs sticking up from the dirt. One leg appeared older than the others. There were five limbs altogether. The squad leader dropped into the hole and pulled at the legs, tossing them out of the crater until he came to one with a sandal still on the foot. He examined the foot closely, noting the decrepit toenails and the withered skin. "Looks like we got us a papa-san and a couple of kids." He reached down and picked up a bloody, furry mass, tossed it out, and said angrily, "And one fucking German shepherd."

"Hell of a body count," Marquez said as he poured water onto a towel and wrapped it around his neck.

Franklin felt sick and wanted to throw up, wanted to kill Vietcong, not old men and children, wanted to go back to that moment and grab the grenade, put the pin back in, and walk away.

But he couldn't. It was too late. Death offers no rehearsal. Casualties of war, they had been told, would be a common experience. See it. Smell it . . . then move out. That's what the brass passed down from on high.

The grunts in the bush had another way of putting it: *"Fuck it . . . don't mean nothing."*

# 12

* * *

Hughes and the others knew the mission had been a bust when they took initial fire from Charlie at the tree line earlier that day. He had decided to push forward, hoping their presence would not compromise the mission, but he knew that would not be the case. The fact the ville was empty only reinforced that notion. Charlie had gone to ground and would not surface so long as he thought there were Americans seeking out his positions, especially if he suspected it was a recon team probing the area.

Hughes contacted the command post and arranged for an "extract" the following morning. He would have called for a daylight pickup but, knowing Charlie would be watching, he chose the early morning darkness when Charles could only hear the rotor thump and not actually see the team being airlifted from the arena. "Let Charles wonder if we're still here," Hughes said, "Maybe he won't sleep too tight tonight."

The team spent the night sleeping in trees high above a trail that meandered through the dense forest. Each man had tied himself to the trunk, straddling a heavy branch, perched on his rucksack for crotch protection. Then they played the "Close Watch" game.

The worst thing a recon specialist can do is lose focus, to forget where he's at and what's going on in the immediate area. Unlike the regular infantry soldier, one hundred yards means nothing to a recce grunt. That may as well be the edge of the earth. To the scout, the game is played out in a matter of feet and inches. Smell is important. A foreigner's smell can be as distinctive as rotting carrion, a trigger mechanism that can set off the alarms. But stealth is the most important, to move unseen in front of the enemies' eyes, and not make a sound.

Sound travels in the darkness like a crash of thunder from the sky, and can have a devastating result. A soldier on ambush patrol takes his turn to sleep, starts snoring, and before long incoming rounds start pulverizing the area. That is when the recon team's job is abruptly finished: when their presence is known to the enemy.

In Nam, word of a recon team's presence carried more swiftly than dry land lightning, or sound in the night. Which was why they knew their job was finished. The team was too small to be a fighting force should contact be made with a Vietcong unit of any size.

Hughes knew that Hackworth had devised a plan to combine the recon and antitank platoons to form a battalion-size "Tiger Force," as he called it, a fast-hitting, power-packed fighting unit that would pounce on Charlie with lightning speed and murderous firepower. Thus far it was theory, but in the works. He hoped it would come about soon, for he and the others were tired of being outnumbered.

Two hours before daybreak the team slithered down from their concealed heights and formed up. With Marquez on point, they slipped quietly through the forest toward the extract point. It took nearly an hour to reach the area, termed "Vegas," where tall elephant grass washed lazily back and forth in a slight breeze. The razor-sharp grass-edges offered a formidable and painful welcome.

Franklin's first experience in the grass was a nightmare he'd never forget. The wind whipped with near gale force, and the grass became what he could only describe as a meat grinder. By the time the team had moved through the field, not an inch of skin was left unblooded on the face and hands of the team.

The men sat waiting, nervous, knowing they had no protection from incoming bullets should Charlie know their presence, and rip off "spray and pray" automatic weapons fire. It was the same technique used by Americans: spray the area with automatic fire and pray that you hit a target.

Hughes sat stolid, his ears tuned for the sound he would recognize. Franklin glanced at him, and asked, trying not to laugh, "How's Butch?"

Hughes grinned and took a rubber doll from his harness. Butch was his good luck charm. Long black hair; no clothes, and uglier than Barbie on her deathbed.

"Butch's doing just fine," Hughes said, then stiffened and looked to the south.

The sound was distant at first, a low, pronounced thump that seemed to rumble overhead, then the distinct slap of the rotors as the Huey flew east of their position, giving the enemy the impression the chopper was bound elsewhere. In the cockpit, the pilot would reach a coordinate, drop low to treetop or paddy level, then run flat out to the rendezvous point.

But in the grass there was no real joy as the Huey flared above the team, turning the sea of elephant grass into a whipping storm of knives.

The men scrambled aboard through both open doors, lay flat, and turned their weapons outward. The nose of the helicopter lowered, the Huey pilot throttled up, then the craft raced across the grass in the first traces of dawn.

During the ride Franklin thought of Has No Horses and

the dead children, and wished again he could change the outcome. He glanced at the Kit, and even felt sorry for the poor bastard. The man had lost his best friend; the team had lost a good friend.

# 13

### ★ ★ ★

Samuel Sharps awoke to the feel of a razor against his face. When his hand touched the thick gauze over his eyes, a woman's voice said, "Please lie still, General. I'm not the greatest in the world when it comes to shaving a man's face."

He found something humorous in this and chuckled. The smell of antiseptic filled the room. "How long have I been here?"

"Three days," the woman said.

His mind flashed back to his last conscious moment. He remembered the explosion but nothing else except the pain. "What's your rank, miss?"

"Captain Jane Caulder, sir. I'm the shift supervisor." She placed the razor in a basin of water and began toweling the residual shaving cream off his face. "There. All done."

He felt his face. "You missed your calling. You should have been a barber. I couldn't have done a better job myself."

He could feel her breath as she leaned close to him. "I think I'll keep the one I have."

He heard the sound of a door open; voices rushed into the room, most of them screams and shouts familiar to a hospital in wartime. "Good morning, General Sharps. I'm Major Dan Eades, chief of ophthalmology."

"Good morning, Major. Pardon me if I don't get up." He went straight to the heart of the matter. "Am I blind?"

There was a pause. "No, sir. But you've suffered damage to your right eye," Eades said.

"What is the extent of the damage?"

"I won't know until the bandages come off and give you an examination."

"When will that be?"

"Now that you're conscious, I'll conduct an exam."

That suited him fine. He wasn't a man who liked surprises or having to wait if there was bad news. He felt a wet cloth wipe at his face, then the slight sting of aftershave on his face. There was the shuffle of feet, the sound of movement nearby, and the physician's voice. "Captain, close the blinds."

The bandage was carefully unwound. Thick pads covered his eyes; when removed, he continued to see only blackness. "I can't see anything," he said.

Suddenly—a burst of light exploded in his brain and he lurched forward. He felt hands pushing him back onto the bed and heard the doctor's voice speaking in a calm, measured tone. "Lie back, sir. This will be uncomfortable for a few moments. But . . . it's good news, General. Your reaction to the light is a positive sign."

Slowly, his eyes adjusted to the light; he could see the light move from one eye to the other. He heard Eades tell the nurse, "Open the blinds. Very slowly."

Gradually, the room filled with light; he began to make out shapes, then objects as the interior clarified. But the light flooding the room was diminished by the relief filling his soul.

He had suffered injuries in life, wounds in France during World War II, airplane crashes, even jet ejections. He had walked away from them all. None were so frightening as this experience.

# 14

* * *

General Sharps was released from the hospital one week after being wounded in the hotel explosion. He went directly to his office at MAC-V Headquarters, where his aide, Major Leif Svenson, was waiting to brief him.

Svenson, a burly Swede from Kenmore, North Dakota, was an F-4 fighter pilot who had been shot down six months before. Injured when he ejected, and spending nearly a week evading the enemy, despite a broken leg, he wanted to complete his tour in Vietnam rather than be shipped stateside for a desk job. Sharps, who had known him as a young lieutenant in his F-88 fighter squadron in Korea, gave him a job as his aide.

The two talked for nearly an hour on the deployment of several air force reserve units that would be arriving in-country in a matter of days from the United States. The war was cranking up; hundreds of thousands more U.S. ground troops were scheduled to arrive from CONUS

(Continental United States), bringing the total number to over 300,000 by the end of August.

Sharps glanced at the photographs on the wall. "What do you hear on the Screaming Eagles?"

Svenson was surprised at the question. In his own round-about way the General was inquiring about his son, which he had never done before. He knew the relationship between the two was strained, but naturally never pursued the matter. "They're still up in the Central Highlands, digging out the Vietcong, clearing the An Khe Pass for the First Air Cav. It's damn rough going up there, General."

Sharps leaned on his desk and rested his chin on hand. His dark eyes seemed to drift back in time. "The monsoon must be beating the hell out of our boys up there."

"It's relentless, sir. The troops on the coast—especially the Marines—are up to their asses in the rice paddies. Air-to-ground support has been mostly ineffective, what with the lousy weather and the VC striking from close range, then disappearing like ghosts."

*Ghosts*, thought the General. Another nickname for the elusive Cong. He glanced over to the corner of his office and saw a pile of clothes that lay neatly folded on a chair. "Is that all that's left of my personal property from the hotel?"

Svenson nodded. "You're lucky to have that much left over. The place damned near burned completely to the ground." He paused, then added, "From where you were found, another thirty seconds and you would have . . ." His voice trailed off.

Sharps rose and went to the window. He stared through the glass for several minutes, saying nothing, watching the throng of mopeds and bicycles stream along the streets like salmon swimming upriver. What he knew—what everyone knew—was that most of them were either Vietcong or sympathizers. He also knew that America had put itself in a situation similar to the French in the 1950s: a one-way street that never ended.

"Do you think we can win this war, Leif?"

Svenson stood and stepped beside the general. He looked out the window at the stream of Vietnamese flowing along the boulevard. "This is their country, sir. They've known nothing but war and invasion for centuries. They see us as no different from the French, the Japanese, or the Chinese. They see us as invaders. We are the Spartans at the gates of Troy, and we don't have a wooden horse."

"Hell," Sharps said, "we don't even have a beautiful Helen to hold hostage. Instead, *we're* being held hostage. What are they thinking in Washington?"

"I understand General Johnson's Linebacker plan has been put on the back burner."

Operating from 8th Air Force Headquarters in Guam, Lieutenant General Johnson had conceived a plan called Linebacker, in which his B-52 Strata-Fortresses would bomb nearly one hundred key industrial and military complexes in North Vietnam, eliminating manufacturing and shipment of valuable war materials, while concurrently destroying national morale and resolve.

Sharps nodded. "Yes, it has. President Johnson doesn't want the United States to appear as some Goliath stepping down hard on the tiny David."

"This David doesn't carry a slingshot, sir. He's well equipped, knows the terrain, and is certain he is right."

The general went back to his desk and began poring over the pile of correspondence that had collected since he was wounded. As always, there were the daily letters from Shania. He opened them first, reading each word as though it were the first he had heard from her. She wrote of Kevin, who was in college, and her recent letters from Franklin, and asked again, "Have you two gotten together yet since he arrived in Vietnam? I truly wish you would, Samuel. I think it would do both of you a lot of good. You're fighting a war together on the other side of the world. He needs his father. You need your son. Can't you find a way?"

He had been invited to Cam Ranh Bay by General

Westmoreland to welcome the 101st Airborne when it arrived in-country, but he had passed on the offer. Knowing the bad blood that still existed between him and his son, he didn't want Franklin to start his tour in the war with an angry beginning. It would be difficult enough in time; no need to make the first day tense because of family problems.

*Christ! How could I have been so stupid! To throw away a family for a romantic fling with a woman half my age!*

He spent the next hour listening to Svenson brief him on the status of the Ho Chi Minh Trail and the ongoing air operations designed to create as much havoc as possible for supplying the Vietcong in the south.

"It's like walking up a muddy slope, General. For every two steps forward, we fall back one. We blow a bridge, the VC rebuilds overnight. We cut one branch of the trail, they use an alternate, or carve out another."

"What's the bottom line on this situation, Leif?"

Svenson shrugged. "We've tried taking away the jungle by defoliation, but that's simply not working. At least, not the way we hoped."

"What do you suggest?"

Svenson went to a map of Indo-China and pointed at the red lines depicting the Ho Chi Minh Trail. "A two-pronged attack, using B-52 bombers for saturation bombing, and lighter aircraft to mine the trail inside South Vietnam, Laos, and Cambodia."

"Mines?" Samuel asked dourly.

"Yes, sir. Antipersonnel mines. We'll put the same fear of God into the little bastards as they have in our people."

"You want to mine nearly fifteen hundred miles of jungle trail?"

Svenson was now getting excited. "Yes, sir, plus we can airborne insert sensor devices to pick up movement of personnel and equipment."

"Sensors?" Samuel was wondering how warfare had

gone from man and machine fighting one another to high technology.

"Yes, sir. The boys in the labs back home are coming up with a lot of new scientific gadgets for us to use in this war. With sensors we don't have to send our people into that hellish place. We can target them through the sensors and send in the bombers to waste them. Our people can sit on the outside and watch the fireworks. Safe and sound. It can be Charlie's worse nightmare."

"Or ours. You know as well as I do that Charlie turns everything against us that isn't nailed down. He'll find the sensors, set them up near our people, and we'll be bombing American personnel or Vietnamese villages. The mines will be added to their already existing inventory of American antipersonnel ordnance they're using to kill and maim our troops. No, Major, forget the sensors and mines. The only way to cut off the trail is to go inside and dig the little bastards out of their holes and tunnels. To do that we'll have to use more ground troops. God help them when they venture into Charlie's living room."

"Is it better to let them venture into ours," Svenson wondered. "At least by fighting them on the trail we can control the action. Keep them busy. Pinned down. That's why the Air Cav is being deployed to An Khe."

All the while he spoke, Sharps had his eyes fixed on the neighboring countries of Laos and Cambodia. If the Ho Chi Minh Trail was shut down, the Vietcong would more than likely use the two neighboring countries as supply depots from which to continue the flow of supplies into South Vietnam. It would be more difficult, but then, the Vietcong understood hardship. That had been proven since World War II.

The question was: Could the American forces endure the same hardships? He doubted that. There was a major difference: the Americans were considered invaders by the Vietnamese. A war of attrition is won by the side willing to give up more than the other side is willing to give up. He knew there would eventually be a watermark the

American people would not allow the government to surpass.

But what was that watermark? How many killed before this war was either fought and won the right way, or abandoned completely? History had taught the United States nothing. The Japanese. French. Now America.

Ten thousand Americans killed in action? Twenty thousand? Thirty? Certainly, no more than that. All Charlie had to do was hold on. He didn't have to defeat the American soldiers. America would do that for him.

# 15

### ✫ ✫ ✫

Franklin Sharps knew Sergeant Bill Trout as about the toughest son of a bitch in the battalion, with the exception of Chassion, Smith, Musselwhite, and a few dozen other top noncoms. As a new sergeant first class and medic platoon sergeant, Trout was continuing in Vietnam the reputation he had begun building at Fort Campbell before deployment: "Do your job, don't whine, and if you've got a personal problem, see the chaplain. If you don't like me, tough fucking shit! Write your congressman. When he contacts me, I'll tell him to talk to my congressman. We're going to war, gentlemen, not to some sorority house party. You're going to see your friends die. You're going to see all sorts of people die. In fact, *you* might die."

When Franklin reported to the battalion aid station to resupply from the last mission, he found Trout sitting in front of the command tent sipping a beer, his M-16 nestled against his chair. His blue eyes narrowed on Franklin as he approached.

"Wilkes was hit yesterday," he said. "Pretty serious shit. He was medevaced to the Third Army Field Hospital in Qui Nhon."

Tommie Wilkes. Franklin's crazy buddy from Airborne school and medic school at Fort Sam Houston and close-in bunkie in the barracks at Fort Campbell. A heartbreaker with the ladies and a hard charger on the battlefield. He'd already been awarded the Bronze Star with Valor and the Purple Heart, the first medic to get hit since arriving in Nam. More important, he was a friend.

The word was that Trout was finding a new reality within himself, one that men often found on the battle-field. Three days before, he had killed a Vietcong sniper with a single shot from over one hundred yards. Franklin figured he was chilling out, letting it all sink in. Real deep. That was never Franklin's problem. He didn't kill for God and country. He killed for revenge. That kept life simple.

Trout pointed toward the brigade commander's tent. "How many whores are standing in front of Colonel Timothy's headquarters?"

Franklin looked. "There aren't any whores in front of Colonel Timothy's tent, Sergeant."

Trout took a swig of beer, shook his head. "Your eyes must be going bad. I'm going to send you to Qui Nhon. I want you to get your eyes examined at the field hospi-tal." He handed Franklin a prepared authorization signed by the battalion surgeon ordering Franklin to report for an eye examination.

He had started to walk away when Trout's voice stopped him. "Tell Wilkes I've written a letter to his fam-ily. I've told them what happened. How he was wounded. How he saved the lives of three American soldiers. Tell him the plat daddy is very proud." He added, "Don't worry about Chassion. I'll square it up with him."

# 16

*★ ★ ★*

The view from the Huey was breathtaking as Franklin studied the scenery stretching from the highlands to the South China Sea. The tall mountains gave way to lush paddies, dotted with Vietnamese tending to the rice crop. Franklin could see Route 19, which was still marked with burned-out French vehicles of Mobile Group 100, the French Foreign Legionnaire task force annihilated eleven years before by the Vietminh. It was common knowledge the Vietcong had purposefully left—even brought in—other derelicts to be a constant reminder to the Americans of what awaited foreign invaders on the stretch of deadly highway.

Sitting across from him was a black trooper from C Company, wearing a grin as large as his helmet. He was going back to the world, his short tour from Campbell to An Khe finished. No more mosquitoes, leeches, land mines, or snipers; hot food and a soft bunk were waiting at the bottom, then the ride back to the world.

Franklin nearly envied the man, who said nothing, but

stared at the passing terrain below, his grin growing ever wider as the mountains disappeared and the thin blue of the South China Sea could be seen in the distance.

"I'm out of this motherfucker!" he suddenly yelled, eyes dancing like two lanterns swinging in the wind. "Yeah! Airborne! Going home to my baby."

Franklin leaned over and extended his hand. The trooper, a buck sergeant, gripped him firmly and long, not seeming to want to let go. "You take care of yourself, young blood," the sergeant said, even looking slightly embarrassed. "Don't go getting your ass shot off."

Franklin shook his head. "I'm going home in one piece. Just like you."

The trooper shifted over beside Franklin, took out his wallet, and began showing photographs of his wife and three children. "They're back home in Alabama. My wife says, 'No more army. No more Nam.' I'm going to college on the GI Bill and going to be somebody." He looked severely at Franklin. "What about you, young blood? You going to college when you get out?"

Over the thump of the rotor slap Franklin shouted, "I don't know. Just trying to get out of here alive. That's all I got on my mind. I'll worry about that river when I get to it, Sarge."

The sergeant slapped him on the back. "The only chance the black man has in this world is to get an education. Without that, we just going to be carrying the Man's load all our lives. Do your tour, put in your time, then get the hell smartened and educated up. That's the package. We done fought for this country all over the world since freedom; now we got to make the big fight back home if we're going to get a piece of the pie."

He had heard it before. The refrain was typical of the philosophy expounded by many black soldiers: Do the time, get the hell out, then get the sheepskin. Work with your mind, not your back. Build from within, not from without.

"We've got to operate like the Cong," the sergeant went

on. "We can't tear down the system from the outside. That won't work. We've got to do it from within. Just like Charlie. Get sneaky, and get smart. One day the white man will wake up, and without warning there we're going to be. Standing tall. Proud. Educated. Ready to take our place. We can only do that with education. That's the ticket that'll get us from the back of the bus to the front. You'll see, young blood. You listen to me. We're not going to be denied our rights any longer."

The war had begun to bring out such attitudes in the black population. What was being called the Civil Rights Movement was growing in the United States, especially in the South, where Jim Crow law still ruled in many states and the races were "separate but equal." Added to that was the expanding antiwar movement, and Franklin could only imagine what the United States would be like if the two ever merged. America could become more violent than Vietnam.

The chopper landed at the airstrip, and the two Screaming Eagles shook hands on the tarmac. The sergeant grinned, then gave Franklin a hurried hug and said, "Take care, young blood. Come home alive. We're going to need young brothers to help in the cause."

Franklin watched him walk toward the operations center, where he'd catch another flight to Ton Son Nhut, then the "freedom bird" back to the "big plantation."

But for Franklin there was the current situation. He was in Vietnam; he wouldn't take that ride for long months to come. He had no idea what he would do when he returned. He had not given it the slightest thought. Right now he was in a war, and he had to say good-bye to a friend.

# 17

* * *

The first thing that struck Franklin's senses when he entered the Third Army Field Hospital was the stench of decaying flesh and antiseptic; the second were the flies, clouds of them in the air, black patches of them on the blood-soaked bandages of wounded soldiers. Moans and screams echoed; metal clanged; flies buzzed.

The beds were lined on each side of the tent; a slight breeze drifted in where the flaps had been raised, but the heat was stifling. He didn't know what he would find, but he didn't expect the heat. It was more torturous than being in the bush. The medical personnel walked around with dour, blanched faces, more mechanical than human. And he could understand why. There were wounds of every type: gunshots, fragmentation grenades, amputations from mines and booby traps, bandaged eyes that would never see again, broken backs and legs, arms and skulls from explosions or dismounting helicopters improperly. But the worst were the burn victims, their bodies covered in heavy white bandages, oozing gel designed to soothe the pain and prevent the skin from scabbing against the dressing.

There were marines, army, air force, and navy personnel in the ward. Officers and enlisted men shared the same space, where rank no longer meant anything, where the common denominator was suffering.

Franklin eased along the aisle, his eyes searching for his friend.

He stood frozen at the sight of his friend. Tommie Wilkes's left arm was heavily bandaged and suspended from an IV pole. Intravenous tubes ran into his feet and one large one into his right bicep, where a "cut-down" had been performed to allow direct insertion of the tube into the artery. A heavy bandage covered his left shoulder and chest area, which Franklin knew was the exit wound of the bullet that had hit Wilkes in the back. Gone was his typical smile; his face muscles were set hard and tight. Gone was the laughter in his eyes; he rarely blinked, but he stared at the ceiling as though expecting God to come through the top and retrieve him from his torture. Gone was his left hand; the blood-soaked bandage covering his stump hung suspended, as though he were raising his hand to ask the teacher a question.

Franklin eased down on the bunk and waved away the flies that stirred from the bandage covering Wilkes's shoulder. The gauze was bluish, seepage from the massive doses of antibiotics he had been given to combat infection. Hard as it was to believe, gangrene was still a potent enemy of the wounded, especially those who had to crawl through the filth and slime of rice paddies after being wounded. Packing wounds with mud often saved the lives of wounded soldiers, but the bacteria introduced set in motion a new set of problems.

Franklin ran his fingers over Wilkes's close-cropped hair, which brought the young trooper out of the trance. A smile threaded across his face, then his lips quivered, and tears suddenly filled his eyes. "Hey, killer. How's my main man?" Wilkes asked.

"Good to go. You?" He knew the answer but wanted to get Wilkes talking.

Wilkes shrugged, then looked at the stump. "Don't mean nothing, man," he replied.

Franklin knew Wilkes was trying to be tough, acting out the bravado of the paratrooper code. But he knew the young man was in a lot of pain, both physically and mentally. And why shouldn't he be? Franklin said to himself. Wilkes was eighteen; he'd been shot to pieces and had lost a part of his body. That's enough to break the strongest. But Wilkes wasn't going to break. Franklin felt and believed that in his heart. Wilkes just needed a little "remindering," as Franklin's great-grandmother used to say.

He tapped Wilkes lightly with his fist on the side of his jaw. "Are we tough?" he asked.

Wilkes's eyes glistened; the smile started to return. "Yeah. We're tough."

Franklin tapped again. "Are we bad?"

Wilkes nodded. "Bad to the bone."

"Are we going home?"

"Home, to drive-in burgers and the pretty girls in short-shorts."

"We going home heroes?"

"Heroes and heartbreakers."

"That's my main man. You're tough. You're bad. You're a hero and a heartbreaker."

Wilkes was now smiling. "Thanks, man. I needed that." He tried to raise up but fell limp onto the pillow.

"Lay still, bro. Don't jerk those tubes out."

Wilkes sighed heavily. "I hate this backside-laying bullshit, Franklin. I wish I could get on my feet and walk around. Anything but lie here and feel these fucking flies chewing on me. I swear, I've fed half the flies in the province since they rolled me out of surgery."

Franklin glanced around and saw the dark clouds rise, then descend again onto the wounded soldiers. "This sucks. Can't the medics do something about this shit?"

Wilkes snickered. "The only time they fan them off is

when the brass tour the place. I hate the flies worse than the Cong."

"You need a smoke. That'll keep them off you for a while."

Wilkes's eyes lit up. "You got one?"

Franklin took out a pack of C-ration cigarettes. He lit the Marlboro and held it to Wilkes's lips. The trooper took a long, slow drag, held it in for what seemed an eternity, then slowly exhaled a cloud of smoke. He giggled as he watched a storm of flies get airborne and fly away to torment someone else.

A few more drags and Wilkes was cruising in the good lane, sounding chipper and talking like they were back in the barracks at Campbell. When they were interrupted by a nurse, who injected him with Demerol, the chatter stopped only long enough for the shot; then it picked back up. They talked about their buddies in the bush, what was up ahead for the brigade, and Wilkes told him what had happened on the day he was wounded.

"Snipers everywhere, man. It was un-fucking-real. Must have been twenty or thirty of them. All of them in the trees. We called in artillery, but that didn't have an effect, so the plat daddy sent everybody forward in two-man teams. One held up stationary while the other advanced drawing fire. The action and delay trip, you know?"

Franklin knew. The action man drew the fire; the delay man sighted on the enemy muzzle flash. A deadly method of taking snipes, but the only effective means in thick terrain.

"One of our guys got hit. I went out to get him. I was just about to him when I took the one here. . . ." Franklin looked down at his thigh. A heavy bandage covered the area between his left knee and hip. "I managed to hobble to the wounded dude and was trying to drag him off when *blam!*" He looked up at his stump. "The fucking bullet hit the outside of the wrist, came out the other side, took it off cleaner than a sharp ax to a chicken's head. That's when I knew I was in trouble. I threw the dude over my shoulder and started running back to our position. Then I took the one in the back. It came out my shoulder and tore me open pretty good." He paused and looked again at the arm suspended from the pole. "I didn't feel any more pain in the hand. The bullet that hit me in the back and came out the shoulder clipped the nerves to the arm. Looks like the whole fucking arm's going to be paralyzed forever."

Franklin reached and held the cigarette again to Wilkes's mouth. The narcotic was starting to take effect. The pupils of his eyes were dilated; his words were becoming slurred as the narcosis began taking hold of his system.

"You did good, buddy," Franklin said, again giving him a hit from the Marlboro. "Trout told me to tell you he's proud of you. He's going to write your folks and tell them what happened."

"Tell him I appreciate that. But I'll probably talk to them before the letter gets home."

"They sending you stateside?"

"Yeah. Walter Reed. I evac tomorrow morning. We get to call home from Clark Air Base in the Philippines."

"Walter Reed's the best. My old man was there during the second big war. They'll take good care of you."

Wilkes scowled as he said, "Right. Then what? A fucking cripple getting in everybody's way?"

"You ain't a cripple, Tommie. You're young and you'll adjust. My grandfather lost his arm in France during World War One. He's dead now, but he rode horses, drove cars, even played golf. He didn't miss out on anything. You just need to rest and heal up. Then you'll come back strong. You're alive, man. That's more than some have, and there's a lot more going back draped in Old Glory. You made it, man. You're a little chewed up . . . but you made it."

This seemed to put some fire back in Wilkes. But there were still other losses to consider. "Guess I'll have to forget about playing pro baseball." He laughed. "Unless they need a water boy."

Franklin knew that Wilkes had been professional baseball material. He had played for the Fort Campbell team, even while in basic training, and had been scouted by the St. Louis Cardinals before the brigade left Fort Campbell.

"Fuck a bunch of baseball. Get well. Go to college. Get married. Have a shitload of kids and enjoy your life, man. You're only eighteen and you've been through more than those Jody fucks back in the world will ever know. You got that going for you: You survived Nam. They're still waiting to get here. You made it, my man. You made it."

Wilkes looked sadly at Franklin. "What about you? You going to make it? Or let that damn hatred get you greased?"

Franklin shook his head. "The hatred's gone, man. Or near about. I just want to stay alive."

"That's a one-eighty reversal. What brought that on? You go and get yourself full of religion?"

"Not religion." Franklin told Wilkes about the grenade and the dead children. "I never meant to kill kids, man. I just wanted Charlie. I got what I come for. I've avenged my brother. I can go home today and never look back on this shit."

The Demerol was bringing Wilkes down hard. He began dozing, and Franklin knew it was time to leave. "I better go, babe. Trout said I could stay overnight. Think I'll hit the enlisted barracks, grab some sleep, and see the city tonight."

Wilkes could only nod. Franklin went to the nurses' station and got a pen and paper. He wrote down his address in Arizona, then nudged Wilkes awake.

"Here's my address and phone number in the world. If you can, call my mother and tell her I'm doing good. She's a great lady. When I get back, I'll come visit you in Georgia."

Wilkes was fading fast, but despite the intravenous tube he raised his right hand. Franklin held it gently, almost lovingly. This was his friend. A white boy from Georgia he had grown to love like a brother.

Franklin leaned over and hugged him. "Stay in touch, my brother."

# 18

## ✯ ✯ ✯

Qui Nhon was a teeming city on the coast, flanked by the South China Sea to the east, the Central Highlands to the west. It was a mecca for every form of entrepreneur in Vietnam, whether the goods were entertainment, libation, narcotics, gambling, or flesh. Pimps patrolled on their mopeds searching for GIs in town for a day or two, eager to help relieve them of their pent-up frustrations and their money. They were called cowboys, or "piss-ants," who should have been patrolling the rice paddies and highlands with M-16s instead of running an ongoing pussy patrol through the streets.

French colonial villas stood as a reminder of the previous war, their stone walls trimmed with barbed wire or broken glass embedded in cement. Old women sold flowers and fruit on the corner; most of them were the Vietcong intelligence-gathering network. Young girls strolled the streets in long silk dresses, looking voluptuous and innocent, carrying multicolored parasols while all the while observing movement of trucks and troops; children

hustled ice-cold soda pop to the grunts used to drinking
from rice paddies and muddy rivers or warm water from
the unit Lister bag.

Franklin bought a bottle of Coke from a kid and
snapped off the top. Before drinking, he put a handkerchief over the mouth of the bottle just in case the kid had
put ground glass in the bottle. As he started to drink he
thought he saw a momentary look of disappointment on
the boy's face, which made him feel good. He started
walking, followed closely by the boy, who was waiting
for him to discard the bottle. When he finished, he sat the
bottle on the sidewalk and continued on his way, drawn
by the sound of rock-and-roll.

The Philadelphia Bar—all the bars had U.S.-flavored
names—was typical, smelling of cheap booze and stale
sex from the whorehouse at the rear. He found a seat near
the front, located near a small stage, where three Vietnamese musicians brutalized Buddy Holly's "Maybe,
Baby" with two guitars and a snare drum. The noise was
deafening, the mangled lyrics lost in the loud talk and
laughter of the troops at the bar.

All the military branches were represented, except the
Vietnamese armed forces. They knew better than to come
on American ground in the city. There was little respect
between the fighting men of the two countries, mainly
because the Americans didn't regard the Vietnamese as
fighters. They considered them cowards, no better than
pimps and laundry boys. Which, for some odd reason
Franklin didn't understand, made him think of the Kit
Carson scout.

At least the sonofabitch showed up for one roll call, he
thought. Which was more than he could say for the "cowboys."

They were a sight to behold, wearing their tight Levi's,
their little asses twitching nervously around hardened men
carrying loaded pistols beneath their jungle fatigue jackets. Most, anyway. M-16s weren't allowed in the cities,

but no GI in his right mind walked the streets anywhere in Vietnam without carrying some heat.

Franklin turned to the bar, spotted several delicious-looking young ladies, then motioned one to join him. She was young, no more than seventeen, he figured, wearing bright red lipstick and a bikini.

Her name was Monique. Odd, he thought, a Vietnamese girl with a French name. She said she was part French. He liked that. Maybe she wasn't all round eyes, but she had some in her, which meant she might be trusted not to shove a crochet needle through his ear and into his brain if they played boom-boom in the back room.

He ordered a drink for the two of them, and they talked; later, they danced on the small floor. The drinks kept coming until he was feeling light-headed and sat back in his chair. He started to order another drink, but she shook her head.

"This place too loud. We go for walk outside." He watched her go to the bar and speak with the bartender, a short, squat man with a wide forehead and broad mouth. Franklin thought he looked like the Buddha statues he had seen in pagodas around the country.

He had seen it coming, and now it was time to talk serious. "How much, for boom-boom?"

Her eyebrows rose seductively; then she whispered in his ear.

"I can handle that." He reached into his pocket and pulled out a roll of piastre, scrip money issued to the GIs. It was forbidden to use American currency in Vietnam. He peeled off the agreed amount, and after she gave the bartender his cut they left.

The night air was muggy and thick with that special heaviness he had known only in-country. Not even in the South, in America, had the air felt so oppressive. Unlike the mountains, where the air was thinner, the coastal regions were known for their humidity.

They walked unsteadily along the street, avoiding children darting about, some offering to shine his boots, others offering their sisters or mothers. Monique shooed them away in Vietnamese, all the while clutching his hand, steering him to wherever she intended to go.

After nearly half an hour they had left the busy city center and were in a small neighborhood of homes. This surprised him, since most of the Vietnamese whores operated from the back rooms of bars or cheap hotels.

"My father was *Légionnaire Etrangère*," she said. He was born in Brussels. I never knew the man since he was killed at Dien Bien Phu. My mother adored him and never remarried. She was Annamese." Franklin understood. Annam was a former French administrative region of central Vietnam, a culture within a culture that included their own language. There was a mystical look of pride in her eyes, as though she were unveiling some great secret in her life.

They reached a wrought-iron gate that opened into a small yard overgrown with weeds and framed by a pond that was drained and darkened by decay. The cement path to the house was cracked and pocked with what appeared to be bullet holes or shrapnel. They were both feeling the effects of the alcohol and moved unsteadily to the heavy front door, where she fumbled with her keys. Finally, she opened a series of three dead-bolt locks and led him inside the house. What struck his senses first was the smell of it, a mixture of dankness, rotting wood, and decrepitude.

The front room was bare except for a chair where she kept a kerosene lantern. When the flame illuminated the room it was clear the house had once been elegant, the walls bearing a vague mural, cracked and peeling and no longer artistically discernible; all the windows were secured by iron bars. Monique locked the bolts and they started up a winding staircase Franklin thought would surely collapse from their weight. But the hard teak structure held solid as they reached the upper level, where the light danced along a neatly painted hallway. Pictures covered both sides of the walls, his eyes noting each one, a small historical tour of the woman's lost past.

"This was my father, Major Henri Ricard." She held

the lantern to a photograph of a dark-haired man dressed in a French Legion uniform. The light drifted to another picture nearby, depicting a woman with long dark hair and deep brown eyes. "My mother's name was Mai Li. She was sixteen when she married my father."

"She was beautiful. How did she die?" Franklin asked.

She shook her head. "She did not die. She was murdered after the Vietminh conquered the French. I was spared because I was a child. I was put in a convent in Da Lat."

Franklin felt the sting of the irony. She had been raised in a convent to become a whore in order to survive. She was as much a second-class citizen in her country as black Americans were in the United States.

He followed her to the end of the hall, where she opened another locked door and entered her light-flooded bedroom. There was the sweet smell of ambrosia and a sudden flutter in the air. He saw a bird flap its wings in a cage beside a window.

It was as though he had stepped from one world into another. From the agony of a persecuting present to the elegance of a forgotten past. She went to her bed, pulled back the mosquito netting draped from the ceiling and lay down, and motioned him to lie beside her.

Franklin sat on the side of the bed and removed his boots, took his .45 pistol and shoved it under the pillow. He undressed, watching her do the same.

They made love, slept, made love again, slept some more, under watchful canary eyes and within hearing distance of sporadic gunfire echoing from beyond the walls.

He felt safe, even if the Vietcong were roaming the streets in search of drunken Americans.

He fell into a deep sleep—and the nightmare began.


He saw himself lying motionless with an agonizing paralysis gripping his mind and body. At first he found the place unfamiliar but gradually began to recognize the surroundings. There was a thick, rich smell of blood in the air. In the distance, a bright light shined through the thin fog that shrouded the ground where he lay, a graveyard, rising like a promontory in the rice paddy.

He was surrounded by men who had been breathing only hours before, but now were stacked like cordwood to give him protection from the evil advancing in the night. He froze, neither thinking nor moving, and watched as a light grew closer, swaying, as though it were dancing or being carried.

From the mist a man appeared, his features growing clearer with each advancing step. The man was short, clad in black pajamas, and stared emptily from dark eyes sunken in a shadowed, pockmarked face expressionless beneath a weathered pith helmet. In one hand the man carried a flashlight, the type used by American troops; in the other, an AK-47 Kalashnikov assault rifle.

Franklin tried to move, to rise—anything but lie there—but he remained frozen to the soggy ground of the graveyard. He wanted to scream, curse, but nothing came out, not even a whimper. He saw the VC's delight in his dilemma, grinning, revealing rotten teeth from behind lips that were no more than a knife wound.

Franklin knew him; knew the leer, the smell, the stench of rotting flesh that clung to the emaciated, malaria-ridden bodies of the men he had hunted and was hunted by.

The soldier stopped near the stack and looked over the bodies of the dead, resting his AK on his hip, weaving like a cobra as the breath strained from his lungs. To Franklin, this particular face was not familiar, although he may have killed this man. But Franklin knew the soldier; he recognized the wiry man who ate rats and rice balls, who spent his days in underground tunnels, then surfaced in the night to hunt Americans.

When the soldier pressed the muzzle of the AK against his face Franklin fought to rise, but to no avail. Then, he saw why: One of his dead comrades' hands had gripped his arm, the man smiling insanely at him, holding him down.

Then the VC began to laugh, his voice joined by the laughter of his dead comrades, their voices rising in a deep, guttural cachinnation that seemed to rise from the bowels of hell. Louder the symphony grew, until Franklin felt lifted by it, swirling upward, as though caught in a tempest.

He tore himself from the terror of the dream and found himself standing in the middle of the bedroom, his pistol clutched in his hand. Monique stared at him from behind the mosquito netting, her eyes wide with fear. The canary was fluttering wildly in the cage, feathers flying.

She eased through the canopy and walked carefully to him, her hand outstretched. He sensed she had been in this situation before, perhaps with other Americans, perhaps with the Vietcong. Qui Nhon was an R and R center for both armies.

Her hand touched the barrel of the pistol, pushed it to his side, and she stepped close and put her arm around him. He felt himself trembling, felt her trembling.

"You are safe here," she whispered.

He picked her up and carried her back to the bed, where they made love again, this time not gently as before.

# 19

★ ★ ★

It was noon when Franklin and Monique left the house
and strolled back to the streets lined with small cafés
and bars. Traffic was heavy, the sidewalks packed with
soldiers hung over from the previous night of carousing.
They had a light breakfast of scones and hot tea. He allowed a boy to shine his boots, never taking his eyes off
the kid. It was a favorite trick of the kids, taught by the
Vietcong, to whip out a straight razor, slash the tendons
behind the knee or the Achilles tendon, and run away and
become lost in the sea of people, leaving the soldier crip-
pled for life.

Charlie was a treacherous bastard, even in childhood.

When they reached the bar, they stood a long moment,
saying nothing. He held both her hands, kissed her lightly
on the cheek, and reached into his pocket. He took a wad
of piastres and added to her payment from the day before.
She didn't refuse him. She needed the money more than
he did.

Rarely did a combat soldier return from a short R and

R with any money. There was no need for currency in the bush. Only bullets, and they came free from Uncle Sam.

He turned and walked away, glancing back once, to see her step into the bar.

He knew they would never meet again.

# 20

★ ★ ★

An hour later he caught a ride on a helo from the brigade's 101st Aviation Battalion that included several "cherries," fresh from Airborne school. Their jungle boots and fatigues were new and clean, camouflage helmet covers sparkling, LC-1 harnesses fresh off the presses.

Fresh meat for Charlie, Franklin thought.

"You with the Screaming Eagles?" a cherry asked, a lanky kid.

He nodded; his thin smile made the inquisitor nervous. "I came over with the brigade from Fort Campbell. What about you guys? You come from Campbell?"

They shook their heads. "Nah," one said, his M-16 shiny and without a scratch. "We all graduated from jump school together." He looked at the others and grinned like a puppy eating shit. "They sent us over to help you guys." He wore his "blood wings"—parachutist wings issued upon graduating from Airborne school—on the retaining band over the cover of his helmet. A five-jump commando.

The third trooper sat also grinning, playing with his bayonet, which he was trying to attach to the stud on the barrel.

Franklin nearly laughed out loud. He looked at the door gunner, who had a big wad of tobacco in his mouth and leaned over and spit toward the opposite door, spraying the cherries' helmets and pretty fatigues.

The three jumped to their feet; the gunner whipped out a .45 pistol and aimed it at the one with the bayonet on his M-16 rifle. He had to shout over the roar of the rotors and the windblast coming through the open doors, but the kid heard him clearly. "Mine's loaded. How about yours?"

The trooper shook his head.

"Then sit your narrow John Wayne ass the fuck down before I throw you out of this fucking bird." He looked at the others and said, "That goes for the rest of you cherries, too!"

Franklin grinned at the gunner, took his pistol out, jacked a round into the chamber, and laid it beside him. The three quickly seated themselves.

Below, the rice paddies were meeting the base of the mountains. Franklin pointed at the French vehicles lining the roads and said to the cherries, "Those were the French Foreign Legion's vehicles. The Cong slaughtered them. I was told you could mark their point of retreat from where the bodies started stacking up near the top. They couldn't go up the highway . . . only down, and the Cong had ambushes waiting for them at every turn in the road." He pointed a finger at the one with the bayonet and said, "You remember that, Cherry. If you do, you just might last out the first day."

The lanky kid looked surprised. "We were told we wouldn't be near combat our first day in the bush."

Franklin shook his head, pointed to the jungle below. "We had a guy come into the unit. He arrived at zero-seven-hundred, was issued his gear at zero-seven-thirty, climbed in a jeep at zero-eight-thirty, which hit a land mine at zero-eight-forty-five, killing him and two others." He paused for effect. "Nobody knew his name. Not the platoon sergeant, not the company commander. They got his name off his dog tags, which they had to dig out of the roof of his mouth. The concussion blew those babies right through his throat and up. They were embedded so deep, the plat daddy had to use a pair of pliers to pull them free." He pointed at his boots. Each of his dog tags was threaded through the bottom lace of each boot. "You wear them like this. Even if you step on a mine, we'll find at least one boot."

The door gunner slapped the lanky kid on the shoulder, spit another stream of tobacco juice, and shouted, "Welcome to the prom . . . ladies!"


When he arrived at his hooch he found Marion sitting alone, reading a letter from his wife. In his lap was a tiny puppy. He was playfully stroking the dog while reading, wearing that special smile a man has when he's hearing good news. He looked up as Franklin dropped onto his rack.

"Hey, brother. You're back soon enough."

"Yeah. Got my business taken care of in fine style."

Marion chuckled. "Was she pretty?"

Franklin smiled just slightly. He rolled over and went to sleep, his thoughts on Monique.

# 21

*   *   *

A few days after Franklin returned from R and R the word came down that the ground element of the First Air Cavalry Division was moving onto the "Golf Course," the huge helicopter complex at An Khe. The name of the massive area that would base the more than four hundred choppers was easy enough to understand. From the air, the distinctive circular helipads uniformly splotching the earth gave the terrain a country club look. It was only natural that the Screaming Eagle troopers began calling An Khe the "Country Club." But on this course, the airmobile couldn't get out of the rough with a five-wood. And there was plenty of rough in which they could lose their balls.

It had been the task of the First Brigade to clear Highway 19 from the coastal city of Qui Nhon through the rugged An Khe Pass, if for no other reason than to ensure that the young cav soldiers wouldn't get their asses shot off before they made it to the top. What pissed off the Screaming Eagles the most? The Eagles had to continue clearing the surrounding pass and Central Highlands since the cav had been promised thirty days to get into position and adjust to the area before beginning operations.

The Eagles had begun operations only days after arriving in-country and were now busting their backs for a full division, three times the brigade's size.

The job had been dangerous and difficult, from the squad level to battalion, with all support elements kicking in and doing a masterful job in a short time. The road was open; engineers had made improvements under the watchful guard of the Airborne infantry placed at key outposts along the route, while the rest of the brigade harassed and chased Charlie, keeping him away from the highway he so loved to violate.

Even the whorehouses flourished around An Khe, indicative of what was laughingly known as "tight security." It had become common knowledge that anyone needing to know anything about anything need only ask the whores. They knew the game schedule before the high command. The mama-sans who ran the joints—which cropped up overnight, with names like Club Arizona, Club Southeast Asia, and Ho's Whores and were typical flesh parlors—were not exotic madams, neither in conduct nor in appearance. Most were repulsive, but they had a product they could sell. After all, one sergeant said, "Even a moron can sell ice in hell."

The whores were young, beautiful in that special Oriental way, many virginal when they hit the bamboo mat the first time with an eager trooper. By sunrise they would be a little older, a few dollars richer, and overloaded with information they would pass along to Mama-san, who in turn passed it along to the Vietcong.

The only respite in Nam was getting laid, and even that required some tactical determination. Sergeant Chassion always reminded the recon troops that "if Uncle Sam wanted you to have pussy, he'd have issued one to your buddy!"

Pussy was amazing in Nam. It bought a few minutes'

pleasure for a trooper who might lose his dick on the next helo assault; it created a flashback for another to the backseat of his Chevy with his girlfriend that last night before reporting back to Campbell. It might generate a few bucks in a trooper's pocket for directing his buddies to a particular *hooch lai* laden with *bambi ba,* cheap scotch, or expensive San Miguel beer. To the married soldiers who indulged, it was a reminder of his wife's refrain: "Don't bring nothing back I can't cook or play with!"

Pussy also got a lot of men killed in Nam. In the long, tedious nights of guard duty at the barbed wire, branches in the distance took on the voluptuous shapes of girls from the past, mesmerizing with their steady advance, eyes soft and glowing from the moonlight. Then the face turned ugly, the outstretched hand held a grenade, and the dick went soft just before everything else in his world turned hard.

"Pussy kills!" one crusty old sergeant warned.

"Yeah," countered a young trooper, "but what a way to go!"

The whores followed the troopers like the laundresses followed the soldiers on the Western frontier in the late 1800s. Hell, they'd even wash your socks and drawers for a few extra piastres. What did the trooper care? He liked being pampered, it was the second best thing to being home with mom. Like soldiers down through the ages, he thought only about three things, besides staying alive: his feet, his stomach, and his dick. And not necessarily in that order.

Everything else was relative to the moment.

But the most incredible thing that had occurred, in Franklin's way of seeing the "Big Picture," as it was called, was the matter of race.

Back in the world, whites and blacks had maintained a distance, friendly for the most part in the barracks, always separate off-post, maintaining that line of demarcation that said: "You can't cross over. Your shade ain't right for the place."

Not in Nam. Race seemed to have stayed aboard the USS *General Eltinge* where the 101st was concerned. A white man stayed alive because the blacks were cooking Charlie with their weapons and looking after the real estate, and vice versa. They drank out of the same canteens, ate from the same tin cups, mixed tears over wounded or dead buddies, and got their asses shot off hauling one another from sure death to safety.

War, thought Franklin, was a dichotomy, a situation of mutual exclusiveness. White hates black; black hates white. Until the shooting starts. Then everybody's the same color: scared birdshit green!

Franklin never saw this to be more true than the day the grunts of the cav started coming up the An Khe Pass. He watched a long, seemingly never-ending string of what appeared to be cattle trucks, loaded with the young "sky soldiers," move steadily upward toward the plateau. It was near sunset and the procession had continued for hours, the sound of double-clutching and grinding gears, and nervous young soldiers trying to look cocky and arrogant, some shouting obscenities at the troopers. The procession would end as dark neared; danger lurked from the blackness like rattlesnakes in the desert: hidden and ready to strike.

Franklin had been assigned to Dawes's team to guard an important bridge over a deep gorge. Charlie had blown the crossing a dozen times in the past, but not since the Screaming Eagles took over the area. The bridge was considered so important, Chassion chose the site for his command post and assigned two teams to the mission. The rest of the platoon was strung along the route doing the same thing at other vital points along the "Highway to Heaven," as it was referred to by some.

Each recon team sat up their M-60s at opposing ends of the bridge and placed claymore mines and trip flares at key points the enemy would have to travel either from the surrounding jungle or from the gorge in order to launch an attack. Sandbags had been filled and stacked to form fighting positions; foxholes were dug and sandbags reinforced on the flanks of each position, giving the two machine-gun teams added protection. Hand grenades and parachute illumination flares were placed in each position for quick access; radios were squelched down, and all was quiet as the sun faded over the western slopes of the mountains.

Then the longest part of the mission began: the long wait through the night.

Franklin and Dawes were together, hunkered beneath the west end of the bridge, when Chassion hurried across the bridge to check on their situation.

"Sit rep?" he whispered.

Dawes spoke softly. "Tighter than a frog's ass underwater, Plat."

Chassion was barely visible, his face painted in green-and-black camouflage. "Good. Keep your people alert. These little bastards want this place out of the action real bad."

"We're good for the night, Sarge," Dawes said.

Chassion whispered to Franklin, "Sharps, you got anything for the runs? I'm shitting like a goose."

"Got some paregoric. It'll tighten you up good, but it might make you drowsy."

"I'll stay awake. Give me some."

Franklin took his red-filtered flashlight and searched his medical aid kit. He handed the bottle to Chassion. "Don't take more than a couple of swigs every four hours."

Chassion patted him on the back. "Thanks, Doc. Damn, I got to go again."

He hurried toward the edge of the gorge. Moments later, they could hear the gurgling sound of his bowels emptying.

Franklin and Dawes chuckled. In the dark sky there was a loud "thud," then another, followed by the most brilliant illuminations the two had ever seen. Flares, fired from artillery or mortar coming from the direction of the Golf Course, exploded.

Franklin and Dawes looked toward Chassion, who was squatting, his pants down to his ankles, steel helmet cocked sideways, his M-16 resting on his knees. "Shit!" he yelled, and at that instant an artillery round crashed beyond him, the concussion pitching him backward. Franklin and Dawes watched in stunned silence as the platoon sergeant disappeared into the darkness below.

"Let's get the fuck out of here!" Dawes shouted to the team. "Under the bridge!"

Artillery rounds began crashing all around the bridge where the troopers, caught in the light of the magnesium flares attached to parachutes drifting to earth, could be seen scurrying for cover.

"What the fuck is going on?" Dawes was shouting into his radio within a heartbeat of him and Franklin rolling out of the foxholes for the greater safety beneath the bridge.

The radio crackled from the command post, but in the din of the artillery and mortar crashing around the bridge, and into the cavernous gorge, Dawes heard nothing he could understand.

Franklin looked toward the gorge, where approximately a hundred yards away, from deep within its darkened bowels, a plume of bright orange flame rose skyward, turning the gorge into a momentary inferno. The tongue of fire burned bright for a few seconds, then extinguished, returning the gorge to darkness.

More flares erupted overhead and Dawes, still on the radio and hearing nothing worthwhile, heard Franklin shout, "Charlie! To the front!"

Three Vietcong soldiers had been flushed from the darkened jungle by the rolling barrage. Their features were clear in the spewing magnesium flares drifting down, giving their shapes an eerie, ghostlike appearance as they ran forward in their familiar bandy-legged stride.

Franklin rose up with his M-16 when Dawes shoved the barrel down and said, in a near-crazed voice, "What's wrong with you, man! Ain't we got enough shit coming down on us without you adding to it!"

Franklin watched as the VC neared the darkness. "Oh, God!" he said and pointed toward the fleeing enemy. In the flare light they saw Chassion had risen from the darkness of the gorge, holding his pants with one hand, his M-16 in the other. The platoon sergeant's helmet was missing, and he was cussing a blue streak.

Chassion and the fleeing Vietcong made eye contact at the same moment. The sergeant dropped his pants, triggered the M-16—but nothing happened.

"His weapon's jammed!" Franklin shouted. At that moment the VCs fired wildly at Chassion, as the tough plat daddy plunged over the gorge edge and again disappeared in the waiting darkness.

By the time Franklin and Dawes had snapped out of the shock, the VC had also disappeared.

There was silence, except for the furious Chassion, rising out of the dark cavern again, cursing a streak so blue even he couldn't understand it.

Dawes started to crawl beneath the bridge. "Where you going?" Franklin said.

"I'm going to hide in the fucking trees! Right now, I'd rather face a platoon of Charlie than Chassion. How about you?"

"I'm right behind you."

The two troopers stayed near the bridge, but out of sight, listening to Chassion bellowing into the radio until the sun came up.

The following day it was learned the "great attack" had been initiated by an overzealous and eager "brown bar" second lieutenant in the First Air Cav. Millions of dollars in taxpayer's money had been pissed away, troopers were terrified and terrorized, but the cav cattle trucks kept coming up the highway, carrying the young soldiers to the waiting battlefields of the Central Highlands.

# 22

\* \* \*

As with all armies, the arrival of mail from home was always the most precious moment for a soldier. Mail call brought letters, "care packages" of nonperishable foods—the most treasured being Kool-Aid to put in the canteens, making the barely potable water tastier—needed items the army was slow on supplying, such as socks, undershirts, underwear, and even sunglasses. For Franklin, the arrival of a certain package from Saigon came to his great surprise: a portable tape recorder.

He read the return address—Brig. Gen. Samuel Sharps—and was tempted to throw it away, but upon seeing several cassettes, from his mother, his brother, and—to his surprise—his sister-in-law, Darlene.

He read the directions, inserted the batteries, put his mother's tape in, and sat back in his hooch and listened.

What he heard made him realize the tapes had not been censored, which was why his mother had sent the recorder and tapes to his father. A general carried more weight than a spec four.

"Hi, baby, it's Mom. I hope this finds you doing well. I think of you every day and pray you are safe. The news here is that more troops are being sent to Vietnam, which means the war is getting bigger. I have spoken to some of our friends who served with your father and their thoughts are that even more soldiers are going to be sent over there.

"I pray about this every day, hoping it won't be true. Back here we are having a sort of war of our own down South, where the civil rights people and a lot of black people are asking, 'Why should our people die for the freedoms of Asians when they don't have freedom in America?'

"It's the same question our people have heard since the end of the Civil War, but I guess you know that.

"Kevin is doing fine, and so is Darlene. She stays busy with the baby, and is nearly finished with her nursing degree at Arizona State. I hope she doesn't move away when she graduates."

His mother went on to talk about the ranch, local events, and other homey things. He rewound the tape and listened to it again, then the one from his younger brother, Kevin.

"Hey, bro, how's the hero doing? Hope this finds you well and safe. I've been following the war on the television and in the newspapers. Looks like you guys are in some pretty rough country. Not so rough here at Berkeley, unless you call getting the clap a hazard of education. Not me, bro. But a few of my dormies."

After a minute or two, Kevin's voice seemed to change, sounding more ominous.

"I don't know what's going on with Mom. Maybe it's just that she's lonely what with you in Vietnam and me in college. But I think she needs to hear from you soon. We sent some extra tapes so you can talk to her. She needs to hear your voice. You need to send them to Pop, so he can get them to her without somebody listening to them."

He talked more about music, summer classes at U.C. Berkeley, and the upcoming football season. Franklin rewound the tape and played it again.

Finally, he listened to the tape from Darlene. Again there was a foreboding concerning his mother.

"Hi, Franklin. Hope this finds you well. I'm here at Sabre Ranch, and Mom has left me alone to talk to you. I'm glad she did. I don't want to burden you because I know you have enough on your mind what with [long pause] . . . everything that's going on over there . . . but I think you should know.

"She's been to Doc Malone a few times and he is sending her to a specialist in Phoenix. She won't tell me anything, except that it's just old age. Maybe it is, I don't know.

"But there seems to be something on her mind and I think you can help. I think it would really help if you would try to make contact with your father. I don't think you know, but he was wounded in a bomb blast in Saigon a while back. He's okay, but the telegram had already been sent to your mom before he could stop it.

"She loves him dearly, as you know, and wishes that you would try to mend your fences, not for her sake, but for yours.

"I hope you will take care of yourself and write to me and send tapes if you can. You are one of the dearest people in the world to me and I can't wait until we can see each other when you get back here."

Darlene went on to talk about Argonne, her daughter, the child Adrian never lived to see or hold; she talked about her final year in nursing college, how the courses were more difficult, and that she hoped to stay in Arizona when she graduated. Franklin played the tape again; the voice of a beautiful woman made him forget, if only briefly, the horror that surrounded him and being so far from home.

In the box with the tapes he found a pint bottle of Jack

Daniel's bourbon. Attached to the bottle was another tape labeled: "From Pop."

He snapped the cassette in half and tossed it into the garbage bucket near his bunk, rose, and walked outside to stare up at the sky. It was nearly dusk, overcast, and muggy, the taste of rain in the air. In the distance he could hear the sound of helicopters in the direction of the cav's Golf Course, and artillery and laughter coming from the hooches of headquarters company, where troopers read their mail for the hundredth time and shared "home life" with their buddies.

He really didn't have anything to share. What was there to say? That his mom may be having a medical problem? That black Americans were struggling for the simple decency of being treated equally? That his dead brother never held his child? That a beautiful woman he had loved secretly since high school was so far from his grasp that he may as well be on the moon?

He looked at the Jack Daniel's, cracked the seal, and took a hit from it. He saw one of the battalion cooks coming his way. He knew the "Spoon," as cooks were called, from pulling KP at Fort Campbell. In the moonlight, the Spoon looked angry. His features were tight, his hands moving nervously.

"Hey, man," Franklin said, "you look like you could use a drink."

The Spoon stopped, reached for the bottle, turned it up, and swigged, throat working, Adam's apple bobbing. Finally, he handed the bottle back. "Thanks, man."

Franklin watched him walk away, his M-16 slapping off his hip, going toward the latrine.

Franklin looked at the bottle: stone empty.

# PART 3

★

## OPERATION GIBRALTAR

# 23

* * *

In early September, after more than a month of deep patrols into the jungles of the Central Highlands, the First Brigade finally got a break. A patrol from the brigade made contact with a small enemy unit on Highway 19, killing one enemy soldier. The soldier was carrying papers identifying him as a member of the 95th Battalion, 2nd Vietcong Regiment.

It was no secret that the 95th was operating in the An Khe area, no secret especially to Major Joe Hicks, brigade S-2 (Intelligence) officer. Hicks was a solid soldier and savvy as they come. He had served with the marines in World War II, the 24th Infantry in Korea—where he survived sixty-nine days, cut off and alone, behind enemy lines—and two Special Forces tours in Vietnam prior to the brigade's deployment from Fort Campbell.

He could smell the presence of the 95th and ordered patrol action to be stepped up, no matter the cost. Tired and pissed off, but smelling fresh opportunity, the brigade began pounding the bush. By day, patrols combed the mountains and sparse rice paddies; by night, ambush patrols set up in every imaginable place the brass suspected Charlie might move upon.

While on one patrol, a soldier from the 502nd Battalion, First Brigade, was scrounging for souvenirs when he accidentally stumbled upon what he thought to be a Vietcong. The soldier, who was actually a cook from Hawaii, had volunteered for the patrol to get a chance to see some action. While interrogating the VC, Hicks discovered he was a PAVN, another name for People's Army Vietnam or, to the grunts, plain old North Vietnamese Army!

The man had come from the north to get his ass captured in the south!

What Hicks and others learned confirmed suspicions that there was a major Vietcong unit in the area and at battalion strength.

All the bells starting ringing; all the lights started flashing.

The prisoner, fearing, no doubt, for his life, wanted to strike a bargain: his life and freedom, including joining the Americans, for information on the 95th. Hicks accommodated, and the man began chattering. Convinced the NVA was for real, Hicks had him put on an aircraft to fly over the area and get an exact fix. What was overlooked was that the man had never flown before and the experience scared him mindless. He recognized nothing from the air.

Hicks was livid, thinking the bastard was just buying time, when another stroke of good fortune surfaced. He picked up a radio intercept from a nearby Forward Air Controller (FAC), whose "bird dog" was taking fire from the ground by a .50-caliber heavy machine gun. The reported area of the firing on the FAC was the same area the NVA had designated to be the Vietcong 95th Battalion's command post.

The First Brigade had found Charlie.

•  •  •

The OPLAN—Operational Plan—was designated Operation Gibraltar, an assault that would utilize air strikes, artillery, and airmobile deployment of troops from the brigade's 2nd Battalion/502nd Airborne Infantry, commanded by Lieutenant Colonel Wilfred Smith, into the village of An Ninh, on September, 18, 1965.

The hardest part of the planning was selecting the unit that would lead the assault. The '02 was chosen because it had found the first hard evidence the 95th was in the highlands. Hackworth had argued hard for 1/327, since it was his opinion the "Above the Rest" battalion was the finest of the three battalions in the brigade, led by the most competent officers and noncoms.

As the word snaked through the brigade, there wasn't a "Screaming Eagle" that didn't want to get into this fight. The troopers were finally going to take it to Charlie and give him a taste of his own medicine, fight him in the open, shoot standing straight up, move forward, and take the enemy where they lived.

Spec Four Franklin Sharps wanted to get on with it and wondered how it was going to get done.

The word came down in whispers, mostly among the noncoms, who chewed hard on their cigarettes, stomped their boots, and wanted to scream to the heavens. Not a one could believe that the 1/327 would be left out of the fight.

Chassion looked like a man chewing steel and ready to shit nails, he was so angry. Trout was even worse, pacing about like a caged tiger, wondering what it had been all about.

*"Hell!"* one noncom from C Company cussed. "We all ought to be in this fight. The whole fucking brigade! Overwhelm the little fuckers and tear them out a new asshole!"

This wasn't the smell of mutiny. These were soldiers who had come to fight and found an enemy who wanted to toy with them. They had come to fight the war and go home. All the troopers had been getting since arriving was a lot of shit many were not prepared to accept in silence. These were paratroopers who had been trained to go behind enemy lines, suffer casualties, and hold their tactical positions, keeping the enemy occupied on more than one front, denying them the opportunity to consolidate their assets on one advancing force, until the infantry came in and mopped up.

Too many of the hardened veterans of Korea, most of whom had served in World War II as well, saw it simply: *"You might leave the dance with a fresh young whore, but while you're there . . . you two-step with the bitch you brung!"*

It wasn't vintage Darryl Royal, the University of Texas coach who coined the phrase, but it was close enough, considering this was war, not football.

The 1/327 had been the vanguard of the brigade and had earned the right to be the first to engage the Vietcong.

# 24

* * *

Franklin had a friend he'd gone to jump school with who was on a chopper with the 101st Aviation Battalion.

He collected up his gear and found Chassion. The platoon sergeant was sitting in his hooch, writing a letter home, using his flashlight to write by.

"Plat, I need a favor."

Chassion looked up, laid down his pen. "What's the problem?"

Franklin shrugged. "I need to get over to brigade HQ, I need to talk to my father in Saigon. I just found out that my mother's sick. I don't know what's going on, but I got a letter from my brother."

Franklin knew he was playing a long shot, but there was no other way.

Chassion nodded but looked suspicious. "I guess a general's son can ask for one favor. But don't ever do it again. Do I make myself clear?"

"Yes, Sergeant."

"How you going to get there?"

"There's a deuce-and-a-half hauling some equipment over to the HQ in an hour. I'll catch a ride back somehow."

The platoon sergeant had a glint of doubt in his eyes. "Make damn sure you are. We're going to have everybody ready for tomorrow, in case we're needed."

Franklin turned and left, breathing relief as he walked toward the battalion command post, praying there was a vehicle going toward brigade headquarters.

At the CP, frustration was boiling over at all levels; even the cooks had a case of the ass. The brigade had not had a hot meal since arriving at Cam Ranh Bay, which meant the Spoons had pulled every shit detail imaginable since their feet touched RVN (Republic of Vietnam) soil. Except for that first day in the field near Bon Me Thuot, when they brewed up banana pudding from local banana trees. While their intentions were only for the men who'd been cooped up on the USS *General Eltinge* for weeks, the result was the largest number of the "toilet trots" in the history of the division. Since then they had probably forgotten how to cook, utilized instead to pull guard duty, unloading ammunition and the tons of C-ration crates required to feed a battalion. Even Colonel Timothy and the entire command staff had lived on C-rations, using their own diet as a means to gauge how the troops were feeling and to show the special leadership required in combat. If his men slept in the mud, "Gentleman Tim," the beacon that lit the path, was deepest in the muck.

At the Golf Course, where the 101st Aviation Battalion was based alongside the incoming First Air Cav. He found a CQ (Change of Quarters) at the command post and asked the whereabouts of one of the crew chiefs on a Huey.

"I'm looking for Spec Five Ronald Douglas," he told the PFC.

The CQ pointed over his shoulder. "You'll find him on the flight line. If you can find him. The oh-deuce is staging, and it's crowded as hell."

The flight line was packed with troopers from the "First Strike" battalion. The mood was nervous as the soldiers, formed into their platoons and companies, were spending the night on the flight line in preparation for the airmobile assault the following morning. The men sat on the ground, using their packs to rest against, their weapons at the ready. Franklin could sense a mixture of moods as he walked through the area—nervous chatter, light laughter, some smoking, others eating C-rations—typical behavior in light of the upcoming assault.

The Hueys sat in a long line, including seven marine heloes brought in to assist, as well as Hueys from Lieutenant Colonel Cody's 52nd Aviation. But it was obvious there were too many troops for the helicopters to accommodate.

Franklin found Douglas, a strapping, redheaded twenty-year-old from Casper, Wyoming. The crew chief was sitting in the open door drinking a can of beer.

"Douglas! Hey, man, how you doing?" Franklin called out.

The man stepped onto the tarmac and stared warily at Franklin. When he recognized him, he stepped forward, his hand extended. "Sharps, my man. What the hell are you doing here?"

"Looking for a cold beer."

"Don't have a cold one. But it's wet."

"That's good enough."

The two drank their beer and made small talk for a few minutes; then Franklin got to the point of his visit. "I need you to get me on this mission."

Douglas stared at him for a moment. "Are you here on orders?"

Franklin shook his head, drained the can of beer. "No. My platoon sergeant thinks I'm over at the commo center at brigade HQ calling my old man in Saigon."

Douglas released a long, low whistle. "Man, you are one crazy motherfucker. You know you're AWOL?"

"I know. But I'm a medic, goddammit. You know there's always room for another doc on one of these operations. Hell, this is the first major American operation to jump off in Nam and I want to be in on the hunt. I've been humping these mountains for weeks trying to rock with Charlie. Here's my chance."

Douglas shook his head and grabbed two more beers, opened them with a church key, and handed one to Franklin. "I don't know, man. You're only about the zillionth dude to pull this shit. Everybody's coming out of the woodwork trying to get in on this op. Personally, I think you're all insane."

"We've been out in the bush hacking away since the get-go, and now that we have Charlie fixed, I want in on the kill. You've been flying around while we've been humping. Walk the bush for three months and see how you'd feel."

Douglas understood. The 101st Av Battalion left Fort Campbell prior to the rest of the brigade. The helicopters were transported on the USS *Iwo Jima*, a helicopter carrier, and were waiting when the troopers arrived at Cam Ranh Bay. Since then, the Av had inserted and extracted the troopers after long-range and deep patrols and medevaced wounded, seeing the frustration the proud brigade was feeling.

Douglas crushed his beer can and threw it into the darkness of the Huey's hull. "OK. I can get you on board with the troops we're ferrying on the first lift—"

"First lift?" Franklin interrupted. "It's not going to be a total assault by the whole battalion?"

"Not enough choppers," Douglas replied. "It's going to be a piecemeal op. Three platoons at a time. We're scheduled for three ferries into an LZ near the village of An Ninh. All this starts after the Skyraiders soften up the area. There's not much room to land in that terrain. If we put troops in another area, they'll be outside the artillery fan, and that'll leave their asses hanging out big time."

Franklin understood. Tactical air support would come from A1-E Skyraiders, a good, low-level air-to-ground support fighter/bomber. However, air support can only stay on station for a limited period of time, due to fuel and ordnance expenditure. No fuel, no bombs, no more air support without returning to base to rearm and refuel. But artillery would be on reserve should it be needed to support the troops once they were on the ground. Artillery operated within a "fan" for maximum firing distance and breadth. Once outside the fan, there would be no support and that could be disastrous.

Douglas hopped off the edge of the chopper. "Throw your gear in the bird and get some sleep. You're going to need it, my man. When the oh-deuce guys start loading up, just act like you're a medic assigned to the chopper. When they insert, go in with them. That's as far as I can get you. After that, you're on your own, good buddy."

Franklin watched Douglas disappear in the darkness toward a string of latrines where long lines were formed by the troopers of the 502nd.

As he loaded his gear into the Huey, he looked again at the lines and wondered how many of them would be dead by this time tomorrow night.

# 25

★ ★ ★

They were going to be the messengers. That certainty was clearly etched on their faces. As the oh-deuce recon team loaded aboard the Huey in total silence, each man carrying an array of weaponry similar to that carried by Franklin's platoon, Franklin sat up from a corner to the dismay of a hulking, tattooed sergeant. On his right shoulder he wore the patch of the 187th Regimental Combat Team. His face, like the faces of the others, was painted with camouflage.

The sergeant looked at Franklin and snapped, "Who are you? Mary fucking Poppins?"

"No, Sergeant. I'm a reporter with *The New York Times*," Franklin said.

The man studied Franklin's gear, looking as though he'd figured it out, then took a bite from a plug of chewing tobacco. "I'd take a fucking medic with combat experience over your lame ass any day of the week. Get out your pen and paper, junior; you're going to war. But first, you might consider covering your family jewels."

Franklin slipped his steel pot under his butt just as the chopper lifted off and, staring past Douglas, who stood behind an M-60 in the open door, watched the darkened tarmac slip away as the chopper rose into the new dawn.

There was the sound of the air rushing through the doors, and the silence in the eyes of the other soldiers. But it was what they had waited for and now that it was about to arrive, there was evident fear. The men didn't look at each other; it was a thing men share in going to war. Don't look the other in the eye; you might see something you don't want to see—maybe your own reflection dancing off the eye of a man who will soon be dead. Maybe the man will be you.

The sergeant nudged Franklin. "What outfit are you with, boy?"

"Recon. First of three-two-seven."

The sergeant looked him in the eye. "Phil Chassion's outfit. You the medic for Recon?"

"Yes."

"I heard he had one. I wanted one myself, but they wouldn't give me one. How did you pull it off?"

"Sheer bravado, Sergeant, and a large measure of charm and bullshit."

"I hope you've got plenty of it, son. You might need it before this day is over."

"I won't let you down."

"That's good to know. When we get on the LZ, you hang tight on my ass and go wherever I go . . . do whatever I tell you. I don't like prima donnas, and no one hangs back."

Franklin stuck out his hand. "Spec Four Sharps. You can count on it, Sarge."

The sergeant shook hands and pointed out the door. In the near distance, an A1-E Skyraider was streaking past, traveling in the opposite direction. "Lock and load!" he shouted, "we're getting close!"

The men locked and loaded ammunition into their rifles. Face muscles were tight, eyes narrowed. Franklin's mouth was dry as salt. The fight was about to be joined.

# 26

* * *

An Ninh was a small village, of little significance in size and importance to the world except to the NVA, the VC, and the approaching First Brigade. The village was nestled at the base of tall mountains, and rice paddies flourished nearby; tall trees gave the hamlet the look of historical elegance.

It was also a staging area and training center, carefully secreted into the mixture of water, rice, and rock.

The most frightening—and ironic—aspect of a battlefield is the silence. The silence of the mind. One expects the noise that shatters the mind and sends courage forward, carrying on foot toward the glory of all that the challenge has created to confront, and turns a human being into an individual. All of which creates heroes and memories never forgotten. It even creates cowards.

But that's not how it works. Not in reality.

There's the silence that awaits the recon element. The point guard is there to ensure there is safety for those who follow.

Franklin stepped off the skids of the Huey and heard nothing except the rotor slap as the helo flew away. There were no birds chirping. There were no old men or women moving about. No one ran for the little shelter the village offered. The village was silent, desolate in appearance, except for a few drifts of smoke that came low, even, across the ground.

That's the warning. The mouth goes dry. The air stands still, even in a strong wind. It's as though nature—and God—has decreed, you're here . . . and there's no way back unless you carve a path through a hell you will never understand in your old age.

And the path begins where Hell opens up. Where youth becomes lost. Children are a dream of the future. That there are no more thoughts of family picnics, or cruising through town with your buddies on weekends. When the faces of pretty girls you've known become memories so distant, pictures carried in wallets, side pouches, or just in reflection, can no longer be brought to mind. When the taste of what once was—that was so wonderful—becomes so bitter you can only taste blood . . . and hear the cries of your comrades, and can't remember their names.

When you realize the ground around you is filled with people who want to kill you! And the fight you have dreamed of—and searched for—is about to become the nightmare you have longed to find!

That's when you know you've found what you've been looking for. That's when you know you're in the deep fucking shit!

And the only way to deal with shit is to put up with more shit than the enemy. You might have to eat some of it for a bit. But, if you can stand the taste . . . you'll survive the smell!


The teams inserted onto smooth, dry ground, as though it had been made especially easy. There was no elephant grass, only clean ground. The blades from the choppers whipped and turned up the surrounding trees, then the choppers pulled back hard and roared away.

Then, again, there was the silence, a sort of life of its own, but one new thing all recognized: the smell of smoke. Smoke has a sort of life of its own. Often, it can't be detected in the heights, for it dissipates quickly. In the trees, it's running away, like a bird fleeing. On the ground, it drifts, moving across the earth as though driven, but when it comes from *beneath* the ground, it has an odor of burnt dirt, acrid, despising to the senses.

Franklin and the others knew they had not landed at the base of a mountain that might hold the enemy in a tight position. They had landed right in their lap!

# 27

* * *

The recon sergeant took the mike. "Hold the second lift. We're in the deep shit. There's something wrong, bad wrong."

But it was too late. The recon unit had spread out on insert, taken position, and saw in front of them that Charlie had set the table and the brigade was the main course.

The first shot was fired, and another; though from a consolidated unit, one from the right, one from the left.

The recce team had landed fifty yards from the underground mess hall of a full regiment.

There is no greater confusion that will ever confront a soldier, no matter how well trained, than to be in a situation he cannot confront, control, or understand. This was the situation the first lift was now caught in.

Franklin saw the first major battle of the Vietnam War, between combined and well-entrenched NVA and VC and approximately thirty-six American soldiers, begin as a major cluster fuck on the American side of the field.

The enemy, who had laid tight during the A1-E bomb preps, taking few casualties, now appeared from nowhere, like the ghosts they had been called, moving low, easy, over ground they knew so well, as though it were a lawn they had mowed from childhood, to slots preselected, to drop in, fire, then move again.

The trees, soft and lush, turned into a fan of ugly gray as the bullets began to spray from the enemies' concealed positions; the crump of mortar fire mixed with the "slap" of the Hueys and din of machine-gun fire, preventing any single sound from being identifiable. Worse, the troopers were caught stone-cold in the open with nowhere to hide, their only hope to move forward and take ground that offered some form of protection.

Franklin saw the fire pattern: cool, calm, coordinated, like a prom night planned by a committee of old teachers who years before had been to the same dance. But now the ballroom was getting deadly.

He looked up and saw two helos take heavy hits of fire, tilt almost simultaneously, and pitch toward the ground. There were no explosions, only the sickening sound of steel scraping against the ground; the screeching of metal being torn from the fuselages as the skids were torn off and the rotors whirled crazily against the earth like egg-beaters, disintegrating in hundreds of deadly flying pieces.

Surviving troopers spilled from the choppers and began running in all directions, disoriented, without leadership, running straight toward the enemy positions, minds dazed.

"Evans! Jackson. Get the sixty trained on that tree line!" The sergeant roared.

The two troopers set up the machine gun and began firing. Red tracers spewed toward a tree line, answered by an equal hail of enemy lead.

The sergeant began organizing his men, pointed at Franklin, and shouted, "You get on my six, boy, and don't lose me for nothing!"

The sergeant grabbed two troopers and flung them forward. "Lay in fire onto that position. We've got to set up a perimeter! There's another lift coming in and we have to give them cover!" He took his M-79 grenade launcher and fired toward the trees. A deep, groaning explosion erupted, followed by a black-gray cloud of smoke.

Franklin looked to his right and saw a soldier running toward them, firing at the enemy from the hip. He was ten yards away when he suddenly stiffened and pitched forward. Franklin crawled to the wounded man, rolled him over, and saw a bullet hole above his right eye.

Along the forward edge of the battle area, the troopers were forming small pockets of resistance but were still trapped in the open.

The sergeant was on the radio, and Franklin heard him yell, "Where's the fucking artillery and air support!"

He could not hear the reply but could read the answer on the sergeant's twisted face as he began grabbing his men and slinging them toward the enemy. "Fire and move! Fire and move!"

Franklin wasn't sure if it was the training taking over or the sheer force of the sergeant's will, but the troopers began moving forward in small groups, one advancing and firing, another laying low, spitting out cover fire until the other team dropped and began firing. They rose and advanced, no more than thirty men, in teams, moving out of the open toward cover.

Not all of them made it. Screams of the wounded stretched from one end of the line to the other and the dead lay crumpled in thick mud, bloody heaps that suddenly took on new purpose.

"Use the dead!" the sergeant yelled. He dropped behind a dead soldier and began rolling the body, its arms and legs flopping crazily, across the open ground, using the corpse for cover while firing over the top. Suddenly a pack became a shield from incoming bullets, helmets a small defense against the enemy.

It was a horror Franklin could not have imagined as he crawled behind the dead soldier and began rolling his body toward covered ground. Like the others he would raise, fire at the bright flash of an enemy rifle, then roll the body forward and repeat the maneuver. All along the line the troopers used their dead comrades to stay alive and try to take command of the fight. None stared into the dead faces; none recognized if their shield was that of a friend or stranger.

Charlie had played his cards right. The trap had not been sprung until the paratroopers were too close for the air support to be deployed without killing American soldiers.

The shouts and screams of the NCOs and the wounded, mixing with the stutter of the M-60s, began setting a rhythm that had something of a settling effect. That and the fire of the M-16s and explosions of grenade launchers were giving the battlefield a violent musical score all its own.

They pushed forward, inching toward the enemies' advance positions. Hand grenades starting flying, exploding, showering the sky with deadly shard. The troopers were so close they were protected from the shrapnel either by being under the mushrooming cloud of flying steel, or by their dead shields.

Finally, the soldiers reached the same terrain giving cover to the enemy. The fight was now going to be close in, each yard to be dearly paid for.

Franklin rolled over the top of his human shield and crawled furiously toward the sergeant, who was on the radio. The voice of Colonel Timothy could be heard talking to the battalion commander over the PRC-25.

"What's your situation?" asked Timothy.

Colonel Wilfred Smith, the battalion commander, shouted, "I'm pinned down on the back side of the landing zone. Behind a rice paddy dike. All my troops are pinned down. We've got a hundred and thirteen dead."

Franklin looked at the sergeant, whose face suddenly screwed up in confusion. Franklin understood: *How could the commander know, in such a short period of time, the*

*number of dead! Especially if he was pinned down behind
the forward element and wasn't really in the fight!*

"Shit!" the sergeant spit. "The BC's panicking!"

"Where's the artillery?" Franklin said.

The sergeant shook his head and pointed to a distant
mountain range. "Stuck in the mud on the other side of
that mountain."

Franklin knew a successful operation would have to
rely on artillery, especially an operation like they were in
now.

The sergeant snapped, "We're outside the artillery fan,
son. So there never was any planned for this operation."

"What about more troops to come in and give us support?"

Again the sergeant spoke the words Franklin didn't
want to hear. "We have another company about eight hundred meters from here. Judging by the sounds from where
they're at, they're in just as deep shit as we are."

Franklin looked around. The troopers were digging in
and were now engaging the enemy from more secured
positions.

The sergeant slapped Franklin on the shoulder. "Welcome to the oh-deuce."

# 28

* * *

The morning wore on with the paratroopers gradually taking small bits and pieces of ground along the battle line, but paying for every bloody inch. Screams of the wounded gradually faded, as most had either died or simply lost the ability to raise their voices. Many of the survivors bore small wounds from shrapnel where grenades were used close in during the move out of the paddy area and into cover.

Franklin was amazed at how smart Charlie had played the Americans into this obvious trap.

What was being heard over the radio was not encouraging. A1-E Skyraiders couldn't provide further fire support due to contaminated fuel back at the airfield in Qui Nhon. All twenty-six troop-carrying helicopters designated for the operation were either destroyed or nonoperational. Most of the officers had been killed on the initial landings, including company commanders and platoon leaders. Then there was a voice over the radio, that of a lieutenant, who said, "We're outnumbered and surrounded. Cut off from other units. Running low on ammunition. We may be forced to go to escape and evasion, sir."

The angry voice of Colonel Timothy came on the radio, telling him, "You're United States paratroopers, Lieutenant. You're supposed to be outnumbered and surrounded, *and* cut off, *and* running low on ammunition! You will not—I repeat—you will not go to E and E! You will fight them, Lieutenant, you will fight them, take ground, and establish contact with smaller units and advance forward. Use the enemies' ammunition. Do I make myself clear? Fight back!"

There would be no relief for some time to come, if it came at all.

They were on their own, without officers, which, Franklin would soon learn, might be their only hope to survive.


The most incredibly hated, despised creature in any military in the history of warfare is without argument the noncommissioned officer. Until there's a battle. All around the village of An Ninh, where young troopers lay pinned down, fighting a well-entrenched enemy, taking acreage in small bits, the NCOs rose to become mammoths of the moment.

Most of the noncoms were combat veterans of Korea, some of World War II, and thus no strangers to the fierceness of fighting for survival. Along the line, the NCOs gathered the men into small fire teams, calmly giving the soldiers instructions on how to take the ground and hold on to it until the support elements could get their act together.

Through his cool professionalism, the sergeant organized a number of fire teams, some from Recon, others from A Company who had straggled into his domain. He pointed toward a hill commanding a superior position over the landing zone. Smoke from the assault rifles, machine guns, and mortar found the enemy positions but Charlie continued his relentless barrage.

"We're going to have to take that fucking hill. If we don't . . . we're dead." He shouted into the radio to other soldiers grouped along the line. His voice was loud, but not panicky.

Quickly, squad leaders or survivors from the company began checking in, requesting orders. The sergeant took inventory of the weaponry at their disposal.

"We've got two M-sixties," one shaky voice said.

"Good. I need them to set up on the flanks. Get one to the left of the smoke."

"What smoke?"

"The purple smoke I'm going to throw to my front. We have one sixty. That'll be the center of the advance. Get one to my left. Thirty meters to the left flank. Do you copy?"

"Yes, Sergeant."

The sergeant threw a smoke grenade to the front of their position. The purple haze drifted upward, then spread in the direction of the hill.

"Do you see it?"

"Roger that," the voice came back. "The sixty's on the way. . . .Wait!"

More gunfire erupted from the hill toward their position. "Go to single shot. Not automatic," the sergeant shouted. "Save your ammunition until you have a target."

The troops were settling down, firing smoothly, but ammunition was becoming critically low and resupply was unlikely for a long time.

Minutes later the radio crackled with the voice of a soldier. "Our sixty's on your left flank."

"Wait one," the sergeant barked as he motioned for Franklin, who slid beside the noncom and listened to his instructions. He nodded at a tall white trooper, a buck sergeant, and told Franklin, "Go with Bartholomew's team." He looked at the squad leader. "Bart, slip into the slot to the right and work forward between the gun on the right flank and ours in the center. Watch for our people coming from the right flank to hook up with your team."

Bartholomew, using hand signals, pointed to the direction of their deployment. Heavy machine-gun fire crackled overhead and explosions spewed dirt and debris into the air, but no one was hit. Franklin knew the other team on the right had been spotted. In what seemed forever, eight troopers suddenly appeared, dirty, some bloodied, their eyes sunken, but appearing eager to fight.

Bartholomew called the sergeant and gave him the sit rep: "We're hooked up on the right!"

"Sit tight!" the order came back. "When we're hooked up on the left we'll open up from there. When you hear the sixty on the left flank open fire, we'll start to swing from your flank! Advance twenty meters and hold your position. When I give the order, lay fire onto the hill to cover the left flank's movement."

"Roger!" Bartholomew yelled as he hand-signaled the others with a balled fist, the sign to wait for his order.

Minutes later, the M-60 at the center opened fire; seconds later, the '60 on the left flank began firing, along with the M-16s and grenade launchers. At that moment the paratroopers, stretched along a seventy-meter line, began moving from the thin cover at the edge of the landing zone toward the hill where enemy fire punished the paratroopers and deprived a landing zone for support elements.

The roar of the fusillade coming from the hill and the guns firing from the center and the left flank of the American line was furious. The right flank began moving fast, firing at VC soldiers who suddenly popped up from concealment, now in the path of the advancing paratroopers.

Franklin fired short three-round bursts, as he had been trained. He heard screams from bushes where moments before an enemy had been firing. Bartholomew, carrying a twelve-gauge pump shotgun, ripped off three quick rounds, killing two enemy soldiers manning a machine-gun position. The scene was macabre, as more smoke was thrown forward to conceal their advance.

Franklin charged over the dead body of a VC and realized they had overrun that part of the Vietcong forward line.

"Down!" Bartholomew screamed. The right flank went down and, as the '60 opened up from the center, swung their line of fire onto the center and left flank of Charlie's front line to cover the advance of the Americans on the left.

Explosions from both hand grenades and M-79s vibrated the ground; heavy gunfire from automatic weapons joined; the air seemed to pulsate from the sound.

Franklin heard a scream from his right, turned to see a man writhing on the ground, holding his stomach. Blood filled his fatigue jacket to the waist. His hands were red, his face ashen. Franklin stared into his empty eyes and watched as his mouth froze open in death. He knew nothing of the man, except that he was white, a paratrooper, dead.

Franklin was not in the 502nd; he was in the 327th. He was among men who, back at Fort Campbell, he and his battalion comrades had engaged against in intramural sports, war games and barroom brawls. He knew none of them! But now, by God, he was one of them.

The battlefield transcends personal animosities, whether over sports rivalry or even a woman. Here they weren't fighting for a flag. Not for an ideal or principle. Not even a nation.

They were fighting for each other! For here they had no one else. Trophies in the battalion trophy case meant nothing. Which battalion had more battle streamers on their guidon meant nothing. Here, on the field of battle, the only thing that meant anything was one immutable fact: If the battalion loses . . . the individual will lose. After that, nothing would be significant.

*"Fight back!"* as the brigade commander had ordered, became the essence of every American at An Ninh. It

became the lifeline to getting back to "the world." Back to Mom and Dad. Back to wives and children. Back to cruising the strip and arguing over music and sports. Back to hamburgers that tasted good. Back to cold beer.

Back to warm, moist pussy!

And fight they did. Like a cornered animal, fearing nothing, for they had nothing left to fear, for they were dead. They just hadn't stopped breathing. Or, as Charlie was now learning, fighting back!

# 29

## ★ ★ ★

By late afternoon, word had come to the beleaguered paratroopers that there were other assets now being brought into play. The First Air Cav had been contacted to provide assistance to bring 101st support troops into the fight via First Cav helicopters, since the 101st had no operational choppers. Falling back on the promise given their division that their troops would be allowed thirty days of preparation time upon arrival before their first combat campaign, the air cav's response was, "No way!"

Hackworth had gone ballistic. From brigade headquarters, he shouted to the cav officer, "An American battalion is fighting and dying, taking casualties, with support nil or nonexistent, so you bastards can sit on your asses at An Khe, eating hot rations and drinking beer in the whorehouses. It was the Screaming Eagles who cleared out your yard for you."

The officer responded with a weak reply, to which Hackworth responded, "I guess it's necessary to inform General Westmoreland that the Screaming Eagles—which

he once commanded—are about to lose the first major
battle of the war because you won't get your people into
the fight!"

That was all it took to get the cav motivated. The word
was sent to the troopers at An Ninh: Hold on. We're coming!

*Fuck them all!* was how the paratroopers felt. *We've
come this far without them. . . .*

# 30

\* \* \*

All along the line, fire elements from different sections were advancing in alternating corridors toward the base of the hill. What had begun as certain slaughter for the Americans hours ago was becoming a battle for survival on both sides.

Both sides! Now, Charlie was fighting for *his* survival. He might control the terrain, thought Franklin, but he was no longer dictating the day. Charles wanted to hug the belt? Wanted to sit in the audience and watch the play being acted out on the stage? Wanted to snipe from concealment? Wanted to booby-trap children to kill Americans?

Not on September 18, 1965.

Despite the fact there was little or no tactical air support, no artillery or heavy weapons support, despite being outnumbered and without further reinforcements, having taken heavy casualties initially and being pinned down in the open terrain and running low on ammunition, on this day, as it neared noon, Sir Charles was learning how to

rock-and-roll with some very pissed-off American paratroopers, whose only dream for the past three months had
been to go eyeball-to-eyeball with them.

What had started out as a nightmare for the paratroopers was turning into a dream come true. With smooth and
precise overlapping fire deployment, the paratroopers,
once in dire straits, were now taking command of Charlie's front doorstep.

The fighting decayed from modern military tactics to pri-
mordial survival tactics: hand-to-hand combat. Neither
side could fire without the fear of killing their own. Even
the enemy on the hill was denied the use of their mortar,
heavy machine guns, and artillery, for fear of killing their
own men. Their wounded were like the wounded troopers,
without assistance, alone, and cut off from their element.

Franklin watched in awe as the soldiers charged into
enemy positions, never stopping, pushing forward, the
rage burning in their eyes. There was no time for chatter,
only the raw, down-into-the-dirt killing that one man does
to another when he's afraid of nothing. Not the Devil . . .
or God Almighty! Neither was on the battlefield.

Especially God, thought Franklin. *If He had been here,
He would have stepped in and stopped this shit.*

Every man knew that for a fact, even the Vietcong.

It no longer mattered how many enemy soldiers the
troopers killed. That's never important. What mattered
was simple: Airborne soldiers are inserted to take and
hold ground. That's their job. If they have to kill, they
will. The Airborne soldier doesn't glorify himself by how
many enemy tanks he knocks out. That's the job of the
armor units. Enemy kills is the job of the infantry, coming
in behind the Airborne in overwhelming numbers. The job
of the Airborne soldier is to provide a point of reference,
a "link-up," for the other units who would ultimately
claim the victory.

Franklin watched in awe as one soldier charged toward

a mortar pit, jumped inside, and with his bare hands ripped the metal sights off the tube and used it to crush the skull of the enemy mortar man.

Another soldier beat back three Vietcong with the remainder of his broken M-16.

Another ripped an AK-47 from a VC's hand, turned it around, and shoved the bayonet through his enemy's throat.

There was no quarter asked, none given, by either side.

Then the incredible happened, so inspiring Franklin could not forget if he lived a thousand years.

The sergeant staggered forward from the smoke and carnage, his body riddled with bullets. He pointed toward the hill and, with his last breath, ordered, "Don't pull back. Don't pull back!"

Franklin screamed, "Take the hill! Take the hill!"

Another trooper screamed, blood running from his mouth, "Take the hill! Take the hill!"

Fear was no longer present in the ranks of the paratroopers.

The Vietcong broke from the onslaught, their confidence overwhelmed by the bravado of the troopers, who breathed their fire of hatred like demons, using rifle butts when ammunition was gone. Helmets as bludgeons. Feet and fists. Knives and teeth. Not to be denied that this was now their moment!

Upward they moved, into a darkness that began to descend as the sun drifted behind the distant mountains, turning the blood-soaked ground from red to a dark purple, then black.


By the time darkness fell, the base of the mountain and its approaches were in the control of the survivors of the morning landing.

The 101st had lost the morning, settled scores in the afternoon, and was preparing to hold on to the night.

Overhead, the flare ships began circling, dropping the large drums of illumination that turned the sky into near-day. Drifting down on parachutes, the glowing canisters created eerie shadows on the terrain, macabre and frightening. The faces of the dead seemed to give off a brief look of surprise as the light touched their faces, then were darkened hulks until the light danced onto them again.

The fighting settled into other pockets the rest of the night, as it became obvious that help truly was on the way. Charlie had broken contact and was fleeing to other holes in the ground to hide to wait for another day.


When morning arrived, elements of the brigade began linking up with the troopers. Vietnamese Army Rangers were blocking one side of the mountain; 2nd Battalion of the 327th infantry—deemed Task Force Collins—was connecting onto both flanks of An Ninh. And the cav had arrived, ferrying in troops in their shiny new helicopters, experiencing their baptism of fire.

The fresh troops advanced past the worn-out troopers of the oh-deuce, in pursuit of the enemy. A young lieutenant stopped near Franklin and saluted him smartly.

Now relieved, the men sat, smoking, fidgeting with their weapons, staring down the hill at the carnage and wreckage spread everywhere the eye could see.

Gradually, those who could walk assisted the wounded toward the LZ, now busy with the arrival and departure of Hueys.

Franklin and the survivors loaded the wounded and the dead onto the choppers on the very LZ where they had landed. As they climbed aboard the choppers, bloodied, but unbeaten, the hills still looked surrounded, but the enemy was disappearing, back into their caves and tunnels.


The brigade won the battle, according to the numbers: 257 dead VC and NVA; 13 dead and 40 wounded Americans. Franklin knew there was nothing really to cheer about, except the fact he was alive. For that he was grateful.

# PART 4

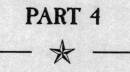

## QUI NHON

# 31

## ★ ★ ★

Tim's Traveling Trouble was given a new mission: to clear Qui Nhon province for the arrival of the elite Korean Capital Division. Much to the brigade's chagrin, the Vietcong had come out only once in regimental size to fight the Screaming Eagles. Except for Operation Gibraltar, Charlie had sat in the bleachers, watching the game being played by the American paratroopers, learning their strategy, remaining patient.

For the Screaming Eagles, the short journey to the rice paddies of Qui Nhon province was as different in purpose and terrain as a ski trip in the mountains of Colorado would be to an alligator hunt in the swamps of Louisiana. The First Air Cav would assume the mission of keeping Charlie's mountain sanctuary under constant threat and harassment, which included shutting down the Ho Chi Minh Trail.

The First Brigade's new mission was to protect the harvest in the vast expanse of rice paddies, which was vital to the national economy, the Vietnamese people, and the

Vietcong. What met the troopers was a terrain as equally deadly as the mountains, though there were no tigers and monkeys; now there was simply nowhere to find protection from the Vietcong snipers, who could disappear without a trace. And of course there were the ubiquitous booby traps, more numerous, sophisticated, and well concealed than in the mountains, since they could be maintained more frequently and deployed over a larger area. Booby traps in the mountains were mostly along trails in the thick jungles, especially punji pits, and more easily detected.

That was not the case in the rice paddies, where every inch of the murky water could conceal punji stakes, poles entangled with rusty barbed wire, land mines, and unexploded artillery ordnance. Petrol was even effective; since gasoline weighs less than water, it floated on the surface and could be ignited, turning a paddy into a raging inferno, leaving a trapped patrol with no direction to run.

He also knew inserts and extracts, especially medevacs, had to operate on limited hard surface, giving the Vietcong more easily recognizable points of reference on where the Americans would land their helicopters. Graveyards were bracketed for artillery and mortar fire and often heavily mined and booby-trapped by the enemy.

Humping the mountains had been physically exacting, but the paddies were a natural nightmare, a place where soldiers would wade through water from their knees to their shoulders, each step forward wearing away their endurance. Under enemy fire, running with the burden of equipment made them easy targets for concealed snipers and automatic weapons crew. Not even the dikes offered a route through the paddies, since the narrow separations between the paddies could be easily mined or boobytrapped and were certainly monitored by enemy snipers.

Streams and rivers were just as lethal, constantly traveled by sampans carrying innocent-looking civilians who could suddenly open fire with a deadly fusillade and disappear into a shoreline of thick reeds, escaping along routes known only to the enemy.

Then there were the snakes, the mosquitoes, and the worst aggravation to most of the troopers, leeches as thick as a man's thumb.

Mosquito repellent did little good to protect the skin since the water quickly rinsed it from the skin. The only alternative was to roll down the sleeves, button the blouse to the collar, and wear a towel around the neck. This added some protection from the leeches and mosquitoes, but not from the relentless heat of the scorching Asian sun, where shade was a luxury; groves of trees, where they existed, were prime zones for Charlie to zero in on with every lethal device at his disposal.

Villages were designed differently in the Central Lowlands, with the structural design mainly bamboo framework, mud siding, bamboo flooring, and palm fronds for roofing—where each bamboo shoot could conceal lethal explosives primed for easy demolition.

The establishment of base camps was made more difficult with limited areas of terrain suitable for a large force to set up a base operation. Vehicles were limited by the fact there were few—if any—passable roads, nearly eliminating the use of gun jeeps, supply "mules," and ammunition caissons. Artillery and mortar squads had to set up in mud and muck, which had a great effect on accurate firing. Patrols were forced to sleep in the paddies, knowing any suitable ground available would probably be mined and targeted by the VC.

Immersion in the water brought added problems for equipment; where clothing, boots, radios, and web gear rotted with such rapidity, the brigade supply officer was under constant pressure to replenish the basic rudiments required by a modern army. Most important, the M-16, already proven to be too delicate and inadequate in Nam, required constant maintenance from jamming, due to the mud and ammunition corrosion. Rifle barrels filled with mud often exploded in the troopers' hands when fired.

But protective cover was the greatest concern: There

was simply nothing the soldiers could lie behind to return fire.

As the First Brigade troopers had learned in the Central Highlands, "walking fire" in the mountainous bush had been a bitch, but walking fire in the rice paddies was a motherfucker!


Where Franklin found the living conditions at An Khe had been at best difficult, Qui Nhon was nightmarish. The rain was endless, overflowing rice paddies, turning the plain into a giant lake that seemed to have no distinctive shores. Roads were nearly impassable, where there were roads; travel by vehicle meant an excursion into a no-man's-land.

The troopers of 1/327 were literally living in mud—if they were lucky. Otherwise, they often slept in water, their nylon camouflage poncho liners their only cover from the elements.

The base camp of headquarters company was a small fort surrounded by barbed wire, minefields, heavy machine guns, mortar, infantry positions manned by the platoons, and the command post at the center. Shade was impossible to find, unless beneath a vehicle or in the hot, steamy bunkers.

Midnight was guaranteed harassment time. One of Charlie's favorite tricks was to mingle with peasants, find a tree or bush, use a stick in the branches that pointed at a bunker within the compound. That night, he would return with a real weapon, place it in the precise branches, squeeze off a few rounds, then hightail it for home. There were few actual hits, but it wreaked havoc on the nerves of the troopers.

Patrols were running on a regular basis, stepped up to a higher level than at An Khe since the area was so vital to the economy.

Moments of respite were relished, although filled with

the constant cleaning of equipment, personal hygiene, and perpetual refortification of the camp.

And then there was the thrill of mail from home.

The arrival of each new tape cassette was a joy for Franklin Sharps, especially those from Darlene. He would sit and listen to her lovely voice and the sound of Argonne chattering in the background. The tapes gave him a sense of belonging to something good and wonderful that he could almost touch.

He had received several by the first week of October, playing them over and over, the voices carrying him to a place that seemed forever lost. The only sadness was listening to those from his mother. He sensed in her voice that something was wrong. She never complained, however, apparently not wanting to burden him with any problem she might have. His mother knew how to suffer in silence. How to endure in private. She was, he often thought, the toughest member of the family.

He was sitting in his hooch, listening to a tape from Darlene when Dawes exploded in, all excited.

"Come on, man; grab your mess kit!"

Franklin looked perplexed. "Mess kit? What do I need a mess kit for?" He wasn't even certain if he could remember where the kit was; they had eaten nothing but C-rations since arriving in-country.

"We got hot chow! Hackworth had hot chow flown in, man." Dawes appeared nearly delirious with joy.

Franklin bolted from his rack and began rummaging through his gear. "Yes!" he shouted, fishing the metal mess kit from his duffel bag.

The two hurried away, joining the swarm of troopers hustling toward the command post, the site of the mess hall.

A long line had formed at the entrance; the smell was nearly overwhelming. Porkchops were cooking on make-shift barbecue grills, as well as chicken, and there was beer. Not cold, but plentiful.

Franklin found himself drifting toward the smell with

the others; there was laughter, chatter, jiving, and music blaring from a hundred transistor radios. Country and western, rhythm and blues, rock-and-roll. The only thing missing was an ocean with bikini-clad babes running along the beach, being chased by hundreds of hungry and horny paratroopers.

"That Hack is some dude, man," Dawes said.

"I wonder how in the hell he managed to pull this off. Hot rations in the bush is beyond belief," Franklin said.

Inside the mess tent, he could see the Spoons dishing out royal portions. They were finally getting to do a real job, and suddenly they were treated like royalty.

Franklin was just about to spear a thick, juicy chop with his fork when there was a flat bang of gunfire. Chicken, chops, mashed potatoes, gravy, biscuits, and beer went flying in every direction as the troopers dropped their mess kits and hit the deck and jacked rounds into the chambers of their M-16s.

From behind the mess tables came a shout: "Medic!"

Franklin stood and hurried around to the rear of the tables. Two Spoons were leaning over the body of a third, who lay on the ground, with a pool of blood forming near his head and his fallen M-16.

Franklin knelt and checked the man. He had a large hole in the top of his head; smoke from the discharged bullet wafted lightly from his mouth.

"He's bought it," Franklin said.

The mess sergeant stood and shook his head. "Poor motherfucker. He got a 'Dear John' this morning. His old lady run off with some college professor back at Fort Campbell."

Franklin looked closer at the dead man and recognized him. He was the cook who had emptied his bottle of Jack Daniel's up at An Khe.

"I never thought he would pull some shit like this," the mess sergeant lamented.

A voice from behind demanded, "What is going the fuck on here!"

Master Sergeant Charlie Musselwhite, from Cordele, Georgia, a tough Korean war veteran and maintenance platoon sergeant, stood over the tables.

Franklin said, "This man shot himself, Sergeant."

Musselwhite glared at the dead body. "Fuck him! Drag his dead ass out of here. Sharps, you can tag and bag him later." He was obviously outraged at the thought the man would commit suicide in front of his comrades while they were being served their first hot meal since leaving the United States. Musselwhite turned to the other men and shouted, "Goddammit, let's eat!"

The event was shocking, and ordinary people might have found the conduct of the men reprehensible, but the troopers were not ordinary people, and these were not ordinary times.

# 32

\* \* \*

The recon gun jeep became instrumental in the Qui Nhon area. A standard jeep, designed for rugged or muddy terrain, it was equipped with radios and a pedestal in the rear. An M-60 or .50-caliber machine gun was mounted on the pedestal, which could hold a standard ammunition box. The man sitting in the right seat was the "scout observer." The driver drove, constantly trying to maintain control over difficult terrain; the observer watched for trouble, and the gunner behind the pedestal was on constant alert.

There was only one problem: the vehicle was road-bound in the Qui Nhon area, making it vulnerable to attack by either land mines or ambush by the Vietcong.

With an operation apparently in mind, the recon platoon was dispatched to reconnoiter a village north of Highway 19, into what was considered known VC-controlled territory. Air reconnaissance—while effective to a point—could minimize the need to acquire more information, and it was always necessary to send in the grunts to root out the story.

Franklin was assigned to Dawes's team, and the group saddled up in three jeeps. Since they were short one man, Franklin was delighted to be given the role of gunner on the jeep with Dawes and Marion.

The small convoy rolled out of the base camp just after daylight and headed east, passing through several checkpoints before turning north, toward what was referred to as "Indian country."


The monsoon had begun, flooding the paddies over the edges of their dikes, making the narrow road, which was no more than a trail, barely visible. The recce troopers were now at full alert, knowing they were beyond the artillery and mortar fan and any tac air support needed would take a good bit of time to arrive.

The jeeps groaned and ground their way slowly, passing peasants knee-deep in the paddies, picking rice and placing it in wicker baskets that floated nearby, or strapped to water buffalo. Children worked alongside the women—there were mostly women or old men, a definite sign the countryside was ruled by Charlie. The younger men were off in other areas planning attacks, recruiting, and training in hidden enclaves.

Franklin tuned his transistor to Armed Forces Radio, transmitting from Saigon, and listened to music while scanning the terrain.

It took nearly an hour to reach the first ville, a hamlet of about one hundred Vietnamese. What they found waiting for them was shocking and appalling.

Huts were burning; children sat in the dirt crying; young women, mostly half-naked, were consoling one another. As the jeeps rolled to a halt, the villagers stared at the Americans with contempt.

Dawes stepped from the jeep and looked around, his face etched with disgust. "What in the name of everything holy has happened here?" he wondered aloud. Then he motioned for the others to stay mounted. "I'm going to see if I can find out what's been going on. You guys sit tight, and keep good eyes."

He walked among the villagers, all of whom appeared in shock and dismay. His Viet language wasn't very good but it was better than the others'. An old man suddenly appeared, his face bloodied, eyes blackened and swollen. He and Dawes spoke out of range of the others, but after several minutes the squad leader joined the team.

"What's going on?" Franklin said.

"Grab your aid bag, man. These people need some attention."

"What's going on?" Marion called from the rear jeep. "Did Charlie do this?"

Dawes motioned them to gather around him. "The village was paid a visit last night by a Korean patrol. I guess they enjoyed themselves with the women and beat the shit out of the old men when they were asked for information about the Cong. They pulled out early this morning." He waved at the burning structures. "They set the fires before skying out. The people were able to get most of them put out, but all their rice stores were destroyed."

"Those motherfuckers," Marion seethed. "From what we've been hearing, they're worse than the Vietcong."

That was the word traveling through the brigade. The Republic of Korea—ROK—army was patrolling the same province and in the short time they had been operational had made a savage reputation in the countryside.

Dawes looked at Franklin. "They need your help, brother."

Franklin grabbed his aid kit and M-16 and went to the center of the ville. Dawes spoke again with the old man— the village "headman"—who began talking to his people. Gradually, the injured began forming a line where Franklin had set up his equipment.

A young woman was first in line. She stood naked from the waist down, where blood ran along the inside of both her thighs. She had been horribly raped. She had her arms crossed over her breasts, and Franklin could see more blood soaking her black pajama top. Her eyes were vacant; she stared emptily at him. Gently, Franklin pulled her arms down and raised her pajama top.

"Those motherfuckers!" he yelled out. He felt the bile rising in his throat.

The nipples on the young girl's breasts had been cut off.

"Holy fuck!" Dawes said. "Look what they done to this child."

Marion started for his jeep. "Let's get those cocksuckers!"

"I'm with you, bro," Burkett said, starting for his jeep.

"Hold it!" Dawes ordered. "You ain't going nowhere."

"Bullshit," Marion said. "This ain't human, man. Those fuckers need to pay. They need to pay with everything they got."

"Right on," Burkett yelled. "Fighting the Cong is one thing. This is . . . man . . . I don't even *know* what this is."

"Goddammit!" Dawes said, "We're not vigilantes." He looked at Franklin. "What can you do for this baby?"

Franklin shook his head. "I'm not a surgeon. She needs a real doctor. In a real hospital." He looked at the others; all were injured beyond the realm of his skills. "I imagine there are others who'll need the same."

Dawes thought for a moment, then walked to his jeep. He radioed the headquarters command post. He spoke for several minutes, then returned to Franklin. "Do what you can for them, Franklin. What I need to know is how many of these folks need a real doctor. Headquarters is going to line up a Chinook."

"Chinook?" He knew an H-47 "banana boat" could carry half the village.

Dawes nodded. "It looks like there's going to be too many for a Huey. We'll set up security at the edges of the ville, just in case Charlie hears about this and takes it out on our asses. Can't say as I'd blame him much." He patted Franklin on the shoulder. "Do what you can. I'll need a count as soon as you can get it on how many we're going to medevac."

For the next hour Franklin did what he could, which amounted to administering morphine to the young girl, bandaging her breasts, and examining her vagina. She had been literally torn apart. There were others in equally bad shape. Dozens of broken bones. One girl had an ear cut off. A small boy had been stomped in the groin to the point his scrotum was so swollen, his penis was not visible. An old woman's nostrils had been slit.

When Franklin was done bandaging, cleaning wounds, and administering the last of his morphine, there were eighteen people in severe enough condition to be evacuated.

He walked over to Dawes, who looked like a man bent on revenge.

"What's the count?"

"Eighteen."

Dawes took the radio and reported back to headquarters. Franklin heard a voice reply, "The Chinook is inbound. Get the place ready. Pop smoke on the LZ."

Marion approached with the headman of the village. The old man's wrinkled face was as worn and weathered as old leather and what few teeth he had were bright red from chewing betel nut, popular among the villagers. There was nothing in his eyes but the look of ancient despair.

"What's up?" Dawes said.

Marion pointed to the old man. "The old guy has something to tell you. I can't understand much of what he's saying. Something about VC."

Dawes and the headman walked and talked. The combination of the old man's broken English and Dawes's fragmented Vietnamese allowed the two a limited communication.

"What did the old man have to say?" Franklin asked,

taping a bandage over the eye of the last villager left to treat.

"The old man is showing his gratitude for our help."

Franklin could detect Dawes's excitement. "What did he have to say?"

Dawes took his map and pointed to a village ten clicks to the north. "He says there are beaucoup Vietcong in this village. He said the VC forced the young men to join their ranks, and that's where they take them for training." He tapped a spot on the map.

Franklin chuckled. "He's probably full of crap."

"We've heard all that shit before, man," Marion said skeptically.

"I don't think so," Dawes said. "The old boy's pretty pissed at Charlie right now. He sent a runner to the village to have the VC send help when the Korean patrol arrived. They didn't lift a finger."

Typical Charlie: Having a village wiped out by the Americans or their allies was more important than the people. The propaganda was priceless.

"You better get on the horn to base camp," Marion said. "Find out what they want us to do."

Dawes went to his jeep and spoke for several minutes with the platoon leader. When he returned he was smiling. "We're to get these people out of here and return to base camp."

That was good news to Franklin and Marion. If there was a large Vietcong force in that village—the next stop on their patrol—they didn't want to go in outnumbered.

"Right," said Franklin. "They're ready to transport." He pointed at the other villagers. "What about them?"

Dawes shook his head. "I guess they're on their own. But we bring the headman back with us."

Franklin knew there would be a Vietnamese interpreter waiting. If the old man was lying, the interrogator would have a better chance of finding out.

• • •

Thirty minutes later, in a cloud of red smoke, the Chinook landed in the center of the village. The prop wash swirled to the dirt, fanned burning embers, causing fires to rekindle. The villagers had to begin a fresh battle to save their village. They had nothing to fight with except buckets of water filled from the rice paddy.

The Americans jumped in to help, but there was little that could be done. What was left standing by the Koreans was now gone.

"Let's mount up!" Dawes ordered. "We can't do anything more for these people." He put the headman in his jeep behind Franklin just as the powerful blades from the helo began to churn up the power.

The Chinook lifted off, and the American gun jeeps pulled out to return to base camp as ordered.

The village was no longer in existence, except in the minds of the villagers, who had nowhere else to go.

The troopers left behind everything they had: three crates of C-rations, poncho liners, and all of the remaining bandages and antiseptic in Franklin's aid kit.

# 33

★ ★ ★

Two days later the battalion was gearing up to return to the area the village headman claimed was a Vietcong training and staging area.

A Company—known as the "ABU" Company—had been selected to lead the assault, with the Recon Platoon in the vanguard.

The mood around Recon was upbeat but not boisterous. The men knew the lessons of the past. Hopes had been raised too many times, only to see them dashed for one reason or the other. They would be landing in the open, moving in water up to their waists, and would be easy targets. The trick was to get in with the element of surprise on their side, take cover, and push Charlie back while the support troops rode to their assistance.

Franklin went to the medical platoon and resupplied his aid kit. He found several of his buddies, many of whom he had not seen since leaving the Nha Trang area.

Spec Four Eddie Carreon, from San Antonio, Texas, was cracking a beer when Franklin arrived. He tossed one to Franklin and said, "Come on, man. Grab some suds and shoot the shit."

Franklin dropped to the ground with the others, sipped his beer, and began listening to the stories they had to tell from the units they were assigned to as medics.

The story seem to be universal: slogging through the mountains, now the water, and no major operation with Charlie. Their blood was up; all were in good spirits. The troopers were eager for a good fight with the Vietcong.

"I just want to get my hands on one of those motherfuckers," said Carreon. He whipped out a switchblade. "Just for a few seconds. That's all I want."

"Bullshit!" said Warner, a young guy from Oklahoma City. "Charlie'll take that knife away from you and cut your dick off with it. Then what will the señoritas do in San Antone?"

"San Antonio will have a day of mourning!" Carreon said.

Everyone laughed. Carreon was so handsome, he was damn near pretty. When he went to combat medic school in San Antone, the telephone rang night and day in the orderly room. To say he was popular with the ladies was an understatement.

Franklin felt good being with the guys from Medical Platoon. Each platoon has its own persona, and the medics were a group of carefree, boisterous young men. They had to have bravado. They weren't there to be heroes, but when the infantry got their asses shot off it was the medics who had to rise to the occasion and go get the wounded, drag their asses to safety, and patch them up. They had earned the respect of every soldier in the battalion.

Franklin left at 2100 to the sound of trucks pulling into the battalion area. The troops would be ferried to the helicopter pads, where they would go through a final check, then mount up and ride.

The moon was full and the weather report solid for the morning assault, but he knew the men would get little sleep, if any. They would lie in their hooches, think about home, family, wives, children, women they planned to have in the future.

Each man would have a thousand things on his mind, but not sleep. Sleep was what a soldier thinks about after he's survived a battle.

# 34

* * *

The sun was rising over the Central Plains, a brilliant orange glow, except where dotted by tiny black specks on the low horizon. To the Vietcong soldier standing guard at the edge of the village, the specks seemed to grow in size until they began to take the shape of giant dragonflies. Within seconds he could hear the faint sound of the rotor whipping the wind echoing from the distance, and he knew what was coming and what to do.

The soldier began running through the village, sounding the alarm. Within seconds huts and other buildings were emptying of soldiers, women, and children, all racing toward their assigned positions. Mortars were uncovered, aimed on the only available landing zone near the village. Crews manned their Goryunov heavy machine guns, the equivalent to the .50-caliber, and the Dekteryovs, the Russian counterpart to the American M-60. Bells were ringing, pans being banged, turning the village into a frenzy of activity.

One young woman, dressed in black pajamas, wore

heavy bandoliers of ammunition strapped over her shoulders; in her arms she carried a baby no more than three months of age. RPG-7 rocket teams scurried through the village to their positions while infantrymen ran on foot to take up positions along the system of dike walls necklacing the ville.

*"The Americans are coming!"* Shouts rang out as the village suddenly turned into an armed encampment and prepared to meet the invaders.


A Company was inbound in heloes with the recon element at the point. Huey gunships flew at the outer flanks, providing air cover for the assault force. The Recon Platoon was at the lead of the assault. Their task: secure the LZ for the incoming company of Airborne infantry.

Franklin was riding with his favorite team, Dawes and the others he'd known since coming aboard back at Fort Campbell. They were all silent now, their butts puckered tight against their helmets, most of them chewing nervously on C-rat chewing gum. Each man carried rations for two days and their standard complement of weapons, ammunition, and water.

They felt the Huey bank sharply, then descend, and the door gunner shouted, "All right, heroes, get your asses ready!" He pointed to the distance.

A village could be seen in the early-morning light. It was a large village by normal standards. It appeared to be on a point of land with a river running through its center. Tall trees surrounded it.

Dawes reached over and high-fived Franklin. "Good luck, man."

"I'm with you!" Franklin shouted. He slipped on his helmet, leaving the chin strap loose, then jacked a round into the chamber of his M-16, checked to see the safety was on, and prepared for the assault.

The team threw their legs over the side and leaned back, their feet braced on the skids. The feel of the water racing past made it seem they were traveling at the speed of sound.

They heard the pitch change in the prop and felt the nose rise as the chopper slowed toward a momentary hover.

Franklin leaned forward and scanned the front. What he saw chilled him. "Damn!" He pointed at the paddies to the front.

Dawes leaned forward and looked. "We're into the shit, brother!"

Mortar fire began falling on the rice paddies selected for the landing. Geysers spewed into the air; tracers streaked long snaking paths of lead from the edge and interior of the village, where heavy machine guns were firing at the troops and helicopters.

The team dropped into the water, which came above even the taller men's waists, and began pushing their bodies through the paddy, their weapons held high above their heads.

Franklin could see Chassion motioning for everyone to move forward.

The Recon Platoon fanned out and charged toward the dikes, their only protection. They were caught in the open—again!—and it was starting to look like a repeat of An Ninh when Franklin heard the thunder of a 105 howitzer artillery round crash into the village.

He saw a ball of smoke and fire rush into the sky; then there was another explosion, then another, this one from an incoming flurry of rockets fired from a Huey gunship.

He looked at Dawes and shouted, "Yeah! This time we've got the firepower!" He raised his weapon and fired, not aiming, just in the direction of the enemy, letting them know life was about to become difficult.

Pushing on, he reached the dike, hugged it close for a moment, then rose up and fired at the muzzle flashes coming from dikes nearly one hundred meters away, near the edge of the village.

More artillery began to fall on the village. Smoke billowed and he could see black-clad VC running in every direction.

Franklin spotted one figure in particular in front of the dike, running from right to left of his line of fire. He took careful aim and squeezed off a round. The bullet cut the water a few feet in front of the target.

He fired a second round. The bullet cut the water short of the target.

He took a deep breath, released slowly, then squeezed.

The target pitched forward and disappeared beneath the water near the wall of the dike.

"Yeah!" he shouted. "Yeah!" It was the best shot he had ever made. And probably the luckiest.

The second wave made its approach south and east of his position, into another line of paddies. A third lift would land north and east, forming a horseshoe at the front of the village. Another element would land north, where they would set up a blocking position. The frontal assault would sweep forward, driving the VC—who would no doubt begin fleeing under the superior firepower—into the waiting guns of the blocking element.

That was the plan.

Chassion motioned the troopers forward, moving in fire teams. Mortar crashed and shook the surface of the paddies; bullets stitched crazy paths of tiny rooster tails across the surface. Miraculously, no one was hit as the team approached the dike wall.

Suddenly, to his right, a VC ran along the top of the dike, then dropped out of sight on the far side. Franklin took a hand grenade, pulled the pin, and lobbed it over the edge. There was an explosion, and in the air above him, framed against the sky, an object was floating down, as though from the heavens. Mud? Tree stump? What?

Only when the body impacted against him did he realize it was a human being. The Vietcong's weight, joined with the weight of his equipment, pushed Franklin beneath the water. He could feel himself drowning; he could feel the VC's body entangled with his, and he knew he was going to die.

There was only silence and, opening his eyes, the brown muck of the paddy water. He was going to die. He was going to—

Then, it dawned on him: *Stand up, fool! You're only in water up to your fucking waist!*

He pushed upward and saw the sun. And the face of the dead man, whose leg was entangled in Franklin's harness. He pulled the leg free and threw the body off just as another VC ran along the dike. He raised his weapon and fired. There was a puff of gray smoke, a loud bang, and he felt something sting his side. He looked at the barrel of the M-16. The muzzle was parted like petals on an open flower. The bottom of the magazine was also missing. He could only figure the barrel was full of mud when he fired and when it exploded the back pressure blew the rounds out of the bottom of the magazine.

He was lucky. But he was without an M-16. He took his pistol and hugged the dike, watching the others as they pushed over it and began driving the enemy back toward the village.

He saw two feet sticking out of the water. The body was head-down. It was the target he had dropped from the first dike. He figured the VC had an AK and ammo strapped to his body and so reached down and felt hair and, as he pulled the VC up, said, "Come here, motherfucker."

The body came up easy, and he saw the bandoliers around the upper torso. He saw the face of a young woman and he saw a baby pop from her arms and bob in the water like a cork floating on a pond.

It was a moment when the sounds of baby Argonne, on the tapes, reached across from one side of the world to the other. When the shame of all that had been done to those children in the mountains surfaced with the same surprising suddenness as with this child.

The mother was the enemy, taking ammunition to those who would kill his comrades.

But the child was not part of the bargain.

He looked at the woman. His bullet had hit her in the right side of her back, come out the left breast, and damn near cut the child in half.

A sudden spray of enemy fire, kicking in the water, broke his reverie. *Grieve later, goddammit! Get your ass moving.*

He stripped off the bandoliers and pushed her body away. He took the towel from around his neck, wrapped the child in it, vaulted over the dike, and raced to a palm tree, where he laid the bundle down, then raced toward the battle.

# 35

**\* \* \***

The advance from the dike to the edge of the village, where Charlie chose to form a line of defense—again hugging the belt and denying tac air and artillery—was where the fighting grew intense. But it allowed the incoming lifts to move across the paddies with little resistance, since the VC heavy weapons assets had been abandoned. Now it was in-close fighting, nerve-wracking, but at least there was cover.

And for the first time since Franklin had been in-country . . . overwhelming odds in the Airborne's favor. At least it looked that way, from the mortar pit where he was hunkered beside Dawes.

The crackle of M-16 fire and AK-47 chatter, mixed with the deep stutter of the M-60s and the M-79 and hand grenade explosions, created an incredible, horrific noise, the sounds echoing off the hard mud huts and rustling the palm trees, at the base of each where Charlie had a bunker and a sniper at the top.

"Slow and easy, slow and easy. No telling what kind

of shit Charlie's got hidden for our ass," Dawes warned.

Both ducked as a spray of AK-47 swept the front of their position, kicking up dirt that flew over their heads.

"See what I mean?" Dawes said.

"Where's the rest of the platoon?" Franklin had been the last one over the dike and into the ville and was disoriented.

Dawes began pointing to where the recce troops were positioned. Chassion had set up a command post near a mud hut at the center of the leading edge of the ville. Three squads on his right flank, three on his left.

For the first time, they had the enemy boxed in, on their ground.

*This is our ground*, Franklin thought.


The recon troopers were the point of the bayonet, shoving it in, but going slow, decisive, making certain it would be a clean thrust. Each step calculated, calm, with precision. Forget about checking the huts. To hell with booby traps. Pull the pin, watch the spoon kick, then throw the grenade inside.

There was no time to check for civilians. This was a war zone. There were no civilians. If they weren't there to fight, they should be somewhere else.

Methodically, the platoon moved through the village, knowing that A Company was following close on their heels, taking out the flanks, shutting off the avenues of retreat.

Charlie was running now, but he was putting up a fight. Sporadic gunfire broke out as he left the house, not giving up an inch without a fight. "This is the way it should be," Franklin said to nobody in particular.

# 36

* * *

Her hair was gray and hung long and loose at her shoulders. Her hands were gnarled like twists of dry vine, her face pleasant, showing nothing of the horror she had known in her life or in her final moments.

She reminded Franklin of his grandmother in Arizona, lying asleep.

He had thrown a hand grenade into the hut, kicked back, waiting for the explosion. When the ground shook and the earth moved, he went inside, firing his rifle.

Then he moved on to the next hut.

He had a grenade, and was about to pitch it inside when he heard the sound of a child crying. He looked in the window. The child was sitting on a bamboo mat, alone, a small cook fire burning nearby. The aroma of the hut caught his nostrils and brought him back to reality. He leaned through the window and saw the door and the mousetrap. He knew there was a bullet beneath the tiny nail planted on the small piece of wood where the lever would strike.

He eased his M-16 through the crude window and fired. The mousetrap tripped and set off an explosion.

*Not today, Charlie. We know your fucking tricks.*

But the child was crying. Another of Charlie's tricks. Get the babies to distract the attention. Dumb-assed, good-natured GI Joe, the sentimental bastard from decades past, always a sucker for a baby. An old woman. Or a skirt.

*Not today!*

He carefully put the pin back into the grenade, securing the spoon. He moved on.

*Not today. Not fucking today!*

It was weakness Charles counted on.

A kid from Iowa with a big heart winds up with his guts in his hands.

*Not today!*

A dumb-ass bar bouncer from New York City—who's never seen trees except in Central Park—is fire-walking the bush. His ass is hanging out all over the place. He just wants to go home, but he's a killer now. A stone fucking killer. You want to bag him, Charles?

*Not today!*

A surfer from Malibu is coming off the paddies, getting his ass shot at, and learning a new 360 on the waves. He's carrying iron. Explosives. Think you can bring him down?

*Not today!*

Want to kill me?

*Not today!*

Franklin moved on, part of the sweep, hoping there would be something—someone—to fight!

"Watch your six!" Dawes shouted. He was at the next hut, and starting to go forward, when there was a single shot.

Franklin ducked instinctively, then looked toward Dawes.

Dawes was sitting by the edge of a hut with a distant look on his face, eyes vacant, as though something had been lost, and he was looking for it but couldn't remember what it was. He was dead.

Franklin realized there was no sympathy left in him. Like Chassion said, "The only place you'll find sympathy in this world is in the dictionary, between suicide and syphilis."

He moved slowly from hut to hut, tossing in the grenades. Firing a killing side burst after each, then moving on.

As he reached the river dividing the village there was an explosion. "What was that?" he shouted.

A voice called back, "Charlie's blown the bridge over the river. Covering his retreat to the other side."

The village was now split into two enclaves.


On this day, Charlie was tough. He wasn't going to give up an inch of ground without a fight.

Franklin saw the figure slip from the side of a hut and start to make a run for the river. He was smaller than Franklin but deadly as a cobra. Franklin cut across his line of flight and dropped behind a well. He watched as the VC came forward, rushing hard, his eyes solid and straight.

He had that special look of fear on his face, the one that's visible on a trapped animal; he was caught, and he knew it. He had no choice but to fight.

Franklin rose up and leveled his M-16 at the enemy soldier. Their eyes joined for a split second, just before Franklin squeezed off a neat three-round burst. The bullets stitched the VC across the chest, sending him into a pirouette like a drunken ballet dancer. He didn't scream. He fell silently to the ground, clutching his AK-47, and lay still.

Franklin moved forward, not thinking or feeling. Move and fire. Reload. Keep moving. His world had been reduced to this tiny microcosm where strangers were joined in the ancient ritual of fighting to the death. He felt the hate boiling up from within his soul.

He had to be cautious, not careful. Careful creates a

pattern the enemy can home in on. Cautious allows latitude while at the same time making one dangerous. They had Charlie on his front porch, and like Franklin's grandfather had said, "You can chase an old cur dog all over the town, but when he gets under his front porch . . . he'll bite your leg off!"

And that's what it came down to.


Overhead, the air whistled as the artillery streaked toward the opposing bank of the river. The sound of the incoming 105 round, followed by impact and a thunderous explosion, meant the howitzers were on target. This was not the time for short rounds.

The crackle of M-16s mixed with the explosions, and all was coming closer. When the troopers reached the river, there was a glorious sight. Approximately twelve Vietcong were swimming toward the far bank!

Franklin raised his rifle to fire, then stopped. He thought he saw what Charlie was up to: Children had been mixed into the group of fleeing soldiers. They were splashing and kicking to the other side, being dragged along by the struggling enemy.

"Hold your fire!" somebody shouted. "There's kids in the line of fire!"

The troopers had to stand helpless and watch as the enemy soldiers crawled up the bank, dragging the children along, using them as human shields.

Within seconds, the VC disappeared into the enclave of huts on the far side, taking the children with them.

Overhead, a gunship banked low, its guns blazing from both doors, bullets spraying the front line of huts facing the river. The mud-and-thatch structures seemed to melt as the gunfire tore at the walls and roofs, tearing huge chunks away with its vicious storm of firepower.

"Slick motherfucker." That's what Marion had to say as he knelt next to Franklin, near the edge of the river, sweat pouring from his face. "Motherfucker knows how to give up something . . . to keep something."

"They killed Dawes," Franklin said acidly.

"Yeah, I know. Guess it just wasn't his day." There was a long pause. "Why have we stopped? We ought to be going after them."

Franklin couldn't understand Marion's lack of compassion for Dawes. It was as though he had not existed.

"Dawes is dead, man, and all you can think about is Charlie."

Marion shrugged it off. "Who the fuck are you to come at me with this shit? You're the guy that wanted to kill Charlie. For your dead brother. That's all I've heard about from you. 'Kill. Kill.' Shit. You come here to kill; I come here to go home. To my wife, kids, my family. You understand the difference?"

Franklin didn't.

Marion went on. "I'm just some dumb-assed nigger from Mississippi that ain't never gonna have shit. That's been my life. I was drafted; I didn't want none of this shit. But there is a GI Bill. I can go to college, get an education, a good job, and buy a home." He waited, got no reaction, and went on. "Charlie ain't nothing but a step I got to cross along the path to where I'm going. He's in my way. You see, brother, the difference between you and me is real simple: You kill for the dead. I kill for the living."

Marion walked away to a position that gave a good view of the enemy on the far side of the river.

Franklin sat alone, listening to Marion's words echo in his brain. Remembering the look on the face of Dawes.

And for a while, the shooting stopped.

# 37

⋆ ⋆ ⋆

By late afternoon the fighting had settled to a stalemate. The concern for civilian casualties on both sides of the river had forced a lull in the conflict. Positions were taken up along the river by both sides, but except for sporadic sniping it was quiet.

Watching the dead Vietcong being counted and gathered made Franklin remember he had something to tend to. He walked to where the baby lay wrapped in the towel and dug a deep hole at the base of a palm tree with his entrenching tool. He placed the child in, covered it over, then patted down the dirt. He knelt, said a short prayer, then took the ET and his weapon and returned to the village.

There were more bodies to deal with, on both sides.

The dead enemy were searched, their weapons stockpiled, and the corpses stacked like cords of wood in a huge net attached to a helicopter. The chopper lifted off and flew away, to deposit the enemy dead in a government-maintained mass grave.

The back side of the village was cleared and used for medevac. Franklin tagged Dawes, stripped his gear from his body, and, with the help of another trooper, placed the remains inside and zipped the body bag. Dawes's remains were loaded up, along with two wounded troopers.

As he stood in swirling purple smoke, watching the Huey depart with his friend, Franklin felt nothing but emptiness.

He walked back to where a command post had been established and there found two nuns had just arrived to work in an orphanage on the other side of the river. He thought that's all the Americans needed, to bring carnage onto a home for victims of the war.

Then the rain began to fall; blinding sheets swept through the village, reducing visibility to zero. Franklin wondered if across the river the Vietcong were taking a break as well.

Franklin had set up a small aid station in a hut and was treating minor injuries suffered by the civilians. The medic from a platoon from A Company—who was now in the village—joined him and the two began treating minor cuts and abrasions. Two wounded Vietcong had been captured and were being interrogated. Information of the VC's position on the far side was critical.

It had grown dark when the most incredible event of the day occurred for Franklin. One of the nuns, plus an old mama-san and a young woman, showed up at the aid station.

The young woman, no more than eighteen, had gone into labor.

"You want me to what?" Franklin asked Chassion.

"You're the medic. You know how to deliver a baby, don't you?" There was a wry look on his face as though he were enjoying Franklin's dilemma.

"I don't know *anything* about delivering babies. Have

the mama-san do it. She's probably done it a hundred times."

Chassion shook his head. "Do you know what a breech birth is, Sharps?"

Franklin knew. The baby was turned feet-down instead of head-down.

The expectant mother was doubled over; blood filled the crotch of her black pajamas.

"The baby's already coming out, goddammit," Chassion yelled. "You might not be much, but you're all she's got."

Franklin looked defeated. "Jesus, Plat. The father of the baby is probably across the river shooting at us right now."

"That's not the baby's fault," Chassion said. "I know this is tough, but you can do it."

"What if I screw up?"

"You won't. We're going to get Doc Benjamin on the horn. He'll talk you through it. Come on, let's get her in one of these hooches."

The woman was taken to a hut where two rough tables had been placed together. Poncho liners provided some comfort, but he doubted if she noticed the difference. She was crying, moaning, occasionally screaming.

He cut away her pajamas, and sure enough, there was a small pair of feet projecting from her vagina. First, he hooked her up to an intravenous solution and gave her an injection of morphine. The battalion surgeon was on the radio, instructing him what to do.

The woman was at full dilation. His hands trembled as he listened to Major Raphael Benjamin's instruction over the radio.

"You'll have to put your hand inside her and feel for the umbilical cord."

Franklin put his fingers inside; he could feel the baby's tiny shoulders and the cord wrapped around its neck.

"Tell him I feel the cord."

The word was passed, and the doctor replied, "Lift it over the baby's head."

The woman screamed and writhed. "Hold her, goddammit," Franklin shouted to Chassion. The burly sergeant clamped down on the woman's legs; another man pinned her shoulders to the table.

He tried again, felt the cord, then slid it over the child's head. "It's done. Now what?" Sweat was streaming from every pore in his body.

"Take the baby by the feet and pull it toward you. Try to help slip the shoulders and arms through the birth canal."

*Jesus!* This was like delivering a foal from a mare.

He began pulling the baby out. The mother was now going ballistic and nearly levitated just as the baby's shoulders became visible, but the two paratroopers pressed her back down.

Blood was flowing as he saw the head suddenly appear, and with a final, determined pull the baby popped out like a cork from a bottle of champagne.

Franklin fell back exhausted, releasing his grip on the child. It was a little girl, purple from the ordeal and covered with creamy and sticky film.

Chassion slapped him on the shoulder. "Way to go, kid. I knew you could do it."

There was a loud applause as the mama-san swept up the child and began cleaning her mouth and nostrils with a grimy towel.

Since the day began, he had seen the life of a friend come to a violent end, taken the life of other human beings, and brought a life into the world.

# 38

* * *

The rain continued to fall, turning the ground slick and deadly, especially for the soldiers who had to cross the open street. A young lieutenant, Harry "the Horse" Godwin, had his fill of the snipers as it turned dark. He was a former marine and a top athlete at Henderson State, and he took his best sharpshooters from A Company and positioned them to have a field of fire along the street and over the river to the Vietcong side. Then, stripped down like a fullback, he would charge across the opening to the other side, dodging and weaving as they tried to kill him. At the moment the enemy snipers fired, Godwin's sharpshooters would fire on the muzzle flashes. Time and again he raced across the street, until gradually the sniper fire stopped and both sides settled in for a long and nervous night.

The night was continually aglow from a combination of flare ships dropping their iridescent load from above, to the mortar squads firing illuminating rounds that aided in lighting up the night, to the individual soldiers shooting their handheld parachute flares into the darkness.

Despite the weather and the bridge being destroyed, the troopers stood watch in case the VC sent a sapper squad or infantry probes across the river. And it still wasn't certain there weren't enemy hiding on the American side. It was that thought that had the nerve cages rattling the most during the night. The flares turned branches and pieces of rubble into human shapes. Each sound was enough to bring a weapon to bear.

Franklin rose from his bunk on the floor, grabbed his weapon, and left the aid hut and went outside to relieve himself. He stepped around the edge of the hut and had started to unbutton his fly when a sound deep and sinister snapped him to full alert. It was coming from the other side of the hut. He eased around the edge, but the darkness was too thick. Then, a flare popped overhead, and nearby there was movement, and a gnawing sound.

His eyes locked onto the creature. Ten feet away, a bamboo rat was holding a coconut in his front paws. The critter seemed the size of a bulldog and, rearing up on his hind legs, grew to an enormous proportion. Franklin had seen bodies the rats had devoured, even dismembered, dragging limbs off to feed on.

He was so scared, he couldn't pull the trigger. All he could do was backpedal, pissing his pants all the way to the inside of the hut. He broke down one of the tables, used the wood to build a small fire on the floor, and climbed on top of the smaller one. *Tonight I sleep off the ground.*

He lay there all night, listening, jerking up at every sound. He stayed on the table, except when it was his turn to pull guard duty with Marion.


The morning brought more disappointment. The weather had broken and a Huey was sent to check out the situation on the opposite side of the river. The sniper fire had stopped. There was no movement. Nothing.

Then a child—a boy—appeared on the bank. The nun was summoned and given binoculars. She recognized the child. A sick feeling began filling everyone's guts.

The chopper didn't take any ground fire, and the scenario was starting to look all too familiar. In less than half an hour, the fear was confirmed. Somehow, Charlie had managed to slip out of the village during the night. There was no known figure on how many had been in the enclave on the other side of the river, and now they were gone. They had even managed to take their dead with them.

A patrol, under the cover of the Americans from their side of the river and the gunship in the sky above the village, crossed toward the debris from the bridge.

The children in the orphanage were safe. What the patrol discovered to be the answer lay in the small building used for the school.

Chassion stood seething at the blackboard, where a crude drawing of a helicopter was still scrawled on the slate.

"The little bastards used this as a classroom, Sarge," Marion said. "Look at all the shit." Human excrement was on the floor.

"The little fuckers kept us busy on the river while they planned their getaway," Chassion said.

Franklin studied the room, scanning the interior for any sign of how the Vietcong might have escaped. There was a fireplace in the wall, which seemed out of the ordinary. More important, there was nothing in the recess to suggest it was recently used for a fire. He took his bayonet and carefully scraped at the front edge. "Look at this, Sarge."

Chassion examined the fireplace for a moment, then ordered, "All of you . . . clear out. Get outside." He took a hand grenade and pulled the pin. There was an open window beside the fireplace; he threw one leg through the opening, then tossed the grenade into the recess.

Chassion rolled out of the window and raced to a tree. The explosion blew the back of the building apart, but not even the rubble could hide the hole that was revealed by the detonation.

The soldiers came back inside and saw how the Vietcong had eluded them. "A tunnel," Marion said angrily. He cleared away rubble with his hands, discovering a larger hole leading into the darkness below.

Chassion got on the radio and called the company commander. He explained the situation, then walked outside. The others followed, and he told them, "They're sending over a tunnel rat. He'll be here in a few minutes. Take a break and have a smoke." He looked at Franklin. "Come with me. Let's check out the orphanage."

The two moved cautiously across the street to a building where children could be seen through the structure. There was no door and no glass on the windows. Inside, nearly two dozen children sat on bamboo mats lined neatly along each side of the wall. It was heartbreaking.

"Poor little bastards," Franklin said.

"Yeah. Life's a bitch. They'll probably grow up to have to kill American soldiers." There was a hard glint in Chassion's eyes; he fidgeted at a grenade on his harness, and for a moment Franklin was scared of what the man might do. Then he said, "Check them out. Do what you can for them."

Franklin gave the children a quick examination. Except for being terrified from the noise and the fighting, none were injured. The nuns arrived a short time later and he went back to the school.

The "tunnel rat" was there, a short, wiry Mexican who looked no bigger than the kids. These were the men who had two primary attributes that allowed them to go into the tunnels and see what Charlie had beneath the ground: they were small and had ice water in their veins.

A rope was tied around his waist, and with a flashlight in one hand, a .45 pistol in the other, he was lowered, headfirst, into the tunnel.

The only way they could tell his progress was to watch the line play out. Gradually, it would move at different increments, mostly slow, sometimes in quick bursts of footage. Franklin helped on the rope and thought he could feel the "rat's" pulse beating from below into the palm of his hands, but knew the pulse was his own. If something happened, he might have to go down and bring him out.

When he thought of the bamboo rat, his skin crawled again; sweat beaded on his forehead, especially when there was a long run on the rope. Whatever was down there was known only to the "rat" and whoever might be lurking in the darkness.

He knew the design of the tunnel: sharp turns and angles, and probably deep, carved-out spaces serving as surgical rooms or barracks, often with shelves carved above the pathway to give a guard a small niche to hide and wait for the "rats."

The tension fell off the rope; it went momentarily slack, and a tug on the line followed. He would back out now, slowly inching his way in reverse to the light.

When the tunnel rat emerged, he was slick with sweat. He sat on the floor for a moment, untied the rope, and lit a cigarette. He didn't say a word for a long time. "It's empty, but lots of sign of activity. They left in a hurry. Blood trails lead toward the north. Then it gets slick and muddy."

"They came out near the bank of the river on the edge of the ville," Chassion said.

"Yeah," the rat replied. "Probably at the tree line to the north. Right under our noses."

Chassion reported to the command post and received orders to return to the other side of the river.

There was nothing but frustration on their faces as they crossed, to return to base camp with little to show for the effort.

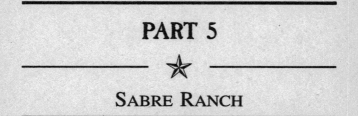

# PART 5

## SABRE RANCH

# 39

The ringing of the telephone jerked Shania Sharps's attention from the television set, where she was watching a political speech by Arizona senator Barry Goldwater, giving his support for President Johnson's decision to commit more troops to Vietnam. The country was beginning to show strong signs of division over the war and now the government was fueling the flames by sending more soldiers, ships, and aircraft.

*This is crazy*, she thought.

The voice was familiar, that of Dr. Jessie Malone, a family practitioner in nearby Willcox. She had been nervous for several days, awaiting tests Malone had made the week before. When he finished giving her the report from a specialist in Phoenix, she cradled the receiver and walked onto the porch. The sun was setting and the sky clear, pristine, and clean, the faint image of the moon already visible overhead.

The world seemed to have gone insane. Vietnam. The Civil Rights Movement in the South. Barriers against

Supreme Court–mandated desegregation of schools, restaurants, and public facilities. Social and economic bankruptcy in Negro communities throughout the country.

*It is all so insane.* She went back inside to get a shawl.

In her bedroom, for some unexplained reason, she found herself opening a cedar chest, where she thumbed through thick packets of old letters written by Samuel to his family and to her during his years overseas.

When her fingers touched one particular envelope, she smiled, feeling the love and history that lay within. The letter sent by Samuel to his parents on his first day upon arriving at Tuskegee.

The day they first met.

# 40

★ ★ ★

He arrived in Macon County, Alabama, on a hot afternoon to the sound of thunder. The sky was cloudless. He noticed a flash of sunlight streak across the horizon and a moment later watched an airplane appear overhead. Samuel pulled off the road as the airplane—it was an A-6—snapped onto its back, then rolled back to straight and level flight. He watched breathlessly; then the A-6 disappeared over a tree line. He took his map and confirmed that he was north of Tuskegee, close to Tuskegee Army Airfield.

He drove for twenty minutes until he came to what looked like a sentry booth. A Negro military policeman stepped out and saluted smartly.

"Can I help you, sir?"

"Is this the airfield?" Samuel stammered.

The MP smiled. "Yes, sir. This is Tuskegee Army Airfield."

"I'd like permission to come onto the field."

The MP straightened. "No, sir. Unless you have official

business, the field is off-limits to civilian personnel."

Samuel looked beyond the MP and saw two airplanes circling in the distance.

"Anything else I can do for you, sir?" the MP asked with an obvious impatience.

Samuel shook his head, backed up, and drove toward Tuskegee. During the drive he made a promise aloud. "The next time I come back I will be on official business."

He couldn't get the roar of that A-6 out of his mind.


Since first telling his family he was going to Tuskegee Institute despite the railings of his grandmother and mother, Samuel had often asked himself, "Why was Tuskegee selected to be the army's training center for Negro pilots?" He knew the hatred that existed in the South. Why, then, did the military select a location in the Deep South? The Negro press claimed it was to guarantee the failure of the program; supporters insisted it was because Tuskegee was a shining example of the Negro's opportunity to succeed in the South.

The campus was smaller than he had imagined; buildings stood in neat rows, their red-brick structure gleaming in the sun. He parked his car and strolled along the campus, stopping at the statue memorializing Booker T. Washington, who had founded the institute in 1881. He stood for a moment staring at the statue, trying to imagine the strength and courage it took for the man to defy so many odds arrayed against him.

He found the administration building and saw a sign directing him toward Admissions. In a tiny office bulging with stuffed bookshelves, he walked up to a small man with wire-framed glasses perched on his nose, sitting at a desk.

"Can I help you, young man?" There was an amused smile on his face, making Samuel uncomfortable as he removed his Western hat.

"My name is Adrian Samuel Sharps. I've been accepted into the fall semester."

The man rose and extended his hand. "My name is Professor LeBaron. I assist with admissions this time of year, but my primary position is professor of agriculture." He scanned a ledger in front of him. "I see you're majoring in agriculture. No doubt you'll take one of my classes."

Samuel nodded. "No doubt." He fumbled with his hat.

LeBaron knew what was going through his mind. "We need to get you enrolled and get you a class schedule figured out." He stopped and looked again at the ledger. "There is one problem—"

"Samuel," he interrupted. "People call me Samuel. What problem is there, Professor?"

LeBaron tapped the ledger. "In your initial application you didn't request dormitory facilities."

"Why is that a problem?"

"Limited facilities, Mr. Sharps. Now that the army has begun training young Colored men to become fighter pilots, our dormitories are overflowing."

Samuel looked dejected. "I never gave it a thought." He looked around, feeling foolish. "I guess I can find a place in town."

LeBaron laughed. "This is Alabama, young man, not Arizona. A young Colored man can't just go and 'find a place in town.'"

For the first time Samuel began wishing he had gone to the University of Southern California.

But LeBaron wasn't a man to let opportunity slip through his fingers. "May I make a suggestion?"

"I'd be grateful."

"I have a place outside of town that I'm preparing for young men in your situation. There're four rooms, two beds to a room. It's clean and away from folks in town. I have one more vacancy. If you don't mind living in the country."

Samuel beamed. "Not at all. I grew up on a ranch in

Arizona. I know all about living in the country."

"Excellent. I think you'll like the accommodations. You'll receive breakfast and supper seven days a week as part of your rent. My daughter will do the cooking, but you'll have to share household chores with your roommates."

"That sounds fine with me, Professor."

They worked together on determining what classes he would need: biology, English, mathematics, and others, until Samuel said, "I'd like to take ROTC."

LeBaron looked at him with surprise. "You want to become an army officer?"

"No, sir, I want to become an army aviator. That's why I chose Tuskegee Institute. I can do both while going to college."

LeBaron sat back. "Do you have a pilot's license?"

"Not yet, but I intend to take primary flight instruction from a man named Charles Anderson." He handed LeBaron the letter he had received from Sparks Hamilton. "I set aside enough money for the training."

LeBaron shook his head gravely. "There's thousands of young Colored men trying to get into the flight program. Most have been rejected for one reason or other. Most all are college graduates and have pilot licenses."

"I think that will change when we get into the war, sir. I want to be ready to do my part."

"You think there will be a war, Mr. Sharps?"

"I do. Our country can't stay out of it much longer."

LeBaron said nothing more. He filled in the last blank with the words: "Reserve Officer Training Corps."

LeBaron handed him the form. "Classes start on Monday," he said, and wrote down the directions to his home. As Samuel left, LeBaron reflected that he had filled his boardinghouse with eight tenants in the last two days. Each one was an agriculture student, all were strong and had worked on farms, and now the last one was a rancher.

Only two were pursuing the ridiculous notion of becoming army aviators.

• • •

Samuel followed the directions to the house, only a few miles from the institute. He parked in front where two other automobiles sat, both with out-of-state license plates. He took his suitcases and had started up the steps when he heard the sound of voices near the side of the house. Two men in their early twenties appeared wearing work clothes. Samuel stood on the porch, saying nothing as they saw him.

"Good afternoon," said one of the men. He was tall and lanky and had a thick mustache. The other nodded, a heavyset man with a shaved head.

"I'm Willis Reeves," the tall man said, offering his hand. "Are you a new tenant?"

"Yes. My name is Samuel Sharps." He extended his hand. "Professor LeBaron sent me here. I'll be bunking with you fellows."

"Daniel Cook," the heavy man said as he shook Samuel's hand. "Looks like you and I'll be sharing a room." Without asking, he took one of Samuel's suitcases and went into the house, with Samuel and Reeves following.

The smell of fresh paint and fried chicken greeted Samuel inside the front room of the boardinghouse. He looked around, pleased with what he saw. There was a parlor, and a hall that led to the bedroom. He put his suitcases beside an empty bed and looked around. He was about to say something when he glanced through the window and saw a woman walking through the backyard carrying a chicken, freshly beheaded and neatly plucked.

"Does she live here?" Samuel said.

Reeves laughed. "You'd think she owns the place. Her father is Professor LeBaron. Her name is Shania."

Samuel whispered her name to himself. She was the most beautiful woman he had seen.

"We better get back to work," Cook said.

Samuel turned to them. "Do you need some help?"

Both smiled at him. "We're digging a hole for the out-house. You sure you want to help?"

"I've dug plenty of outhouse pits in my time."

The two left while Samuel put on his work jeans and boots. When he was dressed he went through the kitchen and saw the young woman standing at the sink. She looked up from the chicken she was preparing. "I hope you like chicken. Poppa called and said we had a new tenant for supper. He said you were a big man and I should prepare another chicken. You look like you could eat a whole fryer by yourself."

Samuel felt his stomach groan; he had eaten little since yesterday morning.

"I could eat a horse."

Shania laughed. "I hope chicken will do."

He took off his hat. "I'm Samuel Sharps."

She wiped her hands on a cloth and shook his hand. "I'm Shania LeBaron. Supper is at six. I hope Poppa told you that he and I take our meals here. It's easier than cooking here and at our home."

"That makes sense." He stared at her for a long moment, still holding her hand. At last, he released his grip and clamped his hat on his head. "I better go help the fellows with the digging."

He found Reeves and Cook digging the trench; a small wooden house stood nearby, the white paint still drying in the heat. A zinc-lined vat lay on the ground. That would serve as the septic tank, preventing contamination of the ground.

The three worked together. Cook dug with a pick while Reeves shoveled the dirt into a wheelbarrow, and Samuel hauled the dirt to a nearby mound. After two hours of digging and shaping, the three hefted the zinc liner into the trench. Finally, the small outhouse was placed over the hole and the three stood looking at the structure with wonderment.

Cook said, "I've never used outdoor facilities before. We had indoor toilets on our farm back in Virginia."

Reeves laughed. "I grew up on a tobacco farm in Kentucky. All we had was privies. You'll get use to the smell. It's the winter that makes you miserable."

"I wouldn't mind the cold right now," Samuel said, wiping the sweat from his face. "Is the humidity always this bad?"

Reeves nodded. "It can even get worse. But in the winter it'll sink into your bones and freeze you half to death."

So many new things, thought Samuel.

"You boys done a good job."

Samuel looked up to see a young man in an army uniform. His hat was cocked to the side and he seemed to swagger as he stepped off the porch. A patch on his left shoulder was that worn by ROTC. He had light skin for a Negro, a thin mustache, and stood as tall as Samuel. "Afternoon, gents. I'm Thomas Guillard, your new roommate." He shook hands with the three and looked around the place. "Reminds me of home back in South Dakota."

"South Dakota?" Reeves said. "I didn't know there were any Negroes in South Dakota."

"Lot of Coloreds have lived up there over the last seventy years. My granddaddy served there in the army."

Samuel looked at him curiously. "Was your grandfather in the cavalry?"

"The Ninth Cavalry. Fought at Milk River along with the Seventh Cavalry. That was the last big battle of the Indian campaigns. There weren't any more threats from Indians, so when he retired he married a Sioux woman, bought a piece of land near Belle Fourche, and started farming."

Samuel felt a bond with this young man. "My grandfather retired a sergeant major with the Tenth. Our family lives in Arizona and raises cattle." He looked at Guillard's uniform. "You're in ROTC."

Guillard grinned. "Just picked up my uniform this afternoon." He straightened in military fashion. "How do I look?"

"Great. You look like the grandson of a soldier," Samuel said.

They heard Shania's voice. "Better wash up, fellows. Supper will be ready in thirty minutes."

The diggers washed while the soldier inspected the outhouse.

The remaining roommates arrived just before supper was served. During the meal LeBaron suggested, "Why don't you gentlemen tell us a little about yourselves?" He looked at one of the new arrivals.

"I'm Delbert Hughes, from Pennsylvania. I'm an agriculture major."

They listened as the others introduced themselves. Austin Braxton from Tennessee, Fillmore Hall from Indiana, and Terrence Spann from Illinois. All raised on the farm.

LeBaron looked at Guillard. "What about you, Thomas?"

Guillard shrugged. "I grew up on a wheat farm in South Dakota. My grandfather was Colored, my grandmother a half-breed Sioux. Her father was a white man." He could see they were curious, for his complexion was almost too light for a Negro. Then he chuckled, adding, "My mother is a white woman. That's why I'm not dark-skinned."

The forks stopped in midair.

"Your mother is white?" asked Reeves.

"White as winter snow."

Cook shook his head. "Down here a white woman seen with a Colored man would be jailed."

"Or lynched," Braxton added.

"Wasn't it difficult growing up with a white mother and Colored father?" Samuel asked.

Guillard shook his head. "Folks in South Dakota aren't prejudiced against Coloreds. Just Indians. They hate them so much they don't have any spare hate or time to use it on Coloreds. We get along just fine."

LeBaron asked Samuel, "What about your family, Mr. Sharps? Are they still living?"

"Yes, sir. At least my mother, father, and grandmother. She's getting old, but she's still spry." Then he told them about his family and the part the Sharps family played in settling the Western frontier. Buffalo Bill Cody. The Rough Riders. His father and uncle in the Great War. He even told them about him beating a tank on a mule.

"Sounds like you gentlemen have already had interesting lives," LeBaron said.

"Wait until classes begin," Shania said. "Life will become very boring."

That night Samuel sat on the front porch oiling his Sharps rifle. He sat looking at the moon, rubbing the stock and barrel, summarizing the day's events. Afterward he wrote a letter to his family, telling them about the trip from Arizona. The best part was the last half of the letter telling them about his first day in Tuskegee: He had seen an army airplane, enrolled at the institute, signed up for ROTC, helped his new roommates dig a hole for an outhouse, made new friends, and eaten dinner with a cultured man and his beautiful daughter.

"Except for the digging and the humidity, I consider my first day at Tuskegee as being perfect," he wrote at the end.

# 41

* * *

Such a beautiful day, Shania thought, when she returned to the front porch. Too beautiful to be ruined by tragic news. She sat there for a long time until the darkness and the slight desert chill drove her inside, again to the telephone.

She dialed a number and waited until she heard her son's voice. "Kevin. Hi, baby; it's Mom."

The reply of Kevin's voice gave her sudden comfort.


An hour later, in his dormitory at Berkeley, Kevin Sharps suddenly felt weak as he hung up the telephone. At nineteen, he was shorter than his brothers, and his skin darker, which he figured was inherited from a branch of his mother's genetic tree.

He sat on the edge of his bed and stared at the wall for what seemed an interminable time until his roommate walked through the door carrying a placard that read: STOP THE WAR!

Desmond Sedgwick, a WASP raised in the San Fernando Valley of Southern California, was a scrawny kid with long, stringy hair to his shoulders and a scraggly, reddish beard. But he was a friend and a fellow member of the local antiwar group raising hell on campus in protest of the war. He propped the sign against his study desk. "What's happening, brother?"

"I'm going to have to go home, Sedge."

Sedgwick detected alarm in his voice. "Problem?"

Kevin's gaze was fixed on the protest sign.

"Not your brother or old man, is it? Nothing's happened to them, has it?"

"They're fine. I guess." He walked to his desk and picked up a letter. The envelope had been made from the sides of a box of C-rations held together by strips of adhesive tape. In the corner was the word FREE where a stamp would normally be placed. Soldiers in Vietnam were allowed free mail service to the United States. He chuckled at the thought of the government's generosity and removed the letter, written in pen on toilet paper that he figured accompanied the C-ration unit, and read the words from his brother again.

When finished he contacted the international operator. It was time to get a message through to his father.

An hour later he had finally reached Saigon Headquarters, Military Advisory Command Vietnam. His father wasn't there, so he left a message to contact him. He made certain the secretary understood the message was marked: URGENT!

Then he contacted the American Red Cross in Oakland and spoke with the night receptionist.

When finished sending a message to his brother in Vietnam, he sat on the bed and cried.

# 42

*** 

**G**eneral Sharps was furious when he came out of the MACV briefing. *More American troops to be deployed to South Vietnam?* He couldn't believe the rush to decision-making that was going on at the higher echelons. He believed the first step should be to shut down the Ho Chi Minh Trail and train the Army of the Republic of Vietnam to defend itself properly. Continual buildup would create more pressure on the country and delay that training. Added pressure would undoubtedly come from the deployment of more troops from North Vietnam. It was becoming Korea all over again.

When he arrived at his office there was a message waiting for him.

PLEASE CONTACT DR. JESSIE MALONE AS SOON AS POSSIBLE.
VERY URGENT. CALL ANY TIME NIGHT OR DAY.
LOVE, KEVIN

It took nearly an hour to get through, and the time difference didn't help. Finally, he heard the sleepy voice of Dr. Malone answer from Arizona.

"Jess, this is Samuel Sharps. What's up?"

Malone's voice was fraught with concern. "Samuel, I assume you've heard from Shania?"

"No, I was contacted by Kevin. He said it was urgent that I contact you."

"I'm glad you did. There's something I need to discuss with you."

"Is it about my family?"

"It's about Shania."

Sharps sat down and listened. The physician spoke for nearly fifteen minutes without interruption. When Malone finished, the general returned the telephone to the cradle, went to the liquor cabinet and uncapped a bottle of Jack Daniel's, poured three fingers from it and downed it quickly, then poured another.

He sat for a long while sipping the whiskey. He wanted to get drunk, but he had to stay sober. At least until he made the call he dreaded to make.

Finally, he contacted the MACV communications center and ordered, "Patch me through to the First Brigade commander of the One-O-First Airborne. Colonel James Timothy."

It took some doing, but he finally reached the brigade commander.

"Colonel Timothy, this is General Sharps at MACV. I need a personal favor. . . ."

When he hung up the telephone a few minutes later, he realized that not only was his wife's life in jeopardy in Arizona, but also his son's life was in jeopardy in South Vietnam.

# 43

***

Franklin was stretched out in his makeshift bed in his bunker at the Screaming Eagles base camp near Qui Nhon. Music played softly, and the rain had stopped, releasing the swarms of malaria-carrying mosquitoes that plagued the camp. His muscles still ached from the long recce, scratches had turned into infected pustules on his face, and his neck still burned from leech bites. What bothered him most were his feet. His soles were wrinkled and cracked, toenails soft from constant immersion in mud and water, and each toe throbbed as he dried them. His ankles were swollen, too, and felt numb.

But his gear was STRAC ("Skilled, Tough, Ready, Around the Clock" or "Shit The Russians Are Coming") clean, his LC-1 harness scrubbed and dried out, jungle boots rinsed and ready, and most important his weapons were spotless and oiled.

He had time to think. Mostly he thought about the last mission. Big-time disappointment. Not much to show for the effort, considering Dawes was dead. The enemy body count was not that high but they did shut down a training facility, at least for the time being. He figured if every search-and-destroy mission achieved that level of success, the war would be over somewhere near the turn of the century.

"Specialist Sharps," a voice called from the entrance.

Franklin looked up to see platoon leader Lieutenant James Gardner.

Franklin snapped to attention and saluted. "Above the Rest, sir!"

"Get your gear and turn it in to Sergeant Hughes. Then report to the command post," Gardner said.

"But, sir, I—"

"Just do as you're ordered, Specialist Sharps." Gardner's voice suddenly took on a gentler tone. "There's someone here from Saigon to see you."

"Yes, sir." He knew his father had finally come to visit.

Franklin reported to Hughes, carrying his M-16, .45 automatic pistol, machete, six hand grenades, four white phosphorus (Willie Peter) grenades, and a twelve-gauge sawed-off pump shotgun, along with his medical aid kit.

Franklin asked Hughes, "Is something wrong, Sergeant?"

Hughes's mouth tightened. "Go on to the CP, son. You'll find out what's going on."

He reported to the CP, a bunker made of railroad ties and sandbags, guarded by machine-gun emplacements. The moment he entered he knew something was wrong. Standing beside his company commander, Captain George Shevlin, was an air force officer.

The grim look on First Sergeant Leo B. Smith's face, coupled with Major Leif Svenson's drooped shoulders and sad face, was all Franklin needed to know. "Is it my father?"

Svenson stepped forward. "I'm Major Leif Svenson. I'm your father's aide at MACV. Come on, son. You're going with me to Saigon."

"Is my father dead?"

The major shook his head. "No. It's your mother. She's very ill and she's requested the Red Cross to have you and your father sent home on emergency leave."

Franklin stared at him a moment, anger building. "So he sent you? Why didn't *he* come?"

The place fell quiet as Svenson's eyes narrowed and he leaned into Franklin's face. "How you feel about your father doesn't mean a fiddler's flying fuck to me, soldier. Hell, without your father's rank and privileges you wouldn't even *see* your mother until after it's too late. So, I suggest you tighten down that smart-ass mouth of yours and follow me to the chopper or I'll have you arrested for insubordination!"

Franklin straightened, his eyes locked to the front. "Yes, sir!"

"Move it out, soldier!"

Franklin stepped smartly toward the chopper, his face burning with anger.

# 44

## ★ ★ ★

General Sharps heard his name called over the public-address speaker in the VIP lounge at Ton Son Nhut Air Base, picked up his service hat and briefcase, and threaded his way through the throng of American military personnel in the transient section. He was amazed at how young they looked, mostly kids of eighteen a year ago, now older in experience but still young, though haggard and gaunt in expression with empty eyes that reflected the "tour of horror," as so many referred to a year in the Vietnamese bush.

He was tired but felt a rush of excitement as he stepped from the air-conditioned building into the hot June sun, where the tarmac seemed to boil beneath his feet. In the distance sat a Boeing 707, where beautiful young stewardesses waited at the top of the steps to welcome each passenger aboard.

In the first-class section, he found his seat near the window and opened his briefcase and removed the message sent by Kevin. Odd, he thought, how urgent messages usually bring tragic news from the war zone to home; it seemed out of the natural order of things for it to be in reverse.

He returned Kevin's note to his briefcase as a colonel sat down beside him. His uniform still smelled new. *Fresh from the bush?* Sharps wondered. He noted the ribbons covering the man's blouse were brightly colored, his combat infantryman badge and parachute wings appeared to have been minted that morning.

Soon enlisted personnel began to board, most wearing khaki's, some still in their jungle fatigues, having only had hours to get from the battlefield to the airport. They could change later, Sharps supposed. Didn't want to miss the bird taking them back to the *world!*

They were of all sizes, shapes, and colors, as different as people could get with the exception of one common denominator: They were going home.

Their faces reflected the emotions of the moment, most of them trying to laugh or smile, others lost in thought, moving past him in slow, funereal fashion, their eyes making momentary contact with his, then turning away quickly, or avoiding him altogether. He knew it was his rank. Most of them probably figured he didn't deserve such a comfortable seat in first class. Why not them? They had suffered the most. He could see their contempt.

Then he saw the soldier he had waited for and stiffened as the face clarified with that special look of the lost returning from war. The young soldier moved aimlessly a few feet, stopping, then continuing down the aisle.

When he stopped next to the general's row, Sharps wanted to reach out and touch his hand, but the soldier said nothing, and his straight-ahead stare signaled Franklin's refusal to give his father the slightest notice.

The captain seated beside Franklin sat up quickly as the general leaned over. "You mind exchanging seats with me in first class? I'd like to ride back to the States next to my son."

The captain nodded, then looked at the soldier sitting beside him, who had already fallen asleep. "My pleasure, General." He rose and with briefcase in hand walked forward as Sharps stowed his briefcase, coat, and hat in the overhead luggage compartment, then paused to remove a blanket. He leaned over his seat and spread the blanket over Franklin.

"What the fuck!" Franklin exploded from sleep, throwing his arms out as though fending off an unexpected attack.

For a moment Samuel saw fear etched on his face. "Easy, Son, easy."

Surprise replaced Franklin's look of momentary fear. He studied his father for a moment, then huddled beneath the blanket as though it were a shield.

"Good morning, sir."

Sharps couldn't hide the indignation he felt at so cold a greeting. " 'Good morning, sir.' Is that any way to greet your old man after all this time?" He extended his hand, which Franklin shook with obvious reluctance.

"Pop, how you doing?"

"You're looking good, Franklin. The bush seems to have toughened you up."

Franklin turned and stared through the window. On the tarmac beneath the wing, a military policeman patrolled with a German shepherd. For a moment he thought of the Kit Carson and his dog and wondered if the Kit was home with his family. If he had a family. If he had a new dog.

"Yeah," Franklin said to his father's image reflecting off the window, "the bush toughened me up. Amazing what a little time in Hell can do for a person."

The air was thick enough to cut with a bayonet. Sharps put his hand on his son's arm. "How have you been, Son?"

Silence.

"Talk to me, Franklin. Let's not fly home treating each other as strangers."

"We are strangers, Pop. Have been most of my life."

"You've changed."

Franklin looked at him incredulously. "What did you expect? One of the Hardy Boys? I've been killing people and living in crap. Yeah. I've changed. Or maybe you've changed—forgotten what combat does to men."

The general's face saddened. "I haven't forgotten. Believe me, I haven't forgotten."

That said, he straightened, tired of his son's belligerence. "What I expect is for you to display some respect. If not as a son, then as a soldier."

Franklin raised his left hand and mock-saluted his father. "Yes, sir . . . General Sharps, sir."

In the seat across the aisle, a lanky white marine sergeant major had been observing the younger enlisted man's disrespect to the general. He leaned across the aisle. "Is there a problem, sir?"

Sharps was embarrassed. "No, Sergeant Major, just a family discussion."

Reluctantly, the marine leaned back in his seat, but not before giving Franklin a scathing look.

Silence followed for what seemed an interminable time. Finally Sharps said, "I'm sorry about your mother, Franklin."

Franklin pulled the blanket over his shoulders. Since his father had sat down, he had barely looked him in the eye. Was it anger? Hatred? He wasn't sure. Yet now there was something to discuss. His father had answers he needed. He lit a cigarette. "What's the situation?"

The general pointed to the overhead NO SMOKING sign. "When did you start smoking?"

Franklin butted out the cigarette. "After my first combat patrol."

"You know it's very bad for your health."

"So are combat patrols. Look, Pop, cease fire for a few minutes. What can you tell me about Mom?"

"I called home last night, spoke with Doc Malone, then called Kevin. Later, I called your mother."

"And?"

"She is dying of brain cancer."

Franklin sank back in his seat. "I knew there was something wrong. Especially in her voice on the tapes. She never mentioned anything about her health."

"I'm sorry I couldn't come up to the highlands and bring you here personally. I had to arrange matters for our trip to the States. That's why I sent Major Svenson."

"Yes, sir," Franklin said. "But there's something I need you to explain."

"What is that?"

"Why are you here? Why are you going back after all these years? You've only been back once in the past five years. When Adrian was buried."

Sharps's tough veneer seemed suddenly fragile. "She's still my wife, the mother of my children." He sighed "She's dying. I have the right to be there. To see her one last time. To be with you and Kevin."

"To ask her forgiveness? Or to soothe your conscience? After what you did to her? Bullshit! She won't forgive you. Kevin won't forgive you. And I sure as hell won't."

"I regret what happened, Franklin. It was a terrible, shameful mistake. Men make mistakes. You'll learn that as you get older."

He could hear his father's words, but the voice sounded different. A voice laced with pain.

"She chose to go back to Arizona and take you and Kevin with her. She said she wanted a home, not a military base to live on. I had my career. Whether you believe this or not, your mother understood. She recognized I had my duty."

"Duty?"

Sharps pointed to the two rows of ribbons on his son's army blouse. "Yes, duty. I'd say you know something about it."

"I'm twenty years old. I've been in combat and seen

more shit that I ever imagined possible. And there's more
to come when I come back. That's not duty. That's a
fucking waste of youth."

At that moment the stewardess's voice came over the
intercom as the Boeing began taxiing to the runway.
"Welcome aboard Flight Nine-Nine-Nine. Please fasten
your seat belts and prepare for immediate departure from
the Republic of South Vietnam to the United States of
America. You're going home, guys!"

At that moment, the inside of the Boeing shook as the
applause and shouts erupted.


Several hours later, Franklin looked through the window
and saw that it would grow light soon, as the Boeing flew
toward the sun. It was dark in the cabin, but not quiet.
The voices of men happy to be alive spoke in low laughter; music purred softly from a hundred transistor radios.
They had survived. What waited was not completely certain, but it was better than the uncertainty they had left
behind.

He even felt a certain admiration for his father, whom
he had worshiped until the terrible day his betrayal to his
family became known. How could he do that? How could
he rip the hearts out of his wife and children?

He rested his head on his pillow and stared through the
window at the stars, at the bright moon, then closed his
eyes and fell to sleep.

# 45

* * *

Franklin found himself in the water, the night as black as tar, except for the occasional flare lighting the sky, drifting slowly to the rice paddy. He was alone, separated from the others, trying not to make any noise. He carried a baby in each arm; they slept, though their bodies trembled from the coldness of the water. He had forgotten what cold water felt like. How it tingled the skin, sank into the bone, and sent a rippling charge of exhilaration through his body.

He was lost but could hear voices. The words were in English, so he knew he was heading in the right direction.

A thick mist had formed on the water's surface; rich and heavy, unlike any fog he had ever seen. He tried to be quiet, but that was not possible. The weight of the two babies was becoming a burden and he began to stumble forward, splashing, nearly falling, as the muddy bottom pulled at his feet.

One of the babies began crying, and there was gunfire

coming at him, tracers leaving their red signatures only inches from his body.

He turned, as though to shield the children, but meat and bone could not prevent a bullet from harming them. Another flare and one of the babies had been struck. The sky became bright and he could see the child's mouth open, as though yawning.

The baby . . . a bamboo rat! Teeth like daggers, mouth seeping blood. The monster had bitten him in the chest. His left nipple was gone. It sank its teeth into his neck, its feet thrashing, clawing at the other baby.

*Argonne!* The baby in his other arm, her face shredded by the razor claws of a beast that was growing by the second, becoming stronger with each slash and tear at his and Argonne's flesh.

He tried to rid himself of the creature, to fling it away, but now it was too big. With a violent swing of one of its front legs, it ripped open the belly of . . . the baby . . . Argonne. . . .


Sharps jerked awake as a stewardess leaned across to Franklin, who was thrashing and screaming, still locked in the throes of the nightmare. He reached up and turned on the overhead light. "Franklin, wake up, Son. Wake up. You're safe."

Franklin began to come around, mumbling like an incoherent child lost in a dark place. Gradually, his voice trailed off and he fell asleep again.

General Sharps sat back in his seat and whispered to the stewardess, "It's over."

# 46

*   *   *

The 707 landed at Travis Air Force Base, California, where the servicemen were processed through Customs and transported to local bus and train stations and to the airport in San Francisco. It was at the airport that Franklin received his first taste of the welcome antiwar demonstrators had for servicemen returning from the war.

Standing behind police barricades, demonstrators carried antiwar placards, shouted obscenities, and jeered at the men who only a few days before had been risking their lives for flag and country in Vietnam.

Franklin carried his duffel bag on his shoulder, trying to ignore the throng, but felt his blood boiling as he entered the terminal.

A fat young woman in a garish muumuu broke past a policeman and swung a placard, hitting Franklin in the back. "Welcome home, hero. How many kids did you kill?" she shouted.

Franklin's arm shot out, as with a life of its own, and his hand smacked her loudly on her face. The placard fell from her hand, and she seemed to dance lightly above the ground, her arms flailing to keep her balance.

"You need a bath, you filthy bitch," Franklin said.

The crowd had grown quiet. A voice shouted, "The motherfucker's crazy!"

Franklin shoved his face close to the woman's. "What's the matter, you ugly bitch? Fly too close to the flame?"

She stared at him, paralyzed with fear. One side of her face bore a scarlet mark. More shouts followed from the crowd, who were stirring from their shock. Franklin ignored them but from the corner of his eye saw a policeman advancing toward him. The woman stumbled backward, then ran drunkenly toward the crowd of demonstrators as the general dragged Franklin toward the entrance, ignoring the shouts of the demonstrators. Just as they reached the open door, Franklin felt something hit his back. He smelled the putrid odor, looked at the sidewalk, and saw the sack of excrement lying at his feet.

They walked into the terminal and Franklin went directly to the men's room, where he stripped off his uniform, his Corcoran jump boots and black beret, and threw the entire ensemble into the garbage can. After changing into his only set of civilian clothes—Western shirt, jeans, and cowboy boots—he tossed the duffel in the trash barrel and walked back into the terminal concourse, where he found his father sitting at a table in the bar.

The general was trembling. "You OK, Son?"

Franklin shrugged. "Yeah. The flower bitch caught me off guard. I should have knocked her fucking head off."

"You can't let those people get to you so easy," the general said. "Hell, boy . . . they're everywhere. What are you going to do? Attack the whole peace movement? You've got to learn to ignore them."

Franklin's fist crashed onto the table. "Christ! Seventy-two hours ago I was in the bush, where all I had to worry about was staying alive. Since then I've been told my mother was dying, reunited with a father I haven't seen in years, flown halfway around the world, and spit on by some scuzzy flower bitch who smelled like my old jungle boots. Now, you say I should lighten up?"

The waitress appeared, pad in hand. "What would you gentlemen like to drink?" She studied Franklin warily.

General Sharps ordered a Rob Roy.

She looked at Franklin.

"I'll take Johnnie Walker Red—a double with water back," he said.

"May I see some identification, please?" she said.

"Identification? You must be kidding me."

"Miss?" Sharps said. "He's just returned from Vietnam."

She shook her head. "The law requires that any patron who purchases alcoholic beverages in the state of California must be twenty-one years of age. That's the law. Please show me your identification if you wish to be served alcohol."

Franklin was seething. He looked at his father. "Old enough to die for my country, but not old enough to buy a Johnnie Red. Welcome back to the real world."

He walked out of the bar and did not look back to witness his father giving the woman a withering lecture on giving a soldier a break.

# 47

✫ ✫ ✫

The pair arrived in Phoenix late that night, their conversation still trapped in the void created by the many wedges that had driven them apart over the years. Franklin realized that had it not been for their common mission—his mother—they would have journeyed together as strangers. This didn't bother him since he was not there to be a benevolent, grateful son. He wanted nothing to do with his father, saw him as just another general, a lifer, not a father who had been there for his family. He had been there mostly in memory, rarely in actuality, arriving for Christmas or an occasional birthday. Now, they were both soldiers, and he was reminded of a time when he was in a park and stood at the feet of a statue of a great general mounted on a charging horse. That's how he viewed his father: the horseback general, sabre thrust forward, dashing toward glory. He saw himself and the other "grunts" as the horse; metaphorically considering himself one of the "stone ponies," the soldiers who took the generals to glory on their backs.

That, as much as anything, angered him. Granted, his father had served his country bravely. But what about his family? On that point, he had never shown up for roll call.

Dr. Jessie Malone was waiting for them at the arrival gate, wearing a somber face, looking disheveled and tired from the drive from Willcox; he also seemed like the Grim Reaper, bearing the burden of news that no one wanted to hear but must be shared.

"Franklin, how are you?" He offered his hand to the general, then wiped his handkerchief at his sweating brow. Overweight and nearly bald, he had known the Sharps family for as long as he could remember. His father had treated the family before he was born.

"How long has it been?" General Sharps said. He held the handshake as if calculating the time.

"Adrian's funeral," Franklin said.

"Of course . . . Adrian's funeral. Seems like ages," Malone said. "We seem to be drawn together by tragedy."

"Too often the case, Jessie. Too often."

Franklin, impatient for the amenities to end, asked, "Dr. Malone, how is my mother?"

The physician motioned toward the BAGGAGE sign. "Let's get your luggage. I'll explain everything on the way to Sabre Ranch."

The drive began with Dr. Malone shifting constantly in the driver's seat of his station wagon. The general sat silently beside him while Franklin sat in the back, aching for answers. Once out of Phoenix, Sharps rolled down the window and said, "My God, smell that sweet desert air."

"Hell, Samuel," Malone said, "that's Fillmont's stockyard. You have been gone for a long while."

The general pointed toward the stockyard, its outline marked by fluorescent lights burning in the rich desert darkness. "My father once did business with the Fillmonts during the Second World War, along with Joaquin Samorran, that Mexican bandit from Hermosillo. What a pair they made. My grandmother was convinced Pop had climbed in bed with the devil."

"Yes, I remember his reputation," Malone added, "Samorran and your father made a lot of money selling beef to the government during that war."

The use of the term "that war" struck Franklin as curious. As though there had been so many, each no longer had its own identity; rather, they were mustered together like apples in a barrel.

"What about my mother, Dr. Malone?"

He saw Malone's eyes in the rearview mirror. It was obvious it was a subject he preferred to ignore. "She has a geoplastoma, Franklin."

"What is that?"

"It's a form of cancer; a brain tumor, to be precise."

"Is it operable?" Samuel asked.

Malone shook his head and again looked at Franklin through the rearview mirror, then to the general. "No. She and I both agreed it would be best for her to spend the rest of her days as normally as possible." He paused and wiped his handkerchief at his forehead. The heat spilling in from the desert was almost unbearable. "She's going to die. That's why I requested the Red Cross bring you both home."

Samuel looked toward the darkened desert flashing by the station wagon. "How long . . ." His voice trailed off.

"No way to know for certain," Malone said. "Two days . . . two weeks . . . two months. Definitely no longer than two months. I have prescribed pain medication, but that's only to keep her comfortable. She's lucid but there are times when she simply cannot get out of bed."

"Will it be quick?" Franklin asked.

"Quick, when it finally comes. She has all her faculties, but she'll sometimes appear confused. She won't wither, but . . ." He appeared to be searching for the right words.

"But what?" Franklin said.

Malone glanced to Franklin through the mirror, and spoke to both of them. "She must not be excited. I can't emphasize this point strongly enough. I know you have a tenuous relationship with your sons. That has to be put aside. If she gets psychologically distressed it could kill her like a bullet." The discomfort in the station wagon was palpable. "I know you two have had a tough time in Vietnam, especially you, Franklin. I was opposed to her requesting that both of you return at the same time. I told her it might be disastrous. But she was insistent. She said she had to have her family together . . . one more time. She said there was something important she had to accomplish. That you both had to be there. You know Shania. She's a fighter . . . and a charmer. He looked over pointedly at the general. "I'll hold you personally responsible at the first sign of conflict between you and your sons."

"She'll not be distressed. I give you my word." Sharps turned to Franklin and offered his hand. "Despite what you might think, my word is good."

Franklin ignored the hand. "Yes, sir," he said.

The rest of the trip was spent in silence.

# 48

★ ★ ★

It was nearly midnight when the station wagon eased through the narrow gate at the family ranch outside Bonita. On the arch above the metal cattle guard at the entrance, three cavalry sabres—joined at the fulcrum—hung beneath a sign that read: SABRE RANCH.

Franklin felt a sudden rush of relief as he stared at the sabres, gleaming in the brilliant moonlight as though branded against the stars. "Kevin put a nice spit shine on the sabres."

General Sharps nodded approvingly. "They never looked better."

The wagon eased through the gate and made the short drive to the house. Flooded in the headlights, Kevin stood waiting for them.

Franklin bolted out the door and bounded onto the porch into the waiting embrace of his brother.

"God, it's good to see you, S-Three." That was one of the nicknames the general had given his sons. "S" for Sharps and a number designating order of birth.

"Welcome home, Franklin." He stood at arm's length and studied his brother. "Man, you look great."

"See what a healthy diet and plenty of exercise will do for you! Makes for a—"

Kevin joined in the chorus. "Lean . . . mean . . . fighting machine!"

At that moment the general stepped onto the porch. Kevin eyed him warily. "Hello, Pop. Welcome back to Sabre Ranch."

Sharps was nearly speechless as Kevin suddenly embraced him. Taking a moment to recover, he returned the vigorous embrace. "Hello, S-Three. How's my young man?"

"Just fine, Pop." Kevin's eyes drifted to Franklin, motioning him to join the embrace. Doc Malone stood on the front step, his head motioning Franklin toward the pair. Franklin shook his head and turned toward the door and saw an image in the bedroom window.

Shania Sharps stood there, wearing her housecoat, watching the reunion. Despite the darkness, Franklin could see the sadness in his mother's eyes. As he crossed the threshold into the house, he heard Doc Malone call aloud, "Good night, fellows. Tell Shania I'll stop by tomorrow. And by the way, welcome home."

Franklin stepped inside and paused momentarily in front of the fireplace. Above the mantel, on wooden pegs embedded in the wall, hung the Sharps rifle carried by his great-grandfather.

He knocked lightly at the half-opened door and heard his mother say, "Come in, Son."

Franklin saw his mother reclined on what appeared to be a hospital bed. He sat down beside her. "Hi, Mom. How's my favorite lady?"

There was a quiver of apology in her voice. "I'm sorry your homecoming has to be so unhappy. It's not what I had planned." She glanced at the door, where the general now stood, looking uncomfortable.

"Don't apologize, Mom. We're all here. Together." His eyes drifted to his father.

She touched his cheek lightly, looking toward the door. "How are you, Samuel?"

General Sharps came to the other side of the bed and kissed her lightly on the mouth. "Franklin and I flew together from Saigon." He sat on the edge of the bed and took her hand. "It was a long journey, but we survived."

"Surviving is all that matters." She glanced at Franklin. "Frankie, may I speak with your father . . . alone? We can sit in the living room a little later."

"No problem. I'll check on S-Three." He leaned over and kissed her on the forehead, then rose and left the room.

When they were alone, Shania said to Samuel, "You look splendid. I never saw a more handsome man in uniform than you. Except for our sons."

He kissed her hand. "You look beautiful."

"You always know the right words, but I never knew you could lie so gallantly."

The general caressed her hands. "I could never lie to you—" He stopped; as a bolt of shame threaded through his body.

Shania smiled. "Oh, Samuel, how could two people have been so wrong? To have wasted so much life?"

"Wrong? You? You're the only right person I've ever known. I was the one who was wrong. Now I have to pay."

She shook her head. "No more. You've already paid dearly. We all have. You. Me. Franklin. Kevin . . . Adrian." She sat up, grimacing in pain.

"Shania, my dear, you mustn't upset yourself. Doc Malone said—"

She sounded strong and reassuring, trying to be resolute, as she always had in crisis. "Please, Samuel. Let's not avoid the truth. I'm dying. Oddly enough, I find consolation—even contentment—in that reality."

He looked at her incredulously. "How?"

"It brought you and Franklin home. I realize you'll both have to go back to Vietnam, but at least we'll have this time together." She sat upright and cupped his face in her hands. "There's a lot that must be accomplished in this short span of time. There's no time to be wasted. This must be a time for healing."

Samuel felt small in the presence of this remarkable woman. "You're incredible; your strength makes me feel embarrassed and ashamed. But mostly, you make me feel proud. I'm the one who committed the wrong to this family, yet it's you . . ."

"No, Samuel. As your mother always said, 'Life treats us all the same. We're all born . . . and then we die. Somewhere in between we're bound to have our hearts broken.' " She took a deep breath. "Now, let's have no more talk about the past. Let yesterday stay where it is. You had your career and I needed a home, where the boys could have stability."

She thought for a moment. "I tire easily, Samuel, but there is one thing I would like to do while we're all together."

"Whatever you want," he said.

"A trip."

"A trip?"

"Yes, all of us together."

"To where?"

"To Quimas. We can rent a villa for a few days."

"Mexico?" He nearly shouted the word and thought she had taken leave of her senses.

"Yes, to Quimas, a place filled with wonderful family memories. We can spend some time there, fish, swim, watch fireworks. Remember, we used to spend Fourth of July in Quimas. We'll celebrate early. You can rent an airplane and fly us there."

He could only smile and nod at her in sheer amazement. "If it's Mexico you want . . . it's Mexico you'll have."

He embraced her gently and could only wonder why

he had been so foolish all those years to cause him precious time lost.

In the living room, Franklin was standing in front of the fireplace, looking at a framed photograph above the mantel of his late brother in his West Point uniform. A black ribbon was attached diagonally across the frame's right-hand corner.

Kevin stepped to his side. "I still can't believe he's dead."

"They've paid for it, Kevin. I made them pay for killing him," Franklin said.

Kevin put his arms around his brother. "What price have you had to pay, brother?"

"It doesn't matter. They paid for the Sharps they killed."

The sound of their mother's voice drew their attention away from the photograph. "Come on, boys. Let's go sit on the porch. Kevin, bring your guitar."

Assisted by Samuel, Shania went onto the porch, followed by their sons. She sat in a swing, where Samuel draped an afghan around her shoulders. He sat beside her while Franklin sat on the other side and Kevin knelt on the steps and began playing "Where Have All the Flowers Gone?"

Samuel looked up at the stars and put his arms around Shania, saying, "My God! What a night." He looked at Franklin. "But a little chillier than what we're used to, isn't it, Son?"

Franklin nodded. "Yes, sir. It feels good." His eyes searched the rich darkness beyond the spray of the porch light.

Shania saw him and understood. She whispered, "There's nothing out there but Sabre Ranch. You're safe at home, Franklin."

When Kevin began singing "Where Have All The Flowers Gone?" Franklin chided, "You still can't sing worth a hoot, little brother."

Shania said, "Beautiful words sung by a beautiful son."

When Samuel rose and stepped off the porch to the edge of the darkness and stared up at the stars, Shania took advantage of the moment and whispered to Franklin, "Kevin's been drafted."

Samuel turned back and saw the look of surprise on Franklin's face. "What are you two plotting?"

Shania said, "I was telling him we're going to Quimas. We'll have a wonderful time. We'll celebrate a real family gathering. Darlene is coming and bringing the baby."

At that, Samuel realized for the first time since arriving that his daughter-in-law and granddaughter weren't at the ranch. "Where are they?"

"In Willcox, at her mother's. They'll be here in the morning."

"You're right, it will be wonderful."

# 49

## ★ ★ ★

At Sabre Ranch sunrise was Franklin's favorite part of the day. Sipping coffee on the front porch, he was moody, even though he was home, because his instincts made him feel like he was still in the bush, keeping him alert and alive. He looked up when he heard the door open and saw Kevin wearing his scrunched-down cowboy hat and boots.

"Want to go for a cavalry charge?"

Franklin jumped to his feet and hurried into the house, returning minutes later wearing his hat and boots. "Let's do it, little brother."

They went to the stable, where three horses were stalled, and saddled two of them. Kevin went to a tack box and pulled out two old cavalry sabres. Unlike the one that usually hung over the fireplace, the blades were scoured, blunt, and chipped along what had once been a sharp edge. These were practice sabres their father had found in an old gas station one summer and used to teach the boys how to ride and fight on horseback.

After attaching the sabres to their saddles they rode a few hundred yards west of the ranch to a stand of cottonwood trees where the family picnicked. A soft breeze blew, and the heat wasn't yet boiling as they spurred their horses and charged through the brush, dodging and ducking branches until they reached an opening where a single tree stood like a promontory.

The "sabre tree," it was called, and for good reason, since it bore more sabre cuts and gouges than could be counted. Franklin spurred his horse and charged, stood in the stirrups, and reached for the blade. He drew it smoothly, extended it over the horse's head, and as he neared the tree brought back his arm and slashed with all his strength. He felt the numbing thud rush up his arm as the blade cut into what was left of the scarred bark. He whirled for another charge.

At the moment he spurred the horse he saw Kevin watching him, both charging at each other like mounted cavalry from an ancient day. Both leaned, extended, then slashed, only the tree separating—and protecting each of them from the other's blade. Splinters of wood flew and both riders wheeled their horses and made another charge.

The air rang with each bite the blades made into the tree, followed by the pounding of hooves and the kicking of dirt with each new attack.

Again and again they charged until the horses were slimy with a white sheen of sweat. Both young men breathed heavily as they brought their horses to a halt, dismounted, and tied off the reins to the tree.

They sat facing each other on the ground, now soft and churned from their horses' hooves, and each stared past the other. Some time passed before Franklin finally spoke. "Mom told me you've been drafted."

Kevin continued to evade eye contact. "I've got to report in two weeks."

"And?"

He shrugged. "And what?"

"Come on, brother. Play it straight with me. What in

the hell are you going to do? Mom's dying . . . you've been drafted . . . we're going to Mexico. What I don't understand is why not Canada?"

"Canada is where I'll probably eventually go. I have friends in Mexico in the peace movement. They'll get me north in due time."

"Due time? Jesus. Mexico to Canada? You're going to be more traveled than me by the time you get to wherever you're going. Does Pop know you've been drafted?"

"Hell, no. Mom wanted to tell him, but I said no. It's my decision. My duty. I'll tell him once we get down there . . . where he can't turn me over to the law."

Franklin nearly laughed. "Duty? You don't know the meaning of the word if you're skying out for Mexico."

"I haven't forgotten. Duty doesn't mean doing something even if you believe it's wrong. Duty means honoring what you believe is right."

Franklin stabbed at the dirt with his sabre. "What the fuck do you know about what's right? You're talking about running away—to Mexico—like the rest of the draft dodgers."

"Don't call me a draft dodger." His fists were balled and he looked ready for a fight. "What about the brothers in Nam? Aren't they part of the program? The white man's program that drafts black kids and uses them as tools of political policy when they can't even vote in some states without bullshit Jim Crow laws stopping them! Shit, man, don't you know about Watts?"

"I know about Watts. A lot of the brothers in my brigade were pissed. Some come from Watts and a helluva lot of them believe that's just the beginning. But, goddammit, man, they didn't run away."

"How do they feel about fighting for a government that still treats them like second-class citizens?"

"Ask yourself that. You were in college. You had a deferment. What happened?"

"Conscience. I couldn't sit in class while our people

were being slaughtered for foreign policy. I joined the movement and my grades suffered."

Franklin listened in disbelief. "You are one self-righteous son of a bitch. And a fool to match. You can avoid all this shit and not become an outcast."

"Oh, yeah. How?"

"You can get Pop to help. He's a general. You can join the fucking Coast Guard. All they do is ride around in boats here in the states and chase pussy."

Kevin didn't find this humorous. "You don't understand. I don't want any part of a military establishment that oppresses our people."

"I'm not the enemy, brother. I want to help you with this problem."

"You don't sound all that helpful. You sound pissed."

Franklin slashed at the ground with the sword. "I am pissed. Pissed that you're running out while other guys—most of them white guys—are dying in that shit. Maybe that's why I'm willing to help. I've been there. I know about duty. Duty doesn't mean standing by with your dick in your hand while your kid brother gets tossed into a meat grinder."

Franklin whistled. "The old man's going to have a case of the ass like we've never seen. He'll go out of his fucking mind. And he's going to fly you there!"

Kevin laughed until tears began to roll.

When they both calmed down, Kevin asked, "What's the war really like?"

His brother looked to the clear sky and with his arms outstretched said, "We were bad to the bone, walked the bush like fucking gods, decided who lived and who died. Man, it was some kind of righteous trip."

His eyes had taken on a shining that suddenly made Kevin uncomfortable. "They say you go crazy after you kill another human being."

"Human being?" Franklin grinned. "They weren't human beings. They were targets. And you don't go crazy afterward, little brother, you go crazy just before you make the kill, just the split second before you come to grips with the fact that it's either that motherfucker or you." He looked around at the pristine beauty and sucked in a lungful of air. "Man, what a place."

Kevin did the same. "Mom used to say this is where God stopped to rest after creating the world. She said He saved the best for last."

Franklin nodded. "He did a helluva good job."

"I'm going to miss her, Franklin. Christ, why her? Why not me? Or you? Or the old man?"

"I don't know. Guess it's her time. I used to wonder the same about guys getting zapped in Nam. Good guys. I always wondered why them and not me. She's a helluva lady. I used to hear her every night in the war. Even felt her right there with me. Looking over my shoulder like some Guardian Angel."

Kevin turned away to wipe at tears. "I know what you mean. The way I still think of Adrian. Always there. Just a step beyond. Like they're waiting, or walking ahead, keeping an eye open for me."

"Like they're covering the point on a patrol. Covering your ass. Not like the old man. Hell, he's never around when you need him."

"He's here now." He patted the horse's neck. "You didn't see him in Nam?"

"Didn't want to. Fuck him."

Kevin sighed. "That's what he'll be saying about me soon."

"Thought about what you'll do when we get to Mexico?"

"I have the phone number of a guy in Cabo San Lucas," Kevin said. "He can get me on a fishing boat to Vancouver. Once there, there's other people who'll help. I'll find a job, get a place to live. I would be there now if it hadn't been for Mom's illness. I was supposed to leave the next day and just drive north. Can't now. Have to stay with Mom to the end."

"Maybe he won't find out."

"Bull. He'll find out. You know Pop. He'll find out. Besides, like I said, I'll tell him. I owe him that much."

"Shit, we don't owe him anything. And don't forget, there's the Coast Guard, the navy, even the air force. Hell, none of those guys actually go to Nam."

"It's not Vietnam. It's the military. I'm no coward. I'll die for my country, but not for this fucking war in Vietnam."

The brothers unsaddled their horses and put away the saddles, sabres, and tack and started for the house. The sun was blistering, the air dry enough to suck water from the body. Franklin wanted a cool drink and knew it was time to pay his respects.

He started around the edge of the house, paused to look back, and saw Kevin step onto the porch. "Aren't you coming with me, little brother?"

Kevin's face was etched with sadness. "No, big brother, you go ahead. All things considered, I don't feel I have a right any longer."

Franklin understood and continued to the back, pausing momentarily when he saw the wrought-iron archway of the family cemetery.

The graves were freshly tended as always, flowers trimming each plot, a gray marker at the head of each, silent sentinels marking the family's passage through time.

He whispered to himself, "The sergeant major, Selona, Grandma Hannah, and all the rest. Heroes all."

He walked directly to a particular marker, whiter than the others.

*Lieutenant Adrian David Sharps*
*Born May 2, 1943*
*Died July 2, 1964, Republic of Vietnam*
*Graduate of United States Military Academy—*
*Class of 1964*

Over a year since he was killed, thought Franklin, as he stood at attention and saluted. "Good morning, sir. Specialist Franklin Sharps, reporting, as promised."

He slowly lowered his hand, then knelt beside the stone, and noting a weed, plucked it from the ground and whispered, "Guess Mom missed this one, big brother."

Tears filled his eyes as he read the headstone over and over. "It's been a long time, big brother. A long time. He wiped at his eyes and continued, saying, "But I made it back. I still have my legs. My hands. All my parts. I took a few hits but nothing serious. I guess you were there looking after me."

He took a deep breath and felt something break away inside like a tree shedding its bark. "I hurt bad, Adrian. Feel empty, alone. I feel like my guts have been ripped out. Sometimes I wish I had come home like you."

He ran his fingers through the soft grass, laid back, and searched the sky as though searching for strength. "I've come home to nothing. Everybody's leaving me! I don't want to be alone. I've been alone for so long. You know what I mean—in the bush. I don't know if I can stay here alone. There'll be no one . . . but you."

He felt his stomach tighten and he thought he would vomit. He felt so weak; so helpless. "Kevin . . . he . . . Oh, Adrian, if you could only hear me . . . tell me what to do."

Franklin fell slowly onto the grave; his lips touched the grass, and though he was joined to the ground he felt a thousand feet above the earth.

He lay there for a long time, the memories of childhood—when it was good, clean, and simple—rippling through his mind. After a time he felt a hand touch his shoulder.

"Don't do this to yourself," Kevin said. He knelt by his brother and they embraced, their bodies trembling, tears mixing at their cheeks.

They did not see their father and mother standing at the corner of the house, both holding each other. Tears streamed down Shania's face; Samuel wore a mask of pain as he stood helpless.

Shania turned and walked to the front of the house; moments later, shoulders stooped and wiping at his tears, Samuel turned and followed his wife.

# 50

＊ ＊ ＊

That afternoon, Samuel found Shania sitting on the living room sofa, staring through the window at Franklin and Kevin, who were repairing shingles on the roof of the stable. He sat down and took her hand and held her for a moment. "Does Fred Turner still have his flight service at the airport?"

She knew what he was up to. "Of course. The man practically lives there since Alice passed away and his son went into the army."

"Excellent. If we're going to Mexico, we're going to need an aircraft. I'll make the arrangements. We can leave tomorrow. Will Darlene and Argonne be going with us?"

"Of course. They'll be here later this afternoon."

"Then I better get busy. Is there anything you need while I'm in town?"

She handed him a list of things. He read it and smiled at her. "You've got everything all planned out, haven't you?"

She flashed her mystery smile. "The keys are in the truck."

At the garage he opened the door and froze. Sunlight filled the garage, where a sedan and truck sat beside another vehicle covered with a tarpaulin. He walked to the vehicle and lifted the tarp, ignoring the dust that had collected since the vehicle was last driven.

"Oh, my Lord." He looked at a green MG sports car and ran his finger along the polished hood. It was just as Adrian had left it before going to Southeast Asia. He sighed, re-covered the MG, and got into the pickup and drove away.

Samuel drove down the long road he once drove in his new DeSoto back in 1941 when he made his journey to Tuskegee. He thought of sleeping on the prairie between Bonita and Fort Davis, Texas, where he visited the graves of his ancestors and where he met another descendant of a Buffalo Soldier who had served with his grandfather Sharps in the 10th Cavalry.

When he turned onto the main road that led to Bonita, his thoughts were so full of that long-ago journey he didn't notice another pickup parked alongside the road. Nor did he notice the driver—a white man in his early twenties, with long, straggly hair and hippie beads—who eased his pickup onto the road and drove in the direction of Bonita.

The main street of Bonita always brought back fond but embarrassing memories for Samuel. It was on that street in 1941 that he saw a column of tanks roll past on the way to an area north of town where the unit bivouacked and began military maneuvers. He chuckled at the thought, recalling how he supplied fresh game for the unit with his Sharps rifle and wound up in a race with a tank on the Fourth of July. The whole town laughed as he rode up on the critter his father selected for him to ride against the Sherman tank—a mule!

He made quite a piece of money that day, crossing the finish line a few yards ahead of the armored challenger.

His first stop was the small airport where he took his first airplane ride in a Stearman, flown by a black aviator named Sparks Hamilton, a veteran of the 92nd Division and of the Great War in France. It was from Hamilton that he learned of the Civilian Pilot Training Program at Tuskegee Institute, in Alabama, where young Negroes were training as pilots in hopes of becoming aviators in the Army Air Corps.

Samuel parked in front of the hangar and walked inside, where he saw an aircraft sitting half-assembled; beneath the fuselage, a pair of legs jutted.

"Are you sleeping or working, Fred?" Samuel called out.

Fred Turner crawled from beneath the aircraft wearing oil-covered overalls. The moment he saw Samuel he started wiping his fingers with a grimy rag. He was in his sixties, tall, with thinning gray hair, deep blue eyes, and a ready smile. He had been a fighter pilot in World War II and nearly lost his leg when hit by a Japanese fighter in the Pacific.

"I'll be damned if it ain't Samuel. How the hell are you, General?"

They shook hands warmly, not just as friends but comrades of a great war.

"I'm fine, Fred. And you're looking fit."

Turner grinned. "The secret is hard whiskey . . . and soft women." They made small talk for a few minutes before Turner got down to cases. "Shania called the other day and said you'd probably be stopping by to talk about renting an aircraft. Christ, Samuel. I'm sorry to hear she's feeling so, so poorly."

"She wants to spend a few days in Mexico. What have you got that'll haul a family of six to Quimas and back?"

Turner, still wiping his hands, said, "Come with me."

They headed toward a lone hangar, the type used to store a single plane.

"This baby belongs to Taylor Carpenter."

Samuel knew the man; they had attended high school together. "Well, well, banker Carpenter."

"He has me rent it out when he's not using it, which is generally most of the time. He doesn't fly much and is a lousy pilot, anyway. It's a repossession he decided to hang on to."

Turner unlocked the door and slid it open. Samuel saw the aircraft and let out an admiring whistle. "What a beautiful sight."

A Cessna 410 Golden Eagle sat within the shadows of the hangar, gleaming where the sunlight danced off its brightly colored fuselage and polished metal.

"Shania called and said you might need a bird with some room."

"She's thought of everything."

"She usually does."

"Do I need to take a check ride?"

Turner frowned. "I doubt that'll be necessary. You still remember how to fly?"

"I think so. Ain't it like riding a bike?" He let that sink in. "By the way, how's Michael?"

A proud smile filled Turner's face. "He's still flying gunships with the First Air Cav."

Michael Turner was a year older than Franklin. The two had played sports together in high school and joined the army on graduation. A rated pilot, he was accepted into the army aviation program while only nineteen.

"He's a fine young man, Fred. I saw him a few weeks ago. He stopped in at my office in Saigon."

"I know. He wrote all about it. Said his squadron commander was scared to say diddly to him for a week, what with him knowing a general and all." His eyes brightened. "I can't wait until he gets out, Samuel. It'll be just like we always planned . . . the Turner Flying Service. God, he's all I've got, and that's more than enough to make my life complete."

Samuel checked his watch. "Better be going. Lots to

do. We'll be here at zero-seven-hundred tomorrow morning."

"She'll be waiting."

Turner went back to the hangar and was surprised to see a young man standing by the airplane he had been repairing. He took one look at the long hair and beads and decided he didn't like the looks of the fellow. "Can I help you?"

The hippie turned and pushed back a long, dark wisp of hair. "Wasn't that General Samuel Sharps?"

Turner picked up an oily rag and looked warily at the man. "That was him. Why?"

"I'm just passing through and thought I'd stop and see his son, Kevin."

"You know Kevin?"

"Yes, sir. We both go to college at Berkeley." He stuck out his hand. "My name is Desmond Sedgwick."

Turner shook hands. "You better call quick. They're all leaving in the morning."

"Oh? Where they going?"

"Mexico. Quimas. Having a family reunion."

"Well, thanks. I guess I'd better get in touch with him soon. Like I said, I'm just passing through."

Turner watched the young man walk away. He had been polite and well mannered, and Turner at least liked that in the young man.


At the ranch, Doc Malone was in Shania's darkened bedroom, where the only light glinted from a penlight he was using to check her eyes.

"Well?" Shania asked, after he opened the curtains. She was seated in a chair near the bed.

"No change for the present," Malone said. "What about the headaches? More frequent? More intense?"

"No worse than usual," she said.

"What about this fool notion of a trip?" he said pointedly.

"What about it? We're going to Mexico."

Malone handed her a bottle of Demerol pain pills. "Have you given any thought to the possibility of a serious attack down there? The consequences? You'll be in an isolated part of Mexico. Medical attention will be limited at best, maybe nonexistent."

Shania smiled in appreciation of his concern. "Would it matter if I was in the parking lot of the UCLA Medical Center?"

She had him there. "No. But there's always the chance—"

"The chance I might die? Jessie, I am going to die. I have this final chance to be with my children and my husband."

He said cautiously, "What about Samuel and the boys? Any problems between them?"

"No, they're perfect gentlemen. Very civil." She took in a deep breath. "That's what worries me. They're keeping their emotions all shoved deep inside. It's like waiting for an explosion."

Malone closed up his medical bag and sat on the edge of the bed. "If you need anything you know how to reach me." He patted her hand and left.

When she heard Malone drive away, she went to the desk in the study and began writing. She wrote three letters and sealed each in a separate envelope and placed them in her jewelry box.

In her heart and mind she knew her life had finally reached the threshold of the end and she felt helpless— but not because she was dying. That, she believed, was God's will. What tore at her the most was the heart-tearing reality that when she was gone, her beloved family would disintegrate.

She allowed herself a luxury thus far denied: She lay on her bed, head on her pillow, and had a good long cry.

• • •

Samuel was coming out of a store in Bonita when he stopped, recognizing an old friend across the street. "Carson!" he shouted as he hurried across the street to greet two high school classmates. "How are you, old friend?"

Carson Johnson was the same age as Samuel, as was his wife, who stepped close to her husband and glowered at the general. She looked hardened and bitter, as though time had eroded her. Johnson didn't look much better, his face reddened by what appeared to be what Shania called "whiskey blossoms."

"Hello, General Sharps," Johnson said. His voice had a hardened edge impossible to miss.

Samuel stiffened; he nodded at Johnson's wife. "Hello, Carson, Carol."

She said nothing but grabbed her husband by the arm and through clenched teeth hissed, "Come on. We're in a hurry."

Johnson ripped away from her grip. "No! I want this black son of a bitch to know what he's done!"

A small crowd was starting to gather by now, and Samuel was burning with embarrassment—and rage. "Carson, I—"

Johnson's voice roared along the street. "Shut up! Damn you, just shut up. You owe me this. You owe me this for Danny."

Samuel looked puzzled. "Danny?"

"Danny! My son, goddammit. I wrote you about him. When he was sent to Vietnam. I begged you to use your position . . . your rank, to keep him out of combat. To find him a safe job where you were." His voice quivered and nearly broke as he sputtered, "You refused!"

Samuel's eyes narrowed. "I couldn't do that for my own sons, Carson."

Carol pulled again at his arm, but he wouldn't be moved. "You killed your son . . . God only knows what that war has done to Franklin. And you killed Danny!"

Samuel was numb. Johnson was shouting, "Danny. They sent him home in a rubber bag!"

Samuel managed to whisper, "I didn't know."

Johnson shrieked, "Pieces of him . . . what pieces they could find."

His wife dragged at him now. She would not allow this to go further. "Carson!" she yelled in his face and yanked him down the street. But as she was leading her husband away, she paused long enough to give Samuel a hate-filled look. "Welcome home, Samuel," she said. "I hope you burn in hell!"

He stood motionless, his head swirling, as he watched two old friends walk away, carrying their mutual misery. Finally, he turned and started for his truck, stopped, and stared at a sign in a store window: PROUDLY DISPLAY YOUR PATRIOTISM—AMERICAN FLAGS SOLD HERE.

# 51

⋆ ⋆ ⋆

*All those medals.* Franklin stared at the rows of decorations displayed in a large, glass-covered shadow box hanging from the wall of the study encasing row upon row of the decorations awarded to his father. He respected the man as a soldier and pilot; however, what once was respect for him as a father had now turned to anger. He recalled what Sergeant Hughes had said: *"Boy, you got a lot of hate in you."* Hardly room for anything else, since he had more than one target. Vietcong. His father. Difference was, he had never loved the Vietcong. They only tried to kill him.

He rubbed harshly at his face, trying to wash away the memory.

The door opened and he turned to see his father. His old man looked shaken. He hadn't seen that since Adrian's funeral.

Samuel walked to a cabinet and poured a large scotch, tossed it down, and poured another. "Care to join me?"

"Sure. Why not?"

Samuel handed his son the drink, raised his glass, and said, "To the profession of arms."

Franklin proposed his own toast. "To the living . . . and the dead."

Franklin raised his glass. "Now that I'll drink to."

Both downed their drinks with one blast. Samuel poured himself another, then—suddenly—threw the glass against the wall.

Instinctively, Franklin's hands went to his face to protect himself from the flying shards.

Shania's voice suddenly exploded from the door. "Samuel! Franklin! What in the world is going on here?"

Samuel walked to a tall gun case, removed an M-1 rifle, sighted down the barrel. Never saying a word, he returned the weapon to the case and removed a Thompson submachine gun. He examined the weapon carefully, as though looking for imperfections. "Carson and Carol Johnson. I ran into them in town."

Shania looked at Franklin, who appeared perplexed. "I see." With an understanding voice, she said, "I thought you knew."

"Thought I knew? That's one of the privileges of rank, my dear. Generals send men into battle; they don't have to review the dead." He bent down and started picking up the broken glass and, looking embarrassed, mumbled, "Waste of damn good scotch."

Franklin goaded him by saying, "Waste of damn good young men."

Samuel roared toward Franklin, his fists balled, his face filled with anger. He stood over his son and said gutturally, "Go ahead, Franklin. Take your best shot. Find yourself someone to blame. The Johnsons did. I'm convenient. It's not a new experience for me. I've buried more good men . . . written more letters to wives and parents—"

Franklin roared back with his own salvo. "But it's the first time you got spit on. Right? Now you know how I felt in the airport." He raised his glass, saying, "Welcome home, General Sharps. Airborne! Above the Rest!"

Franklin walked from the room, feeling the searing heat from his father's angry eyes. Shania walked out knowing her husband's pain.

Later that afternoon Shania was in the kitchen preparing rack of lamb for the evening meal, the favorite of her husband and two sons. She looked up as Franklin came in, walked to the refrigerator, and took out a bottle of beer.

"Smells good, Mom." He took a long pull at the beer. "How do you feel?"

She wiped at a wisp of hair hanging into her face with the back of her hand. "I've felt better."

He leaned against the counter. "Can I do anything?"

"Yes, you can."

"Name it."

"You can treat your father with more respect. This situation is difficult for him, too. It's difficult for all of us."

He shrugged unsympathetically. "Why should he have it easier than the rest of us?"

She looked at him sternly. "Easier? I'm not talking about easier. I'm talking about not making it more difficult. There's a difference. I saw your face and I saw your eyes. You delighted in what happened with the Johnsons."

He sipped from the bottle. "Somebody has to pay."

She slammed down her knife. "The Johnsons have to pay, not your father. He didn't kill Danny Johnson. They have to pay like we have to pay for Adrian, in our own private pain. They have no right to blame your father. He didn't kill Danny Johnson."

Franklin walked to the window and stood staring out at the cemetery. "Everybody has to pay, Mom. Everybody."

She came to him and cupped his face in her hands. "No, Franklin, you're wrong. Everybody has *paid* and the whole country is still paying. The Sharpses, the Johnsons, every person in this country pays whenever one of our boys dies over there."

Franklin had to move into a very delicate area of discussion and wasn't sure how except to forge ahead. "What happened with Kevin?"

"He became involved in outside activities and lost his deferment. Now he's being drafted. Simple as that. He made his choice, just like you."

That wasn't good enough for Franklin. "You mean Pop couldn't—"

"No. He doesn't have that kind of power and even if he did, he wouldn't."

"Yeah. Not for Adrian . . . or Kevin."

"Adrian was his own man. Like you. Kevin is his own man. He knows what his decision will do to the family—to himself."

There it was, he thought. *She knows!* "You know what he has planned?"

"I have a pretty good idea."

"How do you feel about it?"

"I'll support whatever decision he makes. I'll expect the same from you. They'll both need your support."

"Support? For Pop?"

"Yes, for your father. He'll be furious. The humiliation will be unbearable. But that's between Kevin and your father. It's you and your father that worries me. You have to settle your differences."

"How can that happen?"

Shania, her eyes tear-filled, said, "Find a way, Franklin. Find a way. It begins here. Now. With you. He's waiting. He needs it. He needs you. It starts with you taking the first step. He'll take the rest."

"What if I can't?"

She went to the cupboard and took down several plates and glasses. "Then your world will be lonelier than any jungle you've ever seen. Someone has to hold this family together when I'm gone. You're the only one who can. I've been the link between Kevin and your father. If you don't take my place, quit acting the martyr and fool, this family will be destroyed." She stood, hands on her hips, glaring at her son. "I'm not saying it will be easy. It won't. I'm not saying it'll happen overnight. It may take years. But it will never happen if you do not take on the responsibility of keeping the Sharps family . . . a family."

"I don't know if I can. If I can forgive him."

She pointed to the cemetery. "Don't tell me that. Tell that to your family buried out there. They'd forgive anything to hold together what they've fought and sacrificed for. Do you think the sergeant major would have turned his back on his son—forever? Would Selona not have tried with her last breath to find a way? You think about them. And who you are. What you are. And what got you here."

"You might be asking too much of me, Mom."

"Then go ask Adrian. Be the kind of man your brother would have been. He would never have let this family be destroyed by what happened to him. Or for what your father did to me. Besides, that is between your father and me. It's our business. If I can forgive him—and I have—so can you."

There was the sound of a woman's voice calling from the front of the house. "Hello? Are we late for dinner?"

The two walked into the living room and found Darlene standing at the open front door, suitcase in one hand, and holding baby Argonne in her arm.

Franklin hurried forward and hugged the two long and lovingly. "Let me have her." He took the baby and held her high. "Mom, she's got your eyes and mouth."

Darlene hugged Shania. "Not to mention her temper."

Shania looked at Franklin with a raised eyebrow. "All Sharpses have a temper, my dear. It's a genetic thing."

Franklin picked up the suitcase. "I'll put this in Adrian's . . ." He stopped, then carried the luggage to the back bedroom.

Darlene's eyes followed him until he left the room. "He looks well, Mom."

"He's doing well on the outside. But there's a lot of demons on the inside."

"I would think that's to be expected."

Darlene took Shania's hand and held it gently. "How are you doing?"

"I'm doing fine. I just pray that Franklin and Samuel can find some way to settle their differences. It would mean so much to me."

"They will. I have faith in them, their love for you, and the Good Lord. That's a lot of support and strength to count on."

"Let's hope so." Shania stood. "Feel like helping me with dinner?"

That evening, for the first time since Adrian's funeral, the Sharps family sat down together at the dinner table.

# 52

***

Country music blared in the bar in Bonita where Franklin and Kevin found themselves among old friends. Billiard balls cracked, laughter throbbed, and both young men felt good being together again. They found a table in the corner, kicked back, and, like all cowboys, kept their cavalry hats clamped tightly on their heads.

A pretty waitress took their order. "What you guys want to drink?"

"Pitcher of beer, and a shot of whiskey," Franklin replied.

"Make that two shots," Kevin said.

The waitress hurried away just as Franklin heard their names being called through the swelling crowd. "Franklin! Kevin!"

They looked up to see a young man easing his way toward them through the crowd.

"That's Dave Jessup!" Franklin said.

Jessup was Franklin's age; he wore a Marine Corps blouse, and as he drew closer Franklin could see the war in Vietnam had not gone well for his Indian high school classmate. He wore a black patch over his left eye, and a shiny steel hook protruded from the right sleeve.

Jessup threw his arm around Franklin. "Damn, man. You made it."

Franklin looked at him, a painful look on his face. "I have to go back, but I've made it this far, I'll make it the rest of the way." He looked at Jessup's obvious losses. "I'm sorry, Dave. I didn't know."

Jessup was an Apache Indian who grew up in Bonita and had been sent to Vietnam earlier in the year with the first Marines deployed to the war zone. "Fuck it! I'm alive, brother. That's all that matters. Hell, I just got out of the hospital. Home on convalescent leave from the VA hospital in Dago."

They sat down as the beer arrived. Jessup poured, then raised his glass. "Welcome home, brother."

They all took a long drink. "How did you get hit?" Franklin said.

"Land mine. Got hit on my first patrol. Hell, I wasn't in Nam two weeks and I'm on my way home. Didn't see much of anything except the navy hospital in Danang."

Franklin thought about that for a moment. Jessup was in and out before he knew what hit him. "In a way, that might be for the best, man. You didn't have to put up with all the shit before getting the million-dollar wound."

"That's what my uncle told me. He was wounded on D day at Normandy. First time in combat. Out of the landing craft and *zap!* On his way home. War hero and all. Guess that sort of luck runs in the family." He looked quizzically at Franklin. "How does it feel to be back?"

"Don't really know. Just got here last night. Haven't had much time to think about it. Maybe I don't want to."

"You will," Jessup said. "You will."

That sounded odd. "Why's that?"

Jessup poured another glass of beer. "War is hell, son, but the coming home is a motherfucker. You survive the war; then you got to survive the surviving."

"Has it been rough?" Kevin asked.

"Not too bad so far. Most of the guys at the hospital say they just quietly slip back home. Like coming in from a night patrol. The home folks don't want to know where you've been, what you've done, what happened. For the most part you're politely ignored. Except by the war protesters. They want you to join up with their side."

Franklin glanced at Kevin, a slight grin on his lips. "I've been told that by somebody I met." He took another sip of beer. "What're your plans now?"

"College. I'm going to be a big-time Indian. The Vocational Rehab dude at the Phoenix VA told me a grateful nation is going to 're-ha-bil-i-tate' my young ass. Rehabilitate. Shit! I looked it up in the dictionary. It means 'to restore to good or previous condition.' I asked the dude if they were going to give me back my hand and eye. . . . He said I had a lot of attitude. Said a lot of dudes got it worse than me."

Franklin couldn't imagine how, short of being dead. "Do they?"

"Without a doubt. They can't find a job because their brains are full of worms, their hearts full of pain and just plain out of hope. At least I have some money coming in from Uncle." He paused, then tapped the table with his hook and said, "I heard about your mom. I'm sorry, man. She's a great lady."

"Yes, she is."

"She came to the hospital and visited me when she was in the Los Angeles area seeing another doctor about her condition. Brought flowers, fruit, all that good stuff. The guys loved her."

This surprised both of the Sharpses. "I didn't know that."

"Oh, yes, and your old man, too."

This really surprised Franklin. "My dad?"

"In Nam. He came to the field hospital with General Westmoreland and some other big brass. Your dad told the medics they better take good care of me; then he pinned on my Purple Heart. Crazy times. Your mom and dad were the only two people who cared about me."

"What about your family?" Kevin asked.

"Down on the rez!" He laughed sarcastically. "The Indians on the reservation think I'm crazy for fighting the white man's war. They say we fight, then can't find a job. But a lot of Indians are in the service. Volunteers. Draftees. Lot of them getting hit in Nam, too. Just like the black soldiers." He looked at Kevin. "What about you?"

"I've been drafted. I have to report in two weeks."

Jessup stared at him with his one good eye. "So, what are you going to do?"

"What do you mean?"

"When are you booking for north country? Nothing but fools going to Nam. I told my brother the same thing, what the guys in Nam say—'they got me, but not my little brother!'" He downed his beer in two gulps. "Having one fucked-up dude in the family is enough. You better talk to him, Franklin."

Before they could go on, a young man stepped to the table. He was tall, lanky, wore Western clothes, and looked mean. "Howdy, hero," he said to Franklin. "Heard you was back in one piece. Your buddy here wasn't that lucky."

Franklin knew and disliked Bill Taylor. He was the super jock of the area, football scholarship to Arizona, and a righteous pain in the ass. "Hello, Bill, how's the throwing arm?"

Taylor snickered. "Better than your Injun buddy." He looked at Jessup. "Damn, Chief, you look like you tangled with a wildcat."

Jessup rose. "Get the fuck out Jody, you fucking son of a bitch. You weren't invited."

Franklin stepped between the two. He stood close, inhaling Taylor's beer breath. "Bill, you haven't changed a bit. You're still the slimy little sack of shit you were in high school."

That's when Taylor's fist came up, slamming into

Franklin's face. He reeled backward from the punch, and through glazed eyes saw his attacker closing in.

Taylor threw a wild roundhouse punch that hit only the air above Franklin's ducking head; another punch was blocked. Franklin stepped inside Taylor, drove a knee to his groin, then slammed his fist against the back of his neck. Taylor went down like a fallen tree. Moments passed, and he rose, gripping a broken beer bottle in his hand. "I'm going to cut your fucking nigger head off!"

Taylor lunged with the jagged glass extended. Franklin kicked out, driving his hand to the outside, then threw a fist from center field into Taylor's belly. There was a rush of air as the jock was hurled backward into the table and chairs. He rolled on the ground, moaning and clutching his middle, and when he got to his knees, Franklin nailed him behind the ear with the heel of his boot. Only seconds had passed. The football star lay unconscious in a pool of blood, puke, and beer.

In the background, a single loud Indian war cry rose up from the silent, stunned crowd.

An hour later, the telephone rang at the Sharps Ranch. Samuel was sitting at his desk when he answered, listened for a moment, then said, "I'll be there in fifteen minutes." He hung up and sat there shaking his head when Shania came into the study.

"Is something wrong?"

He pushed himself away from the desk and hugged her. "The boys had a little engine trouble with the truck. I better go help them out. Go on to bed, sweetheart. I won't be long."

The parking lot of the bar was lit by the strobing lights of a local ambulance. Samuel could see two attendants wheeling a gurney toward the vehicle. He walked past and recognized the battered face at the bar entrance; he saw a man who resembled the Marlboro cigarette cowboy, Sheriff Wilson Prentice, a tall, burly man who looked tired and irritated.

"Prentice, what the hell's going on here?"

Prentice allowed a slight smile and extended his hand. "I heard you were back in Bonita, Samuel." He looked around, then waved his hand toward the bar. "All hell broke loose in there. According to witnesses, Bill Taylor started throwing punches at Franklin, and got his ass whipped for the mistake." He took a deep breath. "But goddamn, your son near killed that boy. Knocked him flatter than piss on a plate. And they tore the living hell out of the place to boot." There was an uncomfortable pause. "Samuel, I know you've got some personal problems out there at Sabre Ranch. I know about Shania, and I don't want to arrest Franklin, what with him still being in the service. Just do me a favor: Get him the hell out of here. I'd appreciate it if you'd stand for some of the damages, and my report'll show it was started by unknown causes."

Franklin appeared in the custody of a deputy. He was wearing handcuffs and had a bruised face. Samuel said to Prentice, "Get the cuffs off. Have the owner send me a bill. I'll stand for all the damages. I don't want his mother to know about this."

The deputy removed the cuffs and Franklin started to say something to his father, but before the words issued Samuel pointed a hard finger at Franklin, saying, "Not a word! Not a goddamned word. Get your ass in that vehicle."

On the drive home, not a word was spoken between Samuel and Franklin. At the ranch, the two walked in acting as though nothing had happened. Shania asked her son, "What happened to your face?"

"I was checking the engine. You know how that hood doesn't stay up. It slipped from Kevin's hand and caught me on the face. Don't worry, Mom. I'm not hurt." At that moment Kevin came through the front door, looking sheepish.

She kissed them good night. She could smell the beer on their breath but chose not to comment. "You better get some sleep. Tomorrow will be a long day."


Franklin couldn't sleep. It was nearly one o'clock when he went onto the porch and sat watching the full moon. The desert shimmered; he heard birds flitting through the air and reptiles moving about the hard ground, and heard the door open. He figured it was Kevin and said over his shoulder, "We really got our asses in the sling tonight, little brother."

He was surprised at the voice that answered. "Your father said you only had car trouble."

Franklin looked up to see Darlene standing in the moonlight. She was wearing a robe and standing near enough for him to catch her fragrance. "Pop did a good job covering for us but I don't think Mom was fooled."

She listened to him explain and thought the whole incident was childish. "I would think you've had enough fighting to last a lifetime."

"I didn't start it."

"You have to learn to control your temper."

She had him on that point. "I'm trying to fit back in and it's harder than I thought it would be."

"Why? All you have to do is come back to the person you were. A good man with a bright future."

This took him by surprise. "I'm not Adrian. We were two different people. Always were. Even as kids."

"I know. I'm not expecting you to be like him. Just be the person I know you can be." Unexpectedly, she took his hand, and this made him uncomfortable. "What do you think of your niece?"

"She's beautiful. You've done a great job as a mother."

"Sometimes I feel very inadequate." Her eyes drifted off to the distance, a look he recognized. It was one of longing, of not quite understanding how things turned out the way they did.

"Adrian would be very proud." He was looking at her differently now. Not just as his sister-in-law, but as a woman. They were only a year apart in age, but he felt like a fumbling teenager in her presence.

"Do I make you uncomfortable?"

He shrugged. "Darlene, you scare the living hell out of me. You always did. From the first day Adrian brought you home."

Her fingers laced his more tightly. "I never meant to do that."

"It wasn't your fault. There just weren't many black girls around." Which was true. Most of the black people of the area were descendants of military families from the Old West years. Her father had been a porter on the Santa Fe Railroad between Los Angeles and El Paso.

"I'm sure you've had plenty of girls chasing after you."

"Not as many as you might think."

"I find that surprising. You're a very handsome man."

*Jesus! What's going on here?* His brother—her husband—lay buried in his grave not thirty yards away and here he was sitting with his widow and feeling . . . urges . . . that made him ashamed.

"He wasn't supposed to get killed. He was a general's aide. He was on a fact-finding mission, for God's sake. Two months out of West Point and he's killed by a land mine while driving on the outskirts of Saigon." He felt her tremble and put his arm around her. He could only sit helplessly while listening to her sob. "Nobody had even heard of Vietnam this time last year."

"That won't last much longer. Before it's over, the whole world is going to know about Vietnam."

She dabbed at her eyes. "How long do you think it'll take us to win the war?"

"I don't know. Back in July we were thinking we'd all be home for Christmas. I don't think that's the way it'll

work out. Now that the North Vietnamese are into the
fight, I expect it'll go on for quite awhile."

Darlene shuddered and laid her head on his shoulder.
"I watch the news and see so many young people opposed
to what's going on over there. Young men are burning
their draft cards, leaving the country. It's dreadful."

He thought about his buddies, on patrol this very minute while he sat in the darkness with a beautiful woman.
"Can I ask you a favor?"

"Of course."

"Will you keep on sending me tapes when I go back?"

"Yes, I will."

Without knowing what he was doing, he kissed her. He
was helpless. She smelled so wonderful, felt so good in
his arms, and for the moment he forgot who she was.

# 53

*★ ★ ★*

He couldn't be certain of his feelings when he awoke later that morning. He felt ashamed for not controlling his temper at the bar and his feelings for Darlene. It would have been easy to write both off as combat stress. But the truth was, he enjoyed the fight and especially liked being with Darlene.

With sunrise came preparations for the trip. Samuel and Franklin were loading luggage into the back of the family car when they saw a car approaching. Neither had mentioned the events of the night before, both figuring the less said the better. The sun was barely above the eastern horizon, but there was plenty of light to see the dusty rooster tail of the approaching vehicle.

"Looks like someone is up earlier than we are," Samuel said.

Franklin lifted a heavy suitcase into the trunk, then stepped beside his father.

The car stopped and two men got out, both wearing

uniforms, one an officer, the other an enlisted man. They approached and saluted.

The officer said, "Good morning, General Sharps. I'm Major Daniel Swopes, Army Security Agency, Fort Huachuca." He motioned to the enlisted man. "This is Specialist Harold Townes. He's one of our ASA field operatives."

Samuel said, "Look, Major Swopes, my son got into a fight last night. No charges were filed by the sheriff and the damage was paid for. I don't think it's necessary for the ASA to get involved in this."

Swopes shook his head. "I know nothing of a fight, sir. I am not here regarding your son who's in the army."

Samuel was now more perplexed than before. "If not Franklin, then—"

"Desmond?" a voice interrupted from the porch. All turned to see Kevin standing there, a strange look on his face. Shania and Darlene stood at his side. Both looked confused.

Desmond Sedgwick—Specialist Townes—no longer wore his hair in a ponytail; it was cut military close, and he quickly averted his eyes from Kevin.

"General Sharps," the major said, "is there somewhere we can talk in private?"

Kevin stepped down from the porch and started toward the group, staring at Townes.

Samuel said, "Do you know this soldier?"

Kevin stopped beside his father, the stare unrelenting. "Yes, sir. He was my roommate at Berkeley. But he said his name was 'Desmond Sedgwick.' "

Major Swopes stepped in. "Specialist Townes was assigned to the Berkeley campus for field intelligence purposes, General Sharps. I've been sent here to handle this matter personally—and officially."

Samuel was thunderstruck; Franklin glared at Townes. Kevin had told him of his "roommate" and how he offered to help him avoid the draft.

"This doesn't concern my son Franklin?" Samuel asked.

The major removed a letter from the inside of his uniform coat and handed it to Samuel. "This matter concerns your son Kevin Matthew Sharps. He has been drafted into the army, and the ASA has reason to believe he intends to avoid the draft by going to Mexico. Ordinarily, the army wouldn't get this involved. However considering that he is the son of a general officer, the army has ordered me to intervene—to avoid personal embarrassment to you, and political embarrassment for the United States."

Before another word could be said, Kevin lunged forward, crashing his fist against Townes's jaw. The ASA agent flew backward, landing on his back, and stared up through glazed eyes.

"You treacherous son of a bitch!" Kevin shouted at Townes.

Townes started up but met Franklin when he reached his knees. "Stay down, motherfucker," Franklin snarled, his fists at the ready.

Townes slumped back, looking scared and beaten.

Swopes intervened. "Return to the vehicle, Specialist Townes." He looked at Franklin and snapped, "Do not interfere, soldier."

Franklin started to say something, but his father admonished him. "You'll do as you're ordered." To Swopes, he ordered, "Follow me!"

They marched briskly toward the house.

Franklin stepped beside Kevin and said in a low voice, "Well, little brother, I guess Mexico's out of the picture."

Kevin stood silent.


In his study, Samuel sat at his desk, Swopes across from him in a chair. "Now, Major, I'd like a full report on this situation." He watched Swopes take a file from his briefcase; then he sat for fifteen minutes listening to the officer share every detail of the matter.

Samuel twisted anxiously in his chair, but he wasn't totally convinced. "You have offered a pretty good case for your suspicions, Major, but suspicion is all you have. My son has a report date. Until that time he is not in violation of the Selective Service law."

"I realize that, General Sharps. I'm here to inform you of what we believe to be your son's intentions—to avoid the draft by seeking refuge in a foreign country. If he does, it will be a tragedy for your family, and for the rest of the country. The United States is under a great deal of pressure at the present on the issue of draft evasion. Should the son of a general officer evade the draft, it could have monumental ramifications. Hell, every draftee in the country could point at your son and use it for their personal benefit."

Samuel could feel the tide coming in. "And the army isn't prepared to allow that, I assume."

"No, sir, the army is not prepared to allow that. It is clear from Specialist Townes's reports that your son intends to evade the draft by not returning from Mexico, and that he intends to seek refuge in Canada."

"That's speculation on Townes's part."

"No, sir. We have hundreds of undercover agents throughout the United States, on campuses, in political groups, gathering intelligence. A complete network has been established to identify those who intend to evade, and to infiltrate the apparatus for evasion. We don't have the manpower to contact every family of the individual evader, but your case is special."

"You have army personnel spying on the college kids of America?"

"Yes, sir."

"What about active duty personnel?"

Swopes nodded. "We have agents assigned to units for the specific role of trying to identify personnel who might desert before shipment to Vietnam. In this case, Townes happened to be roomed with your son."

Samuel gave it some thought before saying, "When

Kevin came home to visit his mother, Townes assumed he was going to use this opportunity to evade the draft."

"Yes, sir. Townes indicated that was Kevin's purpose."

"What else did Townes report?"

Swopes looked at Samuel directly. "That Kevin was going to tell your family of his intentions."

Samuel stood and walked to the window. He gazed at the luggage sitting beside the car. A few feet beyond the glass, Shania sat in a chair slowly rocking the baby. "Major Swopes, this is a family matter. I appreciate your concern, but I'll handle it from this point."

Swopes stood and gripped his briefcase. "If I can be of help, please don't hesitate to contact me."

The general stood at the window until the officer got into his vehicle and drove from sight.

He went to the porch and stood by Shania. A hundred thoughts swirled through his head. He looked at Franklin. "Find Kevin and meet us at Selona's Bench in the cemetery."


A white wooden bench sat just beyond the entryway of the cemetery, built by Samuel's father for his grandmother decades before. A "place to come to," she would always say; a place to sit and reflect. The paint was cracked and needed sanding and repainting, Samuel thought as he stood by the bench staring at the tombstones.

When all were gathered he came directly to the point. He asked Kevin, "Do you intend to report for your induction?"

Kevin answered nervously, "No, sir. I do not intend to report for induction into the army. I was going to tell—"

His father's features hardened. "When? How? By postcard from Montreal?"

"I was going to tell you in Mexico."

"You miserable coward. You can stand here in this sacred place and speak those words? These people fought—and some died"—he pointed at several graves—"and some were born into slavery, yet they served this country, never enjoying the wonderful bounty you've known because of their sacrifices."

It made little impact on his son. "The war is wrong, Pop!"

"What the hell do you know about what is right or wrong? The very words that come out of your mouth were paid for in blood. This is not about your young, mystic notions about right or wrong. All wars are 'wrong' by definition. Right now we don't have time for philosophy One-O-One; we have a situation we have to deal with head-on, and running away will not solve the problem."

The line drawn in the sand could not have been clearer. Shania watched two men she loved take a stand for their beliefs and felt her heart breaking with every word that passed. It was like watching a battle unfold, one side firing a salvo, the other answering with equal force. But this was not a battlefield. This was her family, and there could be no winner.

"Please, both of you, stop," she pleaded. "Please stop before this goes too far."

Samuel looked at her. "Too far? It's already gone 'too far.' Our son is talking about deserting his country; he's talking about destroying his life and everything we've built. How far is 'too far?' " He looked at Franklin. "You're a combat soldier. How do you feel?"

Franklin was ready for the question; he had been since the night he returned and learned of Kevin's intentions. "I'll buy him the plane ticket with my combat pay. We don't want anybody in the bush who's not willing to be there. They'll get us all killed. If he wants to sky out . . . so be it."

Samuel realized something important. "You knew about this all along."

"I knew. If your family was as important as you say it is to you . . . you'd have seen it coming. But not you. Not the great black general. You have to prove to everyone that you're special. Shit! You're nothing but a nigger with a star on his shoulder." He pointed at Adrian's grave. "My brother is dead for no good reason at all. You pushed him all his life to go to West Point. He never had an option. Kevin does. Now you're not listening to him."

Darlene suddenly began weeping. "Franklin, don't talk like that."

"Why not?" He looked at his father, then his mother. "A few weeks ago I killed a fourteen-year-old kid. He had an old bolt-action rifle with the breech rusted shut. But that didn't matter. He attacked me. You don't know who we're fighting. None of the brass in Saigon know who this enemy really is, how determined they are. They are not going to quit. We are going to lose thousands because we are invading *their* country. Do you think America is the only country that will fight to the death against invaders?"

At that moment, something inside Samuel appeared to snap. His eyes hardened like nothing they had ever seen in the man. He started toward Kevin, as though mechanical, his hands rising up. "You! You're the cause of all this!" His voice was evil, guttural.

Shania had never seen him like this. "Samuel!" She shouted.

Just as Samuel's hands neared Kevin's throat, he was suddenly knocked sideways as Franklin threw his body against his father. They both went down in a tangled heap, thrashing and rolling on the ground shared by their dead family.

"Franklin! Samuel! Please!" Shania shouted. Kevin stood looking shocked; Darlene raced through the gate toward the house.

Franklin rolled Samuel onto his back, pinning his shoulders to the ground with his powerful arms. "He's my brother! Damn you, he's my brother!"

Samuel, wild-eyed, screamed, "He's not my son!"

Franklin shook him. "Why? Because he doesn't want to die in your war?" Franklin shook him again. "That's what we've been fighting for! Goddamn you! His right to make his own choice—right or wrong. My God! I've killed people for his right to make that choice. He'll pay—for the rest of his life—he'll pay! But he has the right—the right to choose!"

"You're wrong." Samuel gurgled. "You're both wrong. This isn't about choice. This is about honor!"

Franklin was now wild in the eyes and heart. "Who do you think you are? God! That's my brother—your son! Haven't we lost enough? How much more do we have to lose before you stand up and say 'no'! How many sons do you have to bury before you say 'that's enough'!"

Shania spoke; the words were barely audible. "Franklin . . . Samuel . . . Kevin . . . please. No more. Please."

"Mom!" Kevin shouted.

Shania, her hands over her ears, stumbled slightly, then slumped to the ground. She lay staring upward, her eyes appearing fixed on the sabres suspended from the archway.

All three men scrambled to her side. Samuel took her in his arms, lifting her head until he was looking into her eyes. "God, oh, God," Samuel muttered, "what have I done to you?"

She seemed to hear him; her eyes fluttered as she gripped his hand. "Don't let me die like this, Samuel. Not like this."

"Call Dr. Malone," he said to Franklin.

"No, Son," she pleaded. "Stay here with me. I'm sorry, Samuel. So very sorry." At that moment she appeared to draw a renewed strength from some inner source. "Don't hate your sons. Promise me . . . you won't hate *our* sons."

He kissed her lightly on the lips. "Not now, my darling. We'll talk later."

She smiled. "There won't be another chance."

Franklin looked sick at hearing his father's words; Kevin could only shake his head in sheer disillusionment.

Shania reached deeper, searching for the words. "You're a father who has sons who will be left alone. They will have to carry their pain without anyone to care.

Franklin will have to deal with his sorrow alone. Kevin won't have a father to help him understand there is a proper—and noble—time for war. A time to die, if need be. Without you he will become an outcast. Without family. Without country. For God's sake, he'll have no meaning."

Samuel pulled her close and whispered, his voice sounding full of plea. "What can I do?"

She looked up at the swords. "You are the weld that holds them together. Like those sabres. Give them strength. Without you they will rust beneath the tears of hatred. Loneliness. And ridicule."

Samuel shook his head. "You ask too much. I could not forgive a son who would betray his country."

She mustered all her strength, and spoke forcefully. "You must help him. I can't, or I would."

Samuel's eyes filled with tears. "That's impossible."

Shania would not give up the fight. She knew she was dying. She knew there would be the living left behind. "I know it's unfair to plead from my position and to use this moment against you. But I have no choice."

Samuel's chest was heaving. In his heart, he could not let go of a lifetime of purpose. "I can't. My son, a draft dodger? Defiling the honor of men who've died? His brother? No!"

"Yes, you can," Shania insisted. "His brother cries from the grave to help the ones alive. I hear him, Samuel. In my sleep. On the wind. Now, at this moment." She paused, collected herself, then continued, her voice now serious and severe. "Why did you come home, Samuel? In search of forgiveness? Or to stand beside your family before what's left of it is destroyed? If so, it doesn't come without a price."

"I came because of you, and the children."

She shook her head, but now she was gentler; forgiving, but still imploring. "No: you came for yourself. Not to ease our pain and suffering, but to ease yours. For once in your life can't you put your family ahead of all other matters? Franklin needs you—he needs someone to help him through the bitterness that's tearing at his soul. Kevin needs you to understand—to be there through this difficult decision and what follows. If you don't, you'll lose everything. You'll die alone, without tears or children and grandchildren to marvel at your achievements. You'll be alone, Samuel."

Tears began to stream down his cheeks. He felt the remaining strength begin to drain from her body. "God, Shania. No. Not like this. Please, dear God, not like this."

"Shhhhhh. I'm so sorry, Samuel, but I must die knowing my family is again joined like those sabres. Please, I beg you, don't let me die a failure."

He sobbed openly now, his body trembling. "God, no, Shania. I won't." He struggled to sit upright. "Tell me what I should do."

Her words were growing fainter. "Hold on to them, Samuel. Find a way." She looked at Franklin and Kevin. "Help him. Please help him."

The two boys sat beside their mother. Franklin said, "We will. We promise."

Her eyes widened, and she reached beyond the three men she loved most on the earth, toward a grave marker, to another she loved, and with one final burst of breath said, "Adrian!"

Shania LeBaron Sharps slumped into her husband's arms, and there was silence beneath the sabres.

# 54

\*\*\*

Four days after her death, Shania was buried beside her firstborn child. Unusual for the time of year, a soft rain had fallen. A thick barricade of clouds hid the sun, and everywhere he looked Franklin saw darkness.

But the darkness of nature was brilliant compared with the darkness he saw standing between his father and brother. Since the moment of her death, neither had said a word to the other.

The following day, Samuel was kneeling at her grave when he heard Franklin's voice. "You're really blowing it, Pop."

Samuel remained silent.

"I expected as much," Franklin went on. "You made a promise to my mother. On her dying breath you made a promise you knew you wouldn't keep."

"People often say things in those moments they know aren't true."

"You are really one self-righteous son of a bitch."

His father turned and walked away.

Kevin was watching from the window. He went to the study and poured a glass of whiskey, his third in less than an hour, and raised it to the shadow box on the wall. "To the profession of arms," he said with a guttural voice, "and the honorable men who fight for duty, honor, and country." He downed the drink, stepped back and saluted with the glass, then threw it against the wall.

Samuel drove away recklessly and uncaring, swerving toward the highway as though drunk. He needed air. Not air in his lungs, air under his body. He needed to fly. To find a private place in the sky, as he had done so often when in need of solace.

When he arrived at the airport, an odd scene awaited him. A sheriff's car sat beside an ambulance. Two attendants were loading a body into the rear of the vehicle.

Doc Malone came out of the hangar. "What's happened, Jessie?" Samuel said.

"Fred shot himself." He handed over a telegraph. "This arrived this morning."

Samuel quickly read the telegram. "Dear God, Michael's been killed in Vietnam."

Malone shook his head sadly. "He was all Fred had. I guess he just couldn't live with the idea of being alone. He climbed into the cockpit of his airplane, stuck a pistol in his mouth, and blew half his head off." Malone put his hand on his old friend's shoulder. "I've got a bad feeling about this war. Is it ever going to end? Or is it going to just keep destroying people's lives?"

Samuel shook his head. "I don't know. It may only just be the beginning."

"I pray that's not the case."

Franklin was packing his suitcase when he heard a strange sound from beyond the house. A hard rain was falling when he stepped onto the porch and saw Kevin near the stable, wearing an old cavalry hat and holding a rusty sword. He was obviously drunk.

"What are you doing?" Franklin shouted.

"Going to the canyon!" Kevin yelled back, spurred the horse, and rode away.

It had been a family tradition, almost a rite of passage, for the Sharps children to make the dangerous ride down the steep canyon not far from the house. Franklin had made the ride, as had Kevin. It was the place where Sergeant Major Augustus Sharps broke his back, lingering several days in a coma before dying. Samuel had made the ride down the precarious slope to test his shattered leg after returning from the war in Europe.

The ride was dangerous to the strong and sober, deadly for someone drunk.

Franklin ran to the stable and saddled a horse; as he mounted up he heard the sound of a truck pulling into the yard. He started to spur the horse when his father rushed toward him and gripped the reins.

"Son, I need to talk to you." There was a desperation in his voice Franklin had never heard.

"I don't have time to hear your confession. Kevin's in trouble."

"What kind of trouble?"

"He's drunk and he's going to ride the canyon."

Samuel reached and grabbed his son and with a quick movement jerked him from the saddle. His eyes blazing, face streaked with rain, he shouted as thunder crashed from the sky, "We don't have time to play any more games. I was wrong. I had to lose my wife and see another man lose his son to understand what your mother tried to spare me. It's not like Adrian. He wanted to serve. Kevin doesn't." He pulled Franklin toward him. "I'm going to keep my promise to your mother."

Franklin could see in his father's eyes he spoke the truth. "I'll saddle you a horse."

Samuel went inside and slipped on his Western boots. On the way out he saw Darlene standing in the living room. He stopped long enough to kiss her on the cheek and say, "I'm going to get this situation straightened out."

He hurried toward the saddled horse.

Echoing in his ears was Shania's final plea: *"Find a way."*

# 55

***

He rode with the wind and the rain tearing at his face and, as when he was a boy, with his father riding beside him. But this time, unlike before, his father did not hold back on the reins and let him appear to win the race.

They rode with a vengeance, as their father and fore-fathers had ridden, heads bent low into the manes, looking neither right nor left, driving the animals with unforgiving harshness to the place all the Sharpses one day had to face. They rode to the canyon and Franklin could hear his father tell the story about when he was a lad sitting by the fire and Sergeant Major Augustus Sharps remembered testing himself when asked by Buffalo Bill Cody to join the Congress of Rough Riders. . . .

After receiving a request to join Cody's Wild West show, Augustus knew he had to face a test if he was to ride with the greatest horsemen in the world. He saddled up and rose through the early-morning darkness and minutes before sunrise sat at attention on a roan stallion named Shiloh. The horse showed a momentary restlessness, throwing his great head forward, then tried to rear up until he was settled by the tightening of the reins. Shiloh snorted and tried to crane his head away from the empty air beyond the rim of the deep canyon.

"It's almost time," Augustus whispered to him.

Augustus sat watching the eastern sky as the sun began to filter through the crackback ridges of the mountains northeast of Bonita. He wore a short-sleeved riding jacket and crisply starched pants that blossomed above his knees before disappearing into tall, highly polished cavalry boots. The dark blue cavalry hat he wore over his close-cropped hair was pulled down tightly at the brim, just above dark eyes that seemed to shine from within the brim's shadow.

The saddle on Shiloh was a McClellan, which he still preferred, what with the open slot in the seat that brought the horse's backbone against his tailbone, giving him the sense he and the horse were melded to each other physically. His Sharps rifle rested in the carbine boot on the right side of the saddle tree; on the left was his three-foot-long sabre.

The sun broke over the horizon; a red flood of sunlight swept the land and flooded into the canyon, running like fast water across hard ground. A narrow trail could be seen in front of Shiloh, a path that disappeared over the rim.

Suddenly, Augustus's arm flashed up; his fingers touched the edge of the brim in a sharp salute. He spurred the horse, stood in the iron stirrups, and leaned back as the stallion bolted over the edge into the redness of the canyon.

Down the stallion plunged, speed building as Augustus's right hand held firm to the reins, checking the power of the animal, while his free hand drew the steel sabre rattling against the saddle. With a smooth movement he extended the blade toward the imaginary enemy that lay waiting at the bottom. At that moment the sun flashed off the burnished blade and he felt the tightness of fear when he realized he was leaning dangerously far over the neck of the charging Shiloh.

He pulled the reins taut, sat back as far as possible, and distributed his body weight evenly, winning for the moment against the forward pull of the horse and gravity.

Down they drove, leaving a spray of dust too heavy to rise in the hot air. The deeper rider and horse descended, the thicker the sheen of the red dust collected, until the two appeared as flaming apparitions. It was only in the final moments of the descent, when the horse dived over the last ledge and he heard Shiloh's hooves crack against the hard floor of the canyon, that he yelled, *"Charge!"*

The canyon came alive with the sound of the stallion's pounding hooves and the rattle of the empty sabre scabbard. Augustus stood in the stirrups, leaned forward while extending the sabre beyond the stallion's rising and plunging head, preparing to receive the enemy charge. At the precise moment he and the enemy would join in battle, the sword flashed forward, narrowly clearing the head of the stallion; then he pulled on the reins, wheeling the horse into the opposite direction.

A scream burst from his lungs as he spurred the animal to full gallop, again stood in the stirrups with the sabre extended. He slashed and cut, parried, and thrust the blade at the enemy as though he were fighting a legion of demons, unaware that he was not alone.

On the ledge above the canyon, another rider sat on a horse, watching the mock battle as she had many times. Selona knew that he came here, to the edge of her small ranch, and made this ride whenever he needed to feel young.

Finally, Augustus drew the horse to a halt and, sitting at attention, saluted smartly with the sabre, then returned the blade to its scabbard with one crisp move.

On the canyon floor, except for man and beast taking in lungfuls of air, there was only silence.

• • •

*A legion of demons.*

His voice came calmly over Kevin's shoulder. "Kevin, Son . . . look at me."

What Samuel saw was a young man astride a horse at the edge of a path, his face tear-streaked, and his eyes fearful.

"I'll make it easy on you, Pop." Kevin's voice was calm, respectful. He took the rusty sword and placed the tip of the blade against his heart. Then he calmly planted the hilt against the saddle horn. "I'll just ride down, at full charge. You'll be proud of me. I'll let you off the hook."

Samuel dismounted. "Trust me, Son. You have to trust me. We're going to find a way out of this situation." He reached up and took the reins and felt the bit tighten in the horse's mouth. The front hooves were close to the edge.

"Easy, Son," Samuel said.

General Sharps put his hand out to Franklin, behind the two and just dismounting, a signal to hold his ground. He released the bit and ran his hand along the horse's neck, over the mane, into the saddle. He touched the rusty sabre, felt its cold steel. He looked up at his son, who sat looking into empty space.

He reached, gripped the sabre, and tore it away from Kevin's chest. At the same moment he pulled a .45-caliber Colt from his belt, laid the muzzle to the horse's head and fired.

Then the blade flashed beneath the sun and horse and rider went to the ground. To Franklin it was all a blur, but he heard Kevin scream and saw the sabre protruding from Kevin's leg just above the kneecap.

Kevin rolled from the saddle, his scream of pain more than his father could endure. "You bastard!" the boy yelled.

Franklin dropped to Kevin's side. "Don't you know what's happened?"

Kevin, wild-eyed in pain, couldn't answer.

Franklin put his hand on his father's shoulder. "You're Four-F, brother. Can't be drafted. Not with that knee." He shook his head in amazement. "You might walk with a limp for a few years. But I'll swear that you fell on the sabre and I'm sure Pop will do the same."

Samuel said, "We need to get medical attention for him. You're a medic; what's your call?"

"Don't take out the sword," Franklin said. He took off his belt, tightened it above Kevin's knee. "He won't bleed to death before I can get to the truck. I'll call Doc Malone." There was a slight grin on his face as he mounted his horse and rode off.

Franklin had only one thought: *The son of a bitch did it!*

# 56

## ✯ ✯ ✯

Following three hours of surgery, Kevin was rolled out of the operating room in the hospital at Willcox. Franklin, Samuel, and Darlene sat in the room waiting.

At last the surgeon came to them.

"The tendons were severed and have been reconnected, but I'm afraid there are many months—perhaps years—of rehabilitation facing that young man. I'll be honest with you. He very likely is going to be walking with a cane from now on."

When Kevin came out from under the anesthesia, the three were allowed a brief visit. They held his hand and tried to comfort him, but Kevin did most of the talking; apologetic and grateful. "Pop, I understand what you did. I know what all this has done to you, and I'm very sorry for the trouble and pain I've caused you. I hope you're not too ashamed of me."

Samuel gripped his hand. "Don't ever speak to me of

shame again, Son. If anyone here deserves to feel shame, it is me. I'm a father who didn't listen to his sons, or to their mother."

After Kevin drifted off to sleep they found a Mexican restaurant and had a quiet dinner. During the drive back to Bonita, Franklin and Darlene sat in the back while Samuel drove, glancing from time to time in the rearview mirror, not oblivious to the affection he saw they had for each other.

It made him feel good. Maybe that was what Franklin needed, he thought. It was what Shania had been to him: a source of personal purpose, someone to come home to. He found a sense of pride in knowing he had changed in so many ways in recent days. *God! If Shania could only have lived to see it.*

What had he learned? That a man is no greater than those who surround him? That he does not have all the answers and will learn few unless he asks many questions? And, most of all, that he must question himself? He had not done that in so long he could not recall the last time. It was as though he suddenly awoke one day knowing everything, and, in recognizing that, knew that for so very long he had known very little about life.

For some strange reason the words of Abraham Lincoln's Gettysburg Address came to mind. Especially the part where he said ". . . *Today we are engaged in a great civil war . . .*"

In a way, America was engaged in a great civil war. Testing whether one part of the nation, or the other part, would prevail or whether the nation could bind itself together.

He thought that impossible in the present. There were too many battles yet to fight, on too many battlefields, both abroad, and, perhaps more important, here at home. The nation would survive the battles abroad, for it was supported by the force of the nation.

The military could not survive battles abroad if there was no nation.

He had learned the importance of a "house divided against itself."

He had no house only a few days ago, and his family had been losing all the battles.

But not anymore! He had made a decision, and by the time they reached Sabre Ranch, while he did not have the solution completely worked out, he had begun to understand what he had to do.

The words of Kevin echoed in his mind . . . *It was time to choose!*

# 57

★ ★ ★

The next morning Franklin saddled two horses and he and Darlene went for a sunrise ride. Argonne was asleep and under the watchful eye of her grandfather, who had risen early to visit Shania's grave and talk about what he had in mind. After detailing as much of his plan as he had devised, he went back inside, checked on the baby, then went into his office.

He spent nearly two hours on the telephone, most of the calls to Washington, one to Saigon. When finished, he sat back in his leather chair and clasped his big hands behind his neck. For the first time in a long while he felt good about himself. He had done something positive for his family. He broke into a wide grin as he saw through the window Franklin and Darlene riding into the yard. He sat watching them; the two seemed to glow in each other's presence.

When he heard them come through the door, he met them in the living room and told Franklin, "I spoke with the Red Cross a few minutes ago. They've extended your leave for three more days."

"Thanks, Pop. I had planned to go back tomorrow."

"Son, you won't be going back. At least, not to Vietnam."

Franklin was stunned.

"Nor will I. At least, not for very long."

"I don't understand," Franklin said.

Samuel went on. "I've contacted the Pentagon and spoken with the vice chief of staff of the air force. He's an old friend of mine. We flew together in Korea. I've informed him it's my intention to retire from military service."

"Retire?" Franklin and Darlene both chorused.

"Yes. I've been through three wars for my country. I think that's enough. I explained the death of your mother, and your brother's injury. The vice chief understands. However, he did ask that I return and get things in order for my replacement. That shouldn't take more than a couple of weeks. Then, it's back home."

"What will you do?" Franklin said. "I mean, all you've known for nearly twenty-five years is being a lifer—"

Darlene laughed. Franklin covered his mouth like a child who had said something bad. "Sorry, Pop. You know what I mean."

"No need to apologize. I know what you mean. There're plenty of things to do. Just because an old warhorse goes to pasture doesn't mean there's nothing to do."

"What about Franklin?" Darlene said.

Franklin was wondering the same thing and saw Samuel looking at him with a glow in his eyes he'd never known from his father.

"What did you mean, when you said I wasn't going back?"

His father shrugged. "Do you want to go back?"

Franklin looked at Darlene. "No, I don't. Not that I'm a coward—"

Samuel cut him off. "You're no coward. I'm a general

and that gives me certain privileges. Not many, mind you, but some. You volunteered for the draft nearly a year ago. That's a two-year hitch, which is nearly half-completed. I spoke with one of the powers in the Pentagon and pointed out to him that you are a combat medic with a lot of experience and expertise in what is now a new and different type of ground war. I also said that your experience could be used more effectively at the combat medic school at Fort Sam Houston, Texas, rather than in Vietnam; that you had been there, in combat, and that you are one of the few medics currently stateside who has seen the situation up close and can better serve your country in an instructor capacity for at least another year. He agreed; as a matter of fact, he thought it was a superb idea. Therefore, you are going to be reassigned to the combat medic school, where you can serve out your enlistment."

Franklin released a long, deep breath. "Pop, I thought you were opposed to any form of nepotism."

"I am. This is not nepotism. What you learned in Vietnam is more valuable here than going back and getting your ass shot off. You can talk with these young medics. Tell them the way the situation really is. I'm sure you learned something in the bush that is not being taught at Fort Sam Houston."

"Yes, sir. Quite a bit. The real thing is nothing at all like what we were taught, especially in the area of medevac and personal hygiene in the bush."

Samuel was already way ahead of him. "That's what I conveyed to the under secretary of defense."

Franklin was impressed. "You know the under secretary of defense?"

"Yes. Six months ago I was assigned to take him all over Vietnam on a fact-finding tour. He's a good man and understands my personal situation as well as the military benefit of this assignment."

"Is that all?" Franklin asked.

"That, and how embarrassing it could be for the government if I retired and wrote a book on why I believe the war is being botched, that more young men are going to die in what is becoming a war we can't possibly win."

There it was, thought Franklin. There's no way the government would want a bronco tromping through their carrot patch, especially when the price of his silence would be to exercise good judgment. Franklin knew he could contribute more as an instructor at the CMS, where his experience could be used to save more men than he could ever hope to save on the battlefield.

Darlene took Franklin's hand and pulled him toward his father. She took Samuel's hand and drew him from his chair and guided both men together.

As she walked out of the room, she turned to see the two embrace.

For the Sharps family, the Vietnam War was over.

# EPILOGUE

★

## 1991

★ ★ ★

At Sabre Ranch, Dr. Franklin LeBaron Sharps sat at his ormulu desk, disinterested in his daily mail, with the exception of one letter that had arrived that morning from Argonne. At forty-seven, he was still sapling lean, his physique strong and durable, like that of a long-distance runner. He continued to wear a paratrooper haircut, his scalp shaved two inches above the ears and close-cropped on top. He allowed himself a narrow mustache, highlighting full lips, and wore a light blue jumpsuit.

When he finished reading the letter, a sudden movement from outside the house caught his eyes. He rose and walked to the French doors and watched a herd of antelope walk lazily through the front yard, ignoring his sudden appearance as he studied them through the glass.

He watched for several minutes, then returned to the letter and read it again. He then glanced to the wall and slowly swiveled his leather chair as he panoramically studied a multitude of family photographs, awards, and decorations. All of which swelled him with great pride. But it was his medical degree that gave him the most satisfaction. After being discharged from the army, he went to college, earned his bachelor's degree, then attended medical school at the University of Texas.

Life had been good to him and Darlene, whom he married in the fall of 1967. They had a child of their own, Jacob LeBaron Sharps, now a first-year medical student at the University of Southern California. Franklin, an orthopedic surgeon, had his practice in Phoenix, where he commuted daily in his private airplane.

Slowly, his eyes scanned the wall carefully, ultimately pausing on one particular frame that gave him a great sense of pride, followed by heartache. As he always felt, when remembering one of the saddest days of his life.

Captured in the frame was a single sheet of paper the size of a dollar bill, bearing the name ADRIAN AUGUSTUS SHARPS II. The paper reminded him of a lightning storm at night, what with the brilliance of the name at the center, then the surrounding dark lead shading from the pencil he used to transcribe his older brother's name from the Wall at the Vietnam War Memorial. There had been other names on the Wall he had recognized on that first—and only—visit in 1983. But his brother's was the only one he had framed. The more than dozen others he had brought back lay within the cover of a book in the bookcase. The book was titled *About Face: The Odyssey of an American Warrior*. The author was Colonel David H. Hackworth, his former commander in the 101st Airborne.

He had visited the memorial with his father, Darlene, their son, Jacob, his younger brother Kevin, now an attorney working for the N.A.A.C.P. in Atlanta, and his stepdaughter, Lieutenant Argonne Sharps, now a graduate of West Point.

Instinctively, his eyes drifted to another photograph on the wall, this one taken four years ago at Argonne's graduation from West Point. She stood at attention, wearing the uniform of a cadet, saluting with her drawn sabre.

Beside her photograph was a picture of his dead brother, wearing an identical uniform, the same sabre salute.

"Tradition." Franklin whispered softly, almost reverently.

Then he heard the front door open and Darlene's voice calling, sounding frightened. He hurried toward the living room, where he found her standing in front of the large front window. She turned, and he could see the worry on her face. He put his arms around her and felt her trembling body weaken against his. "What is it, sweetheart? Aren't you feeling well?"

"You haven't heard?" she asked, her voice nearly frantic. "It's just been announced on the news."

"Heard what? Darlene, you're not making any sense."

She went to the television set and pressed a button on the remote. She quickly switched the channel until she found CNN.

From Baghdad, Bernard Shaw's voice rang with excitement as the greenish picture, filmed with night vision cameras, showed the night sky of the Iraqi capital aglow with the tracer etchings of antiaircraft fire pouring upward from the ground.

He sat heavily on the couch, and the words seemed to be released like a desperate breath. "The air campaign has begun."

"Argonne! My God, Franklin. Her unit is in Saudia Arabia!" Darlene's words shrilled with fear.

Within seconds he was on the telephone to his father, who now lived in Falls Church, Virginia. He was given several numbers by Samuel of influential military men at the Pentagon, called them all, but could reach none of them.

For the next few hours, like most Americans, the two sat in front of their television set, knowing their daughter, along with other sons and daughters, was now journeying into harm's way.

•  •  •

In the desert of eastern Saudia Arabia, First Lieutenant Argonne Sharps sat at the pilot controls in the cockpit of a H-60 Blackhawk helicopter, the tarmac as dark as the night. The four massive blades were churning smoothly toward liftoff revolutions as she flipped down night-vision goggles on her helmet visor and glanced to the rear of the chopper.

Twelve army Special Forces soldiers dressed in desert camouflage sat strapped into the web seats, their faces coated with camouflage beneath their night-vision goggles, their bodies laden with huge packs, ammunition, and explosives. Their hands gripped automatic weapons and heavy machine guns.

Before she increased the throttle and pulled back on the collective, she reached down and touched a metal scabbard lying between her chair and the copilot's seat. The sword had been presented to her by her father when the order came down for her unit to deploy to the Gulf. Now, the sabre's presence gave her a feeling of reassurance, as though five generations of Sharpses were sitting beside her. Guiding and advising her of her duty and responsibility.

Then she heard her copilot's voice break in over the radio and jokingly say, "Pretty tight quarters in here, Argonne. I hope you don't get the cavalry urge and draw that blade. You might slice my head off."

"Not me, Rob. I was raised swinging that old sabre. I can split hairs with it." She could see copilot Lieutenant Robert Shelton's mouth turn upward into a grin. Then, she switched the radio to internal commo mode and said to the Green Beret team, "Hold on, gentlemen. We're on our way to Iraq!"

The sleek, black helicopter lifted off smoothly, creating a tornado of swirling dust and sand on the tarmac, then banked sharply and raced toward the east. In a matter of seconds, the chopper was gone from sight of the ground crews, knifing through the darkness with its cargo of American commandos.

Lieutenant Argonne Sharps was now a seasoned helicopter pilot with her father's former outfit, the 101st Airborne Division. Shortly after the Iraqis invaded Kuwait, the Screaming Eagles were dispatched to the Persian Gulf as part of Operation Desert Shield.

Like her great-great-grandfather, the old 10th Cavalry Buffalo Soldier, she was charging toward battle on a modern-day stallion made of steel and speed, carrying a gleaming, razor-sharp sabre!

# Afterword

★ ★ ★

The following citation for the Medal of Honor was awarded posthumously to the author's platoon leader, First Lieutenant James A. Gardner, U.S. Army, Headquarters and Headquarters Company, 1st Battalion (ABN), 327th Infantry, 1st Brigade, 101st Airborne Division, for action near My Canh, Vietnam, 7 February 1966. For conspicuous gallantry and intrepidity at the risk of his own life above and beyond the call of duty. 1Lt. Gardner's platoon was advancing to relieve "A" Company of the 1st Battalion that had been pinned down for several hours by a numerically superior enemy force in the village of My Canh, Vietnam. The enemy occupied a series of fortified bunker positions which were mutually supporting and expertly concealed. Approaches to the position were well covered by an integrated pattern of fire including automatic weapons, machine guns, and mortars. Air strikes and artillery placed on the fortifications had little effect. 1Lt. Gardner's platoon was to relieve the friendly company by encircling and destroying the enemy force. Even as it moved to begin the attack, the platoon was under heavy enemy fire. During the attack, the enemy fire intensified. Leading the assault and disregarding his own safety, 1Lt. Gardner charged through a withering hail of fire across an open rice paddy. On reaching the first bunker, he destroyed it with a grenade and without hesitation dashed to the second bunker and eliminated it by tossing a grenade inside. Then, crawling swiftly along the dike of a rice paddy, he reached the third bunker. Before he could arm a grenade, the enemy gunner leaped forth, firing at him. 1Lt. Gardner instantly returned fire and killed the enemy gunner at a distance of six feet. Following the seizure of the main enemy position, he reorganized the platoon to continue the attack. Advancing to the new assault position, the platoon was pinned down by an enemy machine gun emplaced in a fortified bunker. 1Lt. Gardner immediately collected several grenades and charged the enemy position, firing his rifle as he advanced to neutralize the defenders. He dropped a grenade into the bunker and vaulted beyond. As the bunker blew up he came under enemy fire again. Rolling into a ditch to gain cover, he moved toward the new source of fire. Nearing the position he leaped from the ditch and advanced with a grenade in one hand while firing his rifle with the other. He was gravely wounded just before he reached the bunker, but with a last valiant effort, he staggered forward and destroyed the bunker and its defenders with a grenade. Although he fell dead on the rim of the bunker, his extraordinary action so inspired the men of his platoon that they resumed the attack and completely routed the enemy. 1Lt. Gardner's conspicuous gallantry was in the highest traditions of the U.S. Army.

Entered Service: Memphis, Tennessee
Place of Birth: Dyersburg, Tennessee
Date of Birth: 7 February 1943
Killed In Action: 7 February 1966
Place of Burial: Murfreesboro, Tennessee

# The White Rose Ball

★ ★ ★

In the writing of these chronicles of a family's dedication in military service to its nation, I have tried to maintain a distance from the events and characters as history has unfolded around them.

However, this book is different. This book represents a part of my life that I chose to share, hoping to shed light onto the shadowed faces of the gallant Vietnam veterans of our nation.

For more than three decades, I have been asked "When are you going to write a book about Vietnam?" I always replied, "It's a personal thing."

I quit high school at sixteen, joined the army two days after I turned seventeen, went into the paratroopers, and when my outfit, 1st Brigade, 101st Airborne Division, received orders in early 1965, I went to war. I was fortunate. Unlike many soldiers who would follow, I was led into battle by the finest officers and noncommissioned officers our service had.

John L. "Dynamite" Hughes is not a fictional character.

He is a real and wonderful man who has once again come into my life as a friend and advisor on the writing of this book. It is his photograph that is used on the jacket of this novel. There were many to chose from, such as Hughes riding an elephant, clenching a rattlesnake between his teeth, or posed in his gun jeep, the one that struck a land mine, and blew John into the branches of a tree (he survived, thank God) . . . but our comrades Sheffield and Vincent were not so fortunate.

Colonel David H. Hackworth, America's most decorated living combat soldier, is a friend and advisor. I was one of his "kids," as he proudly recalls his troopers of "Tiger Force." He retired from the Army to reflect and write the critically acclaimed book *About Face*, became an editor and correspondent for *Newsweek* magazine, and serves as a constant vocal and literary warning to an American government policy that he—through experience—considered fraught with folly and certain death to American soldiers.

Colonel Hackworth is to this day, in my life, the flare drifting down from the flareship—giving light in darkness, the voice telling us, "Fight back!"

Leo B. Smith died in 1997. He was my "First Shirt," and would become the director and curator of the National Medal of Honor Museum. A great friend to all who knew and loved him, to his last breath.

Charlie Musselwhite and his wife Jackie remain true friends. They not only survived three tours of Vietnam, but the terror of the overthrow of Iran when America was forced from that country by the Ayatollah Khomeini. They left Tehran with nothing but their children and the clothes on their back.

Phillip Chassion was killed in Vietnam fighting to save his men, as he always had, tough as ever to the last moment. It's reported there were twenty-six dead enemy soldiers stretched out in front of his position when his body was discovered. It's reported he had twelve bullets in his body. He was one tough son-of-a-bitch who loved his young troops, kicked their asses to make them better, and was always willing to fight and die for them.

Phil Chassion was also a good man, of a wonderful heart. I know. I willingly gave him my beer ration. I don't like beer. I didn't even like Chassion. But I loved him. He kicked my ass one night to get me to the religion of battle. He said: "You might not like where you're at . . . but you asked to be here. Do the job. Die well . . . if you die. But do well while you live. You're a United States paratrooper. Don't piss on the silk!"

When his body was returned to the United States for burial, John Hughes saw to the burial requirements, along with others from the army burial detail detachment. But it was friends who served with him who made certain he was put into the ground with grace and honor. There are a lot of young soldiers who won't know, until now, that he died. In more ways that can be counted, we owe our lives to him.

Lieutenant James Alton Gardner, awarded the Medal of Honor, was killed on his twenty-third birthday, the day before he was to be promoted to the rank of captain. He was a great leader. Died too young. But . . . he died well. I don't know if that could possibly make up for the void he left, but he gave it all in a single, unselfish moment, so that others could have hours, days, weeks, months, years, decades . . . of life.

James Gardner gave it all with valor. Never thinking of himself.

The sergeant depicted in the battle of An Ninh was Herb Dexter, who had served four tours in Vietnam. I never knew the man personally. I only knew of his legendary courage, leadership, and character. What I could not portray in the story can be said now; he was a soldier's soldier. No one can imagine what it is like to be in a situation where there is no hope, and suddenly, you look up to see a sword shining against the enemy fire. To raise the courage of those frightened, to become lions, is a flight among the heavens of the valorous.

Herb Dexter was that sergeant.

And I never shared a beer with the man.

But he was a hero of the day, and that has to mean something. If nothing else, his name won't be forgotten where he died so others would live.

A great soldier.

There is one I wish to remember. Earl Wilson, Memphis, Tennessee. If there was ever a recon soldier, it was Will. I believe he is the essence of the combat soldier. The members of Recon Platoon, 1st Brigade, HHC, 1/327, knew who the best grunt was. It was Earl "Recon" Wilson. The only thing he was afraid of was snakes, and he ate them for breakfast to remind him of his fear.

Everything else was an appetizer . . . or the main course.

History can often be fickle, viewed in one perspective by one generation, considered entirely different by another. Regardless of how the Vietnam veteran may be viewed by history, one critical point will never change: The Vietnam veteran showed up for the roll call!

In 1969, my college fraternity held its annual White Rose Ball. It's a formal affair, and on my white tuxedo coat I wore the miniature medals of my decorations received for valor. It was the only time I've ever done so. I took a break from the festivities and went to the bar and ordered a drink. The bartender eyed the medals, delivered the drink, then snickered, and asked, "Where did you get those medals, kid? In the Boy Scouts?"

I pitched my drink in his face, and replied, "That's goddamned right . . . Above the Rest!"

As Chassion said, "Don't piss on the silk!"

—Tom Willard
July 1999